NATIONAL
GEOGRAPHIC

THE
CIVIL
WAR

NATIONAL GEOGRAPHIC

THE CIVIL WAR

* * *

A Traveler's Guide

EXPERIENCE THE HISTORY, FOLLOW THE BATTLES

Edited by Len Riedel

Executive Director, Blue and Gray Education Society

National Geographic
Washington, D.C.

Contents

✳ ✳ ✳

Introduction

WELCOME TO NATIONAL GEOGRAPHIC'S *THE CIVIL WAR: A Traveler's Guide.* Developed in partnership with the nonprofit Blue and Gray Education Society (BGES), it is National Geographic's most extensive guide to the Civil War. It is also a true collaborative effort, showcasing the strongest elements of each organization: BGES's 50 years of field experience and National Geographic's unmatched team of writers, photographers, and other experts.

The Civil War is the story of America. Yet the fascination with the war does not stop at America's borders. Indeed, many other nationalities share a passionate interest in the Civil War, which was, in reality, a world war. With its more than 225,000 pages of official documents and 10,000 reports of campaigns, battles, engagements, actions, skirmishes, raids, expeditions, affairs, and reconnaissances spread over more than 20 states or territories and countries as geographically diverse as Canada, England, France, and Australia, the war affected thousands of communities around the globe. This book touches on many of them.

Sketch artists during the Civil War rendered historic scenes as they witnessed them or heard them described, like a 19th-century version of a newscast.

The Civil War is often mistakenly presented as "the war fought to end slavery." In fact, the war wasn't fought over slavery, but slavery did cause the war. Hostilities began as a dispute over secession and the Lincoln Administration's commitment to reunite the country following a fractious election. The situation is often represented as an issue of states rights: Should slavery be allowed in the new mineral-rich territories? Why are slaves considered property in one part of the U.S. but not in another? Fearing that decades of compromise and political wrangling could no longer protect Southern interests, key citizens of the South believed they might find common cause in a new confederation of slave states in which all had a common respect for their "Peculiar Institution." The end of slavery was a by-product of wartime decisions made by the Lincoln Administration when other factors, such as possible foreign intervention, intruded.

Living historians re-create the battles of the Civil War through well-attended, scripted reenactments.

Conversely, although the newly elected Lincoln assured Southerners that he had no interest in ending slavery in the states where it currently existed, the people of the South had an entirely different impression. Sponsored by Senator Stephen A. Douglas, the Kansas-Nebraska Act of 1854 reduced the trust that Southerners held in Northern political promises. The bill had opened the Kansas and Nebraska Territories to eventual statehood, suggesting that the settlers in each state could decide for themselves if they would permit slavery, in a process known as popular sovereignty. Southerners, believing they had finally cracked the old Missouri Compromise agreement, flooded into Kansas and, amid much fraud, developed a pro-slavery state constitution. President James Buchanan, anxious to put the slavery question behind him, embraced the constitution. Douglas, however, as head of the Senate Territories Committee and with an eye on the White House himself, sensed the fraud and took issue with Buchanan's acceptance. Enraged, the people of the South believed they had been betrayed.

Artifacts continue to educate us more than 150 years after the war.

In 1860, Douglas could not muster any Southern support, and Lincoln won the election. Soon the states of the Deep South—South Carolina, Georgia, Florida, Alabama, Mississippi, Louisiana, and Texas—would be out of the Union. Kentucky Senator John J. Crittenden made an effort to avert war, but Lincoln rejected his efforts. The peoples' will, Lincoln believed, should not be compromised to satisfy the petulance of the electoral losers. The war came.

This guide represents 19th-century America. The primary theater of operations was, logically, between Washington, D.C., and

Richmond, Virginia—the two capitals. Indeed, nearly 28 percent of the reported actions took place in the Old Dominion and its derivative, West Virginia. Not surprisingly, Tennessee and Missouri, both border states, had the next highest number of clashes, nearly 27 percent. In other words, more than half the battles fought during the Civil War took place in just three states.

Furthermore, since the South had no interest in conquering "free soil," more than 99 percent of all the events related to the war occurred in the South. States along the vital Mississippi River saw 21 percent of the engagements. States such as Alabama, Georgia, South Carolina, and North Carolina did not feel the hard hand of war until 1864 and saw just 15 percent of the activity. States on the periphery of the Confederacy, such as Florida, Texas, the Indian Territory (Oklahoma), California, Idaho, and Minnesota, saw practically no activity—just 4 percent, and much of it the continuation of emerging conflicts with Native Americans that would continue until the 1880s. Key slave states like Maryland and Kentucky experienced 5 percent of the military activity, as the South tried to bring them into the Confederacy. Pennsylvania, Ohio, Vermont, and Indiana experienced infrequent raids.

✳ ✳ ✳

This guide, with its informative sidebar stories and tips for further reading, makes for a pleasant historical excursion. It presents the breadth of the conflict and encourages readers to discover their own Civil War trail. To that end, we have selected a representative sampling of sites and battlefields, all of which have the potential to open more fields of exploration. And we have included 12 walking and 2 driving tours, from Fredericksburg, Virginia, and Gettysburg, Pennsylvania, to London, England—a strong recommendation to allow some time to explore those communities. Let your interest be your guide. Just because a particular town, monument, or engagement is not included

Artists such as Jeff Fioravanti highlight the pastoral beauty of sites such as Burnside Bridge over Antietam Creek, the site of fighting on September 17, 1862.

here, however, does not mean it did not play an important role. As states preserve more of the artifacts, buildings, and battlefields of the Civil War era, future editions of this guide will certainly grow larger. Share your discoveries with BGES at blueandgrayeducation@yahoo .com. Mail us the literature you find so that we can evaluate it against what is already known. You can find the BGES mailing address at the back of the book.

Each person has his or her own level of interest in history. If you want more information or involvement, consider joining a local Civil War roundtable or the Blue and Gray Education Society. BGES's small-group study tours and educational preservation projects contribute much to the journey you are about to experience.

Thank you for purchasing this book.

—Len Riedel
Executive Director, BGES

25 Most Important Battles of the Civil War

The American Civil War is the first great event in redeeming the promise "that all men are created equal." While the war was not fought to end slavery, it had the very desirable outcome of doing precisely that and catapulted the country into the first civil rights era. During the sesquicentennial of the Civil War, historians have revised the number of dead to nearly 800,000. Where was all this blood most constructively shed? Most historians will agree that if you follow these 25 events, you will walk the "critical path" to Union victory.

1. John Brown's Raid at Harpers Ferry (WV)

The threat of slave insurrection is brought to the East.

2. Fort Sumter I (SC)

Lincoln maneuvers the Confederacy into firing the first shot and energizes the North.

3. First Manassas/Bull Run (VA)

The rout of the Union Army disabuses anyone of thoughts of a quick war.

4. Fort Donelson (TN)

Ulysses S. Grant emerges with the first capture of a Confederate army, leading to the fall of the first Southern capital: Nashville.

5. Pea Ridge/Elkhorn Tavern (AR)

Missouri Rebels driven away from the state line lose the state in December 1862.

6. Shiloh (TN)

Nearly destroyed on the banks of the Tennessee, the Union Army is saved by the arrival of reinforcements and the death of Confederate General A. S. Johnston. By blaming others, Grant avoids being fired.

7. New Orleans (LA)

The South loses its largest city and control of the mouth of the Mississippi River.

8. Cross Keys & Port Republic (VA)

In this culminating point of Stonewall Jackson's Valley Campaign, McClellan is denied reinforcements near Richmond.

9. Gaines' Mill (VA)

Lee takes the initiative and drives McClellan from the gates of Richmond.

10. Second Manassas/Bull Run (VA)

Robert E. Lee demolishes John Pope's army, setting the stage to enter Northern territory.

11. Antietam (MD)

Lee is stopped on the banks of Antietam Creek, and the victory allows Lincoln to issue the preliminary Emancipation Proclamation, driving a wedge between adventuresome European nations and Lincoln's attempt to control the rebellion.

12. Perryville (KY)

Confederates discover they have no support in Kentucky, and Braxton Bragg's shortcomings as a commander are revealed.

13. Fredericksburg I (VA)

The catastrophic Union defeat on the heights above this pivotal Virginia city nearly derails Lincoln's military cover for the Emancipation Proclamation.

14. Holly Springs Raid (MS)

His plans derailed, Grant is convinced that he must change his method of supply and operation for the Vicksburg Campaign.

15. Stones River (TN)

This Union victory is reported as Lincoln is releasing the Emancipation Proclamation and the Union is suffering defeats at Fredericksburg and Chickasaw Bayou.

16. Chancellorsville (VA)

Jackson's mortal wounding forces Lee to reorganize his army prior to moving his troops into Pennsylvania.

17. Raymond (MS)

This small battle sets up Grant to place himself between Vicksburg and the Confederate relief army near Jackson.

18. Gettysburg (PA)

The Confederate response to Grant's threat to open the Mississippi River fails to force Grant away and weakens Lee as a strategic adviser to Jefferson Davis.

19. Chattanooga III (TN)

Grant passes the audition to take over the besieged Union Army by routing the Confederate forces.

20. Wilderness (VA)

Grant is attacked by Lee, but rather than retreating as other armies have done, he moves on to Spotsylvania Court House—there is a new spirit confronting Lee.

21. Jonesborough (GA)

This decisive battle allows William T. Sherman to cut the last road into Atlanta, forcing its evacuation and setting Lincoln on the path to an electoral victory in November.

22. Mobile Bay (AL)

This battle closes the last Confederate port on the Gulf of Mexico.

23. Fort Fisher II (NC)

The final Confederate port and Lee's supply line from overseas are closed.

24. Five Forks (VA)

Lee's line is ruptured, and the Confederates abandon Richmond.

25. Appomattox Court House and Station (VA)

Lee's surrender doesn't end the Civil War, but it does send a signal that the war is ending.

Countless sculptures reflect the resolve and deep emotion of people in the Civil War.

Civil War Military Leaders

The Civil War lasted four years, and men usually advanced one or more ranks during the war. This list of leaders mentioned in the book shows their last rank during the war years; however, because Congress promoted dozens of officers for war service after the war ended, it includes those promotions as well.

CS: Confederate States Army
CSN: Confederate States Navy
US: United States Army
USN: United States Navy

* **Anderson,** George W., CS, Maj.
* **Anderson,** Richard H., CS, Lt. Gen.
* **Anderson,** Robert, US, Maj. Gen.
* **Anderson,** William T. "Bloody Bill," CS, Guerrilla
* **Archer,** James A., CS, Brig. Gen.
* **Armstrong,** Frank C., CS, Brig. Gen.
* **Asboth,** Alexander, US, Maj. Gen.
* **Autry,** James, CS, Col.
* **Averell,** William W., US, Maj. Gen.
* **Bailey,** Joseph, US, Lt. Col.
* **Baker,** Edward D., US, Col.
* **Banks,** Nathaniel P., US, Maj. Gen.
* **Barstow,** Hiram E., US, Capt.
* **Basset,** Elisha, US, Capt.
* **Beauregard,** P. G. T., CS, Gen.
* **Bee,** Barnard E., CS, Brig. Gen.
* **Bee,** Hamilton P., CS, Brig. Gen.
* **Benham,** Henry, US, Maj. Gen.
* **Blair,** Francis P., US, Maj. Gen.
* **Bloodgood,** Edward, US, Lt. Col.
* **Blunt,** James G., US, Maj. Gen.
* **Booth,** Lionel F., US, Maj.
* **Bradford,** William F., US, Maj.
* **Bragg,** Braxton, CS, Gen.
* **Branch,** Lawrence O'Bryan, CS, Brig. Gen.
* **Breckinridge,** John C., CS, Maj. Gen.
* **Brown,** Egbert B., US, Brig. Gen.
* **Buchanan,** Franklin, CSN, Adm.
* **Buckner,** Simon Bolivar, CS, Lt. Gen.
* **Buel,** James T., US, Lt. Col.
* **Buell,** Don Carlos, US, Maj. Gen.
* **Burbridge,** Stephen G., US, Maj. Gen.
* **Burnside,** Ambrose, US, Maj. Gen.
* **Butler,** Benjamin F., US, Maj. Gen.
* **Butler,** J. Russell, CS, Col.
* **Butler,** Matthew C., CS, Maj. Gen.
* **Cabell,** W. L., CS, Brig. Gen.
* **Canby,** E.R.S., US, Maj. Gen.
* **Carter,** Samuel P., US, Maj. Gen.; USN, Comdr.

* **Chalmers,** James R., CS, Brig. Gen.
* **Chamberlain,** Joshua L., US, Brig. Gen.
* **Chambliss,** John R., CS, Brig. Gen.
* **Churchill,** Thomas J., CS, Maj. Gen.
* **Cleburne,** Patrick, CS, Maj. Gen.
* **Clingman,** Thomas, CS, Brig. Gen.
* **Cloud,** William F., US, Col.
* **Coburn,** John, US, Col.
* **Coffee,** John T., US, Col.
* **Colcock,** Charles, CS, Col.
* **Cooke,** Philip St. George, US, Brig. Gen.
* **Cooper,** Douglas H., CS, Brig. Gen.
* **Corse,** John M., US, Maj. Gen.
* **Cox,** Jacob D., US, Maj. Gen.
* **Craven,** Tunis A. M., USN, Comdr.
* **Crittenden,** George B., CS, Maj. Gen.
* **Crittenden,** Thomas T., US, Brig. Gen.
* **Crook,** George R., US, Maj. Gen.
* **Curtis,** Samuel R., US, Maj. Gen.
* **Cushing,** William B., USN, Comdr.
* **Custer,** George A., US, Maj. Gen.
* **Dahlgren,** John, USN, Rear Adm.
* **Dahlgren,** Ulric, US, Col.
* **Davis,** Charles H., USN, Rear Adm.
* **Davis,** Jefferson C., US, Maj. Gen.
* **Davis,** Jefferson F., Commander in Chief of the Army and Navy of the Confederate States of America
* **Dorsey,** Caleb W., US, Col.
* **Drake,** Francis, US, Lt. Col.
* **Duffié,** Alfred N., US, Brig. Gen.
* **Dunham,** Cyrus L., US, Col.
* **Du Pont,** S. F., USN, Rear Adm.
* **Early,** Jubal A., CS, Lt. Gen.
* **Echols,** John, CS, Brig. Gen.
* **Elliott,** Stephen E., CS, Brig. Gen.
* **Englemann,** Adolph, US, Col.
* **Ewell,** Richard S., CS, Lt. Gen.
* **Ezekiel,** Moses J., Virginia Militia, VMI Cadet
* **Fagan,** James B., CS, Maj. Gen.
* **Farragut,** David G., USN, Adm.
* **Field,** Charles W., CS, Maj. Gen.
* **Finegan,** Joseph, CS, Brig. Gen.

* **Flournoy,** Thomas, CS, Col.
* **Floyd,** John B., CS, Brig. Gen.
* **Foote,** A. H., USN, Rear Adm.
* **Forrest,** Jeffrey, CS, Lt. Col.
* **Forrest,** Nathan B., CS, Lt. Gen.
* **Foster,** Emory S., US, Maj.
* **Foster,** John G., US, Maj. Gen.
* **Franklin,** William B., US, Maj. Gen.
* **Frazier,** Julian, CS, Col.
* **Fremont,** John C., US, Maj. Gen.
* **French,** Samuel G., CS, Maj. Gen.
* **Fuller,** John W., US, Col.
* **Fry,** Joseph, CSN, Capt.
* **Gano,** R. M, CS, Brig. Gen.
* **Gardner,** Franklin, CS, Maj. Gen.
* **Garfield,** James, US, Maj. Gen.
* **Garnett,** Richard B., CS, Brig. Gen.
* **Gibson,** Randall L., CS, Brig. Gen.
* **Gillem,** Alvan C., US, Maj. Gen.
* **Gillmore,** Quincy A., US, Maj. Gen.
* **Girardey,** Victor J. B., CS, Brig. Gen.
* **Granger,** Gordon, US, Maj. Gen.
* **Grant,** Ulysses S., US, Lt. Gen.,
  Commanding General of the United States
  Armies from March 1864
* **Green,** Thomas, CS, Brig. Gen.
* **Greene,** Colton, CS, Brig. Gen.
* **Gregg,** David M., US, Maj. Gen.
* **Gregg,** John, CS, Brig. Gen.
* **Grierson,** Benjamin, US, Maj. Gen.
* **Grover,** Cuvier, US, Maj. Gen.
* **Hagood,** Johnson, CS, Brig. Gen.
* **Hall,** Albert S., US, Col.
* **Halleck,** Henry W., US, Maj. Gen.
* **Hampton,** Wade III, CS, Lt. Gen.
* **Hancock,** Winfield Scott, US, Maj. Gen.
* **Hannon,** Moses W., CS, Lt. Col.
* **Hardee,** William J., CS, Lt. Gen.
* **Harding,** Abner C., US, Col.
* **Harding,** Chester, Jr., US, Col.
* **Hart,** John E., USN, Lt. Cmdr.
* **Hatch,** Edward, US, Maj. Gen.
* **Hazen,** William B., US, Maj. Gen.
* **Herron,** Francis J., US, Maj. Gen.
* **Heth,** Henry, CS, Maj. Gen.
* **Hicks,** Stephen G., US, Col.
* **Higginson,** Thomas W., US, Col.
* **Hill,** A. P., CS, Lt. Gen.
* **Hill,** Daniel Harvey, CS, Maj. Gen.
* **Hindman,** Thomas C., CS, Maj. Gen.
* **Hoke,** Robert F., CS, Maj. Gen.
* **Holmes,** Theophilus H., CS, Lt. Gen.
* **Hood,** John Bell, CS, Gen.
* **Hooker,** Joseph, US, Maj. Gen.
* **Hopkins,** Charles F., CS, Lt. Col.
* **Howard,** Oliver O., US, Maj. Gen.
* **Hughes,** John T., CS, Col.
* **Hunter,** David, US, Maj. Gen.
* **Hurlbut,** Stephen A., US, Maj. Gen.
* **Jackson,** Claiborne F., CS, Militia Commander,
  CS Governor of Missouri
* **Jackson,** Thomas J. "Stonewall," CS, Lt. Gen.
* **Jackson,** W. H. "Red," CS, Brig. Gen.
* **James,** Jesse, CS, Guerrilla
* **Jenkins,** Albert G., CS, Brig. Gen.
* **Jenkins,** Micah, CS, Brig. Gen.
* **Johnson,** Bushrod R., CS, Maj. Gen.
* **Johnson,** Edward "Allegheny," CS, Maj. Gen.
* **Johnston,** Albert Sidney, CS, Gen.
* **Johnston,** Joseph E., CS, Gen.
* **Jones,** David R., CS, Maj. Gen.
* **Jones,** Sam, CS, Maj. Gen.
* **Jones,** William E. "Grumble," CS, Brig. Gen.
* **Kautz,** August, US, Maj. Gen.
* **Kearny,** Philip, Jr., US, Maj. Gen.
* **Kenly,** John R., US, Maj. Gen.
* **Kilpatrick,** Hugh Judson, US, Maj. Gen.
* **Kimball,** Nathan, US, Maj. Gen.
* **Kirby,** Isaac M., US, Col.
* **Lamb,** William, CS, Col.
* **Lane,** James H., US, Brig. Gen.
* **Lawler,** Michael, US, Maj. Gen.
* **Leake,** W. W., CS, Capt.
* **Lee,** Fitzhugh, CS, Maj. Gen.
* **Lee,** George W. C. "Custis," CS, Maj. Gen.
* **Lee,** Robert E., CS, Gen., General in Chief of
  the Confederate forces from February 1865
* **Lee,** Stephen D., CS, Lt. Gen.
* **Lee,** W. H. F. "Rooney," CS, Maj. Gen.
* **Lincoln,** Abraham, Commander in Chief of
  the Army and Navy of the United States
* **Logan,** John A., US, Maj. Gen.
* **Longstreet,** James, CS, Lt. Gen.
* **Loring,** William W., CS, Maj. Gen.
* **Lyon,** Nathaniel, US, Brig. Gen.
* **Magruder,** John B., CS, Maj. Gen.
* **Mahone,** William, CS, Maj. Gen.
* **Marmaduke,** John S., CS, Maj. Gen.
* **Marsh,** John S., US, Capt.
* **Marshall,** Humphrey, CS, Brig. Gen.
* **Martin,** William T., CS, Maj. Gen.
* **Maxey,** Samuel B., CS, Maj. Gen.
* **McCausland,** John, Jr., CS, Brig. Gen.
* **McClellan,** George B., US, Maj. Gen.
* **McClernand,** John A., US, Maj. Gen.
* **McCulloch,** Benjamin, CS, Brig. Gen.

* **McDowell,** Irvin, US, Maj. Gen.
* **McIntosh,** James McQueen, CS, Brig. Gen.
* **McKay,** James, CSN, Capt.
* **McLaws,** Lafayette, CS, Maj. Gen.
* **McNeil,** John, US, Brig. Gen.
* **McPherson,** James B., US, Maj. Gen.
* **Meade,** George G., US, Maj. Gen.
* **Mendenhall,** John, US, Capt.
* **Merrill,** Samuel, US, Col.
* **Merritt,** Wesley, US, Maj. Gen.
* **Miles,** Nelson A., US, Brig. Gen.
* **Miller,** William, CS, Brig. Gen.
* **Milroy,** Robert H., US, Brig. Gen.
* **Moore,** Absalom B., US, Col.
* **Morgan,** John Hunt, CS, Brig. Gen.
* **Morris,** Thomas A., US, Brig. Gen.
* **Mosby,** John S., CS, Col.
* **Mouton,** Alfred, CS, Brig. Gen.
* **Mower,** Joseph A., US, Maj. Gen.
* **Negley,** James S., US, Maj. Gen.
* **Nelson,** William "Bull," US, Maj. Gen.; USN, Lt.
* **Nethercutt,** John H., CS, Col.
* **Newton,** John, US, Maj. Gen.
* **Olmstead,** Charles H., CS, Col.
* **Opdyke,** Emerson, US, Maj. Gen.
* **Ord,** Edward O. C., US, Maj. Gen.
* **Osborne,** F. A., US, Lt. Col.
* **Parke,** John G., US, Maj. Gen.
* **Parsons,** William H., CS, Col.
* **Patterson,** Robert, US, Maj. Gen.
* **Peck,** John J., US, Maj. Gen.
* **Pegram,** John, CS, Brig. Gen.
* **Pelham,** John, CS, Lt. Col.
* **Pemberton,** John, CS, Lt. Gen.
* **Pendleton,** William N., CS, Brig. Gen.
* **Pettigrew,** J. Johnston, CS, Brig. Gen.
* **Philips,** Pleasant J., CS, Brig. Gen.
* **Phillips,** William, US, Col.
* **Pickett,** George E., CS, Maj. Gen.
* **Pierce,** Ebenezer W., MA, Massachusetts Militia Brig. Gen.
* **Pike,** Albert, CS, Brig. Gen.
* **Pillow,** Gideon Johnson, CS, Brig. Gen.
* **Pleasonton,** Alfred, US, Maj. Gen.
* **Polk,** Leonidas, CS, Lt. Gen.
* **Pope,** John, US, Maj. Gen.
* **Porter,** David D., USN, Rear Adm.
* **Porter,** Fitz John, US, Maj. Gen.
* **Porterfield,** George A., CS, Col.
* **Potter,** Robert B., US, Maj. Gen.
* **Prentiss,** Benjamin M., US, Maj. Gen.
* **Price,** Sterling, CS, Maj. Gen.
* **Purdie,** Thomas J., CS, Col.

* **Quantrill,** William C., CS, Guerrilla
* **Ramseur,** Stephen D., CS, Maj. Gen.
* **Reno,** Jesse L., US, Maj. Gen.
* **Reynolds,** John F., US, Maj. Gen.
* **Reynolds,** Joseph, US, Maj. Gen.
* **Rice,** Samuel, US, Brig. Gen.
* **Richardson,** Israel B., US, Maj. Gen.
* **Ricketts,** James B., US, Maj. Gen.
* **Robertson,** Felix H., CS, Brig. Gen.
* **Rodes,** Robert E., CS, Maj. Gen.
* **Rosecrans,** William S., US, Maj. Gen.
* **Ross,** Lawrence Sullivan "Sul," CS, Brig. Gen.
* **Rosser,** Thomas L., CS, Maj. Gen.
* **Rowan,** Stephen C., USN, Capt.
* **Rust,** Albert, CS, Brig. Gen.
* **Schenck,** Robert C., US, Maj. Gen.
* **Schoepf,** Albin F., US, Brig. Gen.
* **Schofield,** John M., US, Maj. Gen.
* **Scott,** John, US, Lt. Col.
* **Sedgwick,** John, US, Maj. Gen.
* **Seymour,** Truman, US, Maj. Gen.
* **Shackelford,** J. M., US, Brig. Gen.
* **Shaw,** Robert Gould, US, Col.
* **Shelby,** Joseph O., CS, Brig. Gen.
* **Sheridan,** Phillip H., US, Maj. Gen.
* **Sherman,** William Tecumseh, US, Maj. Gen.
* **Shields,** James, US, Brig. Gen.
* **Sibley,** Henry Hastings, US, Brig. Gen.
* **Sibley,** Henry Hopkins, CS, Brig. Gen.
* **Sigel,** Franz, US, Maj. Gen.
* **Singletary,** George, CS, Col.
* **Slemmer,** Adam J., US, Brig. Gen.
* **Slocum,** Henry W., US, Maj. Gen.
* **Smith,** A. J. "Whiskey," US, Maj. Gen.
* **Smith,** E. Kirby, CS, Gen.
* **Smith,** G. W., CS, Maj. Gen.
* **Smith,** William F. "Baldy," US, Maj. Gen.
* **Smith,** William Sooy, US, Maj. Gen.
* **Stanley,** David S., US, Maj. Gen.
* **Steele,** Frederick, US, Maj. Gen.
* **Stevens,** Isaac I., US, Maj. Gen.
* **Stewart,** A. P., CS, Lt. Gen.
* **Stickney,** Albert, US, Lt. Col.
* **Stone,** Charles P., US, Brig. Gen.
* **Stoneman,** George, Jr., US, Maj. Gen.
* **Streight,** Abel, US, Brig. Gen.
* **Stringham,** Silas H., USN, Rear Adm.
* **Strong,** George C., US, Brig. Gen.
* **Stuart,** J. E. B., CS, Maj. Gen.
* **Sturgis,** Samuel D., US, Brig. Gen.
* **Sullivan,** Jeremiah C., US, Brig. Gen.
* **Sully,** Alfred, US, Brig. Gen.
* **Taylor,** George W., US, Brig. Gen.

* **Taylor,** Richard, CS, Lt. Gen.
* **Terry,** Alfred H., US, Maj. Gen.
* **Terry,** B. F., CS, Col.
* **Thomas,** George H., US, Maj. Gen.
* **Thompson,** Gideon W., CS, Col.
* **Thompson,** M. Jeff, CS, Brig. Gen.
* **Tilghman,** Lloyd, CS, Brig. Gen.
* **Toombs,** Robert, CS, Brig. Gen.
* **Torbert,** Alfred T. A., US, Maj. Gen.
* **Turchin,** John Basil, US, Brig. Gen.
* **Tyler,** Daniel, US, Brig. Gen.
* **Tyler,** Erastus B., US, Maj. Gen.
* **Vandever,** William, US, Maj. Gen.
* **Van Dorn,** Earl, CS, Maj. Gen.
* **Wagner,** George D., CS, Brig. Gen.
* **Walcutt,** Charles C., US, Maj. Gen.
* **Walker,** John, US, Capt.
* **Walker,** Lucius M., CS, Brig. Gen.
* **Wallace,** Lew, US, Maj. Gen.

* **Warren,** Gouverneur K., US, Maj. Gen.
* **Washburn,** Cadwallader C., US, Maj. Gen.
* **Watie,** Stand, CS, Brig. Gen.
* **Weitzel,** Godfrey, US, Maj. Gen.
* **Wheeler,** Joseph, CS, Maj. Gen.
* **White,** Moses J., CS, Col.
* **Wild,** Edward A., US, Brig. Gen.
* **Wilder,** John T., US, Brig. Gen.
* **Williams,** James M., US, Col.
* **Williams,** John S., CS, Brig. Gen.
* **Williams,** Thomas, US, Brig. Gen.
* **Willich,** August, US, Brig. Gen.
* **Wilson,** James H., US, Maj. Gen.
* **Winder,** Charles S., CS, Brig Gen.
* **Wise,** Henry A., CS, Maj. Gen.
* **Wright,** Ambrose R., CS, Brig. Gen.
* **Wright,** Horatio G., US, Maj. Gen.
* **Wyatt,** Henry, CS, Private
* **Zollicoffer,** Felix K., CS, Brig. Gen.

Map Key

Road		Union victory	
Railroad		Confederate victory	
Unfinished railroad		Inconclusive battle	
Pontoon bridge		Point of interest	
State boundary		Building, church	
Farm boundary		Woodland	
Walking tour route		Swamp	
Driving tour route		Park or cemetery	

Road
Railroad
Unfinished railroad
Pontoon bridge
State boundary
Farm boundary
Walking tour route
Driving tour route
Interstate highway (20)
Federal highway (61)
State highway (27)
• City
National capital
★ State capital
○ Walking tour city
1 Driving/walking tour stop

Union victory
Confederate victory
Inconclusive battle
□ Point of interest
Building, church
Woodland
Swamp
Park or cemetery

Union	Confederacy	
		Infantry (first position)
		Infantry (second position)
		Cavalry
		Artillery
		Commander's headquarters
		Fort
		Camp
		Vessel
		Line of advance
		Line of retreat
		Fortifications and trenches

CANADA
U.S.

North Dakota p. 404

Idaho p. 456

Bear River 1863

Colorado p. 452

Sand Creek 1864

Kansas p. 398

Glorieta Pass 1862

THE WEST p. 446

New Mexico p. 460

Oklahoma p. 432

Valverde 1862

PACIFIC OCEAN

U.S.
MEXICO

Texas p. 466

WASH. TERR.
OREGON
DAKOTA TERRITORY
MINN.
N.H. VT. ME.
MASS.
N.Y.
R.I. CONN.
MICH.
WIS.
NEV. TERR.
UTAH TERR.
NEBRASKA TERR.
IOWA
PA.
N.J. DEL.
CALIF.
COLORADO TERR.
KANSAS
MO.
ILL. IND. OHIO (Statehood 1863) W.VA. MD. VA.
KY.
Palmeto Ranch 1865
NEW MEXICO TERRITORY
UNORG. TERR.
TENN.
N.C.
Boundary of Confederacy
ARK.
S.C.
TEXAS
MISS. ALA. GA.
LA.
FLA.

Free state, 1861
Slave state, 1861
Border state, 1861
U.S. territory, 1861

18

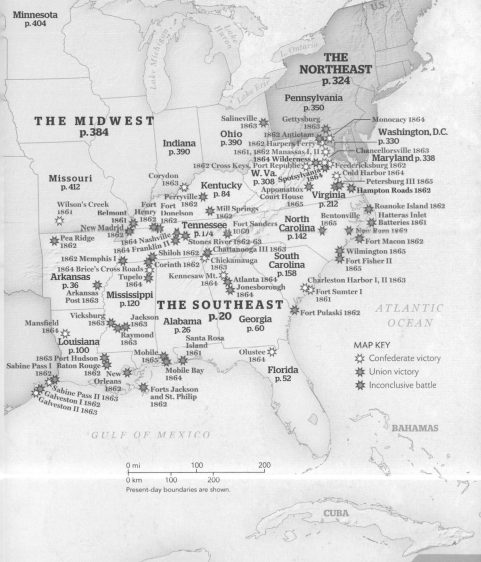

Decisive and Major Engagements of the Civil War

Minnesota
p. 404

CAN.
U.S.

Lake Superior

Lake Huron

Lake Michigan

Lake Ontario

Lake Erie

THE NORTHEAST
p. 324

Pennsylvania
p. 350

THE MIDWEST
p. 384

Salineville
1863
Gettysburg
1863

Ohio
p. 390
1862 Antietam

Monocacy 1864

Washington, D.C.
p. 330

Indiana
p. 390

1862 Harpers Ferry

Maryland p. 338

1861, 1862 Manassas I, II
1864 Wilderness

Chancellorsville 1863

1862 Cross Keys, Port Republic

Fredericksburg 1862

Corydon
1863

W. Va.
p. 308

Spotsylvania
1864

Cold Harbor 1864

Missouri
p. 412

Kentucky
p. 84

Appomattox
Court House
1865

Petersburg III 1865

Hampton Roads 1862

Perryville
1862

Virginia
p. 212

Wilson's Creek
1861

Fort
Henry
1862

Fort
Donelson
1862

Mill Springs
1862

Fort Sanders
1860

Bentonville
1865

Roanoke Island 1862

Hatteras Inlet
Batteries 1861

Belmont
1861

New Madrid
1862

Tennessee
p. 174

North
Carolina
p. 142

New Bern 1862

Pea Ridge
1862

1864 Nashville
1864 Franklin II

Stones River 1862-63

Chattanooga III 1863

Fort Macon 1862

Shiloh 1862

Chickamauga
1863

South
Carolina
p. 158

Wilmington 1865

1862 Memphis I

Corinth 1862

Fort Fisher II
1865

1864 Brice's Cross Roads

Kennesaw Mt.
1864

Atlanta 1864

Charleston Harbor I, II 1863

Arkansas
p. 36

Tupelo
1864

Jonesborough
1864

Fort Sumter I
1861

Arkansas
Post 1863

Mississippi
p. 120

THE SOUTHEAST
p. 20

Fort Pulaski 1862

ATLANTIC
OCEAN

Vicksburg
1863

Jackson
1863

Alabama
p. 26

Georgia
p. 60

Mansfield
1864

Raymond
1863

Santa Rosa
Island
1861

Olustee
1864

Louisiana
p. 100

Mobile
1865

Florida
p. 52

1863 Port Hudson

Baton Rouge
1862

Mobile Bay
1864

MAP KEY

Sabine Pass I
1862

New
Orleans
1862

Forts Jackson
and St. Philip
1862

✶ Confederate victory

Sabine Pass II 1863

✶ Union victory

Galveston I 1862

✶ Inconclusive battle

Galveston II 1863

BAHAMAS

GULF OF MEXICO

0 mi ___ 100 ___ 200
0 km ___ 100 ___ 200
Present-day boundaries are shown.

CUBA

The Southeast

Sunset along the Federal
cannon line at the battlefield
of Raymond, Mississippi

The Southern States Align

Key Southern leaders had long feared the uneasy ramifications of the Missouri Compromise, and while Northern states had adapted to a free-labor economy, Southern wealth and continued prosperity for its most privileged members were anchored on a caste system of chattel slavery. The system was older than the country itself, and its founding fathers, from Washington to Jefferson to Pinckney, had all prospered under it.

The westward expansion and discovery of gold had generated new excitement and opportunity for all; however, the mood of the country had changed. Pennsylvania Congressman David Wilmot had proposed banning slavery in the territories gained from Mexico. Abraham Lincoln had challenged American imperialism with his "spot resolution," and Massachusetts Senator Charles Sumner had been beaten senseless on the floor of the Senate by South Carolina Congressman Preston Brooks for insulting his uncle in a speech about slavery.

Lincoln had given a speech about a "House Divided." Southerners agreed: They and their institution should not stay in such an arrangement. And after Lincoln's election, they didn't.

While stunning plantation homes symbolize the antebellum South for many, secession affected people of all economic levels and backgrounds.

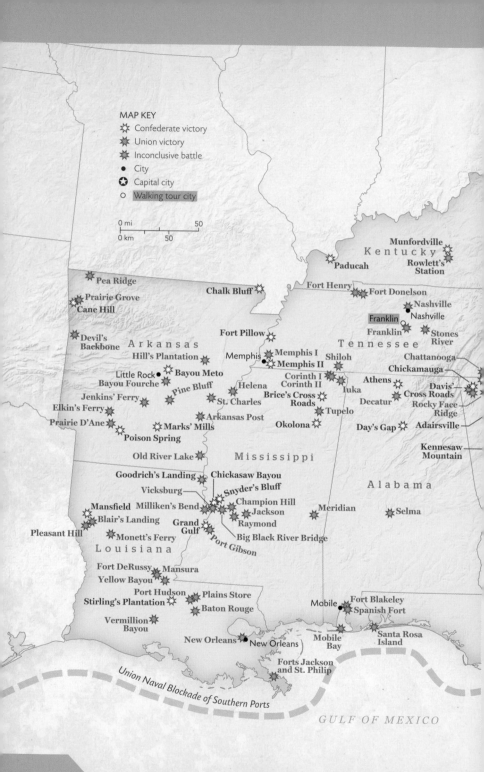

MAP KEY

✦ Confederate victory
✦ Union victory
✦ Inconclusive battle
• City
✪ Capital city
○ Walking tour city

0 mi   50
0 km   50

Kentucky

Munfordville
Paducah
Rowlett's Station

Pea Ridge
Chalk Bluff
Fort Henry
Fort Donelson

Prairie Grove
Cane Hill
Nashville
Nashville

Franklin
Franklin
Stones River

Devil's Backbone
Fort Pillow
Tennessee

Arkansas
Hill's Plantation
Memphis
Memphis I
Memphis II
Shiloh
Chattanooga
Chickamauga

Little Rock
Bayou Meto
Corinth I
Corinth II
Athens
Davis' Cross Roads

Bayou Fourche
Pine Bluff
Helena
Iuka
Rocky Face Ridge

Jenkins' Ferry
St. Charles
Brice's Cross Roads
Decatur

Elkin's Ferry
Arkansas Post
Tupelo
Day's Gap
Adairsville

Prairie D'Ane
Marks' Mills
Okolona

Poison Spring
Kennesaw Mountain

Old River Lake
Mississippi
Alabama

Goodrich's Landing
Chickasaw Bayou

Vicksburg
Snyder's Bluff

Mansfield
Milliken's Bend
Champion Hill
Jackson
Meridian
Selma

Blair's Landing
Raymond

Pleasant Hill
Grand Gulf
Big Black River Bridge

Monett's Ferry
Port Gibson

Louisiana

Fort DeRussy
Mansura

Yellow Bayou
Plains Store

Port Hudson
Mobile
Fort Blakeley

Stirling's Plantation
Baton Rouge
Spanish Fort

Vermillion Bayou
Santa Rosa Island

New Orleans
New Orleans
Mobile Bay

Forts Jackson and St. Philip

Union Naval Blockade of Southern Ports

GULF OF MEXICO

24

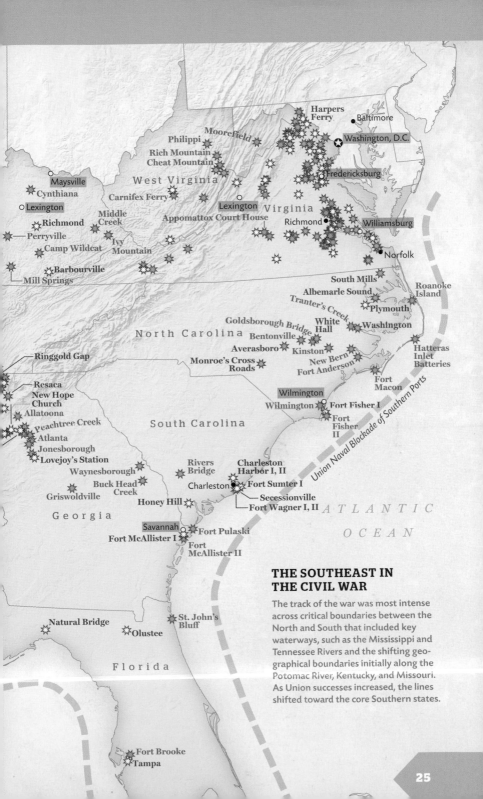

THE SOUTHEAST IN
THE CIVIL WAR

The track of the war was most intense
across critical boundaries between the
North and South that included key
waterways, such as the Mississippi and
Tennessee Rivers and the shifting geographical boundaries initially along the
Potomac River, Kentucky, and Missouri.
As Union successes increased, the lines
shifted toward the core Southern states.

Alabama

ON JANUARY 11, 1861, ALABAMA BECAME THE FOURTH STATE of seven to secede from the Union, following South Carolina, Mississippi, and Florida. The following month, delegates from each state met in Montgomery, Alabama, and created the Confederate States of America. There firebrand William L. Yancey welcomed the new nation's first president, Mississippi Senator Jefferson Davis, proclaiming, "The man and the hour have met." Virginia, Tennessee, Arkansas, and North Carolina soon followed suit, and the Confederate capital shifted to Richmond, Virginia.

Because Union efforts in the West focused on opening the Mississippi River for commerce, Alabama suffered less physical damage during the Civil War than Mississippi. The state established fortifications protecting Mobile Bay and key points along railroads near the Tennessee River. By 1862, its ironworks industry was producing artillery, projectiles, and siding for ironclad vessels like the C.S.S. *Tennessee*. This "Rust Belt" was essential to the Confederate war effort. Even so, by 1865 Alabama had fallen prey to powerful Federal operations.

Jefferson Davis and Alexander H. Stephens—president and vice president of the Confederacy—receive a capital welcome in Montgomery, Alabama.

ALABAMA BATTLES

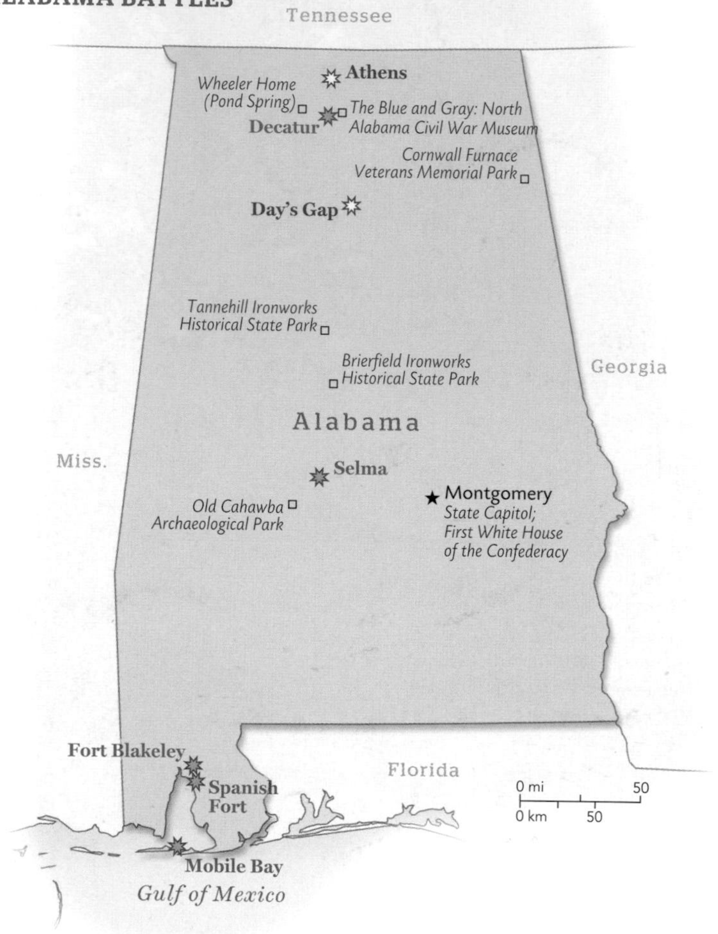

Tennessee

Wheeler Home
(Pond Spring) ☐
✦ Athens
✦ The Blue and Gray: North
Decatur ✦ Alabama Civil War Museum

Cornwall Furnace
Veterans Memorial Park ☐

Day's Gap ✦

Tannehill Ironworks
Historical State Park ☐

Brierfield Ironworks
☐ Historical State Park

Georgia

Alabama

Miss.

✦ Selma

★ Montgomery
State Capitol;
First White House
of the Confederacy

Old Cahawba ☐
Archaeological Park

Fort Blakeley ✦

✦ Spanish
Fort

Florida

0 mi   50
0 km   50

✦ Mobile Bay
Gulf of Mexico

✳ Athens

CAMPAIGN: Operations in North Alabama

OTHER NAME(S): Sulphur Creek Trestle

DATE(S): September 23–25, 1864

Because of its strategic location at the junction of two railroad lines, Athens—possibly the last town in Alabama to take down the Stars and Stripes—passed back and forth between Union and Confederate control.

In January 1864, 600 Confederate cavalry led by Colonel Hannon failed in their attempt to seize control of the town. By the end of September, however, the Rebels under General Nathan Bedford Forrest had reclaimed the town in one of northern Alabama's bloodiest battles. Although guarded, the 73-foot-high wooden trestle at Sulphur Creek was poorly situated, allowing Forrest to attack from the high ground.

LOCATION: Marker on the grounds of the Limestone Judicial Center, 503 S. Jefferson St., Athens. See page 34 for information on a self-guided Civil War driving tour of Athens and Sulphur Creek.

"Fightin' Joe" Wheeler—Confederate officer at age 29, U.S. general at 45

✳ Day's Gap

CAMPAIGN: Streight's Raid in Alabama and Georgia

OTHER NAME(S): Sand Mountain

DATE(S): April 30, 1863

In late April 1863, Colonel Streight led a force of 1,700 Union soldiers across northern Alabama. His goal was Rome, Georgia, ostensibly to cut off the railroad supplying General Bragg's Confederate forces in the middle of Tennessee. In reality, however, Streight aimed to create a diversion for General Grant, who was moving his army south along the west bank of the Mississippi River toward Vicksburg.

The Confederates took the bait. On April 30, General Nathan Bedford Forrest's Rebel brigade caught up with Streight's expedition and attacked its rear guard at Day's Gap on Sand Mountain. Fierce and intimidating, Forrest pursued the outmatched Streight over three days in a series of running skirmishes from Crooked Creek to Gadsden. The battle marker begins a series of Civil War markers leading to Hog Mountain. The Cullman County Museum details Streight's raid.

LOCATION: Marker located next to Hurricane Creek Park in the small community of Battleground, just south of Vinemont, at the intersection of Hwy. 157 and Hwy. 1101. Cullman County Museum, 211 2nd Ave. N.E., Cullman, 256-739-1258 or 800-533-1258, www.cullmancountymuseum.com.

✳ Decatur

CAMPAIGN: Franklin-Nashville Campaign

DATE(S): October 26–29, 1864

Following the fall of Atlanta in September 1864, the Confederates were determined to take the war back to Tennessee. Hoping to draw Sherman north, General Hood marched on Decatur, which was strategically located on the Tennessee River and an

Streight's Raid

Streight's expedition aimed to fix in place Confederate resources that might have helped defend Vicksburg, but the operation was a disaster from the start. Supplied with unbroken mules rather than horses, Streight's mounted infantry had difficulty managing its stubborn charges—a farce amplified by the mules' regular and loud braying.

Nathan Bedford Forrest's relentless pursuit was helped by the intervention of 15-year-old Emma Sansom of Gadsden, Alabama, who had watched Streight's troops abduct her brother and burn the bridge over Black Creek. She guided Forrest to a nearby ford, allowing his pursuit to continue.

Forrest finally surrounded Streight's troops about 20 miles outside Rome, Georgia, and on May 3 forced their surrender by tricking Streight into believing he was vastly outnumbered. In the end, Streight surrendered more than 1,400 men to Forrest's 366. "All's fair in love and war," Forrest reportedly declared.

FURTHER READING

The Lightning Mule Brigade: Abel Streight's 1863 Raid into Alabama by Robert L. Willett. A detailed account of Streight's ill-fated raid

important railroad terminus. After three days of skirmishes against the entrenched Union garrison, Hood turned his forces west to Tuscumbia, where he could draw supplies from nearby Corinth, Mississippi.

The Old State Bank in town still bears scars from rifle and cannon fire. The Decatur Convention and Visitors Bureau has a map of other Civil War sites, while the Morgan County Archives and Blue and Gray museum (see p. 34) also have relevant exhibits.

LOCATION: **Decatur Convention and Visitors Bureau, 719 6th Ave. S.E., Decatur, 800-232-5449 or 256-350-2028, www.decaturcvb.org; Morgan County Archives, 624 Bank St. N.E., Decatur, 256-351-4726.**

✳ Fort Blakeley

CAMPAIGN: Mobile Campaign
DATE(S): April 2–9, 1865

Situated on the banks of the Blakeley River on the east side of Mobile Bay, Fort Blakeley occupied a site chosen less for defensive practicality than for access to the deserted town of Blakeley's infrastructure and the deep water of Mobile Bay. The end came on April 9—hours *after* General Lee surrendered to General Grant at Appomattox (see p. 216)—when Union forces with a four-to-one advantage overwhelmed and captured most of the 4,000 Confederate soldiers who remained.

Although numerous reenactments held here have compromised the battlefield's integrity, it is important as the only remaining battlefield of the spring 1865 offensive to capture Mobile (see sidebar this page).

LOCATION: **Historic Blakeley State Park, 34745 Hwy. 225, Spanish Fort, 251-626-0798, www.blakeleypark.com.**

FURTHER READING

History of the Campaign of Mobile
by Christopher Columbus Andrews
A reissue of the 1889 printing

✳ Mobile Bay

CAMPAIGN: Operations in Mobile Bay
DATE(S): August 2–23, 1864

After the fall of New Orleans in 1862, Mobile Bay was one of the last deepwater ports serving the Confederacy. Confederate defenses were daunting. The mouth of the bay, protected by Fort Morgan to the east and Forts Gaines and Powell to the west, was booby-trapped with pilings and submerged mines designed to force enemy vessels through a channel within point-blank range of Fort Morgan's massive guns. Secondary defenses included three partially clad gunboats, the 1,273-ton ironclad ram C.S.S. *Tennessee,* and several earthen fortifications.

On August 5, as an 18-vessel fleet of Union gunboats and monitors headed into the bay, the lead monitor, U.S.S. *Tecumseh,*

Mobile's Surrender

With the loss of New Orleans in April 1862, Mobile was the closest port on the Gulf Coast for blockade-runners coming from Cuba. The capture of Forts Morgan and Gaines in August 1864, however, cut off access to the city. After the Federals seized Spanish Fort and Fort Blakeley in the spring of 1865, they moved into Mobile with little resistance. Although Confederate forces were present, they abandoned the city without a fight on April 11. The next day, as Union troops moved into the city, bands reportedly played "Yankee Doodle."

Confederate General Taylor (son of President Zachary Taylor) and Union General Canby agreed to a gentlemanly truce on April 30. Once instructions were received from the governments, Taylor surrendered his command of 12,000 men—the last organized forces—to Canby at Citronelle, north of Mobile, on May 5, 1865, officially ending combat east of the Mississippi.

This bronze door panel shows Confederate President Jefferson Davis after taking office.

Incorporated in 1819, the city of Montgomery became Alabama's capital in 1846 and briefly served as capital of the Confederate States of America from February to late May 1861. Although no battles occurred in this central Alabama city, it did play a rather significant role in the Civil War.

On April 11, 1861, Confederate General Beauregard, who was in Charleston at the time, received a telegram authorizing "firing" on Fort Sumter. The telegram's fascinating wording still resonates:

Do not desire needlessly to bombard Fort Sumter. If Major Anderson will state the time at which, as indicated by him, he will evacuate, and agree that in the meantime he will not use his guns against us unless ours should be employed against Fort Sumter, you are thus authorized to avoid the effusion of blood. If this or its equivalent be refused, reduce the fort as your judgment decides to be most practicable.
    From Sec. of War L.P. Walker

Montgomery is home to the First White House of the Confederacy (see p. 35), though not in its original location. Jefferson Davis and his family lived here before the capital of the Confederacy moved to Richmond, Virginia. On the steps of the state capitol, a six-point brass star marks the spot where Davis took the oath of office. Inside is the original Senate chamber where the Confederacy began. Significant information related to the Civil War can also be found at the Alabama Department of Archives and History (www.archives .state.al.us).

FURTHER READING
"A Government of Our Own": The Making of the Confederacy
by William C. Davis
Traces the political forces that shaped the Confederacy

Admiral Farragut watches as battle smoke helps the U.S.S. *Hartford* slip past Fort Morgan.

hit a mine and sank immediately. Unable to back up or turn his fleet around, Admiral Farragut reportedly gave orders to "Damn the torpedoes!, full speed ahead!" The raw courage of Farragut's ship commanders and dense smoke from Fort Morgan's belching batteries provided Farragut's ships with unexpected cover to slip past.

Once past the forts, technological superiority worked in Farragut's favor. The Federal monitor gunboats, touting 360-degree swiveling turrets, could quickly change aim as targets moved, while the fixed cannons of the Confederate ironclad and its sister gunboats required considerable maneuvering to get into firing position. The Union fleet's firepower soon overwhelmed the C.S.S. *Tennessee,* which was forced to surrender. Forts Morgan and Gaines later succumbed to land assault.

Today, panoramic views of the battle area are available from either Fort Morgan or Fort Gaines, both substantially modified during subsequent wars. A yellow buoy in the bay marks the site were the U.S.S. *Tecumseh* sank and still rests today. A self-guided tour map is available on-site or online. Both fortresses may also be viewed from the water via car ferry between Mobile Point and Dauphin Island.

LOCATION: **Fort Morgan, 110 Hwy. 180, Gulf Shores, 251-540-7127, www.fort-morgan.org; Fort Gaines, 51 Bienville Blvd., Dauphin Island, 251-861-6992, www.dauphinisland.org /fort-gaines.**

FURTHER READING

West Wind, Flood Tide: The Battle of Mobile Bay
by Jack Friend
Traces the course of this landmark naval battle and its lasting influence

✳ Selma

CAMPAIGN: Wilson's Raid in Alabama and Georgia

DATE(S): April 2, 1865

Probably the most important military manufacturing center of the Confederacy, Selma was spared the ravages of war until 1865.

Situated along the banks of the Alabama River, this inland city had a thriving naval yard with direct access to Mobile Bay. On April 2, 1865, Selma also proved to be the last battleground for the great Confederate cavalryman General Forrest.

For several days prior, Forrest skirmished with General Wilson's mounted army across Alabama trying to protect Selma's industry, but the die was cast on April 1, 1865, at the battle of Ebenezer Church in Stanton. Forrest's plan to surprise and outflank Wilson's army failed for lack of reinforcements.

Outnumbered and outarmed, Forrest moved on to Selma, 25 miles away, where semicircular earthworks extended for three miles around the town. He arrived with an army only one-fifth of what was needed to properly defend a fort of that size.

Forrest was not blind to the reality of his predicament. By then his mission focused on stalling Wilson's forces long enough to move or destroy supplies that would otherwise fall into Union hands. He failed, and the war ended shortly after Forrest surrendered at Gaylesville.

There is no publicly accessible battlefield in Selma. Explore the Old Depot Museum, built on the site of a Confederate naval foundry destroyed during the battle. At Old Live Oak Cemetery huge oaks covered in Spanish moss shade the graves of many Civil War soldiers, as well as Elodie Todd Dawson, an avid Confederate and half sister of Mary Todd Lincoln. Also in the cemetery find Confederate Memorial Circle and a memorial to the Union dead.

LOCATION: Old Depot Museum, 4 Martin Luther King St., Selma, 334-874-2197; Old Live Oak Cemetery, 110 W. Dallas Ave., Selma, 334-874-2161, www.selma alabama.com.

FURTHER READING

Yankee Blitzkrieg: Wilson's Raid Through Alabama and Georgia by James Pickett Jones First comprehensive account of Wilson's raid

✸ Spanish Fort

CAMPAIGN: Mobile Campaign
DATE(S): March 27–April 8, 1865

Set high on a bluff at the northeast side of Mobile Bay, the massive earthworks of Spanish Fort presented one of Mobile's last defenses. Underwater mines and elevation restrictions on the Union's naval guns helped reduce attacks from the water, but land approaches were more vulnerable.

In late March 1865, Union General Canby slowly and methodically led 32,000 troops up the east side of the bay to lay siege to the fort. For 12 days Spanish Fort withstood the attack. Reeling from a massive Union bombardment late on April 8, however, General Gibson—whose forces had been outnumbered four to one—withdrew his troops silently and under cover of darkness, escaping to Fort Blakeley eight miles away, then on to Mobile. When Canby's forces entered the fort, only a few hundred Confederate defenders remained.

In April 2015, a restored and interpreted Fort McDermott was opened on the right of the Confederate line on the Blakeley River. This impressive site is on Spanish Main Dr. in a Spanish Fort subdivision.

Confederate sergeant's jacket worn at Gainesville surrender

LOCATION: Spanish Fort City Hall, 7581 Spanish Fort Blvd. (Hwy. 31), Spanish Fort, 251-626-4884.

Other Battles and Beyond

✦ "Alabama Civil War Trails"

Updated in 2014, this brochure covers five Civil War trails totaling 35 stops. Trails include Cradle of the Confederacy, Streight's Raid, Ironworks, Last Battle (Mobile Bay), and Tennessee Valley. It is available at welcome centers statewide and online at www .alabama.travel/trails. Or order a free copy by calling 800-252-2262.

✦ Athens and Limestone County Civil War Trail Driving Tour

This self-guided driving tour features the Battle of Athens (Sulphur Creek Trestle). Pick up a tour brochure at the Athens Visitor Center (100 Beaty St. N., Athens, 256-232-5411), or download a copy at www.tour athens.com.

✦ Blue and Gray: North Alabama Civil War Museum

Displays include artifacts, uniforms, photos, letters, drums, and weapons of all kinds.

LOCATION: 723 Bank St., Decatur, 256-350-4018, www.alabamacivilwarmuseum.com.

✦ Brierfield Ironworks Historical State Park

Tour historic ruins of the only iron producer taken over by the Confederacy (1863), which renamed it Bibb Naval Furnaces. The site also includes pioneer-style homes and buildings, hiking trails, and camping.

LOCATION: 240 Furnace Pkwy., Brierfield, 205-665-1856, www.brierfieldironworks.com.

Destroyed by General Wilson's cavalry raid in March 1865, the massive Tannehill Ironworks blast furnaces, now restored, highlight Alabama's industrial wartime role.

✦ Cornwall Furnace Veterans Memorial Park

See a preserved 35-foot Civil War–era cold blast furnace in its original location. Slaves hand dug the canal that powered the furnace, which is now on the National Register of Historic Places.

LOCATION: **Shore of Weiss Lake at 1200 County Rd. 251, Cedar Bluff, 256-927-7275, www .ccparkboard.com.**

✦ First White House of the Confederacy

Tour the fully furnished executive residence of President Jefferson Davis and his family.

LOCATION: **644 Washington Ave., Montgomery, 334-242-1861, www.firstwhitehouse.org.**

✦ Montgomery State Capitol

Self-guided tours are available Monday through Friday. Prearranged guided tours are available on Saturdays.

LOCATION: **600 Dexter Ave., Montgomery, 334-242-3935, www.preserveala.org.**

✦ Old Cahawba Archaeological Park

This park encompasses the site of Castle Morgan Prison, a 200-by-125-foot warehouse that once held 3,000 Union prisoners. Though it was unimaginably crowded, only 2 percent of the prison's population succumbed to disease. After being released, however, many prisoners died on the ill-fated steamship *Sultana*. Pick up the park's Explorer's Guide at the visitor center.

LOCATION: **9518 Cahaba Rd., Orrville, 334-872-8058.**

✦ Tannehill Ironworks Historical State Park

See three blast furnaces that produced 22 tons of iron a day for the Confederate

Rear view of General Wheeler's postwar, 1870 home at Pond Spring

military effort and learn about the process in the park's Iron and Steel Museum. Also enjoy hiking, camping, and seasonal living-history demonstrations.

LOCATION: **12632 Confederate Pkwy., McCalla, 205-477-5711, www.tannehill.org.**

✦ Wheeler Home (Pond Spring)

Period buildings, original memorabilia and furnishings, and gardens grace the 50-acre property that once belonged to Joseph Wheeler and his family. In addition to General Stuart, Robert E. Lee considered "Fightin' Joe" to be one of the two outstanding cavalrymen of the war.

LOCATION: **12280 Hwy. 20, Hillsboro (14 miles west of Decatur), 256-637-8513, www.preserve ala.org.**

Arkansas

THOUGH THE MOST IMPORTANT BATTLES OF THE CIVIL WAR were contested elsewhere, Arkansas was of strategic importance to both sides. Indeed, more than 750 encounters took place within the state. Of chief concern geographically was the Mississippi River: The Union aimed to open the river for commercial navigation, while the Confederacy wished to keep it closed in order to increase economic pressure on the isolated northwestern states. Additionally, both sides struggled for control of neighboring Missouri, with Confederate forces, intent on liberating the state, assembling in Arkansas. In fact, the two decisive battles for Missouri—Pea Ridge and Prairie Grove—were fought on Arkansas soil. Interestingly, Arkansas did not immediately reject the election of Abraham Lincoln and aligned with the new Confederacy only after Lincoln asked for Arkansas soldiers to help subdue the rebellious states. As a frontier border state, Arkansas was more concerned with the threat of Indians to the west than with the Unionists; however, in actuality, Native Americans fought on both sides.

General Parsons' troops attack at Prairie Grove. The Rebels' ultimate withdrawal preserved U.S. control of Missouri and northwest Arkansas.

ARKANSAS BATTLES

Missouri

Pea Ridge

Chalk Bluff

Prairie Grove
Cane Hill

Okla.

Fort Smith National Historic Site

Devil's Backbone

Massard Prairie Battlefield Park

Arkansas

Tenn.

Hill's Plantation

Bayou Meto

Little Rock ★
Little Rock Campaign Driving Tour;
Old State House Museum;
Pratt C. Remmel Park

Bayou Fourche

Helena

Battery C Park;
Freedom Park;
Helena Museum

St. Charles
Pine Bluff

Jenkins' Ferry

Elkin's Ferry

Pine Bluff/
Jefferson County
Historical Museum

Arkansas Post

Nevada County Depot
and Museum

Prairie
D'Ane

Miss.

Historic
Washington
State Park

Poison
Spring

Marks' Mills

Texas

Old River Lake

0 mi   50
0 km   50

Louisiana

✳ Arkansas Post

CAMPAIGN: Operations Against Vicksburg
DATE(S): January 9–11, 1863

This site overlooking the Arkansas River once served as the capital of the Arkansas Territory. In 1863, it was a fortified position protecting the water route toward the new capital at Little Rock. After a failed assault on Vicksburg in December 1862, General McClernand temporarily commandeered General Sherman, along with Admiral Porter, to reopen the Mississippi River for commerce. McClernand drove the Confederate forces back into the fort while also sending ironclad gunboats to hammer the main earthworks at Fort Hindman. Union forces soon overwhelmed the fort's defenders, and on January 11, they took 4,800 Confederate troops prisoner. The battle and the "lost town" are depicted through museum displays, a video, and interpretive signs.

LOCATION: Arkansas Post National Memorial, 1741 Old Post Rd., Gillett, 870-548-2207, www.nps.gov/arpo.

FURTHER READING

Major General John Alexander McClernand: Politician in Uniform by Richard Kiper
A sympathetic account of the controversial leader

This 1849 Colt pocket revolver was used at Fort Hindman in Arkansas Post.

✳ Bayou Fourche

CAMPAIGN: Advance on Little Rock
DATE(S): September 10, 1863

On September 10, 1863, General Steele forced a Rebel rear guard under command of General Marmaduke to evacuate its position north of the Arkansas River and withdraw to Little Rock. In the face of Steele's move to take the capital, the town was evacuated and the state capitol removed to Washington, Arkansas.

Check out the Little Rock Campaign Driving Tour (see p. 50), and visit Pratt C. Remmel Park, where interpretive panels explain how the battle progressed (see p. 51). Then proceed one mile to the stone monument at Fourche Creek. The heaviest part of the battle took place to the northwest, where the Rebels tried to halt the Union advance toward Little Rock.

LOCATION: Monument near 6214 Fourche Dam Pike and E. Roosevelt Rd., Little Rock.

✳ Bayou Meto

CAMPAIGN: Advance on Little Rock
OTHER NAME(S): Reed's Bridge
DATE(S): August 27, 1863

This significant encounter delayed the Union advance on Little Rock and led to a duel between Confederate Generals Marmaduke and Walker, in which Walker was mortally wounded.

The battle began with a Union attack that drove the Confederate forces across the Bayou Meto. The Confederates burned Reed's Bridge as they went, preventing Union troops from following them across the stream. By nightfall, after an artillery

Union ironclads bombard the earthworks of Fort Hindman at Arkansas Post in January 1863.

duel, the Union forces had retreated. This was the last time that Confederate forces successfully repulsed the Union advance on Little Rock.

Despite its roadside location, the battlefield still looks much as it did in 1863.

LOCATION: **Reed's Bridge Battlefield Heritage Park, AR 161 just south of the intersection with Dennis Ln. in Jacksonville, www.reedsbridge battlefield.com.**

✳ Cane Hill

CAMPAIGN: Prairie Grove Campaign

DATE(S): November 28, 1862

This engagement, the prelude to the larger battle at Prairie Grove (see pp. 48–49), was fought in the rugged northwest corner of Arkansas at the northern end of the Boston Mountains. The settlement included three villages and Cane Hill College, the first college in the state.

On November 27, 1862, General Blunt marched 5,000 men rapidly south through rough country, preparing to take on General Marmaduke's Confederate cavalry and claim Cane Hill.

Realizing that his forces were outnumbered two to one, Marmaduke deliberately designed a plan to stretch out the day by withdrawing only one brigade of soldiers at a time. The tactic was successful. Although the fighting lasted for nine hours over more than 12 miles, the relatively bloodless battle ended with fewer than 100 combined casualties littering the field.

Listed on the National Register of Historic Places in 1994, the Cane Hill battlefield extends for more than 5,000 acres around the modern town of Canehill. Although the site has not been preserved, overall it retains much of its 1862 character. Many areas are visible from public roadways, and, while a single sign marks the battlefield site, additional interpretive signs can be found headed into town.

LOCATION: **Marker located near 14311 Hwy. 45, just north of Patterson Rd. in Canehill.**

✳ Chalk Bluff

CAMPAIGN: Marmaduke's Second Expedition Into Missouri

DATE(S): May 1–2, 1863

After his second raid into Missouri failed, General Marmaduke, with Union General Vandever in pursuit, led 5,000 men on a fighting retreat along Crowley's Ridge—a key north-south route above the swamps of northeast Arkansas—toward Chalk Bluff.

Needing to cross the St. Francis River, which forms a boundary between Arkansas and Missouri, Marmaduke's forces built a floating log bridge and raft on the rising water. While crossing on May 1–2, Union troops attacked his rear guard. Although most of Marmaduke's raiders successfully crossed the river during the night, several hundred Rebels from Texas and their horses were not so lucky: They ended up swimming back to Arkansas when the bridge collapsed.

A paved, handicap-accessible riverside trail winds through Chalk Bluff Battlefield Park along the banks of the St. Francis River to an enjoyable view of Crowley's Ridge.

John S. Marmaduke, a Confederate general, became governor of Missouri in 1884.

Interior of the original Fort Curtis, Helena's key earthen defense. The July 4, 1863, Union victory here was dwarfed by those at Gettysburg and Vicksburg.

Interpretive signs describe the battle and the former town of Chalk Bluff.

LOCATION: Chalk Bluff Battlefield Park, County Rd. 368, St. Francis, 870-598-2667.

✳ Devil's Backbone

CAMPAIGN: Operations to Control Indian Territory

DATE(S): September 1, 1863

Hoping to retake Fort Smith from Union forces, General Cabell set an ambush along the base of Backbone Mountain. As the three-hour firefight raged, Union forces commanded by Colonel Cloud began to run out of ammunition, unaware that several hundred Confederate troops had inexplicably fled from the battlefield. General Cabell had no choice but to retreat in the face of certain defeat. In the end, more soldiers ran away than were hurt; combined casualties numbered just 31.

Although located on private property, Devil's Backbone is visible from CR 52 off US 71.

LOCATION: Marker located south of Fort Smith, on US 71 in Greenwood.

✳ Elkin's Ferry

CAMPAIGN: Camden Expedition

DATE(S): April 3–4, 1864

Seeking a ford to cross the Little Missouri River, General Steele's Union troops were attacked by General Marmaduke's cavalry at Elkin's Ferry, a key crossing site south of Okalona. Confederate General Price feared Steele's forces were heading southwest to wage battle at Washington, Arkansas, the new Confederate capital. Angry honeybees ended the first skirmish on April 3. Outnumbered two to one, Marmaduke's efforts ultimately failed, and Union troops proceeded to Prairie D'Ane.

Elkin's Ferry Battlefield extends from Okalona south to the Little Missouri River through an area still fairly undisturbed today. The actual river crossing is an unmarked site with a canoe launch at the end of a gravel road. A state marker is at Missionary Grove Baptist Church en route to the landing. Learn more at the Nevada County Depot and Museum in Prescott (see p. 51).

LOCATION: Elkin's Ferry Crossing is 10 miles north of Prescott, off Hwy. 51 at CR 37, where it ends at the Little Missouri River. A marker stands one mile north of Okalona on CR 55.

✳ Helena

CAMPAIGN: Grant's Operations Against Vicksburg

DATE(S): July 4, 1863

Labeled "Hell in Arkansas" by Union troops because of its muddy, buggy setting, the port city of Helena—which had been occupied by Federal forces in July 1862—was an important staging area for control of the upper Mississippi in 1862 and 1863; Sherman's expedition to Chickasaw Bayou departed from here (see p. 125). It had also become a refuge for thousands of freed slaves, many of whom were recruited into the Union Army.

Unable to attack Federal supply depots at Lake Providence (because of the breech of the Mississippi River levee at Ashton), Confederates under General Holmes attacked Helena in hopes of lifting the siege at Vicksburg. Sadly for the Confederates, Vicksburg was surrendered on the same day of the battle. Furthermore, Helena was no pushover. Indeed, General Prentiss used the topography to his advantage, having developed Fort Curtis and four solid earthen batteries, A–D, built on hills approaching the city.

The Confederates attacked with a two-to-one manpower advantage at dawn on July 4. Though repulsed repeatedly, they gained footholds near some of the batteries. Nevertheless, effective artillery fire and heavy ordnance from the Federal gunboat *Tyler* broke their spirit. The battle ended before noon. With Lee's defeat at Gettysburg and Vicksburg's surrender, July 4, 1863, was a banner day for the Union.

Seven Confederate generals, including Cleburne and Hindman, were from Helena, so the city is awash in Civil War history. Offering wide views over the city, Battery C is the only site breached by the Confederates and the only one of the four battery sites open to the public today (see p. 50). A three-quarter replica of Fort Curtis stands three blocks from the original earthen site. For impressive views of the Mississippi, stroll through Helena River Park, which also has

Confederate Policies Toward Black Soldiers

The issue of manpower affected war efforts in both the North and the South. In the North, the reluctance to use the draft to conscript soldiers led the government to seek other forms of "voluntary manpower." Issued on January 1, 1863, the Emancipation Proclamation opened the path for the enrollment of more than 175,000 black soldiers. While not all of them ended up in combat roles, the physical presence of armed blacks in the Union Army aroused the Confederacy, which declared these soldiers insurrectionists. If captured, they would be executed or returned to bondage. Southern soldiers—who needed little incentive to treat black soldiers harshly—attacked the issue with relish, and black soldiers understood that every Confederate soldier was a potential "slave catcher."

The South did consider enrolling black slaves in its armies with a promise of manumission after the war. The issue was politically and emotionally charged, however, and men such as General Cleburne were muzzled for suggesting black enlistment in 1864. It finally took someone of General Lee's stature to encourage the enrollment of blacks. By April 1865 the first such soldiers were training in Richmond, though they never entered the army.

interpretive signs of the battle. Don't miss the graves of Generals Cleburne and Hindman. The Helena/West Helena Welcome Center offers a "Civil War Helena Tour" brochure of several dozen interpreted spots. It can be downloaded or picked up at the center.

LOCATION: Helena/West Helena Welcome Center, 1007 Martin Luther King Dr., Helena, 870-338-7602, www.civilwarhelena.com.

✳ Hill's Plantation

CAMPAIGN: Pea Ridge Campaign

DATE(S): July 7, 1862

Having arrived too late to ambush Union troops at Cache Creek, the Confederate forces led by General Rust were forced to confront General Curtis's Union troops at Hill's Plantation, about four miles south of Cache Creek near Cotton Plant. Several of the Confederate attacks failed. Nevertheless, Curtis failed to reach the supply ships and turned his force eastward to Helena, where he took command of the city and oversaw Federal operations in Arkansas.

LOCATION: The battle site, which is on private property, is unmarked and not accessible.

✳ Jenkins' Ferry

CAMPAIGN: Camden Expedition

DATE(S): April 30, 1864

After losing large wagon trains to Rebel forces at Poison Spring (see pp. 46–47) and Marks' Mills (see p. 44), General Steele abandoned his campaign for Camden and withdrew to Little Rock. As his forces crossed the Saline River, they encountered knee-deep mud, water moccasins, and floodwater, but the Confederates could not gain the advantage. Protected by log fortifications, Steele's 4,000 Federal infantry beat back an early morning attack and crossed the river on hastily built pontoon boats. The Confederates were unable to follow. Having heard of the alleged massacre of blacks at Poison Spring and Marks' Mills, black members of the 1st Kansas Infantry are said to have murdered a number of Confederate soldiers and captives. Two days later Steele's men entered Little Rock.

Jenkins Ferry Battleground State Park is a small site on the Saline River with several interpretive signs and a picnic area but no restrooms. The actual battlefield, which is located on private property about one mile across the river, is not accessible.

LOCATION: Jenkins Ferry Battleground State Park, 13 miles south of Sheridan on AR 46 at the crossing of the Saline River, 888-AT-PARKS, www.arkansasstateparks.com.

This battle flag was once carried by the 22nd/35th Reg. Arkansas Volunteer Infantry.

☀ Marks' Mills

CAMPAIGN: Camden Expedition
DATE(S): April 25, 1864

Ensconced at Camden and dependent on resupply from Little Rock and Pine Bluff, General Steele suffered a major blow when 240 wagons, empty after a successful delivery, and their escort were cut off by forces more than twice their number under Confederate Generals Fagan and Shelby. The Federals held their own until their commander, Colonel Drake, was wounded. Union resistance collapsed, and 1,000 Federals were captured, along with the entire complement of wagons. It is alleged that of the 300 black freedmen accompanying the column, more than 100 were murdered and 150 taken prisoner.

The destruction of this second major supply train caused Steele to abandon plans to support Banks in Louisiana. He returned to Little Rock on May 2 after fighting a rearguard action at Jenkins' Ferry on April 30.

Marks' Mills Battleground State Park and the nearby cemetery have some interpretive signs but no facilities or staff on-site. A brochure about the battle, as well as the battles of Jenkins' Ferry (see p. 43) and Poison Spring (see pp. 46–47), is available at the park and on the website.

LOCATION: Marks' Mills Battleground State Park, 8 miles southeast of Fordyce at the junction of AR 8 and AR 97, 888-AT-PARKS, www.arkansasstateparks.com.

☀ Old River Lake

CAMPAIGN: Expedition to Lake Village
OTHER NAME(S): Ditch Bayou
DATE(S): June 6, 1864

Throughout the war, Rebel troops often used guerrilla tactics to harass Federal supply and transport ships traveling on the Mississippi River. One such vantage point was Greenville Bend, where, after firing from the riverbank, the Confederates would disappear into the heavy forest, causing much angst for Union troops bent on retaliation.

On June 6, 1864, 3,000 Union troops sent to sack the settlement at Lake Village clashed with 600 Confederates at Ditch Bayou, the last major Civil War engagement in Arkansas. Confederate Colonel Greene ambushed Union troops commanded by General Mower by stationing his men and artillery behind a deep natural fortification, invisible to the mile-wide line of Yankees approaching across an open field.

Though outnumbering the Rebels by more than five to one, Mower's men could not maneuver around them. Greene's aggressive defense sent Mower's troops into temporary retreat before the

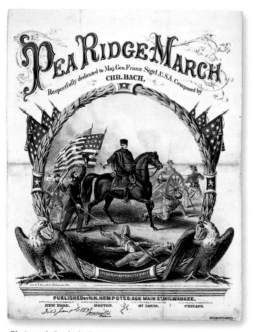

Christoph Bach dedicated "Pea Ridge March" (1862) to Franz Sigel, a Union major general.

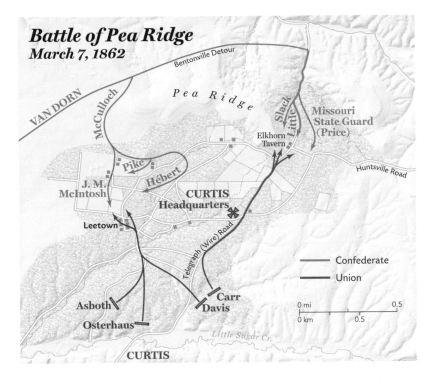

Battle of Pea Ridge
March 7, 1862

Bentonville Detour

Pea Ridge

VAN DORN

McCulloch

Missouri State Guard (Price)

Shack

Little

Elkhorn Tavern

Huntsville Road

Pike

Hébert

J. M. McIntosh

CURTIS Headquarters

Leetown

Telegraph (Wire) Road

Asboth

Carr Davis

Osterhaus

Little Sugar Cr.

CURTIS

Confederate
Union

0 mi   0.5
0 km   0.5

Confederates themselves fell back. Mower's men then advanced to Lake Village, sacked it, and returned to join the remainder of their troops.

The Old River Lake battlefield is now located on private property.

LOCATION: Markers located on US 82, 1.8 miles east of US 65, southeast of Lake Village at Lake Chicot and the mouth of Ditch Bayou.

✳ Pea Ridge

CAMPAIGN: Pea Ridge Campaign
OTHER NAME(S): Elkhorn Tavern
DATE(S): March 6–8, 1862

About 26,000 men fought at Pea Ridge in rugged northwest Arkansas. Noteworthy for the participation of about 800 Cherokee Indians under the command of Confederate General Pike, himself an Indian, this battle helped seal Union control of Missouri and

paved the way for Federal inroads throughout Arkansas.

With an opportunity to catch Federal forces off guard, General Van Dorn, commander of the Army of the West and a cavalryman, sent Generals Price and McCulloch on separate routes around Elkhorn Mountain. Their mission was to attack both flanks of the Union Army. By many accounts, this was a perfect opportunity to crush General Curtis's Army of the Southwest, which was outnumbered in men and artillery. However, Van Dorn failed because he overtaxed his infantry and pushed them beyond the point of exhaustion. Having reached the Union's vulnerable supply line, Van Dorn was unable to seal the deal. Cold, hungry, and without supplies, the Confederate troops performed poorly.

On the morning of March 7, McCulloch's right flank division crossed farmland near

Leetown as Union skirmishers, tucked within a heavy tree line, fired at his troops. In what has been referred to as the Confederate's "crisis in command," McCulloch was killed by a Union sniper. His second in command, James McIntosh, fell immediately after.

General Price's left flank forces attacked from the northern end of the battlefield, near Elkhorn Tavern. Despite earlier losses, the Confederates seemed to be holding their own by the evening of March 7. By the next day, however, Van Dorn's army found itself without sufficient ammunition while Curtis's Union troops had received reinforcements of men and artillery. Van Dorn and his army retreated rather than face certain defeat.

Today, Pea Ridge National Military Park is one of the most pristine Civil War battlefields in the nation. The park's seven-mile interpretive driving tour of battlefield sites includes Leetown and the reconstructed Elkhorn Tavern. Catch living-history demonstrations and explore interactive exhibits.

Objects on display include actual items from the battle such as weapons, artifacts, and General Curtis's coat.

LOCATION: **Pea Ridge National Military Park, 15930 E. Hwy. 62, Garfield, 479-451-8122, www.nps.gov/peri.**

FURTHER READING

Pea Ridge: Civil War Campaign in the West
by William L. Shea and Earl J. Hess
An engrossing campaign history

✳ Pine Bluff

CAMPAIGN: Advance on Little Rock
DATE(S): October 25, 1863

Once Union forces occupied Little Rock, they began reaching deeper into the state. Colonel Powell Clayton and two regiments garrisoned Pine Bluff, 40 miles south on a sharp bend in the Arkansas River. Marmaduke's plans for a surprise attack on the town were thwarted as a Union patrol discovered his approach. Subsequent attacks failed to dislodge the Federals.

LOCATION: **Markers on the grounds of Jefferson County Courthouse, 101 W. Barraque St., Pine Bluff.**

✳ Poison Spring

CAMPAIGN: Camden Expedition
DATE(S): April 18, 1864

By April 1864, Federal forces controlled most of the Arkansas River and areas north but were plagued by food shortages. As a remedy, General Steele's forces in Camden attempted to forage locally but were thwarted by Rebels and their sympathizers, who got to available provisions first.

Having learned that Confederates had 5,000 bushels of corn stored about 20 miles away near White Oak Creek, Steele sent Colonel Williams and 1,100 Union cavalry

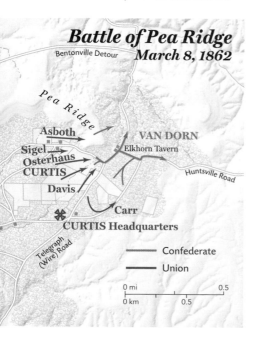

Battle of Pea Ridge
Bentonville Detour **March 8, 1862**

Pea Ridge

Asboth
Sigel
Osterhaus
CURTIS
Davis
VAN DORN
Elkhorn Tavern
Huntsville Road

Carr
✳ CURTIS Headquarters

Telegraph (Wire) Road

— Confederate
— Union

0 mi   0.5
0 km   0.5

Elkhorn Tavern at Pea Ridge got its name from the elk horns on the roof's ridge.

and infantry, including 500 1st Kansas Infantry Colored Volunteers, on a foraging mission. Finding only a partial store of corn remaining, the troops expanded their haul by plundering farms along the way, filling about 198 mule-drawn wagons with corn and other provisions.

Hearing of Williams's expedition, the Confederates pooled five brigades totaling 3,600 men, including Choctaw and Chickasaw Indians, and intercepted the Union supply train on its way back to Camden. The Rebels blocked a section of the Camden-Washington Road, and a fierce battle ensued. In the end, the Confederates captured the wagons and their contents and drove Williams's forces into retreat empty-handed.

What started as a maneuver to deny necessary supplies to Steele's army is still tainted with accusations that many of the black soldiers were brutally murdered as they were retreating or after they surrendered to the Confederate troops. According to some stories, the blacks were massacred and mutilated by some of the Indians, whose way of war included mutilation of defeated foes as a means of denying the enemy a peaceful afterlife.

See interpretive signs and a diorama of the battle and troop positions at the very small, unstaffed park. The walking trail does

not enter the battlefield but does move along the watercourse of Poison Spring.

LOCATION: **Poison Springs Battleground State Park, AR 76, 10 miles west of Camden, www.arkansasstateparks.com.**

✳ Prairie D'Ane

CAMPAIGN: Camden Expedition
DATE(S): April 9–13, 1864

The second battle in the Camden Expedition was a ruse to draw General Price away from Camden so General Steele could take his command, resupply them, and head to Shreveport. Price's army, thinking Steele was aiming for Washington, Arkansas's capital, built defensive earthen fortifications at Prairie D'Ane, a 30-square-mile area of open grassland surrounded by forest. Steele's forces arrived and set up their own defenses, and for two days they enjoyed hunting and relaxing between light skirmishes.

During the night of April 11, Price moved his troops closer to Washington, as Shelby and Marmaduke moved their forces toward modern-day Hope. In the meantime, Steele realized he could not reach Shreveport and occupied Camden, clashing with Price's forces on April 13.

Prairie D'Ane, the largest of Arkansas's battlefields, is still grassland, privately owned, and not open to the public. The Nevada County Depot and Museum has a diorama of the battle (see p. 51).

LOCATION: **Marker at TA Travel Center on Hwy. 371 at I-30.**

✳ Prairie Grove

CAMPAIGN: Prairie Grove Campaign
DATE(S): December 7, 1862

Referred to as the bloodiest battle in Arkansas, this decisive encounter for control of northwest Arkansas and neighboring Missouri resulted in more than 2,500 casualties, fairly evenly split.

The Army of the Frontier was divided into two groups primed to move into Arkansas. General Herron commanded two divisions advancing from Springfield, Missouri, while General Blunt had one holding at Cane Hill.

General Hindman, commander of the Army of the Trans-Mississippi, still had his eye on Missouri, but first he needed to defeat and drive back both Union forces before they joined together. His initial target was Blunt, but as Herron's forces covered 100 miles in just over three days, his priorities changed.

Early on December 7, Hindman tricked Herron into thinking the Rebel troops first encountered near Prairie Grove Church represented his entire force. The bulk of Hindman's two divisions were hidden among trees along Prairie Grove Ridge near the Borden family home and orchard, where they had a sweeping view of the Illinois River Valley. Several times Confederate artillery deterred Herron's efforts to cross the river and take the ridge, but fortunes changed as Blunt's division arrived that afternoon to attack the Confederate's unprotected left flank. Caught between the Union divisions, the Rebels fought tenaciously. One soldier noted afterward that so many dead bodies littered the field and ridge slope that one could walk without touching the ground.

The presumed victor status changed several more times throughout the day, but in reality, the Union's rifled cannons fired farther and more accurately than the Rebels' smoothbore ones. Outgunned, Hindman's dejected

Anthony Thomas's "The Bayonet or Retreat" shows infantry during the Battle of Prairie Grove.

soldiers made a stealthy retreat after midnight, muffling the sounds of their artillery wheels with blankets as they headed south toward Van Buren. The next morning, Union troops, finding the ridge deserted, plundered the Borden house and then set it and several others on fire.

Much of the battlefield remains agricultural land. A must-see, Prairie Grove Battleground State Park protects one-fourth of the original site. Highlights include interactive displays, a one-mile walking trail where the heaviest fighting took place, and a five-mile, 14-stop driving tour extending beyond the park to key battle areas. Also onsite is the Morrow House, where Hindman made final plans for battle.

LOCATION: **Prairie Grove Battleground State Park, 506 E. Douglas St., Prairie Grove, 479-846-2990, www.arkansasstateparks.com.**

FURTHER READING

Fields of Blood: The Prairie Grove Campaign by William Shea A gripping narrative of the fateful clash

✳ Saint Charles

CAMPAIGN: Operations on the White River
DATE(S): June 17, 1862

This Confederate battery above the White River was one of the few Confederate posts remaining in Arkansas after the Battle of Pea Ridge (see pp. 45–46). Indeed, Arkansas was nearly defenseless as many Confederate forces were now east of the Mississippi.

The Saint Charles battery aimed to stop Federal supply ships en route to Jacksonport, headquarters of General Curtis. On June 17, Captain Fry sank three Confederate vessels to block the river. In preparation, the Rebels readied firing positions on a west bank hill. As the Union flotilla came within 600 yards, the U.S.S. *Mound City* suffered a direct hit from a 32-pound cannonball, exploding her steam drum. In what historian

Brown Water Navy

During the Civil War, the term "brown water navy" referred to Federal gunboats that patrolled inland. These were not seaworthy ships like the larger vessels that guarded coastal harbors and fended off blockade-runners. Brown water vessels were required to maneuver in narrow, shallow waters while being strong enough to carry heavy armaments and withstand enemy artillery. Out of practicality, timberclad gunboats soon gave way to ironclads.

The idea of a brown water navy seems to have been spurred by General Scott's Anaconda Plan, which relied heavily on using the Mississippi River and its tributaries to divide the Confederacy and cut off its main supply and transport routes. It demonstrated its utility at Shiloh, Memphis, and during the Vicksburg and Red River Campaigns.

FURTHER READING

Mr. Lincoln's Brown Water Navy: The Mississippi Squadron by Gary D. Joiner The Civil War as fought on the rivers of the West

Ed Bearss called "the most destructive single shot" of the war, more than half of the *Mound City*'s crew perished, many of them scalded.

Union infantry overran the battery and captured Captain Fry. Shallow water stopped naval efforts to continue upriver, so Curtis received his delayed provisions by land.

LOCATION: **See a diorama of the battle and learn about the firing on the U.S.S. *Mound City* at the St. Charles Museum, located inside Town Hall, 608 Broadway St., St. Charles, 870-282-3425. Battle marker located on Belknap Ave. near the intersection with River View Dr. in St. Charles.**

Other Battles and Beyond

✦ Cell-Phone Battlefield Tours

The Department of Arkansas Heritage offers audio tours covering select battlefield sites throughout the state, including Bayou Fourche, Cane Hill, Elkin's Ferry, Prairie D'Ane, Poison Spring, Marks' Mills, Jenkins' Ferry, Ditch Bayou (Old River Lake), and several others. Access the tours online at www.arkansaspreservation.com/learn-more/audio-tours or dial 501-203-3015 and enter the stop number found on the markers.

✦ Little Rock Campaign Driving Tour

Follow the Union approach to Little Rock via an eight-stop route that interprets the fall of the state's capital. Download the brochure at www.littlerock.org/drivingtour.

A monument to the Battle of Bayou Fourche notes Confederate and Union military units.

✦ Battery C Park

See the hilltop site of one of Helena's four Civil War batteries.

LOCATION: **Perry St. off US 49 E. in Helena, www.civilwar.org/civil-war-discovery-trail.**

✦ Fort Smith National Historic Site

Experience the sturdy antebellum grandeur of this fort. Explore barracks and commissary buildings, listen to discussions about Civil War battles via digital videos, and peruse interactive dioramas.

LOCATION: **301 Parker Ave., Fort Smith, 479-783-3961, www.nps.gov/fosm.**

✦ Freedom Park

Part of the National Park Service's National Underground Railroad Network to Freedom, this park's outdoor interpretive exhibits focus on escaped slaves.

LOCATION: **750 S. Biscoe, Helena–West Helena.**

✦ Helena Museum

The museum's collection includes a diorama of the Battle of Helena (see p. 42).

LOCATION: **623 Pecan St., Helena, 870-338-7790, www.helenamuseum.com.**

✦ Historic Washington State Park

Established in 1824, Washington served as the Confederate capital during the Civil War. The park's quaintly restored period buildings house first-rate attractions such as a world-class firearms museum. Serves great lunch.

LOCATION: **Southwest Arkansas, near Hope, Exit 30 (Hope) off I-30, 870-983-2684, www.historicwashingtonstatepark.com.**

Built in 1862, the U.S.S. *Hindman*—a 286-ton tinclad gunboat—was part of the Mississippi fleet.

✦ Massard Prairie Battlefield Park

Tucked into a residential area about five miles southeast of Fort Smith, this well-manicured, unstaffed park has several interpretive signs.

LOCATION: **Red Pine Dr. and Morgan's Way, Fort Smith, 479-784-2368, www.civilwar.org /civil-war-discovery-trail.**

FURTHER READING

The Battle of Massard Prairie: The 1864 Confederate Attacks on Fort Smith, Arkansas
by Dale Cox
The most detailed account of the conflict at Fort Smith

✦ Nevada County Depot and Museum

Learn about the battles of Elkin's Ferry (see p. 41) and Prairie D'Ane (see pp. 47–48) at this museum, which is also spearheading efforts to preserve Elkin's Ferry.

LOCATION: **403 W. 1st St. S., Prescott, 870-887-5821, www.depotmuseum.org.**

✦ Old State House Museum

Built in 1836–1842, the Arkansas statehouse is the oldest standing statehouse west of the Mississippi. Explore Civil War history exhibits and see the chamber where the state's secession convention was held and where Union forces took control after the fall of Little Rock.

LOCATION: **300 W. Markham, Little Rock, 501-324-9685, www.oldstatehouse.com.**

✦ Pine Bluff/Jefferson County Historical Museum

The museum's collection includes an extensive display of Civil War artifacts, including the flag of the Jefferson Guards.

LOCATION: **201 E. 4th Ave., Pine Bluff, 870-541-5402, www.pbjcmuseum.org.**

✦ Pratt C. Remmel Park

The park's interpretive panels explain the Battle of Bayou Fourche (see p. 39). Picnic tables and other facilities are available.

LOCATION: **Exit 4 on I-440, south of the intersection of Lindsey Rd. and Fourche Dam Pike.**

Florida

ON JANUARY 10, 1861, FLORIDA BECAME THE THIRD STATE TO secede. Those who favored immediate withdrawal from the Union— known as fire-eaters—had won out over the cooperationists, who advocated holding off for a multistate exit. Dubbed the "smallest tadpole in the dirty pool of secession" by the Northern press, Florida had a small population and insignificant industry, but its role in the Civil War was anything but peripheral. Fifteen thousand Floridians joined the war effort, and the state's extensive coastline presented a challenge for the U.S. Navy's mission of blockading Confederate commerce.

Like many Southern populaces, Florida's loyalties were split. The Union controlled Key West, the Dry Tortugas, and Santa Rosa Island throughout the war and aimed to recruit the state's blacks—about 40 percent of Florida's population. When the 1863 Declaration of Amnesty and Reconstruction decreed that all would be forgiven if 10 percent of a state's voters pledged allegiance to the United States, the Union scoured the northern part of the state seeking converts. Florida, however, remained in the Confederacy until the war's end.

Located in the Dry Tortugas, Fort Jefferson—the largest coastal fort in the U.S.—served as a Civil War prison. Its walls incorporated an 1826 lighthouse.

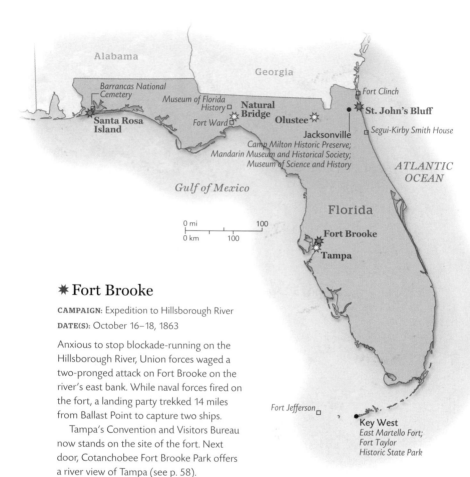

Alabama

Georgia

Barrancas National Cemetery

Museum of Florida History □ **Natural Bridge**

Santa Rosa Island

Fort Ward □ Olustee ※

☀ Fort Clinch

✷ St. John's Bluff

Jacksonville
Camp Milton Historic Preserve;
Mandarin Museum and Historical Society;
Museum of Science and History

Segui-Kirby Smith House

ATLANTIC OCEAN

Gulf of Mexico

Florida

0 mi — 100
0 km — 100

✷ **Fort Brooke**

Tampa

Fort Jefferson □

Key West
East Martello Fort;
Fort Taylor
Historic State Park

✳ Fort Brooke

CAMPAIGN: Expedition to Hillsborough River

DATE(S): October 16–18, 1863

Anxious to stop blockade-running on the Hillsborough River, Union forces waged a two-pronged attack on Fort Brooke on the river's east bank. While naval forces fired on the fort, a landing party trekked 14 miles from Ballast Point to capture two ships.

Tampa's Convention and Visitors Bureau now stands on the site of the fort. Next door, Cotanchobee Fort Brooke Park offers a river view of Tampa (see p. 58).

LOCATION: Convention and Visitors Bureau, 401 E. Jackson St., Tampa, 813-223-1111 or 800-448-2672, www.visittampabay.com.

✳ Natural Bridge

CAMPAIGN: Operations Near St. Marks

DATE(S): March 6, 1865

The last major Confederate victory of the Civil War, this battle began in an effort to protect the state capital at Tallahassee. In

pursuit of the Confederates who had attacked Fort Myers in February, General Newton led his force of nearly 1,000 men to the St. Marks River at Apalachee Bay. Unable to navigate the narrow waterway and finding the crossing at Newport impassable, a contingent of his army moved on to Natural Bridge, a spot where the river dips underground for a quarter mile. Surprisingly, the Confederates, who had quickly mustered a hodgepodge collection of state militia and teen cadets, drove back Newton's troops.

Natural Bridge Battlefield Historic State Park preserves a 64-acre section of battlefield. Interpretive signs, preserved earthworks, and the path across the natural bridge help put the battle into perspective.

LOCATION: **Natural Bridge Battlefield Historic State Park, 7502 Natural Bridge Rd., Tallahassee, 850-922-6007, www.floridastateparks.org.**

FURTHER READING

The Battle of Natural Bridge, Florida
by Dale Cox
A solid historical recounting of the battle

✳ Olustee

CAMPAIGN: Florida Expedition

DATE(S): February 20, 1864

Early in 1864, President Lincoln floated the idea that bringing Florida back into the fold

Key West

This island off the tip of Florida remained under Union control throughout the war, even though the majority of residents supported the Confederacy. Key West was a coaling port for the U.S. Navy's East Gulf Coast Blockade Squadron, based at Fort Taylor (see p. 59).

Fort Taylor never saw action during the war. The squadron was one of several whose mission was to close Southern ports to commerce. The fleet patrolled Florida and Alabama, interdicting blockade-runners from the Bahamas and Havana.

Major improvements were made to Fort Taylor at the end of the 19th century, and it remained active through World War II. Originally located 1,200 feet offshore, Fort Taylor was intentionally landlocked via dredging in the 1960s. A moat was created around the fort in 1985, mostly for aesthetics.

Reenactors represent the many U.S. Colored Troops who served in the Battle of Olustee.

Dr. Samuel A. Mudd, convicted of aiding John Wilkes Booth, was pardoned in 1869.

Today, part of the battlefield is preserved at Olustee Battlefield Historic State Park, where a small museum and mile-long interpretive trail explain the battle.

LOCATION: **Olustee Battlefield Historic State Park, 5815 Battlefield Trail Rd., Olustee, 386-758-0400, www.floridastateparks.org.**

✳ St. John's Bluff

CAMPAIGN: Expedition to St. John's Bluff

DATE(S): October 1–3, 1862

Perched on the south side of the St. John's River, the St. John's Bluff fortification was designed to defend Jacksonville, 18 miles upstream. A two-front Federal assault—one from a gunboat squadron and one from 1,500 Union troops approaching by land—spooked Colonel Hopkins enough that he abandoned the fort during the night of October 2, surrendering it without a fight.

would help him in the upcoming election. In response, General Gillmore organized 6,000 troops to venture into Florida under the command of General Seymour.

Seymour, against orders to stay on the defensive in Jacksonville, seized a railroad bridge over the Suwannee River and began pushing his way into the state. Rather than wait for the Union troops to reach their hastily created earthen fortifications, the Confederate forces under General Finegan moved eastward. The two sides clashed at Ocean Pond in an open pine forest about 50 miles west of Jacksonville and now part of Osceola National Forest.

The Confederate forces continued to outflank Seymour's troops until the Yankees retreated to Jacksonville. Federal efforts to cut off Confederate supply lines, recruit additional men for the U.S. Colored Troops, and bring Florida back into the Union failed at a huge cost of more than 1,800 casualties, twice the number of Confederate losses. General Seymour later described the Olustee devastation as a "devilish hard rub."

Fort Jefferson: The Mudd Connection

This massive six-sided fort is isolated in the Gulf of Mexico, 70 miles west of Key West, on Garden Key in the Dry Tortugas.

Fort Jefferson (see p. 59), the largest all-masonry coastal fort in the U.S., never saw action during the Civil War, but Union troops seeking to stop blockade-runners plied its harbor. Used primarily as a military prison during the war, this is where Dr. Samuel A. Mudd was incarcerated after being convicted for his role in the Lincoln assassination conspiracy. He was later pardoned for his work in fighting an outbreak of yellow fever at the fort.

The ten-acre fort, composed of 16 million bricks, was designed to house 450 guns and 1,500 men. Its surrounding 60-foot-wide moat has helped protect its thick 45-foot-tall walls from waves and enemy attacks.

Gun ports line a long corridor inside Fort Barrancas in Pensacola, Florida.

His commanding officer, General Finegan, thought Hopkins acted too hastily and described the fall of St. John's Bluff as "a gross military blunder."

Fort Caroline National Memorial, which is located 14 miles south of Jacksonville, provides a soldier's-eye view of the river. The best view is from the Ribault Monument, a tribute to the 16th-century French explorer Jean Ribault.

LOCATION: Fort Caroline National Memorial, 12713 Fort Caroline Rd., Jacksonville, 904-641-7155, www.nps.gov/foca.

✴ Santa Rosa Island

CAMPAIGN: Operations of the Gulf Blockading Squadron
DATE(S): October 9, 1861

The largest of Florida's three bay-oriented fortifications, Fort Pickens on Santa Rosa Island had been garrisoned by Union troops almost immediately after Florida seceded from the Union on January 10, 1861. Once the war started, minor dustups occurred between the fort's Union troops and marauding Confederates until General

Anderson and more than 1,200 Rebels launched a surprise nighttime raid against Santa Rosa Island on October 9, 1861.

Although they quickly routed the Union soldiers, the Rebel forces wasted time looting the encampment. With daylight approaching, they began to withdraw as Federals from Fort Pickens responded to the sortie. In less than a year, the Confederates had withdrawn from Pensacola Bay, leaving Fort Pickens and Pensacola under Union control throughout the war. From there, Federals staged their final operations against Fort Blakeley (see p. 30) and Spanish Fort (see p. 33) in Alabama.

Today, Fort Pickens and Fort Barrancas are both part of Gulf Islands National Seashore. Built by slaves in 1829–1834, Fort Pickens is an architectural marvel—a hauntingly eerie site in a beautiful setting on the western tip of Santa Rosa Island. Dramatic changes were made to the fort in the early 20th century. Better preserved is Fort Barrancas, across the bay, which served as General Bragg's headquarters and became the Confederates' primary defensive position for Pensacola Bay against the Union's naval forces. Entrance to Fort Barrancas requires photo identification.

LOCATION: **Fort Pickens, 1400 Fort Pickens Rd., Pensacola, 850-916-5631, www.nps.gov/guis /planyourvisit/fort-pickens.htm; Fort Barrancas (photo ID required), 901 Taylor Rd., Pensacola Naval Air Station, Pensacola, 850-455-5167, www.nps.gov/guis/planyourvisit/fort-barrancas .htm.**

✳ Tampa

CAMPAIGN: Operations Against Tampa
DATE(S): June 30–July 1, 1862

On June 30, the U.S.S. *Sagamore,* patrolling off the west coast of Florida, sent a surrender demand to Confederates manning the fortifications protecting Tampa. The demand was rejected. A bombardment started the next day, but when the town refused to surrender, the attack ceased and the gunboat returned to its blockading duties. Tampa and the fort did not fall under Union control until May 1864. Cotanchobee Fort Brooke Park offers a view over the Hillsborough River from where the Confederates twice defended the city of Tampa against Union naval attack.

LOCATION: **Cotanchobee Fort Brooke Park, 601 Old Water St., Tampa, 813-274-8615, www.tampapix.com/chanside7.htm.**

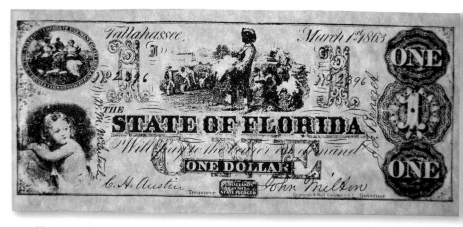

Vignettes of Justice and Ceres, a farm scene, and a portrait of Philadelphia humanitarian Alfred L. Elwyn grace this 1863 Florida Confederate dollar, which had no value at war's end.

Other Battles and Beyond

✦ Florida Civil War Heritage Trail

To request the 80-page guidebook, call 800-245-6300, or visit www.myflorida.com and search for "Civil War."

✦ Barrancas National Cemetery

More than 1,300 Civil War soldiers are interred in sections 1 through 12.

LOCATION: **Naval Air Station, 1 Cemetery Rd., Pensacola, 850-453-4108, www.cem.va.gov.**

✦ Camp Milton Historic Preserve

Interpretive trails detail the history of this Confederate camp.

LOCATION: **1175 Halsema Rd. N., Jacksonville.**

✦ Fort Clinch

Fort Clinch is one of the best preserved forts from the 19th century.

LOCATION: **Fort Clinch State Park, 2601 Atlantic Ave., Fernandina Beach, Amelia Island, 904-277-7274, www.floridastateparks.org.**

✦ Fort East Martello

This citadel-style fort was abandoned, unfinished, when the war ended.

LOCATION: **3501 S. Roosevelt Blvd., Key West, 305-296-3913, www.kwahs.org.**

✦ Fort Jefferson

Accessible only by boat or seaplane, Fort Jefferson served primarily as a Union prison during the Civil War.

LOCATION: **Dry Tortugas National Park, 70 miles west of Key West, 305-242-7700, www.nps.gov/drto.**

✦ Fort Taylor

Fort Taylor played an important role in the Union blockade of the Gulf of Mexico.

LOCATION: **Fort Zachary Taylor Historic State Park, 601 Howard England Way, Key West, 305-292-6713, www.floridastateparks.org.**

✦ Fort Ward

Interpretive trails tell the history of the fort.

LOCATION: **San Marcos de Apalache Historic State Park, 148 Old Fort Rd., St. Marks, 850-925-6216, www.floridastateparks.org.**

✦ Mandarin Museum and Historical Society

Learn about the *Maple Leaf,* a Union paddle steamer sunk by a Confederate torpedo.

LOCATION: **11964 Mandarin Rd., Jacksonville, 904-268-0784, www.mandarinmuseum.net.**

✦ Museum of Florida History

Follow the story of Florida's role in the Civil War through an extensive permanent exhibit.

LOCATION: **500 S. Bronough St., Tallahassee, 850-245-6400, www.museumoffloridahistory .com**

✦ Museum of Science & History

The collection includes a scale model of the *Maple Leaf.*

LOCATION: **1025 Museum Circle, Jacksonville, 904-396-6674, www.themosh.org.**

✦ Segui-Kirby Smith House

This National Historic Landmark site was the home of Confederate General Smith.

LOCATION: **12 Aviles St., St. Augustine, 904-825-2333, www.staugustinegovernment .com.**

Georgia

THE FACE OF THE CIVIL WAR CHANGED ALONG AN imaginary line that stretched diagonally from Georgia's northwest corner to the coastal city of Savannah. Rifled artillery reduced masonry Fort Pulaski to debris, while Generals William Tecumseh Sherman and Joe Johnston danced "a red clay minuet" to Atlanta—with Sherman leading, much to President Davis's consternation. The city's capture heartened the Northern electorate, fueling Lincoln's reelection. Sherman then marched into history by opening a new supply line while fulfilling his pledge to "make Georgia howl." The Confederacy's youthful "seed corn" was decimated at Griswoldville, and Savannah became Lincoln's Christmas present. As Scarlett says in *Gone With the Wind,* she learned to love Tara's red clay because "land is the only thing that matters." Andersonville became a pseudonym for misery, cruelty, and death. Jefferson Davis's fugitive flight from his destroyed nation ended with his capture in a woman's shawl at Irwinville. Yes, from 1861 to 1865, Georgia was indeed on everyone's mind.

William T. Sherman—whose "Hard Hand of War" helped bring the conflict to a decisive end—is perhaps one of the most reviled men of the Civil War.

GEORGIA BATTLES

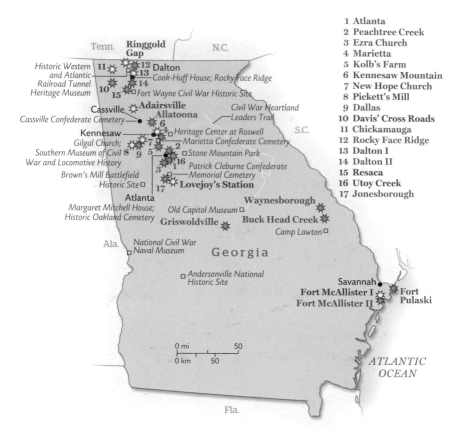

1 Atlanta
2 Peachtree Creek
3 Ezra Church
4 Marietta
5 Kolb's Farm
6 Kennesaw Mountain
7 New Hope Church
8 Pickett's Mill
9 Dallas
10 Davis' Cross Roads
11 Chickamauga
12 Rocky Face Ridge
13 Dalton I
14 Dalton II
15 Resaca
16 Utoy Creek
17 Jonesborough

✳ Adairsville

CAMPAIGN: Atlanta Campaign

DATE(S): May 17, 1864

Following the Battle of Resaca (see p. 78), General Joe Johnston retreated south, with Sherman in pursuit. Johnston's rear guard engaged in skirmishes from Calhoun to Adairsville, where his troops successfully stalled the Federals while he sought a new defensive position. The Oothcaloga Valley was too wide for his usual tactics, however, so Johnston withdrew his forces to Cassville.

Three interpretive signs in the Adairsville Cemetery, which now covers part of the battlefield, describe the battle.

LOCATION: Markers located at the Adairsville Cemetery, intersection of Old US 41 and Cherry St., Adairsville.

✳ Allatoona

CAMPAIGN: Franklin-Nashville Campaign

DATE(S): October 5, 1864

Before his 1864 Tennessee Campaign, General Hood took a swipe at Sherman's vulnerable supply line—the Western & Atlantic Railroad—at Allatoona Pass. Having dispatched General French to fill the pass with debris, Hood then absconded with Union supplies stocked five miles north.

Hood's plans were inadvertently disclosed, possibly the result of public talks given by President Jefferson Davis. Forewarned, Union forces under General Corse fortified each ridge and waited. Corse refused French's bold request that he surrender "to avoid a needless effusion of blood," leading to repeated attacks and 1,600 casualties, about 31 percent of the total combatants.

Allatoona Pass is located just south of Red Top Mountain State Park. The railroad tracks were removed in the 1940s, and today visitors can hike the old railbed through the 60-foot-wide pass between towering ridges. A marked, relatively short dirt trail with interpretive signs leads past Civil War burial sites and trenches. To reach the two superb fortifications overlooking the pass requires a moderate climb.

LOCATION: **Red Top Mountain State Park, 770-975-0055, www.gastateparks.org. Access the Allatoona Pass Battlefield trail (www.georgia trails.com) from exit 283 off I-75, then go east on Old Allatoona Rd. to the small, free parking lot on the left.**

✳ Atlanta

CAMPAIGN: Atlanta Campaign
DATE(S): July 22, 1864

Following the setback at Peachtree Creek (see p. 77), General Hood tightened his line west and south of Atlanta, making a second effort to drive Sherman's forces away from the city. His well-designed plan failed when General Hardee's corps, after a 15-mile overnight march, arrived hours late on the city's east side. There Hardee found General McPherson's prepared forces entrenched on Bald Mountain and farther east than expected.

Caught between two ridges of forewarned Union soldiers, General Hood's Confederate troops suffered a very high casualty rate at the Battle of Allatoona.

Confederates suffered more than 8,000 casualties, but it was the youthful McPherson's last battle. Caught among General Cleburne's skirmishers, the Army of Tennessee commander was shot while trying to avoid capture; he was the highest ranking Union officer killed in combat in the war.

Urban sprawl and meager preservation make the flow of battle here difficult to follow. Start at the Atlanta History Center, whose Civil War collection includes a Union supply wagon, Cleburne's sword, and the flag flying at the time of Atlanta's surrender. Interpretive signs at the southeast corner of the Inman Park Marta station parking lot designate where Federals broke through the Confederate line.

LOCATION: **Atlanta History Center, 130 West Paces Ferry Rd., 404-814-4000, www.atlanta historycenter.com. A monument to General McPherson stands at McPherson Ave. and Monument Ave. in Atlanta.**

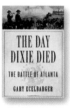

FURTHER READING

The Day Dixie Died: The Battle of Atlanta by Gary Ecelbarger Gripping account of the Atlanta Campaign's most important battle

✴ Buck Head Creek

CAMPAIGN: Savannah Campaign
DATE(S): November 28, 1864

The second skirmish in Sherman's March to the Sea (see p. 74) occurred 53 miles south of Augusta, where General Kilpatrick's cavalry was maneuvering to cut the Rebel supply line and free Union prisoners at Camp Lawton. General Wheeler followed, clashing with Kilpatrick at Buck Head Creek. As Union troops burned the bridge, Wheeler's cavalry crossed upstream, clashing again with Kilpatrick before both retreated.

LOCATION: **Marker located at the creek just past Big Buckhead Church; take US 25 north from Millen, then go left on CR 81 (Big Buckhead Church Rd.) for 3.5 miles. Church entry by appt. only; contact the Jenkins County Chamber of Commerce, 478-982-5595.**

✴ Chickamauga

CAMPAIGN: Chickamauga Campaign
DATE(S): September 18–20, 1863

Marking the end of the Chickamauga Campaign, the Battle of Chickamauga was

---

Winning the Presidency: The Atlanta Campaign

No American president since Andrew Jackson had held two consecutive terms, and with the Civil War dragging on into its fourth year, it seemed certain that the trend would not end with the increasingly unelectable Abraham Lincoln. Prepared to risk his administration— and the war—on one man, Lincoln advanced Ulysses S. Grant to the command of all the Union armies.

As part of his complicated plan to engage the Confederates on multiple fronts, Grant ordered his protégé and friend General Sherman to move against Atlanta, a key railroad and industrial hub. In position after position, Sherman outflanked the highly reputed General Johnston, who was soon replaced by young General Hood. Hood fought aggressively but he could not deter Sherman.

Sherman's capture of Atlanta began a series of Union successes that convinced the electorate that Lincoln could win the war. The election was a landslide.

FURTHER READING

Decision in the West: The Atlanta Campaign of 1864 by Albert Castel Seminal volume on the story of Atlanta

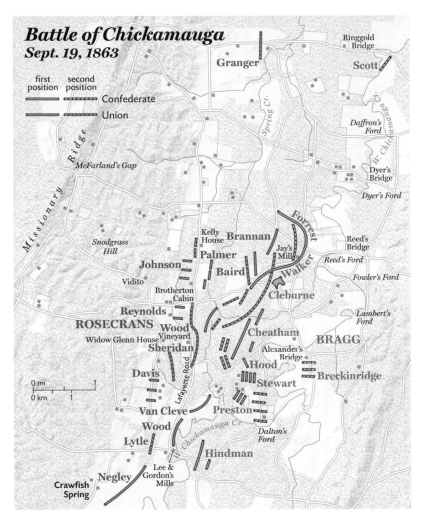

Battle of Chickamauga
Sept. 19, 1863

first position / second position
— — — Confederate
— — — Union

Granger

Ringgold Bridge
Scott

Spring Cr.

W. Chickamauga Cr.

Daffron's Ford

McFarland's Gap

Missionary Ridge

Dyer's Bridge

Dyer's Ford

Snodgrass Hill

Kelly House
Brannan
Palmer
Johnson
Baird
Vidito
Brotherton Cabin

Forrest

Jay's Mill
Walker
Cleburne

Reed's Bridge
Reed's Ford
Fowler's Ford

Lambert's Ford

Reynolds
ROSECRANS
Wood
Widow Glenn House Vineyard
Sheridan

Cheatham

BRAGG

Lafayette Road

Davis

Alexander's Bridge
Hood
Stewart

Breckinridge

0 mi 1
0 km 1

Van Cleve
Wood
Lytle

Preston

W. Chickamauga Cr.

Dalton's Ford

Hindman

Crawfish Spring
Negley
Lee & Gordon's Mills

the largest battle fought in Georgia during the Civil War. It was also one of the few times that Confederate troops outnumbered their Union counterparts on the battlefield.

Determined to take back Chattanooga, which he had lost in early September, General Bragg turned his Confederate troops north on September 18 to meet Union forces commanded by General Rosecrans. Skirmishes between cavalry and infantry from

both sides took place throughout the day, as Bragg's men moved into position. Widespread fighting broke out on the 19th. Although augmented by two divisions of the Army of Northern Virginia's I Corps commanded by General Longstreet, the Confederate soldiers failed to break the Union line. On September 20, however, Longstreet's wing took advantage of a hole in the Union line. The Confederate breakthrough split the

Union troops and sent them fleeing back to Chattanooga. Only the determined resistance of General Thomas's corps saved Union troops from complete and utter ruination.

Explore 5,300-acre Chickamauga and Chattanooga National Military Park via a seven-mile self-guided auto tour or on foot over its extensive trail system. The visitor center features a contoured map, an extensive weapons collection, and an orientation video. Allow several days to understand the enormity of this battle, which covered more ground than is preserved in the park, as well as the battles for Chattanooga (see pp. 178–183).

LOCATION: **Chickamauga and Chattanooga National Military Park, 3370 LaFayette Rd., Fort Oglethorpe, 706-866-9241, www.nps .gov/chch. A brochure and audio tour of the Chickamauga Campaign are available at www.gacivilwar.org.**

FURTHER READING
This Terrible Sound: The Battle of Chickamauga
by Peter Cozzens
Brings to life the battle and the men who fought in it

✳ Dallas

CAMPAIGN: Atlanta Campaign
DATE(S): May 26–June 1, 1864

Unlike at New Hope Church (see p. 76) and Pickett's Mill (see p. 77), Union forces rallied at Dallas, 30 miles north of Atlanta. On May 28, 1864, during the third battle in the "Hell Hole" series, General Logan's well-entrenched Union forces inflicted 3,000 Rebel casualties as Sherman pursued a path eastward to the Western & Atlantic Railroad for supplies. From here, Joe Johnston's forces followed Sherman to Allatoona Pass.

Start at Pickett's Mill for an overview of the "Hell Hole" battles. Then inquire about directions to some unmarked sites related to each.

LOCATION: **Pickett's Mill Battlefield Historic Site, 4432 Mt. Tabor Church Rd., Dallas, 770-443-7850.**

Rock of Chickamauga: George H. Thomas

After Longstreet decimated Rosecrans's right flank, General Thomas was resolute as he "stood like a rock" defending Snodgrass Hill. By cobbling together fragmented Federal forces, fortifying the ridgeline, and fending off repeated Rebel attacks, Thomas—a Virginian—saved Union forces from annihilation. Lincoln noted his "heroism and skill," while his own family turned portraits of him to the wall.

✳ Dalton I

CAMPAIGN: Demonstration on Dalton
DATE(S): February 22–27, 1864

After relieving General Bragg, President Davis reluctantly placed General Joe Johnston in command of the Army of Tennessee. He expected Johnston to attack when spring arrived, but Johnston remained securely entrenched at Dalton. Grant sent General Thomas to probe for and exploit any weaknesses in the Confederate lines. Encounters at Rocky Face Ridge and Dug Gap, and in the Crow Valley, convinced Thomas that a direct assault against the Confederates would fail, and the Union forces withdrew.

A nine-stop driving-tour map for sale at Dalton Freight Depot Welcome Center explores 25 miles of regional Civil War history. Unstaffed Mill Creek Gap Battlefield Park has an Atlanta Campaign relief map.

LOCATION: **Dalton Freight Depot Welcome Center, 305 S. Depot St., 706-270-9960; Mill Creek Gap Battlefield Park, 2401 Chattanooga Rd., Dalton.**

✳ Dalton II

CAMPAIGN: Atlanta Campaign
DATE(S): August 14–15, 1864

Seeking relief from Sherman's siege, General Hood dispatched Wheeler's cavalry to destroy portions of the Western and Atlantic (W&A) Railroad. Approaching Dalton, Wheeler demanded that the garrison surrender but was rebuffed. Failing to beat the garrison, Wheeler brushed aside Union reinforcements as he retreated. Damage to the railroad was quickly repaired.

Visit Dalton Freight Depot to see the location of the W&A line. Also, a marker dedicated to black soldiers stands near Fort Hill Circle and South Green Street in Dalton.

LOCATION: **Dalton Freight Depot Welcome Center, 305 S. Depot St., 706-270-9960.**

❉ Davis' Cross Roads

CAMPAIGN: Chickamauga Campaign
OTHER NAME(S): Dug Gap, McLemore's Cove
DATE(S): September 10–11, 1863

By September 7, 1863, General Rosecrans had maneuvered General Bragg's Confederate forces out of Chattanooga. Then Rosecrans got careless, sending two corps into northwest Georgia to intercept the Rebel forces he thought would be fleeing south. He was wrong.

Armed with intelligence about his opponent's divided forces, Bragg—who was just south of Chattanooga—moved his troops into McLemore's Cove, where, on September 10, he found an isolated division of General Thomas's XIV Army Corps. Bragg ordered Generals Hindman and Daniel Hill to attack, but each hesitated. Union commander Negley discovered his vulnerability and pulled back on September 11. Hindman and Hill also withdrew. Unable to get his orders executed, Bragg displayed a fatal weakness of leadership destined to manifest itself again, to the detriment of the Confederate cause.

LOCATION: **Markers located on GA 193, 9 miles west of LaFayette, at Hog Jowl Rd. in a wayside with a view of Davis' Cross Roads.**

✳ Ezra Church

CAMPAIGN: Atlanta Campaign
DATE(S): July 28, 1864

Having fought several battles for Atlanta, Hood's Confederates were alerted to the march of General Howard's Army of the Tennessee toward the Macon & Western Railroad, a key Confederate supply line. Hood ordered his 30-year-old corps commander, General Stephen Lee, to initiate an attack on

Fort McAllister's massive earth mounds are some of the best preserved of the Confederacy.

an isolated element of Howard's force near Ezra Church. Having arrived first, the Federals were prepared—some soldiers had used the church's pews and their own knapsacks as makeshift breastworks. Although Hood's initiative protected the railroad, Lee suffered nearly 3,000 casualties to the Federals' 600.

LOCATION: Markers located at Mozley Park, 1565 Martin Luther King Jr. Dr. N.W., Atlanta, and Westview Cemetery, 1680 Westview Dr. S.W., Atlanta, 404-755-6611.

✳ Fort McAllister I

CAMPAIGN: Naval Attacks on Fort McAllister
DATE(S): March 3, 1863

Built in 1861 near the mouth of the Ogeechee River, seven miles from the Atlantic Ocean, Fort McAllister, which boasted 17-foot-thick earth mounds, was designed to defend Georgia's interior manufacturing and transportation hubs from naval attack. The fort was attacked seven times during the Civil War before being bombarded by Union ironclads on March 3, 1863. The sandy walls suffered some damage, but, even after eight hours of naval bombardment, the fort was easily repaired and restored.

Today, Fort McAllister State Park—south of Savannah—is home to some of the Confederacy's best preserved fortifications, including a bombproof, barracks, and magazine. The site also includes a museum that shows a video about the fort's history. Guided tours help explain the historic site, which charges an admission fee.

LOCATION: Fort McAllister State Park, 3894 Fort McAllister Rd., Richmond Hill, 912-727-2339, www.gastateparks.org.

✳ Fort McAllister II

CAMPAIGN: Savannah Campaign
DATE(S): December 13, 1864

In 15 minutes on December 13, 1864, Sherman's infantry, under the command of General Hazen, accomplished what eight previous attacks by the Union Navy could not. With Rebel morale and firepower lacking, Hazen's forces, circumventing mines and abatis, attacked the Confederate stronghold from its land side and overwhelmed Major Anderson's 230-man garrison. This was Sherman's final obstacle on his March to the Sea (see p. 74). Here he would find an unfettered supply line that did not fear Nathan Bedford Forrest. So now it was on to capture Savannah, a city that General Hardee had already decided to abandon.

Picturesque Fort McAllister State Park offers river views, playgrounds, picnic areas, and resources for camping, boating, and fishing. The park charges a fee for parking and for admission to the historic site.

LOCATION: Fort McAllister State Park, 3894 Fort McAllister Rd., Richmond Hill, 912-727-2339, www.gastateparks.org. Guided tours help explain the site. Bring bug spray.

✳ Fort Pulaski

CAMPAIGN: Operations Against Fort Pulaski

DATE(S): April 10–11, 1862

Erected in 1829, this imposing five-sided masonry fort features seven-foot-thick walls deemed safe beyond 800 yards. Or so Confederate Colonel Olmstead was informed in 1862, as Federals arrived on Tybee Island a mile away. "They will make it very warm for you with shells from that point," said recent West Point graduate Robert E. Lee, who had partly engineered the fort, "but they cannot breach at that distance." Lee was wrong. The Union's new rifled artillery projectiles traveled farther at greater speeds and penetrated deeper than smoothbore shells.

On April 10, General Gillmore's Union cannons collapsed the fort's southeast corner. Fearing the barrage would explode his

magazine, Olmstead surrendered the following day. A new era in warfare had begun.

Union repairs to the southeast corner of the fort—whose parapets offer sweeping views—are still visible today.

LOCATION: Fort Pulaski National Monument, 15 minutes east of Savannah on US 80, 912-786-5787, www.nps.gov/fopu.

A revolution in warfare occurred in April 1862, when Federal rifled shells reduced Fort Pulaski's thick brick walls to rubble. The fort quickly surrendered, closing Savannah as a port.

Civil War on Foot: Savannah

Of the three "Southern sisters"—Charleston, Savannah, and Wilmington—the city of Savannah is the most authentic. Its historic buildings and design, set around a series of squares, make this a delightful walk filled with Civil War history. Find a parking place along Bay Street and begin your tour at City Hall.

❶ City Hall *(2 E. Bay St.)* With your back to City Hall, look left to see the point where Sherman's troops marched into Savannah. On the corner of Bay and Bull Streets stands the U.S. Custom House, which held revenue gathered before the war. Walk left and take one of the crosswalks over the small alleyway.

The last burial at Savannah's Colonial Park Cemetery took place in 1853.

❷ Commercial Heart
Incoming goods were off-loaded and stored in the riverside buildings until they could be exported or picked up to be sold by local merchants. Return to the intersection of Bull and Bay Streets. Walk south on Bull Street.

❸ Slave Auction Site
An immediate left past the U.S. Custom House leads to an alley. Walk 20 steps; here is where the slave auctions took place, with humans examined and bought like cattle. Return to Bull Street and turn left.

❹ Johnson Square
Delegates met in the Pulaski Hotel (now Regions Bank) to discuss secession, and mourners gathered here after the first battle of Manassas (see pp. 254–256) and also after the assassination of Lincoln. Go south on Bull Street.

❺ Juliette Gordon Low Birthplace *(10 E. Oglethorpe Ave.)* The founder of the Girl Scouts, whose father was a Confederate officer, was a small child during the Civil War. Her family hosted Generals Sherman, Howard, and others. Walk south to Chippewa Square.

❻ Savannah Theater *(222 Bull St.)* From the balcony of this 1818 theater, Alexander Stephens, soon to be Confederate vice president, delivered a stirring defense of secession. Continue south.

❼ Oglethorpe Barracks *(15 E. Liberty St.)* Now the site of DeSoto Hilton, this is where city commander Hardee and General Beauregard decided to evacuate Savannah. Continue on to Madison Square.

8 Madison Square

Sherman's headquarters during the occupation, the Green-Meldrim House is open to visitors. Walk east down West Harris Street to Barnard Street.

9 Bartow House (126 W. Harris St.) Francis Bartow, commander of the Oglethorpe Light Artillery, was killed in the first battle of Manassas. His death was mourned citywide. Walk north on Barnard Street. Turn right on Oglethorpe and walk to Abercorn.

10 Colonial Park Cemetery (201 Abercorn St.) Established in 1750, this cemetery was desecrated during the Union occupation. Burials were looted and headstones altered or used for target practice. After the war the dislocated gravestones were lined up on the far wall and eventually cemented into place.

If time permits, visit the Confederate monument in stunning Forsyth Park at the intersection of Drayton Street and East Park Avenue.

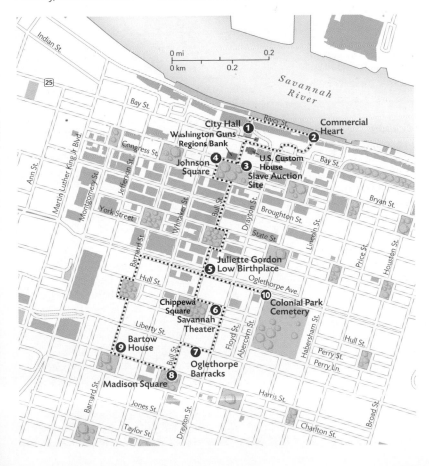

✳ Griswoldville

CAMPAIGN: Savannah Campaign
DATE(S): November 22, 1864

Today's pastoral setting belies the scene of an unsettling attack during the first military encounter of Sherman's March to the Sea (see p. 74). Scouting for enemy lines near Macon, Union General Walcutt's seasoned forces successfully fended off General Wheeler's cavalry before being attacked by a column of several thousand determined Georgia militiamen led by General Philips. When the smoke cleared, the Union's success was soured upon learning the "militiamen" were mostly gray-bearded old men and teenagers, either too old or too young for service in the manpower-starved South.

LOCATION: Markers located at Griswoldville Battlefield, a 17-acre park 10 miles east of Macon on US 80, then follow signs, www.gastateparks.org.

Reality in Fiction: Gone With the Wind

In her 1936 novel *Gone With the Wind*, author Margaret Mitchell shrewdly captures Southerners' ambivalence about the Civil War, from Ashley's loyalty ("If Georgia calls, I go with her but I hope the Yankees will allow us to leave the Union in peace.") to Rhett's warning ("The Yankees are better equipped than we. They've got factories, shipyards, coal mines. All we've got is cotton and slaves, and arrogance."). The novel centers on the tragic love story of a Southern belle and the pragmatic, swashbuckling blockade-runner who loves her even as she pursues another man. Although a product of its time, portraying slaves as happy and loyal, the movie adaptation—condemned by censors as immoral—remains a landmark achievement in American cinematography.

✳ Jonesborough

CAMPAIGN: Atlanta Campaign
DATE(S): August 31–September 1, 1864

General Hood's final effort to defend the Macon & Western Railroad ended here, as Sherman sent General Hardee's forces fleeing south. On September 1, Atlanta's last supply line was severed and the city's evacuation began. Sherman's Atlanta Campaign was all but over, though combat actions continued as both sides headed toward Lovejoy's Station (see pp. 75–76).

The Warren House, now an event facility, borders the battlefield. Eight signs within walking distance of this 1840 home interpret the fighting along the railroad. Fighting along the Flint River is harder to locate.

LOCATION: Warren House, 102 W. Mimosa Dr., Jonesboro, 678-685-1821, www.warrenhouse.net, tours by appointment only.

✳ Kennesaw Mountain

CAMPAIGN: Atlanta Campaign
DATE(S): June 27, 1864

With Richmond on edge, General Johnston traded real estate for time when Sherman foolishly attacked the entrenched Confederates over the difficult terrain of Kennesaw Mountain, 25 miles north of Atlanta. Full frontal assaults at Pigeon Mountain and Cheatham Hill, the battle's epicenter, failed to break Johnston's line.

On June 27, 1864, General Howard's forces stormed up the hill under a barrage of artillery toward the entrenched Rebels. As one bluecoat put it: It was like "charging to death or a southern prison." Like Grant at Cold Harbor three weeks prior, Sherman soon learned a difficult lesson.

"The story of Kennesaw Mountain is the story of earthworks," says chief ranger Anthony Winegar, noting that those dotting the Kennesaw line today are worn by 150 years of weather. The park's visitor center shows a film, "Kennesaw, the Last Mountain," and has a museum that

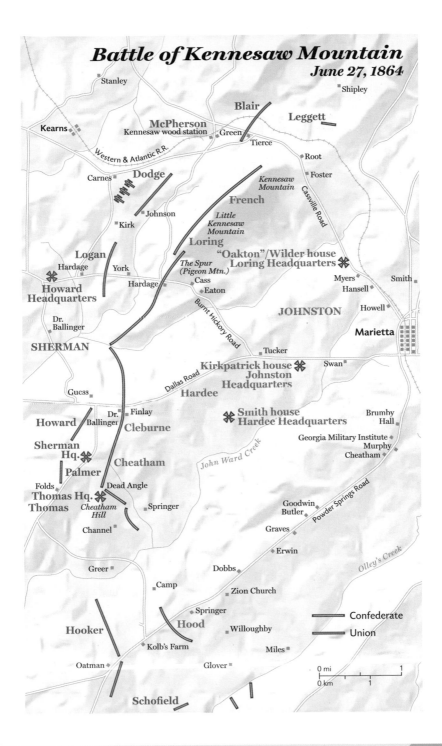

Battle of Kennesaw Mountain
June 27, 1864

Stanley

Shipley

Blair

Leggett

Kearns

McPherson
Kennesaw wood station

Green

Tierce

Root

Western & Atlantic R.R.

Carnes

Dodge

Foster

Kennesaw
Mountain

Cassville Road

Johnson

French

Kirk

Little
Kennesaw
Mountain

Loring

Logan

"Oakton"/Wilder house
Loring Headquarters

Hardage

York

The Spur
(Pigeon Mtn.)

Myers

Smith

Howard
Headquarters

Hardage

Cass

Eaton

Hansell

Howell

JOHNSTON

Marietta

Dr.
Ballinger

Burnt Hickory Road

SHERMAN

Tucker

Kirkpatrick house
Johnston
Headquarters

Swan

Guess

Dallas Road

Hardee

Dr.
Finlay
Howard Ballinger

Smith house
Hardee Headquarters

Brumby
Hall

Cleburne

Georgia Military Institute
Murphy
Cheatham

Sherman
Hq.

Cheatham

John Ward Creek

Palmer

Folds

Dead Angle

Thomas Hq.
Thomas   Cheatham
Hill

Springer

Goodwin
Butler

Powder Springs Road

Channel

Graves

Erwin

Olley's Creek

Greer

Dobbs

Camp

Zion Church

Springer

Hooker

Hood

Willoughby

Kolb's Farm

Miles

Oatman

Glover

0 mi   1
0 km   1

Confederate

Union

Schofield

The Southeast | Georgia   73

With attacks upon his supply line from Louisville through Nashville and Chattanooga, and needing a more secure supply base, General Sherman determined to move to the Atlantic Coast and, with Grant's concurrence, "make Georgia howl." He did just that on a 37-day march covering 300 miles with 60,000 Union troops, who lived off the land. "Uncle Billy," as Sherman was fondly known, instructed them to forage liberally, taking or torching anything of military use to the Rebels. As Henry Hitchcock, his military secretary, later noted, "Never was an army so bountifully supplied."

While Sherman intended to break the Georgia populace's will to resist, he also warned, "Soldiers must not enter the dwellings of the inhabitants, or commit any trespass." Paradoxically, when families without other means pleaded with him to spare food, Sherman turned a deaf ear. "War is cruelty," he said. "The crueler it is, the sooner it will be over." The Union's calling card became "Sherman neckties"—

rails heated and wrapped around trees, thus rendered permanently useless.

Upon arriving on the Atlantic coast to fetch much needed supplies, Sherman messaged Lincoln: "I beg to present you as a Christmas gift the City of Savannah, with one hundred and fifty guns and plenty of ammunition, also about twenty-five thousand bales of cotton."

Sherman, a trusted confidant of Grant, later became chief of staff of the Army. Seen as a liberator by some and a brigand by others, he remains a polarizing figure even today.

FURTHER READING

The March to the Sea and Beyond: Sherman's Troops in the Savannah and Carolinas Campaigns
by Joseph T. Glatthaar
Carefully researched and illustrated study

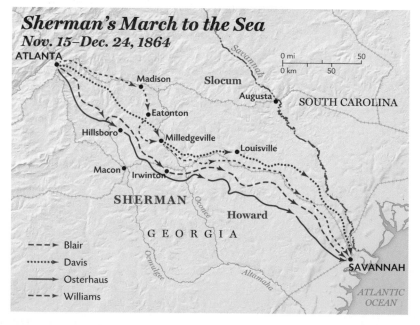

Sherman's March to the Sea
Nov. 15–Dec. 24, 1864

ATLANTA

Madison

Slocum

Savannah

Augusta

SOUTH CAROLINA

0 mi 50
0 km 50

Eatonton

Hillsboro

Milledgeville

Louisville

Macon Irwinton

SHERMAN

Oconee

Howard

GEORGIA

Ocmulgee

Altamaha

SAVANNAH

ATLANTIC OCEAN

- - - ▸ Blair
· · · · · ▸ Davis
——— ▸ Osterhaus
- - - ▸ Williams

highlights the triumphant humanity of the soldiers who felt compassion for their opponents facing death by cremation on the battlefield. The haunting gazes of men and boys speak dramatically from the museum's rear wall. Visitors can hike the Assault Trail below "Dead Angle," and the Illinois monument looms where Union forces nearly breached the Confederate breastworks.

LOCATION: Kennesaw Mountain National Battlefield Park, 900 Kennesaw Mountain Dr., Kennesaw, 770-427-4686, www.nps.gov/kemo.

FURTHER READING

Kennesaw Mountain: Sherman, Johnston, and the Atlanta Campaign
by Earl J. Hess
Illuminating battle account also includes description of modern battlefield park

Hood in Hindsight

The decision to replace General Johnston with General Hood in the Atlanta Campaign seems sound (see sidebar p. 64). Not only did Hood have a strong combat record. He also had been integral to Johnston's plans and had been recommended by Lee. At age 34, Hood became the youngest four-star general in U.S. military history, but because he ultimately failed, the debate over his selection continues to this day.

FURTHER READING

Jefferson Davis and His Generals: The Failure of Confederate Command in the West
by Steven E. Woodworth
Probing study of leadership in the West

✳ Kolb's Farm

CAMPAIGN: Atlanta Campaign
DATE(S): June 22, 1864

In another attempt to protect his supply line following the Battle of Marietta (see p. 76), General Johnston's forces dug in along the Kennesaw Mountain line while Sherman again sought to flank the Confederates on their southern end. Coming upon General Hood's Confederate troops near Kolb's Farm, General Schofield's forces sat behind quickly formed breastworks, planning to take advantage of Hood's tendency to act aggressively. Hood, seeing an opportunity to shatter a part of Sherman's army, launched an attack with two divisions of his corps. Pouring into an open, swampy field, Hood's forces were decimated by troops under the command of General Hooker, resulting in 1,000 Rebel casualties.

Walk part of the unstaffed battlefield on the Kolb's Farm Loop.

LOCATION: Kolb's Farm is located about 7 miles south of the Kennesaw Mountain National Battlefield Park visitor center, on Powder Springs Rd. and Callaway Rd. in Marietta, www.georgiatrails.com.

✳ Lovejoy's Station

CAMPAIGN: Atlanta Campaign
DATE(S): August 20, 1864

After damaging the Atlanta & West Point Railroad, Union General Kilpatrick aimed for the Macon & Western, southeast of Atlanta. At Lovejoy's Station, General Ross's Texas cavalry interrupted Kilpatrick's assault. Surrounded, and with General Cleburne's Confederate infantry on-site, Kilpatrick's 4,500 men, with sabers waving, escaped eastward by breaking through the Confederate line at Nash Farm. The Rebels quickly repaired the damaged railroad.

Nash Farm, where Kilpatrick's cavalry charged across rolling fields and 600 acres of cornfields during harvest season, is now a 204-acre park with a museum located near

Joseph E. Johnston, Army of Tennessee commander, favored defensive stands.

what was the center of the Confederate line. Interpretive signs and site artifacts explain the action here.

LOCATION: **Nash Farm Battlefield Park, 100 Babbs Mill Rd., Hampton, 404-281-8651, www.henrycountybattlefield.com.**

FURTHER READING

Sherman's Horsemen: Union Cavalry Operations in the Atlanta Campaign by David Evans Draws on unpublished material to tell the story of Sherman's raids

✳ Marietta

CAMPAIGN: Atlanta Campaign
DATE(S): June 9–July 3, 1864

After the Battle of Dallas (see p. 66), a monthlong series of combat actions occurred west of town as Sherman pushed Johnston east across Cobb County and forced his Rebel forces to fall back toward Kennesaw. As the urgency to reach Atlanta before the November election increased, Sherman dramatically changed his tactics and attacked at Kennesaw Mountain (see pp. 72–75).

Eight miles west of Marietta's Union and Confederate cemeteries lie the original trench segments.

LOCATION: **Marietta Welcome Center, 4 Depot St. N.E., Marietta, 770-429-1115, www.mariettasquare.com.**

✳ New Hope Church

CAMPAIGN: Atlanta Campaign
DATE(S): May 25–26, 1864

From Adairsville (see p. 62), Sherman forced Johnston to abandon his defensive position in Allatoona Pass's rugged terrain. Johnston quickly and skillfully moved to block Sherman from Atlanta across a ten-mile defensive line from Dallas to Pickett's Mill. Midway, at New Hope Church, the Rebels, outnumbered four to one but holding the high ground, successfully attacked General Hooker's Union forces as they emerged from a steep, wooded ravine they called the "Hell Hole."

LOCATION: **Markers and map at New Hope Church on Hwy. 381 near the intersection with Bobo Rd., northeast of Dallas. The Confederate line ran through the nearby cemetery. Start at Pickett's Mill (see p. 77) for a battle overview.**

General Polk Is Killed

In June 1864, General Johnston formed a ten-mile defensive position along Pine, Lost, and Brushy Mountains in Cobb County. These geographical ridges north and west of Kennesaw blocked Sherman's approach routes to Marietta and Atlanta while also providing excellent observation points. They also severely overextended Johnston's manpower. On June 14, General Polk, an Episcopal bishop turned soldier and a first cousin of former president James K. Polk, joined Generals Johnston and Hardee on the bald crest of Pine Mountain (aka Pine Knob or Pine Hill), where Union cannon fire pierced him through the chest.

Relocated to Pickett's Mill, this 1850s cabin now hosts living-history events.

✳ Peachtree Creek

CAMPAIGN: Atlanta Campaign

DATE(S): July 20, 1864

Jefferson Davis, fed up with Johnston's repeated withdrawals, tapped General Hood to command the Army of Tennessee on July 17, 1864. Sherman, who was closing in on Atlanta's railroads, split his army group. General Thomas approached from the north, while the armies of Generals Schofield and McPherson flanked from the east.

Three miles north of Atlanta, Hood, a very aggressive commander, took advantage of the gap in Sherman's Union forces to attack Thomas's troops at Peachtree Creek. A missed opportunity ensued as fragmented Rebel forces attacked several hours later than planned. Thomas prevailed. The combined casualty toll was more than 6,000 men.

Today, scenic 14.5-acre Tanyard Creek Park features interpretive signs and is traversed by the BeltLine, a one-mile trail that follows the course of the creek.

LOCATION: Tanyard Creek Park, Collier Rd. at Walthall Dr., Atlanta.

✳ Pickett's Mill

CAMPAIGN: Atlanta Campaign

DATE(S): May 27, 1864

Fresh from defeat in the Battle of New Hope Church (see p. 76), Sherman ordered General Howard to strike a perceived weakness on Johnston's right flank. The Rebels had their own version of "Stonewall," as General Cleburne's 10,000 Confederate troops repelled Howard's 14,000, resulting in 1,600 Union casualties.

Through excellent maps and displays, the visitor center at Pickett's Mill Battlefield Historic Site helps connect the battles of New Hope Church, Pickett's Mill, and Dallas (see p. 66), known as the "Hell Hole battles." The trio of battles slowed but didn't stop Sherman's Atlanta Campaign. The 765-acre park still looks much like it did in 1834, with earthworks, thick woodlands, and overgrown ravines that help visitors visualize the challenges faced by both Union and Confederate troops.

LOCATION: Pickett's Mill Battlefield Historic Site, 4432 Mt. Tabor Church Rd., Dallas, 770-443-7850, www.gastateparks.org.

✷Resaca

CAMPAIGN: Atlanta Campaign

DATE(S): May 13–15, 1864

On May 9, General McPherson's forces met stronger than expected resistance near Resaca, preventing them from severing Confederate communication and rail lines—a missed opportunity for sure as they withdrew to Snake Creek Gap. By May 13, Johnston had fortified defenses around Resaca. After that day's skirmishes, fierce fighting raged along Camp Creek and across what is today I-75. The Atlanta Campaign's first real battle left more than 2,500 casualties on each side and no clear winner. Today, a six-mile trail runs through the battlefield. At the Confederate Cemetery, learn how Mary Green created burial sites on her father's plantation.

LOCATION: Resaca Battlefield Historic Site, Battlefield Pkwy., at exit 320 off I-75, Resaca, 800-887-3811, www.resacabattlefield.org.

Reenactments are held on the third weekend of May.

✳ Ringgold Gap

CAMPAIGN: Chattanooga-Ringgold Campaign

DATE(S): November 27, 1863

After Missionary Ridge, Rebels retreated south while General Cleburne staged a rear-guard delaying action to protect Bragg's supply train. Outnumbered three to one, Cleburne used the gap to ambush Union General Hooker. The irony for Hooker's ill-used men is that five miles north, at Parker's Gap, an unguarded cut would have allowed him to bypass Cleburne to the east.

Ringgold Depot has interpretive signs and a good view of the gap. The Old Stone Church nearby is worth a visit for some unique history. Also close by, Confederate Park has a bronze statue of Cleburne and a relief map of the Atlanta Campaign.

After regrouping at Snake Creek Gap, Union forces moved against General Johnston's troops at the Battle of Resaca in May 1864, resulting in heavy casualties on both sides.

LOCATION: **Ringgold Depot, 155 Depot St., Ringgold, 706-935-5290, by appointment only.**

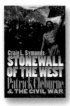

FURTHER READING

Stonewall of the West: Patrick Cleburne and the Civil War
by Craig L. Symonds
First critical biography of the Confederate commander

✳ Rocky Face Ridge

CAMPAIGN: Atlanta Campaign
DATE(S): May 7–13, 1864

General Sherman's opponent in the Atlanta Campaign was General Johnston's Army of Tennessee. On May 7, Union strikes from Mill Creek Gap to Dug Gap distracted Johnston's outnumbered forces perched along this imposing 700-foot-high ridge west of Dalton, leaving them oblivious to Sherman's flanking maneuvers southward. Pelting Union forces below with artillery and rocks, Johnston's men held on for a week before moving to Resaca (see p. 78). By May 9, Union General McPherson, screened by Taylor's Ridge, had cut through Snake Creek Gap toward Johnston's rear.

The remnants of the original stone wall built by the Confederates lie scattered throughout Dug Gap Battle Park. Hike to the crest of Rocky Face via the challenging Disney Trail (see p. 83).

LOCATION: **Dug Gap Battle Park, W. Dug Gap Battle Rd., Dalton, 706-278-0217, www.whitfield-murrayhistoricalsociety.org.**

✳ Utoy Creek

CAMPAIGN: Atlanta Campaign
DATE(S): August 5–7, 1864

Continuing to probe Confederate defenses around Atlanta, Sherman again aimed for the railroads near East Point. General Schofield's Army of the Ohio successfully pushed the Rebels eastward from Utoy

This 1864 sketch depicts Kilpatrick's last charge at the Battle of Waynesborough.

Creek until internal squabbles caused them to halt for the evening. Hood's troops first dug in on a steep incline behind abatis, then moved their defenses east. "The enemy can build parapets faster than we can march," an exasperated Sherman reportedly wrote.

Trench remnants are visible at Cascade Springs Nature Preserve, an unmarked and unstaffed site offering a nice nature walk.

LOCATION: **Marker located at Cascade Rd. (GA 154) and Woodland Terrace, Atlanta; Cascade Springs Nature Preserve, 2851 Cascade Rd. S.W., Atlanta, 404-546-6788.**

✳ Waynesborough

CAMPAIGN: Savannah Campaign
DATE(S): December 4, 1864

In late November, General Wheeler's Confederate cavalry twice drove General Kilpatrick's forces out of Waynesborough, but not before the Federals did considerable damage. The two forces, continually nipping at each other during Sherman's March to the Sea (see p. 74), skirmished 100 miles northwest of Savannah. Kilpatrick's cavalry plowed through three lines of Confederate defenses, forcing Wheeler's outnumbered forces into retreat. The last hurdle for Sherman now was Fort McAllister.

LOCATION: **Marker located at US 25 and GA 24 in south Waynesboro.**

Other Battles and Beyond

✦ Civil War Heartland Leaders Trail

Beginning in Gainesville and continuing south to Milledgeville, this self-guided auto tour highlights Civil War leaders whose homes are preserved within the state, including Confederate Vice President Alexander Stephens. To order the tour brochure, call 800-653-0603, or visit www.civilwaringeorgia.com.

✦ *Crossroads of Conflict*

Crossroads of Conflict: A Guide to Civil War Sites in Georgia by Barry L. Brown and Gordon R. Elwell features more than 350 sites in the state and can be acquired by contacting www.gacivilwar.org.

✦ Georgia Civil War Heritage Trails

For downloadable brochures detailing themed Civil War driving tours throughout the state, visit www.civilwarheritagetrails.org.

✦ "War Comes to Dalton"

Available for purchase at the Dalton Freight Depot Welcome Center (305 S. Depot St., 706-270-9960) in historic downtown Dalton, this driving tour explores 25 miles from Tunnel Hill through Dug Gap to the Resaca battlefield.

✦ Andersonville National Historic Site

A free audio tour helps interpret the prison site and the cemetery.

LOCATION: 760 POW Rd., Andersonville, 229-924-0343, www.nps.gov/ande.

FURTHER READING
Andersonville
by MacKinlay Kantor Pulitzer Prize–winning novel tells the heartbreaking story of the prison and the men who lived there

More than 45,000 Union prisoners entered 26-acre Camp Sumter, notorious for its high mortality rate due to overcrowding, stifling heat, crude shelter, poor food, and bad water.

✦ Brown's Mill Battlefield Historic Site

General Wheeler's successful defeat of General Edward McCook's raiding party on July 30, 1864, and other cavalry failures, helped Sherman realize that he would need to besiege Atlanta if he was to capture it. The site has walking trails and interpretive signs.

LOCATION: **155 Millard Farmer Rd., Newnan, 770-254-2627, www.exploregeorgia.org.**

✦ Camp Lawton

Conditions at this prison—built in 1864 to handle overflow from Andersonville—inspired Sherman to march through South Carolina in early 1865 in revenge. Today, the prison is an archaeological site.

LOCATION: **Magnolia Springs State Park, 1053 Magnolia Springs Dr., Millen, 478-982-1660, www.gastateparks.org.**

✦ Cassville

In May 1864, after the Battle of Adairsville (see p. 62), General Joe Johnston fixed solid defenses on a ridge east of town. As Federals advanced, Hood convinced Johnston to withdraw to Allatoona, something Johnston said he regretted doing.

LOCATION: **Marker on US 41 at Cassville Rd., Cassville.**

✦ Cassville Confederate Cemetery

This is the resting place of 300 unknown Civil War soldiers and General William Wofford, a legislator who, after voting against secession, fought for the cause.

LOCATION: **Cassville-White Rd. at Shinall Gaines Rd. N.W., Cassville.**

✦ Cook-Huff House

General Johnston made his winter headquarters here in 1863–1864. This is also where General Cleburne made a proposal

More than 12,000 Union prisoners are buried in Andersonville's cemetery.

offering freedom to slaves in return for their enlisting in the Confederate Army.

LOCATION: **314 N. Selvidge St., Dalton, 706-278-0217.**

✦ Fort Wayne Historic Site

A mile-long walking trail leads past the last entrenchments created by Georgia militia.

LOCATION: **117 Taylor Ridge Rd., Resaca, 706-625-3200. Visit www.exploregordoncounty .com for a downloadable visitor's brochure.**

✦ Gilgal Church

Miles of breastworks and trenches once surrounded this unstaffed site.

LOCATION: **Near 667 Kennesaw Due West Rd. N.W., Kennesaw.**

✦ Heritage Center at Roswell

Union troops occupied Roswell, a vital mill town for the South, in July 1864. They destroyed the mills and sent 400 workers—mostly women with children—north to move them away from the Federal rearguard areas. Walk the Old Mill Park interpretive trail to Vickery Creek Falls, which powered the mills.

LOCATION: **617 Atlanta St., Roswell, 800-776-7935, www.visitroswellga.com.**

✦ Historic Oakland Cemetery

This garden cemetery is located less than a mile from downtown Atlanta. Call for walking tour availability.

LOCATION: **248 Oakland Ave. S.E., Atlanta, 404-688-2107, www.oaklandcemetery.com.**

✦ Historic Western & Atlantic Railroad Tunnel Heritage Center Museum

The museum offers guided tours of the 1,477-foot rail line, which ran through Chetoogeta Mountain from 1850 to 1928, and the Clisby Austin House, Sherman's headquarters during the first battle of

The Old State Capitol, circa 1807, embodies early Gothic architecture in the U.S.

Dalton (see p. 66). Learn the tunnel's role in the Great Locomotive Chase of 1862.

Dalton (see p. 66).

LOCATION: **215 Clisby Austin Rd., Tunnel Hill, 706-876-1571, www.tunnelhillheritagecenter.com.**

✦ Margaret Mitchell House

Mitchell wrote *Gone With the Wind* here.

LOCATION: **979 Crescent Ave. N.E., Atlanta, 404-249-7015, www.atlantahistorycenter.com/mmh.**

✦ Marietta Confederate Cemetery

Three thousand Confederate soldiers are buried in this 1863 cemetery featuring beautiful statuary.

LOCATION: **395 Powder Springs St., Marietta, 770-794-5601.**

✦ National Civil War Naval Museum

This museum is home to the largest surviving Confederate warship, the C.S.S. *Jackson*, and several full-size replica vessels.

LOCATION: **1002 Victory Dr., Columbus, 706-327-9798, www.portcolumbus.org.**

✦ Old Capitol Museum

Today, a Federalist flavor and robust walking trail make for a pleasant sightseeing excursion. Visit antebellum homes and the old state capitol, where secession got the nod.

LOCATION: **201 E. Greene St., Milledgeville, 478-453-1803, www.oldcapitolmuseum.org.**

✦ Patrick Cleburne Confederate Memorial Cemetery

About 1,000 unidentified Civil War soldiers are buried in this cemetery, which also features a life-size statue of the Confederate general. Headstones are set in the shape of the Confederate battle flag.

Stone Mountain's finely detailed carving (90 by 190 feet) looms 400 feet aboveground.

LOCATION: Intersection of Johnson St. and McDonough St., Jonesboro.

✦ Rocky Face Ridge

The Disney Trail—one of the steepest, most challenging trails in northern Georgia—leads up the mountain where the Battle of Rocky Face Ridge raged in May 1864 (see p. 79). See the grave of George Disney, a Confederate soldier whose burial site was discovered by Boy Scouts in 1912 and given a proper headstone.

LOCATION: Trailhead at rear of the First Church of the Nazarene parking lot, 2325 Chattanooga Rd., Dalton, www.gacivilwar.org.

✦ Savannah

Savor the grace and beauty of the South in this well-preserved antebellum city. Explore via self-guided or commercial walking tours (see pp. 70–71).

LOCATION: Visitor Information Center, 301 Martin Luther King Jr. Blvd., 912-944-0455, www.visitsavannah.com.

FURTHER READING

Civil War Savannah
by Derek Smith
Tales of those who lived and worked in the city during the Civil War

✦ Southern Museum of Civil War and Locomotive History

One sly spy, one stolen train, and one brazen plot equal a hoot of a heist: the Great Locomotive Chase of 1862. The museum's exhibits include the locomotive *General*.

LOCATION: 2829 Cherokee St., Kennesaw, 770-427-2117, www.southernmuseum.org.

✦ Stone Mountain Park

This is the South's Mount Rushmore, with stone carvings of Jefferson Davis, Robert E. Lee, and Stonewall Jackson. There is no cost to hike, but there is a parking fee.

LOCATION: 1000 Robert E. Lee Blvd., Stone Mountain, 800-401-2407, www.stone mountainpark.com.

Kentucky

TWO NATIVE SONS, BORN EIGHT MONTHS AND 100 MILES apart, pitted Kentuckians against one another. At stake for Abraham Lincoln and Jefferson Davis were Kentucky's resources—its young men, horses, agricultural products, the Louisville & Memphis Railroad, and control of the Mississippi and Ohio Rivers. President Lincoln handled the slave state gingerly, lest it jump full bore into the Confederate camp, noting, "To lose Kentucky is nearly the same as to lose the whole game." President Davis understood that, too.

When General Polk seized Columbus to control the Mississippi River passage, Kentucky's "neutrality" ended, as did Lincoln's hesitancy to move troops into the state. Kentucky's divisions deepened as General Grant occupied Paducah, troop buildup soared, and Tennessee became more vulnerable to Union attack. Pro-slavery Unionists were in a bind. Beyond a few significant battles, a host of guerrilla actions, like those of John Hunt Morgan, wreaked havoc across the state. The economic and political divide festered for decades afterward.

Each June since 1987, Georgetown, Kentucky, has hosted a reenactment of John Hunt Morgan's 1862 raid and two-day battle with Federal troops.

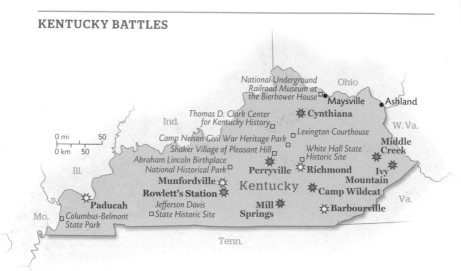

✳ Barbourville

CAMPAIGN: Operations in Eastern Kentucky
DATE(S): September 19, 1861

With Kentucky's feet officially tapping in the Union camp, the Confederates made their battle debut at Barbourville. General Zollicoffer's forces launched a surprise attack against Kentucky state guards at Camp Andrew Johnson but missed catching a batch of Union recruits, who had already been sent to Camp Dick Robinson to complete their training. The excursion was not without reward, however, as marauding Confederates captured abandoned artillery while destroying the camp.

LOCATION: Civil War Interpretive Park, Daniel Boone Dr. and Cumberland Ave., Barbourville. The unstaffed park has murals and markers.

✳ Camp Wildcat

CAMPAIGN: Operations in Eastern Kentucky
OTHER NAME(S): Wildcat Mountain
DATE(S): October 21, 1861

Union troops under General Schoepf held the high ground on Wildcat Mountain as General Zollicoffer led his Confederate forces through Cumberland Gap and along the contested Wilderness Road. While Zollicoffer's men originally outnumbered the Union troops seven to one, Schoepf's soldiers created extensive mountain fortifications. As the Confederates withdrew, the bluecoats savored their first significant victory in Kentucky.

Today, the battlefield is a rural, unstaffed area with three well-maintained gravel trails marked with excellent interpretive signs. Brochures are available on-site, as are restroom facilities and a pavilion.

LOCATION: Camp Wildcat Civil War Battlefield, exit 49 off I-75 and then follow the park signs for 3 miles, www.wildcatbattlefield.org.

✳ Cynthiana

CAMPAIGN: Morgan's Raid Into Kentucky
OTHER NAME(S): Keller's Bridge
DATE(S): June 11–12, 1864

Confederate raider John Hunt Morgan, a romantic figure who would escape from the Ohio State Prison after being captured on a raid, was also a superb cavalry officer and a scion of Lexington society. Here, at Cynthiana, on the banks of the South Licking River, he disrupted Union supply lines. Having already attacked the same location once before, in 1862, Morgan apparently anticipated an easy rout of the Federal infantry and home guards on duty. Instead, the battle grew larger than he could have expected. After setting the town ablaze, Rebels fought a six-hour battle at Keller's Bridge, garnering 1,300 Union prisoners. Morgan's luck ended on June 12, as General Burbridge's 2,400 reinforcements pushed the Rebels back in a bloody engagement.

The 1853 courthouse, from where Federals twice fired on Rebel troops, still stands. There visitors can learn about Morgan's fate in Greeneville, Tennessee, three months later.

LOCATION: **Pick up walking and driving tour maps at the Cynthiana Chamber of Commerce, 201 South Main St., Cynthiana, 859-234-5236, www.cynthianaky.com.**

✳ Ivy Mountain

CAMPAIGN: Operations in Eastern Kentucky
OTHER NAME(S): Ivy Creek, Ivy Narrows
DATE(S): November 8–9, 1861

As Colonel Williams moved through eastern Kentucky seeking recruits, he met Union forces at Ivy Creek. Lacking adequate ammunition and men, Williams sought a defensive position in the mountains. Instead, his men clogged the seven-foot-wide passage. Once they cleared the pass, they fled toward the Virginia state line. Recognizing the risk, Union forces, commanded by General Nelson, a former naval officer, ceased the pursuit, accepting their new foothold in the state's defensible eastern mountains.

A four-lane highway has compromised the battle site, but the terrain still reflects the challenges both sides faced there.

LOCATION: **Interpretive signs and an obelisk are located on the north side of US 460/23, just east of Branham Court Rd.**

Barbourville's reenactors re-create the first Kentucky battle with casualties on each side.

✳ Middle Creek

CAMPAIGN: Offensive in Eastern Kentucky
DATE(S): January 10, 1862

Efforts to rid eastern Kentucky of Confederate training camps found a relatively unknown Ohio college professor, James Garfield, pursuing Rebels over mountainous terrain. Middle Creek, referred to as "the battle that launched a presidency," occurred as General Marshall's Confederate troops, posted on ridges in the narrow valley south of the creek, clashed with Garfield's men. The outnumbered Rebels retreated southeast to Virginia.

This well-preserved, undeveloped site's terrain is similar to how it was in 1862. Two short loop, gravel trails—one Confederate, one Union—are marked with interpretive signs. An informative kiosk with maps and a four-mile driving tour explain this encounter and others nearby.

LOCATION: Middle Creek National Battlefield, intersection of KY 114 and KY 404,

Prestonsburg, 606-886-1312, www.middle creek.org. Signs along US 23 near Prestonsburg point the way to this unstaffed site. Battlefield maps are available on the park website.

✳ Mill Springs

CAMPAIGN: Offensive in Eastern Kentucky
OTHER NAME(S): Fishing Springs
DATE(S): January 19, 1862

Confederate General Zollicoffer established his winter camp on the north side of the Cumberland River, nine miles south of General Thomas's encampment at Logan's Crossroads (the present-day town of Nancy). Faulty assumptions about Union troop strength led Generals Crittenden and Zollicoffer on a night march toward Thomas's camp to make a surprise attack. The Confederates were unaware that the Union forces had been reinforced.

Poor visibility due to weather and thick battle smoke led to tragedy when the near-sighted Zollicoffer strayed into Federal lines and was killed. Having discovered that their waterlogged flintlocks were useless, the poorly armed Rebels fled. The southern-born Thomas had won the first major battle in Kentucky, dashing Rebel hopes of adding a Bluegrass State star to their banner.

The visitor center offers a ten-stop self-driving tour of 100 well-preserved, interpreted acres that allows visitors to imagine Rebels navigating through ravines to avoid detection. Head logs mark the Confederate line. The on-site research library holds first-person accounts of the battle, including General Thomas's battle plans and information on the role of women in the Civil War.

LOCATION: Mill Springs Battlefield Visitor Center, 9020 W. KY 80, Nancy, 606-636-4045, www.mill springs.net.

General Thomas's reinforced troops overwhelmed General Zollicoffer's Rebels at Mill Springs.

✳ Munfordville

CAMPAIGN: Confederate Heartland Offensive
DATE(S): September 14–17, 1862

Munfordville shines as General Bragg's only victory in Kentucky, a moment when the state's control seemed within Confederate grasp. Making an end run around General Buell, Bragg's forces stood between the Union Army and Louisville. When Colonel Wilder refused to surrender the Union garrison at Munfordville, Bragg arrived with reinforcements. Wilder's surrender on September 17 became a footnote in history, as it coincided with the Battle of Antietam (see pp. 340–341).

Bragg's Confederate troops now controlled the 1,200-foot-long Louisville & Nashville Railroad bridge across the Green River, a key north-south supply route. Fearing that his army was too tired and poorly supplied to continue fighting, Bragg made a premature withdrawal north rather than taking the necessary steps to break Buell's army.

Preservation efforts have this unstaffed site which includes a well-interpreted 2.5-mile trail—looking similar to how it did in 1862. See Rowlett's Station (see p. 95) for an orientation.

LOCATION: **Battle for the Bridge Historic Preserve, 1309 US 31 W., Munfordville, 270-524-0101, www.battleforthebridge.org.**

The Awakening

The pen is mightier than the sword, and in *Uncle Tom's Cabin,* Harriet Beecher Stowe, daughter of a fire-and-brimstone preacher, graphically articulated slavery's harsh realities. The story of Simon Legree, who crushed the spirit of Eliza and dominated kind, wise old Uncle Tom, seared the consciences of many. By giving names and faces to the South's "peculiar institution," *Uncle Tom's Cabin* became a rallying cry for emancipation and a worldwide best seller.

Civil War on Foot: Lexington

The blue-blood and bluegrass center of the state was divided like the rest of Kentucky. Federals occupied Lexington in 1861, but less than a year later, after routing the Union at Richmond, Rebel troops entered the city. The visit was short-lived. Following the Battle of Perryville, the Union controlled the city once again.

❶ Henry Clay Law Offices *(176 N. Mill St.)* Henry Clay, the Great Compromiser, practiced law here from 1804 until 1810.

❷ Hunt-Morgan House *(201 N. Mill St.)* This house was built by John Hunt, the first millionaire west of the Allegheny Mountains. He was a relative of John Hunt Morgan, the famous Confederate cavalryman who is reputed to have ridden his horse in the front door of the house, kissed his mother, and continued out the back door while escaping Union soldiers.

❸ Benjamin Gratz House *(231 N. Mill St.)* Built in 1819, this house was purchased by Benjamin Gratz, who preserved the green space after the original buildings of Transylvania University burned down in 1829.

❹ Transylvania University *(301 W. Third St.)* Founded in 1780, Transylvania is the oldest college in Kentucky. Graduates include Cassius Clay, the abolitionist politician, and more than 150 members of Congress. The main building, Old Morrison, served as a Union hospital.

❺ Transylvania University (original site) Originally built in 1780, the college is the 16th oldest in the U.S. After it burned down, the campus moved across the street.

❻ Bodley-Bullock House *(200 Market St.)* Union headquarters during the war, this was also the law office where Mary Todd Lincoln's father apprenticed.

❼ Sayre School *(184 N. Limestone St.)* Originally opened in 1854 as Transylvania Woman's College, this was an all-female boarding school until 1876.

❽ Cheapside and Fayette County Court House Grounds *(215 W. Main St.)* A slave auction block, slave pens, and other

The 170-acre Lexington Cemetery is admired for its historical, natural, and landscape design features.

public facilities once stood on these grounds. Here the slaves of Mary Todd Lincoln were sold to pay off her father's estate. Later, numerous abolitionist speeches were made on the site.

❾ Old Melodeon Hall *(Corner of Upper St. and Main St.)* Tom Thumb, Jenny Lind, and even John Wilkes Booth all played at this 1850 entertainment parlor.

❿ Mary Todd Lincoln House *(578 W. Main St.)* Mary Todd Lincoln lived here from age 13 to 21. Lincoln visited before the Civil War to settle his father-in-law's estate.

⓫ Lexington Cemetery *(833 W. Main St.)* The grounds of this cemetery, which was founded in 1848, are gorgeous, and many luminaries are buried here, including Henry Clay, John Hunt Morgan, Basil Duke, and John C. Breckinridge. Also buried here is Henry Clay's grandson, Andrew Eugene Irwin, who was killed during the siege of Vicksburg in 1863 (see p. 136).

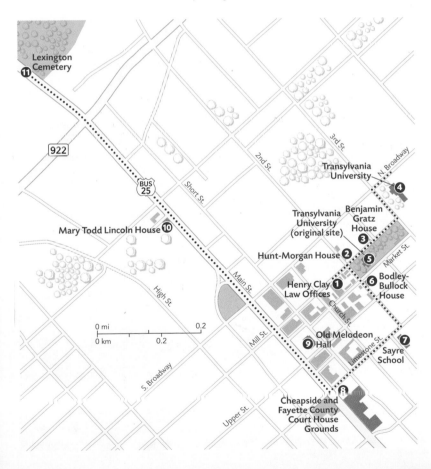

☀ Paducah

CAMPAIGN: Forrest's Expedition Into West Tennessee and Kentucky

DATE(S): March 25, 1864

In 1861, after Confederates had occupied Columbus, General Grant occupied Paducah, primarily for its location at the confluence of the Ohio and Tennessee Rivers just downstream of the Cumberland River. Those water routes were crucial for access to the interior of both Kentucky and Tennessee. Fort Anderson, on Paducah's west end, served as a Federal guard post.

Facing a 650-man Union garrison in 1864, General Forrest's larger force staged a recruitment and supply raid on the town. Forrest met his match, however, while trying to bluff Colonel Hicks into surrendering the town and fort. Hicks's troops successfully drove off the Rebels.

A huge mural on the flood wall at First and Broadway in town depicts Paducah in the Civil War. The home of Lloyd Tilghman, the commander of Fort Henry on the Tennessee River who was killed at the Battle of Champion Hill, is now a Civil War museum.

In this 1927 photo, a boy holds Union and Confederate muzzle-loader balls found on Perryville's battlefield.

LOCATION: Pick up the brochure for a walking tour based on a Union officer's map at the Paducah Visitors Bureau, 128 Broadway, Paducah, 270-443-8783 or 800-PADUCAH, www.paducah.travel. There are numerous Civil War markers in town.

☀ Perryville

CAMPAIGN: Confederate Heartland Offensive

DATE(S): October 8, 1862

In the late summer of 1862, Confederate General Bragg boldly abandoned Mississippi and transported his army south to Mobile, across Mobile Bay, and then to Chattanooga through Georgia, where he sat poised to liberate Confederate Kentucky from the despot's heel. Fearing for the security of Nashville and the Federal supply line from Louisville, Federal Army of the Ohio commander Don Carlos Buell moved north to Louisville. Realizing that Kentucky would not rally to the Rebel banners, Bragg installed a Confederate governor only to carry the government into exile.

The decisive Battle of Perryville was launched as two parched armies found the same small pool of water—and each other. Ironically, an acoustic shadow (sound absorption often caused by topography or wind) deadened the sound waves, leaving

Underground Railroad

Slave management had been a problem since the first slaves were held in America. A person's natural yearning for freedom ensured that as long as there were slaves, there would be people trying to escape slavery. Owners had invested considerable money in their slave property and rightly feared the retribution that might come from slaves becoming educated, independent, or disaffected—or as they called it, "uppity."

Newspapers were filled with announcements of slave auctions and runaways, and a slave catcher could make a good living bringing escapees back to their owners. Powerful slave owners sought and received protective legislation from the states and, more important, from the federal government. Indeed, the Fugitive Slave Law of 1850 put the federal government directly in the business of protecting Southern property and directly in conflict with personal liberty laws passed by the states. General apathy toward the plight of slaves left them few options and fewer friends if they were to be freed.

The Underground Railroad was a quietly known path of friends and sympathetic whites who would receive, hide, feed, and facilitate the next leg of an escaped slave's journey north. Only in Canada could the enslaved truly be free; however, many slaves found welcoming communities in northern and midwestern states like New York, Pennsylvania, Ohio, Indiana, and Michigan, where they would settle. The Quaker faith played a leading role moving slaves to freedom.

The area around Maysville (see pp. 96–97), over to the Ohio River and across to Rankin, Ohio, offers valuable insight into how the Underground Railroad functioned. Documented safe houses, as seen at the National Underground Railroad Museum at the Bierbower House (see p. 99), for example, shed some light on how stationmasters hid fleeing slaves.

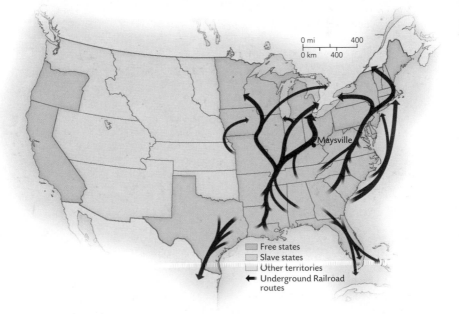

0 mi 400
0 km 400

Maysville

Free states
Slave states
Other territories
Underground Railroad routes

Henry P. Bottom

Well-to-do slave-owning Unionist "Squire" Bottom saw his home and 760-acre farm literally in the midst of the Perryville battle. Afterward, unburied Confederate dead were strewn across his land, being devoured by wild hogs. Bottom arranged for the interment of several hundred in mass graves on his property. This cemetery eventually became the beginning of the Perryville Historic Site. His home has been restored to its wartime appearance on the Perryville battlefield.

General Buell oblivious to the battle, although he was a scant two miles from the front line. The Battle of Perryville was not planned and thus not fought with all the resources of the two armies. Bragg had the tactical advantage and was generally the aggressor, but Federal depth and strength won the day—and earned kudos for an unknown infantry officer, Philip Sheridan, who would achieve greater laurels in 1864–1865 as Grant's cavalry chief.

Following the battle, the cancer that would eat away at the Confederacy's primary western army began to manifest itself. When Bragg asked his subordinates if he should renew the engagement the next day, he accepted their advice to abandon the campaign. Later, however, the same officers worked to undermine his authority, citing his withdrawal from Perryville as an example of his unfitness for command. In 13 months the fruits of that disloyalty would help shatter the Confederate Army in Tennessee. On the Union side, Buell's failure to pursue the withdrawing Confederates would cost him his job after the November midterm elections, when Lincoln resolved to rid himself of Democrat generals.

Today's battlefield topography hasn't changed much. In fact, the small rural town and the preservation of more than 745 acres have produced one of the nation's premier battlefields. Miles of trails with dozens of interpretive signs require hours and some physical agility to explore. The museum is open April to October, but the battlefield grounds, walking trails, and driving tour are accessible year-round. A wall of photos and quotes from soldiers who served at Perryville, many in their mid-teens, help 21st-century visitors understand the human toll of the battle.

LOCATION: **Perryville Battlefield State Historic Site, 1825 Battlefield Rd., Perryville, 859-332-8361, www.perryvillebattlefield.org. Also check out Merchant's Row in town, which is reminiscent of the town's setting in the 1860s.**

FURTHER READING

Perryville: This Grand Havoc of Battle
by Kenneth W. Noe
Award-winning account of the battle and its impact on soldiers and ordinary civilians

✳ Richmond

CAMPAIGN: Confederate Heartland Offensive
DATE(S): August 29–30, 1862

The second largest battle in Kentucky is often a "by the way" battle. And yet it was the most complete Confederate victory in the entire war, as General E. Kirby Smith's experienced forces routed the Union's green recruits. Capturing the bulk of General Nelson's men, artillery, and horses cleared a way north for the Rebels.

The 1811 Federal-style visitor center, known as the Rogers House, survived heavy fighting 700 yards north and a half mile south of its doors. Though modified over time, the building retains some original flooring. The well-interpreted battlefield includes three sites spread over 12 miles. Allow several hours for exploring via a self-guided driving tour.

LOCATION: **Battle of Richmond Visitor Center, 101 Battlefield Memorial Hwy., Richmond, 859-624-0013, www.visitorcenter.madisoncountyky.us.**

FURTHER READING

When the Ripe Pears Fell: The Battle of Richmond, Kentucky
by D. Warren Lambert
Scholarly and highly engaging study

✲Rowlett's Station

CAMPAIGN: Operations in Eastern Kentucky
OTHER NAME(S): Woodsonville, Green River
DATE(S): December 17, 1861

Control of the Louisville & Nashville Railroad over the Green River was the goal here when 500 German immigrants of the 32nd Indiana Infantry used old-world military tactics to repel more than 1,500 Rebel cavalrymen led by Colonel Terry. Colonel Willich, a Prussian native, had trained his forces in German, and, on December 17, he ordered them to form a Roman box or square on the field, with bayonets pointing in all directions. While casualties were low, Terry was killed in that unit's first battle. As the Rebels withdrew, the Union secured the rail line.

That so few Yankees could fend off so many Rebels, followed by Union victories at Mill Springs (see p. 88) and Middle Creek (see p. 88), gave Lincoln hope for success in the West.

Today, the Rowlett's Station battlefield is part of the Battle for the Bridge Historic Preserve in Munfordville (see p. 89). For orientation to both battles, start at the Hart County Historical Museum, where visitors can learn about the original stone railroad bridge piers still in use today.

LOCATION: **Hart County Historical Museum, 109 Main St., Munfordville, 270-524-0101, www.hartcountymuseum.org. Inquire in advance about visiting the earthen remnants of Fort Craig, now on private property, and the Anthony Woodson House's 14-foot scale model of the Louisville & Nashville Railroad, built to 1860 specifications.**

Cannons are set up for the annual reenactment of the 1862 Battle of Richmond.

Civil War on Foot: Maysville

Maysville was the boat dock for the 1786 town of Washington, Kentucky. Explore the early architecture and stories of this historic district, now known as Old Washington, southwest of Maysville. For information on visiting any of the buildings, call 606-759-7411.

❶ Albert Sidney Johnston House *(503 S. Court St.)* A guided tour of the boyhood home of Albert Sidney Johnston, a Confederate general who died in the Battle of Shiloh (see pp. 199–202), reveals period furniture and family photos. Ironically, Union General Nelson spent part of his childhood here years later.

❷ Slavery to Freedom Museum *(2124 Old Main St.)* The brick Georgian town house where Harriet Beecher Stowe visited one of her pupils, Elizabeth Marshall Key, includes educational exhibits on slavery. The accounts of the then 22-year-old Stowe witnessing the slave auction that opened her eyes to the horrors of slavery are not verifiable. She wrote *Uncle Tom's Cabin* (see sidebar p. 89) more than 20 years later.

❸ Washington Courthouse *(2110 Old Main St.)* The limestone foundation of the original 1793 courthouse is still visible under a modern home.

❹ Row Houses *(2117–2121 Old Main St.)* Built starting in 1795, these frame Elizabethan-style row houses are the oldest in Mason County. Three originally served as businesses, and no. 2117 was a town jail.

❺ Paxton Inn *(2030 Old Main St.)* This is where Maysville's movers and shakers met to discuss business and politics. Displays include buttons, artifacts, and antique quilts.

Mefford's Station, a 1787 flatboat-timber cabin, housed 15.

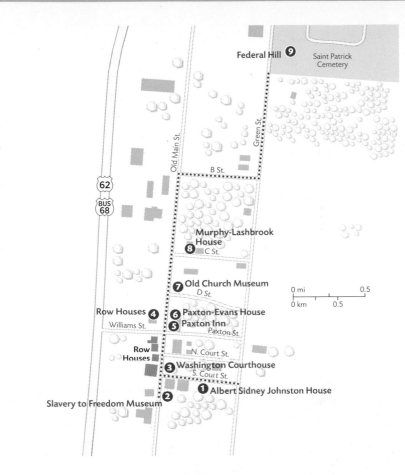

Federal Hill **9**

Saint Patrick
Cemetery

Green St.

Old Main St.

B St.

62

BUS
68

Murphy-Lashbrook
House
8 C St.

7 Old Church Museum
D St.

0 mi   0.5

0 km   0.5

Row Houses **4** **6** Paxton-Evans House
5 Paxton Inn
Williams St.   Paxton St.

Row
Houses   N. Court St.

3 Washington Courthouse
S. Court St.

2 **1** Albert Sidney Johnston House

Slavery to Freedom Museum

6 **Paxton-Evans
House** *(2028 Old
Main St.)* Inquire here for
information about tour-
ing the museums and vil-
lage. Call 606-759-7411
from April to December
or 606-564-9419 from
January–March.

7 **Old Church
Museum** *(2022 Old
Main St.)* Slavery split
the Methodist Episcopal

Church into factions.
The former slave gallery
in this 1848 "South"
church was removed in
the 1970s. It is open by
appointment.

8 **Murphy-
Lashbrook House**
(2014 Old Main St.)
This 1805 brick home
features native wood
throughout, uniting
18th- and 19th-century

architecture. It is now a
private residence.

9 **Federal Hill** *(2004
Green St.)* Now a private
home, this 1800 "House
on the Hill" was built
by Thomas Marshall,
brother of Supreme
Court Justice John
Marshall. Thomas was
a slave owner and the
first clerk of the Mason
County Court.

Other Battles and Beyond

✦ Kentucky Civil War Tour

This driving tour highlights 96 Civil War markers across the state. A list of all the markers included on the tour—with a detailed explanation of each one—is available at http://explorekyhistory.ky.gov.

✦ Abraham Lincoln Birthplace National Historical Park

Established in 1916, this national park is composed of two separate sites within ten miles of each other: Lincoln's birthplace and his boyhood home at Knob Creek. Both locations offer self-guided walking tours and nature trails. Restrooms, a picnic area, and bookstore are located at the birthplace site.

LOCATION: **2995 Lincoln Farm Rd., Hodgenville, 270-358-3137, www.nps.gov/abli.**

Abraham Lincoln's earliest recollection was of his boyhood home at Knob Creek.

✦ Ashland

This was the estate of Henry Clay. Although Clay had died by the time of the Civil War, four of his grandsons served with the Confederates and one with the Union. Although the house is not original, some of the original outbuildings remain.

LOCATION: **120 Sycamore Rd., Lexington, 859-266-8581, www.henryclay.org.**

✦ Camp Nelson Civil War Heritage Park

This park once served as the third largest recruiting and training center for black troops and, later, as a refugee center for former slaves seeking freedom. Today, the 400-acre archaeology site and interpretive center has five miles of walking trails, a video, and the original administrative building.

LOCATION: **6614 Danville Rd., Nicholasville, 859-881-5716, www.campnelson.org.**

✦ Columbus-Belmont State Park

Columbus-Belmont is a massive state park featuring earthworks and a commanding overlook that controlled the Mississippi, which enticed Polk to violate Kentucky's neutrality.

LOCATION: **350 Park Rd., Columbus, 270-677-2327, www.parks.ky.gov.**

✦ Jefferson Davis State Historic Site

A 351-foot obelisk marks the spot where the president of the Confederacy was born on June 3, 1808. Take an elevator ride to the top for a view of the countryside. A presentation on Jefferson Davis is available at the museum by advance request.

LOCATION: **258 Pembroke-Fairview Rd., US 68-80, Fairview, 270-889-6100, www.parks .ky.gov.**

Shaker Village of Pleasant Hill was founded in 1805. Today, the 34 restored structures and living-history programs at this 2,900-acre site help interpret the community's way of life.

✦ Lexington Courthouse

The courthouse has memorials to John C. Breckinridge and John Hunt Morgan.

LOCATION: **273 West Main St., Lexington.**

✦ National Underground Railroad Museum at the Bierbower House

This documented safe house preserves slavery artifacts and period stories.

LOCATION: **38 W. 4th St., Maysville, 606-564-3200, www.kentuckytourism.com.**

✦ Shaker Village of Pleasant Hill

During the Civil War, pacifist residents at this village provided both Northerners and Southerners with food, shelter, and medical services. Today, it is one of the country's largest restored Shaker communities, offering visitors historical reenactments, an inn, miles of trails, and an excellent restaurant.

LOCATION: **3501 Lexington Rd., Harrodsburg, 800-734-5611, www.shakervillageky.org.**

✦ Thomas D. Clark Center for Kentucky History

The center offers Old State Capitol and Military History Museum tours.

LOCATION: **100 W. Broadway, Frankfort, 502-564-1792, www.history.ky.gov.**

✦ White Hall State Historic Site

This 1789 Georgian-style building was once the home of eccentric 19th-century emancipationist Cassius Marcellus Clay, who was born here in 1810. Clay had it remodeled into an Italianate mansion in 1860.

LOCATION: **500 White Hall Shrine Rd., Richmond, 859-623-9178, www.whitehall clermontfoundation.org.**

Louisiana

LOUISIANA WAS THE DEEPEST PART OF THE DEEP SOUTH.
It was no accident that New Orleans, blessed with a labor-intensive
agricultural climate, was the South's largest city. The rich soil generated huge wealth, with half the state's $200 million in annual trade
being in cotton. For the states located along the Ohio, Red, and
Mississippi Rivers, the port was the key to their economic prosperity. In fact, many countries had envoys and banking interests in
New Orleans. Not surprisingly, the government's senior military
adviser devised an economic strategy to defeat the insurgency. By
closing trade routes, Winfield Scott's Anaconda Plan became the
vehicle for the South's economic failure. The war in Louisiana was
composed of three significant operations: the capture of New
Orleans and the restoration of its trade; the surrender of Port
Hudson, which opened trade along the Mississippi River;
and the Red River Expedition, which sought to open Louisiana's
cotton fields to New England factories—it was all political and it
was all about the money.

**An icon of the French Quarter in New Orleans, St. Louis Cathedral boasts
three towering spires. Its 1819 bell still peals.**

LOUISIANA BATTLES

Ark.

0 mi   50
0 km   50

Goodrich's Landing
Grant's Canal Park

Milliken's Bend

Louisiana

Mansfield
Blair's Landing
Pleasant Hill
Monett's   Frogmore Cotton
Grand Ecore Visitor Center   Ferry   Plantation and Gins

Forts Randolph and Buhlow
State Historic Site
Kent Plantation House

Texas

Fort DeRussy   Mansura
Yellow Bayou
St. Francisville
Stirling's Plantation
Opelousas Tourist and
Information Center

Vermillion
Lafayette   Bayou
Alexandre Mouton House/
Lafayette Museum;
Vermilionville

Shadows-on-
the-Teche

Avery Island
Young-Sanders Center

Baton Rouge
Magnolia Cemetery;
Magnolia Mound Plantation;
Old State Capitol

Miss.

Camp Moore Museum
and Cemetery

9   Plains Store
1

4   3 Donaldsonville

2   Metairie   Louisiana's Civil War Museum
Cemetery   10   at Confederate Memorial Hall

8   7   5   6
Fort
Star

Forts Jackson
and St. Philip

Gulf of Mexico

1 Baton Rouge
2 Kock's Plantation
3 Donaldsonville I
4 Donaldsonville II
5 Georgia Landing
6 LaFourche Crossing
7 Fort Bisland
8 Irish Bend
9 Port Hudson
10 New Orleans

✳ Baton Rouge

CAMPAIGN: Confederate Offensive Against
Baton Rouge

DATE(S): August 5, 1862

The state capital fell to the Federals on
May 29, 1862. On August 5, Confederate
General Breckinridge set out to take it back
by attacking General Williams's Union
forces. The Confederate ironclad *Arkansas*
promised protection from the river.
Unfortunately for the Rebel infantry, the
Arkansas's engines failed; it was later
destroyed to avoid capture. The intrepid
Confederates attacked toward the city, using
gravestones for cover in Magnolia Cemetery.
Williams was fatally wounded, as was Mary

Todd Lincoln's brother, a Confederate officer. The Confederates surged ahead until, on
the brink of victory, heavy Federal gunboat
fire drove them away. As the Rebels fell
back, the Yankees evacuated Baton Rouge
two weeks later, though only temporarily;
they would return to the city in September.
In the meantime, the Confederates began to
build Port Hudson, 25 miles upriver.

The Foundation for Historic Louisiana has
a detailed brochure available through local
visitor centers and the state capitol information center. An annual commemorative ceremony of the battle is held every August.

**LOCATION: Baton Rouge Welcome Center, 359
3rd St., 225-382-3564, or download the tour
brochure at www.civilwartraveler.com.**

This small knife is engraved "Baton Rouge 1862."

✳ Blair's Landing

CAMPAIGN: Red River Campaign

OTHER NAME(S): Pleasant Hill Landing

DATE(S): April 12–13, 1864

As word of General Banks's defeat at Mansfield (see p. 109) reached Admiral Porter, the navy—loaded with confiscated cotton and other supplies near Shreveport—began falling back down the Red River, dodging frequent enemy fire from shore. At Blair's Landing, Confederate dismounted cavalry fired from high bluffs on Federal supply vessels stranded because of low water. Porter, describing the action as "this curious affair of a fight between infantry and gunboats," reported that the gunboat *Osage* "opened

a destructive fire on these poor deluded wretches, who, maddened by liquor, and led on by their officers, were vainly attempting to capture an iron vessel." The gunboat's accuracy was enhanced by the first Civil War use of a periscope in Western waters. While there were few Confederate casualties, one was Thomas Green—victor at Val Verde in New Mexico—a loss noted, even by Admiral Porter, as a severe blow to the Rebel effort.

LOCATION: A marker denoting the area where General Green fell is located west of Lake End, off I-49, just beyond the intersection of LA 1 and LA 174; follow the access road to Red River Lock and Dam no. 4.

✳ Donaldsonville I

CAMPAIGN: Confederate Offensive Against Baton Rouge

DATE(S): August 9, 1862

Located where the Mississippi River meets Bayou Lafourche, Donaldsonville was the

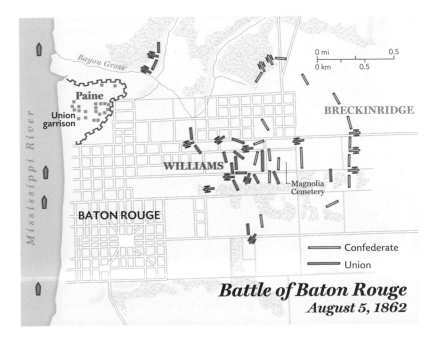

Battle of Baton Rouge
August 5, 1862

temporary state capital in 1830 while the state government moved from New Orleans to Baton Rouge. In 1862, the riverfront was an irresistible perch where Confederates could take potshots at Federal river traffic. After giving the town fair warning, Admiral Farragut lobbed retaliatory artillery onto key buildings and then directed a shore party to burn public facilities. Firings on Union vessels diminished considerably afterward.

Donaldsonville's historic district is worth exploring for the variety of its architecture, which spans antebellum years to 1933 (see p. 117).

LOCATION: The site is unmarked, but Crescent Park overlooks the Mississippi River where artillery fire took place during the battle.

✳ Donaldsonville II

CAMPAIGN: Taylor's Operations in Louisiana West of Mississippi

DATE(S): June 28, 1863

Fort Butler, a star-shaped earthen fort surrounded by a wide brick moat, abatis, and hidden trenches, was built by Federals and fugitive slaves after the August 9, 1862, take-over of Donaldsonville. Seeking to divert Union forces from Port Hudson, Confederate General Taylor ordered General Green to mount an attack on Fort Butler to pave the way for retaking Donaldsonville. The fort's defenders, many of whom were convalescing, numbered about 200. The nighttime attack had Rebels navigating around well-placed outer defensive obstacles, only to be trapped between artillery fire from the fort and from the Union gunboat *Princess Royal*. After about three hours, the Rebels withdrew.

LOCATION: Interpretive signs are located at Historic Fort Butler Commemorative Site, one block from Crescent Park, along a wide, paved river walk at a bend where Mississippi St. becomes Veterans Blvd. in Donaldsonville.

FURTHER READING

Scarred by War: Civil War in Southeast Louisiana
by Christopher G. Peña
Authoritative study of the Civil War's often overlooked battles in the bayou

This Confederate monument and one to U.S. Colored Troops mark the site of Fort Butler.

✸ Fort Bisland

CAMPAIGN: Operations in West Louisiana
DATE(S): April 12–13, 1863

General Banks's objective for the Bayou Teche Campaign was to cut the supply lines feeding the Confederate garrison at Port Hudson. Using the 16,000 men of the XIX Corps, Banks moved against Alexandria. Fort Bisland, the western sentry to Port Hudson, stood in his way several miles upstream of the mouth of Bayou Teche (at present-day Patterson). This earthen fortification was occupied by troops from General Taylor's District of Western Louisiana. Rebel forces captured the well-equipped, 165-foot Union gunboat *Diana* and used it to augment their firepower against the Yankees. After an inconclusive day of skirmishing and learning that the Federals had additional troops on the other side of Bayou Teche, Taylor evacuated Fort Bisland during the night of April 12–13. The two generals would meet again at Irish Bend (see p. 107).

After the battle, Confederate prisoners and fugitive slaves dismantled the fort, which is believed to have stood on the northwest side of today's West Lake Outlet Bridge in Calumet.

LOCATION: A marker is located on US 90 just west of Calumet, before crossing the Wax Lake Outlet Bridge. View the marker safely from Levee Rd., which runs parallel to the right, since there is virtually no traffic there. Sprawling cane fields northeast of the marker denote the main battlefield site, which is now private property.

✸ Fort DeRussy

CAMPAIGN: Red River Campaign
DATE(S): March 14, 1864

This earthen fortification at the mouth of the Red River was the main obstacle for Union forces as they proceeded toward Alexandria. Given it had only 350 defenders, it's no surprise that a Federal force of 10,000 in concert with Admiral Porter's fleet of gunboats easily captured the fort, thought to be impregnable, on March 14, 1864.

David Dixon Porter, an admiral, commanded U.S. Navy forces in the Red River Campaign.

Confederate forces were pushed farther upstream after several skirmishes that culminated in the Battle of Mansfield (see p. 109).

The fort, where earthen fortifications and entrenchments surrounded by open fields are still visible, is open by appointment only.

LOCATION: Fort DeRussy, 379 Fort DeRussy Rd., about 4 miles north of Marksville, www.fort derussy.org. To make arrangements to visit the fort, contact the Forts Randolph and Buhlow site in Pineville, 318-484-2390.

FURTHER READING

Earthen Walls, Iron Men: Fort DeRussy, Louisiana, and the Defense of Red River by Steven M. Mayeux Intimate portrait of the fort and those who lived in and around it

Farragut's fleet bombards Forts Jackson and St. Philip, leading to the fall of New Orleans.

✳ Forts Jackson and St. Philip

CAMPAIGN: Expedition to and Capture of New Orleans

DATE(S): April 16–28, 1862

Forts Jackson and St. Philip stood diagonally across from each other, just north of the mouth of the Mississippi River. Governor Thomas O. Moore had seized both in December 1861. Constructed in 1792, Fort St. Philip, with its high parapets on the east bank of the river, engaged the British fleet in 1815 during the Battle of New Orleans. In 1832, Fort Jackson was added as part of the nation's general upgrade of fortifications known as the Third System. This five-sided masonry fort had thick walls that rose 25 feet above its moat.

War came to Louisiana in April 1862, when David G. Farragut pointed his fleet toward New Orleans. Cooperating infantry under the command of controversial General Butler landed above the forts to cut off the retreat of the garrisons. A sharp bend in the river, obstructed by a chain boom, delayed Union vessels attempting to

pass the forts, exposing them to heavy Confederate artillery fire. After days of heavy mortar ship bombardment, the forts still stood, so Farragut, proclaiming "conquer or be conquered," pushed through the Rebel barriers just after 3 a.m. on April 24. The fleet proceeded on to New Orleans. Isolated and without possibility of relief, the garrison at Fort Jackson mutinied, with many of its defenders deserting. Forts Jackson and St. Philip surrendered on April 28.

Severely damaged by three hurricanes in ten years, historic Fort Jackson is currently closed, though visitors may walk the fort's exterior perimeter.

LOCATION: Fort Jackson, 220 Herbert Harvey Dr. (LA 23), Buras, about 70 miles south of New Orleans, 504-934-6105 or 504-481-7706. For updates on interior access, consult www.plaqueminestourism.com.

FURTHER READING

The Capture of New Orleans, 1862
by Chester G. Hearn
The most complete account of the Union victory

✳ Georgia Landing

CAMPAIGN: Operations in LaFourche District
OTHER NAME(S): Labadieville, Texana
DATE(S): October 27, 1862

Contested 15 miles south of Donaldsonville, this sharp engagement involved two skirmishes, one on either side of Bayou Lafourche at Georgia Landing. Because there was no bridge, the two groups of Confederate troops led by General Mouton were unable to unite on one side of the bayou. Holding the initiative, Union General Weitzel's brigade of 4,000 men attacked the Rebel forces on the east bank and then crossed over the Bayou on a pontoon bridge and attacked the other detachment. Fighting resolutely until their ammunition ran short, the Confederate soldiers retreated eight miles south to Labadieville.

LOCATION: Marker located near intersection of LA 1 and LA 1011 across from Bayou Lafourche.

✳ Goodrich's Landing

CAMPAIGN: Grant's Operations Against Vicksburg
OTHER NAME(S): The Mounds, Lake Providence
DATE(S): June 29–30, 1863

Suffering under siege at Vicksburg, Confederate raiders attempted to relieve the siege by disrupting Union supply depots. Coming from Arkansas, a small Confederate force moved toward the depot at Lake Providence, Louisiana. Here, on several plantations near Lake Providence, Federals hired former slaves to cultivate cotton to be sent north and enlisted others as guards to protect the crops. Rather than lose troops in an attack on a fortified mound, the Confederate commander demanded the garrison surrender. Sadly, the white officers surrendered their force of black soldiers, knowing they would be taken back to slavery. The raiders, led by Colonel Parsons, commandeered Union supplies, fought a skirmish near Lake Providence, and burned the cotton at the Yankee-run plantations. They drew back

when navy transports bringing Alfred Ellet's Mississippi Marine Brigade landed.

LOCATION: This site, 10 miles south of Lake Providence near today's Transylvania, was swallowed by floodwaters decades ago.

FURTHER READING

Ellet's Brigade: The Strangest Outfit of All by Chester G. Hearn
Tells the riveting history of this forgotten brigade

✳ Irish Bend

CAMPAIGN: Operations in West Louisiana
DATE(S): April 14, 1863

General Banks, anticipating a Confederate retreat from Fort Bisland, sent General Grover by river to Grand Lake. General Taylor, needing to protect his retreating troops, sent an advance party of 1,000 soldiers to Irish Bend to block Banks's forces as they traveled up Bayou Teche toward Alexandria. At first, the captured gunboat *Diana* protected the Rebels' right flank, but with Grover's forces attacking, the Confederates destroyed the vessel before making a retreat.

Although the battleground is on private land, it looks much like it did in 1863.

LOCATION: Marker located near 2024 Irish Bend Rd. in Franklin. Face the marker to see Nerson's Woods, where Confederates launched their attack. Other markers are on the courthouse grounds, at the corner of Willow St. and W. Main St., Franklin. Note: The *Diana* marker at the courthouse is outdated. The gunboat's boilers are no longer in Bayou Teche.

FURTHER READING

Thunder Across the Swamp: The Fight for the Lower Mississippi, February–May 1863 by Donald S. Frazier
Second in a series of four books about the war in Louisiana

✴ Kock's Plantation

CAMPAIGN: Taylor's Operations in Louisiana West of Mississippi

OTHER NAME(S): Cox's Plantation

DATE(S): July 13, 1863

Port Hudson was now under Union control (see pp. 112–113), and the Confederates' Louisiana strategy was in disarray. As Federal troops traveling along both sides of Bayou Lafourche were returning to Fort Butler in Donaldson, they clashed with two brigades commanded by Confederate General Green, who had also been posted on both sides of the waterway. Luckily for Green, this battle would turn out better than his last encounter along the Bayou, at Georgia Landing in 1862 (see p. 107).

Heavy skirmishing on July 11 and 12 revealed outnumbered Rebel forces routing the Union at Kock's Plantation (also known as St. Emma Plantation). As the Federal soldiers retreated to Fort Butler, the Confederates seized control over the interior and held it—temporarily.

LOCATION: Kock's Plantation, 1283 S. Hwy. 1, 4 miles south of Donaldsonville. There is a marker in front, but the private house, St. Emma Plantation, is open only to groups of 20 or more by advance appointment. To make an appointment, contact the Ascension Parish Tourist Commission, 225-675-6550, www.louisianadaytours.com/aasemma.htm.

✴ LaFourche Crossing

CAMPAIGN: Taylor's Operations in Louisiana West of Mississippi

DATE(S): June 20–21, 1863

With the siege of Port Hudson under way (see pp. 112–113), Confederate General Taylor made an unsuccessful attempt to draw Union forces away from the siege by sending an expedition to force a Union withdrawal from Brashear City (now Morgan City). Ordered to Brashear City to hold off the Rebels, Colonel Stickney instead led his forces to LaFourche Crossing, where Rebel soldiers swiftly attacked. Although the Confederates were unsuccessful, they regrouped and pressed ahead to the outskirts of Brashear City.

LOCATION: Marker located on the bayou side of LA 308, north of Bartley Ln. and the LaFourche Crossing railroad bridge in Thibodaux.

Federal forces racing to Brashear City (today Morgan City) were attacked short of their destination by Confederates at LaFourche Crossing.

✳ Mansfield

CAMPAIGN: Red River Campaign

OTHER NAME(S): Sabine Cross-Roads, Pleasant Grove

DATE(S): April 8, 1864

In this key battle of the Red River Campaign, General Taylor's Army of Western Louisiana made a stand to halt General Banks's Army of the Gulf and its movement toward Shreveport, the Confederate capital of the state and the military headquarters for all Southern forces west of the Mississippi.

Inadvertently, Taylor was aided by Banks's fateful decision to leave the waterborne supply route of Red River at Natchitoches and head 20 miles west for what he viewed as a more direct approach to Shreveport. With Federal forces stretched in a line for miles along the Old Stage Road (present-day LA 175), Taylor's outnumbered Rebel army was able to deal with Banks's larger force on more equal terms. Taylor's actions netted his forces considerable wagons and supplies.

With Banks's defeat at Mansfield, none of the Union objectives for the campaign were achieved. In addition, the East Texas war production centers of Jefferson, Marshall, and Tyler were saved. The Union defeats at the battles of Mansfield and Pleasant Hill (see p. 112) upset the Federal timetable for the campaign and prevented the Union troops who took part in the expedition from assisting other theaters in a timely manner.

The Mansfield State Historic Site visitor center sits atop Honeycutt Hill, where the opening attack of the battle occurred and where Confederate General Mouton was killed. Walk the battlefield trail or enjoy one of the many interpretive programs offered by the site staff. The visitor center has an orientation film about the battle and displays on the Red River Campaign and the Battle of Mansfield.

LOCATION: Mansfield State Historic Site, 15149 Hwy. 175, Mansfield, 318-872-1474 or 888-677-6267, www.crt.state.la.us /louisiana-state-parks.

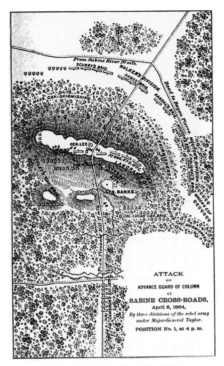

Map of the Battle of Mansfield (aka Sabine Cross-Roads)

✳ Mansura

CAMPAIGN: Red River Campaign

OTHER NAME(S): Smith's Place, Marksville

DATE(S): May 16, 1864

General Taylor's dwindling forces were still trying to stall General Banks's Union troops, this time by blocking their southward route from Alexandria, which Banks had reduced to fiery rubble. This battle is best remembered for its Hollywood-like spectacle over a miles-wide open field flooded with 30,000 troops skirmishing and surprisingly few casualties. Eventually, the Federals drove back the heavily outnumbered Confederates and they completed their escape by crossing the Atchafalaya River toward Simmesport.

LOCATION: The marker located at 2221 L'Eglise St., Mansura, denotes the center of the Confederate battle line.

Now a restaurant, New Orleans's circa 1794 Napoleon House once hosted much intrigue.

✳ Milliken's Bend

CAMPAIGN: Grant's Operations Against Vicksburg

DATE(S): June 7, 1863

Just as the community of Milliken's Bend washed away in floodwaters decades ago, the town's place in history is overshadowed by the siege of Vicksburg (see p. 136), less than 15 miles southeast. During the Civil War, this Union supply post evolved into a recruitment center for freed slaves. On June 7, 1863, newly recruited black regiments joined Iowa soldiers and two Union gunboats in a fierce battle to successfully fend off a Confederate attack.

LOCATION: Marker located at the intersection of Thomastown Rd. and Ashley Plantation Rd., about a mile from the now nonexistent battle site. Hermione House Museum (315 N. Mulberry St., Tallulah, 318-574-0082 or 888-744-8410) has a brochure on the battle.

✳ Monett's Ferry

CAMPAIGN: Red River Campaign

OTHER NAME(S): Cane River Crossing

DATE(S): April 23, 1864

As General Banks was retreating toward the Red River's junction with the Mississippi,

Confederate forces were still nipping at his heels. Although the Rebels held the high ground at Monett's Ferry Hill overlooking the Cane River, the Federals were in no mood for a fight and moved around them, crossing the river at two points. Fearing encirclement, Confederate General Hamilton Bee retreated—too early, according to General Taylor's later report implying that Monett's Ferry was a missed opportunity to destroy or capture Banks's army. Now unimpeded, the Union commander's forces moved on to Alexandria.

LOCATION: The battlefield is an unmarked, undeveloped site located at the intersection of LA 1 and Marco Rd. in Cloutierville. The Cane River crossing is located just south of the intersection; Monett's Ferry Hill is on the right after crossing the bridge.

✳ New Orleans

CAMPAIGN: Expedition to and Capture of New Orleans

DATE(S): April 25–May 1, 1862

The fall of the South's vital and all but undefended seaport was anticlimactic after Farragut's naval flotilla passed Forts Jackson and St. Philip on April 24, 1862 (see p. 106). As Rebels evacuated New Orleans, the city struggled under martial law imposed by General Butler. During his eight-month command, Butler's picture adorned the bottoms of chamber pots, and residents turned their backs on Federal officers.

Look beyond today's well-known French Quarter for a wealth of Civil War sites worthy of your time. The Confederate Memorial Hall Museum's abbey-like architecture hosts one of the largest collections of Confederate Civil War artifacts in the world. Stand on the town hall steps at Lafayette Square, where naval officers demanded the surrender of New Orleans. Visit the grounds of the Old U.S. Mint, where, on June 7, 1862, Butler had local citizen William Mumford hanged for tearing down a U.S. flag, and see the U.S. Customs House on Canal Street—the headquarters of the Union occupying force.

Monuments to General Beauregard, Andrew Jackson, Jefferson Davis, and others dot the city. Reverence for Robert E. Lee shows in a 76-foot-tall monument on St. Charles Avenue at Lee Circle. Generals Taylor, Beauregard, and Hood are interred in Metairie Cemetery (see p. 119), where President Davis was also temporarily interred. The cemetery is located on the old fairgrounds where Confederate soldiers trained for war.

LOCATION: New Orleans Convention and Visitors Bureau, 800-672-6124, www.new orleans.com. Confederate Memorial Hall Museum, 929 Camp St., New Orleans, 504-523-4522, www.confederatemuseum.com. Old U.S. Mint, 400 Esplanade Ave., 504-568-6993. The homes where Jefferson Davis and John Bell Hood died, and the house where General Nathaniel Banks lived while governing in New Orleans are all in the Garden District.

Postwar New Orleans

More cosmopolitan than other Louisiana locales before the war, New Orleans still faced huge challenges adjusting to a new way of life, both socially and economically. The city's robust prewar population of free blacks increased substantially with the influx of freed slaves. Pro- and anti-Union attitudes still clashed bitterly under Federal occupation. The Republican establishment of the Freeman's Bureau to expand rights for blacks—including voting rights—spurred the Black Codes restrictions on lives of African Americans. The New Orleans Massacre at the Mechanic Institute in July 1866 was born of those racial tensions. Fierce Unionists called Radical Republicans became targets as well as blacks, while President Andrew Johnson discouraged Federals from intervening. In 1867 the Republican Party platform included equality for African Americans. Ratification of the 14th Amendment in 1868 failed to quell the strife. Federal troops occupied New Orleans until 1877.

FURTHER READING

An Absolute Massacre: The New Orleans Race Riot of July 30, 1866 by James G. Hollandsworth, Jr. Compelling look at racial tension in New Orleans after the Civil War

FURTHER READING

When the Devil Came Down to Dixie: Ben Butler in New Orleans by Chester G. Hearn Fascinating account of Butler's life and career

The Louisiana Native Guards: The Black Military Experience During the Civil War by James G. Hollandsworth, Jr. A history of blacks in the military in Louisiana during the Civil War

Twelve miles north of Port Hudson and perched above Bayou Sara and the Mississippi, this 1770s town was shelled by Union warships during the siege of Port Hudson. Each June the town commemorates "The Day the War Stopped," a temporary truce called on June 12, 1863, by Confederates so that Union troops could bury John E. Hart, captain of the U.S.S. *Albatross,* at Grace Episcopal Church, a significant gesture since Union vessels had just shelled the church. Hart was a Mason, as was W. W. Leake, the Confederate officer who assisted with the burial arrangements. For just a moment, Masonic brotherhood trumped wartime differences. Take a walk along the historic main street in St. Francisville (see. p. 119) or visit any of the close-by plantation homes and gardens.

✷ Plains Store

CAMPAIGN: Siege of Port Hudson
OTHER NAME(S): Springfield Road
DATE(S): May 21, 1863

Union forces advancing on Port Hudson from Baton Rouge clashed with Rebel pickets about four miles east at a crossroads then known as Plains Store. A skirmish ensued as each side brought in reinforcements, but the outnumbered Rebels' efforts stalled the Federals only long enough to allow Confederate forces to fall back to Port Hudson and Clinton. Within two days, their escape route would be cut off as the siege began.

LOCATION: Marker located near 22929 Old Scenic Hwy. in Zachary. To understand the whole picture, start at Port Hudson State Historic Site (see p. 113).

✷ Pleasant Hill

CAMPAIGN: Red River Campaign
DATE(S): April 9, 1864

Following the Federal defeat at Mansfield (see p. 109), General Banks narrowly escaped a well-planned but poorly executed Confederate attack. Failing to get completely on the flank of the Union army, Confederate General Churchill could not succeed in his plan. Churchill's men were short of water, and so they ceded the battlefield to the Union, which continued to withdraw from the area, not stopping until they got to Alexandria.

The actual battlefield site has a small park with markers denoting the history and street names of the original town of Pleasant Hill, which migrated three miles south to follow the railroad in the 1880s.

LOCATION: The unstaffed Pleasant Hill battle site is 3 miles north of Pleasant Hill at 23271 Hwy. 175. A reenactment is held each April around the time of the battle. For more information, contact the reenactment chairman at www.battleofpleasanthill.com.

✷ Port Hudson

CAMPAIGN: Siege of Port Hudson
DATE(S): May 21–July 9, 1863

While the Union now controlled the upper and lower Mississippi River, miles of territory between the cities of Vicksburg and Port Hudson were still open for Confederate supply and troop movements.

North of Baton Rouge, the 80-foot-high bluffs at Port Hudson hugged a bend in the river, affording good visibility for detecting any Union advance by water. Confederate forces led by General Gardner fortified this natural setting with heavy artillery and parapets a mile along the ridge—a line that is no longer accessible.

The defenses seemed to work well in March 1863, as Confederates took out five of Admiral Farragut's seven ships

General McDowell's forage cap

when he attempted a night run past the fort. Still, his goal to cut off the Confederates' main supply route by blocking the Red River was accomplished with his two remaining vessels. With periodic reinforcements, the blockade held, slowly tightening the stomachs of Gardner's forces.

On May 23, General Banks surrounded Port Hudson, resulting in a 48-day siege, the longest true siege in American military history. As supplies dwindled, soldiers inside the fort consumed horses, dogs, and rats. Banks completed the strangulation Farragut had started. In taking part, the all-black 1st and 3rd Louisiana Native Guards became the first such official black units used in actual assaults against Rebel forces.

After Vicksburg fell on July 4 (see p. 136), Gardner surrendered the last official Confederate stronghold on the Mississippi on July 9. In Lincoln's words, "the Father of Waters again goes unvexed to the sea."

A 640-acre part of the northern quarter of the battlefield has some well-preserved earthworks, museum displays, and six miles of interpreted trails.

LOCATION: **Port Hudson State Historic Site, 236 Hwy. 61, Jackson, 225-654-3775 or 888-677-3400, www.louisianatravel.com/la-civil-war/port-hudson-state-historic-site.**

FURTHER READING

Port Hudson: Confederate Bastion on the Mississippi by Lawrence Lee Hewitt Narrative account of life in the fort and the battle to control it

✳ Stirling's Plantation

CAMPAIGN: Taylor's Operations in Louisiana West of Mississippi

OTHER NAME(S): Fordoche Bridge

DATE(S): September 29, 1863

Intent on marching Union troops across southwest Louisiana to Texas, General Banks posted a unit to guard the approach

Located on the north side of Priest Cap, Port Hudson's Battery K of the 1st Indiana Heavy Artillery Regiment, led by Clayton Cox, used cotton bales to enhance their defenses.

along the Atchafalaya River as he moved toward Texas on Bayou Teche. A skirmish occurred when Confederate cavalry moved to attack the Federals at Stirling's Plantation. While the cavalry attacked, a supporting Confederate force hit a main body of Federal troops, capturing a number of them. The Confederates successfully broke off the engagement and escaped. The small effort had no impact on Banks's operations.

The battlefield is on private property but can be viewed from the road.

LOCATION: **Marker located just past 10118 LA 10, 5 miles north of Fordoche. The bridge crossing—over the now very narrow Bayou Fordoche—is west on Laio Rd.**

Vermilion's living-history museum displays a Cajun pirogue in Bayou Vermilion.

✳ Vermillion Bayou

CAMPAIGN: Operations in West Louisiana
DATE(S): April 17, 1863

Vermilionville (present-day Lafayette) saw the final battle in General Banks's Bayou Teche Campaign. Here, General Taylor's Rebels crossed the Pin Hook Bridge over Vermillion Bayou, and set it ablaze, temporarily severing the route north for pursuing Federals. An artillery skirmish ensued before the Rebels retreated to Opelousas. Banks pressed his advantage and continued on to Alexandria. The river route for Port Hudson's supplies was now cut, and food would need to come from other sources.

While in the area, explore Opelousas (see p. 119). It was the Confederate capital of Louisiana from May 1862 to January 1863 after Baton Rouge was evacuated.

LOCATION: **Marker located on W. Pinhook Rd. (Rte. 183) in Lafayette, at the site of the original bridge crossing.**

✳ Yellow Bayou

CAMPAIGN: Red River Campaign
OTHER NAME(S): Norwood's Plantation
DATE(S): May 18, 1864

The last battle of Banks's Red River Campaign was a rearguard action as the Federals crossed the Atchafalaya River at Simmesport. Typically aggressive General Mower attacked Rebel forces as Federals crossed the river via a hastily built bridge designed by Colonel Bailey. Just as the dam he constructed at Alexandria saved the navy, his engineering feat here saved the Union Army. In allowing the Confederates to disrupt Federal plans, General Banks tied down 10,000 troops so that they were unable to move against Mobile as General Sherman wished. Conversely, the Confederates sent 15,000 reinforcements to Georgia.

The unstaffed site features earthworks that protected the Confederates.

LOCATION: **Yellow Bayou Memorial Park, 15602 Hwy. 1 S., Simmesport, 318-941-2483 or 800-833-4195, www.travelavoyelles.com.**

The Red River Campaign

Raising his sword, General "Whiskey" Smith leads a charge over an abatis in a successful assault on Confederates at Fort DeRussy on March 14, 1864.

After the Mississippi River fell under Union control, the Red River's value rose tremendously. Federal control of that thoroughfare would effectively kill the Confederacy in the west by isolating the state capital at Shreveport and blocking a key access route into Texas. Still, General Grant had mixed feelings about the campaign, fearing the operation would drain resources from Union efforts east of the Mississippi. On the plus side, the Red River flowed through heavy cotton country and could play a major role in saving Northern textile mills desperately in need of raw materials. Increased cloth production would mean increased jobs and a significant boost for Lincoln's reelection prospects.

The Union forces under General Banks and inland navy under Admiral Porter aimed to pacify the state and open the export of cotton north. Grant sought a speedy operation so that General "Whiskey" Smith's infantry could be freed to operate against Mobile and draw away resources that might oppose Sherman's efforts in Georgia. But Banks was neither competent nor efficient. His political priorities plagued the mission, resulting in what Sherman later described as "one damn blunder from beginning to end." Banks's distractions, miscalculations, and insubordination resulted in a resounding rout. Decreasing river depth, helped along by some dam tinkering by the Rebels, almost caused the loss of the Union fleet, whose vessels proved too big and heavy for the winding, shallow Red River. Only the masterful engineering of dams at Alexandria by Joseph Bailey allowed the Federal fleet to escape.

FURTHER READING

Red River Campaign: Politics and Cotton in the Civil War
by Ludwell H. Johnson
Examines how profit and partisanship drove military policy

One Damned Blunder From Beginning to End: The Red River Campaign of 1864
by Gary Dillard Joiner
Details the campaign's detrimental effect on Union strategy

Other Battles and Beyond

✦ Great River Road Driving Tour

A drive along the Great River Road (US 61) reveals a land of cavaliers and cotton fields. More than romantic, the road snakes alongside the Mississippi River, passing through a landscape that still pulses with the enormous wealth and power of Louisiana's antebellum plantations. For information on the route and the sites it includes, visit www .nps.gov/nr/travel/louisiana/riverroad.htm.

✦ Alexandre Mouton House

Once the governor of Louisiana, Alexandre Mouton also served as a U.S. senator and presided over the secession convention in Baton Rouge in 1861. The house is also home to the Lafayette Museum, which displays Civil War relics.

LOCATION: **1122 Lafayette St., Lafayette, 337-234-2208, www.lafayettemuseum.com.**

✦ Avery Island

During the Civil War, salt from the area was critical to the Confederacy. It was used to brine beef and pork and for saltpeter, which was a key ingredient in gunpowder and the percussion caps that fired muskets.

LOCATION: **About 30 miles south of Lafayette on LA 329 (small toll to access the island), 337-365-8173, www.tabasco.com/avery-island.**

✦ Camp Moore Museum and Cemetery

From 1861 to 1862, 25,000 Confederates passed through this training camp north of Lake Pontchartrain. Crowded conditions resulted in high disease and death rates. Many of those who were buried on-site died before ever seeing battle. The museum displays personal items of the common soldier and medical treatments of the time.

LOCATION: **Camp Moore Rd., Tangipahoa, 985-229-2438, www.campmoorela.com.**

See an 1884 Munger steam-powered cotton gin at Frogmore Cotton Plantation and Gins. Robert S. Munger's invention improved ginning by adding suction and a double box press.

Donaldsonville

Visitors can learn about distinctive 19th-century architecture in Donaldsonville's charming historic district.

LOCATION: **Tourist Information Center, 714 Railroad Ave., Donaldsonville, 225-473-4814, www.donaldsonville-la.gov.**

Forts Randolph and Buhlow State Historic Site

This state historic site preserves earthen fortifications and hosts numerous on-site living-history presentations. The former location of pivotal Bailey's Dams—designed in May 1864 by Union Colonel Bailey—can be seen from the park. Without Bailey's engineering genius, the entire Federal fleet would have been isolated and lost to the Confederates because of low water. The dams created enough water flow to get the ships over the rocky bottom of the Red River.

LOCATION: **135 Riverfront St., Pineville, 318-484-2390 or 877-677-7437, www.crt.state .la.us/louisiana-state-parks/historic-sites /forts-randolph-buhlow-state-historic-site/.**

Fort Star

On June 23, 1863, on the banks of the Atchafalaya River at Berwick Bay, Confederate forces seized control of Fort Star (Brashear City), a Federal military depot, from a small Union garrison, capturing wagons, tents, food, and other supplies and taking several hundred prisoners. Today, a historical marker notes the event.

LOCATION: **A small part of Fort Star is visible next to Atkinson Memorial Presbyterian Church, 212 Fourth St., Morgan City.**

Frogmore Cotton Plantation and Gins

Established in the early 19th century, this historic cotton plantation traces the evolution of the cotton industry from circa 1815 to the present day. Living-history displays

The circa 1800 Alexandre Mouton House had two more sections added by 1850.

highlight slave life, while a special permanent program, "The Plantation Civil War—Challenges and Changes," explores the effects of the Federal occupation and Confederate guerrilla activity on Louisiana's cotton plantations, their owners, and slaves in the Old Natchez District.

LOCATION: **11656 US 84, Frogmore (near Ferriday), 318-757-2453, www.frogmore plantation.com.**

Grant's Canal Park

A small part remains of one of two canals created in a failed attempt to bypass the Confederate stronghold at Vicksburg. This canal was designed to provide access from the Mississippi River to Lake Providence. Visit the Byerley House Visitor Center across the street for more information.

LOCATION: **Byerley House Visitor Center, 600 Lake St., Lake Providence, 318-559-5125.**

Grand Ecore Visitors Center

From this perch on an 80-foot bluff overlooking a bend in the Red River, visitors can really understand its strategic importance

Louisiana's Old State Capitol, built in 1849, is known for its Gothic architecture.

and role as a staging point and supply depot for the Union during the Red River Campaign (see p. 115).

LOCATION: **106 Tauzin Island Rd., Natchitoches, 318-354 8770, www.natchitoches.com.**

✦ Kent Plantation House

Built circa 1796, Kent Plantation House is thought to be the oldest standing structure in Central Louisiana. Offering glimpses into the area's rural life, this French colonial structure includes period furnishings, a separate kitchen and milk house, a working sugar refinery, and herb and formal gardens. Programs highlight stories from the owner's journal at the time of the war, when Union troops camped on the grounds.

LOCATION: **3601 Bayou Rapides Rd., Alexandria, 318-487-5998, www.kenthouse.org.**

✦ Louisiana's Civil War Museum at Confederate Memorial Hall

This superb museum in the shadow of Lee Circle and the National World War II Museum has the second largest collection of Confederate memorabilia and artifacts in the world. Here Jefferson Davis lay in state before being taken to Metairie Cemetery. Be sure to visit the great gift shop.

LOCATION: **929 Camp St., New Orleans, 504-523-4522, www.confederatemuseum.com.**

✦ Magnolia Cemetery

Adjacent to Baton Rouge National Cemetery, this was the epicenter of the Battle of Baton Rouge (see p. 102). Look for bullet chips on the gorgeous old monuments.

LOCATION: **422 N. 19th St., Baton Rouge, 225-272-9200.**

✦ Magnolia Mound Plantation

General Grierson's raid started in northern Mississippi and ended in Baton Rouge. Grierson and his men camped in the fields across the street from this site, awaiting new orders. Grierson successfully distracted the Rebels, allowing Grant to march his army down the Louisiana side of the Mississippi River. The house has been restored to the 1800–1830 period. Outbuildings include a kitchen, overseer's house, and pigeonnier.

LOCATION: **2161 Nicholson Dr., Baton Rouge, 225-343-4955, www.brec.org.**

✦ Metairie Cemetery

This cemetery includes monuments to Louisiana soldiers and the graves of Generals Taylor, Beauregard, and Hood.

LOCATION: **5100 Pontchartrain Blvd., New Orleans, 504-486-6331.**

✦ Old State Capitol

Looking like a medieval fortress on the banks of the Mississippi, this 165-year-old state-house was gutted by fire in the Civil War.

LOCATION: **100 North Blvd., Baton Rouge, 225-342-0500 or 800-488-2968, www.louisianaoldstatecapitol.org.**

✦ Opelousas Tourist and Information Center

Get updates on the restoration of the Confederate governor's mansion (now a

The 1792 Magnolia Mound Plantation has gardens and French Creole architecture.

private residence) at 261 North Liberty Street. Jim Bowie of Bowie knife and Alamo fame was also associated with Opelousas.

LOCATION: **828 E. Landry St., Opelousas, 800-424-5442 or 337-948-6263.**

✦ St. Francisville

Visit West Feliciana Parish Historical Society and Museum for a walking tour brochure to explore the history and Civil War stories of this beautiful community. James Audubon did many of his *Birds of America* paintings here.

LOCATION: **11757 Ferdinand St., St. Francisville, 225-635-4224, www.westfelicianahistorical society.org.**

✦ Shadows-on-the-Teche

Offering a fascinating look at antebellum through postbellum life, this 1834 home focuses on the history of the Weeks family. Learn stories told through thousands of family papers, including a note from Mary Weeks Moore to a Federal officer whose troops occupied her Classic Revival–style home in November 1863. "We appeal to you as a gentleman" she wrote, "to protect us against the outrages & annoyances of your men." She is buried in the garden.

LOCATION: **317 E. Main St., New Iberia, 337-369-6446, www.shadowsontheteche.org.**

✦ Vermilionville

Step away from battle sites to learn about Bayou Vermilion life and culture from 1765 to 1890 at this living-history venue.

LOCATION: **300 Fisher Rd., Lafayette, 337-233-4077 or 866-992-2968, www.vermilion ville.org.**

✦ Young-Sanders Center

The center offers a wealth of Civil War information online at its research library.

LOCATION: **104 Commercial St., Franklin, 337-413-1861, www.youngsanders.org.**

Mississippi

MISSISSIPPI HAD SOME OF THE MOST CONTESTED REAL ESTATE in the Civil War. The Mississippi River—described by General Sherman as "the spinal column of America"—forms the state's western border and, during the war, ensured that Mississippi was central to military plans devised by either side. Vital to trade, the wide, muddy channel provided a route directly to New Orleans and the rest of the world.

Cotton was truly king of the state's economy, and by 1860 slaves outnumbered free men in Mississippi. With secession in 1861, Louisiana, Arkansas, Tennessee, and Mississippi controlled the use of the river as a commercial route, denying Northern states access. So vital an artery was the Mississippi River that, by 1863, the United States was in danger of splitting again as the withering economies in western states like Ohio, Illinois, Indiana, and Wisconsin forced state legislatures to consider a separate peace with the South.

Mississippi contributed more than 80,000 men to Confederate armies, while about 17,000 freedmen and escaped slaves from the state joined the U.S. Colored Troops.

Each of the 47 steps at the Illinois Memorial marks a day of the Siege of Vicksburg.

Corinth
*Corinth Contraband Camp;
Corinth Historic Grand
Illumination*

Tenn.

Corinth I
Holly Springs ● Corinth II
Hill Crest Cemetery
Iuka

Ark.

Brice's Cross Roads

Tupelo

Okolona

*Confederate Forts at
Grenada Lake* □

□ *Fort Pemberton*

Mississippi

● Rolling Fork

Ala.

Natchez Trace Parkway

Snyder's Bluff
Chickasaw Bayou
Champion Hill
Vicksburg □
Old Court House Museum
Jackson
Meridian
Raymond
Grand Gulf □
Big Black River Bridge
Windsor Ruins □
Port Gibson

0 mi   50
0 km   50

● Natchez

La.

*Beauvoir:
The Jefferson Davis Home
and Presidential Library* □

└ Ship Island

*Gulf of
Mexico*

✳ Big Black River Bridge

CAMPAIGN: Grant's Operations Against
Vicksburg

OTHER NAME(S): Big Black

DATE(S): May 17, 1863

After their decisive defeat at Champion Hill
(see p. 125), General Pemberton's dejected
troops held open a crossing point for
General Loring with a hastily built thin line
of fortifications along the Big Black River.
Union forces, having discovered a suffi-
ciently deep natural trench, approached
to within a few yards of the Confederate
position. The fight was over in 15 minutes.
After losing nearly 2,000 men, most of
whom were taken prisoner, the remaining
Rebels crossed the river, burning the bridge
behind them, and headed to Vicksburg.

Today, Route 80 bisects the battlefield
area. The meander scar is on the right as
you head west. The river crossing is on the
left as you cross the bridge. The entire site

is private property, with a landscape resembling that of May 1863.

LOCATION: Marker located east of Big Black River near 21080 Old US 80, just before Smith Station Rd. in Edwards. Ask at Vicksburg National Military Park (see p. 136) about closer access to the site.

✳ Brice's Cross Roads

CAMPAIGN: Forrest's Defense of Mississippi
OTHER NAME(S): Tishomingo Creek
DATE(S): June 10, 1864

After his victory at Okolona, General Forrest set his sights on destroying Sherman's supply lines along the Nashville and Chattanooga Railroad. Union General Sturgis, ordered to draw Forrest away from middle Tennessee, lured the Rebels into northern Mississippi in early June 1864.

Challenging Sturgis's forward brigade, Forrest drew the Federals into a navigational trap. As Union infantry approached Grierson's rear, Forrest knew that the marshy, overgrown terrain and June's sweltering heat would take a toll on the Northern troops.

The Brice's Cross Roads memorial marks the spot where the Brice family home stood.

When his third Rebel brigade arrived, Forrest charged the enemy leading with his artillery—a bold, unconventional maneuver. Even with twice the manpower, three times the cannon, and a host of new Colt repeating rifles, Union forces were overwhelmingly defeated. Thoroughly routed, the Yankees rapidly retreated to Memphis, taking only two days and a night to retrace their advance route. Forrest's victory was stunning, for this self-made man without formal education demonstrated the U.S. Army's "Principals of War" (which had yet to be codified) to perfection.

Today, the battlefield covers 1,500 acres. Start at the Mississippi's Final Stands Interpretive Center, which has a detailed model of the battlefield. At "the crossroads" where MS 370 and County Rte. 231 meet in Bethany, two short, paved trails cross the battlefield terrain and 16 interpretive panels explain the action there.

LOCATION: Mississippi's Final Stands Interpretive Center, 607 Grisham St., Baldwyn, 662-365-3969, www.finalstands.com /battlegrounds.

Cavalry Operations in Northern Mississippi

In addition to the major armies, the Confederates also used semi-independent cavalry units. In Mississippi, Okolona, Brice's Cross Roads, and Tupelo saw some of General Forrest's most important and controversial actions in 1864.

FURTHER READING

The Confederacy's Greatest Cavalryman: Nathan Bedford Forrest
by Brian Steel Wills
Detailed study of Forrest's life

FURTHER READING

Forrest at Brice's Cross Roads
by Edwin C. Bearss
Civil War historian's detailed account of this classic battle

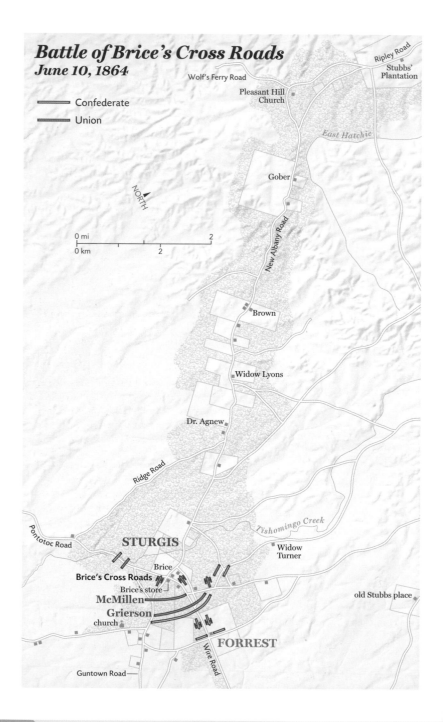

Battle of Brice's Cross Roads
June 10, 1864

Confederate

Union

Ripley Road

Stubbs' Plantation

Wolf's Ferry Road

Pleasant Hill Church

East Hatchie

NORTH

0 mi   2
0 km   2

Gober

New Albany Road

Brown

Widow Lyons

Dr. Agnew

Ridge Road

Tishomingo Creek

Pontotoc Road

STURGIS

Widow Turner

Brice

Brice's Cross Roads

Brice's store

McMillen

Grierson

church

old Stubbs place

FORREST

Wire Road

Guntown Road

✳ Champion Hill

CAMPAIGN: Grant's Operations Against Vicksburg

OTHER NAME(S): Baker's Creek

DATE(S): May 16, 1863

Direct from victory at Jackson (see pp. 128–129), Grant's forces were primed for battle when they found Confederate forces strung out and camped in disorder after an unplanned countermarch to cross Baker's Creek, near Champion Hill (east of Edwards). Grant's well-supplied, organized forces stood in sharp contrast as they approached Champion Hill from the east along three parallel roads. As the Union cavalry crossed Turkey Creek, the Confederates fired the first shots from a nearby plantation and attempted to block the advance of the Union left but failed as the Federal forces advanced toward Coker Ridge and the Coker House.

Grant moved to the offensive, attacking at Champion Hill and pushing through the crossroads while slicing in behind the Confederates and threatening to cut off their supply line. Beaten, Pemberton's troops fled back across Baker's Creek, urged on by heavy enfilading Union artillery. His disorganized force moved back across Big Black River toward Vicksburg; however, a division on his right under the command of General Loring was still isolated beyond Baker's Creek. Rather than be decimated by artillery fire while trying to cross, Loring marched to join General Joe Johnston's forces. Unaware of Loring's desertion, Pemberton held open the Big Black River crossing and paid for it in blood (see pp. 122–123).

Today, open ridges are still somewhat visible in the battlefield area, but the actual ridge where the Confederates faced the main Federal assault has been topped and lowered 20 or 30 feet, and thus does not resemble the field as the soldiers saw it. Half of the battlefield is still owned by the Champion family, who offer private commercial tours. The state owns about 800 acres of additional battlefield, including the antebellum Coker House. Once on the verge of collapse, Coker House has been reconstructed, with the outside left as an exact replica of the structure that was there during the battle. Though unstaffed, interpretive signs explain the action there.

LOCATION: Coker House, 3 miles east of Edwards, near 1245 Hwy. 467, near Adams Ln., www.battleofchampionhill.org.

✳ Chickasaw Bayou

CAMPAIGN: Operations Against Vicksburg

OTHER NAME(S): Chickasaw Bluffs, Walnut Hills

DATE(S): December 26–29, 1862

Knowing that Vicksburg was the key to opening the Mississippi River, Grant planned a two-pronged assault. According to the plan, Grant would come down the Mississippi Central Railroad line while Sherman would commandeer forces recruited by General McClernand in an amphibious assault against the fortified heights above Vicksburg. On December 20, however, Grant was stunned by a surprise attack on his supply base. Additional cavalry raids led by General Forrest further cut his supplies and left him unable to support Sherman, who had departed from Helena, Arkansas, and was now out of communication. Absent Grant, Sherman found the ground swampy and the Confederates ready for his attack. He ultimately launched a frontal attack on December 29, 1862. As Rebel forces held the high ground, they easily beat back Sherman's assault across open fields, inflicting more than 1,700 casualties while suffering about 200. Sherman's report was succinct: "I reached Vicksburg at the time appointed, landed, assaulted and failed."

Today, the 25-square-mile battlefield area lies mostly on private property subject to annual flooding. Get oriented at Vicksburg National Military Park (see p. 136), which offers an inexpensive battlefield driving tour brochure at the visitor center.

LOCATION: Marker located on Hwy. 61 Bus., about 1.5 miles north of Vicksburg National Military Park.

The most intense fighting at the second battle of Corinth took place at Battery Robinett.

✳ Corinth I

CAMPAIGN: Federal Penetration up the Cumberland and Tennessee Rivers

OTHER NAME(S): Siege of Corinth

DATE(S): April 29–June 10, 1862

By early 1862, the Federals occupied most of Tennessee. Then the focus turned to Corinth, the gateway to the entire Mississippi Valley. The expansion of the Federal reach down the Tennessee River to Muscle Shoals, Alabama, presented a major threat to the region's railroad infrastructure. Corinth was at the junction of two key rail lines: the Mobile & Ohio, a prime north-south route, and the east-west Memphis & Charleston. According to General Grant, Corinth was "the great strategic position at the West between the Tennessee and the Mississippi rivers and between Nashville and Vicksburg."

Loss of this junction, described by one Confederate officer as "the vertebrae of the Confederacy," would cripple transportation to eastern Tennessee and into Virginia. Indeed, loss of Corinth would send all east-bound rail traffic on a convoluted route to Mobile, there to detrain and cross Mobile Bay by boat, board another train to Atlanta, and disperse from there. Corinth was indeed the "last ditch to the Deep South."

In early April 1862, Confederate General Albert Sidney Johnston ordered General Beauregard's forces to attack Union troops camped at Pittsburg Landing, near a small country church known locally as Shiloh. Confederates were effectively backing the Federals against the Tennessee River when Johnston was mortally wounded. Failing to capitalize on his gains on the first day's battle, a Union counterattack on the second day caused Beauregard to order a retreat to already fortified Corinth, 22 miles south.

Over the next 30 days, the Federal army, now commanded by General Halleck, inched forward at glacial speed, constructing defensive earthworks at every stop, expecting to rout the Confederate defenders in a single decisive battle. As temperatures soared and supplies dwindled, Beauregard knew his position was untenable so, after much bluff and preparation, he withdrew his army to Tupelo during the night of May 29.

Today, the earthworks are marked so that visitors can follow the methodical nature of this classic Napoleonic siege. Rail Crossing-Trailhead Park, across the tracks from the Crossroads Museum on Filmore Street, also has interpretive signs.

LOCATION: **Corinth Interpretive Center, 501 W. Linden St., Corinth, 662-287-9273, www.nps .gov/shil/learn/historyculture/corinth.htm.**

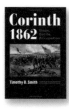

FURTHER READING

Corinth, 1862: Siege, Battle, Occupation by Timothy B. Smith First in-depth account of the battle since the creation of the Corinth Interpretive Center

✳ Corinth II

CAMPAIGN: Iuka and Corinth Operations
DATE(S): October 3–4, 1862

After the September 19 battle at Iuka, the Federals returned to the vicinity of Corinth With Grant away from the army, General Rosecrans was in charge. In the fall of 1862, while Confederates were on the move in Maryland, Kentucky, and Tennessee, General Van Dorn proposed joining General Price in a combined effort to retake Corinth. The idea was to thwart Grant's ability to aid General Buell's efforts against Braxton Bragg, and, as the senior officer, Van Dorn would command the effort.

In early October, while Van Dorn feinted to the north before circling back to Corinth from the east, the Federals expanded the original Confederate earthworks, creating a double layer of outer and inner defenses. Generals Van Dorn and Price succeeded in pushing the Yankees back to their inner works and penetrated the lines all the way to the train depot; however, when a supporting attack was delayed, the Rebel momentum stalled. General Rosecrans held on during two days of vicious fighting.

It's possible to follow the attack routes of Van Dorn, where well-preserved outer earthworks are marked. Within town, walk the route of the Confederate breakthrough from Battery Powell, past the antebellum houses of Union and Confederate generals, through the business district, and to the railroad junction. Some of the most vicious fighting of the battle took place in the field where Battery Robinett stood, as depicted in paintings at the interpretive center. Inquire about seeing Van Hedge's Corinth Civil War Collection—thousands of artifacts and a tabletop map with topographical accuracy showing the fields of battle. Eat at Borrums, with its authentic soda fountain.

LOCATION: **Corinth Interpretive Center, 501 W. Linden St., Corinth, 662-287-9273, www.nps .gov/shil/learn/historyculture/corinth.htm.**

✳ Grand Gulf

CAMPAIGN: Grant's Operations Against Vicksburg
DATE(S): April 29, 1863

The Confederate position here had two fortifications, Fort Cobun high on a bluff and lower Fort Wade. After running his naval fleet past Vicksburg's defenses, Admiral Porter's seven ironclads bombarded the Confederates at this prime cotton port for five hours without success on April 29, 1863. Porter was hoping to secure a landing spot for Grant's army advancing along the west bank of the river. Confederate resistance was so effective, however, that Grant abandoned the effort to land there and moved farther south to Bruinsburg. Once there, he bypassed Grand Gulf in order to capture Port Gibson. As the Rebels evacuated Grand Gulf, Grant built up his supply depot there and kept his forces together, proceeding north toward Vicksburg via Raymond.

Located eight miles north of Port Gibson, Grand Gulf Military Park's museum offers an overview of the naval bombardment and later Union occupation. Its collection includes original artifacts, flags, and authentic Confederate money. Allow at least an hour for the 1.5-mile driving tour over hilly terrain to explore the remnants of Forts Cobun and Wade and other structures. Another route takes visitors to Port Gibson and includes the off-the-beaten-path Shaifer House and Windsor Ruins. A 50-mile route with interpretive "Grant's March" markers begins at Grand Gulf and ends at Raymond Military Park (see pp. 132–133).

LOCATION: **Grand Gulf Military Park, 12006 Grand Gulf Rd., Port Gibson, 601-437-5911, www.grandgulfpark.state.ms.us.**

✳ Iuka

CAMPAIGN: Iuka and Corinth Operations
DATE(S): September 19, 1862

The Confederates had previously pushed the Yankees out of this small town just east of Corinth, and now the Union wanted it back. Generals Ord and Rosecrans were directed to approach Iuka from the west and southwest, respectively, encircle General Price's unsuspecting Rebels, and shut off their escape route. The two-pronged attack didn't synchronize, however, because Ord, instructed to wait until he heard the sound of battle, inadvertently left Rosecrans to strike alone.

Later, Generals Grant and Ord, both positioned within a few miles of Iuka, claimed

that an acoustic shadow kept them from hearing the battle. Attempting but failing to secure the escape route, Rosecrans took heat from Grant, who, though absent from the scene, expressed serious concern about the Ohioan's abilities in the field. After occupying Iuka, Rosecrans failed to pursue the enemy as General Price departed to join forces with General Van Dorn at Ripley.

A detailed two-hour, 35-stop audio tour describes troop maneuvers as well as several antebellum homes used during and after the battle. The research library and Civil War room at the Old Tishomingo County Courthouse Museum offer additional information on the battle.

LOCATION: **Marker located at the intersection of Veterans Memorial Dr. and Heritage Dr. in Iuka. For driving tour information, visit www.battleofiuka.com. Old Tishomingo County Courthouse Museum, 203 E. Quitman St., Iuka, 662-423-3500, www.tishomingohistory.com.**

FURTHER READING

The Darkest Days of the War: The Battles of Iuka and Corinth
by Peter Cozzens
First book-length study of these pivotal 1862 battles

✳ Jackson

CAMPAIGN: Grant's Operations Against Vicksburg
DATE(S): May 14, 1863

Originally planning to proceed directly to Vicksburg after the Battle of Raymond (see pp. 130–131), General Grant instead focused on the state capital of Jackson, a growing Confederate base. He dispatched two corps to destroy the Jackson & Vicksburg Railroad and defeat General Johnston's forces before they could buttress the garrison at Vicksburg or present a danger to Union troops making their way west.

Having learned that Generals Sherman and McPherson were approaching Jackson, Johnston, who arrived from Tennessee on

THE ROAD TO VICKSBURG

On the afternoon of May 3, 1863, Union Gen. U.S. Grant rode west past this intersection to Grand Gulf while Gen. John A. Logan's division turned north toward Vicksburg. Logan was in pursuit of the Confederate force that had abandoned Grand Gulf early that morning. In the early hours of May 4, Grant returned here from Grand Gulf and joined his troops near Hankinson's Ferry, where Logan had captured a raft bridge over the Big Black River, opening the road to Vicksburg.

MISSISSIPPI DEPARTMENT OF ARCHIVES AND HISTORY, 2010

This illustration of the town of Iuka was published in the October 4, 1862, *Harper's Weekly.*

May 13, quickly began evacuating the city while ordering local commander General Gregg to keep a small contingency behind to stall the Federal advance. Grant, surprised to find sparse defenses awaiting him, easily moved into Jackson. His troops occupied and burned the city, which soon acquired the nickname Chimneyville.

Visitors to the Old Capitol Museum can see the House chamber where the ordinance of secession was voted on and where an elderly Jefferson Davis gave his farewell speech. An orientation film and galleries explore the history of the building and area.

LOCATION: Drive by Confederate earthworks on Capitol St. at the entrance to the Jackson Zoo en route to the Old Capitol Museum, 100 S. State St., Jackson, 601-576-6920, www.mdah .state.ms.us.

☀ Meridian

CAMPAIGN: Meridian and Yazoo River Expeditions

DATE(S): February 14–20, 1864

In preparation for his Atlanta Campaign, General Sherman aimed for the interior of the Confederacy, planning to continue to Mobile or Alabama's industrial center in Selma. Operating from Vicksburg, he set out to destroy tracks on the 150 mile route to the three-way rail junction in Meridian, where he would rendezvous with General Smith's cavalry. Smith departed from

Memphis ten days late, however, and found his progress slowed as his 7,500 men wreaked havoc on local farms in north Mississippi and became magnets for hundreds of slaves seeking freedom. While Smith ended up clashing with General Forrest's cavalry in a series of running skirmishes back to Okolona, General Polk responded to feints by Sherman's infantry until, fearing destruction in battle, he marched away, leaving the town to become Sherman's endpoint in a practice run for his scorched-earth March to the Sea (see p. 74). When he was finished, Sherman reported, "Meridian, with its depots, store-houses, arsenal, hospitals, offices, hotels, and cantonments no longer exists."

The Meridian Tourist Bureau has created a detailed Civil War trail that begins at Union Station in Meridian. There is also extended video content about each stop on the town's website.

LOCATION: Meridian Tourist Bureau, 212 Constitution Ave., Meridian, 601-482-8001, www.visitmeridian.com.

☀ Okolona

CAMPAIGN: Meridian and Yazoo River Expeditions

DATE(S): February 22, 1864

In an ongoing series of running battles that began at West Point, General Forrest's cavalry continued to push the Federals north, flanking their more numerous troops at each step. At Okolona, General Smith ran into a cavalry contingent led by Forrest's brother, who was mortally wounded in the fighting that raged over 11 miles. Enraged, Forrest pushed General Smith's troops even harder. A subsequent flanking maneuver forced the Federal horsemen to flee to yet another line, where they charged the Confederates. As the day expired, Smith withdrew. Uncharacteristically, Forrest let him leave as Rebel forces were exhausted and out of ammunition.

LOCATION: **Marker located at the intersection of W. Main St. and N. Gatlin St., Meridian. The Okolona Confederate Cemetery is on S. Church St.**

FURTHER READING

The Battle of Okolona: Defending the Mississippi Prairie by Brandon H. Beck Includes descriptive tour of battle-related sites

✳ Port Gibson

CAMPAIGN: Grant's Operations Against Vicksburg

OTHER NAME(S): Thompson's Hill

DATE(S): May 1, 1863

General Grant's first encounter with Rebel forces after crossing the Mississippi at Bruinsburg began near midnight at a homestead belonging to A. K. Shaifer. Outnumbered and outflanked, the Confederates fell back through Port Gibson, burning the bridge over Big Bayou Pierre. By the evening of May 1, Grant had a victory. The capture of Port Gibson enabled the Federals to force the evacuation of Grand Gulf, where river defenses had been too strong to conquer.

The Shaifer house on Old Rodney Road is still accessible, with on-site interpretation. Nearby is Bethel Presbyterian Church, where Grant regrouped his troops after landing at Bruinsburg. Markers between Windsor Ruins and Port Gibson describe the battle. Check

with Grand Gulf Military Park (see p. 128) for updates on road conditions before heading out.

LOCATION: **Port Gibson Visitor Center, 1601 Church St., Port Gibson, 601-437-4351, www .portgibsononthemississippi.com.**

✳ Raymond

CAMPAIGN: Grant's Operations Against Vicksburg

DATE(S): May 12, 1863

After the Confederate evacuation of Grand Gulf (see pp. 127–128), Grant proceeded

toward Raymond with the goal of cutting the railroad from Jackson into Vicksburg. But a small battle in Raymond completely changed his plans.

As General McPherson's 12,000 men ran into 3,000 of General Gregg's Rebel infantrymen along Fourteen Mile Creek, a confused but determined skirmish ensued. Though McPherson easily scored a victory, Grant theorized that the Confederates must be pooling their manpower resources to protect Vicksburg. He thus changed his plans to attack Jackson (see pp. 128–129) before turning back toward Vicksburg.

Raymond Military Park is the only site in the nation with reproduction cannons that precisely match the number, types, and locations as those used in the battle. A new 0.75-mile paved interpretive trail, as well as a driving tour of the surrounding area, give a good overview of the action. The driving tour brochure is available at City Hall or from local merchants.

LOCATION: Raymond Military Park, intersection of Hwy. 18 and Port Gibson St., Raymond, about 2 miles from Raymond Town Square; City Hall, 110 Courtyard Sq., Raymond, 601-857-8041, www.battleofraymond.org.

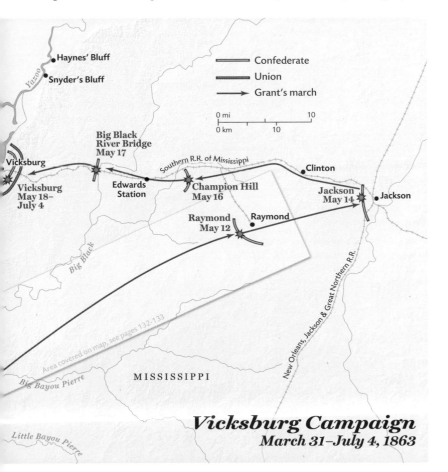

Vicksburg Campaign
March 31–July 4, 1863

Grand Gulf–Raymond Scenic Byway

In May 1863, this road served as the line of communication for General Grant's army. Today, it retains much of its integrity and charm. Follow the "Grant's March" signs to 19 historical markers interpreting the route. If your time is limited, prioritize the 11 markers highlighted below.

1 Start at **Marker 1** in the Grand Gulf town square. Across the square is **Marker 2.** Grant determined to capture Vicksburg rather than support Federal operations against Port Hudson, and he stockpiled two million rations here to supply his army.

2 Climb the winding road out of the Mississippi River Valley on to the loess bluffs. Follow the "Grant's March" markers across Highway 61 for a total of 12.5 miles to **Markers 5 and 6.** Near here Grant made the decision to move against the vital railroad that connected Vicksburg to points east.

3 Continue seven more miles to **Marker 7** at Rocky Springs. Grant headquartered here May 7–10 to await the arrival of Sherman's men. Near here, on May 8, Grant reviewed McClernand's men at Big Sand Creek.

4 Continue 1.6 miles to **Marker 8.** Here the modern road merges with the Old Natchez Trace roadbed. McPherson's men marched along the Trace before passing through McClernand's men at Little and Big Sand Creeks. Take a stroll down the historic sunken road.

5 Continue 8.2 miles to **Marker 11** in Cayuga. Grant headquartered here on May 10 and remained until early on May 12 to allow Sherman to pass from the rear to the center of the army, a move that placed McClernand on the left and McPherson on the right.

6 Drive 10.5 miles to **Marker 15** at Dillon's farm, headquarters for Grant and Sherman during the Battle of

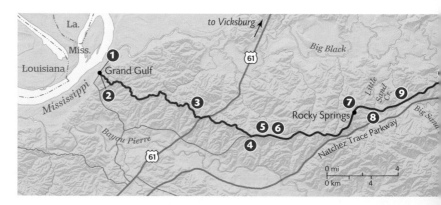

The Old Historic Grist Mill, waterwheel, and dog trot house featured at Grand Gulf State Park

Raymond. Realizing that Confederate forces would be to his left and right if he moved north to the railroad, Grant wheeled his army east to Jackson, in order to drive out Johnston's Rebels, while at the same time sending McPherson north to Clinton to cut the railroad.

7 Drive 7.5 miles to **Marker 17** at the Confederate Cemetery, where 140 Confederate dead from the Battle of Raymond are buried.

8 Drive a half mile to **Marker 19** at St. Mark's Episcopal Church, which was used as a Union hospital.

Cotton spread on the floor served as make-shift mattresses. The Confederate hospital was just across the street in the antebellum court-house **(Marker 18).**

Access I-20 via Clinton-Raymond Road, which exits the Town Square to the north.

✳ Snyder's Bluff

CAMPAIGN: Grant's Operations Against Vicksburg

OTHER NAME(S): Snyder's Mill

DATE(S): April 29–May 1, 1863

Taking place simultaneously with action at Grand Gulf (see pp. 127–128), this battle was another of General Sherman's diversions, designed to keep Confederate troops from interfering with Grant's crossing the Mississippi farther south. As Federal gunboats reached the mouth of the Yazoo River, Sherman aimed to take control of that waterway by outflanking Rebel defenses at Snyder's Bluff. As at Chickasaw Bayou (see p. 125), however, the Confederates held the high ground above the Yazoo, and Sherman's task failed.

LOCATION: Marker located on MS 3, one mile north of US 61 above Redwood.

✳ Tupelo

CAMPAIGN: Forrest's Defense of Mississippi

OTHER NAME(S): Harrisburg

DATE(S): July 14–15, 1864

General Sherman had Atlanta under siege as Federal efforts to keep General Forrest away from Union supply lines in Tennessee continued. The third attempt to beat this "wizard of the saddle," who already had victories at Okolona (see pp. 129–130) and Brice's

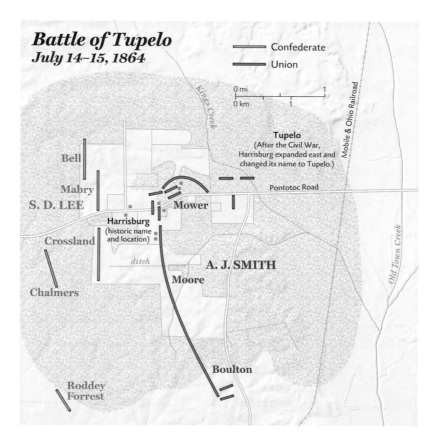

Battle of Tupelo
July 14–15, 1864

Confederate
Union

Tupelo
(After the Civil War, Harrisburg expanded east and changed its name to Tupelo.)

Bell

Mabry

S. D. LEE

Mower

Harrisburg
(historic name and location)

Crossland

Pontotoc Road

ditch

A. J. SMITH

Chalmers

Moore

Boulton

Roddey
Forrest

Kings Creek

Mobile & Ohio Railroad

Old Town Creek

0 mi   1
0 km   1

The Vicksburg Campaign

The red granite Texas Memorial at Vicksburg National Military Park includes 11 steps to honor the other states in the Confederacy and a live yucca plant, native to Texas.

Vicksburg was not one battle, but a series of actions, possibly the most important series in the Civil War. To Jefferson Davis, Vicksburg was "the nail head that holds the two halves of the South together." To Lincoln, "Vicksburg is the key. The war can never be brought to a close until that key is in our pocket."

After months of failed independent attempts by Grant's army and Porter's navy to make inroads on their target, they realized that only with a joint operation would they reopen the entire Mississippi River for commercial navigation—a task essential to the economic vitality of the North.

Vicksburg itself seemed impenetrable. Perched on 200-foot bluffs overlooking the mighty Mississippi, it was bordered by swamps and frequently flooded deltas that seemed to shield it from any land attack during the wet season.

By August 1862, the Union controlled the river from New Orleans to Baton Rouge and from Vicksburg north, but the Confederacy controlled the 250 miles that lay in between. The massive military effort required for the Union to seize control of Vicksburg and the Mississippi River took about 11 months to complete successfully.

Today, many key points in the campaign are accessible to visitors, who are well advised to plan a trip of several days. The key to understanding the campaign is preparation, so do some homework beforehand. The area is a living-history bonanza, with many sites appearing exactly as they did at the time of the war.

The Vicksburg National Military Park visitor center features a film, exhibits, and other information about touring the site. The U.S.S. *Cairo* Gunboat and Museum houses the restored ironclad, sunk by a Confederate "torpedo" in December 1862 and an in-depth look at the naval action at Vicksburg. A 16-mile driving tour weaves past points of interest. Although the entire landscape was practically denuded of trees and cover in 1863, portions of the park have been restored to wartime appearance.

FURTHER READING

Receding Tide, Vicksburg and Gettysburg: The Campaigns That Changed the Civil War
by Edwin C. Bearss and J. Parker Hills
In-depth chronicle of both campaigns by acknowledged experts

Cross Roads (see p. 123), fell to General "Whiskey" Smith, who faced a frontal attack from Forrest and 9,500 Rebels on his way to Tupelo. This time the Federals won the battle, inflicting 1,300 Confederate casualties.

To fully understand the battle, begin at Mississippi's Final Stands Interpretive Center, and then follow the driving tour to Tupelo. Visitors can also see the spot on the north side of the creek where Smith set up camp on July 15 and beat back Forrest's troops after a surprise attack. Located at 3454 Mt. Vernon Road, the 12-acre site has some interpretation.

LOCATION: **Mississippi's Final Stands Interpretive Center, 607 Grisham St., Baldwyn, 662-365-3969, www.finalstands.com.**

✳ Vicksburg

CAMPAIGN: Grant's Operations Against Vicksburg

DATE(S): May 18–July 4, 1863

Since the winter of 1862, strong Confederate defenses and unexpected Union

Eighth Wisconsin volunteers carry their mascot, a bald eagle named Old Abe, into combat at Vicksburg.

missteps had allowed Vicksburg to hold on as the "Gibraltar of the West." But in the spring of 1863, that was all about to change.

Although Confederate troops had fortified Vicksburg's perimeter effectively, General Grant had successfully severed communication lines between Generals Pemberton and Johnston. After May 17, 1863, Rebel supplies and troops could no longer enter or leave the city.

From May 18 to July 4, the Federals made two general attempts to break Confederate lines—on May 19 and May 22—resulting in more than 4,000 casualties for the Union as both efforts failed. Grant then began to dig a series of subterranean mines at different points in front of the Railroad Redoubt, the 3rd Louisiana Redan, the Texas Redoubt, and the Square Fort. Only one was exploded with mixed results for the Union; however, others were to be detonated. Bombardments of the city were incessant, driving civilians into hundreds of hastily dug caves. Food shortages grew as horses, dogs, and rats became meals. Sickness, famine, and despair spread with no hope of relief.

With Sherman covering Grant's rear, Johnston had no chance of relieving Vicksburg and, as the ring of 77,000 Federal troops tightened around Pemberton's army, the soldiers within sent a message to Pemberton: "If you can't feed us, you had better surrender us, horrible as the idea is, than suffer this noble army to disgrace themselves by desertion."

Perhaps recognizing the value to morale of capturing Vicksburg on the Fourth of July, Grant, who usually demanded unconditional surrender, worked some flexibility into his terms in order to secure victory and occupation of the city on Independence Day. For many years after, Vicksburgers, sorrowed by the irony of the surrender, did not celebrate the holiday. For Grant, he had captured his second army of the war—the third, at Appomattox, would be the most significant.

LOCATION: **Vicksburg National Military Park, 3201 Clay St., Vicksburg, 601-636-0583, www.nps.gov/vick.**

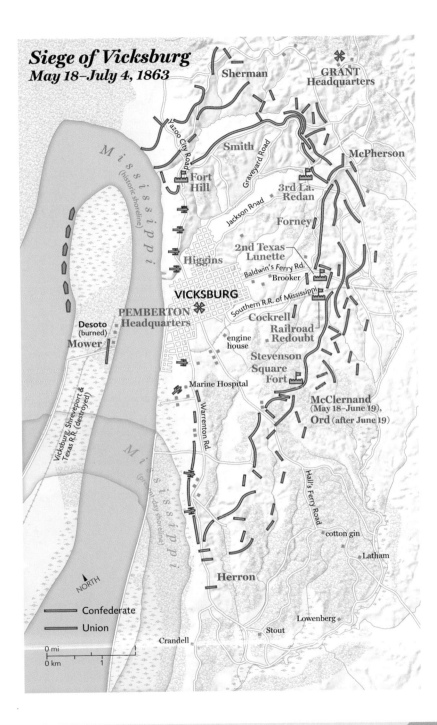

Siege of Vicksburg
May 18–July 4, 1863

Sherman

GRANT Headquarters

Mississippi (historic shoreline)

Yazoo City Road

Smith

McPherson

Fort Hill

Graveyard Road

3rd La. Redan

Jackson Road

Forney

Higgins

2nd Texas Lunette

Baldwin's Ferry Rd.

Brooker

VICKSBURG

Southern R.R. of Mississippi

Cockrell

Desoto (burned)

Mower

PEMBERTON Headquarters

engine house

Railroad Redoubt

Stevenson Square Fort

Marine Hospital

McClernand (May 18–June 19), Ord (after June 19)

Vicksburg, Shreveport & Texas R.R. (destroyed)

Warrenton Rd.

Mississippi (present-day shoreline)

Hall's Ferry Road

cotton gin

Latham

NORTH

Herron

Confederate

Union

Lowenberg

Stout

Crandell

0 mi 1

0 km 1

Other Battles and Beyond

✦ Beauvoir: The Jefferson Davis Home and Presidential Library

Overlooking the Mississippi Sound, Jefferson Davis's writing retreat and refuge after the war offers some fascinating insights into his life. Built on eight-foot-tall brick piers designed for better airflow within, the 1848 house has survived many storms. After Hurricane Katrina filled the first floor with a foot of water, restoration included returning all the paint to original colors.

LOCATION: 2244 Beach Blvd., Biloxi, 228-388-4400, www.beauvoir.org.

FURTHER READING
Jefferson Davis, American
by William J. Cooper, Jr. Definitive, elegant, and humane portrait of the Confederate president

✦ Confederate Forts at Grenada Lake

Part of General Pemberton's Yalobusha Line, this series of eight forts was constructed in 1862 to protect the Confederates' vital rail junction at Grenada. No action took place here, however, because General Grant was diverted back to Holly Springs after General Van Dorn's raid. Two earthen forts, one restored, are open to the public.

LOCATION: 2151 Scenic Loop 333, Grenada, 662-226-5911, www.visitgrenadams.com.

✦ Corinth Contraband Camp

Many escaped slaves (classified by the Union as "contraband") and their families found protection and the beginning of new lives at this encampment. Here they produced food and supplies, created a community, and earned their own wages. Bronze statues note some of their endeavors.

LOCATION: 902 North Pkwy., Corinth, www.nps.gov/shil/planyourvisit/contraband camp.htm.

✦ Corinth Historic Grand Illumination

Luminarias placed during this stunning event honor 12,000 Civil War casualties the first weekend of November each year.

LOCATION: Throughout the town, from Battery Robinett/Corinth Civil War Interpretive Center, through the historic business district, to the Contraband Camp and the historic railroad crossings, www.grandilluminationcorinth.com.

✦ Fort Pemberton

Located between the Yazoo and Tallahatchie Rivers, Fort Pemberton was the culminating action of General Grant's Yazoo River Expedition and 1863 attempt to bring Union soldiers overland behind the fortifications that defended Vicksburg. He failed here in March as the Confederate fort guarded both rivers. Sunken vessels—including the *Star of the West*, the unarmed merchant ship of

Jefferson Davis's presidential library is at Beauvoir house, his postwar home in Biloxi.

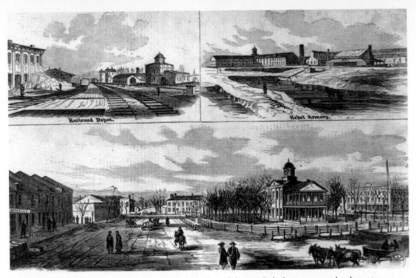

Scenes of wartime Holly Springs include the railroad depot, Rebel armory, and a downtown street view.

1861 Fort Sumter fame—also hampered navigation. The Museum of the Mississippi Delta includes a model of the fort and artifacts from the *Star of the West*. A marker and remnants of Fort Pemberton's earthworks are located west of the museum.

LOCATION: **Museum of the Mississippi Delta, 1608 Hwy. 82 W., Greenwood, 662-453-0925, www.museumofthemississippidelta.com.**

FURTHER READING

Mr. Lincoln's Brown Water Navy: The Mississippi Squadron
by Gary D. Joiner
Clearly written account of the Civil War as it was fought on the rivers in the West

✦ Hill Crest Cemetery

Statues and antebellum iron fences highlight the burial place of notables, including ten Confederate generals and Colonel Autry,

commander of Vicksburg in May 1862, who, when asked to surrender, sent word to the Union flotilla: "Mississippians don't know, and refuse to learn how to surrender."

LOCATION: **380 S. Maury St., Holly Springs, 662-252-2515.**

✦ Holly Springs Raid

General Grant kicked off his two-pronged land approach to Vicksburg here, 40 miles southeast of Memphis along the Mississippi Central Railroad. He followed the rail line toward Jackson, attacking his target from the east, while Sherman attacked from the north. The plan fell apart when General Van Dorn's cavalry column decimated Grant's supply depot in a raid on December 20, 1862. Grant rushed back to Holly Springs, leaving Sherman to attack alone at Chickasaw Bayou (see p. 125).

LOCATION: **Interpretive signage installed. Pick up a tour brochure detailing Van Dorn's raid at the Holly Springs Tourism and Recreation Bureau, 148 E. College Ave., Holly Springs, 888-687-4765, www.visithollysprings.com.**

✦ Natchez

To see Old South architecture in all its glory, explore ten incredible plantation homes here year-round, with more open during the town's annual monthlong spring pilgrimage. Tickets are available at the visitor center.

LOCATION: **Visitor Center, 640 S. Canal St., Natchez, 601-446-6631, www.natchez pilgrimage.com/antebellum-mansions.php.**

✦ Natchez Trace Parkway

Natchez is milepost zero of the 444-mile scenic parkway that cuts diagonally across Mississippi, then into Tennessee, offering access to many Civil War and other historic and scenic sites.

LOCATION: **Find more information at www .natcheztracetravel.com/natchez-trace-park way-maps.html or by calling 800-305-7417.**

✦ Old Court House Museum

Union soldiers raised the flag above this 1860 building on July 4, 1863, after the fall of Vicksburg (see p. 136). The museum's "Confederate and Jefferson Davis" room offers artifacts from the siege and items relating to Davis, with particular emphasis on his political career in Mississippi.

LOCATION: **1008 Cherry St., Vicksburg, 601-636-0741, www.oldcourthouse.org.**

✦ Rolling Fork

The endpoint of Steele's Bayou Expedition in March 1863 was another failed attempt for Admiral Porter's brown water navy and General Sherman's infantry to put Union forces behind Confederate waterfront fortifications. Porter's squadron of gunboats

The 1823 Rosalie Mansion in Natchez is representative of the extraordinary wealth of the traders and planters along the Mississippi River north of New Orleans.

Windsor Ruins, near Port Gibson, recalls the stately 1861 plantation home that burned in 1890. Confederate troops used the cupola for observation, and the view inspired Mark Twain.

became embroiled in narrow, shallow waters not meant for 60-yard-long vessels. At Rolling Fork, one mile from the Yazoo River, dense reeds clogged the fleet's propulsion mechanisms. Porter's skill in backing his gunboats out of the bayou, amid the Confederates' infantry fire and felling of trees to block his way, is one of the dramatic moments of the Civil War. Today, note the reeds growing in the low water, then visit the U.S.S. *Cairo* at Vicksburg National Military Park to learn about the challenges that such large gunboats faced.

LOCATION: **Visitor Center and Museum, 380 Walnut St., Rolling Fork, 662-873-2232. Visitors can pick up a "Steele's Bayou Expedition" driving tour brochure at Vicksburg National Military Park or in Rolling Fork.**

✦ Ship Island

Two thousand Federal troops arrived in December 1861 at Fort Massachusetts, notable now as an 1859 masonry fort that was never re-outfitted for later wars. This barrier island, 12 miles off the Mississippi coast, was the staging area for the Union fleet in the 1862 Battle of New Orleans (see pp. 110–111) and a prison for malcontents banished from New Orleans during the Federal occupation. As part of Gulf Shores National Seashore, it is accessible by concession boat leaving from the Gulfport Marina.

LOCATION: **Fort Massachusetts visitor information, 228-875-9057, www.nps.gov/guis/learn /historyculture/fort-massachusetts.htm.**

✦ Windsor Ruins

This once stately, four-story 1861 plantation home was used as a lookout post for Confederates and later as a hospital for Union troops. Only 23 towering Corinthian columns survived when fire destroyed the home in 1890, and today the site makes for a fascinating, if eerie and isolated, stop.

LOCATION: **About 12 miles south of Port Gibson along MS 552 (Rodney Rd.). For the freshest fried chicken, pork chops, and other Southern delights, stop at the Old Country Store/Mr. D's, 18801 Hwy. 61, Lorman, 601-437-3661.**

North Carolina

"YOU CAN GET NO TROOPS FROM NORTH CAROLINA," SAID Governor John W. Ellis in response to Abraham Lincoln's call for 75,000 volunteers to fight after Fort Sumter. With loyalties narrowly split, North Carolinians opposed a secession convention in January 1861. On May 20, however, the wave of a handkerchief from a state capitol window in Raleigh signaled the vote for independence.

Although two significant amphibious attacks bracketed the Civil War in North Carolina—Hatteras Inlet in 1861 and Fort Fisher in 1865—the state was generally spared major combat operations until the end of the war. And yet, while lacking the heavy industry found in other Southern states, her 300-mile coastline and thriving agriculture were coveted prizes.

Northeast North Carolina fell to the Union early in the war, while the state's western mountains became a haven for Rebel guerrillas and draft dodgers. Mostly small clashes occurred until war's devastation finally hit with General Sherman's advance into the state in March 1865.

North Carolina's Gettysburg monument, by Mount Rushmore sculptor Gutzon Borglum, shows a wounded soldier directing others to charge on. North Carolina provided 14,147 men to that battle and suffered 6,000 casualities.

NORTH CAROLINA BATTLES

✵Albemarle Sound

CAMPAIGN: Operations Against Plymouth

DATE(S): May 5, 1864

After victory at Plymouth (see pp. 150–151), the ironclad C.S.S. *Albemarle* and gunboat *Bombshell* were headed for New Bern, when they were attacked by a fleet of seven heavily armed, wooden Union vessels in Albemarle Sound at the mouth of the Roanoke River. While the *Bombshell* surrendered quickly after being heavily damaged, the *Albemarle* took on the others. After being rammed by the U.S.S. *Sassacus,* a close-range battle ensued between the two ships. The *Albemarle* scored a direct hit to the steamer's boiler and then limped back to the protection of Plymouth. Five months later on October 27, 1864, William B. Cushing and a crew of seven men staged a daring night raid, exploding a torpedo at close range under the vessel's iron casing, sinking the *Albemarle.*

The Penelope Barker House Welcome Center, overlooking Albermarle Sound, offers maps, tours, and information about the battle. Interpretive waterfront panels describe the naval battle site and the Edenton Bell Battery's four cannons, made from locally donated bells because the town lacked sufficient artillery for its defense.

LOCATION: Penelope Barker House Welcome Center, 505 S. Broad St., Edenton, 252-482-7800, www.visitedenton.com/barker-house.

FURTHER READING

Commander William Barker Cushing, of the United States Navy
by Eliza Mary Hatch Edwards
Biography of Cushing written in the late 19th century by one of his near contemporaries

✵Averasboro

OTHER NAME(S): Taylor's Hole Creek, Smithville, Smiths Ferry, Black River

CAMPAIGN: Carolinas Campaign

DATE(S): March 16, 1865

General Sherman's army entered North Carolina in March 1865, ushering in a wave of attacks in the central part of the state. As Union troops proceeded north of Fayetteville toward Goldsborough to join the Federal forces marching inland from the coast, Sherman's left wing clashed with Rebels four miles south of Averasboro. By carefully positioning his troops between the Cape Fear and Black Rivers, General Hardee delayed the Federals' progress for two days, giving General Joe Johnston time to concentrate his forces for the Confederate Army of Tennessee's final battle at Bentonville.

The small, well-interpreted Averasboro Battlefield and Museum anchors the site, originally an 8,000-acre plantation. The landscape of privately owned farmland is similar to how it appeared during the war. Within walking distance is the small Chicora Civil War Cemetery, where 56 Confederates from the battle are interred.

LOCATION: **Averasboro Battlefield and Museum, 3300 NC Hwy. 82, Dunn, 910-891-5019, www.averasboro.com.**

❋ Bentonville

OTHER NAME(S): Bentonville
CAMPAIGN: Carolinas Campaign
DATE(S): March 19–21, 1865

The timing of this battle, less than three weeks before General Lee's surrender at Appomattox, often relegates it to a footnote in history. And yet, it was the state's largest, bloodiest battle, with 80,000 soldiers fighting across 6,000 acres.

While Sherman had moved rapidly through South Carolina into the Tar Heel State with little opposition, he found himself in a considerable battle at Bentonville, where Confederate General Joe Johnston, despite being outnumbered three to one, made an aggressive stand. Johnston, relieved of command during Sherman's Atlanta Campaign, had been recalled to duty at General Lee's insistence to try and stop Sherman from advancing through North Carolina.

The heaviest fighting, on March 19 at Cole Plantation, ended in a tactical draw, but with Sherman's reinforcements arriving the next afternoon, the outcome was predictable. Johnston retreated toward Raleigh and finally surrendered his army on April 26.

Today, about one-third of the battlefield has been preserved. The film and fiber-optic map at the visitor center detail the combat maneuvers of the first day only. The 1850s Harper House, which served as a hospital during and after the battle, is open to

Union General Mower turned the Confederate flank at the Battle of Bentonville.

visitors. The family cemetery and one for Confederate soldiers are nearby. Remnants of original trenches are also visible. Allow a couple of hours for the self-guided, ten-mile driving tour with cell-phone narration. Inquire in advance about private tours.

LOCATION: **Bentonville Battlefield Historical Association, 5466 Harper House Rd., Four Oaks, 910-594-0789, www.nchistoricsites.org /bentonvi.**

FURTHER READING

Last Stand in the Carolinas: The Battle of Bentonville
by Mark L. Bradley
Carefully researched account of an often neglected battle

Surrender at Bennett Farm

Although Jefferson Davis had instructed him to fight on, General Joe Johnston met with General Sherman at the Bennett Farm on April 17, 1865. General Breckinridge, the secretary of war, who agreed that the time for peace had come, accompanied him. In agreeing to peace terms, rather than just the surrender of Johnston's army, Sherman exceeded his authority. His written terms reconstructed Southern governments and granted amnesty for all Southern soldiers now under arms. In contrast, at Appomattox, Lee and his men were paroled, not pardoned. Furious, Secretary of War Edwin Stanton sent Grant to relieve Sherman and secure surrender on the Appomattox terms. Grant did not relieve Sherman but let him understand that the terms of surrender must be a great deal more restrictive without any politics. Sherman did as he was told, and Johnston accepted the new terms on April 26, 1865.

✳ Fort Anderson

CAMPAIGN: Longstreet's Tidewater Operations
OTHER NAME(S): Deep Gully
DATE(S): March 13–15, 1863

During General Longstreet's Tidewater Campaign, Rebels were charged with rounding-up supplies for Lee's Army of Northern Virginia, while keeping Federal forces in North Carolina in check. Aiming to gain the Federal supply depot at New Bern, General Hill waged a successful skirmish at Deep Gully west of town, then ordered General Pettigrew to lead an attack on the garrison at Fort Anderson on the north bank of the Neuse River, opposite New Bern. While the arrival of Federal gunboats on May 15 forced the Rebels to withdraw to Washington, North Carolina, they were able to capture substantial provisions for Lee's army.

LOCATION: **Unmarked site, not to be confused with the Fort Anderson that is located on the Cape Fear River.**

✳ Fort Fisher I

CAMPAIGN: Expedition Against Fort Fisher
DATE(S): December 7–27, 1864

Located on a spit between the Atlantic Ocean and the Cape Fear River, Fort Fisher—22 miles south of Wilmington—protected the Confederacy's last major open port. It extended a mile along the coastline and a third of a mile to Cape Fear River, with massive earth and sand mounds ranging from 12 to 32 feet high anchored on the southern end by batteries towering 45 to 60 feet high. With dozens of internal bombproofs below, its nickname, the "Gibraltar of the South," was quite fitting.

Fort Fisher and its sister forts provided cover for blockade-runners entering and leaving Wilmington through Old and New Inlets. In December 1864, the Federals attempted but failed to take the fort. They returned in January 1865 (see p. 147) and successfully took it after fierce bastion-to-bastion fighting.

Today, about 10 percent of Fort Fisher remains, as erosion and the Atlantic Ocean have taken the eastern face. The northern bastions are still imposing and impressive. The fort's museum includes a 16-foot-long fiber-optic map showing the battle's progression, artifacts from a sunken blockade-runner, and information about the fort's construction.

LOCATION: **Fort Fisher, 1610 Ft. Fisher Blvd. S., Kure Beach, 910-458-5538, www.nchistoric sites.org/fisher/fisher.htm.**

FURTHER READING

The Wilmington Campaign: Last Rays of Departing Hope by Chris E. Fonvielle, Jr. Detailed examination of the battles for Fort Fisher as well as the defense of Fort Anderson

✳ Fort Fisher II

CAMPAIGN: Operations Against Fort Fisher and Wilmington

DATE(S): January 13–15, 1865

After his failed attempt to take Fort Fisher in December 1864, General Butler was replaced by General Terry, who initiated a second operation against the fort, an attack that was the largest U.S. amphibious landing until World War II. Shepherd's Battery guarded the western face, where the main Union assault occurred on January 15, 1865. The Union victory at Fort Fisher opened the door to Wilmington and secured the collapse of the Confederacy.

Walking the grounds within, and looking at the reconstructed mounds with a fully operational 32-pounder seacoast gun perched above, helps visitors experience the fort's immensity. Climb to the top of the mounds for a panoramic view of the Cape Fear River.

LOCATION: **Fort Fisher, 1610 Ft. Fisher Blvd. S., Kure Beach, 910-458-5538, www.nchistoric sites.org/fisher/fisher.htm.**

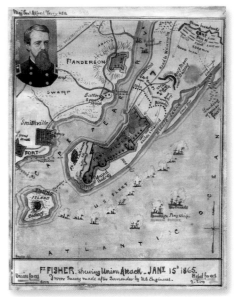

This map shows the Union's two-pronged plan of attack on Fort Fisher in 1865.

✳ Fort Macon

CAMPAIGN: Burnside's North Carolina Expedition

DATE(S): March 23–April 26, 1862

Garrisoned in 1834, this Third System masonry fort protecting Beaufort and Morehead City was surrounded by Union troops on March 23, 1862. The fort's 400 soldiers and outdated artillery stood as the defenders of the state's only deepwater ocean port. General Burnside's siege, led by General Parke, confirmed the vulnerability of such fortifications against new rifled weaponry, a lesson first learned at Georgia's Fort Pulaski (see p. 69) just two weeks prior. Colonel White surrendered after an 11-hour Union bombardment on April 25 breached the fort's walls, causing heavy damage. Since Burnside had successfully shut down three key Rebel coastal defenses, the port of Wilmington offered the only commercial outlet for the Confederacy. Beaufort Inlet became a key Union coaling station.

Fort Macon, a unique belowground fort, has a museum with a film, displays, and first-person accounts of life there during the Civil War. It also offers self-guided or ranger-led tours, reenactments, and cannon firings.

LOCATION: **Fort Macon State Park, 2303 E. Fort Macon Rd., Atlantic Beach, 252-726-3775, www.ncparks.gov.**

✱ Goldsborough Bridge

CAMPAIGN: Goldsborough Expedition

DATE(S): December 17, 1862

General Foster aimed to cut Confederate supplies to Virginia by destroying the Wilmington & Weldon Railroad bridge in Goldsborough. After arriving at the bridge on December 17, his 10,650 troops drove off 2,000 Rebels. The decisive Confederate victory at Fredericksburg (see pp. 237–242), however, spurred the Rebels to reopen the bridge within two weeks.

Today, the unstaffed battlefield site covers 32 acres of the 1862 battlefield and has short walking trails, interpretive markers, and preserved earthworks.

LOCATION: **Goldsborough Bridge Battlefield, 303 Old Mt. Olive Hwy., Dudley, www.goldsboroughbridge.org.**

✱ Hatteras Inlet Batteries

CAMPAIGN: Blockade of the Carolina Coast

OTHER NAME(S): Forts Clark and Hatteras

DATE(S): August 28–29, 1861

Union war strategy proclaimed a blockade on Southern ports but did not have the ships to enforce it. The deepwater port of Pamlico Sound had long sheltered pirates, privateers, and other mariners. As U.S. naval forces increased their inventory of vessels, they sent a small force to close the sound and establish control of traffic off North Carolina's Outer Banks.

The Confederates had built and manned two small forts, Hatteras and Clark, with about 350 men. Soon a joint force of army and navy men under General Butler and Commodore Stringham reduced Fort Clark and compelled the Confederates to surrender Fort Hatteras—the Union's first joint army-navy action and amphibious attack. The victory also gave the North a coaling port in Pamlico Sound.

Displays at the Graveyard of the Atlantic Museum include documents and press clippings from the period and guidance to local markers about the battle. The oceans claimed the fort sites long ago, but the inlet between the Atlantic and Pamlico Sound is navigable via daily free car ferries.

LOCATION: **Graveyard of the Atlantic Museum, 59200 Museum Dr., Hatteras, 252-986-2995, www.graveyardoftheatlantic.com.**

Pickett's Hangings

Like many Confederate leaders, George Pickett wrestled with the problem of desertion in the ranks. So prevalent was Rebel abandonment of station and cause that Robert E. Lee once stated that "nothing but the death penalty, uniformly, inexorably administered, will stop it."

During failed operations to retake New Bern, when Confederate deserters were identified among a group of Union POWs, General Pickett decided to make an example of them. Twenty-two, many from the Rebel brigade of General Nethercutt, were publicly hanged somewhere near the Lenoir County Courthouse in Kinston during the first two weeks of February 1864. A marker about the event is on the 100 block of South McLlewean Street.

FURTHER READING

Combined Operations in the Civil War

by Rowena Reed Provocative modern consideration of Civil War military strategy

Union troops come ashore as the navy opens fire on two Hatteras Inlet forts.

✱ Kinston

CAMPAIGN: Goldsborough Expedition

DATE(S): December 14, 1862

In what is known as the "first battle" of Kinston (Wyse Fork being the second), General Foster's forces set out on December 11, 1862, to march from New Bern to Goldsborough, aiming to disrupt the Wilmington & Weldon Railroad over the Neuse River and cut the flow of Confederate supplies to Virginia. Kinston, the halfway point protected by a semicircle of Confederate outer defenses, got its first taste of war on December 14—a bitter taste that included being plundered by overwhelming Union forces and having a bridge escape cut off too soon.

A 12-stop driving tour of the battle area tells the story in detail and includes the bridge site and interpretive panels along the way. The tour can be downloaded from the Brochure Library on the Kinston-Lenoir County Visitor and Information Center website, as can an audio tour of other key Civil War sites. Private battlefield tours are by appointment only.

LOCATION: Kinston-Lenoir County Visitor and Information Center, 101 E. New Bern Rd., 252-522-0004, www.visitkinston.com.

✲ Monroe's Cross Roads

CAMPAIGN: Carolinas Campaign

OTHER NAME(S): Fayetteville Road, Blue's Farm

DATE(S): March 10, 1865

Known as "Kilpatrick's shirt tail skedaddle," this skirmish began at dawn, when Rebel troops under General Hampton staged a cavalry raid on the Union camp's 1,850 poorly defended troops and the Charles Monroe house, headquarters for General Kilpatrick. As all were jolted from their sleep, Kilpatrick, dressed only in his nightshirt and sharing the company of his mistress, a woman of color, escaped identification and cleverly sent Rebels chasing another soldier on horseback, claiming that was the true Kilpatrick. In the meantime, without lingering to put on proper attire, he fled into the nearby swampland of Nicholson Creek.

Though surprising, the assault by the Confederates lacked the expected punch because they misread the terrain and were bogged down in mud. Then, instead of pursuing Kilpatrick's escaping forces, they plundered the camp's supplies. The Yankees soon regrouped, as General Hampton, knowing that Union reinforcements were on their way, withdrew to Fayetteville with several hundred prisoners.

The battlefield today is on the training grounds at Fort Bragg, so while it's protected from development, visits must be led by a qualified staff guide.

LOCATION: Fort Bragg, 13 miles south of Fayetteville, www.bragg.army.mil. Arrangements to tour the battlefield must be made through the base's Cultural Resources Office (910-396-6680) about a month in advance. Changes in training schedules may affect appointments, so be flexible.

FURTHER READING

The Battle of Monroe's Crossroads and the Civil War's Final Campaign
by Eric J. Wittenberg
The only book-length account of this battle

✷ New Bern

CAMPAIGN: Burnside's North Carolina Expedition

DATE(S): March 14, 1862

With a foothold on Roanoke Island, General Burnside's 11,000 troops joined Commodore Rowan's gunboat flotilla to capture New Bern. Located at the confluence of the Neuse and Trent Rivers, North Carolina's second largest town was protected by Fort Thompson's earthworks and several gun batteries along the Neuse River.

General Branch's 4,500 men were greener and more ill-equipped than their Union opponents, who at least had the victory at Roanoke Island to boast about. But the naval gunboat support tipped the scales to the Federals. On March 14, 1862, Burnside's forces broke through the Confederate line and drove the Federals from town. While evacuating, the Rebels burned bridges and naval stores. Victory here gave the Union control of the state's northeast seaboard and 96 miles of the Atlantic & North Carolina Railroad between Goldsborough and Fort Macon.

While much of the battlefield has been lost to development, 31 preserved acres have original hand-dug earthworks and trenches. Interpretive panels detail the battle. For first-person accounts of life during the subsequent Federal occupation, visit the New Bern Academy Museum (see p. 157).

LOCATION: New Bern Civil War Battlefield Park, US 70 E. and Taberna Way, 5 miles south of New Bern. To arrange a tour, contact the New Bern Historical Society, 252-638-8558, www.newbernhistorical.org/battlefield-park.

✷ Plymouth

CAMPAIGN: Operations Against Plymouth

DATE(S): April 17–20, 1864

Occupied by Union forces since May 1862, Plymouth, 50 miles north of New Bern, was a prime Confederate target. Its location on the Roanoke River gave the Yankees back-door access to Virginia and nearby Tarboro, where the Wilmington & Weldon Railroad continued to supply Lee's Army of Northern Virginia. On April 17, General Hoke led a land attack against the 2,800-man Union garrison. Though outnumbering the Federals by more than two to one, the Rebels were repelled until the arrival of the newly commissioned C.S.S. *Albemarle,* known as the "Iron Monster," on April 19. Working in tandem with Hoke's ground forces, the *Albemarle* sank one Union gunboat and drove another away, prompting the Union garrison to surrender on April 20.

See the *Albemarle*'s bell and a collection of artifacts from the U.S.S. *Southfield,* still submerged in the Roanoke River, at the Port o' Plymouth Museum. A smaller scale but fully operable model of the *Albemarle* is afloat and used for special events like the annual battle reenactment each April.

LOCATION: Port o' Plymouth Museum, 302 E. Water St., Plymouth, 252-793-1377, www.portoplymouthmuseum.org.

✳ Roanoke Island

CAMPAIGN: Burnside's North Carolina Expedition

OTHER NAME(S): Fort Huger

DATE(S): February 7–8, 1862

Known more for the Lost Colony, the English settlers who mysteriously disappeared without a trace in 1590, Roanoke Island was also the first phase of the Burnside Expedition in 1862. Few visitors today realize the magnitude of this early Union victory.

Three Confederate forts, two batteries, and a small "mosquito fleet" protected the island's northern half, the anticipated target for a Union attack. Surprisingly, General Burnside landed 11,500 Union troops at Ashby's Harbor in the less-protected center portion of the island, facing only a three-gun battery manned by 1,500 troops and another 1,000 reinforcements.

From there, the capture of Roanoke Island was easily completed, giving the Union access to Albemarle Sound and other inland waters. Using this route into North Carolina's interior, Burnside was able to circumvent the coastline in his goal of eliminating North Carolina's mainland ports and cutting off Confederate supplies that fed Richmond, Petersburg, and Norfolk. The

island quickly became a safe haven for escaped slaves, resulting in the establishment of a Freedmen's Colony.

Displays at Fort Raleigh National Historic Site detail the battle and Freedmen's Colony. Ask about directions to Confederate earthworks on the island.

LOCATION: Fort Raleigh National Historic Site, 1401 National Park Dr., 252-473-2111, www .nps.gov/fora.

FURTHER READING

The Battle of Roanoke Island: Burnside and the Fight for North Carolina
by Michael P. Zatarga
Detailed account of this critical battle written by a local Civil War historian

✳ South Mills

CAMPAIGN: Burnside's North Carolina Expedition

OTHER NAME(S): Camden

DATE(S): April 19, 1862

The Great Dismal Swamp canal near Elizabeth City was a backdoor route for Confederates to ferry supplies and reinforcements from Norfolk, where they were building ironclads. Fearing this route could threaten the Union fleet via Albemarle Sound, General Burnside directed General

Burnside's army and Goldsborough's gunboats capture Roanoke Island.

Reno to destroy the South Mills lock, where Rebels had established defensive batteries. Although Reno's 3,000 troops dwarfed Colonel Wright's 750, the Federals balked after the initial skirmish three miles southeast of the lock and returned to New Bern without destroying the lock.

LOCATION: Interpretive panel by the canal on Canal Dr., a third of a mile south of Main St. (US 17), South Mills. There's another marker at the skirmish point, 3 miles southeast on Rte. 343, a quarter mile south of Nosay Rd., South Mills.

✳ Tranter's Creek

CAMPAIGN: Burnside's North Carolina Expedition

DATE(S): June 5, 1862

As Confederates camped along this narrow deep creek near the Tar River, their commander, Colonel Singletary, was planning a raid on Washington, eight miles away (see below). Learning of the proposed action, Colonel Osborne's regiment and the gunboat *Pickett* launched a preemptive strike. Colonel Singletary was killed in the attack, and the Rebels withdrew as the Union troops returned to Washington.

LOCATION: Interpretive panel in the parking lot at 6149 US 264 W., Washington.

✿ Washington

CAMPAIGN: Longstreet's Tidewater Operations

DATE(S): March 30–April 20, 1863

Federals occupied this small town at the junction of the Tar and Pamlico Rivers for a year, following their capture of New Bern (see p. 150). In order to contain the Union troops there as Rebels rounded up supplies for Virginia, General Hill's Confederate forces surrounded the town on March 30 and staged a nearly monthlong siege, preventing Federal supplies and reinforcements from getting through. The Confederates withdrew on April 19 after a Union ship ran the blockade and resupplied General Foster's garrison.

Wilmington's Blockade-Runners

Geography helped protect Wilmington until February 1865, when the city ceased being "the lifeline of the Confederacy." Prior to that, blockade-runners were adept at navigating two routes from the Cape Fear River, routes challenging to Union vessels trying to cover both while circumventing the hazardous shoals between. Fort Fisher protected the river's upper inlet and Fort Caswell the southernmost. Once blockade-runners delivered their wares to Wilmington, the Wilmington & Weldon Railroad provided a direct supply line to Lee's Army of Northern Virginia.

Washington has several marked sites around town. Check at the visitor center for maps and tour information. Several of the period homes that survived the Union burning of the town in 1863 are open to the public on special occasions.

LOCATION: Washington Visitor Center, 102 Stewart Pkwy., Washington, 252-946-9168 or 800-546-0162, www.pamlico.com.

✿ White Hall

CAMPAIGN: Goldsborough Expedition

OTHER NAME(S): Whitehall, White Hall Ferry

DATE(S): December 16, 1862

The C.S.S. *Neuse* was under construction when General Foster's troops, en route to destroy the Wilmington & Weldon Railroad, clashed with Confederate cavalry across the Neuse River about 18 miles south of Goldsborough. The *Neuse* was damaged in the skirmish but quickly repaired.

A small park on the Neuse River has interpretive signs and a view of the north bank, where the *Neuse* was being built.

LOCATION: Whitehall Landing, W. River St. and New St., Seven Springs.

✳ Wilmington

CAMPAIGN: Operations Against Fort Fisher and Wilmington

OTHER NAME(S): Fort Anderson, Town Creek, Forks Road, Sugar Loaf Hill

DATE(S): February 12–22, 1865

A month after the fall of Fort Fisher (see p. 147), after the Union blocked the entrance to the Cape Fear River, the Confederates made their last stand to try to save Wilmington's vital port from capture.

Located on high ground on the west side of the Cape Fear River where the thriving colonial town for Brunswick once stood, Fort Anderson was the largest of the remaining Confederate defenses along that waterway. After three days of being surrounded by Union infantry and bombarded by Admiral Porter's navy, the outnumbered Rebels made an overnight evacuation on February 19 but continued futile stands at Confederate batteries on their way to Wilmington. Additional military operations took place against General Hoke's division on the east side of the river. Three days later, General Bragg evacuated Wilmington after destroying everything of military value. The Union occupied the city on February 22.

Brunswick/Fort Anderson offers layers of history, with the earthworks of the Civil War fort built over the town site in 1862. Wilmington boasts 200 antebellum homes, cemeteries, and other Civil War sites—some open to visitors. The Cape Fear Museum (see p. 156) has several Civil War exhibits.

LOCATION: Wilmington and Beaches Convention and Visitors Bureau, 505 Nutt St., Wilmington, 910-341-4030, www.wilmington andbeaches.com/civil-war-attractions; Wilmington History Tours, www.wilmington historytours.com/civil-war-wilmington.html.

FURTHER READING
General Robert F. Hoke: Lee's Modest Warrior
by Daniel W. Barefoot
Sympathetic portrait of the often neglected Confederate commander

✳ Wyse Fork

CAMPAIGN: Carolinas Campaign

OTHER NAME(S): Second Kinston

DATE(S): March 7–10, 1865

At the start of this fluid three-day battle six miles east of Kinston, the Confederates, supported by the ironclad C.S.S. *Neuse*, briefly gained the advantage and took 1,500 prisoners, the last mass capture of Union soldiers in the war. With the arrival of Union reinforcements and General Schofield, the Rebels fell back to Kinston. In what was her first and last battle, the ram *Neuse,* one of only 22 Confederate ironclads, was scuttled by her crew to prevent her capture.

Part of the battlefield is preserved with earthworks and interpretive signs. The C.S.S. *Neuse* Civil War Interpretive Center displays the remains of the Confederate ironclad. A 12-stop Wyse Fork driving tour can be found in the Brochure Library on the Kinston-Lenoir County Visitor and Information Center website (see p. 149).

LOCATION: C.S.S. *Neuse* Civil War Interpretive Center, 100 N. Queen St., Kinston, 252-522-2107, www.nchistoricsites.org/neuse.

Drowned by Gold

Rose O'Neal Greenhow—a well-connected socialite turned Confederate spy—is credited with helping General Beauregard win the first battle of Manassas (see pp. 254–256). Even during imprisonment, she managed to pass accurate notes to Confederates via women visitors. On October 1, 1864, she was aboard the blockade-runner *Condor* when it ran aground at the mouth of the Cape Fear River near Wilmington. Fearing recapture by a pursuing Union ship, she escaped via a rowboat, which then capsized in the rough water. It has been said that Greenhow, weighed down by the gold she was carrying, drowned.

Civil War on Foot: Wilmington

Founded in 1732, Wilmington had become North Carolina's most populated town and most active seaport by 1840. During the Civil War, it also became the most important seaport in the Confederacy by 1863. It was the last open port to fall to Union forces in 1865.

❶ Market Street During the Civil War, sleek, swift blockade-running vessels lined the waterfront docks, unloading military and civilian cargoes and loading cotton and naval stores for the return trip to Bermuda or Nassau. Stand on the waterfront and look across the river to the Confederate Navy Yard, also known as Beery's Shipyard. There, workers built two submarines and an ironclad, the C.S.S. *North Carolina.*

Another uncompleted ironclad, the C.S.S. *Wilmington,* was burned when Wilmington fell in late February 1865.

❷ Site of Slave Boat Launch On September 21, 1862, eight slaves launched a boat from the foot of Orange Street and rowed it to the mouth of the river, where they were rescued. The wartime diary of one of the slaves, William B. Gould, is exceptionally interesting.

❸ DeRosset House *(23 S. 2nd St.)* Built about 1847, this was the residence of Armand John DeRosset, a physician and commission merchant with DeRosset and Brown, a blockade-running firm.

❹ St. Thomas Preservation Hall *(208 Dock St.)* This 1847 building across

from DeRosset House was, during the Civil War, the Church of St. Thomas the Apostle, the first Roman Catholic Church in Wilmington.

❺ Confederate Monument *(Intersection of Dock St. and 3rd St.)* The granite base of this 1924 statue dedicated to Cape Fear Confederate soldiers was designed by Henry Bacon, architect of the Lincoln Memorial in Washington, D.C.

❻ St. James Episcopal Church *(25 S. 3rd St.)* Union forces seized this 1839–1840 church and made it a hospital in 1865 when Rev. Alfred A. Watson, a native of Brooklyn, New York, refused to pray for President Lincoln.

❼ Burgwin-Wright House *(224 Market St.)* Built in 1770–1771 by English-born merchant John Burgwin, this house served as General Cornwallis's

Wilmington's Confederate monument depicts courage and sacrifice.

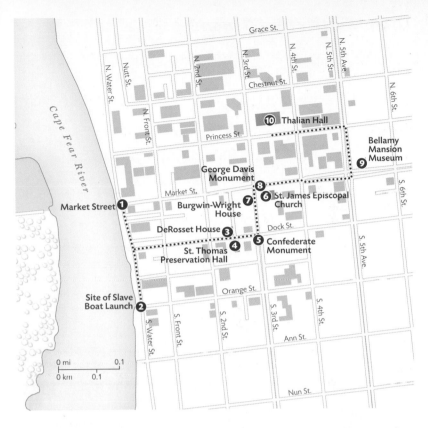

headquarters during the British occupation of Wilmington in 1781. Purchased by Thomas Grainger Wright in 1799, the house was rented during the Civil War. One account claims English blockade-running crews enjoyed raucous parties here.

❽ George Davis Monument (Intersection of 3rd St. and Market St.) A prominent

Wilmington lawyer, Davis (1820–1896) was the last attorney general of the Confederacy.

❾ Bellamy Mansion Museum (503 Market St.) Built in 1859–1860, this impressive building was the family residence of Dr. John D. Bellamy. The on-site slave quarters are worth viewing.

❿ Thalian Hall (310 Chesnut St.) Citizens and

soldiers alike enjoyed nightly performances in Thalian Hall, known then as the Wilmington Theater. Major Dawson surrendered the city on the steps of City Hall, across the street, on February 22, 1865.

If you have a little extra time, walk east on Market Street and read the numerous historical markers along the way.

Other Battles and Beyond

✦ Civil War Trails

For information about interpreted Civil War trails, visit www.nccivilwar150.com and www.civilwartraveler.com.

✦ Asheville

This remote western mountain town suffered economically but remained rather unscathed physically until the end of the war. Its location along the Buncombe Turnpike, then a heavily traveled 75-mile route from South Carolina to East Tennessee, made it an ideal hub for livestock drovers. Confederate deserters also flocked to the area's rugged terrain. Asheville was considerably damaged on April 26, 1865, when General Stoneman's 6,000 raiders plundered the town in a final act of Federal destruction. Visible earthworks and a marker on the grounds of the University of North Carolina at Asheville campus are remaining reminders of the war's turmoil.

LOCATION: Start your exploration of the area at the Smith-McDowell House Museum, on the A-B Tech Campus, 283 Victoria Road, Asheville, 828-253-9231, www.wnchistory.org.

FURTHER READING
Cold Mountain
by Charles Frazier
Best-selling novel traces the trek of a disillusioned Confederate soldier through the Blue Ridge mountains

✦ Attmore-Oliver House

This home of the New Bern Historical Society houses many artifacts from the Battle of New Bern (see p. 150).

LOCATION: 511 Broad St., New Bern, 252-638-8558, www.newbernhistorical.org.

✦ Bennett Place State Historic Site

The museum traces the surrender negotiations of 1865 and the aftermath, while highlighting what life was like for the Bennetts, a non-slave-owning yeoman farm family.

LOCATION: 4409 Bennett Memorial Rd., Durham, 919-383-4345, www.bennettplace historicsite.com.

FURTHER READING
This Astounding Close: The Road to Bennett Place
by Mark L. Bradley
Detailed study draws on eyewitness accounts

✦ Cameron Art Museum

Beyond the parking lot are two Confederate trenches, a walking trail, and interpretive signs about the U.S. Colored Troops. Check with the museum for Civil War events.

LOCATION: 3201 S. 17th St., Wilmington, 910-395-5999, www.cameronartmuseum.org.

✦ Cape Fear Museum

Exhibits include a large-scale model of the waterfront during the Civil War and a diorama of Fort Fisher. Check the calendar for special programs related to the war.

LOCATION: 814 Market St., Wilmington, 910-798-4370, www.capefearmuseum.com.

✦ C.S.S. *Neuse* II

This intriguing full-scale replica of the 158-foot gunboat that took part in the Battle of Wyse Fork (see p. 153) offers boardings on Saturdays and by appointment.

LOCATION: 118 W. Gordon St., Kinston, 252-560-2150, www.cssneuseii.org.

✦ Hillsborough

This small town, ten miles from Bennett Place, has antebellum homes, churches, and cemeteries, and hosts Civil War–related events.

LOCATION: **Start at the Visitor Center, 150 E. King St., 919-732-7741, www.visithillsborough nc.com, where General Johnston and Secretary of War Breckinridge discussed surrendering the army to General Sherman.**

✦ Mendenhall Plantation

Richard Mendenhall actively supported the abolitionist movement. Visitors to his Quaker home can view a false-bottomed wagon used to transport slaves to freedom.

LOCATION: **603 W. Main St., Jamestown, 336-454-3819, www.mendenhallplantation.org.**

✦ Museum of the Cherokee Indian

Displays at this museum include information about Thomas's Legion, a regiment composed partly of Cherokee Indians.

LOCATION: **589 Tsali Blvd., Cherokee, 828-497-3481, www.cherokeemuseum.org.**

✦ New Bern Academy Museum

This 1809 former schoolhouse gives details about the battle (see p. 150) and life in town during the Union occupation.

LOCATION: **Intersection of Hancock St. and New St., New Bern, 800-767-1560, www.tryon palace.org/new-bern-academy-museum.**

✦ Oak Grove

This circa 1793 home is one of three plantation homes that survived the Battle of Averasboro (see pp. 144–145) and the only one open for tours by appointment.

LOCATION: **8640 Burnett Rd., Godwin, 910-489-2907.**

✦ Raleigh

The state capitol—where secession was declared on May 20, 1861—was used as a signal station in April 1865, and the official monuments on the grounds include one to the first Confederate soldier killed in the war, Henry Wyatt. Other attractions include the North Carolina Museum of History, which has a permanent exhibit on the war, and Oakwood Cemetery, which holds the graves of Confederate generals, former governors, and nearly 3,000 soldiers.

LOCATION: **Start at the Greater Raleigh Visitor Center, 500 Fayetteville St., Raleigh, 919-834-5900 or 800-849-8499, www.visitraleigh.com.**

✦ Salisbury National Cemetery and Confederate Prison Site

Nearly 12,000 Union soldiers who were prisoners at the Salisbury Confederate Prison are buried in 18 trenches here.

LOCATION: **202 Government Rd., Salisbury. Visitors can pick up a free self-guided driving tour brochure or purchase a tour CD at the Visitor Information Center, 204 E. Innes St., Salisbury, 704-638-3100 or 800-332-2343.**

✦ Wilmington National Cemetery

There are a significant number of Civil War burials here. Read the fascinating job titles on some of the soldiers' tombstones.

LOCATION: **2011 Market St., Wilmington.**

Hillsborough's Dickson House has period gardens and General Johnston's 1865 office.

South Carolina

DURING HIS INFAMOUS MARCH THROUGH THE STATE, General Sherman noted that he feared for the fate of South Carolina. Indeed, the state reaped a terrible harvest for its open advocacy of disunion—towns were burned and civilians fled. South Carolina was the cradle of the rebellion, and Union soldiers intended to sow salt in her furrows so that secession could never take root again.

The seacoast cotton plantations on Hilton Head Island and near Beaufort and Edisto Island reflect an idyllic time when cotton was king. For generations, the white gold flowed into and out of Charleston, "that place where the Ashley and Cooper Rivers came together to form the Atlantic Ocean."

Reduced by bombardment, modification, and hurricanes, Fort Sumter lowered its flag in submission in April 1861 and raised it again in triumph in April 1865. The fort commands the view even today as people stand on the Charleston Battery or on the beaches of Morris, Johnson, or Sullivan's Islands. South Carolina is the epicenter of America's Civil War.

Today, pastel-colored antebellum houses line the Battery in Charleston. Installed as a coastal defense during the Civil War, it is now a promenade.

1 **Fort Wagner I**
2 **Fort Wagner II/Morris Island**
3 **Grimball's Landing**

✳ Charleston Harbor I

CAMPAIGN: Operations Against the Defenses of Charleston

DATE(S): April 7, 1863

Union leadership pushed for an attack on the city of Charleston with the hope that a resounding success would lift the flagging national spirit and renew enthusiasm for the war effort. Charleston had been chosen primarily for its symbolic role as the birthplace of the rebellion.

On April 7, 1863, a Union naval force of nine ironclad warships commanded by Admiral Du Pont attacked Confederate forces near the entrance to Charleston Harbor. Unable to penetrate even the first line of Confederate defenses with the slow and unwieldy ships, they withdrew when the tide turned, after less than two hours. A Union land force under the command of General Hunter had been in motion to cooperate with the naval bombardment, but this effort was abandoned. Struck more than 90 times by Confederate fire, the iron-clad warship *Keokuk* sank the next day. Four other monitors were significantly damaged. While the armored ships could withstand a fair bit of artillery fire, their ability to deliver effective fire against fortifications was limited by their inability to elevate the encapsulated heavy guns in the monitor's turrets. Criticized for his failure to capture Charleston, Du Pont was relieved of command at his own request in July 1863. He returned home to Delaware, awaiting orders that never came.

The site where this battle took place can best be observed and interpreted from the ramparts of Fort Sumter.

LOCATION: Fort Sumter National Monument, Charleston Harbor, 843-883-3123, www.nps .gov/fosu, accessible by concessioner boat (Fort Sumter Tours, 800-789-3678, www .fortsumtertours.com).

✳ Charleston Harbor II

CAMPAIGN: Operations Against the Defenses of Charleston

OTHER NAME(S): Fort Sumter

DATE(S): September 7–8, 1863

Starting August 17, 1863, Fort Sumter came under regular fire by Union troops. By August 23, most of the fort's guns had been rendered ineffective, and the impressive masonry structure was reduced to rubble.

Meanwhile, on August 21, Union General Gillmore sent an ultimatum to General Beauregard to surrender Fort Sumter and Battery Wagner (on Morris Island) or he would fire on the city of Charleston. When the Confederates did not respond, Union troops began firing the Swamp Angel (a 200-pound Parrott rifle) at the city, using the steeple of St. Michael's Church for a bearing. Outraged that the Union would target the civilian population, the Confederates

asked for time to evacuate Charleston's nonmilitary residents. Gillmore gave them a day, but claimed that Charleston was a legitimate target. The next day, firing resumed, but the Swamp Angel burst after the 36th shot and was not replaced. This encounter marked the first time during the Civil War that a civilian population was deliberately targeted for military purposes.

On September 6–7, after 60 days of holding off the larger Union forces while being constantly bombarded, Beauregard finally ordered troops to abandon Battery Wagner and Battery Gregg on Morris Island. On September 7, Union forces occupied Battery Wagner. On September 8, a storming party of about 400 Union marines and sailors attempted a surprise attack on Fort Sumter. The Confederates had been tipped off and were prepared, however, and they easily repulsed the Union attack. Though the Union had finally captured a position at the

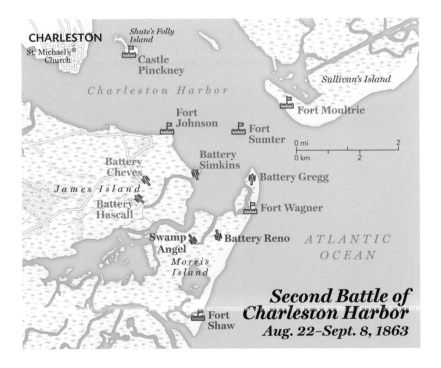

Second Battle of **Charleston Harbor**
Aug. 22–Sept. 8, 1863

mouth of Charleston Harbor and nearly reduced Fort Sumter to rubble, both Charleston and Fort Sumter remained in Confederate hands until Sherman's campaign in 1865.

The site and platform of the Swamp Angel are inaccessible today. During the war, this location was reached via causeway from Morris Island, which has lost much of the landmass that existed at the time, with the north site of Battery Wagner about a mile from the tip of the island.

LOCATION: **Morris Island can be accessed on nature boats that run tours to the island (Sandlapper Tours, 10 Wharfside St., Charleston, 843-849-8687, www.sandlappertours.com).**

FURTHER READING

Gate of Hell: Campaign for Charleston, 1863
by Stephen R. Wise
An exploration of the fierce, bloody siege of Fort Sumter and Charleston

✳ Fort Sumter I

CAMPAIGN: Operations in Charleston Harbor
DATE(S): April 12–14, 1861

Fearing that a Federal effort to resupply the garrison would extend Union occupation of the fort, Confederate General Beauregard demanded the surrender of the Union

CHARLESTON

Shute's Folly Island

Castle Pinckney

Folly Channel

Charleston Harbor

South Channel

Fort Johnson

James Island

First Battle of Fort Sumter
April 12–14, 1861

Light House Creek

Morris I

garrison at Fort Sumter on April 10, 1861. Garrison commander Major Anderson refused. On April 12 at 4:30 a.m., the Confederates opened fire on the fort—the first shots of the Civil War. The Union garrison was not well supplied with ammunition, however, and could not reply effectively. On the afternoon of April 13, after nearly 36 hours of continuous bombardment, Anderson surrendered and evacuated the fort. Although there were no casualties during the many hours of bombardment, a Federal soldier was killed when a gun at the fort firing a salute exploded. When Union troops returned to the North, they were greeted as heroes. They took their flag with them. In April 1865, Anderson raised the same banner as the Federals again took possession of the now ruined fort.

To find the original sally port, walk outside the fort, where artillery shells are also visible embedded in the walls.

LOCATION: Fort Sumter National Monument, Charleston Harbor, 843-883-3123, www.nps .gov/fosu, accessible by concessioner boat (Fort Sumter Tours, 800-789-3678, www .fortsumtertours.com).

FURTHER READING

Days of Defiance: Sumter, Secession, and the Coming War by Maury Klein A dramatic narrative filled with insights into the character of many dynamic leaders

❋ Fort Sumter II

CAMPAIGN: Operations Against the Defenses of Charleston

DATE(S): August 17–August 23, 1863

The Federal batteries on Morris Island fired on Fort Sumter from August 17 through August 23. More than 1,000 shells were fired on the first day alone. By August 23, most of the fort's guns had been dismounted from their carriages and the masonry reduced to rubble. Still, Fort Sumter's garrison held out, and the Federals considered other ways to open access to Charleston Harbor.

LOCATION: Fort Sumter National Monument, Charleston Harbor, 843-883-3123, www.nps .gov/fosu, accessible by concessioner boat (Fort Sumter Tours, 800-789-3678, www .fortsumtertours.com).

❋ Fort Wagner I

CAMPAIGN: Operations Against the Defenses of Charleston

DATE(S): July 10–11, 1863

Morris Island was advantageously positioned to control the main shipping channel into

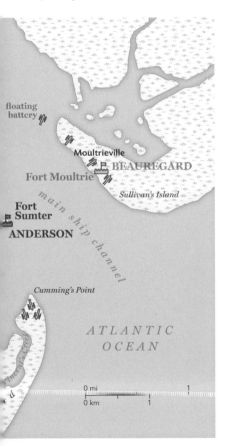

floating battery

Moultrieville

Fort Moultrie BEAUREGARD

Sullivan's Island

Fort Sumter

ANDERSON

main ship channel

Cumming's Point

ATLANTIC OCEAN

0 mi 1

0 km 1

South Carolina Secession Trail

The wealth of the region produced a very strong states' rights attitude that gave birth to an independent streak. Seven-term congressman Robert Barnwell Rhett, Sr., was one of the earliest and most extreme of the Southern fire-eaters. Follow this trail to see sites informally known as the South Carolina Secession Trail.

Colleton County Courthouse

❶ Barnwell-Gough House (*705 Washington St., Beaufort*) Rhett, the "Father of Secession," lived here with his grandparents as a young man.

❷ Old Beaufort College Building (*University of South Carolina Beaufort, 801 Carteret St., Beaufort*) Rhett briefly attended college on this campus.

❸ Milton Maxey House (*1113 Craven St., Beaufort*) Referred to as the "Secession House," the home of Edmund Rhett (brother of Robert Barnwell Rhett, Sr.) served as the site for secession meetings. It was not, as rumored,

the place where the Ordinance of Secession was written; that took place in Columbia.

❹ Secession Oak (*1263 May River Rd., Bluffton*) On July 31, 1844, Rhett inspired a younger generation to form the Bluffton Movement, dedicated to the Secession of South Carolina. This 350- to 400-year-old oak tree stands on private land on the Stock Farm development. Visit Stock Farm Antiques (843-757-8046) or call 843-304-1922 for directions and permission to visit.

❺ Holy Trinity Episcopal Church (*Intersection of SC 13 and SC 29 or 1.1 miles east of US 278 on E. Main St., Grahamville*) On July 4, 1859, Rhett made a stirring pro-secession speech here, predicting the 1860 presidential election would determine the fate of the Union. This church is

all that remains of this antebellum town.

❻ Gillisonville (*Old Courthouse Sq., marker on US 278, 0.1 mile north of SC Rte. 462, Gillisonville*) The Southern Rights Association of the Beaufort District (primarily Rhett and William Ferguson Hutson) met here and drafted a constitution calling on the slaveholding South to secede. In this town burned by Federals, only the Baptist Church still stands (less than 200 yards away from this important spot).

❼ Stony Creek Presbyterian Chapel (*About one block north of SC Rte. 17, McPhersonville*) This chapel served the planters of upper St. Luke's Parish. Among its members were William Ferguson Colcock, U.S. congressman and secession advocate, and William Ferguson Hutson, one of the authors of the Ordinance of Secession.

❽ Colleton County Courthouse (*101 Hampton St., Walterboro*) On June 12, 1828, Rhett began his public, pro-secession career here by calling on South Carolinians to resist the oppression of the federal government and, if need be, to become a "Free, Sovereign and Independent People."

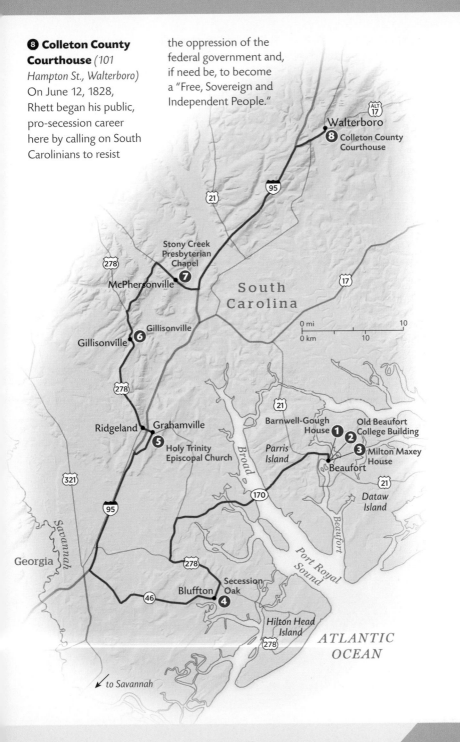

Charleston Harbor. On July 10, 1863, Union artillery on Folly Island, together with an iron-clad fleet commanded by Admiral Dahlgren, bombarded Confederate defenses on Morris Island. This action provided cover for General Strong's brigade, which crossed Lighthouse Inlet and landed on the southern tip of the island. Strong's troops advanced, capturing several batteries that day until they were within range of Battery Wagner, a sand forti-fication also known as Fort Wagner. At dawn on July 11, Strong and his men attacked. Although some Union soldiers reached the parapet and entered the fortification, the Union effort was ultimately repulsed.

LOCATION: Today, Battery Wagner is in the surf of the Atlantic Ocean. You can visit Morris Island by taking a nature tour boat (Sandlapper Tours, 10 Wharfside St., Charleston, 843-849-8687, www.sandlappertours.com). The location of the battery is unmarked, about 1,500 paces south from the boat drop-off point; the attack came from the south.

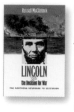

FURTHER READING

Lincoln and the Decision for War: The Northern Response to Secession
by Russell McClintock
An analysis of the decision-making process from partisan rancor to consensus

✳ Fort Wagner II/Morris Island

CAMPAIGN: Operations Against the Defenses of Charleston

DATE(S): July 18, 1863

After the failed July 11, 1863, Union assault on Battery Wagner, General Gillmore reinforced his beachhead on Morris Island. At dusk on July 18, he ordered an assault led by the 54th Massachusetts, a regiment composed of free blacks from Boston and New England. Despite incurring heavy losses as

Union troops on Morris Island fired on Charleston using the Swamp Angel, a 200-pound Parrott rifle, which ultimately burst after its 36th shot.

they neared the fort, the surviving members of the 54th scaled its earthen walls and engaged in bloody hand-to-hand combat with the Confederates before being driven out. Subsequent assaults by other regiments gained temporary footings but also failed. Union soldiers retreated to their positions late in the evening, after suffering more than 1,500 casualties, compared with 174 Confederate casualties. Then the Federals settled into position for a lengthy and costly siege that ultimately led to the Confederates abandoning their position under cover of darkness on September 7. Black soldiers were hailed for their valor in this battle, which led the Union to increase their recruitment.

LOCATION: Today, Battery Wagner is in the surf of the Atlantic Ocean. You can visit Morris Island by taking a nature tour boat (Sandlapper Tours, 10 Wharfside St., Charleston, 843-849-8687, www.sandlappertours.com). The location of the battery is unmarked, about 1,500 paces south from the boat drop-off point; the attack came from the south.

FURTHER VIEWING

Glory

Award-winning film that is the most historically accurate representation of this event

☼Grimball's Landing

CAMPAIGN: Operations Against the Defenses of Charleston

DATE(S): July 16, 1863

This engagement on James Island was one of two feints directed by Union General Gillmore in an attempt to create a diversion from the primary Federal forces preparing to attack Battery Wagner. General Terry and his troops landed on the island on July 8, 1863, and set up camp at Grimball's Landing. On July 16, the Rebels tried to attack but soon aborted the assault because of the marshy conditions and poor leadership. Before they could try again, the Union troops withdrew from the island on July 17.

The Grimkés: Abolitionist Sisters

Born into an upper-class slaveholding family in Charleston, Sarah and Angela Grimké both left their Southern plantation way of life to join the abolitionist movement. These former Southern belles turned Quakers became some of the first female public speakers in the country, daring to speak to mixed crowds of men and women about their experience with slavery and, ultimately, delivering antislavery testimony to a committee of the Massachusetts legislature. They also published some of the most powerful antislavery tracts of the time. In response, South Carolina officials closed the mail system to incendiary antislavery tracts. This was part of the reason the South rejected Lincoln, whose patronage appointments threatened the mail embargo. Their childhood home is at 329 East Bay Street in Charleston.

The location where this battle occurred is currently privately held farmland, but plans for residential development in tandem with site preservation are imminent.

LOCATION: Southwestern side of James Island along the Stono River.

✳ Honey Hill

CAMPAIGN: Savannah Campaign

DATE(S): November 30, 1864

When Union General Hatch and his force left Hilton Head and steamed up the Broad River, his plan was to cut the Charleston & Savannah Railroad near Gopher Hill (Ridgeland, South Carolina) in support of Sherman's projected arrival in Savannah. After disembarking at Boyd's Landing, they headed inland, where they encountered Colonel Colcock's troops at Honey Hill.

54th Massachusetts: The First U.S. Colored Regiment

Commanded by a 25-year-old white colonel named Robert Gould Shaw, the 54th Massachusetts was formed after more than 1,000 black volunteers responded to a call to duty from the governor of Massachusetts. The 54th is revered for the great valor it displayed during the second battle of Fort Wagner/Morris Island (see pp. 166–167), when more than 40 percent of the regiment, including Shaw, were killed, wounded, or captured. The Confederates buried Shaw with his fallen soldiers, considering this the ultimate insult; however, Shaw's abolitionist parents insisted just the opposite was true. By the end of the war, more than 180,000 blacks would serve in the Union armies. And the 54th would add many campaigns in the region to its legacy.

Determined attacks by U.S. Colored Troops (including the 54th and 55th Massachusetts) failed to dislodge the Confederates. Realizing the impossibility of success, the Union troops withdrew after dark.

There is no public access. Excellent fortifications remain, and plans are under way to open the site to visitors.

LOCATION: Marker located 1.8 miles east of Grahamville on US 278.

✳ Rivers Bridge

CAMPAIGN: Carolinas Campaign

DATE(S): February 3, 1865

This battle was one of the Confederacy's last stands in Sherman's sweep across the South. Wanting to bypass the Salkehatchie River crossing, which was guarded by Confederates under General McLaws, Federal troops began to build bridges. McLaws and his men delayed the Union soldiers for only

one day. When Union troops attacked their right flank, the Confederates withdrew toward Branchville, and Union forces continued on toward Columbia.

The state historic site features a 0.75-mile self-guided trail with interpretive panels, occasional ranger-led tours, a Confederate cemetery, and earthen fortifications.

LOCATION: Rivers Bridge State Historic Site, 325 State Park Rd., Ehrhardt, 803-267-3675, www.southcarolinaparks.com.

FURTHER READING

Rehearsal for Reconstruction: The Port Royal Experiment
by Willie Lee Rose
An analysis of some of the war's noblest hopes and greatest tragedies

✳ Secessionville

CAMPAIGN: Operations Against Charleston

DATE(S): June 16, 1862

Under the immediate direction of Union General Benham, General Hunter transported divisions led by Generals Wright and Stevens to James Island. They entrenched at Grimball's Landing and Sol Legare Island, near the southern flank of the Confederate defenses, and marched toward Charleston. Before dawn on June 16, 1862, they attacked Tower Battery (later renamed Fort Lamar) at Secessionville, which was held by about 500 Confederate soldiers with heavy artillery. After an intense battle in the marshy terrain and the arrival of about 1,000 additional Rebel troops, the Confederates prevailed. The Union would try again in 1863 and 1864.

While insignificant in the war overall, this Confederate victory boosted flagging Confederate morale. Benham, who had acted against orders in his attempt to take James Island, was relieved of his command.

Managed by the South Carolina Department of Natural Resources, the site on James Island features a self-guided walking trail that passes original earthworks. An annual commemoration takes place on the Saturday closest to June 16.

LOCATION: **Fort Lamar Heritage Preserve, Fort Lamar Rd., Charleston, 803-734-3893, www.scgreatoutdoors.com/park-fortlamarhp.html.**

FURTHER READING

Secessionville: Assault on Charleston
by Patrick Brennan
An account of the Northern attempt to capture the city

✳ Simmon's Bluff

CAMPAIGN: Operations Against Charleston
DATE(S): June 21, 1862

A few days after Secessionville, Union forces were still eager to capture Charleston. To accomplish this, an amphibious expedition was mounted with the goal of severing the Charleston & Savannah Railroad. After

Sherman's March Through South Carolina

After taking Savannah in December 1864, General Sherman was ordered to march north to join with Grant in defeating Lee and ending the war. Sherman's columns moved into South Carolina along supportive routes toward Columbia. In addition to the fighting at Rivers Bridge, key sites include Broxton Bridge, Orangeburg, and Congaree Creek.

Union troops landed near Simmon's Bluff at Wadmalaw Sound, they routed and burned the Confederate camp, and then returned to their ships, having failed in their original objective. There were no casualties in this raid, one of many such encounters that occurred along the South Carolina coastline.

LOCATION: **Wadmalaw Island, a mostly rural and undeveloped area, is privately held today.**

The Charleston & Savannah Railroad was vital to protecting Savannah and getting supplies to Confederate troops. This made it a target for General Sherman.

Other Battles and Beyond

✦ Civil War Sites Vacation Guide

This self-guided tour takes in more than 70 sites relating to the Civil War in seven South Carolina counties. The guide is available as a downloadable PDF at www.oldeenglish district.com or by calling 800-968-5909.

✦ Historic Cheraw Cell-Phone & Walking Tours

Don't miss this charming, antebellum Southern town, a haven for refugees during the Civil War and the unwilling host to many of General Sherman's troops in 1865. The cell-phone tour features 25 local sites, many relating to secession or Sherman's March, and the walking tour includes many more. For information on both tours, visit the Cheraw Visitor's Bureau at 221 Market St., Cheraw, or call 843-537-8425. Details are also available online at www.cheraw.com.

FURTHER READING

Sherman's March Through the Carolinas by John G. Barrett A good story as well as a scholarly account

✦ The Battery

While visiting Charleston, stroll past pastel-colored houses along what is known as The Battery. The wall was installed for coastal defense during the Civil War. Today, it is lined with stately, antebellum homes and monuments. It also affords a good view of Fort Sumter and Fort Moultrie from the High Battery (Cooper River side).

LOCATION: **Located at the point where Charleston Harbor begins.**

✦ Boone Hall Plantation and Gardens

A large colonial revival house has replaced the original house on this antebellum plantation. Notable features are the Avenue of Oaks, a one-mile drive lined with mature, stunning live oaks, and Slave Street, where you can take a self-guided tour of eight original slave cabins.

LOCATION: **1235 Long Point Rd., Mt. Pleasant, 843-884-4371, www.boonehallplantation.com.**

✦ Charleston Museum

A stop here is an excellent way to get oriented for a Civil War visit to Charleston. The exhibit "City Under Siege" is an exploration of the events leading up to secession through the firing on Fort Sumter. Civil War–era objects on display include weapons, uniforms, and medical kits.

LOCATION: **360 Meeting St., Charleston (across from the main Charleston Visitor Center), 843-722-2996, www.charlestonmuseum.org.**

FURTHER READING

Confederate Charleston: An Illustrated History of the People and the City During the Civil War by Robert N. Rosen A history of the city during the war illustrated with many seldom seen pictures

✦ Citadel, the Military College of South Carolina

Established in 1843, the Citadel educated many Civil War leaders. Today, it enrolls more than 3,400 students in undergraduate and graduate programs. Enjoy the impressive military parade most Friday afternoons when school is in session. Check the website or call for the current parade schedule. Campus tours are also available.

LOCATION: **The modern campus is at 171 Moultrie St., Charleston, 843-225-3294, www.citadel.edu. The Civil War campus is now the Embassy Suites Hotel (337 Meeting St., Charleston).**

✦ Confederate Museum

Owned by the United Daughters of the Confederacy, this former 1841 Market Hall is now a small and intimate museum with an old-fashioned feel dedicated to the Confederacy. Items such as the first Confederate flag to fly over Fort Sumter and the first "secession" flag to fly over Charleston are on display, along with other personal artifacts from the period.

LOCATION: **188 Meeting St., Charleston, 843-723-1541, www.confederatemuseum charlestonsc.com.**

✦ Congaree Creek

Union and Confederate forces met at a half-mile-long earthwork in the four-hour battle that took place at Congaree Creek on February 15, 1865, in the waning days of the Civil War. The Union prevailed, and Sherman's army advanced to Columbia two days later. A paved trail helps interpret the event.

LOCATION: **Near I-77, where Congaree Creek crosses Old State Rd., Cayce, www.battleat congareecreek.com.**

✦ First Baptist Church

This still active church was the site of the first South Carolina secession convention on December 17, 1860. Fear of a smallpox outbreak quickly moved the meeting to Charleston, where the work was completed. A small museum displays the table where the secession document was drafted.

LOCATION: **1303 Hampton St., Columbia, 803-256-4251.**

✦ Florence Stockade Trail and Memorial Park/Florence National Cemetery

Interpretative signs and walking trails tell a vivid story of life at this significant site, where more than 18,000 Northern troops were imprisoned.

LOCATION: **803 E. National Cemetery Rd., Florence, 843-669-8783, www.schistorytrail .com.**

Still operating as a military college today, the Citadel educated many Civil War leaders.

View Fort Sumter from the Confederate perspective at Fort Moultrie National Park.

✦ Fort Moultrie National Park

A trip to Fort Moultrie allows visitors to see Fort Sumter from the perspective of the Confederacy. Take a self-guided tour to learn about the history of this fort, which stretched from the late 1700s through World War II, and enjoy the harbor view from the beach.

LOCATION: 1214 Middle St., Sullivan's Island, 843-883-3123, www.nps.gov/fosu. Accessible by car.

FURTHER READING
Lifeline of the Confederacy: Blockade Running During the Civil War
by Stephen Wise
The definitive work on the impact of blockade-running operations on the conduct of the war

✦ H. L. Hunley Project and Submarine Tours

During the week, this laboratory works to preserve the Confederate submarine *H. L. Hunley*. On weekends only, visitors can tour and learn about this history-making, technological marvel.

LOCATION: 1250 Supply St., North Charleston, 843-743-4865, www.hunley.org.

✦ Magnolia Cemetery

Established in 1850, this cemetery contains many wonderful examples of 19th-century architecture, sculpture, and funerary art. The expansive grounds contain a lake and ponds and are shaded by live oaks and intertwined with Spanish moss. It is the burial site for more than 2,200 Civil War veterans, 14 signers of the Ordinance of Secession (including Robert Barnwell Rhett, Sr.), and two crews of the Confederate submarine *H. L. Hunley*. A Confederate Ghost Walk takes place annually on the second weekend of October.

LOCATION: **70 Cunnington Ave., Charleston, 843-722-8638, www.magnoliacemetery.net.**

✦ McLeod Plantation Historic Site

Located on James Island across the Ashley River from downtown Charleston, this antebellum sea cotton plantation later served as a campsite for Confederate and Union troops. It also housed black soldiers. After that, it served as a Freedmen's Bureau. This 36-acre estate includes particularly interesting slave quarters. Owned by the Charleston County Park and Recreation Commission, the plantation offers guided tours, self-guided tours, and a cell-phone app.

LOCATION: **325 Country Club Dr., Charleston, 843-762-9514, www.ccprc.com/1447/mcleod -plantation-historic-site.**

✦ Parris Island Museum

A short drive away from the Beaufort Historic District, which absolutely should not be missed, is this exceptional museum located at the famous Marine Corps Recruit Depot, an active military base, on Parris Island. See recruits mastering their training. Graduation parades are held on Fridays.

LOCATION: **At the corner of Panama St. and Olongapo St., Beaufort, 843-228-2951, www.parrisislandmuseum.com.**

✦ Potter's Raid

After Sherman passed through South Carolina, he instructed his cavalry operating out of Georgetown under the command of General Potter to destroy the railroads and infrastructure that his march in February had missed. The raid, conducted from April 8 to April 21, 1865, resulted in two small-scale

skirmishes, at Dingle's Mill on April 9 and at Boykin's Mill on April 18.

LOCATION: **The Boykin's Mill battlefield is 8 miles south of Camden at the junction of SC 261 and County Rd. 2 at 73 Boykin Mill Rd., Rembert. A tour brochure can be found at the kiosk at Dingle's Mill Memorial located on the west side of US 521 at Turkey Creek Bridge in Sumter.**

✦ Rose Hill Plantation State Historic Site

This is the Southern plantation home of William Henry Gist, the "Secession Governor." Gist became governor of South Carolina in 1858 and believed that the institution of slavery in South Carolina could be protected only if the state seceded from the Union. Tour the house or walk the lovely grounds and rose gardens.

LOCATION: **2677 Sardis Rd., Union, 864-427-5966, www.southcarolinaparks.com/rosehill.**

FURTHER READING

When Sherman Marched North From the Sea: Resistance on the Confederate Home Front by Jacqueline Glass Campbell
A study of the impact of Sherman's March on civilians in South Carolina and North Carolina

✦ South Carolina Confederate Relic Room and Military Museum

Dedicated to preserving the military history of South Carolina from the Revolutionary War to the present, this museum has a great display on the occupation and burning of Columbia. See the battlefield flag collection, weapons, and uniforms.

LOCATION: **301 Gervais St., Columbia, 803-737-8095, www.crr.sc.gov.**

Tennessee

ONE OF THE MOST FOUGHT-OVER AREAS IN THE CIVIL WAR, Tennessee saw nearly 1,500 different engagements or encounters. The state's rivers, roads, and mountain passes were important transportation arteries to the Deep South and, thus, the source of many conflicts. Tennesseans themselves were quite divided in their support. Those who lived in the eastern part of the state—hearty people without a large vested interest in the issues of Civil War—generally remained loyal to the Union. During the war, Tennessee provided more than 186,000 troops to the Confederacy and more than 31,000 troops to the Union, more Union troops than all other Confederate states combined. With this in mind, Lincoln selected Tennessean Andrew Johnson to be his vice president in 1864. Nevertheless, three years earlier, in June 1861, Tennessee had voted to secede from the Union, making it the last state to do so. From Knoxville to Memphis and Fort Donelson to Chattanooga, the state has done a laudable job of preserving and presenting its Civil War heritage.

Stones River National Battlefield is the site of an important Union victory, where more than 20,000 soldiers were killed, wounded, or captured.

TENNESSEE BATTLES

1 Memphis I
2 Memphis II
3 Fort Henry
4 Fort Donelson
5 Dover
6 Johnsonville

7 Franklin I
8 Franklin II
9 Thompson's Station
10 Spring Hill
11 Columbia
12 Hoover's Gap

13 Nashville
14 Brentwood
15 Stones River
16 Murfreesboro I
17 Murfreesboro II
18 Vaught's Hill

19 Chattanooga I
20 Chattanooga II
21 Chattanooga III
22 Fort Sanders
23 Campbell's Station
24 Mossy Creek

25 Fair Garde
26 Dandridge
27 Bean's Stat
28 Bull's Gap
29 Blue Sprin
30 Blountsvill

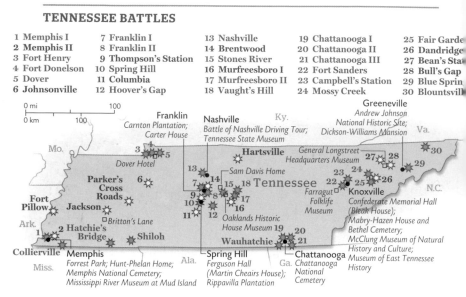

✳ Bean's Station

CAMPAIGN: Longstreet's Knoxville Campaign

DATE(S): December 14, 1863

In this last engagement of the Knoxville Campaign, General Longstreet ordered Confederate cavalry troops to surround General Shackelford's Union infantry. He intended to surprise them and cut off their retreat, but after two days of fighting, the Union troops made a fighting retreat. While this battle was a Confederate victory, it had little long-term effect on the war.

There are future plans for an interpretive park. In the meantime, don't miss the General Longstreet Headquarters Museum, a few miles away in Russellville (see p. 210).

LOCATION: Marker located at the intersection of US 11 and Bean's Station Cemetery Rd.

✳ Blountsville

CAMPAIGN: East Tennessee Campaign

DATE(S): September 22, 1863

Loyalist eastern Tennessee was an area of special interest to President Lincoln, who wanted to protect the residents at any cost. Union General Burnside, district commander in Cincinnati, undertook an expedition into eastern Tennessee to clear the roads and gaps to Virginia. In a four-hour battle, his troops forced the Confederates, led by General "Grumble" Jones, to withdraw from Blountsville and ultimately from eastern Tennessee altogether.

The battle is reenacted annually, and plans for an interpretive park are under way.

LOCATION: Marker located on Blountville Cemetery Rd., just north of County Hill Rd., in Blountville. Five additional markers are within walking distance. See also Tennessee Civil War Trails (see p. 207).

✳ Blue Springs

CAMPAIGN: East Tennessee Campaign

DATE(S): October 10, 1863

Representative of the vicious nature of the fighting in this area, this battle near the present town of Mosheim centered on control of the critical Virginia & Tennessee Railroad connecting Virginia with Chattanooga. General Williams and his Confederate cavalry set out to disrupt Union communications and logistics. His forces fiercely fought the Union cavalry unit led by General Carter. Surprisingly bloody, this last major engagement in the area was but another example of the contentious war in eastern Tennessee.

Interesting markers from the Tennessee Civil War Trails program (see p. 207) can be found within ten miles of the battlefield, including two bridge burners sites and the Andrew Johnson National Cemetery.

LOCATION: Two markers located on W. Andrew Johnson Hwy. (US 11E) in Mosheim. Others are located west of Emerald Rd. and on Mt. Pleasant Rd.

FURTHER READING

War at Every Door: Partisan Politics and Guerrilla Violence in East Tennessee, 1860–1869
by Noel C. Fisher
Detailed examination of the struggle for political and military control of this hotly contested region

✳ Brentwood

CAMPAIGN: Middle Tennessee Operations
DATE(S): March 25, 1863

In moving against the Brentwood railroad station, which was held by Union Colonel Bloodgood and 400 of his men, Confederate General Forrest ordered telegraph lines cut and railroad tracks torn up. He eventually forced Bloodgood to surrender. Then he forced a second surrender about two miles south at the Union stockade commanded by Captain Basset. This enabled the Confederates to burn the bridge over the Little Harpeth River, capture many supply wagons, and take about 800 Union prisoners.

These sites are rapidly disappearing because of the relentless growth of the Nashville metropolitan area.

LOCATION: Marker located on US 31 near Brentwood in Williamson County.

✳ Bull's Gap

CAMPAIGN: Breckinridge's Advance Into East Tennessee
DATE(S): November 11–13, 1864

During this battle, which involved a composite of sites, the opposing forces struggled for control of the road and railroad that opened communications between southwestern Virginia and extreme northeastern Tennessee. General Breckinridge

Andrew Johnson

"When I die, I want no more winding sheet than that of the brave old flag . . . and no softer pillow than the Constitution of my country."

These are the words of Andrew Johnson, the 17th U.S. president, who was buried atop Monument Hill in Greeneville, Tennessee, on August 3, 1875. Johnson—who had been Lincoln's choice to replace Maine's Hannibal Hamlin on the 1864 ticket—became president after Lincoln's assassination. On February 24, 1868, Johnson was impeached, but not convicted, when he challenged the authority of the Radical Republicans running Congress. He was charged with violating the Tenure of Office Act of 1867 by trying to remove strongman Secretary of War Edwin Stanton. He would remain the only president impeached until President Clinton was nearly 130 years later. A strong loyalist, Johnson prescribed that he be buried wrapped in a U.S. flag with a copy of the Constitution resting beneath his head. His wife, Eliza, is buried beside him under a stately monument erected here by the family in 1878. Their immediate family members and many descendants are also buried in this family plot. The cemetery is now part of Andrew Johnson National Historic Site, which includes several places of interest (see p. 207).

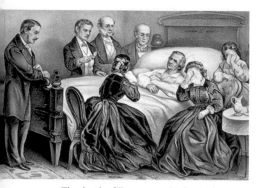
The death of Tennessean Andrew Johnson, 17th president of the United States

and his Confederate troops sought to close the channel and, at the same time, make the area safe for foraging by attacking the Federal troops led by General Gillem at the gap; however, they approached the position from behind, having marched through Taylor's Gap and to a crest east of Bull's Gap in the same Bays Mountain area. After two days of fighting, the Federals held the position but eventually withdrew to resupply themselves. The Confederates pursued and continued to snipe at the Federals, causing about 240 casualties. Confederate losses were not reported. The pursuit ended near Strawberry Plains.

LOCATION: **Marker located in Russellville about 700 yards north of Andrew Johnson Hwy. (US 11E), near the Bethesda Cemetery gate.**

✳ Campbell's Station

CAMPAIGN: Longstreet's Knoxville Campaign
DATE(S): November 16, 1863

Confederate General Longstreet's independent operation against Knoxville very narrowly missed its greatest opportunity when a substantial portion of General Burnside's troops successfully evaded Longstreet's effort to cut them off from Knoxville. Burnside's forces made a stand at Campbell's Station and held off the

attacking Confederates before withdrawing back to Knoxville.

While in the area, don't miss the Farragut Folklife Museum and its collection of items related to Admiral Farragut in nearby Farragut, Tennessee (see p. 209).

LOCATION: **Marker located on the grounds of Farragut Town Hall, 11408 Municipal Center Dr., Farragut.**

✳ Chattanooga I

CAMPAIGN: Confederate Heartland Offensive
DATE(S): June 7–8, 1862

This engagement was merely an exchange of artillery fire in which approaching Federal troops from Huntsville, Alabama, placed artillery on Stringer's Ridge overlooking the

David Glasgow Farragut

Born in Campbell's Station (now called Farragut) on July 5, 1801, David Glasgow Farragut became a midshipman at age nine and served until his death 60 years later. He served in the War of 1812 and, despite his strong Southern ties, continued to serve in the Union Navy and became a hero during the Civil War. He was victorious at the Battle of New Orleans (see pp. 110–111) and, more famously, at Mobile Bay (see pp. 30–32), which successfully closed the last major Confederate port in the Gulf of Mexico. Although the statement is generally regarded as apocryphal now, he is perhaps best known for demanding of the U.S.S. *Hartford*'s commander: "Damn the torpedoes! Full speed ahead!"

Farragut was the first U.S. naval officer to be named a full admiral. An informative monument erected in his honor can be found in Farragut Memorial Plaza by Farragut Town Hall (see p. 209), just a few miles from his birthplace.

Reenactors engage at Chickamauga and Chattanooga National Military Park. The battle here marked the end of the Union offensive in the region, forcing Union soldiers back to Chattanooga.

town and opened fire. Confederate return fire came from Cameron Hill. The Federals' movement lacked purpose, and they were soon drawn off by Confederate General Bragg's invasion of Kentucky in early September 1862.

The Federal artillerymen were posted on Stringer's Ridge, which is across the Tennessee River facing Cameron Hill to the southeast. They surely would have fired from the area at the nearest pass through the mountains.

LOCATION: An informative marker outlining changes in the Chattanooga waterfront is located on River St., west of Tremont St., and a marker for Cameron Hill is located on I-24 on the Olgiati Bridge.

✳ Chattanooga II

CAMPAIGN: Chickamauga Campaign
DATE(S): August 21, 1863

This event, small in scope but huge in effect, was a precursor to the massive Chickamauga Campaign and battle (see pp. 64–66). Eager to satisfy President Lincoln's demand that Federal troops protect East Tennessee, General Rosecrans set

his sights on Chattanooga as a means of securing the state. He deployed his army in three major columns, one of which was to take and dominate the Cumberland Plateau northwest of Chattanooga (of which Stringer's Ridge is the last portion). Once again, the Federals opened fire on the city from Stringer's Ridge. When General Bragg realized the Federals were passing him to the west, he abandoned Chattanooga.

LOCATION: See location info for Chattanooga I.

✳ Chattanooga III

CAMPAIGN: Chattanooga-Ringgold Campaign
DATE(S): November 23–25, 1863

The struggle for Chattanooga comprises three different battles under one umbrella. They all take place within the same operational time frame in November 1863. By the time they ended, Union forces had driven away the Confederates, Bragg had lost his command, and the Federals had already begun planning their spring offensive.

On the banks of the Tennessee River, the city of Chattanooga stood at the opening of the gateway to the Deep South. Initially

Union troops under General Thomas capture Orchard Knob during the battles for Chattanooga.

important because of the railroads, which ran to Memphis, Lynchburg, and Atlanta, Chattanooga became the object of General Buell's post-Corinth march in the summer of 1862 and was spared attack only by General Bragg's move into Kentucky. By September 1863, however, the city had become the refuge for General Rosecrans's beaten and dispirited army. War Department envoys had reported that Rosecrans was ineffective and, if left in command, would surely lose his army to starvation. This was a possibility because Rosecrans had the Confederate Army on Missionary Ridge in front of him, the Confederate Army on Lookout Mountain with artillery commanding the city and the Tennessee River below him, and the rugged Cumberland Plateau behind him. The meager supplies for his forces came to Bridgeport, Alabama, and had to be transported out of Confederate artillery range across the Tennessee River and behind Stringer's Ridge, as many as 60 miles north of Chattanooga, where they were vulnerable to capture or destruction by Confederate

cavalry. By the end of October, a month after Chickamauga (see pp. 64–66), General Grant was ordered to Chattanooga with authority to replace Rosecrans with General Thomas—a move he quickly made. Using plans developed by Rosecrans, Grant established a "Cracker Line," which guaranteed the army would not starve. He then summoned his friend William T. Sherman to join him. Chattanooga had now become center stage, and Grant stood in the wings.

Fearing the Confederates might dispatch soldiers to help General Longstreet capture Knoxville, Grant ordered Thomas to make a demonstration against a forward Confederate outpost at Orchard Knob. The attack on November 23 was successful, and the Federals overran the position with a vastly superior force. This would become Grant's and Thomas's headquarters for the operations against Lookout Mountain and the eastern portion of Missionary Ridge. Grant hoped to uncover the Confederate position and then sweep the Confederates from the ridge overlooking Chattanooga.

With the opening of the Cracker Line, the commanding position atop Lookout Mountain served as a strong left flank for Bragg's army on the ridge. Grant had brought his trusted subordinate General Sherman to Chattanooga, and Sherman's force stealthily moved on the north side of the Tennessee River to a point opposite the eastern flank of Bragg's line on Missionary Ridge. Grant did not want a full-out attack from General Hooker, whom he did not trust. Hooker's men moved with purpose on November 24 and moved up the mountain to fight a vicious action on a plateau just below the summit, where a fight raged around the Craven House. That evening the Confederates abandoned Lookout Mountain and moved to augment the forces on Missionary Ridge.

November 25 was the day of decision, and it unfolded as no one expected. In an effort to fix the Confederates in position while Sherman attacked the Confederate right, Thomas was ordered to attack and carry rifle pits at the base of the ridge; however, the Union soldiers were not to be denied. When the Confederates fled, the Federals spontaneously followed up the side

Rhea County Spartans

In the summer of 1862, a group of 30 prominent young women living in Rhea County, Tennessee, formed the first and only all-female cavalry unit of the Civil War. These Confederate women in their teens and twenties named their nonmilitary unit the Spartans. Led by Mary McDonald and her sister-in-law, Caroline McDonald, these "sidesaddle soldiers"—as they were sometimes called—aided the Confederate cause by carrying food and clothing to fathers, brothers, and sweethearts while they patrolled the countryside. Some historians believe that the Spartans also carried out limited espionage for the Confederacy. In 1865, a zealous, local Union captain named John Walker arrested the Spartans and sent the women miles away to Chattanooga. There, Walker was reprimanded for wasting Union time and resources, and the Spartans were sent back home.

of the precipitous ridge in a crude form of "King of the Hill." While Sherman faltered in the face of rugged terrain while facing a worthy foe in Confederate General Cleburne, Thomas's men carried the ridge and swept the Confederates away in a disorganized retreat that would not stop until they reached Dalton, Georgia. The siege of Chattanooga was over, and Grant was identified as the man who could win the war. He was summoned to Washington for a promotion to lieutenant general and given command of all the Union armies.

To visit, start at Orchard Knob Reservation, part of Chickamauga and Chattanooga National Military Park; the area contains several interesting monuments. Then drive up to and along the length of beautiful Missionary Ridge. The National Park Service maintains several reservations on the ridge where you can park and walk along the line

George H. Thomas, a Union general, was nicknamed "The Rock of Chickamauga."

to read interpretive signs and see homes with artillery pieces still in their front yards. For a short video and other information to help orient you, stop at the visitor center atop Lookout Mountain. From there, cross the street to Point Park, the 3,000-acre location of the "Battle Above the Clouds." These ample grounds are populated with cannons, monuments, and sweeping views of the Tennessee River and valley below. Make sure

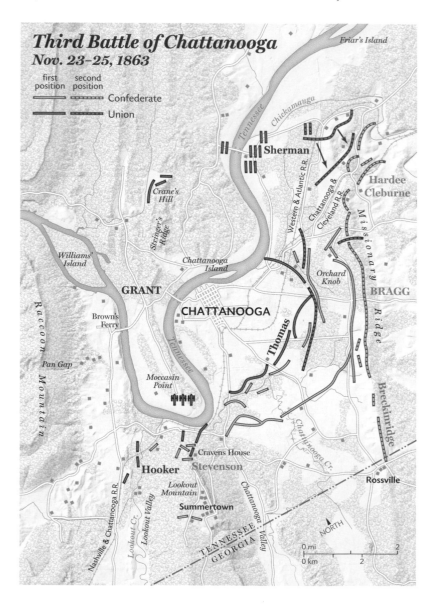

Third Battle of Chattanooga
Nov. 23–25, 1863

first position
second position
Confederate
Union

Friar's Island

Tennessee
Chickamauga

Sherman

Crane's Hill

Hardee
Cleburne

Stringer's Ridge

Western & Atlantic R.R.

Chattanooga & Cleveland R.R.

Missionary Ridge

Williams' Island

Chattanooga Island

Orchard Knob

BRAGG

GRANT

CHATTANOOGA

Brown's Ferry

Thomas

Breckinridge

Raccoon Mountain

Pan Gap

Moccasin Point

Tennessee

Chattanooga Cr.

Cravens House

Stevenson

Rossville

Hooker

Lookout Mountain

Chattanooga Valley

Nashville & Chattanooga R.R.

Lookout Cr.

Lookout Valley

Summertown

NORTH

TENNESSEE
GEORGIA

0 mi 2
0 km 2

you also visit Cravens House, partway down Lookout Mountain.

LOCATION: **Chickamauga and Chattanooga National Military Park, Lookout Mountain Visitor Center, 1110 East Brow Rd., Lookout Mountain, 423-821-7786, www.nps.gov/chch; Orchard Knob Reservation, 500 N. Highland Park Ave., 706-866-9241; Missionary Ridge Reservations, North Crest Rd.**

FURTHER READING

The Shipwreck of Their Hopes: The Battles for Chattanooga
by Peter Cozzens
Third book in an acclaimed trilogy about the war in the West

✳ Collierville

CAMPAIGN: Operations on the Memphis & Charleston Railroad

DATE(S): November 3, 1863

Because the Memphis & Charleston (M&C) Railroad was a major communications route, the Confederate cavalry sought to disrupt its operations and, thus, throw into disarray General Sherman's plans to move Union troops into Chattanooga. During the course of the war, four encounters between the two sides took place in and around Collierville; however, this battle was the most important. Believing that the M&C Railroad was inadequately defended, Confederate forces commanded by General Chalmers planned to break it up.

This commemorative sculpture stands at Chickamauga and Chattanooga National Military Park.

As Chalmers and his men approached the railroad, Union reinforcements led by Colonel Hatch arrived on his flank. Rather than escalate the fight, Chalmers withdrew his Confederate troops back into Mississippi.

LOCATION: **Several markers can be found at or near the town square on West Poplar Ave. in Collierville, including two from Tennessee Civil War Trails (see p. 207).**

☀ Columbia

CAMPAIGN: Franklin-Nashville Campaign

DATE(S): November 24–29, 1864

After being delayed in northern Alabama, General Hood made his long-awaited advance into Tennessee. Volunteer Staters in his command were overjoyed to be returning home. Hood moved aggressively, and Union soldiers posted at Pulaski fell back to Columbia, with the Duck River at their backs. Sensing an opportunity, Hood advanced artillery and a corps under the command of General Stephen D. Lee to hold General Schofield in place. Meanwhile, Confederate cavalry under the command of General Forrest chased Union General Wilson away from crossing points east of Columbia. Schofield fell back across the river as Hood's two divisions crossed behind him and moved toward Spring Hill—a point that would allow Hood to encircle and perhaps capture Schofield's corps. Discovering his perilous position, Schofield retreated toward Nashville with Lee, following along present-day Route 31.

LOCATION: **Markers located at the intersection of North Hood Rd. and Waynesboro Hwy. (US 64) in Lawrenceburg; on US 43, 5 miles north of Lawrenceburg; and on Collinwood Hwy. (TN 13), north of Sunny Acres Dr. in Waynesboro.**

☀ Dandridge

CAMPAIGN: Operations About Dandridge

DATE(S): January 17, 1864

The few days of conflict around Dandridge began near the East Tennessee & Virginia

Railroad when Union troops commanded by General Parke forced General Longstreet's Confederate forces to fall back. With the goal of pushing the Confederates out of their winter encampment and key foraging area entirely, Park advanced on Dandridge with the hope of occupying the area. In the meantime, however, Longstreet had summoned Rebel reinforcements. Although Park and his Union soldiers briefly succeeded, they were soon pushed back by Longstreet. The Confederates pursued as far as Strawberry Plains; however, no decisive outcome was achieved because of the lack of cannons and ammunition—and shoes.

LOCATION: **Marker located across from the Jefferson County Department of Education, 780 TN Rte. 92, Dandridge.**

☀ Dover

CAMPAIGN: Middle Tennessee Operations

DATE(S): February 3, 1863

General Wheeler and his Confederate cavalry set out to disrupt Union shipping on the Cumberland River at Palmyra. In response,

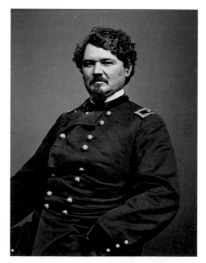

General Sturgis commanded Federal forces at the Battle of Mossy Creek.

At Fort Donelson, Grant demanded an "immediate and unconditional surrender."

the Federals simply stopped all shipping. Realizing he couldn't wait around indefinitely, Wheeler instead planned an attack at Dover on the 800-man garrison under Colonel Harding. But before he could execute the assault, General Forrest mounted a failed attack that incurred many casualties. The two Confederate generals and their men retired, leaving the Union in control of Middle Tennessee. Forrest was so bitter about this encounter that he refused to serve under Wheeler again.

LOCATION: **Fort Donelson National Battlefield, 120 Fort Donelson Rd., Dover, 931-232-5706, www.nps.gov/fodo.**

✳ Fair Garden

CAMPAIGN: Operations About Dandridge
DATE(S): January 27–28, 1864

This engagement exemplifies the thrust-and-parry pattern of battle during this severely cold winter period. The Confederates sought additional food and supplies by foraging in the vicinity of the French Broad River. Union cavalry under General Sturgis sought to deny them and successfully attacked General Martin's

Confederate forces on Fair Garden Road. The next day, the Union forces pursued the Rebels until they observed General Longstreet's infantry brigades crossing the river. At this point, they withdrew and decided to attack General Armstrong's cavalry division a few miles away. After intense fighting, the Federals, though victorious, were forced to withdraw because of fatigue and a lack of supplies and ammunition.

LOCATION: **Sevier County; no public access.**

✳ Fort Donelson

CAMPAIGN: Federal Penetration up the Cumberland and Tennessee Rivers
DATE(S): February 12–16, 1862

This is one of the most important small battles of the Civil War. Here General Grant earned the nickname "Unconditional Surrender" by forcing encircled Confederate troops to surrender. One of the first victories for the embattled Union, it led directly to the capture of Nashville—the first Confederate state capital to be captured.

Earlier in the month, Grant had participated in the practically bloodless capture of Fort Henry (see pp. 187–188) on the

Tennessee River. Rather than await the arrival of his departmental commander, General Halleck, Grant promised to quickly capture Fort Donelson, which guarded the Cumberland River above Clarksville.

Inland naval forces, under the command of Commodore Foote, attempted to bombard the fort into submission but fell back when the Confederate batteries proved more of a match than those at Fort Henry. The Confederate forces were poorly led by Generals Floyd, Pillow, and Buckner. After attempting a breakout, which should have succeeded, Floyd and Pillow deserted with their forces, leaving Buckner to surrender. Colonel (soon to be General) Forrest

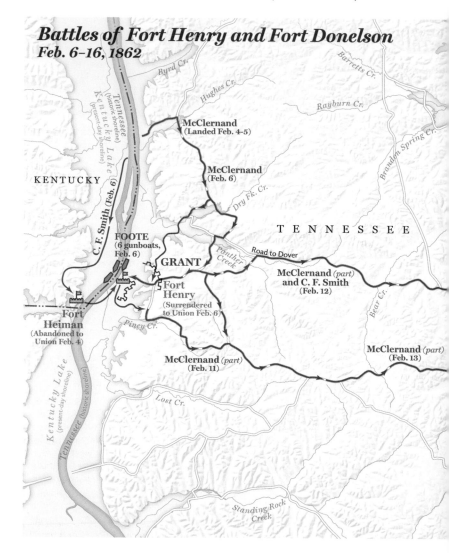

Battles of Fort Henry and Fort Donelson
Feb. 6–16, 1862

refused to accept the decision and led his cavalry out through icy waters in a daring escape. Buckner then asked for terms and was told by Grant that no conditions other than immediate and unconditional surrender would be accepted.

This small national park and its expansive grounds are a hidden treasure. From its interpretative stops you can learn much about Grant and his operations. Don't miss the Dover Hotel (see p. 209), the site of the famous "unconditional and immediate surrender" of the Confederates to General Grant, who immediately earned a promotion to major general.

LOCATION: Fort Donelson National Battlefield, 120 Fort Donelson Rd., Dover, 931-232-5706, www.nps.gov/fodo.

FURTHER READING

Where the South Lost the War: An Analysis of the Fort Henry–Fort Donelson Campaign, February 1862
by Kendall D. Gott
An examination of this pivotal campaign and its overall impact on the war

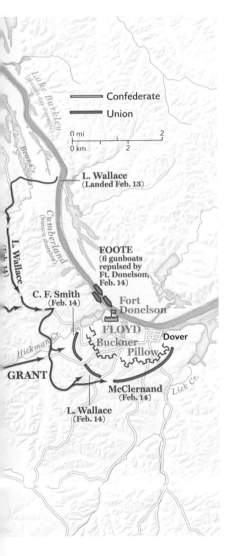

✳ Fort Henry

CAMPAIGN: Federal Penetration up the Cumberland and Tennessee Rivers

DATE(S): February 6, 1862

The first battle of the war to use ironclad gunboats, the Battle of Fort Henry was also the first significant Union victory and the beginning of General Grant's road to Appomattox. Poorly engineered, the fortification on the Tennessee River was flooding with the rising river when Commodore Foote landed Grant's infantry above the fort. Before the infantry could march overland, the Confederates under General Tilghman surrendered to naval officers, who rowed through the front entrance to the fort. Most of the Confederate troops made their way to Fort Donelson, which was next in Grant's sights. Fort Henry's fall meant the Tennessee River was open to Union gunboats and shipping as far south as Muscle Shoals, Alabama. Today, some outer works survive, but the fort is in the Tennessee River.

LOCATION: Markers located at the intersection of Donelson Pkwy. (US 79) and Fort Henry Rd.,

and on Fort Henry Rd. near Land Between the Lakes Rd., both in Dover.

FURTHER READING

Forts Henry and Donelson: The Key to the Confederate Heartland
by Benjamin Franklin Cooling
A rare detailed analysis of this important campaign

✳ Fort Pillow

CAMPAIGN: Forrest's Expedition Into West Tennessee and Kentucky

DATE(S): April 12, 1864

Fort Pillow, an earthen fortification overlooking the Mississippi River, had been an important part of the Confederate river defense until the Union captured it in 1862. Forty miles north of Memphis, the fort was being held by about 600 Union soldiers, approximately half black and half white (most of these Tennesseans). General Forrest and his Confederate cavalry planned to seize the fort commanded by Major Booth. Booth was killed early in the day and replaced by Major Bradford. Forrest demanded an unconditional surrender, which Bradford refused. Injured, Forrest stayed back after ordering his troops to overrun the fort.

The Confederates were successful, but confusion reigned as negotiations for surrender began while some Union soldiers (perhaps unaware of the flag of truce) attempted to escape to the river, where a Union gunboat was anchored. Marksmen fired at them from the bluffs. Some drowned. Many accounts report that Confederates continued to kill Union soldiers, even after they had thrown down their weapons and surrendered. A disproportionate number of black Union soldiers were killed during this battle, while white Union soldiers were mostly taken as prisoners of war. Northern newspapers labeled it the "Fort Pillow Massacre." While some insist

that the Confederates intentionally murdered the blacks, others point out that the soldiers who were shot violated the flag of truce. Still others note Forrest's battle reputation, saying that if he had ordered the black soldiers massacred, none would have escaped. This battle remains one of the most controversial events of the Civil War.

Covering 1,600 rural acres, Fort Pillow State Park has several markers and a visitor center that shows a short movie.

LOCATION: Fort Pillow State Park, 3122 Park Rd., Henning, 731-738-5581, www.tnstate parks.com/parks/about/fort-pillow.

FURTHER READING

An Unerring Fire: The Massacre at Fort Pillow
by Richard L. Fuchs
Examines Forrest's role in the events that followed the battle

The River Was Dyed With Blood: Nathan Bedford Forrest and Fort Pillow
by Brian Steel Wills
Different examination of the most controversial episode of the Civil War

✳ Fort Sanders

CAMPAIGN: Longstreet's Knoxville Campaign

DATE(S): November 29, 1863

Having lost the opportunity at Campbell's Station (see p. 178) and hoping to prevent General Burnside's army from heading to Chattanooga, General Longstreet and his Confederates laid siege to Knoxville. Their predawn attack did not take into account the ditches that surrounded the earthen fort. Even before reaching the ditches, many Rebels became entangled in telegraph wire strung at knee height, making them easy targets. Although the attack was quickly called off, it was one of the most lopsided defeats of the war, with an estimated 70

Nathan Bedford Forrest

General Forrest, a charismatic and controversial Confederate leader, takes a hostage.

A roughly raised Westerner, Forrest is one of the great names of the Civil War. He made a fortune in slave trading and management, jobs a "gentleman" would not do. When war broke out, he enlisted as a private, but his natural leadership traits quickly led to a commission. Using his own money, he purchased weapons and uniforms for his Tennessee recruits and quickly earned a reputation for riding to the sound of the guns. Although a mere lieutenant colonel, he refused to join in the surrender of Fort Donelson (see pp. 185–187), instead leading his men out through icy waters. At Shiloh (see pp. 199–202), he led his men from a meaningless post guarding a bridge into combat, and he maintained a heroic and singularly spectacular defense against pursuing Federals at Fallen Timbers. Forrest did not work well under direct supervision; however, his independent operations led to multiple successes, and he earned a fearsome reputation for his actions against Federal garrisons and supply centers. He had multiple horses shot out from under him, killed 19 Union soldiers in direct combat, and was wounded several times. In fact, the "Wizard of the Saddle" so concerned General Sherman that he designed a campaign to keep Forrest away from his supply lines during the Atlanta Campaign. Forrest operated primarily in Tennessee, Alabama, and Mississippi. Tarred by the incident at Fort Pillow (see p. 188), Forrest was defeated at the Battle of Selma in 1865 and surrendered shortly thereafter. Following the war, Forrest briefly accepted an invitation to head what would be known as the Ku Klux Klan. He resigned after a year and took over the presidency of a railroad. He died a repentant and humble man. He and his wife are buried in Memphis, Tennessee.

FURTHER READING

The Confederacy's Greatest Cavalryman: Nathan Bedford Forrest
by Brian Steel Wills
A biography of one of the war's most colorful and controversial figures

Confederate and 100 Federal casualties. Eastern Tennessee remained under Union control for the remainder of the war.

LOCATION: **The battle took place in present-day Knox County; however, the sites related to the campaign no longer exist.**

FURTHER READING

The Knoxville Campaign: Burnside and Longstreet in East Tennessee
by Earl J. Hess
A vivid account of the vital campaign that tested the heart of East Tennessee

✳ Franklin I

CAMPAIGN: Middle Tennessee Operations
DATE(S): April 10, 1863

Confederate cavalry under General Van Dorn moved north from Spring Hill to determine if the Federals had occupied Franklin. While moving along Lewisburg Pike near the Harpeth River, General Forrest was attacked by Federal forces under General Stanley, who had crossed behind Forrest's force at Hughes Ford. Stanley achieved an initial success before Forrest's men drove him back. The Confederate cavalry withdrew, and Van Dorn reported that Franklin was indeed occupied.

LOCATION: **Williamson County; no public access.**

✳ Franklin II

CAMPAIGN: Franklin-Nashville Campaign
DATE(S): November 30, 1864

Confederate General Hood awoke on the morning of November 30, 1864, to discover that Union forces under the command of General Schofield had passed his lines during the night and were well on their way to escaping to Nashville. Deeply disappointed, Hood reportedly railed against his subordinates' failure to seal off the retreat route. Indeed, Confederate forces had camped within a few hundred yards of the Columbia-Nashville Pike (US 31). Realizing the lost opportunity, Hood ordered a pursuit, which caught up with the Federal forces at Franklin.

The Federals were constructing temporary bridges across the Harpeth. Hood, realizing their vulnerability, ordered an assault, hoping to smash the Union against the river. The Federals were better prepared than he expected, and the 4 p.m. assault—the largest Confederate charge in the war—was heavy work indeed. At one point, Hood's men breached the Union lines near the Carter House but were driven back. As twilight turned to dark, Hood continued the effort, but the Union lines were too strong. Multiple attacks were all beaten back, and six Confederate generals were killed. The Federals continued their retreat to Nashville, leaving Hood with a bloody battlefield. Hood pursued the Union forces to Nashville, where, two weeks later, he and his army were decisively beaten.

Postwar analysis has been hostile to Hood's decision to attack the Union lines. Many suggest he should have attempted another flanking maneuver. Others note that Franklin was an elusive final opportunity to destroy Schofield that would have been available only as an

Frock coat of General Cleburne, who died in the Battle of Franklin

The largest private military cemetery in the United States is at Carnton Plantation in Franklin.

immediate attack. Regardless, the casualties here ensured that the South would never smile again.

The Lotz House sponsors a walking tour that captures the essence of the battle, and a good interpretation is present throughout the town. Other essential stops include the Carter House (see p. 208) and the Carnton Plantation (see p. 208). A campaign to preserve the Franklin battlefield is ongoing. One could easily spend three days covering sites in Franklin, Spring Hill, Columbia, and Nashville.

LOCATION: **Lotz House, 1111 Columbia Ave., Franklin, 615-790-7190, www.lotzhouse.com.**

FURTHER READING

For Cause and Country: A Study of the Affair at Spring Hill and the Battle of Franklin
by Eric A. Jacobson
Profiles once ignored battle that was a watershed moment at war's end

The Lost Papers of Confederate General John Bell Hood
by Stephen M. Hood
More than 200 documents shed light on some of the war's lingering mysteries and controversies

✳ Hartsville

CAMPAIGN: Stones River Campaign
DATE(S): December 7, 1862

Yet another of the Confederacy's seemingly endless supply of effective cavalrymen, Colonel Morgan crossed the Cumberland River under cover of darkness and surprised a Federal force guarding the crossing. Union Colonel Moore reported after the fact that the Rebels had approached wearing blue uniforms, fooling the Union vedettes. During the 75-minute battle, one of Moore's units ran, causing chaos and forcing the Federals to fall back. During the course of battle, Morgan captured more than 1,800

Civil War on Foot: Franklin

Long overlooked, the 1864 Battle of Franklin (see pp. 190–191) is seeing renewed interest. Of the two pedestrian-friendly historic areas, the six-stop route along Columbia Avenue, also known as Columbia Pike (US 31), is more important. Follow these numbered stops to retrace soliders' steps as the battle raged through town.

❶ Carter House
(1140 Columbia Ave.)
Orient yourself here, and acquire tickets if you wish to tour the house and visit the small museum. During the battle, civilians cowered in the basement here as the grounds in front of the house witnessed the decisive counterattack that broke the Confederates' momentum. More than 100 bullets ripped through the office and wooden smokehouse, which still stand today. Blood soaked the front steps. Head south on Columbia Avenue.

❷ Union Forward Position *(Intersection of Columbia Ave. and Fairground St.)* Here in a signposted stop, the Union Army found itself poorly positioned with two brigades of General Wagner's division dangerously exposed to attack on three sides. When the massive attack came at roughly 4 p.m., the line broke

Lotz House survived the bloody Battle of Franklin to become a field hospital.

and fled to the Federal main lines near the Carter House. In doing so, they helped screen some of the onrushing Rebels, who were able to advance to the sally port entrance of the main Federal line.

❸ Academy Park
(120 Everbright Ave.)
Wagner's retreating men tried to make a stand on this ground (now home to the city library), only to be swept away by a massive charge by General Frank Cheatham's corps. Take Columbia Avenue north to Cleburne Street.

❹ Cotton Gin Site
From the point of the small park with a cannonball pyramid, you are in the area of the primary assault and death site of Patrick Cleburne. Cleburne's division was destroyed attacking earthworks across Cleburne Street, and Cleburne himself was killed a short distance to the right of the cannonball monument. Continue straight (east) on Cleburne and Stewart Street 300 yards to the Lewisburg Pike, where Cleburne's and French's divisions attacked. Go right on the Lewisburg

Pike for 300 yards to the Collins Farm, where the railroad and Osage orange trees hampered the assault. Return to Columbia Avenue, turn right, and then turn left on Strahl. Continue on Strahl, parallel to Brown's attack, to Carter.

❺ Brown's Attack As you walk along Strahl Street, look to the right, where scenic vistas are being cleared. You are walking parallel to Brown's attack; he was in Cheatham's Corps. Here General Strahl was killed in the assault. General Carter was mortally wounded and died on December 10 at a home near Winstead Hill. Return to Columbia Avenue and turn left, heading north toward Fowlkes Street.

❻ Lotz House (*1111 Columbia Ave.*) This building is the architectural gem of Andrew Lotz, who rode out the battle in the basement of the neighboring Carter House, where the walking tour began.

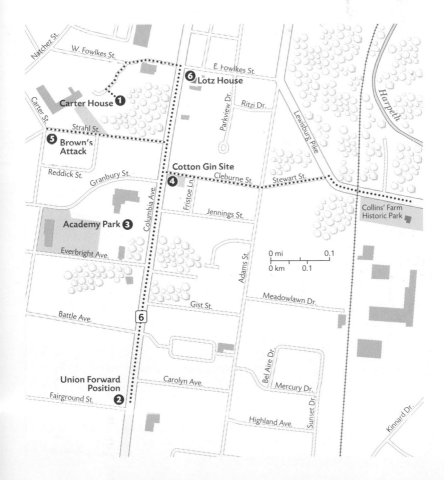

Union soldiers. His great success here led to a promotion to brigadier general.

LOCATION: Markers located at the intersection of Broadway and White Oak St., and on River St. (TN Rte. 141) on the right when traveling north, both in Hartsville.

FURTHER READING
Rebel Raider: The Life of General John Hunt Morgan
by James A. Ramage
A balanced biography of a celebrated Confederate leader

✳ Hatchie's Bridge

CAMPAIGN: Iuka and Corinth Operations

OTHER NAME(S): Davis Bridge

DATE(S): October 5, 1862

With his disappointing defeat at Corinth (see p. 127), General Van Dorn and his battered Confederates fell back, intending to return to Holly Springs, Mississippi. Unfortunately for the Rebels, General Grant ordered supporting reinforcements to intercept Van Dorn and hold him east of the Hatchie River, where General Rosecrans, who was in pursuit, might smash the remnants of the Confederate Army.

Not realizing the developing trap, the Confederates crossed the Hatchie River at Davis Bridge near Pocahontas and moved along State Line Road toward the Mississippi and Tennessee state line. Briefly occupying the high ground with the river about a mile to the rear, the Rebels quickly retreated to a natural earthwork, which cut across the field and is still visible today. Here the advancing Federals under General Ord pushed the Rebels back, capturing four pieces of artillery and approximately 200 soldiers. The Confederates successfully evaded the trap, however, and crossed to the high ground east of the Hatchie River, some five miles above Davis Bridge, leaving the tardy Rosecrans to report to Grant that the Rebels

At Davis Bridge on the Hatchie River, General Van Dorn's army evaded Union capture.

were escaping. Grant ignored Rosecrans's protests and ordered the pursuit terminated.

Currently, little of this site, which is part of Tennessee Civil War Trails (see p. 207), is developed. There are plans for future development of this battlefield in conjunction with Shiloh (see pp. 199–202), however. Visitors can drive to the top of Metamora Hill, where Union troops placed guns after forcing the Rebels off the commanding position. From here the entire battlefield is in view. Or take a half-mile walk through the woods, starting at the National Park Service gate and ending at the former bridge site on the Hatchie River. Several markers and a Confederate monument along the way provide historical context.

LOCATION: **Davis Bridge Battlefield, Essary Springs Rd., Pocahontas, 731-658-6554.**

FURTHER READING

The Darkest Days of the War: The Battles of Iuka and Corinth by Peter Cozzens An illuminating book about the 1862 Confederate offensive

✱ Hoover's Gap

CAMPAIGN: Tullahoma or Middle Tennessee Campaign

DATE(S): June 24–26, 1863

With General Grant holding Vicksburg firmly in his grasp, General in Chief Halleck encouraged General Rosecrans to attack General Bragg's forces and keep him from sending troops to help break the siege. Not anxious to advance before he was ready, Rosecrans had plans of his own. He decided to march toward and capture Chattanooga. As his forces moved out, Colonel Wilder's mounted infantry—known as the Lightning Brigade—reached Hoover's Gap, nearly nine miles ahead of the Union forces under General Thomas. Armed with new Spencer repeating rifles (see sidebar this page), the Lightning Brigade occupied the gap and

Spencer Repeating Rifle

A reliable weapon on the battlefield, the Spencer repeating rifle could fire about 14 to 20 rounds of ammunition per minute. In contrast, most soldiers carried muzzle-loading rifled muskets, which fired about two or three rounds per minute. First used in 1863 by the Union Army's "Lightning Brigade," the Spencers were most famously employed by the Union in the Battle of Hoover's Gap and by General Custer's Brigade of Michiganders during the Gettysburg Campaign.

then beat back the Confederate cavalry under Colonel Butler, who had attacked them. A division of Confederate infantry then attacked, also to be driven back. After Thomas's Union corps arrived, the fighting continued until June 26, when the Confederates abandoned the entire Duck River line from Shelbyville to McMinnville.

The Union victory started the campaign that stripped the Rebels of their foothold in Middle Tennessee. Rosecrans's subsequent movements maneuvered Bragg out of Tennessee to the banks of Chickamauga Creek in mid-September 1863.

The battlefield site today includes interpretive signage, numerous monuments, and a Confederate cemetery.

LOCATION: **Beech Grove Confederate Cemetery and Park, 116 Confederate Cemetery Rd., Beech Grove, 931-571-7311. For information about an 11-stop driving tour of the Tullahoma Campaign, see p. 207.**

✱ Jackson

CAMPAIGN: Forrest's Expedition Into West Tennessee

OTHER NAME(S): Salem Cemetery

DATE(S): December 19, 1862

General Forrest was in West Tennessee on a mission to disrupt the rail supply line to

General Grant's army. Forrest smashed the Union cavalry at Lexington on December 18 and continued on toward Jackson the next day. At Salem Cemetery, infantry troops under Colonel Englemann waited to attack Forrest and his mounted troops in an attempt to slow their progress through the region. Instead, the Confederates pushed the Union troops back to their fortifications at Jackson and withdrew. Meanwhile, this diversion allowed two of Forrest's other mounted columns to successfully disrupt railroad tracks and communication lines north and south of town.

A self-guided tour of this minimally developed battlefield is available at the main gate. Included are three monuments, two cannons, and a historical marker.

LOCATION: **Salem Cemetery and Battleground, Cotton Grove Rd., Jackson, 731-424-1279.**

✳ Johnsonville

CAMPAIGN: Franklin-Nashville Campaign
DATE(S): November 4–5, 1864

Attempting to check the Union advance through Georgia, General Forrest led a 23-day raid that culminated in an attack on the Yankee supply base at Johnsonville. Undetected, his soldiers positioned artillery across from the base. When the Union gunboats and land batteries began engaging the Confederates, they didn't last long because the Rebels were so well positioned. Fearing a capture of their boats by the Confederates, the Union set fire to them. Wind spread the fire to the supply warehouse. Forrest captured the Union gunboats but that evening withdrew to execute orders to cooperate with General Hood, who was in northern Alabama preparing to invade Tennessee.

The visitor center at the 2,000-acre Johnsonville State Park features exhibits and a film, two original earthen fortifications, and a reproduction of a Union soldier's hut.

LOCATION: **Johnsonville State Park, 90 Nell Beard Rd., New Johnsonville, 951-535-2789, www.tnstateparks.com.**

✳ Memphis I

CAMPAIGN: Joint Operations on the Middle Mississippi River
DATE(S): June 6, 1862

The position of Memphis on the Mississippi River made it important in the movement of supplies and warships south. On June 6, 1862, the Union flotilla, led by Flag Officer Davis, destroyed the Confederate river defense fleet in an hour and a half, capturing or sinking seven of eight Confederate boats and incurring only one Union casualty. Poor command structure on both sides and an assortment of vessels, some ill-equipped for war, contributed to the chaos and melee that characterized this battle. Ultimately, it resulted in the surrender of Memphis to the Union and left the Confederates without a significant naval presence on the Mississippi for the rest of the war.

LOCATION: **Marker located at the Memphis-Gateway-Shelby County Visitor Center, 12036 Arlington Trail, Arlington, 901-543-5333. Tennessee Civil War Trails includes four additional related sites (see p. 207).**

✳ Memphis II

CAMPAIGN: Forrest's Defense of Mississippi
DATE(S): August 21, 1864

The second event in Memphis was a night raid by General Forrest. He had three objectives for his raid: capture three Union generals, release Southern prisoners from Irving Block Prison, and recall Union troops from northern Mississippi. He failed at his first two objectives, narrowly missing the capture of General Washburn, who escaped wearing his nightshirt. But Forrest succeeded in drawing Union troops back to Memphis and away from Mississippi, allowing him to plan his raid on General Sherman's supply lines. And when he withdrew from Memphis after his two-hour, predawn raid, he cut telegraph wires and took 500 prisoners and a large quantity of supplies, including horses.

LOCATION: **Shelby County; no public access.**

General Forrest's night raid on Memphis was one of his many raids in the region.

✳ Mossy Creek

CAMPAIGN: Operations About Dandridge

DATE(S): December 29, 1863

In December 1863, Union troops set up their winter encampment at Mossy Creek. On learning that the Confederates had arrived at Dandridge, General Sturgis sent most of his troops there. Meanwhile, a Confederate cavalry unit led by General Martin attacked Sturgis's remaining garrison force at Mossy Creek. The early Confederate success turned into quite the opposite, however, when the main body of Federal troops returned and drove the Rebel forces away. The Union continued to hold the line around Talbott's Station.

LOCATION: **Marker located on E. Old Andrew Johnson Hwy., just south of Municipal Dr. in Jefferson City.**

✳ Murfreesboro I

CAMPAIGN: Confederate Heartland Offensive

DATE(S): July 13, 1862

In July 1862, General Forrest and Colonel Morgan, both Confederate cavalrymen, engaged in simultaneous raids to distract

Federal infantry. Of the two, Forrest's raid into the center of the old town of Murfreesboro proved more dramatic. There, he overran a Union hospital and forced the surrender of all the camps and sites under the command of General Crittenden. Next, the Confederates destroyed Union supplies and tore up railroad track. More important, this encounter set the stage for Confederate General Bragg's invasion of Kentucky and diverted Union forces from a drive toward Chattanooga.

LOCATION: **Stones River National Battlefield, 1563 N. Thompson Ln., Murfreesboro, 615-893-9501, www.nps.gov/stri. Also, several markers tell this story, including one near the pre–Civil War courthouse in Murfreesboro and five along US 70 S.**

✳ Murfreesboro II

CAMPAIGN: Franklin-Nashville Campaign

DATE(S): December 5–7, 1864

After his terrible loss at Franklin, General Hood dispatched an infantry division and General Forrest's cavalry to attack the Federal supply depot at Fort Rosecrans, outside present-day Murfreesboro. On the first day, two Union garrisons surrendered to

Forrest, and other Union soldiers retreated inside the fort. Fighting continued over the next few days as Confederate reinforcements arrived. In the end, though, the fighting along the Wilkinson Pike favored the Federals, and the Confederates fell back. Forrest continued to harass the Yankees and destroy railroad track and blockhouses, but, ultimately, this endeavor was just a minor Union irritation. A week later the entire Confederate army under General Hood was routed at the Battle of Nashville.

Part of the massive Fortress Rosecrans can be viewed today as part of Stones River National Battlefield.

LOCATION: **Stones River National Battlefield, 1563 N. Thompson Ln., Murfreesboro, 615-893-9501, www.nps.gov/stri.**

✳ Nashville

CAMPAIGN: Franklin-Nashville Campaign
DATE(S): December 15–16, 1864

After a devastating loss at Franklin (see pp. 190–191), General Hood and the Confederates pressed on toward Nashville, hoping a victory would force General Sherman out of Georgia. However, the Confederates were outnumbered from the start by almost two to one. Plus, the Union had been constructing defensive works around the city since 1862.

Hood's plan was to entrench and hope that General Thomas would attack. In an effort to lure Thomas's troops out of the city, Hood sent several brigades to attack the railroad between Nashville and Murfreesboro, and he sent General Forrest's cavalry to harass the Federal garrison in Murfreesboro. But Thomas patiently bided his time. A little too patiently for the Union High Command, who pushed for immediate action.

An ice storm and subzero temperatures had subsided by December 15, when the Union attacked. At the end of the first day, the Confederate right flank held, but the left flank had imploded. With a smaller battle line, Hood confidently fortified Shy's Hill

Confederate Martyr: Sam Davis

Sometimes called the "Boy Hero of the Confederacy," 21-year-old Sam Davis (1842–1863) was a Rebel scout working behind enemy lines when, in the fall of 1863, he was captured by Union soldiers near Minor Hill, Tennessee. Davis was found to be in possession of Union battle plans and other items intended for General Bragg. Although his captors offered to spare his life if he would reveal his network, the young man refused and was widely reported to have said to them, "If I had a thousand lives to live, I would give them all rather than betray a friend"— words reminiscent of Nathan Hale's during the Revolutionary War. Davis was executed, and his death became a rallying point for the Southern cause. His home in Smyrna, Tennessee, can be visited (see p. 211), and you can follow the Sam Davis Trail in Pulaski, Tennessee.

and Overton's Hill. But the next day, the Union took both hills, and Hood's army fled.

This, the culminating battle of Hood's 1864 Tennessee Campaign, resulted in the loss of 4,500 more Confederate soldiers and marked the end of the Army of Tennessee. It was also one of the most decisive battles in history, which ended with the Confederate forces, lucky to escape at all, retreating all the way to Mississippi. There, Hood resigned, and the Deep South was now left more open to the Union than ever before.

Little of the original battlefield remains in this urban area. However, the informative Battle of Nashville Driving Tour (see p. 206) can guide you to many sites of interest, such as Fort Negley, Shy's Hill, and Mount Olivet Cemetery. And don't miss the Tennessee State Museum (see p. 211).

LOCATION: **Davidson County; no public access.**

FURTHER READING

The Decisive Battle of Nashville
by Stanley F. Horn
A well-written, definitive volume on the Battle of Nashville

✳ Parker's Cross Roads

CAMPAIGN: Forrest's Expedition Into West Tennessee

DATE(S): December 31, 1862

General Forrest's West Tennessee raid against General Grant's supply lines was drawing to a conclusion, and General Sullivan wanted Forrest and his Confederate cavalry cut off from crossing the Tennessee River. Forrest and his men encountered Colonel Dunham and his Union soldiers at Parker's Cross Roads. The Confederate artillery gained an early advantage, and Forrest sent Dunham a demand for unconditional surrender. Dunham refused and was preparing his troops for the next attack when Colonel Fuller's Union brigade surprised the Confederates with an attack at their rear. Caught between two Union brigades, Forrest boldly ordered: "Charge 'em both ways." And they did. In fact, the Rebels repelled Fuller's troops and rushed past Dunham's, withdrawing south to Lexington and across the Tennessee River. Both sides claimed victory, but the Confederates are usually given the victory since they were able to escape what should have been the perfect trap.

The battlefield itself is bisected by I-40; however, it has been well preserved. You can walk more than two miles of paved walking trails with interpretive signs. To learn more about Forrest's earlier raids in the area, start at the Gibson County Courthouse in Trenton, Tennessee.

LOCATION: Parker's Crossroads Battlefield Visitor Center, 20945 Hwy. 22 N., Wildersville, 731-968-1191. For a brochure on hiking, biking, or the 10-mile self-guided driving tour, stop at the battlefield visitor center or visit www .parkerscrossroads.com. Gibson County Courthouse, 295 N. College St., Trenton, 731-855-7615.

Reenactors stand at the ready at Parker's Crossroads Battlefield.

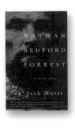

FURTHER READING

Nathan Bedford Forrest: A Biography
by Jack Hurst
Informative and anecdotal biography that not only humanizes this controversial figure but also is immensely readable

✳ Shiloh

CAMPAIGN: Federal Penetration up the Cumberland and Tennessee Rivers

DATE(S): April 6–7, 1862

Following the Union successes at Forts Donelson and Henry (see pp. 185–188), the

This monument at Shiloh National Military Park is one of many memorials there.

Union forces were able to penetrate Mississippi and Alabama. Soon the key railroad community of Corinth, Mississippi, came into sight. Initial efforts to enter Corinth failed, and Union troops under the overall command of General Sherman set up an unfortified position on the banks of the Tennessee River near a little wooden church called Shiloh, a Hebrew word meaning (ironically) "place for peace." They were waiting for General Buell's Army of Ohio before attacking Corinth. Meanwhile, 40,000 Confederates led by General Albert Sidney Johnston advanced, undetected, from Corinth to a position just two miles away.

Early on April 6, the Confederates attacked, surprising Sherman and his fellow Federals. A raging battle ensued. By afternoon, a battle line had been established near a sunken road that earned the name the Hornet's Nest, from the intensity of the fighting. While leading an attack, Johnston was unknowingly wounded behind his knee. Soon after, he swooned and fell from his horse, his boot filling with blood. He died on the battlefield. Though the Confederates

had been successful in moving back the Union line, they had begun the battle hungry and tired, and now were exhausted as the day's fighting petered out. Grant arrived on the field from Savannah and began to form a last line near the river. A miscommunication with Grant caused General Wallace to march by a different road and then countermarch to reach the battlefield late. Grant would have his revenge, and Wallace's military career was practically ended. A stormy night rolled in, causing both sides to hunker down and wait until morning. Meanwhile, thousands more Union troops arrived, including 15,000 commanded by Buell.

The Federals attacked early on April 7 and used their fresh troops to drive back the Confederate line. Now, they outnumbered the Rebels by about 10,000 soldiers. By afternoon, General Beauregard, now in command of the Confederates, determined that he could not win. Knowing they had already sustained massive casualties, he ordered a Confederate retreat and marched his troops south toward Corinth.

The next day, Union troops were ordered to pursue. At Fallen Timbers they ran into the Rebel rear guard under the command of General Forrest. Forrest's aggressive tactics persuaded the Union troops to quit their pursuit and return to Pittsburg Landing. Forrest himself was seriously wounded during this encounter; however, he went home to recover and was fighting again several weeks later.

With more than 100,000 troops engaged in the battle, and more than 23,000 total casualties, Shiloh was one of the biggest battles of the Civil War. And, for a time, it was also the bloodiest, until surpassed by Gettysburg (see pp. 352–357) a year later. While it was declared a Union victory, nothing substantial was earned for all the sacrifices made by both sides.

Stop at the visitor center in this rural area for the movie and excellent bookstore. The 12.7-mile driving tour around the 5,000-acre battlefield features 20 stops including the Hornet's Nest, Bloody Pond, and the Albert Sidney Johnston death site. Don't

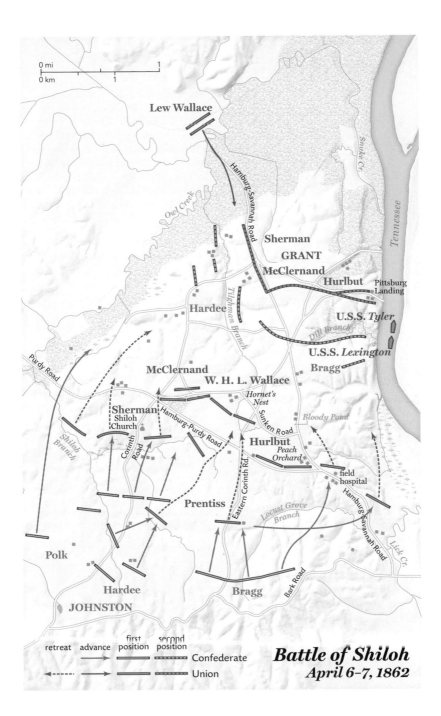

0 mi 1
0 km 1

Lew Wallace

Hamburg-Savannah Road

Owl Creek

Tennessee

Snake Cr.

Sherman
GRANT
McClernand

Hurlbut

Pittsburg
Landing

Tighman Branch

Hardee

U.S.S. Tyler

Dill Branch

U.S.S. Lexington

Purdy Road

McClernand

W. H. L. Wallace

*Hornet's
Nest*

Bragg

Bloody Pond

Shiloh
Branch

Sherman
Shiloh
Church

Hamburg-Purdy Road

Sunken Road

Corinth
Road

Hurlbut
*Peach
Orchard*

field
hospital

Eastern Corinth Rd.

Hamburg-Savannah Road

Prentiss

*Locust Grove
Branch*

Polk

Hardee
JOHNSTON

Bragg

Bark Road

Lick Cr.

retreat advance   first   second
                    position   position

Confederate

Union

Battle of Shiloh
April 6–7, 1862

The Dramatic Death of Van Dorn

In the spring of 1863, Earl Van Dorn (1820–1863), the handsome, blue-eyed Confederate general, was headquartered at the Martin Cheairs home, now known as Ferguson Hall, in Spring Hill. An amateur poet, dedicated romantic, and excellent horseman, Van Dorn was also a serial adulterer. While there, he carried on an affair with a beautiful, young married woman named Jessie Peters. On May 7 of that year, her angry husband, Dr. George Peters, entered the house and fatally shot Van Dorn in the head. That same night, Peters gave a complete confession to the police, but he was never prosecuted for the murder.

miss the cemetery and the walk down to the landing. Ranger-led programs and other events are seasonally available. The Corinth Civil War Interpretive Center, which is about a 22-mile drive from the Shiloh visitor center, is also part of the park and worth a visit.

LOCATION: **Shiloh National Military Park, 1055 Pittsburg Landing Rd., Shiloh, 731-689-5696, www.nps.gov/shil.**

FURTHER READING
Shadow of Shiloh: Major General Lew Wallace in the Civil War
by Gail Stephens
A biography of this fascinating, multifaceted American character with a spotlight on Shiloh

Shiloh, 1862
by Winston Groom
A thrilling narrative account of this unforgettable battle

✳ Spring Hill

CAMPAIGN: Franklin-Nashville Campaign
DATE(S): November 29, 1864

Late in November 1864, Confederate General Hood moved his army into Tennessee, making for the rear of the Union forces at Pulaski under General Schofield. As the Union troops fell back to Columbia, Hood bluffed in his front and moved around the east side of Columbia, crossing the Duck River. By November 29, Hood had a loose hold on the main transportation artery along Columbia Pike (US 31). Union soldiers successfully fought to hold open the road. Although more Confederates arrived on the field as the sun set, they failed to block the pike. During the night, with Confederate soldiers a stone's throw away, the Union troops escaped north toward Franklin, where they would have to cross the Harpeth River en route to Nashville. Severely disappointed, Hood ordered his army to pursue the fleeing Federals.

Today, visitors can still see Oaklawn, where Hood spent his evening, and tour Rippavilla Plantation (see p. 211), where General Hood gave out orders for the battle at Spring Hill. There is also a driving tour and a historic homes tour for Maury County and the city of Spring Hill.

LOCATION: **A walking tour with interpretative signs exists along Rally Hill Turnpike. Turn into the parking lot and enjoy a walk to overlook the scene of the Battle of Spring Hill. More interpretative markers are north on Rally Hill Turnpike and also at Rippavilla Plantation.**

FURTHER READING
Twenty-five Hours to Tragedy: The Battle of Spring Hill and Operations on November 29, 1864, Precursor to the Battle of Franklin
by Jamie Gillum
Eyewitness testimony linked by narrative outlines the tale of this blunder

✳ Stones River

CAMPAIGN: Stones River Campaign
DATE(S): December 31, 1862–January 2, 1863

December 1862 was disastrous for the Union cause: Fredericksburg (see pp. 237–242) had been devastating, and General Sherman had lost 1,775 men at Chickasaw Bayou (see p. 125). With the controversial Emancipation Proclamation set to take effect on January 1, military success was essential to avoid the perception of desperation. Lincoln needed a victory from General Rosecrans's Army of the Cumberland.

The Confederates struck at dawn on December 31, attacking while some Union soldiers were still in nightclothes cooking breakfast. They began driving the Union line back; however, brutal fighting in an area that soldiers dubbed the Slaughter Pen or Hell's Half Acre held off a further retreat. Scores of soldiers on both sides lost their lives here, and bodies quickly piled up. Meanwhile, Union reinforcements arrived, and Rosecrans repositioned his line along Nashville Pike. The battle ended at dusk on New Year's Eve, and both armies rested on January 1.

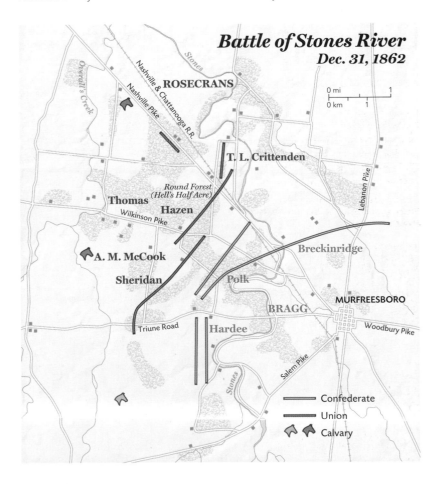

Battle of Stones River
Dec. 31, 1862

General Bragg had assumed the Union troops would retreat after December 31. Instead, they surprised him with a devastating attack on his right flank in the late afternoon of January 2. Bragg ordered his men to drive the Union troops across the Stones River. As the Confederates neared the river, however, they encountered a deadly surprise: Union Captain Mendenhall had 57 guns facing their approach. Within minutes, the Confederate charge had turned into a sad retreat.

One of the bloodiest battles of the war, the encounter at Stones River ended with more than 13,000 Union and more than 10,000 Confederate casualties. Bragg left Murfreesboro, and Rosecrans claimed Union victory. The rich farmland of Middle Tennessee would now feed Union soldiers.

Although the National Park Service has preserved only about a fifth of the original battle site as Stones River National Battlefield, the battlefield walking tour is nonetheless very good. You will also find a driving tour with historical markers and several other points of interest, including the Hazen Brigade Monument, the oldest intact Civil War memorial in the nation.

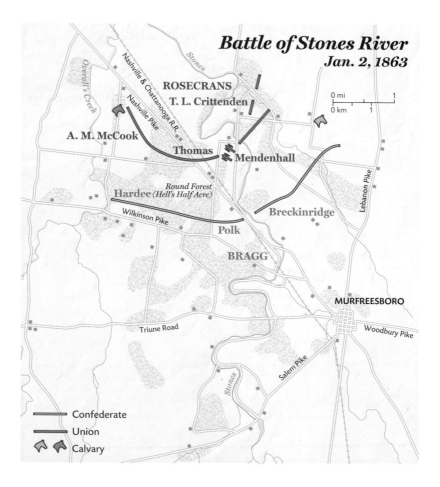

Battle of Stones River
Jan. 2, 1863

Overall's Creek

Stones

Nashville & Chattanooga R.R.

Nashville Pike

ROSECRANS
T. L. Crittenden

0 mi 1
0 km 1

A. M. McCook

Thomas

Mendenhall

Lebanon Pike

Round Forest
Hardee (*Hell's Half Acre*)

Wilkinson Pike

Breckinridge

Polk

BRAGG

MURFREESBORO

Triune Road

Woodbury Pike

Stones

Salem Pike

Confederate
Union
Calvary

LOCATION: **Stones River National Battlefield, 1563 N. Thompson Ln., Murfreesboro, 615-893-9501, www.nps.gov/stri.**

FURTHER READING

No Better Place to Die: The Battle of Stones River by Peter Cozzens
A detailed account of the late 1862 campaign and battle

✳ Thompson's Station

CAMPAIGN: Middle Tennessee Operations
DATE(S): March 5, 1863

There had been little activity in the war since the slaughter at Stones River (see pp. 203–205). On March 5, 1863, Colonel Coburn and his Union infantry brigade left Franklin to reconnoiter toward Columbia. About four miles north of Spring Hill, they attacked a Confederate force and were repelled. Next, Confederate General Jackson made a frontal attack on Coburn's troops while General Forrest's division attacked from the left and rear. After hours of hard fighting, Coburn ran out of ammunition and was completely surrounded. He surrendered himself and more than 1,000 troops. Thompson's Station was a major embarrassment for the Union Army.

LOCATION: **Markers located in Thompson's Station: one at the intersection of Thompson's Station Rd. W. and School St., and another on Columbia Pike (US 31) on the left when traveling north.**

✳ Vaught's Hill

CAMPAIGN: Middle Tennessee Operations
OTHER NAME(S): Milton
DATE(S): March 20, 1863

All day, a brigade of Union infantry under the command of Colonel Hall held off a Confederate cavalry attack led by General Morgan. The Confederates sustained heavy casualties and finally withdrew late in the afternoon, when Union reinforcements began to arrive from Murfreesboro. The Union forces continued to gather strength in Middle Tennessee.

LOCATION: **Marker located on Lascassas Pike, on the right when traveling north, near Milton.**

✳ Wauhatchie

CAMPAIGN: Reopening of the Tennessee River
DATE(S): October 28–29, 1863

Union forces had recently seized control of Brown's Ferry on the Tennessee River just west of Chattanooga. The site was an important part of the "Cracker Line," the essential Union supply route into Chattanooga. Union forces had secretly floated downriver and built a pontoon bridge, allowing their troops to cross and establish a strong defensive position.

The Confederates under General Jenkins attacked around midnight, though night attacks were rare and risky. The Union troops were well entrenched and reinforcements were already on the way. One of the few battles fought at night, Wauhatchie protected the newly won Cracker Line and cleared the way for the third battle of Chattanooga later that fall (see pp. 179–187).

LOCATION: **Marker located on Cummings Hwy. (US 11) on the left when traveling east in Tiftonia.**

Other Battles and Beyond

✦ Battle of Nashville Driving Tour

This free, 17-stop driving tour created by the Battle of Nashville Preservation Society is available at all tour stops and local tourism facilities in Nashville. Call 615-780-3636 to order a copy of the tour brochure, or download it at www.bonps.org. Guided tours are also available for a fee.

✦ Civil War Heritage Trail

Published by the Tennessee Wars Commission, the Civil War Heritage Trail includes 62 sites across the state. The trail, which is outlined in a free brochure titled "A Path Divided," identifies five themes: Invasion by River, Fight for West Tennessee, Contest for Middle Tennessee, East Tennessee's Mountain War, and Hood's Tennessee Campaign. The brochure is available at state welcome centers and online at www.tn.gov.

✦ From Bridge to Bridge

This driving tour covers 40 miles in East Tennessee and includes 23 stops, beginning with Strawberry Plains Bridge over the Holton River and ending at Lick Creek Bridge. The tour's theme is the fight for control of the critical East Tennessee & Virginia Railroad. To request a copy, contact the Rose Center Museum (442 W. 2nd North St., Morristown, 423-581-4330, www.rosecenter.org).

This drawing shows the first Union dress parade in Nashville, including the 51st Regiment Ohio volunteers, in March 1862.

✦ Tennessee Civil War National Heritage Area

Links to multiple driving tours can be found on this organization's site (www.tncivilwar .org), including the battles of Franklin, Cumberland Valley, and Collierville.

✦ Tennessee Civil War 150 Documentaries

Nashville Public Television and the Renaissance Center created this fascinating series of documentaries and short films focused on the human stories of the Civil War in Tennessee. A few of the topics included are faith, rivers and rails, and women. Visit www.nptinternal.org/productions/civilwar /home for more information.

✦ Tennessee Civil War Sesquicentennial

Created by the Tennessee Department of Tourist Development, the Tennessee Civil War Sesquicentennial website offers a wealth of information about the people, places, and artifacts of the war in the state, along with wonderful photos. Access it at www.tnvacation.com.

✦ Tennessee Civil War Trails

This excellent map-guide identifies more than 270 Civil War sites throughout the state. Part of a five-state trails system with more than 1,000 sites, it is available at any state welcome center, by calling 615-532-7520, and online at www.civilwartrails.org.

✦ Tullahoma Campaign Civil War Trail

With the help of a brochure, visitors can trace the Tullahoma Campaign. The 11-stop drive goes from Hoover's Gap to Sewanee and includes Fairfield, Wartrace, Bell Buckle Gap, Liberty Gap, Shelbyville, Tullahoma, Manchester, Winchester, and Cowan—a total of 130 miles. Call 800-799-6131.

View this restored bedroom at the Andrew Johnson National Historic Site in Greeneville.

✦ Andrew Johnson National Historic Site

Greeneville is the home of the 17th president, Andrew Johnson, who became president after Lincoln was assassinated (see sidebar p. 177). Visit the museum and original tailor shop in the visitor center, then see the early home, the homestead, and the cemetery where he is buried.

LOCATION. 101 N. College St., Greeneville, 423-638-3551, www.nps.gov/anjo.

✦ Britton's Lane

On September 1, 1862, near the village of Denmark, a Confederate cavalry brigade commanded by General Armstrong carried out a raid on a Federal force of cavalry, infantry, and artillery commanded by Colonel Elias S. Dennis. The result was the capture of 213 prisoners, a large Union wagon train, and two pieces of artillery. Eighty-seven of these Union soldiers were imprisoned in the Denmark Presbyterian Church, where their graffiti can still be seen. Maintained by the Britton Lane Battlefield Association, this battlefield includes interpretive signs.

LOCATION: Britton Lane Battlefield, 4707 Steam Mill Ferry Rd., Medon, 731-989-7944, www.brittonlane1862.madison.tn.us.

Reenactors gather outside Carnton Plantation in Franklin, near where some of the bloodiest fighting of the Civil War took place, around Carter House and Lewisburg Pike.

✦ Carnton Plantation

This plantation home served as a temporary field hospital for hundreds of Confederate soldiers wounded in the bloody Battle of Franklin (see pp. 190–193), which raged right outside. Upstairs rooms served as operating rooms, and bloodstains can still be seen on the wooden floors. The bodies of four Confederate generals were laid out on the back porch. Adjacent to Carnton is the McGavock Confederate Cemetery, where 1,481 Confederate soldiers are buried.

LOCATION: **1345 Eastern Flank Cir., Franklin, 615-794-0903, www.boft.org.**

✦ Carter House

Before the Battle of Franklin began, Union General Cox used the parlor here as headquarters. Later, this brick house became the battle epicenter, with thousands of soldiers clashing all around it. The morning after the battle, the Carters' son, Tod Carter, was found mortally wounded in the yard. Still scarred by more than 1,000 bullet holes, the house offers daily, guided tours. See pages 192–193 for more information.

LOCATION: **1140 Columbia Ave., Franklin, 615-791-1861, www.boft.org.**

✦ Chattanooga National Cemetery

This 75-acre cemetery contains three significant monuments and is the burial site for nearly 13,000 Civil War soldiers. Don't miss the memorial to Andrews' Raiders, who inspired the establishment of the Congressional Medal of Honor and were commemorated in the 1956 movie *The Great Locomotive Chase*.

LOCATION: **1200 Bailey Ave., Chattanooga, 423-855-6590, www.cem.va.gov.**

✦ Confederate Memorial Hall (Bleak House)

This antebellum mansion served as headquarters for Confederate General Longstreet during the siege of Knoxville. A Union cannon took out the tower, killing three Confederate sharpshooters. Bloodstains remain, and two cannonballs are still embedded in the walls. Today, it is owned by the United Daughters of the Confederacy and guided tours are available on a somewhat limited basis.

LOCATION: **3148 Kingston Pike, Knoxville, 865-522-2371.**

✦ Dickson-Williams Mansion

This Federal-style mansion hosted many famous guests, including three presidents, the Marquis de Lafayette, and Davy Crockett. It served as headquarters for both Confederate and Union officers when they were in Greeneville. Union General Morgan spent his last night here before being ambushed in the garden.

LOCATION: **108 N. Irish St., Greeneville, 423-787-0500.**

✦ Dover Hotel

On the banks of the Cumberland River, this historic hotel was the site of the Confederate headquarters where General Grant's demand for the "unconditional and immediate surrender" of Fort Donelson was received (see pp. 185–187). An exhibit room and the grounds are open to the public. A living history movie dramatizes the Confederate commander's debate.

LOCATION: **101 Petty St., Dover, 931-232-5706, www.nps.gov/fodo.**

✦ Farragut Folklife Museum

A highlight of this free museum is a collection of items pertaining to Admiral David Glasgow Farragut (see sidebar p. 178), hero of the battles of New Orleans and Mobile Bay. Items include personal china, letters, family photographs, and uniform ornamentation. A map of the Battle of Campbell's Station (see p. 178) is also on display. And don't miss Farragut Memorial Plaza, which is located right outside the museum.

LOCATION: **Farragut Town Hall, 11408 Municipal Center Dr., Farragut, 865-966-7057, www.townoffarragut.org.**

✦ Ferguson Hall (Martin Cheairs House)

Built in 1853, this high-ceilinged, white-columned antebellum house in Spring Hill was the site of the sensational murder of Confederate General Van Dorn (see sidebar p. 202). Its construction inspired the Rippavilla Plantation (see p. 211), which was owned by Martin Cheairs's brother. Van Dorn's room is currently being refurbished to its original state. Tours are available.

LOCATION: **Hwy. 31, Spring Hill, 931-486-2274. Visit www.antebellum.com for printed brochures about numerous antebellum sites and the Battle of Spring Hill.**

Scarred by more than 1,000 bullets, the Carter House stands as a silent witness.

✦ Forrest Park

The legendary General Forrest and his wife are buried here beneath a majestic equestrian statue honoring him.

LOCATION: **Union Ave. and S. Dunlap St., Memphis, 901-636-4200, www.tnstateparks .com/parks/about/nathan-bedford-forrest.**

✦ General Longstreet Headquarters Museum

Originally the Nenney family home, the building served as the headquarters of General Longstreet during the unusually cold winter of 1863–1864. Enjoy a guided house tour or the annual Civil War Christmas celebration.

LOCATION: **5915 E. Andrew Johnson Hwy. (US 11E), Russellville, 423-438-0968, www .longstreetmuseum.com.**

✦ Hunt-Phelan Home

The oldest home in Memphis, the Hunt-Phelan Home served as a headquarters for General Polk as he planned for the Battle of Corinth (see pp. 126–127) and for General Grant as he planned for Vicksburg (see p. 136). Later, it became a Union hospital.

LOCATION: **533 Beale St., Memphis, 901-786-8801, www.civilwartraveler.com/WEST/ TN/W-Memphis.html.**

✦ Mabry-Hazen House and Bethel Cemetery

Located on the highest hill in downtown Knoxville, this house hosted soldiers from both sides during the war. Guided tours include more than 2,000 family artifacts and a nice Civil War display. It's best to call in advance. The nearby Bethel Cemetery is the burial site of more than 1,600 Confederate and 50 Union soldiers killed during the Battle of Fort Sanders.

LOCATION: **1711 Dandridge Ave., Knoxville, 865-522-8661, www.mabryhazen.com.**

✦ McClung Museum of Natural History and Culture

The collection at this University of Tennessee museum is anchored by a 3-D topographic re-creation of an 1864 map of the defenses of Knoxville and includes an engaging 28-minute video. Other museum highlights include a drum found in Longstreet's camp and the original pardon written by President Andrew Johnson for Frank H. McClung.

LOCATION: **1327 Circle Park Dr., Knoxville, 865-974-2144, mcclungmuseum.utk.edu.**

✦ Memphis National Cemetery

Nearly 14,000 Civil War soldiers are buried here, including many of those killed in the 1865 *Sultana* riverboat disaster, in which hundreds of former prisoners from Southern camps perished.

LOCATION: **3568 Townes Ave., Memphis, 901-386-8311, www.cem.va.gov.**

FURTHER READING

Disaster on the Mississippi: The* Sultana *Explosion, April 27, 1865 by Gene Eric Salecker An exploration of the worst maritime disaster in U.S. history as seen through the eyes of survivors and rescuers

✦ Mississippi River Museum at Mud Island

Five galleries in this museum—which showcases 10,000 years of history in the Lower Mississippi River Valley—are devoted to events of the Civil War. Check out the simulated battle between a gunboat and a river battery (very near where a real one happened) and a reproduction of the front third of a Union gunboat.

LOCATION: **125 N. Front St., Memphis, 901-576-7232, www.mudisland.com.**

✦ Museum of East Tennessee History

The permanent collection includes items from both Confederate and Union Armies and deals frankly with the dilemma faced by loyal U.S. citizens in that area of the country.

LOCATION: **601 S. Gay St., Knoxville, 865-215-8830, www.easttnhistory.org.**

✦ Oaklands Historic House Museum

Both Union and Confederate officers stayed in this Italianate mansion, but the most famous guest was Confederate President Jefferson Davis in 1862. Inside, the Confederates accepted the surrender of Murfreesboro (see pp. 197–198). The museum offers guided tours.

LOCATION: **900 N. Maney Ave., Murfreesboro, 615-893-0022, www.oaklandsmuseum.org.**

✦ Rippavilla Plantation

Built in 1855, this plantation home was originally owned by the Nathaniel Cheairs family.

On a guided tour you can see family artifacts and an assortment of Civil War weaponry.

LOCATION: **Rte. 31N, just south of Spring Hill, 931-486-9037, www.rippavilla.org.**

✦ Sam Davis Home

This beautiful 168-acre plantation home was once the home of Sam Davis, who was captured and executed as a Confederate spy (see sidebar p. 198). See a film, visit the museum, and take a guided tour.

LOCATION: **1399 Sam Davis Rd., Smyrna, 615-459-2341, www.samdavishome.org.**

✦ Tennessee State Museum

A large section of this museum is dedicated to the role of the Volunteer State in the Civil War. Collection highlights include: a hand-drawn map of the Shiloh battlefield, Nathan Bedford Forrest's revolver, and Sam Davis's boot, slashed by Union troops in their search for hidden papers.

LOCATION: **505 Deaderick St., Nashville, 615-741-2692, www.tnmuseum.org.**

The plantation home Rippavilla was built by Nathaniel Cheairs and his wife, Susan, in Spring Hill. It was completed in 1855 and can be visited today.

Virginia

NO OTHER STATE WAS AS VITAL TO THE CONFEDERACY AS Virginia. With the South's largest population, the Confederacy's capital and most industrialized city, and a vulnerable border along the Potomac River, the Old Dominion experienced more major battles and engagements than any other state.

Although Virginia initially voted against joining the Deep South states in rebellion, that changed after Fort Sumter, when Lincoln demanded Virginians mobilize to help restore order in their sister slave states. For Southern strategists, Virginia was the ideological linchpin of a new slave nation, with a symbolic connection to the founding fathers Jefferson, Madison, Monroe, and Washington that Southern fire-eaters mistakenly believed would foster widespread acceptance of this Second War of Independence.

Today, Virginia is home to a vast number of key Civil War battlegrounds and other sites that have been preserved and opened to visitors—from the first major battle at Manassas to its effective end with the surrender of Lee at Appomattox.

Robert E. Lee on his beloved horse, Traveler, surveys Gettysburg from the Virginia monument, the largest of the battlefield's Confederate monuments.

VIRGINIA BATTLES

1 Cedar Creek
  Fisher's Hill
  Tom's Brook
2 Guard Hill
3 Front Royal
4 Upperville
5 Manassas Gap
6 Aldie
  Middleburg
7 Dranesville
8 Chantilly
9 Thoroughfare Gap
10 Buckland Mills
11 Bristoe Station
12 Blackburn's Ford
  Manassas I
  Manassas II
  Manassas Station Operations
13 Rappahannock Station II
14 Brandy Station
  Kelly's Ford
  Rappahannock Station I
15 Auburn I
  Auburn II
16 Aquia Creek
17 Chancellorsville
  Fredericksburg I
  Salem Church
18 Mine Run
  Morton's Ford
19 Cross Keys
  Port Republic
20 Wilderness
21 Fredericksburg II
22 Trevilian Station
23 Hanover Court House
24 Haw's Shop
25 Totopotomoy Creek/Bethesda Church
  Beaver Dam Creek
26 Chaffin's Farm & New Market Heights
  Darbytown & New Market Roads
  Yellow Tavern
  Old Church
27 Cold Harbor
28 Gaines' Mill
  Mantapike Hill (Walkerton)
29 Garnett's & Golding's Farms
30 Oak Grove
  Savage's Station
  Seven Pines
  Glendale/White Oak Swamp
31 Saint Mary's Church
  Darbytown Road
32 Drewry's Bluff
  Proctor's Creek
33 Amelia Springs

34 Cumberland Church
35 High Bridge
36 Rice's Station
  Sayler's Creek
37 Namozine Church
38 Chester Station
  Swift Creek
39 Deep Bottom I
  Deep Bottom II
  Fair Oaks & Darbytown Road
  Ware Bottom Church
40 Fort Stedman
  Petersburg III
  Port Walthall Junction
41 Wilson's Wharf
42 Five Forks
  Globe Tavern
  Hatcher's Run
  Lewis's Farm
  Peebles' Farm
  Sutherland's Station
  White Oak Road
43 Boydton Plank Road
  The Crater
  Dinwiddie Court House
  Petersburg I
  Petersburg II
  Ream's Station I
  Ream's Station II
  Jerusalem Plank Road
44 Williamsburg
45 Yorktown
46 Big Bethel
47 Hampton Roads
48 Sappony Church
49 Hill's Point/Suffolk
  Norfleet House/Suffolk

Pa.

Ohio

West Virginia
see page 310

McDowell—

0 mi   50
0 km   50

Hot Springs

After Virginia seceded from the Union in 1861, the
northwestern part of the state then separated from
Virginia. It was admitted to the Union as the new
state of West Virginia in 1863.

Ky.

Buchanan
Peaks of Otter □

Hanging Rock

Bedford
Liberty

Cloyd's Mountain ✳

✳ Cove Mountain

Museum of the
Middle Appalachians □   Saltville II
Saltville I ✳✳   ✳ Marion

Martha Washington Inn □

□ Laurel Hill

Tenn.

✵Aldie

CAMPAIGN: Gettysburg Campaign

DATE(S): June 17, 1863

After Lee's decisive victory at Chancellorsville (see pp. 224–227), he led his army north through the Blue Ridge, screened by J. E. B. Stuart's cavalry. With concern over Lee's intentions, Federal cavalry under General Pleasonton were instructed to gain intelligence at any cost. Aldie's strategic location at the junction of two roads led to an indecisive confrontation after several cavalry attacks by both sides. Today, the town features more than 400 acres of preserved battlefield, an antebellum mill, and multiple battlefield markers and monuments.

LOCATION: Marker and a monument to the 1st Massachusetts located on Snickersville Tpke., just over a mile north of Rte. 50. There are additional battlefield markers along Rte. 50 in Aldie and in the parking lot of the historic mill at 39401 John Mosby Hwy., Aldie.

✵Amelia Springs

CAMPAIGN: Appomattox Campaign

DATE(S): April 5, 1865

Early on April 5, 1865, Union cavalry encountered a Confederate wagon train filled with much needed food supplies. In the ensuing fight, they destroyed about 200 wagons and captured nearly 600 soldiers and teamsters. Cavalry sent by General Lee to repair the damage failed. Robbed of

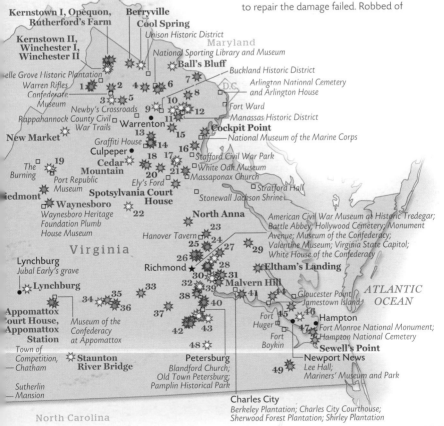

Kernstown I, Opequon, Rutherford's Farm

Berryville

Kernstown II, Winchester I, Winchester II

Cool Spring

Unison Historic District

Maryland

Belle Grove Historic Plantation

National Sporting Library and Museum

Warren Rifles Confederate Museum

Ball's Bluff

Buckland Historic District

Newby's Crossroads

Arlington National Cemetery and Arlington House

Rappahannock County Civil War Trails

Warrenton

Fort Ward

Manassas Historic District

New Market

Graffiti House

Cockpit Point

Culpeper

National Museum of the Marine Corps

The Burning

Cedar Mountain

Stafford Civil War Park

White Oak Museum

Port Republic Museum

Ely's Ford

Massaponax Church

Piedmont

Spotsylvania Court House

Stratford Hall

Waynesboro

Stonewall Jackson Shrine

Waynesboro Heritage Foundation Plumb House Museum

North Anna

American Civil War Museum at Historic Tredegar; Battle Abbey; Hollywood Cemetery; Monument Avenue; Museum of the Confederacy; Valentine Museum; Virginia State Capitol; White House of the Confederacy

Hanover Tavern

Virginia

Lynchburg

Jubal Early's grave

Richmond

Eltham's Landing

Lynchburg

Malvern Hill

ATLANTIC OCEAN

Appomattox Court House, Appomattox Station

Museum of the Confederacy at Appomattox

Gloucester Point

Jamestown Island

Fort Huger

Hampton

Town of Competition, —Chatham

Staunton River Bridge

Fort Boykin

Fort Monroe National Monument; Hampton National Cemetery

Sewell's Point

Sutherlin —Mansion

Petersburg

Blandford Church; Old Town Petersburg; Pamplin Historical Park

Newport News

Lee Hall; Mariners' Museum and Park

North Carolina

Charles City

Berkeley Plantation; Charles City Courthouse; Sherwood Forest Plantation; Shirley Plantation

irreplaceable transportation for his supplies, Lee moved on to Jetersville.

LOCATION: Marker located 3 miles north of Jetersville on Amelia Springs Rd. Enjoy a great meal at Hatcher's Dining, 16420 Court St., Amelia Court House.

✳ Appomattox Court House

CAMPAIGN: Appomattox Campaign

DATE(S): April 9, 1865

After a final, desperate attempt to break through the Union lines, General Lee ran out of options. Although he claimed he "would rather die a thousand deaths" than surrender, his 27,000 men were hungry, outnumbered, and nearly encircled. Given famously lenient terms, the Confederate forces were saluted and fed by Union troops, who only days before had been their sworn enemy.

A re-created village contains the McLean House. Here Lee surrendered his army to General Grant. The site also includes a walking trail, a theater showing two movies, a museum with original artifacts, and many buildings accessible to the public. Don't miss the Museum of the Confederacy at Appomattox (see p. 303).

LOCATION: Appomattox Court House National Historical Park, 111 National Park Dr., Appomattox, 434-352-8987, www.nps.gov /apco. If using GPS, specify "Appomattox Courthouse Historical Park" to avoid visiting today's nearby courthouse by mistake.

FURTHER READING

A Stillness at Appomattox
by Bruce Catton
A moving account of the end of the war and Lee's surrender

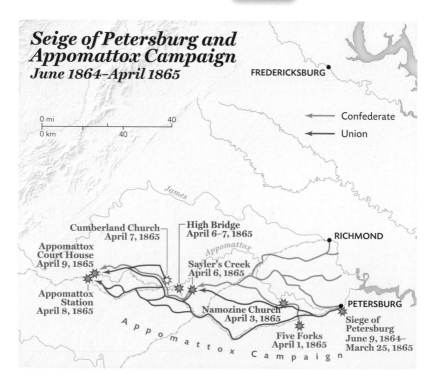

Seige of Petersburg and Appomattox Campaign
June 1864–April 1865

FREDERICKSBURG

0 mi — 40
0 km — 40

← Confederate
← Union

James

Cumberland Church
April 7, 1865

High Bridge
April 6–7, 1865

RICHMOND

Appomattox
Court House
April 9, 1865

Appomattox

Sayler's Creek
April 6, 1865

Appomattox
Station
April 8, 1865

Namozine Church
April 3, 1865

PETERSBURG

Five Forks
April 1, 1865

Siege of
Petersburg
June 9, 1864–
March 25, 1865

Appomattox Campaign

✳ Appomattox Station

CAMPAIGN: Appomattox Campaign

DATE(S): April 8, 1865

Although Lee believed his night marches had outpaced pursuing Union forces, cavalry under General Custer struck Confederate artillerymen at Appomattox Station, burning three trains of desperately needed rations and closing off a potential escape route. Most important, this action further reduced the options for General Lee, leading first to his final breakout attempt the next day, and soon thereafter to surrender.

There is a postwar train station, now a visitor center, with a marker commemorating the battle and additional markers in Appomattox Court House National Historical Park.

LOCATION: Visitor center and marker located at the intersection of Church St. and Main St. in Appomattox. Additional markers on Old Courthouse Rd., at the western end of Appomattox Court House National Historical Park (see p. 216).

✵ Aquia Creek

CAMPAIGN: Blockade of the Chesapeake Bay

DATE(S): May 29–June 1, 1861

Early in the war, Union ships traded fire here with Confederate cannons, whose position on the Potomac enabled the Rebels to attack boat traffic, albeit to little practical effect. After the Confederates withdrew in 1862, Aquia Creek's strategic location as the northern terminus of the important Richmond, Fredericksburg & Potomac River Railroad made it valuable as a Union supply depot. This region was the staging area for a number of Federal operations including Fredericksburg and Chancellorsville, and served as a camp for the Union Army in the winter of 1862–1863. Notably, more than 10,000 slaves escaped to freedom through this area.

There are multiple markers in Aquia Landing Park and a museum nearby.

LOCATION: Aquia Landing Park, 2846 Brooke Rd., Aquia, 540-658-5019.

Ulysses S. Grant sat in this chair while accepting Lee's surrender at Appomattox.

✴Auburn I

CAMPAIGN: Bristoe Campaign
DATE(S): October 13, 1863

Sent by General Lee on a scouting mission, General Stuart's cavalry inadvertently entered a gap in the Union Army, itself an accident caused by General Meade's order to change direction. After a minor skirmish, the Rebels realized they were trapped between Union columns. Stuart sent couriers dressed in Union uniforms asking Lee for help. The Confederates spent a tense, sleepless night hidden in a wooded ravine less than half a mile from the camping Federals.

LOCATION: Marker located on Old Dumfries Rd. less than a mile north of the intersection with Longwood Ln. and nearly 4 miles north of the intersection with Catlett Rd. in Catlett.

✴Auburn II

CAMPAIGN: Bristoe Campaign
DATE(S): October 14, 1863

General Stuart's cavalry, trapped by Union forces, staged an early-morning attack to break out. Unaware, Union General Caldwell's men were making breakfast and brewing coffee when Rebel artillery opened fire. The site has been known as Coffee Hill, for all the hastily spilled coffee, ever since. Despite the initial confusion, Union forces repulsed Stuart's initial attack. Nevertheless,

---

The "Ride Around McClellan"

J. E. B. Stuart made his reputation with a daring three-day ride around McClellan's army in June 1862, suffering only one casualty. In the process, he captured more than 150 Union prisoners and gathered important intelligence that enabled Lee to plan the destruction of the larger Union Army in the Seven Days Battles. Stuart received high praise in the Confederate press for this innovative and bold mission.

Stuart's cavalry broke through the Federal lines, escaping their precarious position of the previous night.

LOCATION: Marker located at the intersection of Old Auburn Rd. and Rogues Rd., nearly 4 miles east of the Fauquier County Fairgrounds off Rte. 29 in Warrenton.

✴ Ball's Bluff

CAMPAIGN: McClellan's Operations in Northern Virginia
DATE(S): October 21, 1861

After a patrol mistook a line of trees for an unguarded Confederate camp, General Stone ordered a Union assault against the "Rebels" the next morning. This farcical assault on a nonexistent camp became a tragedy when real Confederates appeared nearby and routed the hapless Federals, driving many into the Potomac River. Lincoln's friend, Senator Edward Baker, an army colonel, was killed—the only sitting U.S. senator to die in the war. Although minor in military significance, this battle led to the creation of a highly politicized and meddlesome congressional committee to oversee the war.

The preserved battlefield and cemetery include walking trails, guided tours, and many interpretive signs.

LOCATION: Ball's Bluff Battlefield Regional Park, east end of Ball's Bluff Rd. outside Leesburg, off US 15, 703-737-7800.

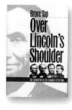

FURTHER READING

Over Lincoln's Shoulder
by Bruce Tapp
A look at the controversial oversight committee

✴ Beaver Dam Creek

CAMPAIGN: Peninsula Campaign
DATE(S): June 26, 1862

With McClellan's Army of the Potomac within sight of Richmond's church spires,

Two soldiers earned the Medal of Honor for refusing to retreat at Blackburn's Ford.

Lee took the offensive. Vastly outnumbered, Lee nevertheless created a masterful plan: In placing the majority of his army on his left, he intended to destroy the isolated Federal V Corps under General Porter. The plan promptly fell apart when Stonewall Jackson's troops failed to arrive on time and an impatient General A. P. Hill initiated the attack without his support. Although the Confederates suffered many more casualties, McClellan ordered Porter to fall back, ceding ground to Lee.

See multiple markers and walking trail at the preserved battlefield site.

LOCATION: Richmond National Battlefield Park, 7423 Cold Harbor Rd., Mechanicsville, 804-226-1981, nps.gov/rich.

❋ Berryville

CAMPAIGN: Sheridan's Valley Campaign
DATE(S): September 3–4, 1864

Given orders to crush Confederate General Early and lay waste to the fertile Shenandoah Valley, General Sheridan sparred with a small Confederate force at Berryville.

Early prepared for a counterattack the next morning, only to find the Federals dug in behind eight miles of earthworks, leading to a Rebel withdrawal.

LOCATION: Two markers located across from Clarke County High School on W. Main St., Berryville. Marker about Lee's famous horse, Traveller, on N. Church St. by Clarke County General District Court.

❋ Big Bethel

CAMPAIGN: Blockade of the Chesapeake Bay
DATE(S): June 10, 1861

Although merely a skirmish by later standards, this battle is usually considered the first land battle of the Civil War. Union forces under militia General Pierce initially ran into each other, alerting the Confederates to their approach. The Confederates manned the defenses near Big Bethel Church, holding off a subsequent attack.

Although much of the battlefield lies underwater today, there are multiple signs in Bethel Park, as well as a small monument to 19-year-old Henry Wyatt of the 1st North

Carolina Infantry, the first Confederate private killed in combat.

LOCATION: **Rightmost portion of Bethel Park, 123 Saunders Rd., Hampton, 757-766-3017. There is also an obelisk on Big Bethel Rd. just north of the park.**

✷ Blackburn's Ford

CAMPAIGN: Manassas Campaign

DATE(S): July 18, 1861

A few days before the first battle of Manassas (see pp. 254–256), Union reconnaissance under General Erastus Tyler and Colonel Isaac Richardson decided to test a Rebel position at Blackburn's Ford. After artillery fire and an inconclusive infantry engagement, the Federals retreated, handing the South a small victory. This area also saw action during the first battle of Manassas when General Jones's troops attempted to flank Northern forces.

LOCATION: **Two markers located just off southbound Centreville Rd., immediately before the bridge over Bull Run.**

✷ Boydton Plank Road

CAMPAIGN: Richmond-Petersburg Campaign

DATE(S): October 27–28, 1864

In an attempt to cut Southern supply routes, General Hancock ordered an assault on Boydton Plank Road and the Southside Railroad. After initially occupying the road, the Federals retreated in the face of a Confederate counterattack. Made of wood planks, Boydton Plank Road was an important all-weather route. By expediting the movement of crops to market, this 73-mile road helped increase southern Virginia's crop revenues by up to 100 percent.

LOCATION: **Marker located less than half a mile north of the intersection of Boydton Plank Rd. and White Oak Rd., Petersburg.**

Although famous as a cavalry battle, several thousand infantry fought at Brandy Station.

Jubal A. Early

Although born into a plantation family, Jubal Early (1816–1894) stridently lobbied for Virginia to stay in the Union. When Virginia left, however, Early, like Lee, under whom he served for much of the war, remained loyal to his home state. Despite his legal training, he fought in many battles in the eastern theater. After taking independent command, Early reached Washington in July 1864 only to be defeated. After the war, he fled to Mexico. An influential writer, Early—whom Lee affectionately called his "bad old man"—was the father of the "Lost Cause" movement.

❖ Brandy Station

CAMPAIGN: Gettysburg Campaign
DATE(S): June 9, 1863

Following a grand review of Confederate cavalry by General Lee, and after the lead elements of his army had started northward on a raid into Pennsylvania, a dawn attack by General Pleasonton's Union cavalry took J. E. B. Stuart's Confederate cavalry by surprise, leading to a dramatic—but ultimately inconclusive—all-day back-and-forth battle.

Brandy Station was the largest cavalry engagement of the war and the end of Confederate cavalry dominance in the eastern theater. It became personal for Lee when his son, cavalry brigade commander W. H. F. "Rooney" Lee, was wounded.

Although Union cavalry did not uncover the secret movement of Lee's infantry toward the Shenandoah Valley, this battle was an important boost to Federal cavalry morale. From then on, they knew they could meet the Southerners on equal terms.

Today, there is a driving tour (see p. 295) and a partially preserved, although wooded, battlefield. The antebellum Graffiti House (see p. 300) holds a wealth of information about the battle. And recently, Fleetwood

Hill, a key location on the battlefield, was restored to its wartime appearance.

LOCATION: Brandy Station Battlefield Park and multiple markers located just after the intersection of St. James Church Rd. and Beverly Ford Rd. and directly across from Culpeper Regional Airport.

FURTHER READING

Brandy Station, 1863: First Step Towards Gettysburg
by Dan Beattie
An illustrated guide to the seminal cavalry battle of the war

✳ Bristoe Station

CAMPAIGN: Bristoe Campaign
DATE(S): October 14, 1863

As General Meade withdrew toward Washington, D.C., General A. P. Hill's corps attacked the retreating Union rear without proper reconnaissance. This mistake cost them dearly as General Warren's V corps were hidden behind a nearby railroad embankment to the right, which protected Union forces. Struck by a surprise volley of fire, the Rebels "fell thick as leaves," according to a soldier who witnessed the battle. The Confederates lost around 1,300 men and five valuable cannons, while the North suffered about 500 casualties. This fiasco was widely criticized in the South, including by Jefferson Davis. General Lee is said to have told Hill to "bury these poor men, and let us say no more about it."

The battleground is now part of a pleasant country park that boasts more than two miles of walking and

This sword was used by Surgeon General Thomas Lawson Barraud, killed at Bristoe Station.

equestrian trails, informative brochures, and many interpretive markers.

LOCATION: **Bristoe Station Battlefield Heritage Park, 10708 Bristow Rd., Bristow, 703-792-4754.**

✳ Buckland Mills

CAMPAIGN: Bristoe Campaign

DATE(S): October 19, 1863

As J. E. B. Stuart's cavalry shielded Lee's retreating army, General Kilpatrick's Union cavalry trailed, looking for an opening. General Custer was surprised by Fitzhugh Lee's sudden assault from the south, driving them back on a cavalry chase known to the victorious Confederates as the Buckland

Early's defeat at Cedar Creek destroyed Confederate capabilities in the valley.

Races. This, the last large Confederate cavalry victory in Virginia, was a humiliating defeat for Custer, who called it "the most disastrous this division ever passed through."

Today, there are several markers and a preserved historic village, the Buckland Historic District (see p. 297).

LOCATION: **Marker located near the intersection of Rte. 29 and Buckland Mill Rd.**

✳ Cedar Creek

CAMPAIGN: Sheridan's Valley Campaign

DATE(S): October 19, 1864

Shielded by the Blue Ridge Mountains, the Shenandoah Valley had long been used by the Confederacy as a supply source and avenue to attack the North. Determined to put an end to this, Union General Sheridan led an army of more than 30,000 men on a trail of destruction, destroying the "Breadbasket of the Confederacy." Yet General Early was not ready to give up without a fight. His ragged army of 15,000 attacked Union positions at Cedar Creek, routing the Federal forces, capturing more than 1,000 prisoners, and taking much needed supplies.

Initially unaware of his army's rout at the hands of a much weaker foe, Sheridan rode in from Winchester, rallied his troops, and ordered them to prepare a counterattack. At 4 p.m., the Federals attacked, driving the

George Armstrong Custer

Famous for his 1876 death at the Battle of Little Big Horn—known as Custer's Last Stand—Custer (1839–1876) also played an important role in the Civil War. Flamboyant in both the risks he took and the clothes he wore, Custer, a brash officer, gained quick promotions and distinguished himself throughout the war, playing an important role at crucial junctions in the conflict. In the Battle of Gettysburg, he prevented J. E. B. Stuart from attacking the Union rear, while he was also responsible for cutting off Lee's last possible escape route at Appomattox. The seeds of Little Big Horn could be seen during the Civil War in several instances when his forces could have, and should have, been annihilated.

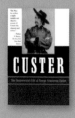

FURTHER READING

Custer: The Controversial Life of George Armstrong Custer by Jeffry D. Wert Definitive account of this quixotic soldier

John Singleton Mosby

Legendary as the "Gray Ghost" for his ability to strike Union forces then fade into the country-side, John Singleton Mosby (1833–1916) was one of the most pursued Confederate officers of the war. While he actively opposed secession, once Virginia left the Union, Mosby enlisted in the Confederate army. In 1863, he took command of the 43rd Virginia Partisan Rangers, whose missions included raids behind enemy lines, kidnapping key officials, and intercepting intelligence dis-patches—each mission had the death penalty as a reward if he or his men were captured. Once, Mosby cap-tured a sleeping Union brigadier general, woke him up, and asked him if he had heard of Mosby. "Yes! Have you got the rascal?" the Union com-mander responded. Mosby replied, "No, he's got you!" So powerful and feared were Mosby's Raiders that the area he operated in was known as Mosby's Confederacy. Almost as remarkable as his wartime exploits was his postwar conversion to the Republican Party, where Mosby not only became Grant's personal friend but also helped chair his election campaign in Virginia.

Confederates from their lines north of Middletown and dealing the final blow to Early's army. Sheridan called it "a victory turned from disaster."

Today, Cedar Creek features more than 1,500 acres of preserved land, although it is broken up by private property. There is a self-guided driving tour (see p. 295), battle apps available for download, and multiple markers and monuments. Start at the visitor center to understand the many ways to experience this magnificent park. Don't miss the nearby antebellum Belle Grove Historic Plantation (see p. 296) or the XIX Corps trench lines marked with interpretative signs—ask at the park visitor center or at the Cedar Creek Foundation visitor center. A reenactment on the grounds of the actual battle is held every October.

LOCATION: Cedar Creek and Belle Grove National Historical Park, 7712 Main St., Middletown, 540-869-3051, www.nps.gov/cebe; Cedar Creek Battlefield Foundation, 8437 Valley Pike, Middletown, 540-869-2064, www.ccbf.us.

FURTHER READING

From Winchester to Cedar Creek: The Shenandoah Campaign of 1864 by Jeffry D. Wert
A dramatic account of Sheridan's campaign in the Shenandoah

☀ Cedar Mountain

CAMPAIGN: Northern Virginia Campaign
DATE(S): August 9, 1862

After a back-and-forth artillery battle led to the death of General Winder, Federal troops under General Banks attacked disorganized Southern forces near Cedar Mountain. Just as the Union forces were on the cusp of victory, Stonewall Jackson—riding with his sword and battle flag—personally rallied the Rebel troops.

Although much of the battlefield is pri-vate land today, a public walking trail covers more than 150 acres of preserved land.

LOCATION: Markers located at the intersection of James Madison Hwy. and Madison Rd., www.friendsofcedarmountain.org. For the battle-field, take a left at the intersection of James Madison Hwy. and Rte. 657 (General Winder Rd.). The preserved portion of the battlefield will be on your right.

FURTHER READING

Stonewall Jackson at Cedar Mountain by Robert K. Krick
A look at Jackson's last independent campaign

✳ Chaffin's Farm and New Market Heights

CAMPAIGN: Richmond-Petersburg Campaign
DATE(S): September 29–30, 1864

A battle for control over several forts guarding Richmond, this encounter is most notable for the gallant performance of black soldiers, 14 of whom received the Medal of Honor, and did a great deal toward eliminating the then widely held belief that black soldiers were inferior fighters. The capture of forts forced General Lee to spread his forces more thinly to continue protecting Richmond. Today, a self-guided walking tour leads through the remains of Fort Harrison, which was captured in the assault.

LOCATION: Remains of Fort Harrison, and many markers, located at 8621 Battlefield Park Rd., Richmond, 804-226-1981.

FURTHER READING

The Battle of New Market Heights: Freedom Will Be Theirs by the Sword
by James S. Price
A look at the black soldiers who fought at New Market Heights

Fort Harrison and the Battle of Chaffin's Farm: To Surprise and Capture Richmond
by Douglas Crenshaw
A fresh take on this overlooked battle

✳ Chancellorsville

CAMPAIGN: Chancellorsville Campaign
DATE(S): April 30–May 6, 1863

Although initiated by General Hooker, Chancellorsville was Lee's masterstroke, his "perfect battle," and ranks as one of the most important battles of the war.

While marching the majority of his army north and west of the Rappahannock River, Hooker feinted an assault on Lee's position at Fredericksburg, crossing behind Lee in the wilderness of Spotsylvania. Hooker expected Lee either to attack him in his trenches or to

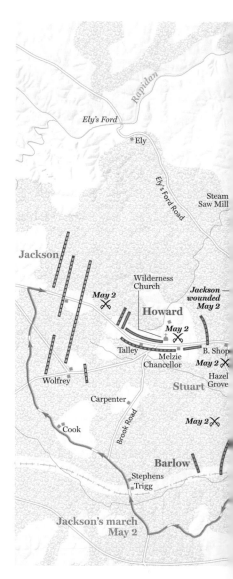

flee toward Richmond. "My plans are perfect," Hooker boasted. "May God have mercy on General Lee for I will have none."

Hooker, believing Lee was conforming to his expectations of directly attacking, pulled back to fortifications he was constructing near the crossroads of Chancellorsville. Instead, Lee took the offensive, sending Jackson to move completely around the Federal army to attack the unprotected Federal XI Corps. Hooker, confident that the Rebels were in fact retreating, dismissed

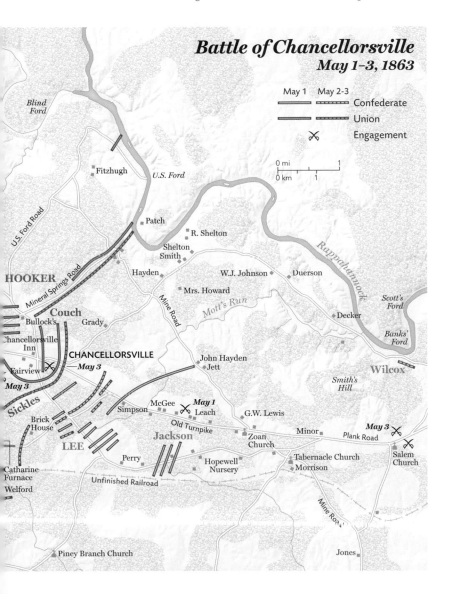

Battle of Chancellorsville
May 1–3, 1863

May 1 May 2-3
Confederate
Union
Engagement

0 mi   1
0 km   1

early warnings of a possible Confederate attack. Near dinnertime, Jackson struck, routing the Union right. This victory, arguably the grandest of his career, would be his last. While reconnoitering the lines that dark night, he was fired on in confusion by his own men, whose bullets pierced his left arm, soon resulting in its amputation. As Lee famously said when he was notified, "He has lost his left arm; but I have lost my right." Jackson was removed to Guinea Station, where he developed pneumonia and "crossed over the river and rested under the shade of the trees" on May 10.

Still, Hooker had great opportunities, and on May 3, General Sedgwick broke through the Confederate lines at Fredericksburg and began to move west, to fight a battle at Salem Church. Hooker, not realizing Lee's plans, voluntarily withdrew from key terrain in Hazel Grove, allowing Lee to reunite his forces and crush his positions near the Chancellorsville intersection. Hooker was quite literally dazed by Lee's continued attacks when a cannonball

Stonewall Jackson wore this hat during the war.

struck a post he was leaning against, knocking him unconscious.

Understanding the risk to his army by Sedgwick's advance, Lee once again made the risky choice of splitting his troops, sending reinforcements to halt Sedgwick.

Despite these setbacks, Hooker still had a large numerical advantage. In fact, a majority of Union corps commanders voted for a counterattack. Yet, Hooker overruled them and insisted on a retreat, carried out during a rainstorm the night of May 5. This epic battle sealed Lee's now legendary reputation, as Hooker became the fourth Union commander he had defeated in less than a year.

Today, the well-preserved battlefield is part of Fredericksburg and Spotsylvania National Military Park. It features a driving tour, walking paths, and many monuments and markers. Don't miss the walking trail of the first day's fighting, the Chancellorsville driving tour (see p. 295), Jackson's wounding site near the visitor center, the Stonewall Jackson Shrine at Guinea Station (see p. 305), or the

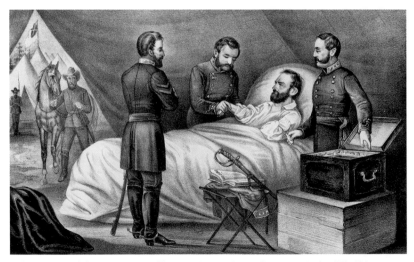

Jackson survived the amputation of his arm—it was a bout of pneumonia that killed him.

antebellum Salem Church (see pp. 275–276), used as a hospital by both North and South. You can even visit the grave of Jackson's amputated arm at the restored Lacy House.

LOCATION: Chancellorsville Battlefield, 9001 Plank Rd., Spotsylvania, 540-786-2880, www.nps.gov/frsp.

FURTHER READING

Chancellorsville, 1863: The Souls of the Brave
by Ernest B. Furgurson
A seminal account of this major battle

✲Chantilly

CAMPAIGN: Northern Virginia Campaign

DATE(S): September 1, 1862

In an attempt to cut off the Union retreat from the Second Manassas battlefield (see pp. 256–257), General Jackson sent two divisions to attack Federal forces near Ox Hill. During ferocious fighting in the middle of a thunderstorm, Union Generals Kearny and Stevens were both killed, although they halted the Confederate advance.

LOCATION: Multiple monuments located at the very small Ox Hill Battlefield Park, 4134 W. Ox Rd., Fairfax, 703-324-8702, www.fairfaxcounty.gov/parks/oxhill.

✲Chester Station

CAMPAIGN: Bermuda Hundred Campaign

DATE(S): May 10, 1864

Here General Butler's attempt to cut Confederate communications between Richmond and Petersburg was thwarted by a Southern attack in 100-degree heat. Artillery fire set the woods ablaze, risking the lives of the wounded until an evening truce allowed for their evacuation.

LOCATION: Marker located on W. Hundred Rd., 1 mile east of the intersection with Parker Ln. There are two other markers within half a mile at the Chester YMCA on W. Hundred Rd.

✷Cloyd's Mountain

CAMPAIGN: Crook-Averell Raid on the Virginia & Tennessee Railroad

DATE(S): May 9, 1864

Ordered by Grant to sever the Virginia and Tennessee Railroad to disrupt supplies arriving in Lynchburg and supporting Lee's army,

Philip Kearny

An international man of mystery and adventure before the term was coined, Philip Kearny (1815–1862) lived an incredible life that seems more fitting for Hollywood than a history book. Grandchild of the last royal recorder of New York City and son of a founder of the New York Stock Exchange, Kearny was born into wealth. Despite his aristocratic birth and an inheritance that made him a millionaire, he desired an army life. He served in Algeria with the French army, where he was given the nickname "Kearny the Magnificent" for his bravery. He lost his left arm in the Mexican-American War, where he outfitted his men at personal expense with 120 matching horses and uniforms. In 1859, after embarking on a world tour, he served Napoleon III and became the first American to be awarded the French Legion of Honor. During the Civil War, he again served with distinction, fearlessly charging into battle with memorable quotes such as "I'm a one-armed Jersey son-of-a-gun, follow me!"

Renowned in both North and South, Kearny met an untimely death at the Battle of Chantilly by attempting to escape after he had refused to surrender. "You've killed Phil Kearny," said Southern General Hill. "He deserved a better fate than to die in the mud." In fact, at the time of Kearny's death, some expected him to replace McClellan as commander of the Union Army.

General Crook advanced to southwest Virginia, near present-day Roanoke, attacking Confederate defenders near Cloyd's Mountain. Brutal hand-to-hand combat resulted in the death of 23 percent of the Southerners, including General Jenkins, who lost the battle. The extensively damaged railroad was soon repaired.

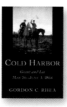

Badge of George Upton, killed at Cold Harbor

LOCATION: Marker located on the median on Cleburne Blvd., a third of a mile south of the intersection with Cloyd's Mountain Rd.

✦Cockpit Point

CAMPAIGN: Blockade of the Potomac River
DATE(S): January 3, 1862

With 37 heavy guns at various spots on the Potomac, the South attempted to cut off the North's use of the river. This battle was an inconclusive engagement between Union ships and Confederate batteries at Cockpit Point, withdrawn by the time the North returned on March 9.

LOCATION: No current public access. Visitors can see a similar battery built at the same time at Leesylvania State Park, 2001 Daniel K. Ludwig Dr., Woodbridge.

✳ Cold Harbor

CAMPAIGN: Grant's Overland Campaign
DATE(S): May 31–June 12, 1864

One of the bloodiest battles of the Civil War, and Lee's final large victory, the battle consisted of a series of Union assaults against

What's in a Name?

Cold Harbor was named after the Cold Harbor Tavern, which offered cold meals and "harbor," an old way of saying shelter. Despite the confusing name, it was an inland town, not a port.

entrenched Confederates at a rural crossroads named Cold Harbor. Believing Lee's army to be "whipped," Grant thought that an audacious attack could potentially end the war. The assault on June 3, 1864, led to approximately 7,000 Union casualties and earned Grant a reputation as the "fumbling butcher." Still, the relentless number of previous battles from May 5 onward had bled Lee and moved Grant into position to assault Richmond directly. Lee understood the looming threat, noting, "We must destroy this army of Grant's before he gets to the James River. If he gets there, then it will be a siege, and then it will be a mere question of time." Following Cold Harbor, Lee's fears were realized when Grant stole a march on him and moved south against the key transportation network of Petersburg.

Today, significant elements of the battlefield are preserved and offer a wealth of information, including a very small visitor center, walking path, driving tour, and many monuments.

LOCATION: Cold Harbor Battlefield, 5515 Anderson-Wright Dr., 5 miles southeast of Mechanicsville on Rte. 156, 804-226-1981.

FURTHER READING

Cold Harbor: Grant and Lee, May 26–June 3, 1864
by Gordon C. Rhea
A vivid account of the battle

✳ Cool Spring

CAMPAIGN: Early's Raid and Operations Against the B&O Railroad
DATE(S): July 17–18, 1864

After General Early's surprise attack on Washington, D.C., General Crook's Union forces pursued him to the Shenandoah River, meeting skirmishers at Cool Spring

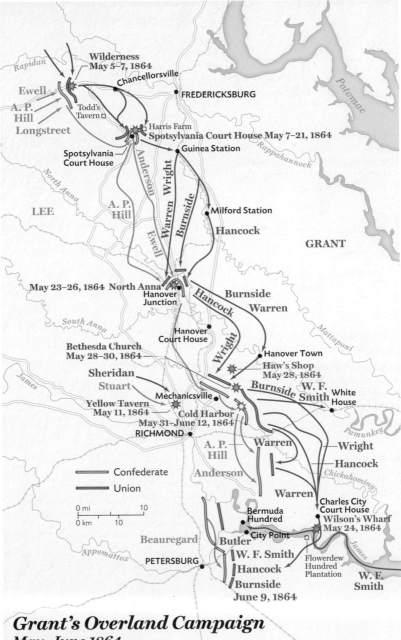

Wilderness
May 5-7, 1864

Rapidan

Chancellorsville

FREDERICKSBURG

Ewell

A. P. Hill

Longstreet

Todd's Tavern

Harris Farm
Spotsylvania Court House May 7-21, 1864

Spotsylvania Court House

Guinea Station

Rappahannock

North Anna

LEE

A. P. Hill

Ewell

Anderson

Warren

Wright

Burnside

Milford Station

Hancock

Potomac

GRANT

May 23-26, 1864 North Anna
Hanover Junction

Hancock

Burnside
Warren

Wright

South Anna

Hanover Court House

Mattaponi

Bethesda Church
May 28-30, 1864

James

Sheridan
Stuart

Yellow Tavern
May 11, 1864

Mechanicsville

Cold Harbor
May 31-June 12, 1864

RICHMOND

Hanover Town

Haw's Shop
May 28, 1864

Burnside W. F. Smith White House

Pamunkey

A. P. Hill

Anderson

Warren

Warren

Wright

Hancock

Chickahominy

— Confederate
— Union

0 mi   10
0 km   10

Beauregard

Appomattox

Bermuda Hundred

City Point

Butler

PETERSBURG

W. F. Smith

Hancock

Burnside
June 9, 1864

Charles City Court House

Wilson's Wharf
May 24, 1864

Flowerdew Hundred Plantation

James

W. F. Smith

Grant's Overland Campaign
May-June 1864

plantation. A flanking maneuver by General Rodes threw the Northern forces into disarray, ending the attack. Today, the original plantation house is a Catholic monastery. Visitors maintain a respectful silence when walking their grounds.

LOCATION: **Marker located at the intersection of Castleman's Rd. and Harry Byrd Hwy. Monastery located at 901 Cool Spring Ln., Berryville, 540-955-1425. Irregular hours; call for an appointment.**

FURTHER READING

Shenandoah Summer: The 1864 Valley Campaign
by Scott Patchan
A fresh take on Early's impact on the Confederacy

✲Cove Mountain

CAMPAIGN: Crook-Averell Raid on the Virginia & Tennessee Railroad

DATE(S): May 10, 1864

In this minor engagement, General Jones's Confederates repulsed Union General Averell's attacking soldiers and then counterattacked, driving the Federals from the field of battle near Cove Mountain.

LOCATION: **No public access.**

✲ The Crater

CAMPAIGN: Richmond-Petersburg Campaign

DATE(S): July 30, 1864

During the siege of Vicksburg in 1863 (see p. 136), Grant had used tunnels to burrow under Confederate lines, expecting to blow them up and destroy the forces defending them. He brought that same innovative thinking to Petersburg and authorized the 48th Pennsylvania—a regiment of coal miners—to dig a mine shaft under Confederate positions manned by South Carolinians under General Elliott. They loaded the shaft with gunpowder and exploded a large gap in Southern defenses. Union soldiers ran down into The Crater, not around it, giving the rallying Confederates the high ground. "Like shooting ducks on the pond," Grant said, calling this "the saddest affair I have witnessed in the war."

The Crater is largely filled in now, although there are many markers and the area has been preserved. Blandford Church (see p. 297) stands nearby.

LOCATION: **Petersburg National Battlefield, 5001 Siege Rd., Petersburg, 804-732-3531, www.nps.gov/pete. Park at Siege Rd., a third of a mile east of the intersection with Rte. 301.**

The Crater

A technical marvel, the explosion that preceded the Battle of the Crater was, at that point, the largest in human history and offered the Union a chance to seize the high ground near Petersburg and, perhaps, win the war. Why did it all fall apart? Black troops under the command of IX Corps commander Ambrose Burnside had trained for the attack, only to be removed by Meade with Grant's approval. Many believe Meade lacked faith in the black troops, although Grant later testified that he feared a disaster would lead to charges he had set the black soldiers up to be slaughtered. At the last minute, command was turned over to the typically drunk General James Ledlie, who drank rum in the trenches while his men were slaughtered, ironically leading to the disaster Grant had feared.

✲ Cross Keys

CAMPAIGN: Jackson's Valley Campaign

DATE(S): June 8, 1862

This was the first of two battles of a masterful one-two punch ending General Jackson's famous Shenandoah Valley Campaign, which

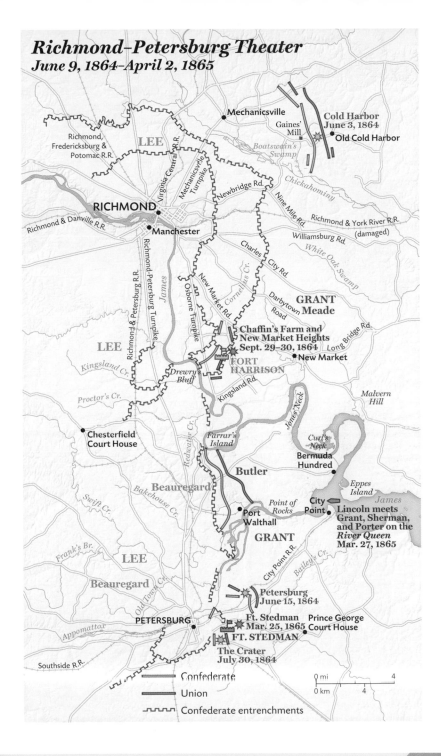

Richmond–Petersburg Theater
June 9, 1864–April 2, 1865

Mechanicsville

Cold Harbor
June 3, 1864
Gaines' Mill
Old Cold Harbor

Richmond, Fredericksburg & Potomac R.R.

LEE

Boatswain's Swamp

Virginia Central R.R.

Mechanicsville Turnpike

Newbridge Rd.

Chickahominy

Nine Mile Rd.

Richmond & York River R.R.

RICHMOND

Richmond & Danville R.R.

Manchester

Williamsburg Rd. (damaged)

White Oak Swamp

Charles City Rd.

Richmond-Petersburg Turnpike

James

Osborne Turnpike

New Market Rd.

Cornelius Cr.

Darbytown Road

GRANT
Meade

Richmond & Petersburg R.R.

LEE

Long Bridge Rd.

Chaffin's Farm and
New Market Heights
Sept. 29–30, 1864

New Market

Kingsland Cr.

Drewry's Bluff

FORT HARRISON

Kingsland Rd.

Malvern Hill

Proctor's Cr.

Redwater Cr.

Farrar's Island

Jones' Neck

Curl's Neck

Chesterfield
Court House

Bermuda
Hundred

Eppes Island

Butler

Beauregard

Bakehouse Cr.

Point of Rocks

City Point

James

Lincoln meets
Grant, Sherman,
and Porter on the
River Queen
Mar. 27, 1865

Swift Cr.

Port Walthall

Frank's Br.

GRANT

LEE

City Point R.R.

Bailey's Cr.

Beauregard

Old Town Cr.

Petersburg
June 15, 1864

Appomattox

PETERSBURG

Ft. Stedman
Mar. 25, 1865

Prince George
Court House

FT. STEDMAN

The Crater
July 30, 1864

Southside R.R.

Confederate

Union

Confederate entrenchments

0 mi 4
0 km 4

Troops rush toward The Crater after the explosion that created the mounds in the middle of this drawing. Visible in the distance are the inner Confederate lines.

forced two Union armies to retreat, tied up Federal forces in the valley, prevented Lincoln from releasing soldiers to support McClellan's siege of Richmond, and allowed Jackson to come to Lee's aid. Although the battlefield is not open to the public, markers describe the action.

LOCATION: **Battle video and printed driving tour available at the Hardesty-Higgins House Visitor Center, 212 S. Main St., Harrisonburg, 540-432-8935. Markers located on Goods Mill Rd., half a mile south of the intersection with Bluff Rd. in Harrisonburg.**

✳ Cumberland Church

CAMPAIGN: Appomattox Campaign

DATE(S): April 7, 1865

With the Federals closing in, Southern troops at Cumberland Church, trying to defend the road to Appomattox Station, repulsed a Union attack before withdrawing under cover of darkness. Here, General Lee

rejected Grant's first request for surrender, still hoping he could eventually escape and join with Johnston's army in North Carolina.

LOCATION: **Multiple markers located at the entrance to Cumberland Presbyterian Church, 1835 Cumberland Rd., Farmville.**

✳ Darbytown and New Market Roads

CAMPAIGN: Richmond-Petersburg Campaign

DATE(S): October 7, 1864

Lee's second attempt to retake Fort Harrison found initial success and routed Union cavalry at Darbytown Road. However, the attempt on Union lines at New Market Road was not successful, forcing the Confederates to draw back toward Richmond.

LOCATION: **Multiple markers located near the intersections of Darbytown Rd. and Lost Country Ln., and Darbytown Rd. and Monohan Rd., in Richmond.**

Darbytown Road

CAMPAIGN: Richmond-Petersburg Campaign

DATE(S): October 13, 1864

Grant's relentless efforts to take Richmond continued here, as Union forces under General Terry probed Confederate defenses in a sharp and bloody skirmish with troops under General Anderson. Badly mauled by the Confederates, Northern forces retreated to their lines at New Market Road.

LOCATION: **No markers for the October 13 engagement, although a marker discussing the defense of Richmond in general can be found on Darbytown Rd., a fifth of a mile east of S. Laburnum Ave., Richmond.**

Deep Bottom I

CAMPAIGN: Richmond-Petersburg Campaign

DATE(S): July 27–29, 1864

General Hancock's Union forces assaulted Southern defenses south of Richmond. Largely a diversion to weaken Lee's forces before the botched Battle of the Crater near Petersburg (see p. 230), this unsuccessful attack achieved its limited goal, although final Union victory was still months away.

LOCATION: **Markers located on New Market Rd., three-quarters of a mile after the intersection with Long Bridge Rd., and at the end of Deep Bottom Rd., facing the James River.**

FURTHER READING

The Petersburg Campaign, Volume 1: The Eastern Front Battles, June–August 1864
by Edwin C. Bearss
An incisive look at this crucial campaign

Deep Bottom II

CAMPAIGN: Richmond-Petersburg Campaign

DATE(S): August 16, 1864

Two weeks after the first battle of Deep Bottom, Union troops under General Terry attacked Southern forces, breaking through their defensive lines. A Rebel counterattack led by General Field sealed the breach, however, and forced the Northern soldiers to retreat. Although the Confederates prevailed, their lines continued to weaken. The battle is notable for the deaths of two high-ranking Confederates: John R. Chambliss and Victor J. B. Girardey.

LOCATION: **Marker located at the intersection of Darbytown Rd. and Fussells Ridge Dr. in Henrico.**

Dinwiddie Court House

CAMPAIGN: Appomattox Campaign

DATE(S): March 31, 1865

In an attempt to stop Union General Sheridan's flanking maneuver, General Pickett's infantry and Fitzhugh Lee's cavalry attacked the Union vanguard near Dinwiddie Court House, pushing them back. This was the last victory of the war for the Army of Northern Virginia. From this position the Confederates moved to the end of their lines at Five Forks, where Federal attacks broke them on April 1.

The antebellum Dinwiddie courthouse is now a museum, with several historical markers outside.

LOCATION: **Dinwiddie Courthouse, 14101 Boydton Plank Rd., Dinwiddie, 804-469-5346.**

Dranesville

CAMPAIGN: McClellan's Operations in Northern Virginia

DATE(S): December 20, 1861

A minor battle between General Stuart's troops, who were protecting a foraging mission, and Pennsylvanian soldiers under General Ord, this engagement is important as the first Union victory south of the Potomac River.

LOCATION: **Marker located outside Dranesville Tavern (open for private events only), 11919 Leesburg Pike, Herndon, 703-750-1598.**

✳ Drewry's Bluff

CAMPAIGN: Peninsula Campaign

DATE(S): May 15, 1862

After the retreating Confederates destroyed their ironclad the *Virginia,* Federal gunboats steamed up the James River, looking to seize Richmond. They were stopped by Confederate batteries at Drewry's Bluff. Ironically, the Union's newly built ironclad monitors, although strong, were unable to aim their cannons high enough to attack Southern defenses. Facing strong artillery fire, sniping, and heavy damage to the ironclad *Galena,* the Federal ships withdrew.

The battlefield is now part of Richmond National Battlefield Park. Visitors will find a short trail, several markers, and a river view at Drewry's Bluff.

LOCATION: **Richmond National Battlefield Park, 804-226-1981, www.nps.gov/rich. Take Bellwood Rd. to Fort Darling Rd. and then go left for half a mile. When the road diverges, veer right and park in the cul-de-sac at the end of the road.**

FURTHER READING

Ironclads and Big Guns of the Confederacy: The Journal and Letters of John M. Brooke edited by George M. Brooke, Jr. A firsthand description of Confederate ordnance operations during the war

❊ Eltham's Landing

CAMPAIGN: Peninsula Campaign

DATE(S): May 7, 1862

As the Confederates at Williamsburg retreated from the narrow Virginia Peninsula, Union forces under General Franklin sailed up the York River, attempting to cut off the Southern retreat. After disembarking at Eltham's Landing, they faced troops led by General G. W. Smith in a minor engagement that prevented Union forces from cutting off the Rebel army. Confederate General Hood

earned praise for his aggressive performance and would later earn more at the Battle of Gaines' Mill (see p. 244).

LOCATION: **Marker located at the intersection of Farmers Dr. and Plum Point Rd., West Point.**

✳ Fair Oaks and Darbytown Road

CAMPAIGN: Richmond-Petersburg Campaign

DATE(S): October 27–28, 1864

While other parts of the Union Army moved against the Boydton Plank Road (see p. 220), General Butler led the X Corps against defenses at Darbytown Road, while the XVIII Corps attacked Fair Oaks. General Grant hoped to draw some of Lee's forces away from his primary effort south of Petersburg. The attacks failed, with a stunning 16 Union casualties for every Confederate casualty, while the South took around 600 prisoners.

LOCATION: **No public access.**

Family Feud

J. E. B. Stuart's father-in-law, Phillip St. George Cooke, although a Virginian, remained loyal to the Union and fought for the North. As his legendary son-in-law famously remarked, "He will regret it only once, and that will be continually." Following Stuart's death in May 1864, after the Battle of Yellow Tavern, Cooke's daughter wore black for the rest of her life. Cooke's own son also sided with the Confederacy, although he survived the war and later reconciled with his father. Such family disputes were common during the Civil War, even among those at the highest ranks of leadership. Stonewall Jackson's sister, for example, was a staunch Unionist.

Confederate soldiers captured 11 Union flags at Fair Oaks and Darbytown Road.

✳ Fisher's Hill

CAMPAIGN: Sheridan's Valley Campaign
DATE(S): September 21–22, 1864

LOCATION: Fisher's Hill, 540-740-4545, www.shenandoahatwar.org. Parking lot on Battlefield Rd., a half a mile west of the U.S. Post Office at 2753 Battlefield Rd.

After General Early's defeat at Opequon on September 19, 1864 (see pp. 266–267), his troops assumed seemingly strong defensive positions at Fisher's Hill. As the Union forces advanced, they drove back the Rebels and captured valuable high ground. Around 4 p.m., the Federals, who had by that time outflanked Early's men, attacked. Outnumbered around three to one, the Confederate defense collapsed, and Early retreated toward New Market. This defeat made General Sheridan's scorched-earth campaign through the Shenandoah Valley possible.

Large portions of the battlefield are preserved, and signs are installed to help visitors understand the action on this wide and high hill.

A Union Color Guard uniform worn at Five Forks

General Sheridan's charge at Five Forks turned the Confederate line.

✳ Five Forks

CAMPAIGN: Appomattox Campaign
DATE(S): April 1, 1865

Five Forks was crucial to the defense of the Southside Railroad, and thus crucial to the survival of Richmond, so Lee ordered General Pickett to hold it at all costs. Around 1 p.m., General Sheridan held the Rebel right flank in place with dismounted cavalry, attacking with rapid small arms fire. Around 4:15, General Warren's massed infantry attacked the Confederate left flank, capturing many prisoners. Due to an effect called acoustic shadowing, Pickett and Fitzhugh Lee could not hear the battle going on nearby and were eating a late lunch far away from the front lines while their divisions were being destroyed. About half the Rebel force of 10,000 fled, while the other half surrendered. This loss led directly to the abandonment of Richmond.

Two major military controversies arose from this battle: the deteriorating reputation of Pickett, who had fallen mightily in Lee's eyes, and the relief of Union V Corps Commander Gouverneur Warren by General Sheridan, a controversy that would last until 1880.

The well-preserved Five Forks battlefield features many markers, an impressive new visitor center, and a driving tour.

LOCATION: Petersburg National Battlefield, Five Forks Unit, 9840 Courthouse Rd., Dinwiddie, 804-469-4093, www.nps.gov/pete.

✳ Fort Stedman

CAMPAIGN: Richmond-Petersburg Campaign
DATE(S): March 25, 1865

The Confederate attack on Fort Stedman was a desperate attempt to break out of Grant's encirclement. Full of intrigue, it began with a stream of "deserters," who later turned on the Union forces and seized the fort. Although achieving initial success, the attack soon faltered when surrounding Federal forces poured a devastating fire into the Confederate advance. Soon Union reinforcements retook the fort and sent the Confederates back to their trenches. Lee had discovered how weak his offensive capabilities had become. A Southern soldier taken prisoner in the battle recalled his surprise when he saw Lincoln and Grant, who "rode by us seemingly not the least concerned . . . as if nothing had happened."

Located on the Petersburg National Battlefield driving tour, the stop has a loop trail that permits visitors to walk the Confederate attack.

LOCATION: Petersburg National Battlefield, 5001 Siege Rd., 1.5 miles south of the intersection with Oaklawn Blvd., Petersburg, 804-732-3531, www.nps.gov/pete.

✳ Fredericksburg I

CAMPAIGN: Fredericksburg Campaign
DATE(S): December 11–15, 1862

After Lincoln's firing of General McClellan, newly appointed commander Ambrose E. Burnside decided to move south with speed and outrace Lee to Richmond by crossing multiple rivers. Although a good plan on paper, Burnside lost the initiative waiting for pontoon boats when his infantry could have crossed with little difficulty. By the time the crossing materials arrived a week late, Lee's army was waiting behind defenses on the high ground of Marye's Heights just beyond the town. In one of the worst mistakes of the war, Burnside assumed that "the enemy will be more surprised by a crossing immediately in our front." Indeed, Lee was surprised, but only by the recklessness of such a doomed assault.

A doll given by a Confederate officer

After minor engagements, including a skirmish between Confederate snipers and

Jackson commanded from Fredericksburg's Prospect Hill, where earthworks are still extant.

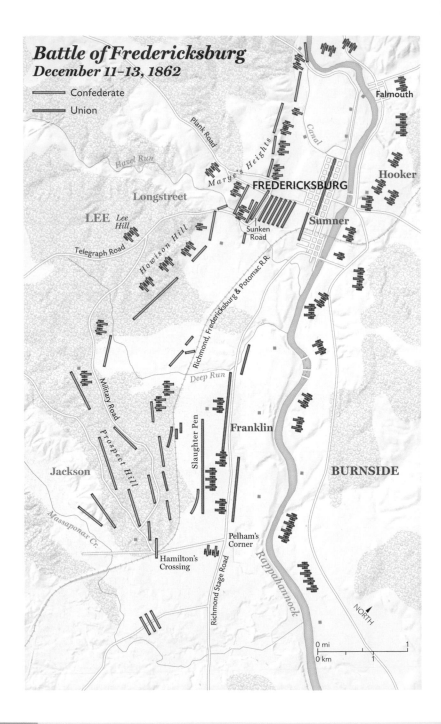

Battle of Fredericksburg
December 11–13, 1862

- Confederate
- Union

Falmouth

Plank Road

Hazel Run

Canal

Marye's Heights

FREDERICKSBURG

Hooker

Longstreet

LEE

Lee Hill

Sumner

Sunken Road

Telegraph Road

Howison Hill

Richmond, Fredericksburg & Potomac R.R.

Deep Run

Slaughter Pen

Franklin

Military Road

BURNSIDE

Prospect Hill

Jackson

Massaponax Cr.

Rappahannock

Pelham's Corner

Hamilton's Crossing

Richmond Stage Road

NORTH

0 mi 1
0 km 1

Union pontoon engineers, and looting in the town of Fredericksburg, the assault on Lee's army began in earnest on December 13, 1862. The one bright spot, General Meade's breach of Stonewall Jackson's Confederate defenses on Prospect Hill, was wasted when Meade never received reinforcements and Rebels filled the gap. Watching the action, Lee uttered one of his famous quotes: "It is well that war is so terrible—we should grow too fond of it!" Meade's valiant soldiers had won so much, only to be cut down in a Confederate counterattack, and Meade responded in horror, "My God, General Reynolds, did they think my division could whip Lee's whole army?"

Elsewhere on the battlefield, the mass of Southern troops behind a stone wall cut down waves of doomed Union attacks. Realizing the magnitude of his defeat, Burnside despondently considered personally leading a charge on Confederate lines, before realizing the foolishness of even more bloodshed. Although the Rebels

suffered around 5,000 casualties, the Federals suffered far more, and the staggering loss of around 13,000 Union troops for absolutely no gain was a disaster for morale, both in the army and in the North in general. "If there is a worse place than Hell," Lincoln noted, "I am in it."

Today, Fredericksburg is a jewel of a park and features a visitor center with videos, walking and driving tours, many markers, monuments, and the antebellum Chatham plantation house, all amid a largely preserved battlefield. Don't miss the newly added Slaughter Pen, the area over which the Federals' Left Grand Division charged. Also be sure to see the small interpretative display featuring a 12-pounder Napoleon cannon at Pelham's Corner, where the young artillerist fired into the Union flank, distracting and delaying the advance of the Union left against Jackson's position.

LOCATION: **Fredericksburg and Spotsylvania National Military Park, Fredericksburg Battlefield Visitor Center, 1013 Lafayette Blvd.,**

Carnage and Confederate dead after the second battle of Fredericksburg on May 3, 1863

Civil War on Foot: Fredericksburg

Fredericksburg is one of the nation's great cities, with roots to George Washington and his family, so a walk here is a walk through America. This tour passes by many other sites downtown with historical markers and interpretative signs, so give yourself at least half a day to fully discover the area.

❶ Visitor Center *(706 Caroline St.)* At the time of the war, this was the Town Hall and Market Square. During the battle, slaves hid around here. Turn left on Hanover Street.

❷ Federal Hill *(510 Hanover St.)* You are walking in the footsteps of the Federal soldiers, who marched out of town to assault Marye's Heights to the west. The building here housed Union casualties, and Union artillery used its yard as a firing position. If you look carefully at the chimney, you can see shell damage. Retracing your steps, you will pass at least 14 antebellum homes: No. 401 was the mayor's home during the war.

❸ St. George's Church *(810 Princess Anne St.)* Turn left on Princess Anne Street and walk past the 1852 courthouse to the Presbyterian church on the left, which was

Completed in 2007, the multimillion-dollar restoration of Federal Hill returned the structure to its Civil War look.

severely damaged in the battle. Clara Barton and Walt Whitman nursed Union soldiers here. Continue to the intersection of William and Charles Streets.

❹ Slave Auction Block Slave auctions were held here on the outskirts of town. Easily accessible from the countryside, it was a perfect location.

❺ Site of the Upper Crossing Turn right on Charles and then right again on Amelia, past the Baptist church. Continue to the river.

As you walk, look down the alleys and at the homes. From between and inside the houses, Confederates kept up a harassing fire on engineers building the bridge and Union infantry trying to secure the landing site.

❻ Old Stone Warehouse Walk south along Sophia Street and turn right on William Street. To your left you will see the Old Stone Warehouse, which was used as a storage facility for goods and cargo being unloaded from the river.

❼ Caroline Street

Turn left on Caroline Street, which served as the Confederates' main line in town, and walk along the rows of antebellum row houses and businesses in the 500 to 800 blocks. Forming the center of commercial operations in 1862, these buildings were looted before and after the battle.

❽ Lower Caroline Street

Continue under the antebellum railroad tracks, passing the home of James Monroe on the left (No. 301). As Federals forced their way up Rocky Lane, Confederates defended the section between 207 and 205 Caroline. Shells damaged the Sentry Box House (No. 133). Cross the street and return up Caroline. The houses at 132, 134, 136, and 138 Caroline have Federal graffiti on the walls. Oceanographer Matthew Fontaine Maury, who served as a naval agent in Europe, lived at No. 214, while the owner of No. 306 was imprisoned for refusing to take the oath of allegiance in 1862.

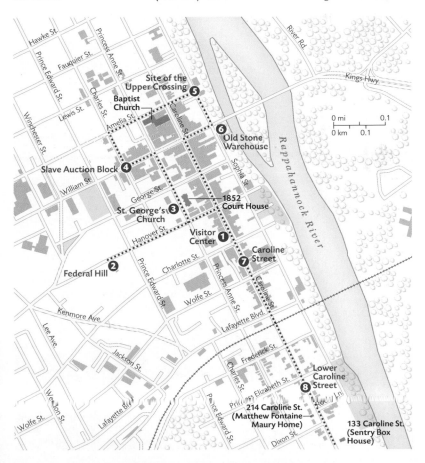

Fredericksburg, 540-654-5121, www.nps.gov /frsp. Slaughter Pen located at 11190 Tidewater Trail, Fredericksburg, 800-298-7878. Pelham's Corner located at the intersection of Jim Morris Rd. and Schumann St., Fredericksburg.

FURTHER READING

Fredericksburg! Fredericksburg!
by George C. Rable
A fascinating account of the battle of Fredericksburg

The Fredericksburg Campaign: Winter War on the Rappahannock
by Francis Augustín O'Reilly
A gripping and vivid account of this campaign

✳ Fredericksburg II

CAMPAIGN: Chancellorsville Campaign

DATE(S): May 3, 1863

To cover his move around Lee, Union General Hooker left the VI Corps and a division of the II Corps under General Sedgwick to fool Lee into believing that a spring attack would be made on Confederate lines at Fredericksburg. After Sedgwick demonstrated at Fredericksburg, he was to join the main Union Army. A portion of the force that had been left behind was to close Hooker's open right flank, down from the Orange Turnpike to Ely's Ford. Facing a hard division under Confederate General Early, Sedgwick required two assaults to carry the lightly manned Confederate position. He and Early both then moved westward to join in the fighting around Chancellorsville.

Ask at the visitor center for information about this second battle of Fredericksburg.

LOCATION: Fredericksburg and Spotsylvania National Military Park, Fredericksburg Battlefield Visitor Center, 1013 Lafayette Blvd., Fredericksburg, 540-654-5121, www.nps.gov /frsp.

✳ Front Royal

CAMPAIGN: Jackson's Valley Campaign

DATE(S): May 23, 1862

Attacked by Stonewall Jackson during his famous Shenandoah Valley Campaign, Colonel Kenly's Union forces holding Front Royal were forced into retreat, and finally broken, by a cavalry charge led by Major Flournoy. In this battle, the 1st Maryland C.S.A. fought against the 1st Maryland U.S.A., making this a jarring "brother against brother" battle in a war already defined by the division of families, friends, and the very country itself.

LOCATION: Two markers located at the intersection of N. Royal Ave. and Chester St., Front

Balloons

Gaines' Mill (see p. 244) was the first battle in which both sides simultaneously used observation balloons. Although a quaint technology by today's standards, balloons were yet another example of the vast technological changes that were revolutionizing American trade, industry, and war. With more than 3,000 balloon flights, the Civil War witnessed the first large-scale use of balloons in any war, while the U.S.S. *George Washington Parke Custis*, used as a launching platform, was arguably the world's first aircraft carrier.

Although the Union balloon program was canceled in 1863 because of cost and political infighting, one Confederate source claims that their presence on the battlefield caused great headaches for Rebel forces, noting, "Even if the observers never saw anything, they would have been worth all they cost for the annoyance and delays they caused us in trying to keep our movements out of their sight." The Confederacy also had a nascent balloon program, although limited resources kept it from being a factor.

Jackson's Reputation

Late in life, Robert E. Lee pays a visit to his old comrade Stonewall Jackson.

homas J. "Stonewall" Jackson (1824–1863), one of the great figures of the Civil War, was the "stone wall" that anchored the line at Manassas—giving him his famous nickname. He was also the general who confounded multiple Federal armies in the Shenandoah Valley, marching so rapidly that his men were known as Jackson's Foot Cavalry. His firm defense of the Confederate right at Fredericksburg (see pp. 237–242) was prelude to his romantic great triumph and tragic death at Chancellorsville (see pp. 224–227).

Today, Jackson is lionized as one of the greatest legends in U.S. history. But he did have battlefield failures: Kernstown, Cedar Mountain, and, most notably, the Seven Days Battles around Richmond.

At the Battle of Savage Station, for example, Confederate General Magruder asked for Jackson's support. Jackson responded that he had other important duties to perform. A similar occurrence took place at the Battle of White Oak Swamp, where Jackson did not respond to nearby gunfire.

Critics and analysts have made a range of excuses and charges—he was fatigued, he wouldn't fight on Sundays, he was too pious, he was eccentric. Some historians believe that Jackson's seemingly poor positioning and timing during the Seven Days Battles were actually the result of a secret directive given to him by Lee—to ensure that McClellan was boxed into an area where he could be destroyed.

That Lee does not chastise or demote Jackson—despite multiple failures—indicates that he was not unhappy with Jackson's performance. Indeed, despite these significant failures, Lee never lost confidence in Jackson or his capabilities. At Chancellorsville, he risked the fate of the Confederacy by allowing Jackson to march away with the vast majority of his army. Regardless of whether Jackson had a secret mission from Lee or not, he proved himself one of the war's greatest commanders. In fact, many historians believe the South might have won at Gettysburg (see pp. 352–357) if Jackson had lived.

FURTHER READING

Stonewall Jackson: The Man, the Soldier, the Legend
by James I. Robertson, Jr. A biography of the enigmatic and talented Southern general

"McClellan is to me one of the great mysteries of the war," said Ulysses S. Grant about the Union general.

Royal, 800-338-2576, www.discoverfrontroyal.com. The Warren Rifles Confederate Museum is on Chester St. (see p. 307).

Gaines' Mill

CAMPAIGN: Peninsula Campaign

DATE(S): June 27, 1862

The third of the Seven Days Battles began when Lee sent multiple assaults against General Porter's dug-in V Corps on the Union's right flank. He intended to destroy the V Corps and rout the other 80 percent of the Union Army. Stonewall Jackson was not in place when Lee wanted to attack; however, once he arrived, the Confederate assault of more than 30,000 men led by General Hood's Texas brigade swept the field in this largest battle in the East.

Although a great victory by any measure, Southern forces failed to follow and destroy the retreating Federals. This decisive Confederate victory convinced McClellan to change his base of operations to the more secure James River. In the sense that this battle saved the Confederate capital, whose fall in 1862 could have ended the war much earlier, this battle ranks as one of the most important of the war.

Today, the preserved battlefield is part of Richmond National Battlefield Park and offers many markers and a walking trail.

LOCATION: Richmond National Battlefield Park, 6283 Watt House Rd., Mechanicsville, 804-226-1981, www.nps.gov/rich.

Garnett's and Golding's Farm

CAMPAIGN: Peninsula Campaign

DATE(S): June 27–28, 1862

While fighting raged at Gaines' Mill north of the Chickahominy River, Rebel forces commanded by General Magruder executed a very important diversion by demonstrating against the Union forces south of the river at Garnett's and Golding's Farm on June 27, 1862.

Magruder made his force appear much larger than it was, successfully deceiving Union observers and McClellan that he faced the larger threat. However, Magruder's subordinate, General Toombs, nearly blew his cover. Toombs, a political general, attacked a Federal position with too much exuberance, risking a major counterattack that would have exposed the charade and opened Richmond to capture that day. Fortunately, McClellan did not bite. An unrepentant Toombs responded to his dressing down by calling Magruder "that old ass." Confederate forces were driving the Federals south toward the Chickahominy River and Grapevine Bridge.

LOCATION: Marker located just after the intersection of N. Airport Dr. and Hanover Rd., Highland Springs.

✾ Glendale/White Oak Swamp

CAMPAIGN: Peninsula Campaign
DATE(S): June 30, 1862

As Federal forces retreated from just outside Richmond, action took place at Glendale, the fifth of the Seven Days Battles. Lee wanted to trap retreating Federals and crush them. Generals Longstreet and Hill assaulted forces under Generals McCall and Kearny. In the heat of battle, the Confederates seemed to be gaining ground until a bayonet charge made by the 69th Pennsylvania crashed into Longstreet's men, turning the tide of the battle for the Union, which evaded destruction.

Meanwhile, as fighting at Glendale raged to the south, General Franklin's Union rear guard engaged Stonewall Jackson's men in an artillery battle at White Oak Swamp. Jackson's failure to support his fellow Confederates in a more meaningful way remains controversial today. The conventional interpretation is that Jackson was fatigued and unsure of what he could or should do. But was that true? The historical debate rages on.

Visitors should start at the Glendale/Malvern Hill Visitor Center in Richmond National Battlefield Park.

LOCATION: **Richmond National Battlefield Park, Glendale/Malvern Hill Visitor Center, 8301 Willis Church Rd., inside Glendale National Cemetery, 804-226-1981, www.nps.gov/rich.**

✸ Globe Tavern

CAMPAIGN: Richmond-Petersburg Campaign
DATE(S): August 18–21, 1864

Unable to take Petersburg by direct assault, Grant decided to slowly strangle the Confederates. As a diversion, Grant attacked to the north in the second battle of Deep Bottom. As Lee and his men were preoccupied, he moved to cut Lee's supply line from Weldon, North Carolina. Union General Warren seized the Weldon Railroad and destroyed miles of track. Several days of Confederate assaults attempted to retake the railroad, but a deadly Northern artillery assault on August 21 ended all hope of this

An oversize Union flag flies atop the Globe Tavern, used as the headquarters of General Meade at the Battle of Malvern Hill.

happening. This loss meant the Rebels had to unload their supplies from Halifax station, then carry them 30 miles by wagon. This was a sign of things to come. It was also the Union's first victory during the Richmond-Petersburg Campaign and is a classic example of Grant's strategy of strangulation and attrition.

LOCATION: **Markers at the intersection of Halifax and Flank Rd., in the off-site Fort Wadsworth unit of Petersburg National Battlefield, 804-732-3531, www.nps.gov/pete.**

⚜ Guard Hill

CAMPAIGN: Sheridan's Valley Campaign
DATE(S): August 18, 1864

On their way to reinforce Jubal Early's forces in the Shenandoah Valley, General Anderson's men were surprised while crossing the Shenandoah River. Although 300 Rebels were captured, the Confederates counterattacked and drove the Union forces back to Cedarville.

LOCATION: **Markers located at the intersection of Rte. 340 and Riverton Rd., in Front Royal. Another marker and river viewing point is accessible by going east on Riverton Rd. after the intersection and taking the first right.**

⚜ Hampton Roads

CAMPAIGN: Peninsula Campaign
DATE(S): March 8–9, 1862

The advent of modern naval combat began here, near Fort Monroe (see p. 299) and Fort Wool on March 8, 1862, when Confederate ironclad C.S.S. *Virginia,* outfitted with 12 guns and a ram, battled five wooden Federal ships with a total of 219 guns, sinking one, grounding another, and nearly finishing off a third. On March 9, the Federal ironclad U.S.S. *Monitor,* with its innovative swiveling turret design, battled the *Virginia* to a draw before withdrawing.

LOCATION: **Markers located in Monitor-Merrimac Overlook Park, 16th St. (VA 167), Newport News.**

✳ Hanover Court House

CAMPAIGN: Peninsula Campaign
DATE(S): May 27, 1862

Union General Porter's V Corps moved north to protect General McClellan's right flank, which straddled the Chickahominy River. They aimed to disrupt the railroad line and open Telegraph Road as a route for Union reinforcements coming south from Fredericksburg. Near the colonial-era Hanover Court House, they were confronted by Confederates troops, which they defeated in a fierce battle. The Union reinforcements never arrived, however, because by this time, Stonewall Jackson had begun his remarkable Valley Campaign, and the federal government, fearing for the security of Washington, D.C., had ordered them to hold in place in the event they were needed to repel Jackson.

LOCATION: **Marker and monument to Confederate soldiers located outside historic Hanover Court House, 13182 Hanover Courthouse Rd., 804-537-5815. The colonial-era Hanover Tavern is nearby (see p. 300).**

Ironclad Ships

The Civil War marked the first use of ironclad ships in combat. International reaction was swift. In Britain, the world's largest naval power, which had built two experimental ironclads, the *London Times* opined, "Whereas we had available . . . one hundred and forty-nine first-class warships, we have now two." Ironically, the North never fielded an oceangoing ironclad, and the Confederates' problems with propulsion systems limited theirs to coastal waters and inner harbors. The Confederates secured a single oceangoing ironclad commissioned as the C.S.S. *Stonewall Jackson.* The war ended before it engaged Union vessels. It was docked in Havana, Cuba, and eventually sold for scrap.

The battle between the U.S.S. *Monitor* and the C.S.S. *Virginia* revolutionized naval warfare.

✴ Hatcher's Run

CAMPAIGN: Richmond-Petersburg Campaign

DATE(S): February 5–7, 1865

One of several repeated efforts to take the important Boydton Plank Road (see p. 220), Hatcher's Run was an attempt by Grant to cut off Rebel supplies during the Siege of Petersburg. Although Union forces did not take the road, they gained ground, while Confederate casualties could not be replaced, and Southern lines became increasingly weaker.

LOCATION: Markers, parking area, and battlefield located on Dabney Mill Rd., half a mile west of the intersection with Duncan Rd. in Petersburg.

✴ Haw's Shop

CAMPAIGN: Grant's Overland Campaign

DATE(S): May 28, 1864

While covering the Army of the Potomac as it advanced across the Pamunkey River toward Totopotomoy Creek, General Gregg's cavalry engaged Southern cavalry near Enon Church, to inconclusive results. General Custer added to his reputation at this fight, capturing 80 Confederates using dismounted cavalry.

LOCATION: Two markers located at Enon Church, 6156 Studley Rd., Mechanicsville, point visitors across the field to where the Federal attack took place.

✷ High Bridge

CAMPAIGN: Appomattox Campaign

DATE(S): April 6–7, 1865

As Lee's army retreated toward Lynchburg, a small Union force seized High Bridge, which was necessary to cross the Appomattox River. They attempted to burn the bridge and trap the Confederates. On April 6, 1865, Southern cavalry waged a desperate fight to secure the bridge, lest their army be divided in two. They seized the bridge and captured around 800 Federals. With Union forces in hot pursuit, on April 7 it was the Confederates' turn to try to delay the opponent by burning the

bridge. Northern troops put out the fire before too much damage was done, however. As a result, Lee's men could not take their rations at Farmville. This put Lee, already in a race against time, in an even more desperate position.

Today, High Bridge is part of a beautiful and extensive walking trail known as High Bridge Trail State Park. Visitors who take the trail, which has good interpretation, will enjoy both the exercise and the story while being rewarded with a wonderful view. The bridge is located 4.5 miles east of Farmville. The easiest way to see it is to park at the lot on River Road, 3.5 miles east of Farmville and then walk on the trail, one mile east toward the bridge.

LOCATION: **High Bridge, 3.5 miles east of Farmville, 434-315-0457. Park in the lot at the intersection of River Rd. and the trail.**

Lee's Retreat

As Lee retreated from Petersburg to Appomattox, desertions, casualties, and captures drained the strength of his army from more than 50,000 to fewer than 30,000 troops. After suffering catastrophic losses at the Sayler's Creek fight, Lee was severely undermanned. Although stragglers caught up days after the surrender, Lee's parolees numbered no more than 27,000 soldiers.

When it was built in the 1850s, High Bridge was "perhaps the largest bridge in the world." Today, it is a fantastic recreational attraction.

✳ Hill's Point/Suffolk

CAMPAIGN: Longstreet's Tidewater Operations

DATE(S): April 11–May 4, 1863

Sent by Lee to protect Richmond from a possible attack by Union reinforcements at Norfolk, and also to gather supplies in preparation for a planned raid into the north, General Longstreet moved against Union-controlled Suffolk on April 11, 1863, besieging the Union Army there. The siege lasted

Taunting Messages

Fitzhugh Lee (Robert E. Lee's nephew and Southern brigadier general) and Union General Averell had been close friends at West Point. Now the Civil War had placed them on opposite sides of the conflict.

Before the Battle of Kelly's Ford, Fitzhugh Lee sent his old pal a taunting message: "I wish you would put up your sword, leave my state, and go home. You ride a good horse, I ride a better. If you won't go home, return my visit, and bring me a sack of coffee." A furious Averell sought revenge at Kelly's Ford and left a sack of coffee and note with wounded Confederates: "Dear Fitz, here's your coffee. Here's your visit. How do you like it?"

After the war, Lee became governor of Virginia and Averell became rich by helping invent modern asphalt. Both men also became consul generals, Averell to British North America (which became Canada) and Lee in Havana, Cuba. At the outbreak of the Spanish-American War, Lee joined the U.S. Army and became military governor of Havana. Despite their mutual success, similar diplomatic roles, and Lee's abandonment of the Confederate cause symbolized by his service in the Federal Army, there is no evidence suggesting these estranged friends ever met again.

nearly a month, and while neither side gained the upper hand, Union forces were stuck in Suffolk, preventing them from threatening Richmond and also allowing the Confederates time to forage for food.

The battlefield has been lost to development, but markers are scattered throughout the town. The headquarters of Union General Peck, an antebellum Greek revival house known as Riddick's Folly, stands nearby. Also nearby is newly restored Fort Huger (see p. 299). Like its companion Fort Boykin (see p. 299), Huger is an earthen fort open to visitors.

LOCATION: **Two battle markers located on N. Main St., the first at the intersection with Godwin Blvd., the second one a third of a mile south of Edgewood Ave., just after Holly Lawn Cemetery.**

✳ Jerusalem Plank Road

CAMPAIGN: Richmond-Petersburg Campaign

DATE(S): June 21–24, 1864

Attempting to destroy the Weldon Railroad, Union forces suffered heavy casualties when a counterattack by General Mahone drove them from the field of battle and secured the railroad. Despite this loss, Federal forces extended their lines west, foreshadowing Grant's strategy of extending Union lines and cutting off the Southern supply that would lead to Richmond's fall in 1865.

LOCATION: **Markers and the remains of Fort Davis located at the intersection of Crater Rd. and Flank Rd., Petersburg. Jerusalem Plank Rd. was later renamed Crater Rd. (US 301).**

✳ Kelly's Ford

CAMPAIGN: Cavalry Operations Along the Rappahannock

DATE(S): March 17, 1863

Determined to crush Fitzhugh Lee's Confederate cavalry, General Averell crossed the Rappahannock River and hid behind a stone wall, where he fended off several Confederate assaults. He failed to press his

With the area's only macadamized road, Kernstown—named after German-American Adam Kern—was a gateway to the important city of Winchester. Thus, Kernstown was the site of three battles in the war: Kernstown I, Kernstown II, and the second battle of Winchester, which began here.

advantage, however, and the Confederates escaped destruction. Notable for the colorful backstory of the commanding generals and also as a prelude to the Battle of Brandy Station (see p. 221), the battle is, nevertheless, overshadowed in history by the death of young artillerist John Pelham.

LOCATION: **Markers and battlefield view located on Newbys Shop Rd., half a mile northeast of the intersection with Kellys Ford Rd., Remington, 540-371-1907.**

✳ Kernstown I

CAMPAIGN: Jackson's Valley Campaign
DATE(S): March 23, 1862

Designed to threaten the security of Washington, D.C., Jackson's legendary campaign began inauspiciously. Relying on false intelligence, he ran into a much larger Federal force at Kernstown and was forced to retreat after Colonel Kimball's men attacked his left flank. Jackson was furious that the commander of his old Stonewall Brigade, Richard Garnett, had retreated without permission. He pressed charges, which hung over Garnett's head for 16 months and went to the grave with him during Pickett's Charge at Gettysburg.

Kernstown was notable as Jackson's only defeat during the war; nevertheless, the outcome achieved Lee's purpose by compelling Lincoln to withhold reinforcements from McClellan's Peninsula Campaign. McClellan suffered from bad intelligence. Lacking

combat instinct, he specialized in organizing and was unwilling to unleash his army until he had perfected his plans. Lincoln had removed McClellan as general in chief two weeks prior, and the general had begun to suspect a plot against him in the administration. Jackson would feed that fear.

Kernstown Battlefield Park offers walking tours, historical markers, and the antebellum Pritchard House.

LOCATION: **Kernstown Battlefield Park, 610 Battle Park Dr., Winchester, 540-869-2896, www.kernstownbattle.org.**

FURTHER READING
"We Are in for It!":
The First Battle
of Kernstown
by Gary L. Ecelbarger
A readable and interesting look at this battle

Upon Lee's advice, John Pelham was posthumously promoted to lieutenant colonel.

✳ Kernstown II

CAMPAIGN: Early's Raid and Operations Against the B&O Railroad

DATE(S): July 24, 1864

Under the false impression that wily General Early no longer posed a threat to the Shenandoah, Union troops left to reinforce Grant at Petersburg. To stop them, Early attacked General Crook's men near Winchester and, after routing them, moved north to fight battles at Monocacy and Fort Stevens outside Washington, D.C. In retaliation for the burning of the Virginia Military

Union forces captured this Confederate battle flag at Kernstown.

Institute, Early burned Chambersburg, Pennsylvania, on July 30. This had the intended effect, and Grant ordered the Union VI and XIX Corps to the Valley.

LOCATION: Kernstown Battlefield Park, 610 Battle Park Dr., Winchester, 540-869-2896, www.kernstownbattle.org.

✳ Lewis's Farm

CAMPAIGN: Appomattox Campaign

DATE(S): March 29, 1865

Determined to destroy Lee's army or force him out of his defenses, Grant sent troops to turn Lee's right flank. General Chamberlain's brigade met General Johnson's Confederates at Lewis's Farm, turning back the Rebels after being reinforced by an artillery battery and two additional regiments. This is considered by some as the first battle of the Appomattox Campaign and, thus, the beginning of the war's end.

LOCATION: Marker located on Quaker Rd. (VA Rte. 660), 1 mile south of US 1. While the battlefield is private property, a drive on Quaker Rd. provides some outline of the action.

✳ Lynchburg

CAMPAIGN: Lynchburg Campaign

DATE(S): June 17–18, 1864

General Hunter advanced toward Lynchburg, an important Confederate city with

Lynchburg

A vital transportation hub, Lynchburg in the 1850s was the second wealthiest city per capita in the entire United States. Trade ties to the north made Lynchburg, like the rest of Virginia, relatively slower to embrace the Confederate cause. The city's key location as a transportation hub supported multiple hospitals. Indeed, it was the only major city in Virginia never to fall to Union forces. Lee and the Confederate Army found themselves supplied by the Southside Railroad that ran across the state along the south side of the James River. The James River Canal paralleled the river and was part of the route of Stonewall Jackson's funeral procession back to Lexington in 1863. Lynchburg connected to the Virginia & Tennessee Railroad and had a spur from the Orange & Alexandria Railroad, which brought supplies from Tennessee and Northern and Central Virginia. When Hunter burned Lexington and the Virginia Military Institute, the cadets were marched to Lynchburg, where General Early placed them far from the front. The war ended with the capital of the state in Lynchburg, which was also the site of a military prison camp.

Civil War on Foot: Lexington

Noteworthy for its strong ties to the Confederacy, Lexington was the home of Governor John Letcher, whose home was burned along with the Virginia Military Institute (VMI) during Hunter's Raid in 1864. After the war, Lee became president of what is now Washington and Lee University. He and Jackson are buried here.

❶ Jackson Memorial Hall/VMI Museum *(415 Letcher Ave.)* Constructed with funds paid in reparations for the burning of VMI, this building houses the museum, which explores the history and life of Jackson and the Corps of Cadets. The magnificent painting in the chapel shows the charge of the cadets at the Battle of New Market.

Dedicated in July 1895, this statue of Jackson stands over his gravesite.

❷ VMI Barracks Proceed across the road and bear right to Washington Arch, the primary entry to the barracks, which were burned in 1864. The statue of Washington was relocated to Richmond during the war. The area in front of the arch is known as The Bricks. From here, the cadet formation departed for war. Proceed to the left and look up at the corner of the barracks. The second-floor room was Jackson's classroom and where he lay in state prior to his burial. Look ahead to see the statue of Jackson. Jackson's horse, Little Sorrel, was cremated and the remains were buried at the statue's base.

❸ Sir Moses Ezekiel's Statue "Virginia Mourning Her Dead" New Market Day is sacred to the Corps, and a memorial parade is held every year on May 15. The graves of some of the Cadets who "Died on the Field of Honor, Sir" are here.

❹ Lee-Jackson House *(4 University Pl.)* Walk down the road off the VMI campus. Now the home of the president of Washington and Lee University, this is where Jackson and his first wife lived before the war and where Robert E. Lee lived and died as president of Washington College after the war.

❺ Robert E. Lee Episcopal Church *(123 W. Washington St.)* Known as Grace Episcopal when Lee was here, this impressive stone church was renamed in his honor. Here he served as a vestryman and attended his last meeting before his death.

❻ Stonewall Jackson Memorial Cemetery *(314 S. Main St.)* Jackson is buried here along with two Virginia governors, his sister-in-law, Margaret Junkin Preston, and more than 100 Confederate veterans.

❼ Lexington Presbyterian Church
(120 S. Main St.) Jackson was defined by his strong religious beliefs, and he and his family worshipped in this Lexington church. Here also he defied state law and taught slave children to read.

❽ Stonewall Jackson House *(8 E. Washington St.)* Jackson lived here with his second wife, Anna, while he taught at VMI. In 1861 he left his home, never to return again.

❾ Lee Chapel *(11 University Pl.)* Dominated by the magnificent "Lee Recumbent" statue, this tranquil setting is the final resting place of Robert E. Lee and his family. He is buried below the chapel in the crypt across from his office, which is as it was the day he died. His famous horse, Traveller, is buried just outside.

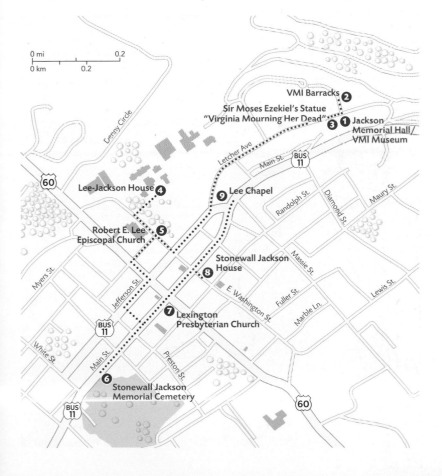

rail and canal transport and a hospital. General Early's II Corps thwarted attempts to take the city, forcing Union troops, short of supplies, to withdraw from the fighting.

The town visitor center offers information about the many monuments and cemeteries, including Jubal Early's grave (see p. 301), and traces the path of the battle. There are interpretive signs near Fort Early and near Early's grave.

LOCATION: **Lynchburg Visitor Center, 216 12th St. at Church, Lynchburg, 800-732-5821, www.discoverlynchburg.org.**

✳ Malvern Hill

CAMPAIGN: Peninsula Campaign
DATE(S): July 1, 1862

Despite the hard fighting of the previous six days, Lee still hoped to destroy McClellan's army. This led him to make one of the worst decisions of the war. Believing a coordinated infantry assault could take Malvern Hill if Union artillery were suppressed, he ordered

FURTHER READING

Extraordinary Circumstances: The Seven Days Battles by Brian K. Burton A detailed look at this important campaign

Confederate artillery to bombard the hill. He was unable to bring sufficient fire on the hill to justify attacking, and the Rebels suffered 5,000 casualties. The Federal position was so strong that less than one-third of the Union army saw combat on this day. The final battle of the Seven Days Battles was a Confederate disaster not duplicated until Pickett's Charge at Gettysburg (see pp. 355–356). That night the Federals slipped away to their new supply base at Berkeley Plantation on the James.

Today, the battlefield is nearly restored to its 1862 appearance, with walking trails and many markers. While the battlefield is open year-round, the Malvern Hill Visitor Center is open in the summer only.

LOCATION: **Malvern Hill Visitor Center, 8301 Willis Church Rd., inside Glendale National Cemetery, Richmond National Battlefield Park, 804-226-1981, www.nps.gov/rich.**

✳ Manassas I

CAMPAIGN: Manassas Campaign
DATE(S): July 21, 1861

The first major battle in Virginia, often seen as the first large battle of the Civil War, Manassas is a dramatic story rife with legend. Believing his troops unprepared, Union General McDowell resisted the battle, but political pressure forced him to move south to meet the equally unprepared Rebel army at Manassas.

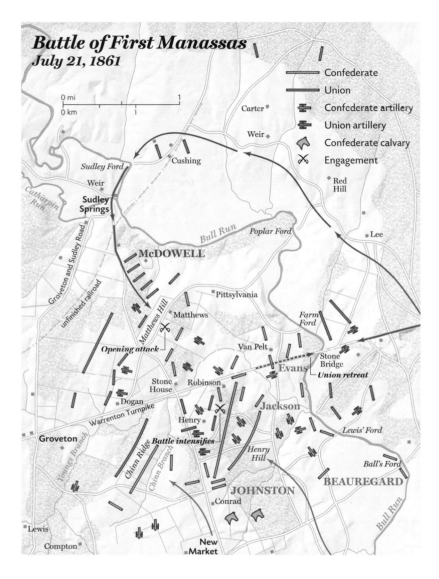

Battle of First Manassas
July 21, 1861

Confederate
Union
Confederate artillery
Union artillery
Confederate calvary
Engagement

0 mi 1
0 km 1

Carter
Weir

Cushing

Sudley Ford
Weir
Sudley Springs

Catharpin Run

Groveton and Sudley Road

unfinished railroad

Red Hill

Bull Run

Poplar Ford

Lee

McDOWELL

Pittsylvania

Matthews

Matthews Hill

Opening attack

Van Pelt

Farm Ford

Stone Bridge

Evans

Union retreat

Stone House

Robinson

Dogan

Warrenton Turnpike

Henry

Groveton

Young's Branch

Chinn Ridge

Chinn Branch

Battle intensifies

Jackson

Henry Hill

Lewis' Ford

Ball's Ford

BEAUREGARD

JOHNSTON

Conrad

Lewis

Compton

New Market

Bull Run

Initial Union attacks on the Confederate left flank put them near victory, until Rebel reinforcements in the afternoon turned the tide on the Union right with a charge and bloodcurdling scream soon to be known as the "Rebel yell." The overwhelming defeat shocked the North, whose politicians demanded answers. Nonstandard uniforms worn by new recruits created confusion for friend and foe and produced the design of the Rebel battle flag. Not only did this battle create the legend of Stonewall Jackson, but it also featured other men who would become famous, including J. E. B. Stuart and

William Tecumseh Sherman. Jefferson Davis arrived at the moment of Southern victory.

The well-preserved battlefield features trails, an excellent movie in the visitor center, a driving tour, and more.

LOCATION: Manassas National Battlefield Park, 6511 Sudley Rd., Manassas, 703-361-1339, www.nps.gov/mana.

FURTHER READING

A Single Grand Victory: The First Campaign and Battle of Manassas
by Ethan S. Rafuse
A comprehensive narrative of the battle

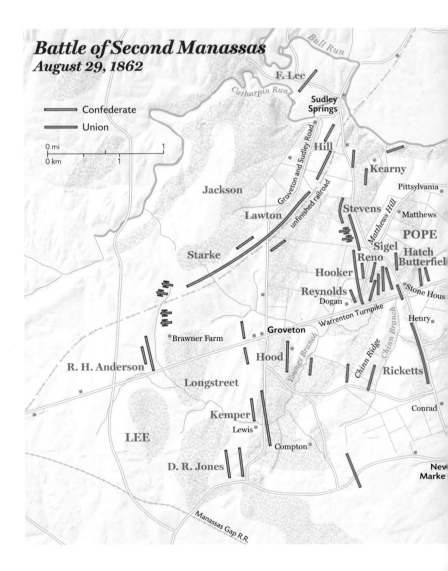

Battle of Second Manassas
August 29, 1862

Bull Run

F. Lee

Catharpin Run

Sudley Springs

━━ Confederate
━━ Union

0 mi   1
0 km   1

Hill

Kearny

Pittsylvania

Jackson

Groveton and Sudley Road

unfinished railroad

Stevens

Matthews Hill

Matthews

Lawton

POPE

Starke

Sigel
Reno

Hatch
Butterfiel

Hooker

Reynolds

Dogan

Stone Hous

Warrenton Turnpike

Henry

Groveton

Youngs Branch

Chinn Branch

Chinn Ridge

Brawner Farm

Hood

R. H. Anderson

Longstreet

Ricketts

Conrad

Kemper

Lewis

LEE

Compton

New
Marke

D. R. Jones

Manassas Gap R.R.

✳ Manassas II

CAMPAIGN: Northern Virginia Campaign

DATE(S): August 28–30, 1862

Although overshadowed by the more famous first battle of Manassas, the second battle was both larger and more important. After McClellan's failure to take Richmond, Lincoln appointed John Pope, who had been successful in the West, to take the fight to the South. Pope's aggressiveness got him into trouble on August 28, 1862, when a small attack from General Jackson, designed to draw him in, did just that. Convinced that he had cornered Jackson, Pope attacked—only to be surprised by 28,000 of General Longstreet's troops, who had reinforced Jackson midday on August 29, in one of the largest simultaneous mass assaults of the war. This assault crushed the Union line, producing a memorable victory that led to Lee's first raid into the North.

LOCATION: Manassas National Battlefield Park, 6511 Sudley Rd., Manassas, 703-361-1339, www.nps.gov/mana.

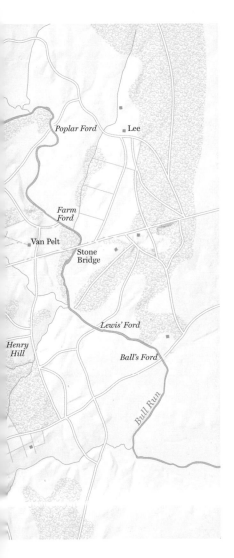

FURTHER READING

Return to Bull Run: The Campaign and Battle of Second Manassas by John J. Hennessy The definitive account of Second Manassas

Stonewall Jackson

For years, historians have debated the meaning behind "Stonewall"—one of the most famous nicknames in American history. According to the legend, General Bee rallied his faltering troops by saying, "There is Jackson standing like a stone wall! Rally behind the Virginians!" One observer, however, claimed that he angrily said, "Look at Jackson standing there like a damned stone wall!" He was referring to Jackson's supposed inaction while Bee's men fought. Killed in battle shortly after he spoke those words, Bee himself could never clarify the issue. Whatever the nickname's intended meaning, Jackson unquestionably proved himself one of the greatest commanders of the Civil War.

Pictured are the remnants of a railroad turntable at Manassas Station that was destroyed by retreating Confederates.

Manassas Gap

CAMPAIGN: Gettysburg Campaign

DATE(S): July 23, 1863

Notable as the last encounter of the Gettysburg Campaign, this battle was a small rearguard action as General Lee returned to Virginia following defeat at Gettysburg (see pp. 352–357). Today, visitors can trace the lines of the battle from Route 647 and Highway 55. A marker explains the shape of the battle and allows drivers to tour the battle's location.

LOCATION: Marker explaining the battle at the Linden Park and Ride on Rte. 647, a half mile west of the intersection of Rte. 647 and Hwy. 55, 540-636-1446, www.warrenheritage society.org.

Manassas Station Operations

CAMPAIGN: Northern Virginia Campaign

DATE(S): August 25–27, 1862

Seizing an opportunity to fall on General Pope's unprotected supply line, Stonewall Jackson attacked the railroad at Bristoe Station and moved to take the Union supply depot at Manassas Junction. On August 27, 1862, Jackson caused one train to derail and another to back up, which spread word of the raid. During the encounter, Jackson defeated men under the command of General Taylor, who was mortally wounded in the scrap. Meanwhile, Richard S. Ewell's Confederate forces fought a battle at Kettle

Run against General Hooker's men, while Jackson's men helped themselves to the boxcars of sumptuous supplies at Manassas Junction, which included hams, canned lobster, and German wine. Jackson so feared the effect of liquor on his men that he ordered the casks broken open, only to witness the spectacle of soldiers dipping their canteens at the curb to catch the demon rum. The day's fighting over, Jackson dug in near an unfinished railroad just north of the First Manassas battlefield, awaiting Pope's certain arrival.

LOCATION: **Bristoe Station Battlefield Heritage Park, 17674 Main St., Dumfries, 703-792-4754. There is a related marker at the intersection of Nokesville Rd. and Aden Rd., a mile and a half away. Signage is also posted at the Manassas Railroad Station, 9431 West St., Manassas.**

✷ Mantapike Hill

CAMPAIGN: Kilpatrick-Dahlgren Raid
OTHER NAME(S): Walkerton
DATE(S): March 2, 1864

From their camp at Stevensburg, General Kilpatrick and Colonel Dahlgren led 4,000 Union soldiers on a botched raid on Richmond, intending to attack the Confederate capital from the rear and rescue Union prisoners at Belle Isle. Poor coordination meant that Kilpatrick, having trudged through snow and rain to reach the city's inner defenses, decided to withdraw when he could find no sign of Dahlgren's men. Meanwhile, Dahlgren was forced to retreat after meeting resistance before being ambushed by the 9th Virginia Cavalry. Dahlgren was killed in the battle, and papers on his body allegedly suggested that he had orders to assassinate Jefferson Davis, leading to much controversy.

LOCATION: **Marker where Dahlgren died, located at the intersection of Bunker Hill Rd. and Stevensville Rd. in Dahlgren's Corner. Another marker, referencing early movements toward Richmond, is located at the intersection of River Rd. W. (VA Rte. 6) and Dover Rd. in Manakin Sabot.**

✷ Marion

CAMPAIGN: Stoneman's Raid Into Southwest Virginia
DATE(S): December 17–18, 1864

This raid, which was executed by General Stoneman on December 17, 1864, to further weaken the Confederate infrastructure, overwhelmed weak Confederate defenses protecting the lead and salt mines near Marion and Saltville.

LOCATION: **Two markers located at the intersection of N. Main St. and Medical Park Dr., in Marion. There are also several markers outside Marion and a Confederate monument in the town itself. The antebellum Martha Washington Inn is in nearby Abingdon (see p. 302).**

✷ McDowell

CAMPAIGN: Jackson's Valley Campaign
DATE(S): May 8, 1862

Jackson and his 10,000 men moved rapidly into the Allegheny Mountains to drive away 6,000 Federal soldiers near McDowell. After seizing Sitlington's Hill, Jackson had Virginia Military Institute cadets disassemble cannons and drag them to the top of the hill

John Pope lost his army's trust after implying that Easterners could not fight.

The Plot Against Jefferson Davis

Ulric Dahlgren stands over an interesting cast of characters, including Count Zeppelin from Germany and a Swedish observer and aide to several Union generals.

Ulric Dahlgren, a Union colonel, never made it to Richmond. He attempted to cross the James at Dover Mills, but the river was swollen with rainwater. He blamed a local black guide for this misfortune and summarily hung him. Meanwhile, Southern resistance east of Richmond forced Dahlgren to retreat, but he was ambushed and killed by Confederates, who allegedly found papers on his body with orders to assassinate Jefferson Davis and burn Richmond. This revelation caused a political furor in both North and South. General Meade assured Lee there was no such order. Historians have long debated the letter's authenticity, with some contending it was a Confederate forgery while others believe the orders came from near the top of

Union command. The original order was apparently turned over to Union Secretary of War Edwin Stanton in 1865—whom some believe had a role in the plot. Many believe Stanton burned the letter to avoid incriminating himself, further fueling the conspiracy theory. In any event, the document has been lost to history—although many so-called copies survive. Some speculate the outrage resulting from this "plot" led to Lincoln's assassination, but that seems a stretch. In one of the many ironies of the war, Dahlgren was already famous for the seizure of secret letters. He had captured important Confederate letters sent from Jefferson Davis to Robert E. Lee on July 2, 1863.

Dahlgren was wearing this glove and bloody sash when he was killed (note the bullet hole).

where, reassembled, they added considerable firepower. Jackson was "King of the Hill" when General Schenck attacked, leading to a four-hour battle.

Sitlington's Hill is a demanding but rewarding climb. Bring water and allow time.

LOCATION: Battlefield trail and marker located at the intersection of Rte. 250 and Rte. 678, McDowell.

FURTHER READING

Stonewall in the Valley: Thomas J. "Stonewall" Jackson's Shenandoah Valley Campaign, Spring 1862
by Robert G. Tanner
A full account of Jackson's famed Valley Campaign

✵Middleburg

CAMPAIGN: Gettysburg Campaign

DATE(S): June 17–18, 1863

As the Army of Northern Virginia marched north to Gettysburg, General Stuart's cavalry screened Lee's army, hiding his movements and intentions from the curious Federals. Stuart engaged Union forces near Middleburg, routing Colonel Duffié's 1st Rhode Island Cavalry. Although forced to fall back by continued Union pressure, Stuart's Rebel troops protected Lee's movements from being discovered.

LOCATION: "Pink Box" visitor center, 12 N. Madison St., Middleburg, 540-687-8888. The equestrian-focused National Sporting Library and Museum (see p. 303) features a sculpture of an abused and malnourished Civil War horse. Unison Historic District (see pp. 306–307) is also located nearby.

FURTHER READING

Bold Dragoon: The Life of J. E. B. Stuart
by Emory M. Thomas
The life story of one of the war's most interesting figures

✵Mine Run

CAMPAIGN: Mine Run Campaign

OTHER NAME(S): Payne's Farm

DATE(S): November 27–December 2, 1863

With two-thirds of Lee's I Corps under Longstreet in Tennessee, Union General Meade planned on smashing Lee before winter. His surprise march through the wilderness was intended to destroy the right flank of the Southern army; however, after several minor engagements, Lee and his men dug in on commanding ground near Mine Run. Meade (an engineer by training) in consultation with another engineer, V Corps Commander Warren, determined that Lee's lines were too well laid for a direct assault and withdrew.

LOCATION: Multiple markers and a walking trail located across from Zoar Baptist Church, 31334 Zoar Rd., Locust Grove.

✵Morton's Ford

CAMPAIGN: Demonstration on the Rapidan River

DATE(S): February 6–7, 1864

Although neither side gained ground in this halfhearted demonstration, the Union troops successfully diverted the Rebels and then withdrew the night of February 7.

LOCATION: No public access.

✵Namozine Church

CAMPAIGN: Appomattox Campaign

DATE(S): April 3, 1865

With Lee's abandonment of Petersburg, Federal cavalry aggressively attempted to cut off a portion of Lee's fleeing forces. Here the men led by brash young General Custer clashed with Fitzhugh Lee's cavalry and some infantry in the fields near Namozine Church.

LOCATION: Markers and antebellum church located at the intersection of Namozine Rd. (Rte. 708) and Greenes Rd. (Rte. 622), Amelia County. This is part of Virginia Civil War Trails' "Lee's Retreat" tour (see p. 295).

✳ New Market

CAMPAIGN: Lynchburg Campaign

DATE(S): May 15, 1864

Despite its small size, this was one of the more romanticized battles of the war. While Grant waged a spring offensive against Lee, General Sigel was ordered to disrupt the key Confederate supply base and communications network at Lynchburg. Since the war's inception, cadets from the Virginia Military Institute had filled various roles as instructors and reserve forces at many sites in the valley; however, they had not seen combat. At New Market, around 4,100 Confederates attacked Sigel's 10,000 men. A split in the Confederate lines put the 257 young cadets in the front, near a Union battery. Immortalized for their bravery, the cadets charged through boot-sucking mud in a rainstorm and captured the battery.

The preserved battlefield features the Virginia Museum of the Civil War. The Virginia Military Institute in Lexington (see pp. 252–253) holds an annual commemorative parade and ceremony on May 15.

LOCATION: New Market Battlefield Historical Park, 8895 George R. Collins Pkwy., New

An annual event at New Market re-creates the drama and tragedy of battle.

Market, 866-515-1864; Virginia Museum of the Civil War, www.vmi.edu/vmcw.

✵ Norfleet House/Suffolk

CAMPAIGN: Longstreet's Tidewater Operations

DATE(S): April 13–15, 1863

As the siege of Suffolk began, General Longstreet's men pushed toward the Union lines, erecting a battery at Hill's Point on April 13, 1863, that threatened Union shipping on the James River. The next day, Union ships attacked a similar battery at nearby Norfleet House, but the U.S.S. *Mount Washington* grounded. On April 15, newly built Union batteries opened fire on the unfortunately positioned Norfleet House works and forced a Confederate withdrawal.

LOCATION: No public access to the battlefield. Siege of Suffolk marker located on N. Main St., less than a mile north of the intersection with US 58 Alt. in Suffolk. Cedar Hill Cemetery, which features a Confederate monument, is located nearby.

The New Market Cadets

Possessing the fervor and unconditional enthusiasm of youth, the charge by the Virginia Military Institute (VMI) cadets—many whom had been students of Professor Stonewall Jackson—was truly a unique occurrence in American history. Never before or since has an American college student body participated in a battle as an independent unit and won. The youngest cadet to take part was a mere 15 years of age. Five years after witnessing his best friend die from battle wounds, one survivor, Moses Ezekiel, went on to create the statue "Virginia Mourning Her Dead," which stands at VMI over the graves of six of those killed in action on that day. For more than 150 years, cadets and alumni of that prestigious school have been inspired by the "spirit of VMI."

Pontoon bridges, like this one erected at North Anna, were important tools.

✵ North Anna

CAMPAIGN: Grant's Overland Campaign

DATE(S): May 23–26, 1864

In an effort to catch Lee's army outside its entrenchments, Grant decided to move south and threaten Richmond. Lee moved cautiously but decisively to maintain his defensive advantage. After abandoning the lines at Spotsylvania, he moved to the line of the North Anna River while protecting the critical Hanover railroad junction. Grant carelessly moved across the river on May 23, penetrating the Southern lines. Lee turned this initial defeat into a masterful trap when he repositioned his army and dug earthworks in an inverted V anchored on the river. As Grant's different corps advanced and crossed the river, they unwittingly split into three independent groups not easily supported by any other. Lee had an opportunity to destroy all or a major part of Grant's army; however, ill in his tent and with unreliable subordinate leadership, he was unable to strike, making this one of the greatest what-ifs of the war.

The battlefield of Ox Ford has Blue and Gray Walking Trails with 23 interpretive signs. The Blue Trail is an official bird-watching site.

Widely regarded as the most important battle in the Shenandoah Valley, Opequon marked the beginning of the end of Jubal Early's fighting power, before his ultimate defeat one month later at Cedar Creek.

ocated near the Maryland border, Winchester changed hands a remarkable 72 times. Sitting at the foot of the Shenandoah Valley and used as a staging area for movements into the Ohio Valley, the city was an important transportation center screened by mountains to the east and west. Those who lived there suffered greatly under Union rule. One occupier, General Milroy, a "radical" abolitionist, wrote, "My will is absolute law . . . the secesh here have heard many terrible stories about me before I came and supposed me to be a perfect Nero for cruelty and blood . . . I confess I feel a strong disposition to play the tyrant among those traitors." Winchester Medical College, the first medical school in Virginia, was burned to the ground on the orders of Union General Banks because the body of one of John Brown's sons had been dissected there to train students. Later, as he was burning the Shenandoah Valley, General Sheridan said, "The crow that flies over the Valley of Virginia must henceforth carry his rations with him." Caught between two armies, Winchester suffered greatly for it.

FURTHER READING

The Last Battle of Winchester: Phil Sheridan, Jubal Early, and the Shenandoah Valley Campaign, August 7– September 19, 1864
by Scott Patchan
A chronicle of the largest battle in the Shenandoah

LOCATION: **North Anna Battlefield Park, 11576 Verdon Rd., Doswell, 804-365-7150. For the trail map and interpretive guide, visit www .hanovercounty.gov/RP/North_Anna_ Battlefield_Park_Trail_Map_and_Guide.pdf.**

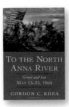

FURTHER READING

To the North Anna River: Grant and Lee, May 13–25, 1864
by Gordon G. Rhea
A riveting narrative of this crucial period

today's Richmond Airport. Attacking across swampy ground, Union forces found little success. Much to Lee's relief, the Federals pulled back and did not renew the assault.

Today, the grounds of the Richmond Airport cover the battlefield, although there is a small marker, surviving earthworks, and an artillery piece located just outside the airport.

LOCATION: **Marker and replica artillery gun located at the intersection of South Airport Dr. and Clarkson Rd. in Richmond.**

✷ Oak Grove

CAMPAIGN: Peninsula Campaign
DATE(S): June 25, 1862

As Lee prepared to use 80 percent of his army on the other side of the Chickahominy River to destroy 20 percent of McClellan's exposed army, McClellan unexpectedly launched a probing attack on Lee's under-manned and exposed right flank near

✴ Old Church

CAMPAIGN: Grant's Overland Campaign
DATE(S): May 30, 1864

Following the fighting at North Anna (see pp. 263–265), with Union and Confederate forces arrayed along Totopotomoy Creek, Union cavalry under General Torbert tested Confederate positions to the south and east. They encountered General Butler's Rebel

Union General Torbert's victory over Butler's Confederates at Old Church set the stage for one of the bloodiest battles of the war, Cold Harbor.

horsemen and drove them toward Old Cold Harbor, which was seized by Federals the next day.

LOCATION: Marker referencing Confederate positions on Mechanicsville Tpke., located a tenth of a mile before the intersection with Pebble Path Pkwy. in Mechanicsville.

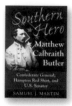

FURTHER READING

Southern Hero, Matthew Calbraith Butler: Confederate General, Hampton Red Shirt, and U.S. Senator by Samuel J. Martin A biography of this overlooked general and senator

✳ Opequon

CAMPAIGN: Sheridan's Valley Campaign
OTHER NAME(S): Third Winchester
DATE(S): September 19, 1864

After weeks of warily engaging Jubal Early's forces in the Shenandoah, Sheridan learned from a local Union sympathizer that Lee had ordered one of Early's divisions to return to the Petersburg fortifications. He seized this opportunity to strike Early's remaining forces. To blunt the oncoming Federal

Robert E. Rodes

One of the most underrated generals to serve in the Civil War, Robert E. Rodes (1829–1864) graduated from the Virginia Military Institute (VMI) and was rapidly advancing in reputation as a brigade commander in an army led by many from West Point. Just before Stonewall Jackson ordered the attack at Chancellorsville (see pp. 224–227), he looked over the staging army led by many VMI graduates and said to Rodes, "The Institute will be heard from today." Jackson, lying on his deathbed, endorsed Rodes's promotion to major general. Like Jackson's, however, Rodes's aggressive battlefield leadership led to his own death at the Battle of Opequon.

Many military leaders were killed at Opequon, including two generals—Robert Rodes and David Russell—and the Confederate grandfather of World War II hero George S. Patton, Jr.

The Union V Corps assaults a Confederate fort during the Battle of Peebles' Farm. Northern victory brought Grant closer to his goal—seizing the Boydton Plank Road.

assault, the Southerners attacked first, although that only delayed the Union wave to come. Early action saw heavy casualties as the Confederate line was pushed back toward Winchester. The battle culminated in a massive 6,000-man Union cavalry charge, arrayed one mile wide and three men deep, described by George Custer as "one moving mass of glittering sabers." He noted this charge was "one of the most inspiring as well as imposing scenes of martial grandeur ever witnessed upon a battle-field." It was one of the rare decisive cavalry charges of the Civil War.

A bloody fight with more than 8,600 casualties, Opequon led to the deaths of two Confederate generals and the wounding of three more. The encounter also significantly weakened Early's force, and a subsequent battle at Fisher's Hill (see p. 235) just two days later seemingly destroyed it, only to see it resurrected later in October at Cedar Creek (see pp. 222–223).

Today, the battlefield is well preserved and features more than five miles of walking and bike trails. The town visitor center has a great deal of information about the Battle of Opequon and the other two battles contested over Winchester (see p. 264).

LOCATION: Winchester-Frederick County Visitor Center, 1400 S. Pleasant Valley Rd., Winchester, 877-871-1326, www.visit winchesterva.com.

FURTHER READING
From Winchester to Cedar Creek: The Shenandoah Campaign of 1864 by Jeffry D. Wert
A riveting take on the 1864 Shenandoah Campaign

✳ Peebles' Farm

CAMPAIGN: Richmond-Petersburg Campaign
DATE(S): September 30–October 2, 1864

Grant continued to stretch Lee's thinning lines by ordering attacks on both the eastern and western ends of Lee's earthworks. This western battle was one of many attempts to take Boydton Plank Road and control the Southside Railroad. Initial Federal movements on September 30, 1864, seized Fort Archer, forcing the Southerners out of their lines near Squirrel Level Road. An October 1 counterattack by Confederate General Hill was repulsed, although it limited Union gains. The next day, Federal forces took

Fort MacRae, extending their lines farther. These incremental extensions of the Federal lines to more than 35 miles would be the eventual undoing of Lee's army.

LOCATION: **Petersburg National Battlefield, 5001 Siege Rd., Petersburg, 804-732-3531, www.nps.gov/pete. Battle marker located at the intersection of Flank Rd. and Church Rd.**

✳ Petersburg I

CAMPAIGN: Richmond-Petersburg Campaign

DATE(S): June 9, 1864

Seeking redemption after his failure during the Bermuda Hundred Campaign (see sidebar p. 274), General Butler sent General Gillmore to attack the sparsely manned Confederate Dimmock Line near Petersburg. Despite Federal forces having 2,000 more men than the defending Confederates, the Union infantry refused to attack until after a cavalry assault.

Though spread out, the 2,500 defenders repulsed the cavalry assault, a defeat made more embarrassing because the defending Confederate home guard was made up of old men, young boys, and wounded soldiers, thus earning this battle the nickname Old Men and Young Boys. Confederate reinforcements soon arrived, and this chance to take Petersburg was lost. Gillmore's complete failure here led to his arrest, although no charges were ever brought against him.

LOCATION: **Petersburg National Battlefield, 5001 Siege Rd., Petersburg, 804-732-3531, www.nps.gov/pete. Part of the Dimmock Line can be seen near the visitor center and early in the Petersburg driving tour.**

✳ Petersburg II

CAMPAIGN: Richmond-Petersburg Campaign

DATE(S): June 15–18, 1864

Six days after the Union loss at the first battle of Petersburg, the Army of the Potomac arrived and attacked General Beauregard's defenses. His force was small—a mere 5,400 men. Unable to hold off the Union assault,

Re-created infantry fortifications, like these at Petersburg National Battlefield, give visitors a feel for Civil War–era defenses.

Ulysses S. Grant

Grant only narrowly escaped being assassinated with Lincoln. He had been invited to Ford's Theatre with the president but had to decline because of plans to visit Philadelphia.

Born into modest circumstances as the son of a tanner, Ulysses S. Grant (1822–1885) seemed destined for obscurity. Indeed, his life was a string of failures and mediocrity until the Civil War. Yet despite these hardships, he saved the nation by leading the Union Army to victory and then was twice elected president.

Although he didn't want to go, Grant attended West Point, where he graduated in the middle of his class. He served in the Mexican-American War, but afterward, poor assignments, business ventures gone wrong, a drinking problem, and failure as a farmer resulted in Grant working as his father's clerk—a humiliating blow.

The Civil War presented an opportunity, and here Grant finally succeeded. He rejoined the army and quickly won major battles, including the first major Union victory at Fort Donelson (see pp. 185–187), where he became famous for demanding "unconditional surrender." He later won the campaigns of Vicksburg and Chattanooga, which catapulted him to the rank of lieutenant general, the first since George

Washington to occupy this position. Using a combination of superior strategy, relentless aggression, and brute firepower, Grant overpowered the Confederates to win the war, ultimately taking Richmond after the herculean siege of Petersburg.

After victory in the war, Grant was elected president in 1868 and oversaw an administration committed to civil rights, though riddled with corruption. After leaving office, Grant became bankrupt when a Wall Street business partner's corrupt dealings destroyed his investment firm. Dying from throat cancer, and racing to raise money for his family, Grant finished his memoirs, a best seller published two months after his death in 1885.

Despite the greater pedigree or prior success of many of Grant's contemporaries, it was the humble son of a tanner who saved the Union. Both for the role he played in saving the Union, and also for his fulfillment of the American ideal that any one can rise to the highest office in the land, Grant remains one of the most important figures in American history.

they withdrew to their second lines near Harrison Creek. Fearing all was lost, Beauregard noted that "at that hour [Petersburg] was clearly at the mercy of the Federal commander, who had all but captured it."

Despite early success and an overwhelming manpower advantage, Union forces under General Smith failed to finish the job, even though they could and should have seized the city. Historians have debated whether a bout of malaria, sheer hesitation and fear, or both led to such timid moves by Smith. More Union attacks on June 16 resulted in minor gains, although the Confederate position was already developing backbone and a Southern counterattack captured some Union prisoners. On June 17, a morning attack by General Potter was initially successful but crested when Union forces encountered another line of Southern earthworks. By the next day, Lee had sent

two divisions to reinforce the Confederates; the crisis was past. Assaults on the Confederate positions were bloody and ineffective, and Grant called them off. Facing incredible odds, the city of Petersburg was saved.

Although in disfavor with President Davis, this was Beauregard's finest moment in the war. This was also the Union's last best chance to seize Petersburg without a siege. The failure to capitalize on this golden opportunity meant the next nine months of the war would be fought in the trenches.

LOCATION: **Petersburg National Battlefield, 5001 Siege Rd., Petersburg, 804-732-3531, www.nps.gov/pete. Petersburg remains a jewel of a park and is very well interpreted. Pleasant old town Petersburg (see p. 304) is also well worth a visit, as is Grant's Headquarters at City Point (1001 Pecan Ave., Hopewell, 804-458-9504). Located on the water, his headquarters is part of Richmond National Battlefield Park (804-226-1981, www.nps.gov/rich), although not contiguous with other parts of the park.**

Union soldiers and freedmen cheer President Lincoln during his visit to City Point, Virginia.

✳ Petersburg III

CAMPAIGN: Appomattox Campaign
DATE(S): April 2, 1865

"I mean to end the business here." Those were Grant's thoughts as he pondered this, his final attack on Petersburg—and one of the most important battles of the entire war. His well-supplied Union army of 120,000 faced off against a ragged force of 55,000 tired Confederates. This was the endgame to four years of national division.

Lee was well aware of his precarious position. He knew that his lines would soon break and Richmond would be lost. He intended to move south to link up with Joseph Johnston's Army of Tennessee, attack Sherman, and then turn to face Grant. Failure at Fort Stedman and Five Forks (see pp. 236–237) had reduced the size of his army and limited his options. Sensing victory was at hand, Grant ordered a general assault on Petersburg.

At dawn, Union forces advanced at multiple locations. General Sheridan's recently arrived cavalry penetrated Petersburg's defenses at several points. General Wright and his VI Corps broke through multiple defenses manned by Georgians and North Carolinians. As he rode along his lines, Confederate General Hill was killed by a Federal bullet, a fitting end for a man who had famously said he would rather die than witness the end of the Confederacy.

Desperate fighting by the outnumbered Confederates merely delayed the inevitable. During the fighting, Lee sent a telegram to President Davis: "I advise that all preparation be made for leaving Richmond tonight." Lee and his army escaped in the middle of the night, abandoning Richmond. Grant's hounding of Lee caused Lee's surrender one week later.

Today, a visit to Petersburg National Battlefield is essential to understand the enormity and importance of both the siege of Petersburg and this battle, so crucial to the end of the war. The park offers a wealth of interpretive signs, walking trails, exhibits, and a visitor center. Many monuments and forts—like Fort Gregg, Fort Wadsworth, and the imaginatively named Forts Hell and Damnation—are worthwhile visits. Other locations integral to this story—such as where A. P. Hill died, marked by a monument within woods near Pamplin Historical Park (see p. 304)—are open to visit.

LOCATION: Petersburg National Battlefield, 5001 Siege Rd., Petersburg, 804-732-3531, www.nps.gov/pete.

FURTHER READING

The Final Battles of the Petersburg Campaign: Breaking the Backbone of the Rebellion
by A. Wilson Greene
A detailed look at the campaign that won Richmond

✳ Piedmont

CAMPAIGN: Lynchburg Campaign
DATE(S): June 5, 1864

Seeking to crush Confederate resistance in the Shenandoah Valley, General Hunter attacked the Southern army near Piedmont. An attack on its right flank resulted in a retreat that soon became a total collapse when General Grumble Jones, attempting to stop the retreat, was killed. More than 1,000 Rebels were taken prisoner. Largely preserved, the battlefield is privately owned and can be viewed only from Battlefield Road.

LOCATION: Interpretive marker outside New Hope Community Center, 691 Battlefield Rd., New Hope. Small battlefield marker on Battlefield Rd., 1 mile north of New Hope.

FURTHER READING

The Battle of Piedmont and Hunter's Raid on Staunton: The 1864 Shenandoah Campaign
by Scott C. Patchan
A worthy take on Piedmont and its consequences

✷ Port Republic

CAMPAIGN: Jackson's Valley Campaign

DATE(S): June 9, 1862

Although General Shields's men were able to repulse the initial attacks made by the Stonewall Brigade, General Taylor's reinforcements assaulted the Union artillery at the Coaling and successfully forced a retreat. Fremont's army arrived on the scene too late and only had time to witness the rout of their Federal comrades across the river. This victory, along with a victory at the Battle of Cross Keys (see pp. 230–232), gave the Confederacy control of the valley, which allowed Jackson to come to Richmond with his valley army and reinforce Lee. A free printed driving tour of both battles is available at the Harrisonburg visitor center. The Port Republic Museum (see p. 305), in an antebellum house, is nearby.

LOCATION: **Battlefield and markers located at the intersection of SE Side Hwy. (Rte. 340) and Ore Bank Rd. in Port Republic; Harrisonburg Tourism and Visitor Services, 212 S. Main St., Harrisonburg, 540-432-8935, www.visit harrisonburgva.com.**

✷ Port Walthall Junction

CAMPAIGN: Bermuda Hundred Campaign

DATE(S): May 6–7, 1864

As Grant embarked on his Overland Campaign, General Butler's Army of the James landed at Bermuda Hundred (see sidebar p. 274) with the intention of cutting off the Richmond-Petersburg Railroad. Although General Hagood's men repulsed light Federal action the day before, on May 7, they were routed and the railroad was cut at Port Walthall Junction. The Confederates retreated to Swift Run Creek.

LOCATION: **Marker located at the Bermuda Hundred landing site, at the east end of Bermuda Hundred Rd. Markers and earthworks remains located at R. Garland Dodd Park, 201 Enon Church Rd., Chester, 804-530-2459. A driving tour is available through *Blue and Gray* magazine; call 800-248-4592 and ask for issue no. 181, "The Bermuda Hundred Campaign."**

✳ Proctor's Creek

CAMPAIGN: Bermuda Hundred Campaign

DATE(S): May 12–16, 1864

Although General Butler had 30,000 troops, his reluctance to confront Beauregard's 18,000 would be his undoing. After a hesitant attack on Drewry's Bluff on May 12, 1864 (see p. 234), Butler's caution and inability to seize the initiative hampered a successful assault on the Confederate right. On May 16, a Rebel attack routed the Union right, whose defeat would have been greater if a heavy fog had not arrived, making further Confederate attacks ineffective.

LOCATION: **Markers located at the intersection of Jefferson Davis Hwy. and VA Rte. 288.**

✵ Rappahannock Station I

CAMPAIGN: Northern Virginia Campaign

DATE(S): August 22–25, 1862

With Richmond saved by the Seven Days Battles, Lee moved north to face General

---

Lincoln's Conundrum

Union general "Black" David Hunter became famous during the Civil War for a May 9, 1862, order emancipating slaves in Georgia, Florida, and South Carolina. He was not authorized to give such an order, and Lincoln immediately rescinded it—but why? Although remembered as the great emancipator, Lincoln was also a canny political operator. Too early of a move toward emancipation, Lincoln believed, would hurt the Union cause in the pro-slavery border states and also open the Republican Party to attacks from political opponents who, even in 1862, were not ready for the collapse of slavery. After the war, David Hunter was the president of the military commission in charge of trying Lincoln's assassins.

Pope. The two sides faced off across the Rappahannock River. While the main armies skirmished for several days, J. E. B. Stuart's cavalry raided Pope's headquarters on August 23. Several subsequent minor skirmishes involved portions of the two armies along the Rappahannock River, including at Waterloo Bridge. Meanwhile, Stonewall Jackson moved to destroy Union supplies at Manassas Junction. Today, you can drive over a new Waterloo Bridge and cross the Rappahannock just as the soldiers did, only in the comfort of your car.

LOCATION: **Marker and bridge located at the intersection of Waterloo Rd. and Old Bridge Rd. in Amissville.**

✳ Rappahannock Station II

CAMPAIGN: Bristoe Campaign

DATE(S): November 7, 1863

Lee positioned his army at a strategic location on the Rappahannock River, hoping to force General Meade to divide his army. In a case of "be careful what you ask for," Meade's divided army launched surprise assaults on Lee's positions at Rappahannock station and Kelly's Ford, overwhelming the startled Confederate defenders and resulting in the capture of more than 1,600 men from Jubal Early's division. Put in an indefensible position after this embarrassing defeat, Lee was forced to winter farther south, in Orange County.

LOCATION: **Marker located on James Madison St., a fifth of a mile south of the intersection with W. Main St. in Remington. A driving tour is available through Virginia Civil War Trails (see p. 295).**

✳ Ream's Station I

CAMPAIGN: Richmond-Petersburg Campaign

DATE(S): June 29, 1864

Early in the Richmond-Petersburg Campaign, General Wilson and General Kautz led a Union cavalry raid on the Confederate railroads linking Lynchburg to Petersburg.

The Federals believed Ream's Station to be controlled by Union troops. But when they arrived, they found themselves split in two and nearly surrounded. Fierce fighting ensued as the desperate Federals discarded artillery, burned supply wagons, and abandoned the wounded as they attempted to break free. Although the raid succeeded in tearing up around 60 miles of track, critical supplies and artillery were lost, and about one-third of the Federal force was captured or killed.

LOCATION: **Multiple markers located in front of Oak Grove Church, 12715 Acorn Dr., Petersburg. Adjacent Civil War Trust land with interpretation located at the intersection of Halifax Rd. and Ream's Dr. in Petersburg.**

✳ Ream's Station II

CAMPAIGN: Richmond-Petersburg Campaign

DATE(S): August 25, 1864

On August 25, 1864, the day after they destroyed part of the Weldon Railroad, General Hancock's Union II Corps encountered Rebel forces led by General Heth.

The Confederate troops overwhelmed the Federals, who were poorly positioned. Those who were not captured were routed. Hancock withdrew, leading his remaining troops to the Jerusalem Plank Road.

LOCATION: **There is a walking trail with interpretation on the land near the intersection of Halifax and Reams Rd. near Oak Grove Church, 12715 Acorn Dr., Petersburg.**

Union soldiers attempt to take the Weldon Railroad during one Battle of Ream's Station.

✷ Rice's Station

CAMPAIGN: Appomattox Campaign

DATE(S): April 6, 1865

As the rest of the Army of Northern Virginia fought at Sayler's Creek, General Longstreet's men screened the army and dug in to guard the wagon trains at Rice's Station. A brief engagement with Union skirmishers was inconclusive. With Lee's defeat at Sayler's Creek, Longstreet moved across the High Bridge to Farmville that night.

LOCATION: Marker located at 202 Pisgah Church Rd. in Rice.

✷ Rutherford's Farm

CAMPAIGN: Early's Raid and Operations Against the B&O Railroad

DATE(S): July 20, 1864

After initially surprising Federal forces with a minor ambush, the poorly positioned left flank of General Ramseur's Confederates was assaulted by General Averell's Union forces at Rutherford farm, resulting in a Confederate rout. In the end, more than 300 Southern soldiers and four artillery pieces were captured.

LOCATION: Multiple markers and parking located just off Martinsburg Pike (Rte. 11) at the eastern end of the Rutherford Crossing shopping complex. After the intersection of Nursery Ln. and Martinsburg Pike, head southwest on Martinsburg Pike, taking the second nonresidential right turn; if you reach the intersection with Merchant St., you've gone slightly too far. For visitor information, contact Winchester-Frederick County Convention and Visitors Bureau, 1400 S. Pleasant Valley Rd., 540-542-1326, www.visitwinchesterva.com.

✷ Saint Mary's Church

CAMPAIGN: Grant's Overland Campaign

DATE(S): June 24, 1864

Union General Gregg was guarding a train of supplies when he was attacked by General Hampton in this cavalry engagement a little north of Westover Church on Virginia Route 5. Around 600 men were killed, wounded, or captured, although the Union supplies were protected and safely carried across the James River.

LOCATION: Marker located on Old Union Rd., three-quarters of a mile west of the intersection with Barnetts Rd.

✷ Salem Church

CAMPAIGN: Chancellorsville Campaign

DATE(S): May 3–4, 1863

En route to join Hooker's Union forces after his victory at second Fredericksburg (see p. 242), General Sedgwick's men were beaten back by Confederates at Salem Church. A Union attack in the afternoon of May 3 was repulsed, and Lee sent reinforcements during the night. Southern assaults

Salt

A necessity before refrigeration and modern preservatives, salt was used to preserve food and cure leather. Saltville, Virginia, was the eastern Confederacy's largest natural source of this vital mineral. Noting the importance of salt, William Tecumseh Sherman famously said, "Salt is eminently contraband, because of its use in curing meats." As the war continued, Confederate diarists noted their desperation not only at the lack of food but also at the lack of salt. One soldier found an inventive way to salt his meat—by rubbing it in the dirt and grime on a meat-house floor. By "taking up the dirt out of the meat houses," he wrote, "and leaching it—a fair article of salt could be made." Salt was so important that those involved in its production were immune from the draft. As the war dragged on, prices surged throughout the Confederacy, largely due to the Union blockade, which prevented the import of cheap foreign salt.

During reenactments, soldiers fire at an angle toward the sky. Although the guns are unloaded, an occasional ramrod is fired. This aiming technique is for safety.

on May 4 were defeated. That evening, Union forces retreated across the river at Banks Ford while Hooker's army withdrew at U.S. Ford near Chancellorsville, ending the Chancellorsville Campaign.

LOCATION: **Fredericksburg and Spotsylvania National Military Park, multiple sites, 540-786-2880, www.nps.gov/frsp. The center of the Confederate line, the church (4054 Plank Rd., Fredericksburg) is open sporadically; call for details.**

FURTHER READING

Chancellorsville
by Stephen W. Sears
The definitive account of this important Civil War campaign

❋ Saltville I

CAMPAIGN: Burbridge's Raid Into Southwest Virginia

DATE(S): October 2, 1864

To damage the Southern economy, Union forces led by General Burbridge moved to destroy the vital Confederate saltworks near Saltville (see sidebar p. 275) but were delayed by Confederates at Clinch Mountain

and Laurel Gap. This gave General Robertson time to reinforce his men and successfully resist the Union assault on October 2. This battle is infamous for the slaughter of wounded black soldiers by Confederate guerrilla Champ Ferguson in the aftermath. He was executed after the war for this crime.

LOCATION: **Civil War Battlefield Overlook, 275 Buckeye St., Saltville, 276-496-5342, www.saltville.org/tourism.**

❋ Saltville II

CAMPAIGN: Stoneman's Raid Into Southwest Virginia

DATE(S): December 20–21, 1864

This second raid to capture Saltville was more successful than the first, coming on the heels of Union victory at Marion. The scattered and outnumbered Rebels were unable to stop the determined advance of General Stoneman, who took Saltville and destroyed the saltworks industry. The nearby Museum of the Middle Appalachians (see p. 303) has an exhibit on both battles that took place in Saltville.

LOCATION: **Civil War Battlefield Overlook, 275 Buckeye St., Saltville, 276-496-5342, www.saltville.org/tourism. There's no interpretation for this battle.**

✳ Sappony Church

CAMPAIGN: Richmond-Petersburg Campaign
DATE(S): June 28, 1864

As General Wilson and General Kautz's cavalry raided behind Confederate lines, tearing up railroad track, they were confronted by Confederates under Generals Hampton and Lee at Stony Creek Depot. Hounded by the Southern cavalry, Union horsemen withdrew in the night to Ream's Station (see pp. 273–274), where battle would commence the next day. Don't miss the prerevolutionary Sappony Church.

LOCATION: Marker located at the intersection of Concord Sappony Rd. and Sussex Dr. in McKenney.

A Confederate in the Virginia Heavy Artillery at the Battle of Sayler's Creek

✳ Savage's Station

CAMPAIGN: Peninsula Campaign
DATE(S): June 29, 1862

As the bulk of the Union Army withdrew toward the James River, General Magruder followed, striking the Union rear guard under General Sumner. When Magruder asked him to assist, Stonewall Jackson replied that he had other business to attend to, leading some historians to criticize Jackson and others to speculate that Lee had given him a special role to stay above the fray and then entrap McClellan's army when the time was right. The day's inconclusive fighting ended as Union forces continued to withdraw.

LOCATION: Multiple markers located on Meadow Rd. just east of the intersection with Grapevine Rd. in Sandston. The core of the battlefield sits in the I-64 and I-295 interchange. Critical parts of the battlefield are visible on VA Rte. 156 just beyond Grapevine Bridge.

✳ Sayler's Creek

CAMPAIGN: Appomattox Campaign
OTHER NAME(S): Sailor's Creek
DATE(S): April 6, 1865

After the fall of Richmond, Grant continued to hound Lee, giving his army no rest. General Sheridan's cavalry, assisted by the II and VI Corps, cut off around a quarter of the Army of Northern Virginia near Sayler's Creek. Although technically three separate but related engagements, the Battle of Sayler's Creek was the death knell of the Army of Northern Virginia. Not only was a fourth of the army destroyed, but also many Confederate generals were captured, including Robert E. Lee's eldest son, George Washington Custis Lee. This was Lee's last major battle. Upon witnessing streams of retreating troops, he famously remarked, "My God, has the army dissolved?" In private correspondence with Jefferson Davis, Lee noted, "a few more Sailor's Creeks and it will all be over." The next day, Grant began correspondence with Lee, beginning talk of

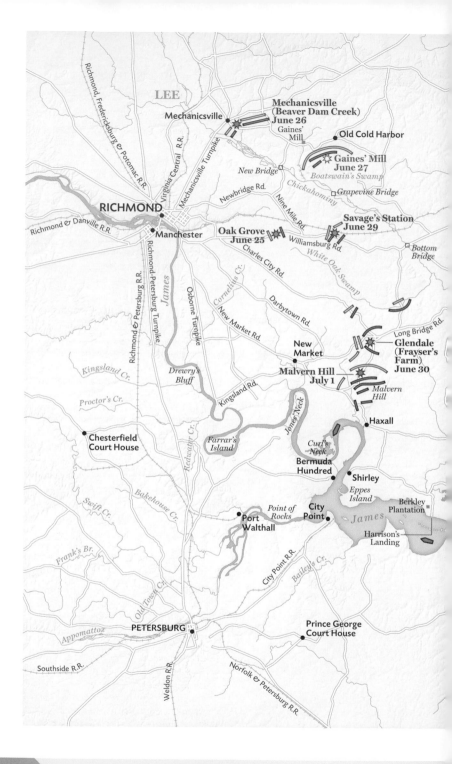

LEE

Mechanicsville

Mechanicsville
(Beaver Dam Creek)
June 26

Gaines'
Mill

Old Cold Harbor

Gaines' Mill
June 27

New Bridge

Boatswain's Swamp

Chickahominy

Grapevine Bridge

RICHMOND

Virginia Central R.R.

Mechanicsville Turnpike

Newbridge Rd.

Nine Mile Rd.

Savage's Station
June 29

Manchester

Oak Grove
June 25

Williamsburg Rd.

Bottom
Bridge

White Oak Swamp

Charles City Rd.

Cornelii's Cr.

Darbytown Rd.

Long Bridge Rd.

New Market Rd.

Glendale
(Frayser's
Farm)
June 30

New
Market

James

Osborne Turnpike

Malvern Hill
July 1

*Malvern
Hill*

*Drewry's
Bluff*

Kingsland Rd.

Kingsland Cr.

Jones's Neck

Haxall

Proctor's Cr.

*Farrar's
Island*

*Curl's
Neck*

Chesterfield
Court House

Bermuda
Hundred

Shirley

*Eppes
Island*

Berkley
Plantation

Bakehouse Cr.

Point of
Rocks

City
Point

James

Harrison's
Landing

Swift Cr.

Port
Walthall

Frank's Br.

City Point R.R.

Bailey's Cr.

Old Town Cr.

PETERSBURG

Prince George
Court House

Appomattox

Southside R.R.

Weldon R.R.

Norfolk & Petersburg R.R.

Richmond, Fredericksburg & Potomac R.R.

Richmond & Danville R.R.

Richmond & Petersburg R.R.

Richmond-Petersburg Turnpike

Redwater Cr.

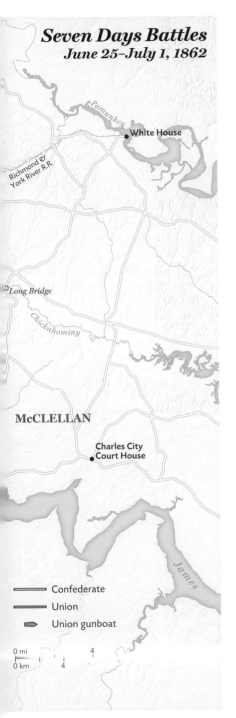

Seven Days Battles
June 25–July 1, 1862

White House

Richmond & York River R.R.

Pamunkey

Long Bridge

Chickahominy

McCLELLAN

Charles City
Court House

James

—— Confederate
—— Union
⬧ Union gunboat

0 mi   4
0 km   4

surrender that would effectively end the war on April 9.

Part of the Virginia Civil War Trails' "Lee's Retreat" tour (see p. 295), the well-interpreted battlefield park has a visitor center and the antebellum Hillsman House.

LOCATION: Sailor's Creek Battlefield State Park, 6541 Saylers Creek Rd., Rice, 804-561-7510, www.dcr.virginia.gov/state-parks/sailors-creek.shtml.

❖ Seven Pines

CAMPAIGN: Peninsula Campaign
DATE(S): May 31–June 1, 1862

With McClellan dangerously close to Richmond, Joe Johnston, general in chief of the Confederate Army, launched disjointed attacks against Federal forces south of the Chickahominy River. Both sides poured more and more troops into the battle, making it the largest in the eastern theater to that point. On the first day of fighting, Union forces were driven back, with both sides suffering heavy casualties. Southern attacks continued on June 1, but to little effect for either side.

Although an important battle in its own right—with around 11,000 men killed or wounded—Seven Pines's real impact on history comes from the wounding of General

Union soldiers pose with their artillery shortly after the Battle of Seven Pines.

Johnston. He was replaced by Robert E. Lee. Soon Lee would plot a massive assault—the Seven Days Battles—that would drive the Federals away from Richmond and, if properly executed, destroy the Union Army.

LOCATION: Multiple interpretive markers line E. Williamsburg Rd., from the intersection with Naglee Ave. west to the intersection with Early Ave. in Sandston. Two other markers located on nearby Casey St.: The first, going east, is just before the intersection with Rodes Ave.; the second, continuing on the road for one-fifth mile, is just before the intersection with Hunters Wood Ln.

Freeman Markers

In the early 1920s, Richmond residents Douglas S. Freeman and J. Ambler Johnston noted that "the fields were completely unmarked, overgrown with timber, no roads, no markers, nothing to indicate where the engagements were." So they founded the Battlefield Markers Association, raising $10,000 and erecting 59 roadside markers. Johnston was a noted architect and son of a Confederate veteran. Both he and Freeman owned land with important Civil War historic value that they donated to the National Park Service. Freeman, the editor of the *Richmond News Leader,* and also the son of a Confederate veteran, wrote text for the markers, which helped invigorate the movement to preserve and remember Civil War history. He later won the Pulitzer Prize for biographies of George Washington and Robert E. Lee.

FURTHER READING
Echoes of 1861 to 1961
by J. Ambler Johnston
A look at battlefield preservation with recollections from Douglas S. Freeman

☼ Sewell's Point

CAMPAIGN: Blockade of the Chesapeake Bay
DATE(S): May 18–19, 1861

A minor duel between Confederate batteries located at Sewell's Point and Union gunboats, this battle is notable as the first outbreak of fighting in Virginia. Nearby Fort Monroe (see p. 299) and Fort Wool offer interpretation of Civil War naval operations in the Chesapeake Bay.

LOCATION: Naval Station Norfolk, Norfolk; no public access.

☼ Spotsylvania Court House

CAMPAIGN: Grant's Overland Campaign
DATE(S): May 7–21, 1864

After the Battle of the Wilderness (see pp. 288–289), Grant moved southeast, attempting to steal a march on Lee. His goal was to beat Lee to Spotsylvania Court House or draw him into a fight where Union numerical superiority would dominate.

The Confederates reached the high ground outside Spotsylvania Court House literally minutes before the Northern soldiers and began digging in. On May 8, forces led by General Warren and General Sedgwick attacked Confederates at Laurel Hill. A sniper killed Sedgwick from long range after Sedgwick unfortunately predicted they couldn't hit an elephant at such a range; however, history tells us they could hit a Union major general—the VI Corps commander was dead.

On May 10, Grant ordered a series of attacks along the more than four miles of Confederate defenses. Limited success at an area known as the Mule Shoe convinced him to try again. Two days later, Grant followed up earlier success by ordering 20,000 men to attack at 4:30 a.m. Lee mistakenly believed Grant was preparing to retreat and had withdrawn artillery from his defenses. This mistake was costly but not fatal, as the attack in heavy fog ruptured the Confederate lines but was stymied by

Robert E. Lee

Robert E. Lee (1807–1870) is a study in paradoxical contrasts. A patrician who was reserved in polite company, he was a savvy gambler in battle, willing to risk all in bold moves that usually paid off. He opposed secession, saying "I can anticipate no greater calamity for the country than a dissolution of the Union." Yet he could not bring himself to raise arms against his native state of Virginia. "I am rejoiced that slavery is abolished," Lee claimed after the war. Nevertheless, he was willing to fight for a rebellion intent on preserving that horrible injustice.

Despite all the contradictions in his life, one thing was clear: Robert E. Lee was destined for greatness. Although scandal and debts incurred by his father tarnished the family name, he was nevertheless born into American royalty. His father, "Light Horse" Harry Lee, was a hero of the Revolutionary War and governor of Virginia; his wife, a descendant of Martha Custis Washington.

Lee excelled both at West Point and in the Mexican-American War, and he was offered command of all Union armies in 1861. Instead, he resigned his commission, answered Virginia's call, and was commissioned into the Confederate Army as one of its senior officers. Pressed into action in late 1861, he failed in western Virginia, took over the construction of fortifications in South Carolina, and was summoned from his advisory position by the president to take command of the Army of Northern Virginia. Immediately successful, he won a series of stunning victories against a larger and better-equipped foe.

Despite his mythical reputation, Lee's aggressiveness got the better of him on several occasions, notably at Antietam (see pp. 340–341) and especially with Pickett's Charge at Gettysburg (see pp. 355–356). Lee met his match in Grant, who, years later, recalled Lee's total control over his emotions, even during surrender at Appomattox, noting "He was a man of much dignity . . . whatever his feelings, they were entirely concealed from my observation."

After the war, Lee became president of what is now Washington and Lee University. He supported the cause of

After the war, Lee briefly met President Grant at the White House.

national reconciliation, telling a fellow Southerner, "Don't bring up your sons to detest the United States government . . . we form one country now. Abandon all these local animosities, and make your sons Americans." His commitment to reconciliation meant he gained popularity in the North, and strident abolitionist Henry Ward Beecher raised funds for Lee's university, as did Northern industrialist Cyrus McCormick. The *New York Herald* even endorsed Lee to run for president in 1868.

Although remembered by some as a heroic figure, Lee felt the weight of defeat, saying near the end of his life, "The greatest mistake of my life was taking a military education." Literally a son of the American Revolution, yet also a man whose success would have torn the country in two, Lee holds a unique place in American history, full of victory and defeat, patriotism and betrayal. His legend has grown to such proportions that the federal government he fought against has honored him on two stamps, while one U.S. military base bears his name. In 1975 President Ford signed a joint congressional resolution that pardoned Lee and restored his citizenship retroactive to June 13, 1865.

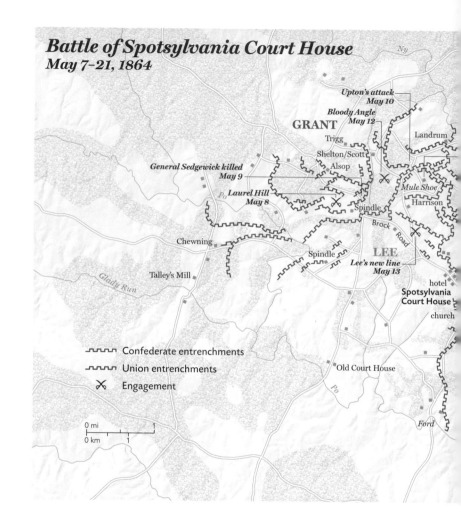

Battle of Spotsylvania Court House
May 7–21, 1864

Ny

Upton's attack
May 10

Bloody Angle
May 12

GRANT

Trigg

Landrum

Shelton/Scott

Alsop

General Sedgewick killed
May 9

Po

Mule Shoe

Harrison

Laurel Hill
May 8

Spindle

Brock Road

Chewning

Spindle

LEE

Lee's new line
May 13

Glady Run

Talley's Mill

hotel

Spotsylvania
Court House

church

Confederate entrenchments

Union entrenchments

Engagement

Old Court House

Po

0 mi   1
0 km   1

Ford

rallying Confederate reinforcements sent by Lee to breach the gap. As the Federal soldiers charged toward the Confederates at the break of dawn, a defending Southerner yelled, "Look out, boys—we will have blood for supper." There was much blood, but very little time to eat. Characterized by hand-to-hand combat and point-blank fighting, all in the pouring rain, the battle dragged on for 22 hours, making it possibly the longest and certainty one of the most brutal engagements of the entire war. Lee constructed

new defenses during the battle, which Grant, looking to take the Confederate left, unenthusiastically assaulted on May 18. Again Grant had been repulsed; he would need to find another way. Grant left the field of battle after a final fight at Harris farm before moving closer to Richmond.

Today, the earthworks are preserved in the Spotsylvania Unit, which also has interpretive signs and miles of trails. The unit is part of Fredericksburg and Spotsylvania National Military Park.

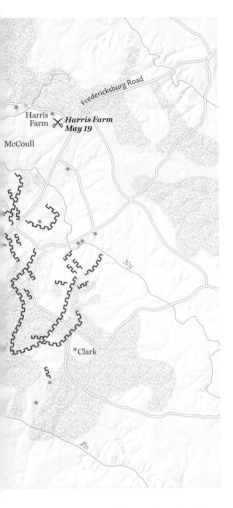

LOCATION: Fredericksburg and Spotsylvania National Military Park, Spotsylvania Battlefield Exhibit Shelter, 9550 Grant Dr. W., Spotsylvania, 540-373-6122, www.nps.gov/frsp.

FURTHER READING

The Battles for Spotsylvania Court House and the Road to Yellow Tavern: May 7–12, 1864 by Gordon C. Rhea New analysis covering the Wilderness to Bloody Angle

✳ Staunton River Bridge

CAMPAIGN: Richmond-Petersburg Campaign

DATE(S): June 25, 1864

The Wilson-Kautz raid behind Confederate lines continued as Union troops destroyed railroad tracks and supplies. On June 25, 1864, they destroyed track near the Staunton River Bridge, but Confederate home guards prevented them from destroying the bridge itself. Meanwhile, General W. H. F. Lee's cavalry closed in on the Federals, setting the stage for the Battle of Sappony Church three days later (see p. 277). Today, the nicely preserved battlefield park offers walking trails that cross the bridge, earthworks, two visitor centers, and more.

LOCATION: **Staunton River Battlefield State Park, Clover Visitor Center, 1035 Fort Hill Trail, Randolph, 434-454-4312, www.stauntonriver battlefield.org.**

✳ Sutherland's Station

CAMPAIGN: Appomattox Campaign

DATE(S): April 2, 1865

Following the April 1 victory at Five Forks (see p. 236), Union troops under General Miles moved toward Petersburg, seizing the South Side Railroad, the city's last supply line, thus sealing Richmond's fate. Today, the battlefield area is the start of the Lee's Retreat Civil War Driving Tour. Nearby Fork Inn, an antebellum plantation house and war hospital, is open for visitors.

LOCATION: **Multiple markers at the intersection of Cox Rd. and Namozine Rd. in Sutherland. Fork Inn, 19621 Namozine Rd., Sutherland, 804-265-8141, www.civilwartraveler.com.**

✳ Swift Creek

CAMPAIGN: Bermuda Hundred Campaign

DATE(S): May 9, 1864

As Union General Butler advanced toward Petersburg, his forces met with a brash Confederate attack at Arrowfield Church, later described as "brave to madness." After repulsing the attack, and inflicting heavy casualties in the process, Union forces destroyed rail tracks instead of pushing their advantage, while Federal gunboats and troops moved on Fort Clifton. Failing to gain meaningful ground, both the boats and troops were recalled.

LOCATION: **Markers located along Jefferson Davis Hwy. (US 1), on the right heading north. The first is just before the road crosses over Swift Creek, and the last is less than half a mile north, just before the intersection with Aldridge Ave.**

✳ Thoroughfare Gap

CAMPAIGN: Northern Virginia Campaign

DATE(S): August 28, 1862

Union forces led by General Ricketts skirmished with General Longstreet's Confederates near Chapman's Mill in the Thoroughfare Gap. The mill changed hands three times, with Confederate and Union sharpshooters occupying the structure. The Rebels seized the nearby high ground, partially due to very poor Union leadership, and this allowed Longstreet's men to carry the position and join Stonewall Jackson's forces.

This would be decisive in the forthcoming battles at Manassas (see pp. 254–257). Today, the remains of Chapman's Mill can be viewed, but walk with caution as poisonous snakes are frequently sighted.

LOCATION: **Chapman's Mill, 17504 Beverly Mill Dr., Broad Run, 540-253-5888, www.chapmans mill.org.**

✳ Tom's Brook

CAMPAIGN: Sheridan's Valley Campaign

DATE(S): October 9, 1864

Tired of Confederate harassment, General Sheridan looked for a hammer blow to destroy his opponent's resistance in the Shenandoah Valley. He got what he wanted at Tom's Brook, when General Torbert's men attacked the Rebels that had been following them. Considered to be the largest Union cavalry victory in the east, this crushing blow forever altered the balance of cavalry power in the valley. The battlefield is now part of Shenandoah County Park, which has an interpretive sign.

LOCATION: **Shenandoah County Park, 380 Park Ln., Maurertown, 540-984-3030, www .shenandoahcountyva.us/parks/county-park.**

James Barbour Terrill, a Confederate brigadier general, was killed at Bethesda Church.

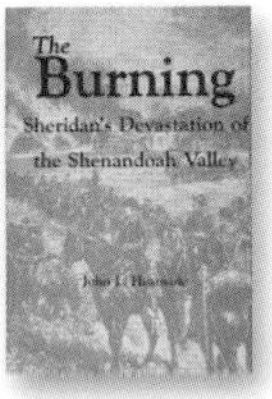

FURTHER READING

The Burning: Sheridan's Devastation of the Shenandoah Valley
by John L. Heatwole
Vivid civilian and military accounts of Sheridan's campaign

✲Totopotomoy Creek/ Bethesda Church

CAMPAIGN: Grant's Overland Campaign
DATE(S): May 28–30, 1864

Unlike Federal commanders before him, Grant was a true fighter. Despite the heavy death toll, Union forces kept moving toward Richmond. A cavalry engagement on May 28, 1864, led the Confederates to construct breastworks at Totopotomoy Creek, blocking the path to Richmond. The next day, Federal forces probed Southern lines, attempting to cross to the east of the Confederate lines and bypass Rebel fortifications. Union forces climbed atop a farmhouse known as Rural Plains, using it as an observation post to direct artillery fire, while the owners, the Shelton family, huddled in the basement. On May 30, the II Corps seized the section of the Confederate lines but was prevented from making further gains. By June 1, the armies had begun moving toward Cold Harbor (see p. 228).

LOCATION: Totopotomoy Creek Battlefield and Rural Plains, 7273 Studley Rd., Mechanicsville. Note: At the time of publication, Totopotomoy Creek Battlefield and Rural Plains are newly acquired sites undergoing restoration. Access may be limited. You can walk a trail to the Confederate lines. For updates, contact Richmond National Battlefield Park, 804-226-1981, www.nps.gov/rich.

✲Trevilian Station

CAMPAIGN: Grant's Overland Campaign
DATE(S): June 11–12, 1864

In order to occupy Confederate cavalry while he maneuvered to take Richmond, Grant sent General Sheridan on a diversionary raid west toward Charlottesville. After the raid, Sheridan would unite with General Hunter's Union troops and turn to threaten the Southside Railroad and the city of Lynchburg.

Sheridan attacked General Hampton's Confederate cavalry with moderate success at Trevilian Station on June 11, 1864. On the following day, however, the Confederates turned the tables on their Union attackers, beating them back with dismounted men behind a defensive line. This reversal prevented Sheridan from linking up with Hunter's Union Army as planned. This battle is widely regarded as Custer's first "Last Stand." Mismanagement of his forces nearly led to his destruction.

Today, there is no public battlefield access, but visitors can still see across the fields. There are on-site markers as well as a great driving tour available online.

LOCATION: Markers located on Louisa Rd. (US 33), one at the intersection with Trevilians Square Rd. and another slightly farther on Louisa Rd., a tenth of a mile east of the intersection, in Louisa. For more information, consult the Trevilian Station Battlefield Foundation, www.trevilianstation.org.

✲Upperville

CAMPAIGN: Gettysburg Campaign
DATE(S): June 21, 1863

Attempting to gather information on Lee's movements, Federal cavalry ran into J. E. B. Stuart's cavalry screen, forcing him to retire to a defensible position at Ashby Gap. At the same time, Confederate infantry began crossing the Potomac into Maryland. Stuart then moved east, intending to go around the Union Army to meet Lee in Pennsylvania. Many argue that Stuart's ride led to Lee's defeat at Gettysburg (see pp. 352–357).

LOCATION: Markers located at the intersection of John Mosby Hwy. and Hill Rd. (also known as Trappe Rd. or Rte. 619), and on Hill Rd., 1 mile north of the intersection with Mosby Hwy.

FURTHER READING

Receding Tide: Vicksburg and Gettysburg—The Campaigns That Changed the Civil War by Edwin C. Bearss and James Parker Hills
Analysis of two of the Civil War's most important campaigns

☀ Ware Bottom Church

CAMPAIGN: Bermuda Hundred Campaign
DATE(S): May 20, 1864

General Beauregard attacked General Butler's Union forces near Ware Bottom Church on May 20, 1864, forcing the Federals back. The Rebels then reinforced the Howlett Line, a long line of earthworks stretching from the James to the Appomattox River, which, due to unique positioning, made it nearly impossible to take. Butler, too, was behind extremely strong fortifications, creating a

Union General Warren fortifies his lines at the Weldon Railroad.

standoff. In his memoirs, Grant described the situation: "It was therefore as if Butler was in a bottle. He was perfectly safe against an attack; but . . . the enemy had corked the bottle and with a small force could hold the cork in its place." The Confederates held the Howlett Line until Lee evacuated on April 2.

Ware Bottom Battlefield Park features many markers, a walking path, and preserved earthworks.

LOCATION: Ware Bottom Battlefield Park, 1600 Old Bermuda Hundred Rd., Chester.

☀ Waynesboro

CAMPAIGN: Sheridan's Expedition to Petersburg
DATE(S): March 2, 1865

The last remnants of Jubal Early's forces were crushed here after a brief engagement. Although the Confederate general escaped, more than 1,500 Rebels were captured. General Sheridan continued to Charlottesville and then joined the Army of the Potomac near Petersburg on March 26. Modern development has overtaken the battlefield, although there is a monument to Confederate Colonel John Harman, a battle marker, and the Waynesboro Heritage Foundation Plumb House Museum (see p. 307).

LOCATION: Marker located at the intersection of Dupont Circle and Main St. in Waynesboro. Harman monument located in Constitution Park, alongside McElroy St.

☀ White Oak Road

CAMPAIGN: Appomattox Campaign
DATE(S): March 31, 1865

Lee's army was stretched to the breaking point. On March 30, 1865, he had rearranged his forces to meet Federal threats on his right flank. The next day, having learned that the Union left flank was exposed, he planned an attack. The Union seized the initiative, however, turning the Rebels' planned assaults into counterattacks. General Sheridan moved on Dinwiddie

Custer's Colorful Rivalry

Custer revealed his fearlessness in a letter, writing, "As the country is concerned I, of course, must wish for peace, and will be glad when the war is ended, but if I answer for myself alone, I must say that I shall regret to see the war end."

The Battle of Tom's Brook (see pp. 284–285) pitted George Armstrong Custer against his close friend and West Point classmate Thomas Rosser. At the beginning of the battle, Custer—ever the showman—bowed deeply to his rival, an action widely reported in the Union press. Not only did Custer win the battle, but he also captured his rival's headquarters wagon and ostentatiously wore Rosser's captured uniform.

After this loss, Rosser sent Custer a message: "You may have made me take a few steps back today, but I will be even with you tomorrow. Please accept my good wishes and this little gift—a pair of your draws captured at Trevillian [sic] Station."

To which Custer replied: "Dear friend, Thanks for setting me up in so many new things, but would you please direct your tailor to make the coat tails of your next uniform a trifle shorter."

Unlike Fitzhugh Lee and William Averell—two friends caught on opposite sides of the Civil War who likely never met again—Custer and Rosser did meet again, this time in 1873, during an expedition near Yellowstone.

As Custer described it, the experience "seemed like the time when we were cadets together, huddled on one blanket and discussing dreams of the future." Rosser, now working for a railroad, helped his old friend out of a bind by convincing Custer's superior, David S. Stanley, to drop charges of insubordination.

After Custer's untimely death at the Battle of Little Bighorn in June 1876, Rosser wrote a strident editorial defending his friend and blaming others for the embarrassing massacre. Rosser went on to become rich through speculation related to his railroad work and retired to Charlottesville, Virginia.

Court House, while General Warren attacked Confederates at White Oak Road. Although Warren's forces gained some ground, they were repelled by troops under General Johnson. Confederates punched out of their defensive works and struck elements of the V Corps. While checking the Federals, Lee was unable to break them. After a number of hours of fighting, his men returned to their trenches. Much of the battlefield has been preserved, and many markers line the wooded walking trail.

LOCATION: Parking lot and entrance to walking trail at the intersection of White Oak Rd. and Claiborne Rd. in Sutherland.

✲Wilderness

CAMPAIGN: Grant's Overland Campaign
DATE(S): May 5–7, 1864

Lee and Meade had wintered on opposite sides of the Rapidan River, mere miles apart. When Grant arrived as general in chief, he wanted to use Meade's 115,000-man army to crush Lee's 64,000 battle-hardened troops in the open. Lee had other plans and intercepted Union forces moving south in a densely wooded area known as the Wilderness, where Grant's superior size and artillery could not be realized.

Fierce fighting did not dislodge the Federals from two crucial road intersections they needed to keep moving south. On May 6, Union attacks nearly destroyed the Confederate right, until General Longstreet's Corps pushed the Federals back. This was costly: Lee lost 11,400 men and Longstreet was seriously wounded in the confusion of battle, although, unlike Jackson (see pp. 224–227), he would survive. Portions of the dense forest caught on fire, leading to chaos and confused fighting, dooming some wounded soldiers to be burned to death, while others got lost in the smoke. On May 7, after suffering more than 18,000 casualties, Grant left the field of battle but did not retreat—unlike previous Union generals in his position—and instead continued south. This was a crucial morale-booster for his troops, who thus far were accustomed to retreating in the face of Lee's army.

The battlefield has been well preserved in some sections. The exhibit shelter, which is sporadically manned by the National Park Service, features information on the many walking trails and interpretive markers. There is also a driving tour available online. General

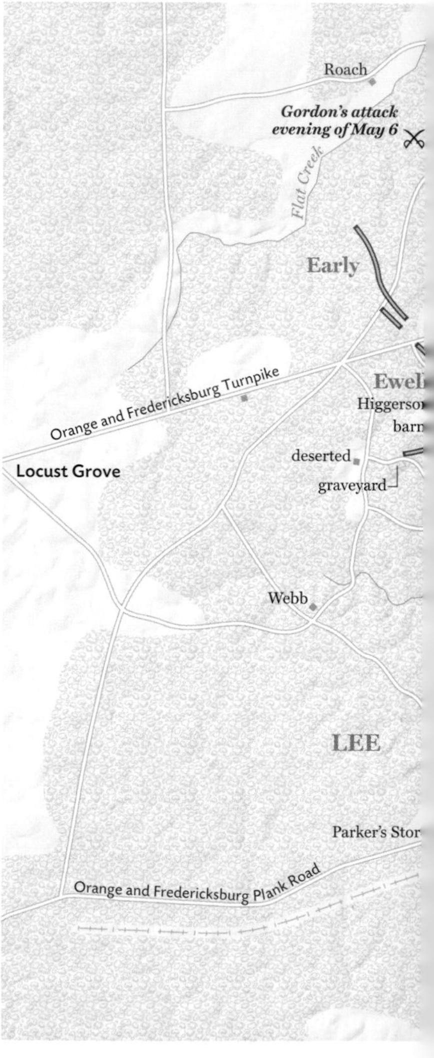

Warren's headquarters at the restored Lacy House is nearby. Guided walking tours begin at the exhibit shelter on weekends and holidays. Check at the Chancellorsville Battlefield visitor center (see p. 227) for times.

LOCATION: **Fredericksburg and Spotsylvania National Military Park, Wilderness Battlefield Exhibit Shelter, Rte. 20, 2 miles south of the intersection with Rte. 3 in Locust Grove.**

The driving tour is available at www.nps.gov /frsp.

FURTHER READING
The Battle of the Wilderness: May 5–6, 1864
by Gordon C. Rhea
An illuminating account

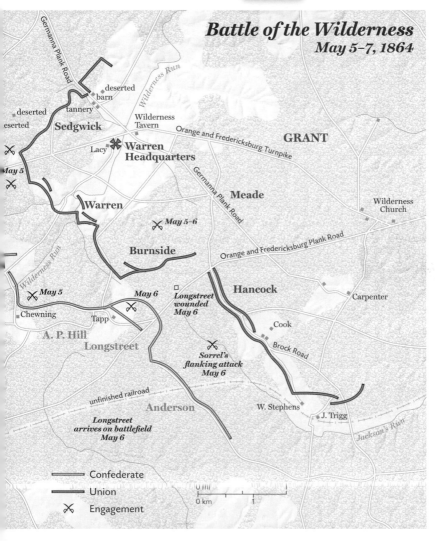

Battle of the Wilderness
May 5–7, 1864

Germanna Plank Road

Wilderness Run

deserted barn

deserted
tannery
deserted
deserted

Wilderness Tavern

Sedgwick

Lacy

Warren Headquarters

Orange and Fredericksburg Turnpike

GRANT

May 5

Germanna Plank Road

Meade

Warren

Wilderness Church

May 5–6

Wilderness Run

Burnside

Orange and Fredericksburg Plank Road

May 5

Chewning

May 6

Tapp

Longstreet wounded May 6

Hancock

Carpenter

Cook

Brock Road

A. P. Hill

Longstreet

Sorrel's flanking attack May 6

unfinished railroad

Anderson

Longstreet arrives on battlefield May 6

W. Stephens

J. Trigg

Jackson's Run

Confederate
Union
Engagement

0 km   1

New Yorkers pause by an exploded Confederate battery at Yorktown.

✦ Williamsburg

CAMPAIGN: Peninsula Campaign
DATE(S): May 5, 1862

As the Confederates retreated from York-town, Union General Hooker attacked the Southern rear guard while assaulting Fort Magruder. General Kearny thwarted strong counterattacks by Longstreet, and General Hancock seized unmanned portions of the Confederate left, although Federal forces did not follow up on these gains. The Rebels retreated in the night.

Williamsburg today has a number of Civil War sites, including Bassett Hall (see p. 293). Soldiers camped on the campus of William and Mary and used Wren Chapel as a hospital. If visiting nearby Jamestown Island (see p. 301), ask about the Confederate batteries on-site. In winter, a drive along the Colonial Parkway to Yorktown will reveal Confederate earthworks overlooking the York River. The enhanced earthworks at Yorktown are from this Civil War campaign.

LOCATION: Remains of Fort Magruder with markers located at the intersection of Queens Creek Rd. and Penniman Rd. in Williamsburg. Fort Magruder marker and redoubt in the courtyard of the Fort Magruder Hotel, 6945 Pocahontas Trail, Williamsburg, 757-220-2250. Multiple battle markers located at the intersection of Hwy. 60 and 5th Ave. in Williamsburg.

FURTHER READING

Defend This Old Town: Williamsburg During the Civil War
by Carol Kettenburg Dubbs
A look at Williamsburg's role in the war

✳ Wilson's Wharf

CAMPAIGN: Grant's Overland Campaign
DATE(S): May 24, 1864

When Fitzhugh Lee attacked a Union supply depot at Wilson's Wharf, black troops under the command of General Wild drove him back. The military significance of this battle is overshadowed in history by the identity of the people who took park in it, namely, free blacks who fought and defeated Rebel forces determined to preserve slavery.

Today, large portions of the battlefield are interpreted at Fort Pocahontas and also at the nearby Sherwood Forest Plantation (see p. 305), the home of the pro-secessionist tenth president of the United States, John Tyler, whose grandson still lives at Sherwood Forest. An annual reenactment is conducted at Fort Pocahontas in May.

LOCATION: Fort Pocahontas, 13500 Sturgeon Point Rd., Charles City, 804-829-9722, www .fortpocahontas.org.

✳ Winchester I

CAMPAIGN: Jackson's Valley Campaign
DATE(S): May 25, 1862

Stonewall Jackson moved toward Winchester from the south and defeated Union forces at Bowers Hill. Meanwhile, General Ewell's men approached from the southeast, attacking Camp Hill. The Confederates overran the Union forces, who streamed through Winchester in disorganized retreat. Today, Winchester is a beautiful town with much history, although this particular engagement is not adequately preserved or interpreted.

LOCATION: Civil War Orientation Center and Winchester-Frederick County Visitor Center, 1400 S. Pleasant Valley Rd., Winchester, 877-871-1326.

✳ Winchester II

CAMPAIGN: Gettysburg Campaign
DATE(S): June 13–15, 1863

Planning to move north, Lee ordered General Ewell to rid the Shenandoah of Union soldiers in preparation for the upcoming Pennsylvania campaign. Ewell attacked Winchester and West Fort on June 13 and 14, and finished the job by cutting off General Milroy's retreat before daybreak on June 15.

LOCATION: Civil War Orientation Center and Winchester-Frederick County Visitor Center, 1400 S. Pleasant Valley Rd., Winchester, 877-871-1326.

✳ Yellow Tavern

CAMPAIGN: Grant's Overland Campaign
DATE(S): May 11, 1864

During the Battle of Spotsylvania Court House (see pp. 280–283), General Sheridan moved to raid Richmond. On May 11, he engaged the outnumbered Stuart, who was mortally wounded in the battle. Development has overtaken the battlefield, though there is a monument to J. E. B. Stuart near where he was shot in the gut. Nearby Old

Telegraph Road is well worth riding just to understand what a "major road" in the Civil War looked like.

LOCATION: J. E. B. Stuart Monument located on Telegraph Rd., a fifth of a mile south of the intersection with Virginia Center Pkwy. in Glen Allen. To drive on Old Telegraph Rd., head north on Washington Hwy. (US 1) from Glen Allen. Veer right about a third of a mile past the intersection with Sliding Hill Rd.

✵ Yorktown

CAMPAIGN: Peninsula Campaign
DATE(S): April 5–May 4, 1862

With the aim of taking Richmond, General McClellan moved from Fort Monroe and encountered a small Confederate force at Yorktown. Wrongly, he believed that the Southern defenses and manpower were stronger than they really were. He dug in, with siege guns and heavy fortifications.

On April 16, McClellan's troops staged a successful attack at Dam 1, but the wary Union general did not commit sufficient forces to exploit his gains. Instead, McClellan prepared for a heavy full assault on May 4. The Rebels, however, had other plans: They evacuated in the dark, late on May 3.

Although Yorktown is most famous as the field where the Revolutionary War was won, most of the fortifications extant today were shaped by this Civil War battle. While in the area, don't miss Lee Hall (see pp. 301–302), which was Generals Magruder's and Johnston's headquarters, or Edgeview Plantation.

LOCATION: Yorktown Battlefield Visitor Center, 1000 Colonial Pkwy., Yorktown, 757-898-2410, www.nps.gov/york.

FURTHER READING
John Bankhead Magruder: A Military Reappraisal
by Thomas M. Settles
A biography of Virginia's third highest ranked officer

Civil War on Foot: Williamsburg

The old colonial capital had fallen into decay with the movement of the state government to Richmond in 1780. Anchoring the town was the College of William and Mary, located at the head of Duke of Gloucester Street and dividing Jamestown and Richmond Roads. Park and walk to Duke of Gloucester Street.

❶ John Blair House *(W. Duke of Gloucester St.)* The ovens here were used to bake bread for Union soldiers.

❷ Bowden-Armistead House *(Corner of N. Nassau and W. Duke of Gloucester Sts.)* This was the home of Lem Bowden, a Union sympathizer who became mayor during the Civil War. The home retains its wartime appearance.

❸ Bruton Parish Church *(W. Duke of Gloucester St.)* Used as a hospital and burying grounds for Confederate soldiers, the church was closed when the pastor made disloyal statements and refused to pray for Lincoln's health.

❹ Robert Carter House (Paige House) *(Palace Green St.)* The owner, Robert Saunders, owned more slaves than anyone else in town. The Federals used the house as the office of the provost marshal.

❺ St. George Tucker House *(W. Nicholson St.)* A border here named Charles Minnegerode introduced a German-style Christmas tree, the first in Virginia. Minnegerode became religious minister for Jefferson Davis.

❻ Market Square The magazine served as a jail and armory, while the courthouse was a barracks, hospital, and morgue. The grounds were used as a field hospital after the Battle of Williamsburg (see p. 290) and as a general encampment area.

❼ Ludwell-Paradise House *(W. Nicholson St.)* Philip Barziza, warden at Eastern Lunatic Asylum, raised ten children here. One child, Dessie, served in Hood's Texas Brigade and marched past his birthplace on May 4, 1862.

❽ Palmer House *(Blair St.)* Known as the Vest Mansion, this was headquarters for Confederate General Magruder, who hosted social functions here, and Union General McClellan. After the war it housed the local Freedman's Bureau.

Robert Saunders was not only president of the College of William and Mary but also the two-time mayor of Williamsburg.

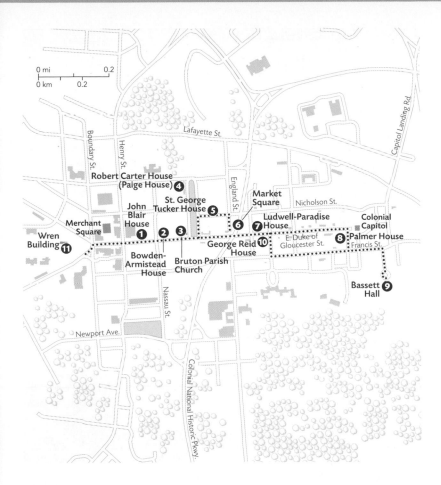

❾ Bassett Hall *(Francis St. E.)* Here Custer served as the best man at the wedding of his classmate John Lea, a wounded but recovering Confederate officer.

❿ George Reid House *(Corner of Colonial and W. Duke of Gloucester Sts.)* As Confederate soldiers headed into battle, they received biscuits and meats at this shop.

⓫ Wren Building *(College of William and Mary)* This is one of the country's oldest academic buildings. College president Benjamin S. Ewell became Joseph E. Johnston's chief of staff during the Civil War and returned afterward to reopen the school. Make sure to see Wren Chapel.

If you have built up an appetite, head for the Cheese Shop *(410 W. Duke of Gloucester St.)* in Merchant's Square, which offers fresh bread and a wonderful variety of sandwiches.

Other Battles and Beyond

✦ Battle Companion Apps

NeoTreks offers a series of free companion apps for the iPhone. Featuring information on several crucial battles, the info-packed apps use GPS to show your location in relation to the battle lines. Battles with apps include Antietam, Bull Run, Cedar Creek, Chancellorsville, Fredericksburg, Gettysburg, Petersburg, Second Manassas, Vicksburg, and others. Neotreks created the apps in partnership with the Civil War Trust (www.civilwar.org), which works to save battlefields across the nation. To find the apps, search the name of the battle and the words "Battle App" in the App Store.

✦ Louisa County Civil War Trail

From the Battle of Trevilian Station (see p. 285) to the mines of Tolersville, Louisa County, Virginia, played an important role during the Civil War. The Louisa County Civil War driving tour incorporates a wide variety of related sites. For tour details, contact the Louisa County Historical Society (540-967-5975, www.louisacountyhistoricalsociety.org). A map can also be found at www.civilwartraveler.com.

✦ Mosby's Confederacy

One of the Confederacy's most popular figures, John Singleton Mosby earned a reputation for daring and reliability (see sidebar p. 223). Authorized to organize a ranger regiment, the 43rd Virginia Partisans were one of a kind. The Mosby Heritage Area Association (www.mosbyheritagearea.org) has published "Drive Through History: The John Mosby Highway US Route 50," a wonderful driving tour. Call 540-687-6681 to order.

Danville's elegant Sutherlin Mansion is considered the last capitol of the Confederacy. Originally completed in 1859, it now houses the Danville Museum of Fine Arts and History.

✦ "150th Anniversary Civil War Scenic Roads in Virginia"

Created by the Virginia Department of Transportation, this valuable map offers a great overview of the many sites in the Old Dominion. The map can be found at Virginia welcome centers or obtained directly from the Virginia Department of Transportation (401 E. Broad St., Richmond, 800-367-7623). It is also available online at www.virginiadot.org.

✦ Rappahannock County Civil War Trails

Rappahannock County, Virginia, played a key role during the Civil War. Learn about the many events that took place in the area by following the Rappahannock County Civil War Trails. Find details about the trails at the Rappahannock County Visitor Center (3 Library Rd., Washington, 540-675-3153) or in the online guide, available at http://civilwar.visitrappahannockva.com/trails.html.

✦ Virginia Civil War Tourism

With information about the history of the Civil War in Virginia, travel packages, battle reenactments, and special events, the Commonwealth of Virginia's official tourism website has everything you need to plan your Civil War trip. Access the website at www.virginia.org/civilwar, or call 800-847-4882 for more information.

✦ Virginia Civil War Trails

The go-to resource for touring sites large and small all across the state, Virginia Civil War Trails offers detailed maps, numerous driving tours, valuable site information, and more. Call 888-248-4592 to obtain brochures and maps, or pick them up at Virginia welcome centers and battlefield visitor centers. They are also available on the excellent companion website, www.civilwartrails.org. For a full list of Virginia welcome centers, visit www.virginia.org.

Reenactors, encamped, commemorate the 150th anniversary of the war.

✦ American Civil War Museum at Historic Tredegar

Located at the historic Tredegar Ironworks—the industrial base of the Confederacy—the American Civil War Museum offers a full account of the conflict from three different perspectives: Union, Confederate, and African American. With great exhibits, the center is well worth a visit, especially in conjunction with other stops in the Richmond area. The museum also maintains the White House of the Confederacy (see p. 307) and the Museum of the Confederacy at Appomattox (see p. 303).

LOCATION: **500 Tredegar St., Richmond, 804-649-1861, www.acwm.org.**

✦ Arlington National Cemetery and Arlington House

Once the plantation of Robert E. Lee, Arlington National Cemetery has become America's most revered resting ground for those who served their country. It was founded in an act of spite: Federal officials elected to bury soldiers in Mrs. Lee's rose garden so they would never forget their role in the great war. Now a museum dedicated to the life of Lee and his family, Arlington House still stands in the middle of the cemetery grounds. Nearby, the Confederate

Belle Grove's 7,500 acres held a distillery, multiple mills, and many crops and cattle.

section features a sculpture by Sir Moses Ezekiel, a Virginia Military Institute cadet.

LOCATION: **Visitor Center, 1 Memorial Ave., Fort Myer, 877-907-8585, www.arlington cemetery.mil. The cemetery is also accessible from the Arlington National Cemetery station on Metro's Blue Line. Unauthorized vehicles cannot drive inside the cemetery.**

✦ Battle Abbey

Originally built for the Confederate Memorial Institute but now owned by the Virginia Historical Society, the building known as the Battle Abbey has been significantly expanded over the years and today covers all Virginia's history. The epic four-part paintings "The Four Seasons of the Confederacy" by French artist Charles Hoffbauer are still on display.

LOCATION: **428 N. Boulevard, Richmond, 804-358-4901, www.vahistorical.org.**

✦ Belle Grove Historic Plantation

This 1797 historic manor, built by Nelly Madison Hite—sister of James Madison—and her husband, is an excellent way to experience the plantation life of Virginia's upper crust in the 1800s. You can also learn about the Battle of Cedar Creek (see pp. 222–223), which took place on the plantation's front lawn. Stephen Dodson Ramseur, a Confederate general, died here. Guided tours of the house are available, and a commemoration of the battle is held annually.

LOCATION: **336 Belle Grove Rd., Middletown, 540-869-2028, www.bellegrove.org. Note: There is another historic plantation—the birthplace of James Madison—with the same name that is now a bed-and-breakfast. The two sites are more than 100 miles apart, so if you are using GPS, be sure it is taking you to the correct one.**

✦ Berkeley Plantation

Famous as the site of the first Thanksgiving celebration in 1619, Berkeley Plantation is one of the oldest estates in America and the ancestral home of the Harrison family, two of whose members, William Henry Harrison and Benjamin Harrison, were elected president. During the Civil War, Union forces occupied the house and Lincoln visited twice. Today, the house offers a stunning look into a bygone era of colonial glamour. Tours of the grounds are self-guided.

LOCATION: **12602 Harrison Landing Rd., Charles City, 804-829-6018, www.berkeley plantation.com.**

✦ Blandford Church

Stunningly beautiful, the prerevolutionary Blandford Church was restored by the Ladies Memorial Association of Petersburg in the early 20th century and dedicated as a monument to the soldiers who fought for the Confederacy. The hallmark attractions here are the 15 original Louis Comfort Tiffany stained-glass windows. Despite its historic status, the church still conducts burials.

LOCATION: **244 N. Market St., Petersburg, 804-733-2400, www.virginia.org/listings /historicsites/blandfordchurch.**

✦ Buchanan

On June 13, 1864, General Hunter marched through Buchanan, driving out Confederate troops who burned the local covered bridge and also much of the local town, destroying nearly 30 buildings. Hunter, for his part, ordered the burning of the house of Confederate Colonel Anderson.

LOCATION: **Marker located outside 653 Lowe St. in Buchanan.**

✦ Buckland Historic District

Appearing largely the same as it did during the Civil War era, this picturesque village—now a National Historic District—features a 19th-century tavern, gristmill, and church. It is also home to the prerevolutionary Buckland Hall. The first inland town in Prince William County, Buckland was an important wagon stop between Alexandria and the Blue Ridge Mountains.

LOCATION: **Intersection of Rte. 29 and Buckland Mill Rd., Buckland, 703-754-4000, www.buck landva.net.**

✦ "The Burning"

As Sheridan engaged in a campaign to destroy food in the Shenandoah Valley that

Visitors find the Confederate section of the cemetery at Blandford Church humbling.

was being used to feed Lee's army, his "bummers" experienced an act of retaliation that precipitated an outrage typical of the war in its most vile form. On October 3, 1864, Confederate scouts killed the son of the quartermaster general of the Union Army, Montgomery Meigs. Believing that a local resident was responsible, Sheridan ordered the entire town of Dayton burned within a five-mile radius. The next day he limited his order to merely burning the area around Dayton, including homes and farms.

LOCATION: **Marker located at the intersection of John Wayland Hwy. and Main St. in Dayton.**

✦ Charles City Courthouse

Built in the 1730s and used continuously for more than 250 years, the Charles City Courthouse witnessed both the Revolutionary War and the Civil War. Here J. E. B. Stuart's June 1862 ride around the Union Army concluded with Stuart returning west along modern-day Route 5 to Richmond,

reporting to Lee that the Federal supply line was vulnerable.

LOCATION: **10702 Courthouse Rd., Charles City, 804-652-4702.**

✦ Culpeper

With its strategic location, Culpeper and its surroundings were hotly contested in the Civil War. Individual Southern states maintained hospitals in and around the town and provided supplies to run the hospitals for their native sons in the Confederate Army. This history is brought to light by a walking tour of the town that can be acquired at the very impressive downtown visitor center.

LOCATION: **111 Commerce St., Culpeper, 540-727-0611, www.visitculpeperva.com.**

✦ Ely's Ford

Site of many important crossings by the Federal Army, Ely's Ford played an important

During the Civil War, Fort Monroe was a beacon of freedom for escaping slaves. Yet 250 years prior, Old Point Comfort (Monroe) was the landing site of the first slave ships to visit America.

though underappreciated role in the tides of the war. In August 1862, the Federals crossed this ford to reach Second Manassas. During the Chancellorsville Campaign, both Confederate and Union soldiers passed through. The ford also witnessed the crossing of Union soldiers during the Overland Campaign in May 1864.

LOCATION: **From the Chancellorsville Visitor Center at 9001 Plank Rd. in Spotsylvania, head north on Bullock Rd. At the intersection, take a left onto Ely's Ford Rd., following the road for just over 4 miles. Just before the river, turn right to reach a very small road that will take you to Ely's Ford; if you cross the Rapidan River, you have (barely) gone too far.**

Now ruins, Chancellor House was Hooker's initial headquarters during Chancellorsville.

✦ Fort Boykin

With a rich history dating back to 1623, Fort Boykin offers visitors a chance to experience multiple eras of American history. During the Revolution, it was used to defend the James, and in the War of 1812, troops here successfully beat back a British landing force. In the Civil War, the superior range of the Union ironclad U.S.S. *Galena* rendered the fort useless and it was soon abandoned.

LOCATION: **7410 Fort Boykin Trail, Isle of Wight, 757-357-2291, www.co.isle-of-wight.va.us /historic-resources/fort-boykin.**

✦ Fort Huger

Along with Fort Boykin, Fort Huger—named after the commander of the Confederate garrison in Norfolk—was constructed to prevent Union boats from sailing up the James to the Confederate capital. Today, tourists can walk along the fort, getting a glimpse of Confederate fortifications of the time.

LOCATION: **15080 Talcott Terrace, Rushmere, 757-357-2291, www.historicisleofwight.com /fort-huger.**

✦ Fort Monroe National Monument

The much larger twin of Fort Wool, Fort Monroe is the largest stone fort built in the United States. Also built after the War of 1812, the seven-sided fort—which took the place of Fort Algernon, its 1608 wooden precursor—offers a spectacular look at past military technology. During the Civil War, Fort Monroe stayed in Union hands and was a beacon for escaping slaves who sought freedom by running to Union lines, thus earning it the nickname the "Freedom Fortress." Jefferson Davis was imprisoned here after his capture in 1865, an event depicted in the Casemate Museum.

LOCATION: **20 Bernard Rd., Hampton, 757-722-3678, www.nps.gov/fomr.**

✦ Fort Ward

Of the many forts built to defend Washington, D.C., from the Confederacy, Fort Ward in Alexandria is the best preserved. This historic 35-acre site illuminates the defense of Washington while also informing visitors of the everyday life of soldiers and civilians in and around the fort.

LOCATION: **4301 W. Braddock Rd., Alexandria, 703-838-4848, www.alexandriava.gov /fortward.**

✦ Gloucester Point

The site of the first fighting after the fall of Fort Sumter, Gloucester Point, across from Yorktown, helped close the deepwater York

River and was manned by Confederate artillery from early 1861. During the American Revolution, Cornwallis planned to escape his encirclement at Yorktown here, but was thwarted by a storm. Today, Gloucester Point is preserved as a park under its original name, Tyndalls Point. Civil War earthworks can be viewed at the site.

LOCATION: **Tyndalls Point Park, 1376 Vernon St., Gloucester Point, 804-693-0014, www .virginia.org/Listings/HistoricSites/Tyndalls PointPark.**

✦ Graffiti House

Named for the messages, drawings, and signatures scrawled on the walls by soldiers of the time, this antebellum building is replete with extremely rare, preserved historical messages from participants in the Civil War—a vivid and humanizing reminder that participants in the war may have lived in a different era but were fundamentally just like us. The building also serves as the headquarters of the Brandy Station Foundation and features information about the Battle of Brandy Station (see p. 221).

LOCATION: **19484 Brandy Rd., Brandy Station, 540-727-7718. Irregular hours; call for openings.**

✦ Hampton National Cemetery

This cemetery was founded in 1862 as the final resting place for soldiers who died during the Peninsula Campaign. The site features Union and Confederate graves and monuments to both sides.

LOCATION: **Intersection of Cemetery Rd. and Marshall Ave., Hampton, 757-723-7104, www.cem.va.gov.**

✦ Hanging Rock

General Hunter's Army of Western Virginia retreated from Lynchburg to the Mountain State and was engaged in a small battle at Hanging Rock on June 21, 1864. Two future presidents, Rutherford B. Hayes and William

McKinley, were present in the engagement. Markers to the fight are accompanied by a walking trail and small commemorative park in the bucolic town of Hanging Rock, outside Salem.

LOCATION: **Marker located on Dutch Oven Rd., just after the intersection with N. Electric Rd. in Hanging Rock.**

✦ Hanover Tavern

One of the few extant colonial taverns in Virginia, Hanover Tavern has hosted such esteemed figures in American history as George Washington, the Marquis de Lafayette, and the man they would defeat at Yorktown, Lord Cornwallis. Today, you can dine at the tavern and see the oldest continuously operating dinner theater in America. Cavalry actions during the Civil War took place around the tavern and in the Court House area across the street.

LOCATION: **13181 Hanover Courthouse Rd., Hanover, 804-537-5050, www.hanovertavern .org.**

✦ Hollywood Cemetery

This large Richmond cemetery is the final resting place of President James Monroe, President John Tyler, and Confederate President Jefferson Davis. Twenty-eight Confederate generals are also buried here, among them J. E. B. Stuart and George Pickett. Historic walking tours are held once daily April through November. Segway tours are by appointment only.

LOCATION: **412 S. Cherry St., Richmond, 804-648-8501, www.hollywoodcemetery.org.**

✦ Hot Springs

Boasting one of the few truly hot springs on the East Coast, the town of Hot Springs was used as a relaxation retreat by Confederates after the war. Robert E. Lee and his wife visited the springs in 1866, and a host of other notable figures have passed through, seeking relaxation in the mineral water. Today, the springs are open for visitors, with Homestead Resort as the centerpiece.

LOCATION: **Hot Springs at the Omni Homestead Resort, 7696 Sam Snead Hwy., Hot Springs, 800-838-1766, www.omnihotels.com /hotels/homestead-virginia.**

✦ Jamestown Island

Site of the first successful English colony in the New World, the island is also home to Confederate earthworks and batteries erected to prevent a land approach toward Richmond. Be sure to ask your tour guide or park staff for their exact location.

LOCATION: **1368 Colonial National Historic Pkwy., Jamestown, 757-229-4997, www .historicjamestowne.org.**

✦ Jubal Early's Grave

One of the many interesting figures of the war, Jubal Early opposed secession yet, when war broke out, ardently fought for his native state of Virginia. He was key in promoting the "Lost Cause" view of the Civil War. His impressive grave can be seen at Spring Hill Cemetery in Lynchburg. This also was the vicinity of his headquarters during the 1864 Battle of Lynchburg (see pp. 251–254).

LOCATION: **Spring Hill Cemetery, intersection of Oakley Ave. and Fort Ave., Lynchburg.**

✦ Laurel Hill

Markers and walking trails guide visitors around this bucolic 75-acre property, revealing the history of J. E. B. Stuart—who was born here—and his family, the area's Native Americans, and the slaves who worked on the farm.

LOCATION: **1091 Ararat Hwy., Ararat, 276-251- 1833, www.jebstuart.org.**

✦ Lee Hall

One of the few antebellum houses still extant on the Virginia peninsula, Lee Hall was the home of planter Richard Decauter Lee. During the Civil War, Confederate Generals Magruder and Johnston headquartered here, and a small skirmish was fought on the property as the Confederates

Richmond's Hollywood Cemetery was named after the many holly trees on the site.

Lee Hall's owner, Richard D. Lee, was not directly related to the famous Confederate.

retreated on May 4, 1862. The on-site museum houses artifacts from the 1862 Peninsula Campaign.

LOCATION: **163 Yorktown Rd., Newport News, 757-888-3371, leehall.org.**

✦ Manassas Historic District

The Manassas Historic District encompasses the site of the original Manassas Junction and includes a beautiful array of preserved 19th-century buildings.

LOCATION: **9431 West St., Manassas, 703-361-6599, www.visitmanassas.org.**

✦ Mariners' Museum and Park

A must-see for Civil War naval enthusiasts, this museum brings to life the drama of the world's first ironclad battle, with personal artifacts, documents, and virtual exhibits made possible by modern technology. Visitors can tour a replica of the C.S.S. *Virginia* and view the remains of the original as well

as a replica of the U.S.S. *Monitor*'s famous turret. A movie illustrates the battle.

LOCATION: **100 Museum Dr., Newport News, 757-596-2222, www.marinersmuseum.org.**

✦ Martha Washington Inn

Built for Francis Preston in 1832, the antebellum Martha Washington Inn has played many roles throughout history: as a mansion, Civil War hospital, women's college, and hotel. Today, it is valuable as an example of 19th-century American architecture. Civil War enthusiasts who desire a luxurious break can book a stay here. Local tradition holds that a number of ghosts haunt the hotel—be sure to ask at the front desk.

LOCATION: **150 W. Main St., Abingdon, 276-628-3161, www.themartha.com.**

✦ Massaponax Church

Built shortly before the war, this antebellum church was used as headquarters and a hospital. Generals Grant and Meade met here after the Battle of Spotsylvania Court House (see pp. 280–283). Wall scrawling by Civil War soldiers is preserved inside. Today, the church is used by an active congregation, and Sunday worshippers are welcome. Call to see if other visits are possible.

LOCATION: 5101 Massaponax Church Rd., Fredericksburg, 540-898-0021, www .massaponaxchurch.com.

✦ Monument Avenue

Replete with statues of Jefferson Davis, Robert E. Lee, Stonewall Jackson, J. E. B. Stuart, and others, beautiful Monument Avenue is a must-see on any visit to Richmond. Listed on the National Register of Historic Places and flanked by historic mansions, this is, in more ways than one, a testament to a bygone era.

LOCATION: Begin at the intersection of Monument Ave. and N. Thompson St. in Richmond and go southeast until you reach N. Allen Ave. Statues line the route from beginning to end.

✦ Museum of the Confederacy

With an unmatched collection covering figures both major and minor, this essential museum—which is located just steps from the White House of the Confederacy (see p. 307)—presents the diversity of figures involved in the Southern rebellion.

LOCATION: 1201 E. Clay St., Richmond, 804-649-1861, www.moc.org. The museum recommends that visitors park nearby at 550 N. 12th St.

✦ Museum of the Confederacy at Appomattox

This informative museum displays several irreplaceable artifacts from the surrender, including General Lee's dress uniform and Paris-made battle sword, inscribed in French with the phrase "God helps those who help themselves." Featuring a dozen audiovisual stations and more than 400 photographs,

documents, and other items, this is a must-visit destination to understand the larger picture of what was essentially the end of the war.

LOCATION: 159 Horseshoe Rd., Appomattox, 434-352-5791, www.acwm.org.

✦ Museum of the Middle Appalachians

Exhibits here include artifacts illuminating the role Saltville played in the Civil War, most especially as the Confederacy's crucial supplier of salt (see sidebar p. 275). Postwar exhibits further detail the town's role as a vital manufacturing space for the mineral.

LOCATION: 123 Palmer Ave., Saltville, 276-496-3633, www.museum-mid-app.org.

✦ National Museum of the Marine Corps

Documenting, preserving, and displaying more than 230 years of Marine Corps history, this fine museum includes a special exhibit on Marines in the Civil War.

LOCATION: 18900 Jefferson Davis Hwy., Triangle, 877-635-1775, www.usmcmuseum .com.

✦ National Sporting Library and Museum

Notable for the statue of the haggard Civil War horse out front, the National Sporting Library and Museum preserves the history and culture of horse and field sports. With more than 26,000 books and works of art, this is a mecca for equestrian enthusiasts.

LOCATION: 102 The Plains Rd., Middleburg, 540-687-6542, www.nsl.org. The library is free to enter, but the art museum has a small fee.

✦ Newby's Crossroads

Newby's Crossroads was the site of Custer's first "Last Stand" (there would be others), in which an outmaneuvered Custer escaped from Confederates by hacking his way through dense forest to Amissville in July 1863.

LOCATION: **Marker located at the intersection of Laurel Mills Rd. and Richmond Rd. in Amissville.**

✦ Old Town Petersburg

Although Petersburg dates back to 1750, making it one of Virginia's older cities, the historic brick buildings that stand today were constructed after an 1815 fire burned the town's wooden center. Full of cafés, antique shops, boutiques, and restaurants, Old Town Petersburg offers a wealth of charming heritage and modern convenience. An important site in its own right, this charming Virginia town also makes for a great stop for lunch or dinner when visiting Petersburg National Battlefield.

LOCATION: **216 N. Sycamore St., Petersburg, 804-732-0700, www.historicpetersburg.org.**

✦ Pamplin Historical Park

With two museums and four antebellum houses, there is much to see here. Artifacts and costumed interpreters help bring history to life, creating a vivid and unforgettable learning experience. The park also offers a weekend camp for kids and adults to experience life as a Civil War soldier.

LOCATION: **6125 Boydton Plank Rd., Petersburg, 804-861-2408, www.pamplinpark.org.**

✦ Peaks of Otter

As General Hunter moved toward Lynchburg, he crossed the Peaks of Otter, arduously hacking his way through thick forest. The mountain view, then as now, impressed him so much that he wrote, "The Peaks of Otter is the finest sight for mountain scenery." Hunter continued to modern-day Bedford before advancing to Lynchburg.

Informative living-history exhibits at Pamplin Historical Park bring home the full reality of day-to-day life during the Civil War.

The modern visitor can experience the view just as he and his men did by visiting the Peaks of Otter Visitor Center.

LOCATION: **Peaks of Otter Visitor Center, 85919 Blue Ridge Pkwy., Bedford, 540-586-4496. Consult www.huntersraid.org for more information on the Peaks of Otter and the rest of this exciting historical journey.**

✦ Port Republic Museum

Exhibits at this museum describe the Battle of Port Republic (see p. 272), as well as the town's history before and after the war. The collection includes artifacts from the period and hundreds of historical documents.

LOCATION: **8691 Water St., Port Republic, 540-249-0040, www.portrepublicmuseum.org.**

✦ Sherwood Forest Plantation

Said to be the longest frame house in America, this was the home of former president John Tyler, a vocal supporter of the South, who used his slaves to help build the fortifications that protected the peninsula. Although the tenth president's grandson lives here, the beautiful house is open to visitors.

LOCATION: **14501 John Tyler Hwy., Charles City, 804-829-5377, www.sherwoodforest.org.**

✦ Shirley Plantation

Founded in 1613, this is Virginia's oldest plantation and has been owned by the same family for 11 generations. Robert E. Lee's mother was born here, and during the Civil War, it was used as a Union Army field hospital. Today, it is open for tours.

LOCATION: **501 Shirley Plantation, Charles City, 804-829-5121, www.shirleyplantation.com.**

✦ Stafford Civil War Park

Easily accessible by car, this recently opened site offers a wealth of historic information and sites, including an Army of the Potomac winter camp, three artillery batteries, an

Jackson wished to die on a Sunday—and he did.

18th-century sandstone quarry, and portions of two corduroy roads.

LOCATION: **400 Mt. Hope Church Rd., Stafford, 540-658-4864, www.staffordparks.com.**

✦ Stonewall Jackson Shrine

The plantation building where the famous general suffered and died features a number of original artifacts and some reproductions to give visitors a flavor not only of Jackson's last moments but also of the practice of medicine in the 19th century. Although he lost his arm in battle, Jackson actually died of pneumonia, which was difficult for doctors to treat. The use of unscientific treatments, such as bloodletting, only exacerbated his condition.

LOCATION: **12019 Stonewall Jackson Rd., Woodford, 804-633-6076, www.nps.gov/frsp /learn/historyculture/js.htm. Call for opening hours.**

✦ Stratford Hall

Built in the late 1730s, Stratford Hall— home of the Lee family and birthplace of

The monumental classical-style Virginia State Capitol was recently restored and reopened.

Robert E. Lee—is one of a precious few truly grand prerevolutionary houses in Virginia. Although worth seeing for the plantation house alone, Stratford Hall also includes walking trails, a mill, and even a beach.

LOCATION: 483 Great House Rd., Montross, 804-493-8038, www.stratfordhall.org.

✦ Sutherlin Mansion

Sutherlin Mansion served as the "Last Capitol of the Confederacy" from April 3 until April 10, 1865. Here Jefferson Davis and his cabinet awaited the arrival of Robert E. Lee's retreating army, and from here Davis issued his last presidential proclamation and departed for Greensboro, North Carolina, after Lee surrendered at Appomattox. A Virginia Historic Landmark, the mansion is now occupied by the Danville Museum of Fine Arts and History and features interpretation of its Civil War heritage in addition to modern art exhibits.

LOCATION: 975 Main St., Danville, 434-793-5644, www.danvillemuseum.org.

✦ Town of Competition

The county seat of Pittsylvania County was known as Competition during the war. An antebellum courthouse adorns Main Street, and army recruits camped on the grounds around Courthouse Springs near the playing fields of Hargrave Military Academy. Colonel Martin of the 53rd Virginia was wounded and captured at the Angle during Pickett's Charge at Gettysburg (see pp. 355–356). After the war he returned and practiced medicine in Chatham, where he bought Oak Hall, an 1840 mansion. He died in 1912 and is buried in the Old Chatham Cemetery.

LOCATION: Oak Hall (private), intersection of Franklin Pl. and S. Main St., Chatham.

✦ Unison Historic District

This beautiful and quaint Virginia town has good examples of antebellum and 19th-century architecture. Site of the minor 1862 battle of Unison, this town also bore witness to the ravages of the Civil War. Once named

Union, the town changed to Unison because postal regulations stipulate that two towns in the same state cannot share a name.

LOCATION: **Intersection of Unison Rd. and Foxcroft Rd., Unison, www.unisonva.org.**

✦ Valentine Museum

Located in the antebellum Wickham House, the Valentine Museum was Richmond's first private museum. Today, it focuses on the city's history both before and after the Civil War, interpreting the story with an expansive collection of more than 1.6 million objects.

LOCATION: **1015 E. Clay St., Richmond, 804-649-0711, www.thevalentine.org.**

✦ Virginia State Capitol

Designed by Thomas Jefferson and Charles-Louis Clerisseau, the Virginia State Capitol is the home of the oldest legislative body in the Western Hemisphere, tracing its roots back to the 1619 House of Burgesses. During the Civil War it was the Capitol of the Confederacy, and it was toured by Lincoln after the fall of Richmond. Today, the Capitol is open for visitors in addition to still being the seat of Virginia's government.

LOCATION: **1000 Bank St., Richmond, 804-698-1788, www.virginiacapitol.gov.**

✦ Warren Rifles Confederate Museum

Filled with Civil War–era uniforms, battle flags, buttons, letters, and personal artifacts, this small museum is well worth a stop during a visit to Front Royal.

LOCATION: **95 Chester St., Front Royal, 540-636-6982, www.vaudc.org/museum.html. Visits in winter require an appointment.**

✦ Warrenton

Frequently occupied by soldiers on either side, Warrenton was central to the 1862 Second Manassas Campaign. Today, historic Main Street in Old Town Warrenton preserves the charm of a bygone era, with brick sidewalks and preserved architecture.

LOCATION: **Main St., Warrenton, www.virginia .org/cities/warrenton.**

✦ Waynesboro Heritage Foundation Plumb House Museum

This museum hosts a wide variety of Civil War and Native American artifacts, illuminating the history of the area. Built at the turn of the 19th century, the house is the oldest frame dwelling in Waynesboro and was caught in the middle of the March 2, 1865, Battle of Waynesboro (see p. 286).

LOCATION: **1012 W. Main St., Waynesboro, 540-943-3943, www.waynesboroheritage foundation.com/plumb-house-museum.**

✦ White House of the Confederacy

Although best experienced in conjunction with a visit to the neighboring Museum of the Confederacy (see p. 303), the White House of the Confederacy—which was inhabited by Jefferson Davis during the Civil War—is well worth a visit on its own merits. Built in 1818, the restored house has been called by the *Washington Post* as "second only to Mount Vernon among restorations of historic American dwellings." Many of the furnishings inside are original.

LOCATION: **1201 E. Clay St., Richmond. The museum recommends that visitors park nearby at 550 N. 12th St.**

✦ White Oak Museum

The museum's collection includes weapons, coins, ammunition, and other artifacts of the U.S. Army's extended base of operations in Virginia. There is also a fascinating presentation of camp structures used by soldiers.

LOCATION: **985 White Oak Rd., Falmouth, 540-371-4234, www.whiteoakmuseum.com.**

West Virginia

WEST VIRGINIA WAS BORN IN THE CIVIL WAR. WHEN Virginia left the Union, the mountainous western portion of the state—long culturally distinct from the aristocratic plantation system present in the east—voted to leave Virginia. Few had slaves, and Wheeling, Western Virginia's largest city, was well over 300 miles from Richmond, but only 60 miles from Pittsburgh. In 1863, West Virginia was admitted to the Union as a state, thus, in one of history's many ironies, ensuring that the only state to successfully secede did so from the Confederacy.

Although West Virginia saw only scattered fighting during the war, in the run-up to the conflict, it bore witness to a crucial event: John Brown's raid on Harpers Ferry. No other action evoked such sympathy in the North, or condemnation in the South, as Brown's attempt to begin a slave uprising. Today, West Virginia has preserved several notable battlefields and other associated sites, making it a worthy destination for Civil War travelers.

John Brown's raid on Harpers Ferry inflamed tensions in both North and South, helping start the war. U.S. Army officers Robert E. Lee and J. E. B. Stuart captured Brown and his supporters.

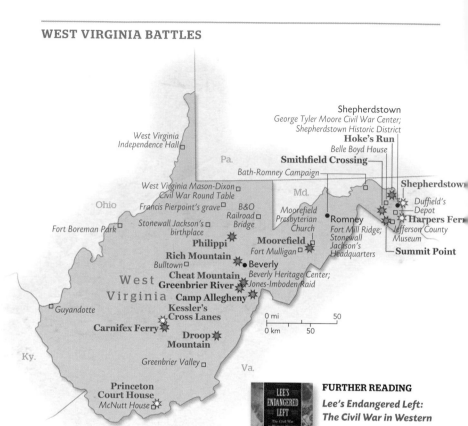

Shepherdstown
George Tyler Moore Civil War Center;
Shepherdstown Historic District
Hoke's Run
Belle Boyd House
Smithfield Crossing
Bath-Romney Campaign

West Virginia
Independence Hall □

Pa.

Md.

Shepherdstow

Ohio

West Virginia Mason-Dixon □
Civil War Round Table
Francis Pierpoint's grave □ B&O
Railroad □
Stonewall Jackson's *Bridge*
birthplace
Philippi ✶

Moorefield
Presbyterian
Church □ **Romney**
Fort Mill Ridge;
Stonewall
Jackson's
Headquarters

Duffield's
Depot
Harpers Fer
Jefferson County
Museum
Summit Point

Fort Boreman Park □

Moorefield ✶
Fort Mulligan □

Rich Mountain ✶
Bulltown □ ● **Beverly**

West **Cheat Mountain,** ✶ *Beverly Heritage Center;*
Greenbrier River ✶ *Jones-Imboden Raid*
Virginia **Camp Allegheny** ✶
Kessler's
Cross Lanes
Guyandotte □ ✶

Carnifex Ferry ✶
Droop ✶
Mountain

Ky.

Greenbrier Valley □ Va.

0 mi   50

0 km   50

Princeton
Court House ✶
McNutt House □

✷Camp Allegheny

CAMPAIGN: Operations in Western Virginia
DATE(S): December 13, 1861

To defend the Staunton-Parkersburg Pike—
an important transport route—Colonel
Johnson's Confederates seized the high
ground on Allegheny Mountain. Federals
under General Milroy attacked but were
repulsed and pushed down the mountain.

Remains of earthworks and other structures present at the time of engagement are
still visible.

**LOCATION: Marker and battlefield on Old Pike
Rd. (County Rte. 3), 2 miles west of US 250,
near Bartow.**

FURTHER READING

Lee's Endangered Left:
The Civil War in Western
Virginia, Spring of 1864
by Richard R. Duncan
Vivid account of military
actions in the eastern
theater late in the war

✶ Carnifex Ferry

CAMPAIGN: Operations in Western Virginia
DATE(S): September 10, 1861

Union General Rosecrans attacked General
Floyd's men at Carnifex Ferry, with fighting
stopped only by the onset of darkness. Floyd
retreated in the night, blaming his loss on
co-commander General Wise.

Confederate failure to control the
Kanawha Valley meant that West Virginia's
bid for statehood would not be actively contested by the Confederates.

The large, well-preserved state park offers hiking trails and interpretation of the battle.

LOCATION: **Carnifex Ferry Battlefield State Park, 1194 Carnifex Ferry Crossing, Summersville, 304-872-0825, www.carnifexferrybattle fieldstatepark.com.**

✴ Cheat Mountain

CAMPAIGN: Operations in Western Virginia

DATE(S): September 12–15, 1861

A poor start for a general who would soon become great, this battle is most notable as Robert E. Lee's first of the war. He attempted to overpower General Reynolds's position at Fort Milroy on Cheat Mountain. Poor

Alfred Napoleon Alexander Duffié

Born in Paris, Duffié was a promising soldier in the French army who served in Africa and in the Crimean War. Yet, in 1859, just two months after accepting a promotion, he attempted to resign. He had fallen in love with Mary Ann Pelton, an American woman. When his resignation was angrily rejected, he deserted and fled to New York, where the two were married. Duffié exaggerated his background and military service, claiming to be the son of a count and to have been wounded eight times in combat. He joined the Union Army and, despite a poor combat record, was promoted to brigadier general. He was en route to help with operations in Texas when the war ended. Quick to anger, he once challenged General Porter to a duel. His poor English and foreign manners were both amusing and infuriating to contemporaries. He once famously ordered a charge by saying, "You all have got to die someday anyway. If you die now you wont have to die again. Forward!" He became a U.S. citizen in 1867.

intelligence and uncoordinated attacks doomed the Confederates' efforts, even though the Union position was guarded by a mere 300 men.

Today, the remnants of Union Fort Milroy lie within Monongahela National Forest.

LOCATION. **Monongahela National Forest, 304 636-1800, www.fs.usda.gov/mnf. From Durbin, head northeast on US 250 for 6.5 miles, then take a left onto Rte. 245 (White Top Rd.) and stay on the road for 1 mile until you reach the summit. At the fork in the road, be sure to take a right to remain on White Top Rd.**

✴ Droop Mountain

CAMPAIGN: Averell's Raid on the Virginia & Tennessee Railroad

DATE(S): November 6, 1863

Generals Averell and Duffié (see sidebar this page) led men to destroy the Virginia & Tennessee Railroad. While Duffié demolished Confederate property, Averell met General Echols's forces at Droop Mountain, defeating them and ending Confederate resistance in West Virginia.

The well preserved state park offers a range of interpretive and athletic activities.

LOCATION: **Droop Mountain Battlefield State Park, multiple entrances on Rte. 219 nearly 4 miles southwest of Hillsboro, 304-653-4254, www.droopmountainbattlefield.com.**

❊ Greenbrier River

CAMPAIGN: Operations in Western Virginia

DATE(S): October 3, 1861

General Reynolds moved to test the Confederate lines at Camp Bartow. Reynolds tried to hold the Rebels' attention in their front with a skirmish line while attempting to turn the Confederates' right flank. Even supported by artillery, he was unable to make any progress and subsequently returned to Cheat Mountain.

LOCATION: **Marker on Old Pike Rd., just east of the intersection with Potomac Highlands Trail (Rte. 28), Bartow.**

✳ Harpers Ferry

CAMPAIGN: Maryland Campaign

DATE(S): September 12–15, 1862

After defeating the Federals at the second battle of Manassas (see p. 257), Lee decided to bring the war to the North and invaded Maryland. When Marylanders did not treat them as liberators, he determined to enter Pennsylvania; however, with a large Federal garrison on his supply lines, he boldly split his army in two, with one wing under Longstreet staging to Hagerstown and covering the South Mountain passes while

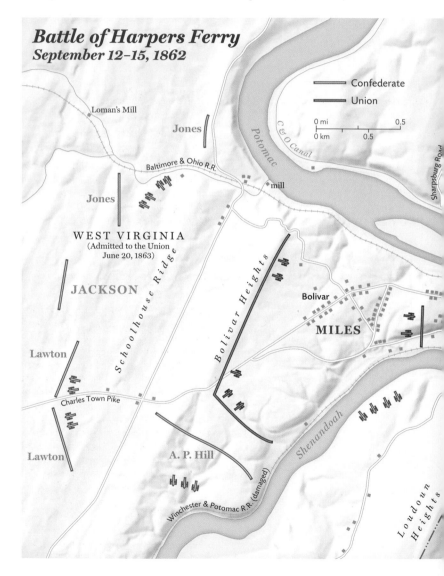

Battle of Harpers Ferry
September 12–15, 1862

Confederate

Union

Loman's Mill

Jones

Baltimore & Ohio R.R.

Potomac

C & O Canal

Sharpsburg Road

0 mi   0.5
0 km   0.5

mill

Jones

WEST VIRGINIA
(Admitted to the Union
June 20, 1863)

JACKSON

Schoolhouse Ridge

Bolivar Heights

Bolivar

MILES

Lawton

Charles Town Pike

Lawton

A. P. Hill

Shenandoah

Winchester & Potomac R.R. (damaged)

Loudoun Heights

Stonewall Jackson moved against Harpers Ferry. Jackson surrounded the Federals on three sides, holding the high ground at each, and unleashed an artillery barrage and morning infantry attack. The outcome was never in doubt. More than 12,000 Union soldiers surrendered, the largest surrender of American soldiers until Bataan and Corregidor in World War II.

Much of the presentation at Harpers Ferry National Historical Park focuses on John Brown's raid. The Kennedy Farm, where Brown planned his attack, is located nearby in Maryland. Fully interpreted and preserved, the Schoolhouse Ridge battlefield occupied the high ground just outside the park. The Maryland Heights battlefield is a challenging but rewarding climb best made after the first freeze, as the mountain is heavily forested and infested with poisonous snakes.

LOCATION: **Harpers Ferry National Historical Park, 171 Shoreline Dr., Harpers Ferry, 304-535-6029, www.nps.gov/hafe.**

FURTHER READING

Midnight Rising: John Brown and the Raid That Sparked the Civil War by Tony Horwitz The story of John Brown's raid

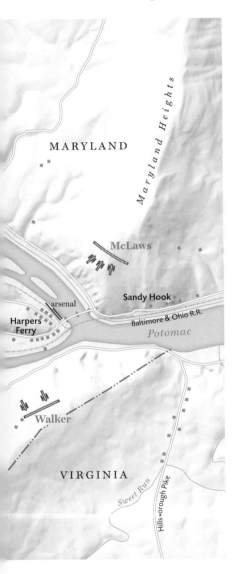

✳ Hoke's Run

CAMPAIGN: Manassas Campaign

DATE(S): July 2, 1861

Almost three weeks before First Manassas (see pp. 254–256), Jackson's men, who would soon be immortalized as the "Stonewall Brigade," fought forces under General Patterson near Hoke's Run. The outnumbered Confederate forces had orders to delay the Federal advance—and they did precisely that. Although seemingly inconsequential, Patterson's subsequent withdrawal to Charles Town and Harpers Ferry allowed Jackson and other Confederates to reinforce the main army at Manassas, turning a near loss into the first great victory of the war.

Today, development has overtaken the battlefield. Nearby Martinsburg offers the Belle Boyd House (see p. 319), home of the famous spy.

LOCATION: **Markers located at 5006 and 5453 Williamsport Pike, at 5715 Hammonds Mill Rd.,**

John Brown's Raid

"John Brown's Body" and "The Battle Hymn of the Republic" are songs inspired by the raid.

John Brown's raid on Harpers Ferry is one of the most important events leading up to the Civil War. Brown, a staunch abolitionist, had come from Kansas, where he had led bloody attacks and committed cold-blooded murder against slaveholders. A fanatic with a gleam of insanity in his eye, Brown believed that forceful intervention and a slave uprising were needed to end the injustice of slavery.

Bringing that passion to the east, on October 17, 1859, Brown's band, including five blacks, seized the firehouse at Harpers Ferry. They carried long pikes to help arm the slave army he planned to form. Instead, forces led by future Confederate generals Robert E. Lee and J. E. B. Stuart broke into the firehouse killing or capturing Brown and most of his men, although five managed to escape.

While planning the raid, Brown met important antislavery leaders, including Frederick Douglass, whom he tried to convince to join his raid. Douglass refused, believing it would be suicidal and counterproductive to the cause. Harriet Tubman, however, agreed to participate, although she luckily missed it because of an illness at the time of the raid.

Brown also had support from a small group of very wealthy Northerners known as the Secret Six, including Gerrit Smith—a millionaire member of Congress—and Thomas Higginson, who would later be an officer in the U.S. Colored Troops. Henry David Thoreau, John Quincy Adams, Ralph Waldo Emerson, and many others all voiced support for Brown. His broad support among intelligent and successful Northerners undermined the Southern claim—that Brown was a fringe lunatic not to be taken seriously. Both derided and feared in the South, Brown's execution made him a martyr in the North. Although he failed to see slavery abolished in his lifetime, his actions set the stage for secession and emancipation only a few years later.

FURTHER READING

Fields of Honor: Pivotal Battles of the Civil War
by Edwin C. Bearss
First chapter provides a stirring narrative of John Brown's raid

and on Embankment Rd., just east of the intersection with Williamsport Pike. For more information, consult the Falling Waters Battlefield Association, www.battleoffallingwaters.com.

✳ Kessler's Cross Lanes

CAMPAIGN: Operations in Western Virginia
DATE(S): August 26, 1861

General Floyd attacked Union Colonel Tyler's men at Kessler's Cross Lanes, taking them by surprise and ousting them. After this victory, Floyd moved to Carnifex Ferry (see pp. 310–311). Robert E. Lee would soon arrive and take command of Confederate forces in western Virginia but with mediocre results. The two politicians turned generals—John Floyd, a former Virginia governor and secretary of war for President Buchanan, and Henry A. Wise, former governor of Virginia—were more interested in competing with each other than in fighting Yankees. "Granny" Lee proved unable to control them and returned to Richmond.

LOCATION: **Two markers located at the intersection of Summersville Lake Rd. (Rte. 129) and Cooper Creek Rd. (Rte. 9), Kessler's Cross Lanes. Another marker is located half a mile south of that intersection on Summersville Lake Rd.**

✳ Moorefield

CAMPAIGN: Early's Raid and Operations Against the B&O Railroad
DATE(S): August 7, 1864

After the burning of Chambersburg, General McCausland returned south and was driven back by Federal artillery on high ground near New Creek, near what is now Keyser, West Virginia. Retiring to Moorefield and camping outside the town, McCausland's men were attacked in their camps around 3 a.m. The surprise was complete, and the Rebels fled, leaving a disorganized mass of horsemen who would no longer be effective in the war.

Interpretive signs from the West Virginia Civil War Trails program tell the story of the engagements at New Creek and Moorefield.

LOCATION: **Marker located on US 220, a third of a mile south of the U.S. Post Office at 165 Old Fields Rd., Old Fields.**

✳ Philippi

CAMPAIGN: Operations in Western Virginia
DATE(S): June 3, 1861

Notable as the first land battle in the eastern theater, this clash began when Colonel Morris

Lee's early losses might have sidelined him were it not for Johnston's wounding.

attacked Colonel Porterfield's Confederate forces at Philippi. The Union troops surprised the Confederates by attacking from two directions and sending them fleeing after a single volley, earning this battle the nickname the "Philippi Races." Ultimately, the Rebels were forced to retreat to Huttonsville.

LOCATION: Blue and Gray Park, at the intersection of Rte. 250 and Rte. 119, next to the covered bridge in Philippi. There is an informative marker located on the campus of Alderson Broaddus College. Take Circle Drive East; when going north, it will be on your right. Stonewall Jackson's birthplace (see p. 323) is in nearby Clarksburg.

✳ Princeton Court House

CAMPAIGN: Jackson's Valley Campaign
DATE(S): May 15–17, 1862

General Marshall's Confederates defeated General Cox's Union forces in three days of fighting. Union forces then retreated to Camp Flat Top. It is a representative engagement of the fighting in the mountains—a

Frederick Lander, Union colonel and poet, rides into action at Philippi.

running fight of little real significance in the grander scheme of the war.

LOCATION: Marker on S. Walker St., a tenth of a mile south of the intersection with Airport Dr. in Princeton. The antebellum McNutt House (see p. 320) is nearby.

FURTHER READING

West Virginia and the Civil War: Mountaineers Are Always Free
by Mark A. Snell
The story of West Virginia in the Civil War

✳ Rich Mountain

CAMPAIGN: Operations in Western Virginia
DATE(S): July 11, 1861

After assuming command of Union forces in the area, General McClellan moved to take on the Rebels. Union forces under General Rosecrans attacked Colonel Pegram's rear, stampeding his force and capturing more than 500 men. This success caused Garnett to retreat from his other positions; he was killed in a skirmish at Corrick's Ford. The decisive victory reinforced the legitimacy of West Virginia's Unionist Wheeling legislature and raised McClellan's national profile.

More than 400 acres of the battlefield are preserved and interpreted for visitors. The nearby Beverly Heritage Center has information on the battle (see p. 319).

LOCATION: Rich Mountain Battlefield Park, located on Rich Mountain Rd., 5 miles west of Beverly, 304-637-7424, www.richmountain.org.

✳ Shepherdstown

CAMPAIGN: Maryland Campaign
DATE(S): September 19–20, 1862

After the Battle of Antietam (see pp. 340–341), equally wary Union and Confederate Armies faced off as Lee moved south back to Virginia. General Porter attacked General Pendleton's rear guard, taking four of his artillery pieces. On September 20,

Pickets fire across a ford in the river at Shepherdstown. Counting only dead and wounded, the Battle of Shepherdstown was the bloodiest in West Virginia.

a Confederate counterattack decimated a Federal attempt to establish a bridgehead.

LOCATION: Visitor Center, 129 E. German St., Shepherdstown, 304-876-2786, www .shepherdstown.info. Markers at the intersection of S. King St. and E. German St. Don't miss the Bavarian Inn on the banks of the Potomac River. It was a favorite of Nancy Reagan in the 1980s.

FURTHER READING

Shenandoah Summer: The 1864 Valley Campaign by Scott Patchan An engaging and detailed look at Early's underappreciated campaign

❋Smithfield Crossing

CAMPAIGN: Sheridan's Valley Campaign

DATE(S): August 25–29, 1864

General Merritt's Federal forces faced Confederates under General Early across Opequon Creek. On August 29, Rebels crossed at Smithfield, pushing the Northerners toward Charles Town. Union reinforcements halted the Confederate push, resulting in an inconclusive end to this minor skirmish.

LOCATION: No markers or public access; however, taking WV 51 over Opequon Creek will take you through the general battle area.

❋Summit Point

CAMPAIGN: Sheridan's Valley Campaign

DATE(S): August 21, 1864

In the second battle in General Sheridan's Valley Campaign, Union forces gathered at Charles Town were assaulted by two columns of Confederates, one led directly by General Early, which moved east, while General Anderson went north against Federal cavalry. The Northerners delayed and repulsed the Confederates before withdrawing the next day.

LOCATION: Much of the battle took place around 2 miles west of Charles Town, although the land is not open to the public.

Other Battles and Beyond

✦ West Virginia Civil War Trails

With driving tours, historical background, and more, West Virginia Civil War Trails is an invaluable resource for planning excursions. While there are many worthy tours, be sure not to miss the Battle of Laurel Hill driving tour. For more information, visit www.civil wartraveler.com.

✦ West Virginia in the Civil War

Frequently updated, the West Virginia in the Civil War website—accessible at www.wvcivil war.com—is the most up-to-date source on upcoming events, reenactments, and more.

✦ West Virginia Mason-Dixon Civil War Round Table

This group of Civil War aficionados holds a worthwhile meeting in Morgantown every third Thursday of the month. They also produce an online newsletter available at www .wvmasondixoncwrt.org.

✦ West Virginia Tourism

The best place to plan a trip of any type to the Mountain State, West Virginia Tourism collects information on hotels, tourist attractions, restaurants, history, and more. Access it at www.wvtourism.com.

✦ B&O Railroad Bridge

Targeted in the 1863 Jones-Imboden raid (see p. 322), Rowlesburg's crucial bridge on the Baltimore & Ohio Railroad presented a rich target for Confederates, particularly because its large size and remote location meant repairs would be difficult. After a day of stubborn fighting, it was successfully

The Potomac River as seen from Harpers Ferry, West Virginia. "Potomac" is believed to have meant "trading place" in Algonquin.

defended by the Union troops—the only location attacked during the raid that survived mostly unscathed. Today, a new bridge marks the site.

LOCATION: **East end of E. Main St., Rowlesburg, www.rowlesburg.info.**

✦ Bath-Romney Campaign

In an effort to keep control of western Virginia, Jackson waged a harrowing winter campaign in January 1862. Known as the Bath-Romney Campaign because the Confederate commander seized both towns, the expedition was a success despite the terrible weather, with more than 100 miles of the Baltimore & Ohio Railroad destroyed. In the end, however, this early success did little to reinforce Virginia's diminishing claim to its western counties.

LOCATION: **Historic marker at the Hampshire County Courthouse Square, Confederate Memorial at Indian Mound Cemetery, Romney, www.cometohampshire.com/history.**

✦ Belle Boyd House

Known as the "Siren of the Shenandoah," Belle Boyd is perhaps the most famous spy of the entire war. She charmed her way into receiving Union information and rode through enemy lines with false papers to alert Jackson of Union plans. For this, she was awarded the Southern Cross of Honor. Featuring displays that re-create that bygone era, Boyd's onetime home is available to visit. She was married in London, England, and that church is included on the city's Civil War walking tour (see p. 484).

LOCATION: **126 E. Race St., Martinsburg, 304-267-4713, www.bchs.org.**

✦ Beverly Heritage Center

The Beverly Heritage Center describes the July 11, 1861, Battle of Rich Mountain, the importance of the Staunton-Parkersburg Turnpike, and the everyday life of the residents of Beverly in Civil War times. With four

A spy before age 18, Belle Boyd used her age and gender to evade suspicion.

historic buildings, artifacts, guided cemetery tours, reenactments, and more, this is a worthwhile stop.

LOCATION: **4 Court St., Beverly, 304-637-7424, www.beverlyheritagecenter.org.**

✦ Bulltown

In autumn 1862, William L. Jackson, Stonewall Jackson's cousin, led a raiding party of around 800 men to take Fort Bulltown, a small fortification in Bulltown. They lost the element of surprise, however, when a Confederate fired his gun, alerting the Union troops to their advance. In 12 hours of light fighting, the Confederates lost eight men, while the North emerged almost completely unscathed. For this, William was given the derisive nickname "Mudwall," in contrast to his dashing and brilliant cousin. Today, the earthworks are preserved and there is an interpreted trail at the Bulltown Historic Area.

LOCATION: **1 Burnsville Lake Rd., Burnsville, 304-452-8170. Camping can be reserved at www.recreation.gov.**

✦ Duffield's Depot

Known as the "oldest purpose-built combined freight and passenger station" in the United States, this depot was captured by Mosby's Raiders in 1864 in an attempt to disrupt the Baltimore & Ohio Railroad. Mosby took prisoners and burned most of the buildings, sparing the depot.

LOCATION: **14 Melvin Rd., Shenandoah Junction. Information about the depot can be found at www.civilwartraveler.com.**

✦ Fort Boreman Park

Fort Boreman Park is the site of an abandoned Union fort named for West Virginia's first governor, Arthur I. Boreman. Union forces established the fort in 1863 to protect the Baltimore & Ohio Railroad.

LOCATION: **Parkersburg, 304-424-1976, www .woodcountywv.com. To reach the park from Parkersburg, take WV 68 S and briefly merge onto US 50 before taking the immediate exit for County Rte. 9. Then turn left onto Fort Boreman Dr., following it to the park.**

✦ Fort Mill Ridge

Constructed by Confederate forces to defend the town of Romney, these are arguably the best preserved Civil War trenches still extant anywhere in the nation. The museum and visitor center—with information on the trenches—are located in historic Taggart Hall in Romney.

LOCATION: **To reach the fort from Mechanicsburg, take US 50 (Northwestern Pike) east for one mile, and then turn right onto Core Rd. After crossing the river, turn left onto Fort Mill Ridge and follow that road until it ends at the park. Taggart Hall Visitors Center, 91 S. High St., Romney, 304-822-4320, www.wvcommerce .org.**

✦ Fort Mulligan

The well-preserved Civil War–era Fort Mulligan sits atop a hill with great views of Petersburg and the surrounding mountains. Built by Union soldiers in 1863, the fort was intended to shore up the Federal position in an area that was still dangerous for Union men. Not only are the earthworks impressive, but there is also a great walking tour available that will only enhance your understanding of the site.

LOCATION: **To reach the fort from Petersburg, take 28 (N. Fork Hwy.) east for 1 mile. Turn left onto Hospital Dr., and then veer right to the fort. Information and the walking tour are available from www.grantcountypress.com/ft _mulligan.html, or call 304-257-1844.**

✦ Francis Pierpoint's Grave

Widely known as the Father of West Virginia for his role in securing the state's admission to the Union, Pierpoint is buried at Woodlawn Cemetery in Fairmont. Ironically, he was never technically governor of the state of West Virginia. Instead, in 1861 he was elected governor of the "restored state of Virginia" by a Unionist legislature in Wheeling that rejected secession and represented Virginia in the Union during the war. In 1863, when West Virginia was admitted as a state, Arthur Boreman was elected governor, and Pierpoint continued to serve as the governor of the "restored" Virginia, with its capital based in Alexandria.

LOCATION: **335 Maple Ave., Fairmont, 304-657-1813, www.historicwoodlawncemetery.org.**

✦ George Tyler Moore Civil War Center

A special place of research affiliated with Shepherd University in Shepherdstown (see p. 323), the George Tyler Moore Civil War Center has a series of seminars, summer fellowships, and educational programs. With a wide range of information, including a database of Civil War soldiers, this is a great resource for anyone looking to do deep research on the Civil War.

LOCATION: **136 West German St., Shepherdstown, 304-876-5429, www.shepherd.edu /gtmcweb.**

A view of German Street in the Shepherdstown Historic District. Confederates burned the local covered bridge in 1861.

✦ Greenbrier Valley

The town of Lewisburg, in Greenbrier Valley, witnessed a number of Civil War battles and their aftereffects, with buildings serving as hospitals for wounded soldiers and some engagements taking place in and around the town itself. The Greenbrier Public Library has preserved Civil War graffiti on a section of wall, and there is a Civil War cemetery in the town. The visitor center offers information on several walking tours. Request the free guide on the website.

LOCATION: **Greenbrier County Convention and Visitors Bureau, 200 W. Washington St., 800-833-2068, www.greenbrierwv.com.**

✦ Guyandotte

Supposedly the only town on the Ohio River to vote for secession, Guyandotte was a hotbed of disunion in an otherwise Unionist state. The choice to secede had tragic

consequences when the 9th West Virginia infantry set up a Union recruitment camp. On November 10, 1861, a Confederate raid encircled the town. In the ensuing fight, 10 Union soldiers were killed and 20 others wounded. Unionist sympathizers were rounded up and imprisoned. In retaliation, Union forces burned nearly the entire town the next day. The Madie Carroll House, which can be visited today, was one of the few structures to survive the inferno.

LOCATION: **Marker and Madie Carroll House at 234 Guyan St., Huntington, 304-736-1655, www.madiecarrollhouse.org.**

✦ Jefferson County Museum

With more than 2,000 artifacts, multiple exhibits, and a wide range of information on the Civil War and the general history of life in Jefferson County, the Jefferson County Museum is a good place to begin learning about Charles Town and the hanging of John Brown (see p. 314). A walking tour that focuses on black history in the region is available online.

LOCATION: Jefferson County Museum, 200 E. Washington St., Charles Town, 304-725-8628, www.jeffcomuseumwv.org. Visit www.jeffcty wvblackhistory.org to access the black history walking tour.

✦ Jones-Imboden Raid

With fears of a successful split from Virginia coming to fruition, the Confederacy attempted to stop West Virginia's bid for statehood while simultaneously weakening the Northern supply lines in the state. In April and May 1863, Confederate forces led by Grumble Jones and John D. Imboden separately attacked and destroyed crucial infrastructure of the Baltimore & Ohio Railroad in West Virginia. Their efforts to keep western Virginia in the Confederacy failed, however, as the new state was admitted to the Union just a few weeks later on June 20, 1863. Although Confederate Captain Harding shot and nearly killed the local sheriff, there were no hard feelings— the sheriff helped him get a pension.

LOCATION: Marker located outside the old Randolph County Jail, at the intersection of Walnut St. Extended and Court St. in Beverly. Other markers related to the raid are scattered across the state.

✦ McNutt House

Built in 1840, this antebellum house is notable as the only Civil War–era structure still standing in the town of Princeton—it was one of the lucky few to escape burning by retreating Confederates. Equally notable is the fact that the house was used by two future presidents, Rutherford B. Hayes and William McKinley. Today, the house is the home of the Princeton-Mercer County Chamber of Commerce. It has been listed on the National Register of Historic Places since 2001.

LOCATION: 1522 N. Walker St., Princeton, 304-487-1502, www.frontiernet.net/~pmccc.

✦ Moorefield Presbyterian Church

Used as a hospital for both Union and Confederate wounded, this antebellum church was built around 1847. Northern soldiers used the church's pews as firewood

The Jones-Imboden Raid targeted this B&O Railroad bridge at Rowlesburg, West Virginia.

and stabled horses inside. Its minister, William W. Wilson, was an ardent Confederate who became a chaplain in the Rebel army. Today, the church houses an active modern congregation.

LOCATION: **109 S. Main St., Moorefield, www.moorefieldchurch.org.**

✦ Shepherdstown Historic District

Founded in 1762, Shepherdstown is the oldest town in West Virginia, with many buildings dating from the 1700s and 1800s, including the Weltzheimer Tavern, Baker House, and Sheetz House. The core of the town is now known as the Shepherdstown Historic District, concentrated mostly along German Street. Notably, the town was once proposed as a location for our nation's capital. One of the world's first steamboats was tested in the river nearby, and after the Battle of Antietam (see pp. 340–341), nearly the entire town was used by the Confederates as a hospital.

LOCATION: **Shepherdstown Visitors Center, 129 E. German St., Shepherdstown, 304-876-2786, www.shepherdstown.info. A walking tour of the town is available at www.historicshepherds town.com/walking_tour.**

✦ Stonewall Jackson's Birthplace

The house where Stonewall Jackson was born no longer stands; however, two markers identify and commemorate the legendary general's birth. One, a small metal plaque, stands on the exact location of the house. A second, much more informative marker is a block or so away. It details Jackson's tough childhood of poverty and how both of his parents had died by the time he was seven years old.

LOCATION: **The first marker is on W. Main St. at the intersection with Court St in Clarksburg. The second is on W. Main St. at the intersection with S. 5th St. in Clarksburg.**

The Bulltown battlefield was named after the Delaware Indian chief Bull.

✦ Stonewall Jackson's Headquarters

On January 14, 1862, during the Bath-Romney Campaign (see p. 319), Stonewall Jackson made his headquarters at the John Baker White House. The biting winter cold had demoralized General Loring and his men, who were fighting under Jackson. Loring undermined his commander by convincing Richmond officials to order Loring's men out of Romney. For this interference, Jackson resigned his post, although he was later convinced to stay. Today, the house still stands, although it is not open to visitors.

LOCATION: **Marker and house at 235 E. Main St., Romney.**

✦ West Virginia Independence Hall

West Virginia Independence Hall bore witness to the historic Wheeling Convention and the West Virginia Constitutional Convention, which proclaimed and secured statehood for the Mountain State.

LOCATION: **1528 Market St., Wheeling, 304-238-1300, www.wvculture.org/museum/wvih mod.html.**

The Northeast

At the Battle of Antietam, casualties amounted to more than 22,000 soldiers in a single day.

Milestones

> FEBRUARY 6-16, 1862
Ulysses S. Grant is nicknamed "Unconditional Surrender" after dual victories at Forts Henry and Donelson.

> FEBRUARY 27, 1862
The Confederate Congress grants Davis the right to suspend habeas corpus.

> MARCH 7-8, 1862
Defeat at Pea Ridge dampens hope that Missouri will be governed by the Confederacy.

> MARCH 8-9, 1862
The age of wooden warships ends with the battle of ironclads *Monitor* and *Virginia*.

> APRIL 5-JULY 1, 1862
The first grand Federal offensive sputters out in front of Richmond; Confederate General Lee takes the initiative.

> APRIL 24, 1862
The Federal fleet passes Forts Jackson and St. Philip; New Orleans will soon surrender.

> JUNE 17, 1862
The U.S. Congress passes the Morrill Act, which will be a major source of growth in higher education.

> AUGUST 14, 1862
Black leaders at the White House reject Lincoln's plea to support African colonization outside the United States.

> SEPTEMBER 22, 1862
Lincoln uses the Battle of Antietam to justify announcing the Emancipation Proclamation on January 1, 1863, disrupting Union armies.

> NOVEMBER 4, 1862
Lincoln's war policy is rebuffed in the midterm elections. Lincoln fires several commanders who are Democrats.

Bedrock of the Union

The United States Army was barely 16,000 men strong when the Civil War started. By war's end it had grown to more than 2.2 million, due in part to Northern mobilization, which would involve significant numbers of immigrants and eventually nearly 200,000 African-American soldiers. With the firing on Fort Sumter, President Lincoln called for volunteers to help quash the rebellion. New York and Pennsylvania alone enrolled hundreds of regiments. In addition to combat troops, Northern states also raised and frequently mobilized troops to protect the land within their own borders. Indeed, state militia were the only line of defense during General Lee's 1863 raid into Pennsylvania. Other forces protected critical junctions such as bridges and railroads.

While the Northern states were generally spared the ravages of war, they did suffer ravages of the heart, as hundreds of thousands of soldiers came home maimed while others lay, unknown, in countless Southern cemeteries.

After the war, Northern communities marked the victory and celebrated their heroes with parades, monuments, and museums—artifacts that tell the story of the North's Civil War experience.

As if to symbolize a state of disunion, the Capitol dome loomed incomplete over President Lincoln during his inauguration on March 4, 1861.

C A N A D A

Lake Huron

Lake Ontario

New York

Lake Erie

P e n n s y l v a n i a

Williamsport
Hancock

Gettysburg

Trenton
Philadelphia

Folck's Mill

Hanover
Boonsboro
Frederick

Wilmington

Antietam
South Mountain

Baltimore

Maryland

Monocacy
Fort Stevens

Washington, D.C.

District of
Columbia

Delaware

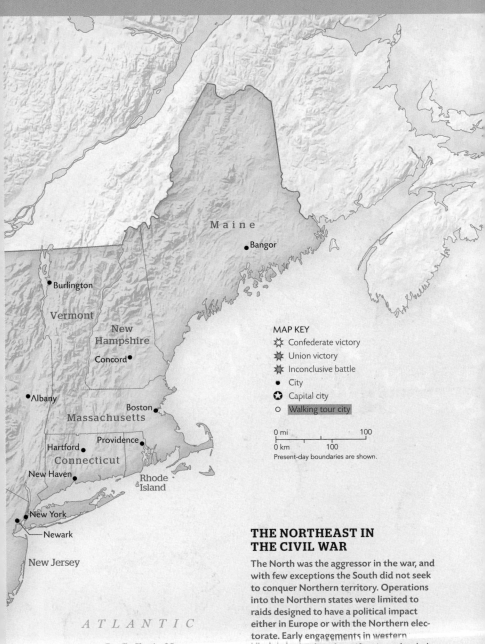

M a i n e

•Bangor

•Burlington

Vermont

New
Hampshire

Concord•

•Albany

Boston•

Massachusetts

Providence•

Hartford•

Connecticut

New Haven•

Rhode
Island

New York•

Newark

New Jersey

MAP KEY
✷ Confederate victory
✸ Union victory
✸ Inconclusive battle
• City
✪ Capital city
○ Walking tour city

0 mi   100
0 km   100
Present-day boundaries are shown.

A T L A N T I C

O C E A N

THE NORTHEAST IN
THE CIVIL WAR

The North was the aggressor in the war, and
with few exceptions the South did not seek
to conquer Northern territory. Operations
into the Northern states were limited to
raids designed to have a political impact
either in Europe or with the Northern electorate. Early engagements in western
Virginia had political ramifications that led
to the formation of West Virginia.

Washington, D.C.

WHEN PRESIDENT GEORGE WASHINGTON ENVISIONED A
national capital centrally located on the banks of the Potomac River
between Virginia and Maryland, he never imagined that it would be
on the front lines in a civil war between the states. When Virginia sided
with the South, Washington, D.C., was suddenly vulnerable. Only Fort
Washington stood guard over the city, but as the war expanded, so did
the city's defenses. By the end of the war, 68 forts surrounded the
nation's capital. The heavy defenses successfully deterred the
Confederates and, in 1864, provided a source of reinforcements for
the Army of the Potomac, which was heavily engaged in Virginia.

Civil War–era Washington, D.C., was a work in progress. The Capitol
Building was receiving a dome, and additional funding was sought to
finish the monument to President Washington. Countless private structures housed dignitaries and power brokers. The Smithsonian "Castle"
provided a stunning view of the surrounding countryside, but the
National Mall was still a smelly, tidal pool. After the war, monuments
commemorating the victory were erected all over the city.

**President Lincoln rides with his predecessor, James Buchanan, to his
1861 inauguration.**

✶ Fort Stevens

CAMPAIGN: Early's Raid and Operations Against the B&O Railroad

DATE(S): July 11–12, 1864

With General Grant's forces laying siege to Rebel armies at Petersburg, Virginia, Lee sought to draw some of the Union soldiers away from his front. After fending off a threat to the Confederate logistics network along the James River, Southside Railroad, and Virginia & Tennessee Railroad at Lynchburg, Lee unleashed his old Valley Army, which was now under the command of General Early, to launch a disquieting assault into Maryland and perhaps Pennsylvania.

By July 10, Early's army had come within ten miles of Washington, D.C., but the Confederate soldiers were exhausted from the Battle of Monocacy (see p. 343), near Frederick, Maryland. This battle and Early's summer movements allowed the Federals to scrape together enough soldiers to repel the invaders. When the Confederates attacked on July 11, the Union troops easily repelled their weak effort.

President Lincoln himself visited Fort Stevens during the battle to demonstrate to panicked citizens that the threat to the capital was minimal. While visiting, however, the lanky president came under fire from enemy sharpshooters, prompting an officer to grab him and pull him down, saying, "Get down, you damned fool." Though the president escaped injury, a bullet struck an officer within a mere three feet of him.

LOCATION: See a partial reconstruction of Fort Stevens with interpretive marker at the corner of 13th St. and Quackenbos St. N.W.

Union soldiers await the Confederates in a field sketch of the Battle of Fort Stevens.

FURTHER READING

A Guide to Civil War Washington
by Stephen Forman
A helpful guide to expand a tour of D.C.

Reveille in Washington, 1860–1865
by Margaret Leech
A contemporary look into Civil War Washington

Other Battles and Beyond

You could commit a day or a week to exploring the Civil War in and around Washington, D.C. Antebellum sites relating to the war number in the hundreds, and with the numerous monuments, museums, and historic sites and the Library of Congress, passing tourists and dedicated students of the Civil War alike will find that they've hit the mother lode of Civil War history here in the Union capital.

✦ Civil War to Civil Rights Heritage Trail

The self-guided 60-minute "Neighborhood Heritage Trail" features 21 interpretive signs that tell the stories of several little-known historical sites pertaining to both the Civil War and the civil rights movement. The trail begins in front of 1317 G Street N.W., between 13th and 14 Streets. Visit www.culturaltourismdc.org for a map and a downloadable audio tour, or call 202-661-7581.

✦ African American Civil War Memorial and Museum

More than 180,000 black men fought for the Union Army throughout the Civil War, and many of their triumphs and struggles as soldiers, sailors, and volunteers are told here, along with the stories of those who did not fight but played a role in the abolition of slavery. The nearby memorial sculpture, along with its Wall of Honor containing more than 200,000 names, serves as a reminder of the courageous story of the U.S. Colored Troops.

LOCATION: 1925 Vermont Ave. N.W., 202-667-2667, www.afroamcivilwar.org.

✦ Battleground National Cemetery

In the Battle of Fort Stevens (see p. 332)— the only battle to take place in the Union

capital—a combined total of more than 900 men were killed or wounded. Here at Battleground National Cemetery, just half a mile from Fort Stevens itself, 41 Union soldiers who died in the battle have been laid to rest. Also on-site are two Civil War–era cannons, which stand at the cemetery entrance, as well as a collection of monuments commemorating the units that participated in the battle. At half an acre, this small plot is one of the country's smallest national cemeteries.

LOCATION: The cemetery entrance is located on Georgia Ave. N.W., between Whittier Pl. and Van Buren St. Multiple markers can be found along Georgia Ave. and within the cemetery.

✦ Ford's Theatre

The place where Lincoln was shot during Act III of *Our American Cousin* has long been a popular tourist site containing a wealth of historical activities and significant artifacts. In addition to the Ford's Theatre Museum, whose collections include the clothes the president wore the night he died, a boot worn by John Wilkes Booth the night of the assassination, and the pistol used to do the deed, the campus also includes a tour of the Petersen House, where Lincoln was carried and tended to after being shot, as well as a walking tour of the neighborhood around Ford's Theatre.

LOCATION: 511 10th St. N.W., 202-347-4833, www.fordstheatre.org.

✦ Frederick Douglass National Historic Site

One of the best known abolitionists, orators, and social reformers of the Civil War era, Frederick Douglass was born a slave in Maryland in 1818 and died a free man in 1895. He spent the last 17 years of his life here in the house he named Cedar Hill.

Ranger-led tours of the house allow visitors to see a variety of Douglass's personal belongings, including books, photographs, and the rolltop desk where the former slave wrote numerous speeches as well as his final autobiography, *The Life and Times of Frederick Douglass.*

LOCATION: **1411 W St. S.E., 202-426-5961, www.nps.gov/frdo. The visitor center and a free parking lot are located at the intersection of W St. and 15th St. S.E.**

✦ Historical Society of Washington, D.C.

The historical society of the nation's capital covers more than 200 years of local history with its substantial collection of maps, photos, and manuscripts chronicling the city's social, political, and physical development into the metropolis it is today.

LOCATION: **801 K St. N.W., 202-249-3955, www.dchistory.org.**

✦ Lincoln Memorial

One of the most enduring and iconic national monuments, the Lincoln Memorial was built, designed, and dedicated in the

IN THIS TEMPLE
AS IN THE HEARTS OF THE PEOPLE
FOR WHOM HE SAVED THE UNION
THE MEMORY OF ABRAHAM LINCOLN
IS ENSHRINED FOREVER

Daniel Chester French carved the colossal statue inside the Lincoln Memorial.

1920s. Aside from the 19-foot-tall statue of Abraham Lincoln that sits in the middle of the memorial's main chamber, additional features include an inscription of Lincoln's Second Inaugural Address inscribed on the memorial's north wall and his Gettysburg Address inscribed on the south wall. The 36 columns supporting the exterior of the memorial represent the number of states in the Union at the time of Lincoln's assassination in April 1865.

LOCATION: **2 Lincoln Memorial Circle N.W., 202-426-6841, www.nps.gov/linc.**

✦ National Archives Museum

Famously home to the Declaration of Independence, the Constitution, and the Bill of Rights, the National Archives Museum also allows visitors to take a virtual journey through its extensive stacks and vaults with its "Public Vaults" exhibition. Accessible Civil War documents include telegrams from Lincoln to his generals and records that belonged to the 54th Massachusetts Infantry Regiment.

LOCATION: **700 Pennsylvania Ave. N.W., www.archives.gov.**

✦ National Museum of American History

Perhaps no other museum contains a more extensive collection of artifacts pertaining to the heritage of the United States than this branch of the Smithsonian. Artifacts in the museum's collections include the original Star-Spangled Banner, President Lincoln's top hat, Confederate General Stuart's pistol, and chairs used by Generals Grant and Lee during Lee's formal surrender at Appomattox. Museum exhibits highlight information on American wars and politics, American ideals, and African-American history.

LOCATION: **14th St. and Constitution Ave. N.W., 202-633-1000, www.americanhistory.si.edu.**

The Willard Hotel has been visited by every U.S. president since Franklin Pierce.

✦ National Museum of the U.S. Navy

The Civil War brought great changes in naval technology and tactics as both sides made use of ironclads and submarines for the first time in history. Located on the grounds of the Washington Navy Yard, this museum's Civil War exhibit explains how those changes affected the outcome of the war and tells the stories of several pivotal naval battles, including New Orleans, Mobile Bay, and Hampton Roads. Other museum highlights include a model of the U.S.S. *Monitor* and artifacts recovered by underwater archaeologists from the Confederate commerce raider *Alabama*.

LOCATION: 736 Sicard St. S.E., 202-433-6826.

✦ President Lincoln's Cottage at the Soldiers' Home

The seasonal home for the first family, this historic cottage provided President Lincoln an escape from the political pressure, the blistering summer heat, and occasionally the terrible smells of downtown Washington, D.C., from 1862 to 1864. In fact, during his first summer at the cottage, the relative peace and quiet afforded Lincoln an opportunity to write a preliminary draft of the Emancipation Proclamation. The visitor center includes an award-winning, interactive gallery and rotating special exhibits featuring original artifacts. Guided tours are available to visitors.

LOCATION: 140 Rock Creek Church Rd. N.W., 202-829-0436, www.lincolncottage.org.

✦ Willard Hotel

The primary hotel for official business in the 1860s was the Willard, which remains a popular and thriving D.C. hotel today. It was here that Ulysses S. Grant arrived in winter of 1864 to be announced as the new general in chief of the United States Armies, and in 1861, it also provided president-elect Lincoln with a discrete place to stay before his first inauguration.

LOCATION: 1401 Pennsylvania Ave. N.W., 202-628-9100. Visit the lobby.

Civil War on Foot: Washington, D.C.

Washington has always had two centers of power: the Capitol and the White House. During the Civil War, the drama of the crisis was focused on Lincoln and the White House. This tour displays the wealth of related and important sites surrounding life at the White House as Lincoln experienced it.

❶ Pedestrian Mall
Unlike today, security at the White House during the Civil War was lax, with the doors open to all comers and the president liable to leave at any time to visit trusted colleagues in the surrounding area. Soldiers' tents would have filled the grounds.

❷ Winder Building
(600 17th St. N.W.) Here were housed a number of agencies, including the War and Navy Departments, and the surgeon general. A signal station allowed signaling to locations outside the city.

❸ Blair House *(1651 Pennsylvania Ave. N.W.)* This set of three properties includes the Renwick Gallery, which served as the headquarters of the Army Quartermaster Corps; the home of Samuel Phillips Lee, who commanded the North Atlantic Blockading Squadron; and the home of Montgomery Blair, whose family were powerful political players. Today, this is the president's guesthouse.

❹ Rathbone House *(712 Jackson Pl. N.W.)* Army officer Henry Rathbone, who accompanied his fiancée to Ford's Theatre as the Lincolns' guests on April 14, 1865, was wounded in the attack on the president.

❺ Decatur House *(1610 H St. N.W.)* Commodore Stephen Decatur died here after a duel before the Civil War. Slave quarters are still attached to the rear of the building. Across the street is St. John's, where practically every president, including Lincoln, has worshipped.

❻ Dolley Madison House *(1520 H St. N.W.)* George B. McClellan, commander in chief of the U.S. Army, used this house

The Dolley Madison House (aka Cutts-Madison House) was home to First Lady Dolley Madison.

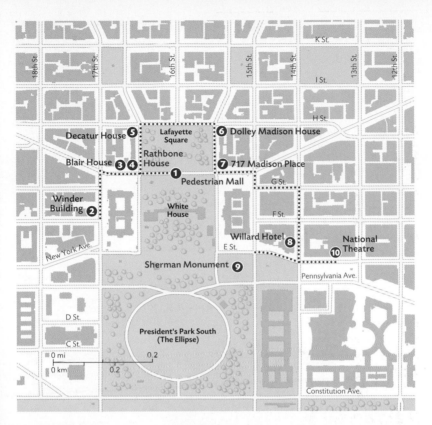

as his headquarters in Washington, D.C.

❼ 717 Madison Place Secretary of State William Seward used a house on this site similar to the Decatur House and was attacked here as part of the Lincoln assassination.

❽ Willard Hotel *(1401 Pennsylvania Ave. N.W.)* This was the center of political Washington during the Civil War. Lincoln stayed here prior to his inauguration, and it is the place where Julia Ward Howe wrote the stirring lyrics to the "Battle Hymn of the Republic."

❾ Sherman Monument *(15th St. and E St. N.W.)* This lavishly and appropriately appointed monument honors William T. Sherman, Grant's right-hand man. His words were tough and his actions tougher—no man except perhaps Lincoln has been more reviled in the South.

❿ National Theatre *(1321 Pennsylvania Ave. N.W.)* John Wilkes Booth expected Lincoln to be here on the evening of April 14, but the president had decided to go with his wife to Ford's Theatre instead to see the last performance of Laura Keene in *Our American Cousin.*

Maryland

IN SOME WAYS, MARYLAND'S CIVIL WAR HISTORY CAN BE bookended by two major events: the Baltimore Riot of 1861, where the first bloodshed of the war occurred, and the search for John Wilkes Booth, which took place over two weeks in southern Maryland in April 1865.

In the four years between the two events, Maryland was the site of several major battles, due in part to its strategic location on the Potomac River, which both the Union and Confederate Armies would cross numerous times throughout their campaigns, and also to its status as a loyal slave state. The high traffic led at least one Maryland city, Hagerstown, to claim the label "the Crossroads of the Civil War."

Indeed, geographically and culturally, the slave state and border state of Maryland was very much at the crossroads of the war, with the eastern half generally sympathetic to the South and the western counties loyal to the Union. This state perfectly epitomized the reality of a "divided union."

Several dead soldiers lie in front of the Dunker Church—an iconic site on the Antietam battleground and the focal point of several Union attacks.

Potomac River
Hancock   Hagerstown   Pa.
Folck's Mill
          3 4 1
Sharpsburg   Frederick
Kennedy Farmhouse   2
W. Va.   Antietam   Baltimore
Harpers Ferry National Historical Park
          U.S. Naval Academy Museum
Crampton's Gap   Maryland   Del.
          D.C.   Surratt House Museum
          Va.

1 South Mountain
2 Monocacy
3 Williamsport
4 Boonsboro

ATLANTIC
OCEAN

0 mi   50
0 km   50

✳ Antietam

CAMPAIGN: Maryland Campaign
OTHER NAME(S): Sharpsburg
DATE(S): September 16–18, 1862

The single bloodiest day in American history began at dawn on September 17, 1862, with a sequential attack of three Federal corps on the command of Stonewall Jackson. Fighting moved from north to south along Hagerstown Pike. The first phase of the fierce battle raged for more than four hours from the North and East Woods through farmer Miller's 30-acre cornfield toward the West Woods, Confederate artillery positions, and a church of pacifists known as Dunkers.

As midday approached, the focus of the battle shifted to the center of the Confederate line, where Rebel brigades situated in a sunken country lane attempted to hold their crucial central position. Numerous Union assaults faced a terrifying sheet of flame whenever they crested the undulating hills in front of the Sunken Road. The line was broken only after Union troops discovered they could fire into the flank of the defending force, holding a bend in the road that exposed their right flank. When the Confederates abandoned their position, they exposed other defenders in what would hereafter be known as Bloody Lane. Once the Federals had occupied Bloody Lane, they halted and failed to press their advantage.

Farther to the south, General Burnside's corps carried a stone bridge over Antietam Creek (later dubbed Burnside Bridge) on the third attempt, only to squander time boiling coffee. Pressing their advantage, they nearly

**Wooden tombstone of Confederate soldier
J. H. Slade, mortally wounded at Antietam**

entered the town of Sharpsburg, only to be smashed and sent back to the bridge crossing by the timely arrival of General Hill's division from Harpers Ferry. Lee awaited a renewal of the fighting on September 18 before returning to Virginia on the following day. Along the way, he would fight a rear-guard action at Shepherdstown. Although Lincoln was dissatisfied with McClellan's performance, the battle gave the president the victory that his cabinet suggested was needed to issue a preliminary Emancipation Proclamation.

Administered by the National Park Service, the battlefield visitor center shows a wonderful movie. The battlefield itself has numerous informative and challenging trails following key battle events. McClellan's headquarters at the Pry House—located on the east side of the battlefield—also houses a branch of the National Museum of Civil War Medicine.

LOCATION: **Antietam National Battlefield, 5831 Dunker Church Rd., Sharpsburg, 301-432-5124, www.nps.gov/anti.**

FURTHER READING

Landscape Turned Red: The Battle of Antietam by Stephen W. Sears
The most readable work on the war's bloodiest battle

✳ Boonsboro

CAMPAIGN: Gettysburg Campaign
DATE(S): July 8–14, 1863

Following the Union victory at Gettysburg (see pp. 352–357), the Confederate wagon

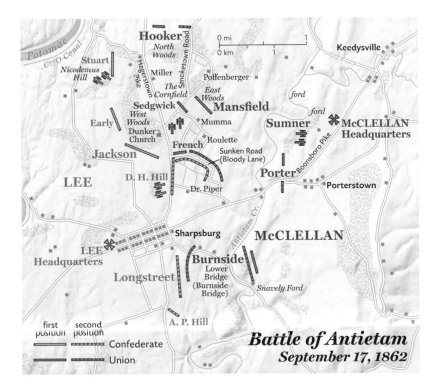

Battle of Antietam
September 17, 1862

Confederate forces clash with Union cavalry at Falling Waters in the Battle of Boonsboro.

train carrying supplies, prisoners, and wounded soldiers stretched for miles, making it vulnerable to capture or destruction. Confederate General Stuart and his five cavalry brigades were tasked with covering the retreat. Once the wagon train had reached Williamsport (see p. 345), the Confederate cavalry rode north, driving back marauding Union cavalry. Stuart's soldiers engaged with Federal cavalry at Beaver Creek Bridge, just north of Boonsboro, but were forced to withdraw after the arrival of Union infantry late in the evening. Although the battle was small, it secured time for Lee. Within a week, his forces were able to cross the Potomac over the newly constructed pontoon bridge at Falling Waters. During the withdrawal, the Federals captured some 700 men but lost the larger prize, as Lee had escaped.

LOCATION: **The battle occurred primarily along present-day Old National Pike/Alt. US 40. The battle marker half a mile north of the intersection of Rte. 40 and Lappans Rd. includes a battle map and explanation.**

FURTHER READING

Retreat From Gettysburg: Lee, Logistics, and the Pennsylvania Campaign
by Kent Masterson Brown
A comprehensive history of the Confederate retreat

✲Folck's Mill

CAMPAIGN: Early's Raid and Operations Against the B&O Railroad

DATE(S): August 1, 1864

On July 30, Confederate cavalry under General McCausland set fire to the town of Chambersburg, Pennsylvania, after the town failed to meet a Confederate ransom demand. Riding west with the intent to take Cumberland, Maryland, in similar fashion and disrupt the town's Baltimore & Ohio Railroad supply hub, McCausland's cavalry met Federal resistance two days later at Folck's Mill, two and a half miles east of Cumberland. Atop a ridge near the mill, General Kelley and a small force of Union soldiers halted McCausland's advance. After five hours of skirmishing, the Confederates withdrew, sparing the town of Cumberland.

LOCATION: **Markers located on the grounds of Ali Gran Shriners Hall near I-68 exit 46. Access via Ali Ghan Rd. N.E., east of Evitt's Creek.**

FURTHER READING

Shenandoah Summer: The 1864 Valley Campaign,
by Scott C. Patchan
A detailed history of the campaign focusing on General Early

✤ Hancock

CAMPAIGN: Jackson's Operations Against the B&O Railroad

DATE(S): January 5–6, 1862

With several thousand men under his command, Jackson launched a campaign on January 1, 1862, to disrupt supply lines on the Baltimore & Ohio Railroad and the Chesapeake & Ohio Canal. Marching north from Winchester, Virginia, through a brutal winter storm, Jackson and his men confronted the Federals on the banks of the Potomac outside the garrisoned town of Hancock. From across the river, the Confederates opened fire on the Union batteries stationed around St. Thomas Episcopal Church. Despite two days of bombardment, General Lander refused to hand over the town. Unable to locate a safe place to cross the Potomac and force a surrender, Jackson withdrew to Romney, Virginia.

LOCATION: Markers dedicated to St. Thomas Episcopal Church located at the intersection of Main St. (Rte. 144) and Church St., on the right when traveling west on Main St.; and on Church St. south of Main St. (Rte. 144), on the left when traveling south.

✳ Monocacy

CAMPAIGN: Early's Raid and Operations Against the B&O Railroad

DATE(S): July 9, 1864

Known as the battle that saved Washington, the Battle of Monocacy was a delaying tactic on the part of the Union Army. With General Early's forces of 20,000 only a few days' march from the Union capital, General Wallace hastily scrounged up troops to halt the Confederates in their tracks, meeting Early's army on the banks of the Monocacy River, outside Frederick.

Though the battle was the northernmost military victory for the South, it ultimately proved crucial for the Union, as it granted the Federal Army enough time to reinforce its defenses in Washington, D.C. The strategy came at a cost, however, with nearly 2,000 Union casualties. Rebel casualties amounted to fewer than 700—not enough to stop Early's advance.

The National Park Service site has numerous interpretive walking trails. Don't miss the site where Lee's orders were found in September 1862 (see map p. 344).

LOCATION: Monocacy National Battlefield, 5201 Urbana Pike, Frederick, 301-662-3515, www.nps.gov/mono. Consult www.visit maryland.org for a map of Early's 1864 raid.

FURTHER READING

Shadow of Shiloh: Major General Lew Wallace in the Civil War by Gail Stephens Focuses on Wallace's Civil War career

---

Emancipation: Not What It Seemed

The Civil War was fought to preserve the Union; freedom for the slaves was a by-product. The Emancipation Proclamation was, in fact, a political document, threatening Southerners with the loss of their slave property if they were still fighting or in rebellion on January 1, 1863. Yet Lincoln had no ability to enforce the order. Slaves in New Orleans and other places where Union forces had reestablished a Federal presence were still slaves, as were slaves in border states. Always the politician, Lincoln was not prepared to push emancipation on loyal citizens. The directive disrupted the country and the Union Army. Still, the recruitment of black soldiers helped the North win the war. Within two years, Lincoln had a change of heart and supported a constitutional amendment abolishing slavery, though he would not live to see it implemented. It passed in January 1865, and Lincoln was dead three months later. The civil rights era had begun.

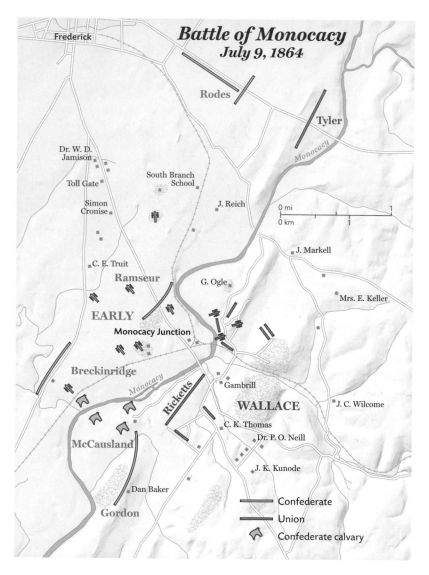

Battle of Monocacy
July 9, 1864

Frederick

Rodes

Tyler

Monocacy

Dr. W. D. Jamison

South Branch School

Toll Gate

Simon Cronise

J. Reich

0 mi   1
0 km   1

J. Markell

C. E. Truit

Ramseur

G. Ogle

Mrs. E. Keller

EARLY

Monocacy Junction

Breckinridge

Monocacy

Ricketts

Gambrill

WALLACE

J. C. Wilcome

C. K. Thomas

McCausland

Dr. P. O. Neill

J. K. Kunode

Dan Baker

Gordon

— Confederate
— Union
⤶ Confederate calvary

✳ South Mountain

CAMPAIGN: Maryland Campaign

DATE(S): September 14, 1862

It had been ten days since Confederate soldiers began crossing the Potomac River into Union territory. When Marylanders did not flock to his banners, Lee made plans to enter Pennsylvania. The plans went awry, however, when Union soldiers discovered a mislaid copy of Lee's operational orders while rummaging through abandoned Confederate camps near Monocacy Junction. The plans quickly made their way to General McClellan,

Ohio regiments engage with North Carolina regiments at the Battle of South Mountain.

who marched his troops to South Mountain, where pitched battles were fought at Crampton's, Turner's, and Fox's Gaps. After a full day's worth of fighting and more than 2,000 casualties on both sides, the Union Army gained possession of all three mountain passes, boosting morale after their recent string of losses. But the much needed victory came at a price, as the delay at South Mountain allowed Lee to capture Harpers Ferry and prepare for the Battle of Antietam (see pp. 340–341), which would begin in just three days.

LOCATION: Markers are part of the Maryland Civil War Trails program. Interpretive signs and maps are located in and around Turner's, Fox's, and Crampton's Gaps. The house in Turner's Gap was there during the battle. North Carolinians have placed a bronze monument a quarter mile south of Reno Monument Rd. and the Appalachian Trail.

FURTHER READING
Antietam, South Mountain and Harpers Ferry: A Battlefield Guide
by Ethan S. Rafuse
A guide to sites in Maryland and West Virginia

To Antietam Creek: The Maryland Campaign of September 1862
by D. Scott Hartwig
A study of the campaign and its major battles

❊ Williamsport

CAMPAIGN: Gettysburg Campaign
DATE(S): July 6–16, 1863

With his decision to return to Virginia after the Battle of Gettysburg (see pp. 352–357), Lee had to move his combat forces and supplies to Williamsport, where he planned to cross the Potomac River. The bridges there had been destroyed by high water, and Lee had to hold his position until the river cooperated. Federal cavalry tried to cut off his forces, but with the arrival of infantry, Lee was able to construct nearly nine miles of defensive earthworks.

LOCATION: Interpretive markers at 205 W. Potomac St., Williamsport, opposite the park visitor center, and on the grounds of the C&O Canal Towpath.

Civil War on Foot: Frederick

A major crossroads of the war, Frederick contains more than two dozen sites showcasing the community's rich Civil War heritage. Start at the city's visitor center, where you can find more destinations within walking distance in addition to the ten listed here.

❶ National Museum of Civil War Medicine (*48 E. Patrick St.*) The unprecedented casualties of the Civil War led to vast improvements in medicine. This museum tells the uplifting and heart-wrenching stories of the doctors, nurses, and surgeons who helped build a viable medical system.

Barbara Fritchie waves the Union flag from her home, as depicted in John Greenleaf Whittier's poem.

❷ Barbara Fritchie House (*154 W. Patrick St.*) The story that Fritchie taunted Jackson's hardened troops as they marched out of the city is most likely apocryphal. Poet John Greenleaf Whittier immortalized the tale in his 1864 poem "Barbara Fritchie."

❸ Ramsey House (*119 Record St.*) After the Battle of Antietam (see pp. 340–341), Lincoln visited the army. On the return trip, he stopped here to visit a wounded general and treated a curious crowd to an impromptu speech.

❹ City Hall (*101 N. Court St.*) No other Marylander had more impact on the antebellum period than Chief Justice of the Supreme Court Roger B. Taney, whose majority decision in the Dred Scott case energized abolitionists, Republicans, and Southerners. See a bust of Taney here and read the interpretive plaques about the case.

❺ Evangelical Reformed Church (*15 W. Church St.*) While encamped around the city, General Jackson attended services here.

❻ Kemp Hall (*4 E. Church St.*) The Maryland state legislature met twice here to take up the case of secession and twice voted not to secede. The decision was critical to Lincoln's plans: Had Maryland joined Virginia, the capital in Washington, D.C., would have been isolated and untenable.

❼ Evangelical Lutheran Church (*35 E. Church St.*) Frederick was a logical place to collect and treat casualties from engagements like Antietam, South Mountain, Monocacy, and Gettysburg. This church was one of many that served as hospitals.

❽ Mt. Olivet Cemetery
(515 S. Market St.) Here in this fine resting place you will find the graves of Francis Scott Key and Barbara Fritchie, along with a memorial to unknown Confederate soldiers.

❾ B&O Railroad Station
(Corner of All Saints St. and Market St.) Not only did Lincoln pass through here on the train to and from Antietam, but he also gave a speech to the people assembled. In addition, militia and fire brigades had been rushed to Harpers Ferry through this station

in response to John Brown's Raid of 1859.

❿ Roger B. Taney House
(121 S. Bentz St.) The chief justice's home is now a museum to his tenure, which involved many confrontations with Lincoln over civil rights and the authority of the president in times of war.

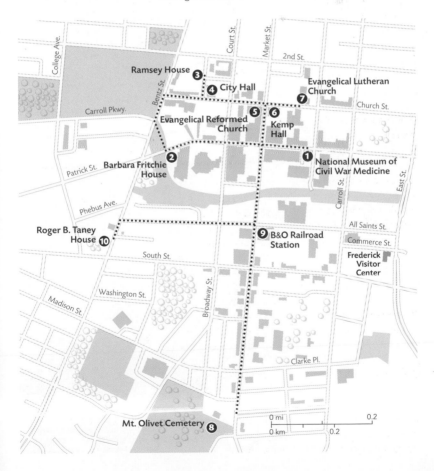

Other Battles and Beyond

Noteworthy Civil War–era sites abound throughout Maryland, from western cities like Hagerstown, which served as a staging area during four separate military campaigns, to the state's southern region, where John Wilkes Booth attempted his escape into Virginia. Dozens of towns, museums, and monuments both in the state and along its critical borders pay tribute to Maryland's essential role in the Civil War. Maryland Civil War Trails offers several Civil War walking tour brochures that can be picked up at any visitor center or downloaded at www.visit maryland.org.

✦ Baltimore

With the B&O Railroad Museum, Fort McHenry, and Greenmount Cemetery, where John Wilkes Booth is buried along with several Confederate generals, Baltimore contains plenty of Civil War sites worth visiting. For an overall history of how the war affected the state, a good place to start is the Maryland Historical Society's museum, which contains thousands of artifacts, provides historical tours, and interprets the state's participation in the Underground Railroad. See the Maryland Civil War Trails brochure.

LOCATION: **Maryland Historical Society, 201 W. Monument St., Baltimore, 410-685-3750, www.mdhs.org.**

✦ Crampton's Gap

Crampton's Gap saw intense fighting during the Battle of South Mountain (see pp. 344–345). Follow the action at this fiercely defended site using the interpretative markers erected by the Blue and Gray Education Society. The War Correspondents Memorial Arch commands the site; however, it should not distract from the fairly clear lines where the battle took place.

LOCATION: **Gathland State Park, 900 Arnoldstown Rd., Jefferson, 877-620-8367, dnr2.maryland.gov.**

✦ Hagerstown

Claiming the title "The Crossroads of the Civil War," Hagerstown fell under Confederate occupation during the 1862 Maryland Campaign and the 1863 Gettysburg Campaign. The town also witnessed a cavalry raid and an invasion by General Early in 1864. Local literature tells the town's Civil War history, as do strategically placed interpretative signs. The Hagerstown Convention Visitors Bureau provides a Civil War walking tour of the city that includes the street-to-street cavalry battle of July 6, 1863.

LOCATION: **Hagerstown Convention Visitors Bureau, 16 Public Sq., 301-791-3246, www .marylandmemories.org.**

✦ Harpers Ferry National Historical Park

Located at the picturesque confluence of the Potomac and Shenandoah Rivers, Harpers Ferry was the scene of some of the most dramatic events in American history. In addition to being the target of abolitionist John Brown's famous raid in 1859, it was also the site of the 1862 siege and surrender of the Federal garrison that precipitated Lee's decision to remain in Maryland, thus spurring the Battle of Antietam (see pp. 340–341). In all, Harpers Ferry changed hands eight times between 1861 and 1865, and much of the history explaining the town's significance can be found on interpretive signs located within the park. Walking trails are marked for both Loudon and Maryland Heights but can be strenuous. Allot several hours to see the earthworks midway and atop Maryland Heights, and wait for the first frost before attempting the climb to avoid the poisonous snakes that heavily infest the mountain.

LOCATION: **171 Shoreline Dr., Harpers Ferry, West Virginia, 304-535-6029, www.nps.gov /hafe.**

✦ Kennedy Farmhouse

In 1859, in an effort to incite a slave revolt, John Brown and his followers used this home to quietly plot their raid on the Federal arsenal that sat several miles to the south in Harpers Ferry. Tours are available.

LOCATION: **2406 Chestnut Grove Rd., Sharpsburg, 301-370-6850, www.johnbrown.org.**

✦ Potomac River

A geographic and symbolic barrier between North and South, the river factored heavily into military tactics for both sides. Interpretive signs mark key crossing sites such as Boteler's Ford, Edward's Ferry, Rowser's Ford, Shepherdstown, and Williamsport. Interpretive signs at White's Ford and White's Ferry mark the spot where the majority of Lee's army crossed during the Maryland Campaign in September 1862.

LOCATION: **Start at White's Ferry, 24801 White's Ferry Rd., Dickerson, 301-349-5200.**

✦ Sharpsburg

Sharpsburg contains a handful of sites that help paint a more vivid picture of the Battle of Antietam (see pp. 340–341). Just outside the city, on Shepherdstown Pike (Rte. 34), lies Antietam Station, through which hundreds of soldiers passed on their journey home. A sign on the left as you head east into Sharpsburg marks the site of Lee's battle headquarters. Visit National Cemetery.

LOCATION: **A mile south of Antietam National Battlefield on Sharpsburg Pike (MD 65).**

✦ Surratt House Museum

John Wilkes Booth stopped here during his escape from Washington, D.C., to retrieve hidden weapons and supplies. The site is now home to a museum dedicated to Lincoln's assassination. The Surratt Society, which also operates the museum, offers tours of Booth's escape route on select dates. A driving tour (unaffiliated with the museum) traces Booth's route along Route 5 through Maryland and into Virginia.

LOCATION: **9118 Brandywine Rd., Clinton, 301-868-1121, www.surrattmuseum.org.**

✦ U.S. Naval Academy Museum

Recognizing Maryland's strong sympathies with the South, the Federals moved the U.S. Naval Academy from Annapolis to Fort Adams in Newport, Rhode Island, in 1861. Throughout the war, the Annapolis grounds served as a Union Army hospital, and students and faculty did not return until after the war ended. The museum here tells the story of the U.S. Naval Academy's fascinating past and covers U.S. naval history from its beginnings in the Revolutionary War to the modern day fleet.

LOCATION: **118 Maryland Ave., Annapolis, 410-293-5261, www.usna.edu/museum.**

Daguerreotype of abolitionist John Brown, leader of the infamous raid on Harpers Ferry

Pennsylvania

THE STATE OF PENNSYLVANIA WAS RICH NOT ONLY IN
manpower but also in natural resources and crops, making it a
desirable destination for Confederate operations. Lee knew that
deep penetrations could severely affect communications and commerce here, and he intended to do just that when he entered the
state in June 1863. After losing track of the Army of the Potomac's
movements, Lee was required to bring his forces together for battle. That concentration took place around Gettysburg, where the
war's most famous battle was fought over three days in July 1863.
But while Gettysburg may be the most familiar battle site to many,
a number of cities in the Keystone State showcase the impact of
the war in the North, including Chambersburg, Cashtown,
Harrisburg, Carlisle, and York—the largest Northern city to experience Confederate occupation.

**General Meade stands in front of his tent in June 1864. Although the
Pennsylvania native defeated Lee at Gettysburg, President Lincoln criticized
his hesitance in pursuing the retreating Confederates.**

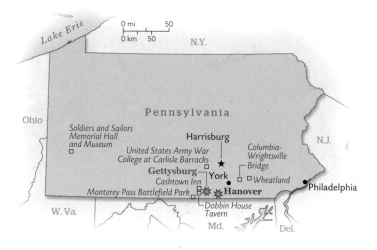

✳ Gettysburg

CAMPAIGN: Gettysburg Campaign
DATE(S): July 1–3, 1863

Lee had planned to enter Pennsylvania to relieve war-weary Virginia and capitalize on the abundance of food that would be available. Lee knew that if he could disrupt Union supplies and commerce he would force the Union government to respond and perhaps release troops from other threatened areas like Vicksburg, Mississippi, to chase him away. Lee intended to capture Harrisburg and perhaps threaten Philadelphia or Baltimore. With a long supply line, he authorized impressment of items the army needed while issuing IOUs to the suppliers. His soldiers were under strict orders to avoid plundering, but an exception was made when the Caledonia Ironworks, owned by abolitionist congressman Thaddeus Stevens, was burned. The remains of the furnace and the mill can still be seen along Route 30 in Fayetteville, Pennsylvania.

Lee had detached his cavalry with discretionary orders to rejoin him in Pennsylvania and, as a result, was unaware of the movement of the Army of the Potomac to the area around Frederick, Maryland. With elements of the Union Army within 30 miles of his logistics trail and 60 miles of his troops, Lee called for his dispersed forces to assemble near Gettysburg. Lee's III Corps under the command of General A. P. Hill was at Cashtown, eight miles northwest of Gettysburg. The Cashtown Inn served as headquarters for Hill, who, disregarding Lee's orders to avoid bringing on a battle, allowed a subordinate division commander, Henry Heth, to stumble into the biggest battle of the war.

For nearly a month, Confederates had chased state militia from site to site. When scouts reported Federal troops in Gettysburg, Heth aimed to prove that was not true by sending a force far greater than was necessary. What he found was indeed regular Federal troopers under the command of General John Buford.

Buford defended the town using Knoxlyn, Herr, and McPherson Ridges, each one parallel to the next, thus buying time for the arrival of Union infantry, including the now famous Iron Brigade—composed mainly of "westerners" from Wisconsin, Indiana, and Michigan. The brigade attempted to defend the Union position, but this was to be General Lee's day. The continual arrival of additional forces under General Ewell overlapped Federal defenses and drove them back through town to high ground near the city's Evergreen Cemetery. Here the Union Army regrouped, bolstered by the arrival of General Hancock as temporary commander.

Total casualties after the first day of battle amounted to 15,000, including General John Reynolds, who had been shot dead as he reached McPherson Woods to begin his troop deployment.

By dawn on July 2, the majority of both Lee's and Meade's armies had reached Gettysburg, and with remaining corps arriving throughout the day, Confederate totals reached about 70,000 men, and Federal totals about 90,000—the largest number of soldiers that would gather for any battle throughout the war. With ample manpower

Chambersburg 1863

Chambersburg, Pennsylvania, lies about 25 miles northwest of Gettysburg and was the site of Lee's and Longstreet's headquarters prior to the start of the Battle of Gettysburg. The town suffered the indignity of being burned in July 1864, after refusing to fill a cash ransom demand made by Confederate General McCausland. The burning was in retaliation for Federal burnings that had taken place in the Shenandoah Valley. A monument dedicated to Corporal Rihl—the first Union soldier killed in Pennsylvania—was erected south of Chambersburg on the west side of US Route 11 toward Maryland, just north of Greencastle.

on both sides, and with Lee and Meade both setting up headquarters on-site to direct battle strategy (Lee at the Thompson House on Seminary Ridge and Meade at the Leister Farmhouse on Cemetery Ridge), day two at Gettysburg proved to be a bloody one.

Lee reopened the battle by attacking the Union flanks, which formed the ends of the

The Battle of Gettysburg unfolds amid a violent swirl of cannon and musket fire.

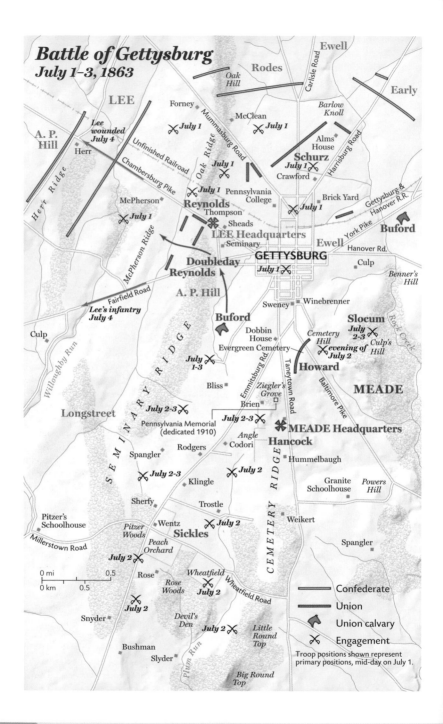

Battle of Gettysburg
July 1–3, 1863

Ewell

Rodes

Early

Oak Hill

LEE

Forney

Mummasburg Road

McClean

⚔ July 1

⚔ July 1

Barlow Knoll

A. P. Hill

Lee wounded July 4

Unfinished Railroad

Herr

Oak Ridge

⚔ July 1

Alms House

Carlisle Road

Schurz

⚔ July 1

Crawford

Harrisburg Road

Chambersburg Pike

McPherson

⚔ July 1

⚔ July 1

Pennsylvania College

Brick Yard

⚔ July 1

Gettysburg & Hanover R.R.

Herr Ridge

McPherson Ridge

Reynolds

Thompson

⚔ Sheads

LEE Headquarters

Seminary

York Pike

Buford

Fairfield Road

Doubleday

Reynolds ▶

A. P. Hill

GETTYSBURG

⚔ July 1

Ewell

Hanover Rd.

Culp

Benner's Hill

Lee's infantry July 4

Willoughby Run

Culp

SEMINARY RIDGE

Buford

Dobbin House

Sweney

Winebrenner

Cemetery Hill

Slocum

July 2-3 ⚔

Rock Creek

Evergreen Cemetery

⚔ evening of July 2

Culp's Hill

⚔ July 1-3

Bliss

Ziegler's Grove

Howard

⚔ July 2-3

Brien

⚔ July 2-3

Emmitsburg Rd.

Taneytown Road

Baltimore Pike

MEADE

Longstreet

Pennsylvania Memorial (dedicated 1910)

Angle

Codori

✺ MEADE Headquarters

Spangler

⚔ July 2-3

Rodgers

Hancock

Hummelbaugh

Klingle

⚔ July 2

CEMETERY RIDGE

Granite Schoolhouse

Powers Hill

Sherfy

Trostle

Weikert

Spangler

Pitzer's Schoolhouse

Pitzer Woods

Wentz

⚔ July 2

Millerstown Road

Peach Orchard

Sickles

⚔ July 2

Rose

Wheatfield

⚔ July 2

Wheatfield Road

0 mi   0.5

0 km   0.5

Rose Woods

⚔ July 2

Devil's Den

⚔ July 2

Little Round Top

━━━ Confederate

━━━ Union

Snyder

Plum Run

🐴 Union calvary

⚔ Engagement

Bushman

Slyder

Big Round Top

Troop positions shown represent primary positions, mid-day on July 1.

Northern army's defensive fishhook-shaped line centered along Cemetery Ridge. Fierce fighting took place near both ends of the formation, and many Gettysburg landmarks—including Devil's Den, Little Round Top, Rose Farm, the Peach Orchard, the Wheatfield (later known as the Bloody Wheatfield), East Cemetery Hill, and Culp's Hill—would become infamous as the armies clashed in and around the sites.

Late in the afternoon, Confederate General James Longstreet and his divisions launched an attack centered on the Peach Orchard but ranging from a point opposite the Devil's Den (a rock formation at the eastern edge of the Union lines to a spot near today's Pennsylvania Monument on Cemetery Ridge). Controversy surrounded General Daniel Sickles, who had positioned his corps on higher ground bordering the Emmitsburg Road rather than on the low ground on the south end of Cemetery Ridge. The Confederate attack swept to the right of Sickles's formation up undefended Little Round Top,

A Confederate lieutenant's jacket

whose position commanded the entire Union line, and then into the teeth of his defensive works, compelling Lee's men to turn and fight in a different direction than Lee had intended. While Lee's men briefly crested Cemetery Ridge, they failed to gain Little Round Top, where the 20th Maine and Colonel Chamberlain gained fame, and the attack faded out as the last units Lee had committed to it proved inadequate to hold the gain. Near Culp's Hill, Lee had hoped a simultaneous attack might handcuff Meade and allow Lee's soldiers to gain a dominant position astride Baltimore Pike and at a point where they could force the Union to evacuate East Cemetery Hill. They failed. Uncoordinated attacks after dark gained the hill, and fighting spilled into Evergreen Cemetery before the Confederates were forced back.

July 3 did not get off to the start that Lee had hoped for. While his original plan had been to continue the Confederate assault on the Union flanks, a dawn strike by the Federals on Culp's Hill allowed the Union to regain the ground lost the night before. By mid-morning, Culp's Hill was once again in the hands of the Northerners.

Rethinking his battle strategy, Lee shifted his focus to the Union center. Under the new strategy, General Longstreet—despite his disagreement with Lee's plan—would lead an assault on the Union line at Cemetery Ridge using three divisions, including that of General Pickett. In what would become known as Pickett's Charge, more than 12,000 infantry advanced three-quarters of a mile or more over the open field between the Confederate position and the Union line on Cemetery Ridge. Their objective was the copse of trees atop the ridge near Ziegler's Grove—the center of the Union position. However, overnight

Benner's Hill

Lying close to a mile east of the center of Gettysburg, Benner's Hill served as a platform for Confederate artillery to fire on the Union batteries on Cemetery Hill on July 2, 1863. The two sides fired at one another for nearly an hour and half, and when the smoke cleared, the battery commander, former Virginia Military Institute cadet Major Latimer—just 19 years old—had suffered a severe wound to his right arm. Latimer died nearly a month later from his injury.

A group of Civil War reenactors marches during a reenactment of the Battle of Gettysburg.

a redistribution of infantry and artillery along the length of the ridge changed Lee's odds of a successful attack dramatically for the worse.

Around 1 p.m., under Lee's orders, more than a hundred cannons began bombarding the Union center in what would be the largest concentration of artillery amassed throughout the Civil War. Despite the enormous firepower of the cannonade, however, the shelling did little to weaken the Federals as Lee had hoped. Roughly two hours later, the nine brigades of infantry composing Pickett's, Pettigrew's, and Trimble's Charge marched in long gray lines—more than 12,000 men strong—toward the enemy. Although some soldiers succeeded in breeching the low stone wall that the Union had held on Cemetery Ridge—a site memorialized by the High Water Mark of the Rebellion Monument—the assault failed to dislodge the Union position because of the massive destruction caused by enfilading artillery and infantry lines during the approach to the Emmitsburg Pike. More than half of the 12,000 Confederates who had crossed the shallow valley in the charge did not return. The Federals,

by comparison, suffered no more than 1,500 casualties.

Two cavalry battles were fought in the hours that remained on July 3, including one east of Gettysburg in an area off the Hanover Road known as the East Cavalry Field, but the collapse of Pickett's Charge essentially marked the end of the Battle of Gettysburg. The total casualty count over the three days reached 28,000 Confederates and 23,000 Federals—the highest total of any engagement throughout the war.

On July 4, amid a heavy rain, General Lee waited for an attack from Meade that never came. The two armies, both positioned in defensive lines of their own, stared at each other through the downpour, and as evening fell, the Confederate general ordered the Army of Northern Virginia's retreat from Gettysburg. Although Meade pursued him in the days that followed, the cautious general was too slow to trap and destroy the army as President Lincoln hoped. By July 14, the Confederates had slipped over the Potomac River back into Confederate territory.

Four and a half months later, Lincoln delivered his Gettysburg Address at the official dedication ceremony for the National Cemetery of Gettysburg. His 273-word speech honored the fallen soldiers and the sacrifices they had made to preserve the Union and the principle of human equality.

LOCATION: Gettysburg National Military Park, 1195 Baltimore Pike (Rte. 97), Gettysburg, 717-334-1124, www.nps.gov/gett.

FURTHER READING

Flames Beyond Gettysburg: The Confederate Expedition to the Susquehanna River, June 1863
by Scott L. Mingus, Sr.
A study of General Ewell's II Corps and their role at Gettysburg

Pennsylvania Civil War Trails: The Guide to Battle Sites, Monuments, Museums and Towns
by Tom Huntington
Provides visitor information to key sites

Receding Tide: Vicksburg and Gettysburg, the Campaigns That Changed the Civil War
by Edwin C. Bearss and J. Parker Hills
The history surrounding the two pivotal campaigns that ended on July 4, 1863

Roads From Gettysburg
by John W. Schildt
A handy guide for any Gettysburg visitor

❋ Hanover

CAMPAIGN: Gettysburg Campaign
DATE(S): June 30, 1863

Under orders from General Lee, Confederate General Stuart and his cavalry screened the movement of Lee's army into Maryland. Left to his discretion, Stuart rode north through and then around the Union Army, heading north to rejoin Lee in Pennsylvania. Having captured more than 100 new wagons, Stuart found his path back to Lee blocked by the Union Army, now under the command of General Meade. When Stuart arrived in Hanover, he was met with resistance by a Federal rear guard under General Kilpatrick. Fighting ensued in the streets as the Confederates drove the Federals through town. The arrival of Federal reinforcements, including General Custer, forced the Confederates to flee, and Stuart himself was nearly captured. Markers along Frederick, Broadway, and other city streets designate key points during the battle.

LOCATION: Hanover Area Chamber of Commerce, 146 Carlisle St., 717-637-6130, www.hanoverchamber.com.

Extraordinary Men of Pennsylvania

Pennsylvania was home to a good number of Civil War leaders, from John Reynolds, a native of Lancaster, to Union Army Commander Meade, who, although born in Spain, lived and died after the war in a house given to him in Philadelphia. The city was also the location of the family home of early Union Army General in Chief McClellan. Other Pennsylvania natives include Winfield Scott Hancock, Samuel Heintzelman, and Congressman David Wilmot, sponsor of the Wilmot Proviso, which sought to restrict slavery in the 1840s.

Civil War on Foot: Gettysburg

The most overlooked aspect of Gettysburg's history is the impact the Civil War had on the town itself. Start in the town square, where roads led east to York and Hanover, south to Baltimore, west to Chambersburg, and north to Carlisle. This crucial transportation nexus is why the battle took place at Gettysburg.

❶ 11 York Street
The Confederates did not fire into the town, but over- and undershooting did lead to some damage, like the Confederate shell embedded on this building's second floor.

❷ David Wills House
(8 Lincoln Sq.) Lincoln stayed here the night before he gave his Gettysburg Address.

❸ Intersection of Middle Street and Baltimore Street On July 1, 1863, the triumphant Confederates consolidated their gains here as the Federals rallied on Cemetery Hill.

❹ Presbyterian Church (208 Baltimore St.) This was used as a hospital during and after the battle, and Lincoln stopped here for a rally after he delivered his Gettysburg Address.

❺ 242 Baltimore Street Jennie Wade, the only civilian killed in the Battle of Gettysburg, was born here.

❻ 1863 Inn of Gettysburg (516 Baltimore St.) On the other side of the inn

is the house where Jennie Wade was killed by a stray bullet, now a museum. Continue to the top of the hill and Evergreen Cemetery to see Wade's grave, marked by an American flag. Also in Evergreen Cemetery is the site where Lincoln gave his Gettysburg Address.

❼ Dobbin House
(89 Steinwehr Ave.) Eat in the room used by Confederate snipers to pick off officers on Cemetery Hill.

❽ Farnsworth House Inn (401 Baltimore St.) While walking north on Steinwehr back to Baltimore Street, notice the proliferation of bullet marks on the south side of the Civil War–era Farnsworth House Inn. Continue walking past the Shriver House, where Confederates used the cupola for sniping at Union soldiers, and the house of Tillie Pierce, who wrote a civilian's diary of the experience.

Lincoln arrived at the Gettysburg Railroad Station in November 1863 before delivering the Gettysburg Address.

Stop finally at the Prince of Peace Episcopal Church. Here Civil War veterans erected more than 300 plaques inside the church to fallen foes.

❾ Fahnestock House

(47 Baltimore St.) With Union forces fighting west and north of town, General Howard observed his corps' defense and collapse from this spot. Here he also learned that General Reynolds had been killed.

❿ Scott House

(43–45 Chambersburg St.) Return to the town square and turn west on Chambersburg Road. The house at No. 43–45 was owned by the Scott family, whose mistress hung a red shawl from the second-story window during the Civil War to designate it as a hospital. Now known as the James Gettys Hotel, the building was also used as a hotel.

⑪ Railroad Station

Head north on Carlisle Street to the railroad station, where a small museum commemorates Lincoln's arrival at the station and his famous remarks.

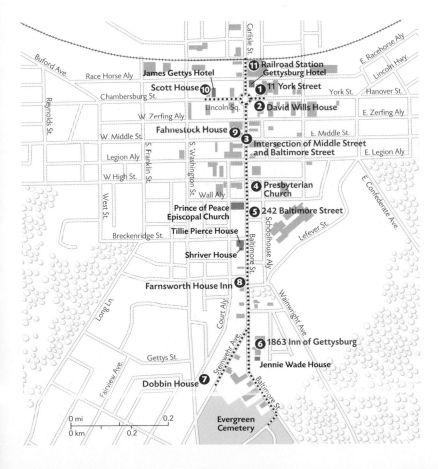

Other Battles and Beyond

✦ Cashtown Inn

In 1863, General A. P. Hill used the inn in this town, just a few miles northwest of Gettysburg, as his headquarters. Ignoring Lee's instructions, Hill permitted a division under General Heth to march into Gettysburg. Heth ran into General Buford's Union vedettes, however, thus setting off the first day of the Battle of Gettysburg.

LOCATION: **1325 Old Rte. 30, Cashtown, 717-334-9722, www.cashtowninn.com.**

✦ Dobbin House Tavern

An excellent view of activities on Cemetery Hill allowed Confederates perched in the upstairs windows of this restaurant to pick off careless Union officers for three days. Highly recommended tavern and restaurant.

LOCATION: **89 Steinwehr Ave. (Bus. Rte. 15 S.), Gettysburg, 717-334-2100, www.dobbinhouse .com.**

✦ Columbia-Wrightsville Bridge

Despite its architectural prominence, this bridge spanning the Susquehanna River—once the longest covered bridge in Pennsylvania—was burned by retreating Union militia as General Early and his forces advanced from the Wrightsville side. Today, it is officially Veterans Memorial Bridge.

LOCATION: **PA Rte. 462 between Columbia and Wrightsville.**

✦ Hanover

Hanover was the site of a cavalry engagement involving George Custer on June 30, 1863. There are interpretive signs and a monument to Custer. Eat at Famous Hot Weiner near the town square.

LOCATION: **Hanover Visitor Information Center at Guthrie Memorial Library, 301 Carlisle St., 717-632-5183, www.yorkpa.org.**

✦ Harrisburg

Although the Confederates did not occupy the city of Harrisburg, the state capital was a symbolic and strategic objective for them. In addition to the National Civil War Museum, don't miss the mansion of Lincoln's first Secretary of War, Simon Cameron.

LOCATION: **National Civil War Museum, 1 Lincoln Circle, 717-260-1861, www.national civilwarmuseum.org; Simon Cameron Mansion, 219 S. Front St., 717-233-3462, www.dauphin countyhistory.org/mansion.**

✦ Monterey Pass Battlefield Park

Site of an engagement between Union cavalry and retreating Confederate wagon trains, this park has interpretive markers and a self-guided driving tour.

LOCATION: **14325 Buchanan Trail E., Waynesboro, www.montereypassbattlefield .org.**

✦ Philadelphia

Philadelphia has numerous important Civil War–related memorials, artwork, and museums, including the Grand Army of the Republic Museum and Library and the Historical Society of Pennsylvania. Independence Hall—where Lincoln spoke en route to his inauguration—also served as a major waypoint on the Underground Railroad.

LOCATION: **Visit Philadelphia, www.visitphilly .com; Grand Army of the Republic Museum and Library, 4278 Griscom St., 215-289-6484, www.garmuslib.org; Historical Society of Pennsylvania, 1300 Locust St., 215-732-6200, www.hsp.org; Independence National Historical Park, 41 N. 6th St., www.nps.gov/inde.**

✦ Soldiers and Sailors Memorial Hall and Museum

The nation's only military memorial dedicated to honoring the men and women of all branches of service, this museum includes Civil War uniforms, equipment, paintings, and personal diaries and letters.

LOCATION: 4141 5th Ave., Pittsburgh, 412-621-4253, www.soldiersandsailorshall.org.

✦ United States Army War College at Carlisle Barracks

This was the site of a skirmish between Confederate cavalry and Union militia prior to General Stuart's ride to Gettysburg. There is some shell damage on the columns of the Cumberland County Courthouse, and interpretive signs help tell the story of the Confederates who camped in Carlisle, including General Ewell and his troops. The U.S. Army Heritage and Education Center—the army's primary historical research facility—contains a well-constructed outdoor museum while also offering a priceless photographic collection and extensive archives. Helpful staff will assist in uncovering important primary source materials.

LOCATION: 122 Forbes Ave., Carlisle, 717-245-3131, www.carlisle.army.mil; U.S. Army Heritage and Education Center, 950 Soldiers Dr., Carlisle, 717-245-3972, www.carlisle.army.mil/ahec.

✦ Wheatland

Just west of downtown Lancaster sits President James Buchanan's Wheatland—the historic home, grounds, and gardens of the 15th U.S. president. Buchanan ran his presidential campaign from the library here in 1856, and he returned to Wheatland after his presidency. He is buried close by.

LOCATION: 1120 Marietta Ave., Lancaster, 717-392-4633, www.lancasterhistory.org.

✦ York

When General Early and his division occupied York in late June 1863, it became the largest Northern town occupied by the Confederates. The hospital—which treated thousands of soldiers after the Battle of Gettysburg—was located on the grounds of present-day Penn Park, where interpretive signs, along with a soldiers and sailors monument, pay tribute to York's role in the war.

LOCATION: York Convention and Visitors Bureau, 60 E. North St., www.yorkpa.org; Penn Park, 100 W. College Ave., www.yorkcity.org/parks. Monument at the intersection of W. College Ave. and S. Beaver St.

Union militia burned a wooden, covered version of the Columbia-Wrightsville Bridge on June 18, 1863.

Other Northeastern States

Connecticut, Delaware, Maine, Massachusetts, New Hampshire, New Jersey, New York, Rhode Island, and Vermont

IN 1861, WHEN PRESIDENT LINCOLN INITIALLY CALLED FOR 75,000 volunteers to serve for 90 days, he could not have envisioned a war that would last more than four years and cost more than 800,000 lives. In the end a total of more than 7 million men, including more than 180,000 African Americans, fought on both sides. While the North did institute a draft, governors had wide latitude to coerce "volunteers" to join. Unit designations were state-based not federal. The North showed itself capable of waging war and sustaining a thriving economy. Its well-armed soldiers feasted on canned goods in the field, and clothing was plentiful. Unlike the destitute South, the North assimilated its casualties, welcomed the victors home, and commemorated their triumph.

Impressive monuments abound in the Northern states, but Grant's Tomb in New York City befittingly stands as one of the most iconic.

Connecticut

Connecticut's contributions to the war effort came in a variety of forms. Thousands of weapons made by Colt's Manufacturing Company and the Winchester Repeating Arms Company found their way onto every battlefield, while local abolitionists like Harriet Beecher Stowe fought great moral battles in ways of their own. The Connecticut Freedom Trail (www.ctfreedomtrail.org) includes many of the state's historic sites, providing a vivid picture of African-American struggles throughout the 19th century.

✦ Confederate Bell

Originally cast in Cincinnati, Ohio, this bell was reportedly captured during the war by Confederate troops. Connecticut Colonel Warner eventually recaptured the bell, which some say bore the words of an eager Confederate: "This bell is to be melted into a cannon—may it kill a thousand Yankees!"

LOCATION: **Ridgefield Community Center, outside Lounsbury House, 316 Main St.,** Ridgefield, 203-438-6962, www.lounsbury house.com.

✦ Fort Trumbull

Rebuilt from 1839 to 1852 as part of the country's coastal defense system, Fort Trumbull served as headquarters for the 14th Infantry Regiment during the war. Tours of the facility and the 19th-century living quarters are available. The visitor center and interpretive markers provide information on the fort's history.

LOCATION: **Fort Trumbull State Park, 90 Walbach St., New London, 860-444-7591.**

✦ General Mansfield House

Once the home of Joseph K. F. Mansfield, who was mortally wounded at the Battle of Antietam, the house commemorates the lives of more than 950 Middletown citizens who fought in the war. The permanent exhibit also contains a section on women's lives in the Civil War.

LOCATION: **151 Main St., Middletown, 860-346-0746, www.middlesexhistory.org.**

American author and short-lived Confederate soldier Samuel Clemens (aka Mark Twain) resided here while writing many of his most popular works.

✦ Harriet Beecher Stowe Center

Though Stowe published more than 30 books, her 1852 antislavery novel, *Uncle Tom's Cabin,* is her most memorable; the book is often cited as a key element of the growing abolitionist sentiment of the 19th century. The center offers tours of Stowe's house and the neighborhood.

LOCATION: **77 Forest St., Hartford, 860-522-9258, www.harrietbeecherstowecenter.org.**

✦ John Brown's Birthplace

Though the building itself no longer stands, the Torrington Historical Society maintains the plot of land where John Brown was born (the original building was destroyed by fire in 1918). A granite monument marks the site, along with an interpretive marker.

LOCATION: **192 Main St., Torrington, 860-482-8260, www.torringtonhistoricalsociety.org.**

✦ Leverett Beman Historical District

These five acres were home to several prominent leaders of Connecticut's abolitionist movement, including Pastor Jehiel Beman; son Amos Beman, an abolitionist who frequently contributed to several black newspapers; and daughter-in-law Clarissa Beman, who founded the Middletown Colored Female Anti-Slavery Society.

LOCATION: **Triangle formed by Cross St., Vine St., and Knowles Ave. in Middletown.**

✦ Mark Twain House and Museum

Samuel Clemens (Mark Twain was the satirist's pen name) joined the Confederate militia in his home state of Missouri in 1861. His two-week stint was enough for him to piece together a fictionalized account of his experiences several years later titled "The Private History of a Campaign That Failed." Visitors can see where Twain lived when he wrote *Adventures of Huckleberry Finn* and *The Adventures of Tom Sawyer.*

LOCATION: **351 Farmington Ave., Hartford, 860-247-0998, www.marktwainhouse.org.**

✦ Museum of Connecticut History

The museum's military collection includes uniforms, flags, portraits, weapons, memorabilia, and other mementos that once belonged to Connecticut soldiers imprisoned in Andersonville. Small arms produced by the Connecticut-based Colt's Manufacturing Company are also on display.

LOCATION: **Collocated with the Connecticut State Library, 231 Capitol Ave., Hartford, 860-757-6535, www.museumofcthistory.org.**

✦ New England Civil War Museum

The museum's collection is made up largely of personal artifacts donated by Colonel Burpee of the 21st Connecticut Infantry as well as the Hirst brothers of the 14th Connecticut Volunteer Infantry, which helped defend against Pickett's Charge at Gettysburg (see pp. 355–356).

LOCATION: **14 Park Pl., Rockville, 860-870-3563, www.newenglandcivilwarmuseum.com.**

✦ 29th Colored Regiment Monument

More than 900 soldiers fought with the 29th Colored Regiment—the first all-black regiment in Connecticut. The veterans are honored here on their 1863 training grounds with a monument erected in 2008.

LOCATION: **West side of Criscuolo Park in New Haven on the banks of the Mill River.**

Delaware

A slave state and a border state, Delaware remained loyal to the Union and played a crucial role in the continued success of the Underground Railroad. Although most Delawareans who took up arms fought in blue uniforms, some soldiers went south to join the Confederacy.

✦ Admiral Du Pont Monument

Samuel Francis Du Pont played a significant role in orchestrating the Federal naval blockade of Southern ports. Sadly, his greatest opportunity was a failure. The monitor attack on Charleston in April 1863 delayed Robert E. Lee's invasion, which led to the Battle of Gettysburg. Du Pont was relieved of command at his own request in July 1863.

LOCATION: **Intersection of W. 19th St. and Tower Rd. at the entrance to Rockford Park in northwest Wilmington, 302-577-7020, www .destateparks.com.**

✦ Appoquinimink Friends Meeting House

This Quaker meetinghouse was serviced by Underground Railroad stationmasters, who hid runaway slaves between the floorboards of this small two-story structure.

LOCATION: **SR 299, west of US 13 in Odessa, 302-652-4491. Open by appointment only.**

✦ Delaware Soldiers and Sailors Monument

Dedicated to the fallen Delawarean soldiers of the Civil War, this monument features an eagle sitting atop a column with the serpent of rebellion in its talons.

LOCATION: **Triangle formed by Delaware Ave., W. 14th St., and N. Broom St. in Wilmington, a quarter mile southeast of Trolley Sq.**

✦ Fort Delaware

Perhaps the most significant element of Delaware's Civil War legacy, this fort housed some 30,000 Confederate and political prisoners over the course of its four years as a prison camp. Following the Battle of

Gettysburg (see pp. 352–357), the fort held nearly 12,000 prisoners—the highest number of soldiers held there at any one time. The fort is open seasonally, and a walking tour showcases its features and history.

LOCATION: **Fort Delaware State Park, Pea Patch Island, Delaware City, 302-834-7941, www.destateparks.com.**

✦ Friends Meetinghouse

As many as 2,700 slaves may have passed through this historic Quaker meetinghouse, including Harriet Tubman. Abolitionist Thomas Garrett, who lived nearby, was so revered that, upon his death, freed blacks carried him on their shoulders to his burial site on the meetinghouse grounds.

LOCATION: **401 N. West St., Wilmington, 302-652-4491, www.wilmingtondefriendsmeeting .org.**

FURTHER READING

Harriet Tubman: The Road to Freedom by Catherine Clinton A biography of the Underground Railroad's most famous conductor

✦ Hagley Museum and Library

Delaware's greatest contribution to the war effort came in the production of black powder for ammunition, and the Du Pont family was the first name in the gunpowder business. Aside from the actual library and museum, you can also visit the powder yards and the Du Pont family home.

LOCATION: **200 Hagley Creek Rd., Wilmington, 302-658-2400, www.hagley.org.**

✦ New Castle Court House Museum

Located in the heart of historic New Castle, the courthouse was the site of the 1848 trial of abolitionists Thomas Garrett and

Local history is preserved at the Old Library Museum in New Castle, Delaware.

John Hunn, stationmasters on the Underground Railroad. The guilty verdict resulted in a crippling fine of $4,500. Tours and other interpretive programs take place during normal operating hours.

LOCATION: 211 Delaware St., New Castle, 302-323-4453, www.history.delaware.gov/museums.

FURTHER READING
"Dear Friend": Thomas Garrett and William Still, Collaborators on the Underground Railroad by Judith Bentley Explores the friendship of Garrett and Still, a free black man

✦ Wilmington and Brandywine Cemetery

This cemetery serves as the final resting place for the majority of Civil War soldiers who hailed from Delaware, including four Medal of Honor recipients.

LOCATION: 701 Delaware Ave., Wilmington, 302-652-5770, www.wilbrancem.weebly.com.

Maine

More than 70,000 men of Maine put on the Federal uniform over the course of the Civil War. The state began erecting monuments to its war dead as early as 1863, resulting in more than 140 monuments in communities large and small.

✦ Bangor Museum and History Center

This museum and history center features a variety of artifacts from the Civil War, including several swords and a 12-pound Dahlgren boat howitzer, which is located on the lawn of the Thomas A. Hill house—home of the Bangor Historical Society.

LOCATION: 159 Union St., Bangor, 207-942-5766, www.bangormuseum.org.

✦ Bar Harbor Civil War Monument

This impressive granite memorial dedicated to Maine's Civil War dead was erected in 1882 in the cemetery next to St. Saviour's Episcopal Church.

LOCATION: St. Saviour's Episcopal Church, 41 Mt. Desert St., Bar Harbor, 207-288-4215.

✦ Eighth Maine

Originally built as a summer vacation home for veterans and families of the Eighth Maine Volunteer Regiment, this building now serves as both a museum and a 15-room lodge. The on-site library offers information on the regiment's service.

LOCATION: 13 8th Maine Ave., Peaks Island, 239-789-7859 or 207-329-3530, www.8thmainepeaksisland.com.

✦ Fort Knox

The first fort in Maine to be built of granite, Fort Knox served primarily as a training ground for Maine troops who were garrisoned here and would later go to war at

Maine troops—mostly volunteers—trained at Fort Knox before heading to battle.

Lincoln's call. The fort is open from May to October 31; the grounds are open year-round.

LOCATION: **740 Fort Knox Rd., Prospect, 207-469-6553, www.fortknox.maineguide.com.**

✦ Fort Preble

The only Civil War battle in Maine took place just beyond Fort Preble's ramparts in Portland harbor—a naval fight that ended with the capture of Confederate raiders.

LOCATION: **East side of the Southern Maine Community College campus, 2 Fort Rd., South Portland, 207-741-5500.**

✦ Hannibal Hamlin House/ Mount Hope Cemetery

After his long political career, Hamlin returned to his Bangor home in 1882. He is interred at Mount Hope Cemetery, about four miles northwest of the house.

LOCATION: **Hannibal Hamlin House, 15 5th St., Bangor; Mount Hope Cemetery, 1048 State St., Bangor, 207-945-6589, www.mthopebgr.com.**

FURTHER READING

Team of Rivals
by Doris Kearns Goodwin
A Pulitzer Prize–winning study of President Lincoln and his cabinet

✦ Joshua L. Chamberlain Museum

Chamberlain earned the Medal of Honor for his bravery at the Battle of Gettysburg. Later he served as governor of Maine and president of Bowdoin College.

LOCATION: **226 Maine St., Brunswick, 207-729-6606, www.pejepscothistorical.org.**

FURTHER READING

The Twentieth Maine: A Classic, the Story of Joshua Chamberlain and His Volunteer Regiment
by John J. Pullen
A history of Chamberlain's regiment and their battles

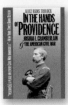

In the Hands of Providence: Joshua L. Chamberlain and the American Civil War
by Alice Rains Trulock
A biography of Chamberlain and his wartime career

✦ Maine Maritime Museum

Here you will learn of the powerful shipbuilders and guild of sea captains who faced Confederate privateers and raiders.

LOCATION: 243 Washington St., Bath, 207-443-1316, www.mainemaritimemuseum.org.

✦ Maine State Museum

The museum's Civil War artifacts include several battle trophies and the first collection of Civil War flags in the nation to have been conserved and exhibited.

LOCATION: 230 State St., Augusta, 207-287-2301, www.mainestatemuseum.org.

✦ Washburn-Norlands Living History Center

Once the estate of the prominent Washburn family, the site—which hosts an annual Civil War reenactment—is now a living-history museum and working farmstead that provides insight into 19th-century rural life.

LOCATION: 290 Norlands Rd., Livermore, 207-897-4366, www.norlands.org.

Massachusetts

The leadership of the state of Massachusetts during the Civil War fully embodied hearty New England values. Citizen soldiers quickly responded to the nation's call, and political leaders like Nathaniel Banks and Benjamin Butler were joined by young idealists like Charles Lowell and Robert Gould Shaw on the front lines. Paul Revere's descendants fought on the fields at Chancellorsville, and free blacks charged on the beaches of South Carolina. Key figures like abolitionists William Lloyd Garrison and Charles Sumner brought pride to the state for their oratory skills, while others like Clara Barton made great strides in battlefield medicine.

✦ Boston African American National Historic Site

Points of interest here include the Robert Gould Shaw and 54th Massachusetts Regiment Memorial, along with several other sites pertaining to the Underground Railroad, the abolitionist movement, and early struggles for civil rights.

LOCATION: Charles St. (Rte. 28) to Boston Common, Boston, www.nps.gov/boaf; Museum of African American History, 46 Joy St., Boston, 617-725-0022, www.maah.org.

FURTHER READING

Blue-Eyed Child of Fortune: The Civil War Letters of Colonel Robert Gould Shaw
The correspondence of Colonel Shaw of the 54th Massachusetts

✦ Charles Sumner House

A staunch opponent of slavery, Massachusetts Senator Charles Sumner counted among his acquaintances President Lincoln, Henry Wadsworth Longfellow, and many leading black abolitionists, who lived near Sumner's brick town house here in Boston's Beacon Hill community.

LOCATION: 20 Hancock St., Boston. The house is a private residence.

FURTHER READING

Charles Sumner and the Coming of the Civil War
by David Herbert Donald
Prize-winning biography of Sumner and his influence on prewar politics

✦ Clara Barton Birthplace Museum

A nurse, teacher, humanitarian, and most famously the founder of the American Red Cross, Barton tended wounded soldiers and delivered much needed medical supplies at several famous battles including Antietam (see pp. 340–341) and Fredericksburg (see pp. 237–242). Open seasonally and by appointment only, this museum—the site of Barton's childhood home—pays tribute to her pioneering career.

LOCATION: **66 Clara Barton Rd., North Oxford, 508-987-2056 ext. 2013, www.clarabarton birthplace.org.**

FURTHER READING
A Woman of Valor: Clara Barton and the Civil War
by Stephen B. Oates
A biography of Barton and her active role in the war

✦ Concord Museum

In the mid-19th century, Massachusetts was the epicenter for progressive American thinkers like Ralph Waldo Emerson and Henry David Thoreau, who both strongly supported the abolitionist movement. This museum houses several impressive artifacts from their lives, including Emerson's study and the desk on which Thoreau wrote *Walden* and "Civil Disobedience."

LOCATION: **53 Cambridge Turnpike, Concord, 978-369-9763, www.concordmuseum.org.**

✦ Faneuil Hall

Abolitionists and orators like Frederick Douglass, William Lloyd Garrison, and Lucy Stone took the podium at this famed marketplace and meeting hall to denounce the institution of slavery.

LOCATION: **1 Faneuil Hall Sq., Boston, 617-635-4500, www.cityofboston.gov.**

FURTHER READING
Civil War Boston: Home Front and Battlefield
by Thomas H. O'Connor
A study of Boston's role in the war and the impact it had on the city

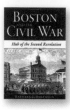

Boston and the Civil War: Hub of the Second Revolution
by Barbara F. Berenson
An in-depth account of the abolitionist movement in Boston

✦ Fort Warren

Completed just before the beginning of the war, the granite stronghold built to defend Boston also functioned as a prison for Confederate military and political prisoners. The arrest of two envoys, James Mason and John Slidell, during what was known as the Trent Affair nearly persuaded Great Britain to intercede in the war, which could have provided much needed foreign support for the South. Today, the fort offers tours and has multiple interpretive markers.

LOCATION: **Georges Island, 7 miles from Boston, 617-223-8666, www.bostonharbor islands.org. Ferries depart from several main-land piers, namely Long Wharf North (66 Long Wharf) in Boston. Open seasonally.**

✦ Harvard University

The Civil War–era sites to see on Harvard's historic campus include Memorial Hall, built in the late 1860s as "a symbol of Boston's commitment to the Unionist Cause and the abolition movement in America." Several marble tablets in the building honor Harvard's Union dead, including Robert Gould Shaw. Portions of Soldiers Field Athletic Area were donated by Henry Lee Higginson, who served as a lieutenant dur-ing the war. A monument at the entrance to

Soldiers Field lists the names of Higginson's comrades who lost their lives in the war.

LOCATION: 45 Quincy St., Cambridge, 617-495-2420, www.fas.harvard.edu.

✦ Louisa May Alcott's Orchard House

Perhaps best known as the author of *Little Women,* Louisa May Alcott was also a stationmaster on the Underground Railroad and a nurse during the war. Her writing was heavily influenced by the likes of her father, abolitionist Amos Bronson Alcott, as well as Transcendentalists Ralph Waldo Emerson and Henry David Thoreau. Although the Alcotts moved frequently, their most permanent home was this house in Concord.

LOCATION: 399 Lexington Rd., Concord, 978-369-4118, www.louisamayalcott.org.

The Union Club of Boston

Boston's intellectual and civic leaders met frequently during the Civil War to discuss the issues surrounding the conflict, including slavery, politics, and the future of a nation less than a century old. Recognizing the need for a formal gathering place to meet and talk, a small group of Boston's most prominent and powerful thinkers founded the Union Club of Boston (8 Park St., Boston, 617-227-0589, www.union club.org)—a gentleman's association formed to bolster support for the Union cause. Early members included Ralph Waldo Emerson, Oliver Wendell Holmes, and abolitionist and former Massachusetts governor Edward Everett, who served as the club's first president. Today, Boston's elite (men *and* women) continue to gather at the club, and new members sign the same book that has preserved the signatures of almost 500 members since the group's founding.

✦ Lowell National Historical Park

Throughout the 19th century, Northern mills—like Lowell's water-powered textile mills located along the Merrimack River—depended heavily on Southern cotton plantations to produce high-quality cloth. As the war raged on, however, local mills eventually broke ties with their Southern suppliers.

LOCATION: 246 Market St., Lowell, 978-970-5000, www.nps.gov/lowe.

✦ Mount Auburn Cemetery

A number of Civil War figures are buried here in this rural cemetery, including abolitionist Edward Everett; Edwin Booth, famous actor and brother of John Wilkes Booth; Dorothea Dix, superintendent of Army nurses; Senator Charles Sumner; and poet Henry Wadsworth Longfellow.

LOCATION: 580 Mount Auburn St., Cambridge, 617-547-7105, www.mountauburn.org.

✦ Park Street Church

A historic stop on the Freedom Trail, Park Street Church played a significant role in downtown Boston as a gathering place for devout Christians. In 1826, Edward Beecher, brother of Harriet Beecher Stowe, became pastor of the church, and in 1829, abolitionist William Lloyd Garrison delivered one of his most notable speeches, in which he outlined his arguments against slavery.

LOCATION: 1 Park St., Boston, 617-523-3383, www.parkstreet.org.

✦ Sojourner Truth Memorial Statue

In 1843, the famed abolitionist, women's rights advocate, and former slave Sojourner Truth joined the Northampton Association of Education and Industry, whose positions on women's rights and religious tolerance aligned with her own. There she met fellow abolitionists like William Lloyd Garrison and Frederick Douglass. She later purchased a home in Northampton, which has been incorporated into a self-guided walking tour.

LOCATION: Intersection of Park St. and Pine St. in Northampton, www.sojourner truthmemorial.org.

FURTHER READING

Narrative of Sojourner Truth
by Sojourner Truth
Powerful narrative of a remarkable life

✦ Springfield Armory National Historic Site

The Springfield Armory produced rifles and muskets for soldiers in every American war until 1968. The armory reopened as a national historic site in 1978 and now houses the world's largest collection of historic American military firearms, including hundreds of Civil War–era muskets and rifles.

LOCATION: 1 Armory Sq., Springfield, 413-734-8551, www.nps.gov/spar.

✦ U.S.S. *Constitution* Museum and Charlestown Navy Yard

Sandwiched between Boston National Historical Park and Charlestown Navy Yard, this museum is dedicated to preserving artifacts and archives related to "Old Ironsides." Perhaps most famous for its role in the War of 1812, the ship also served as a training vessel for the U.S. Naval Academy during the Civil War. The shipyard built the U.S.S. *Cumberland,* sunk by the Confederate ironclad *Virginia (Merrimac);* U.S.S. *Harford,* Admiral Farragut's flagship at New Orleans and Mobile Bay; and the U.S.S. *Housatonic,* which was sunk by the Confederate submarine *H. L. Hunley.*

LOCATION: Bldg. 22, Charlestown Navy Yard, Charlestown, 617-426-1812, www.ussconstitu tionmuseum.org. Tours of the ship are operated separately from the museum.

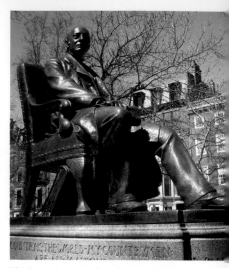

This bronze statue of abolitionist William Lloyd Garrison is in Boston's Back Bay.

✦ William Lloyd Garrison Statue

One of the founders of the American Anti-Slavery Society, William Lloyd Garrison is perhaps best known for his role as editor of the antislavery newspaper the *Liberator,* which he published in Boston from 1831 to 1865. His stirring words are inscribed on one side of the statue.

LOCATION: Along the Commonwealth Avenue Mall between Dartmouth St. and Exeter St. in Boston's Back Bay.

New Hampshire

A total of 18 infantry regiments, two cavalry units, two artillery units, and several companies of sharpshooters were sent from the Granite State to defend the Union, and their contributions are remembered in museums, historical societies, and monuments found throughout the state. Aside from military history, New Hampshire also boasts unique sites commemorating local Civil War–era pioneers like balloonist Thaddeus S. C. Lowe and sculptor Augustus Saint-Gaudens.

✦ Exeter Historical Society

Exhibits at this historical society highlight Exeter's involvement with the Civil War, as well as Abraham Lincoln's historic visit to Exeter in 1860. The Historical Society has pieced together a walking tour that traces Lincoln's visit.

LOCATION: 47 Front St., Exeter, 603-778-2335, www.exeterhistory.org.

✦ Fitts Museum

Established by the Fitts brothers, one of whom was present at Gettysburg, the museum displays a flag and barometer saved from a Civil War–era ship, as well as a sword that belonged to Lieutenant Robie, an infantryman awarded the Medal of Honor.

LOCATION: 185 High St., Candia, www.fitts museum.org. Open only on select dates.

✦ Fort Constitution

Fort Constitution was part of a system of forts built to defend Portsmouth Harbor. Several New Hampshire units trained here on the fort grounds, and others remained garrisoned here during the Civil War. Updates to the fort were begun during the war, but like many other forts in the North during this time period, construction was never completed.

LOCATION: 25 Wentworth Rd., New Castle, 603-271-3556.

✦ New Hampshire Historical Society

The society maintains a library and a museum whose collections contain Civil War badges, drums, military equipment, and currency from the time period.

LOCATION: 30 Park St., Concord, www.nh history.org.

✦ Portsmouth

Portsmouth contains a wealth of Civil War history. Start at the Strawbery Banke Museum, which oversees a number of historical homes. Another local highlight is the Soldiers and Sailors Monument, which commemorates the U.S.S. *Kearsarge* and its sinking of the C.S.S. *Alabama.*

LOCATION: Strawbery Banke Museum, 14 Hancock St., Portsmouth, 603-433-1100, www.strawberybanke.org; Soldiers and Sailors Monument, Goodwin Park, Islington St., Portsmouth.

✦ Saint-Gaudens National Historic Site

American sculptor Augustus Saint-Gaudens created many famous Civil War monuments and statues, including the Robert Gould Shaw Memorial in Boston, the "Standing Lincoln" statue in Chicago, and many statues in New York. Here, visitors can tour Saint-Gaudens's home, as well as the galleries, which contain more than 100 of his works.

LOCATION: 139 St. Gaudens Rd., Cornish, 603-675-2175, www.nps.gov/saga.

✦ Thaddeus S. C. Lowe Birthplace

An inventor, scientist, and ballooning pioneer, Lowe was appointed chief aeronaut of the Union Army Balloon Corps by President Lincoln. The corps' role was to provide aerial reconnaissance of Confederate troops, and it participated in major battles, including Antietam, Yorktown, and Fredericksburg.

LOCATION: Marker at the intersection of Presidential Hwy. (US 2) and Turnpike Rd., in Jefferson.

✦ Woodman Museum

The museum's collection contains several notable Civil War artifacts, including a saddle used by President Lincoln shortly before he was assassinated. The John P. Hale House, also owned by the Woodman Museum, once belonged to John P. Hale, an abolitionist and prominent member of the Free Soil Party. Hale's daughter, Lucy Lambert Hale, was engaged to John Wilkes Booth, and letters between the two are included among the items in the museum's collections.

LOCATION: **182 Central Ave., Dover, 603-742-1038, www.woodmanmuseum.org.**

New Jersey

New Jersey may have provided more than 80,000 soldiers for the Union Army, but the majority of the state disagreed with Lincoln's leadership. In the 1864 presidential election, the state chose New Jersey native George B. McClellan over the sitting president. McClellan's burial site is located here, as are several other significant Civil War figures, including immortal writers Walt Whitman and Stephen Crane.

✦ Absecon Lighthouse

The Grand Army of the Republic (GAR) convened only once in New Jersey, in 1910, when 18,000 veterans gathered in Atlantic City for the 44th national GAR convention. A marker on the lighthouse grounds commemorates the event. Visitors can climb the lighthouse, which, as the tallest in the state, offers tremendous views.

LOCATION: **31 S. Rhode Island Ave., Atlantic City, 609-449-1919, www.abseconlighthouse .org. Marker can be reached from Vermont Ave.**

✦ Essex County Courthouse Plaza

Seated on a bench in the plaza is a bronze statue of President Lincoln designed by sculptor Gutzon Borglum, of Mt. Rushmore fame. Nearby in Military Park are several more Borglum statues, including the impressive "Wars of America" monument.

LOCATION: **50 W. Market St., Newark, 973-693-5700. Military Park is on Broad St.**

✦ Finn's Point National Cemetery

Confederate soldiers are generally not permitted burial in national cemeteries; however, there are nearly 2,500 Confederates buried at Finn's Point, having died while in the Federal prison at nearby Fort Delaware. More than 100 Union soldiers are also buried here, and handsome monuments memorialize soldiers from both sides.

LOCATION: **Fort Mott State Park, 454 Fort Mott Rd., Pennsville, 215-504-5610, www.cem.va.gov.**

✦ Hamilton's Civil War and Native American Museum

Spanning several centuries of American history, this museum features Civil War swords and muskets, as well as Native American knives and dream catchers. It is sustained by the Camp Olden Civil War Round Table.

LOCATION: **2202 Kuser Rd., Hamilton, 609-585-8900, www.campolden.org.**

The New England Emigrant Aid Company

In response to the Kansas-Nebraska Act, which allowed the residents of a territory to determine the status of slavery in the states to be formed from the Kansas and Nebraska Territories, a group of New England businessmen led by Massachusetts congressman Eli Thayer developed the New England Emigrant Aid Company—a transportation company that would assist antislavery emigrants to settle in Kansas in hopes they could influence a free state constitution. Although the company didn't profit from the business venture, as it originally hoped, the emigrants that it helped place in Kansas in and around Lawrence were fully involved in all the politics and violence of "Bleeding Kansas" (see sidebar p. 401).

✦ National Guard Militia Museum of New Jersey

In its mission to preserve the military history of New Jersey, this site houses numerous manuscripts, photographs, and other artifacts. Two unique pieces on display include a Civil War–era submarine prototype and the state's only Civil War cannon.

LOCATION: **Sea Girt Ave. and Camp Dr., Sea Girt, 732-974-5966, www.nj.gov/military /museum.**

✦ Peter Mott House

Located in the historically black town of Lawnside, this was the home of preacher Peter Mott, a free black man and an agent on the Underground Railroad. Tour guides are on duty every Saturday. Weekday visits can be arranged by appointment.

LOCATION: **26 Kings Ct., off Moore Ave., Lawnside, 856-546-8850, www.petermott house.org.**

✦ Riverview Cemetery

The tallest monument in this cemetery marks the burial site of George B. McClellan. After being relieved of command from the Army of the Potomac in 1862, McClellan ran unsuccessfully against President Lincoln in the 1864 presidential election.

LOCATION: **870 Centre St., Trenton, 609-396-9540.**

✦ Stephen Crane Gravesite

In perhaps his best known work, *The Red Badge of Courage,* Stephen Crane penned the story of a Union soldier's abandonment and eventual return to the Civil War battlefield. Well received in the late 1890s, the novel remains a key text in the American literary canon today.

LOCATION: **Evergreen Cemetery, 1137 North Broad St., Hillside, 908-352-7940.**

The 1st Regiment Vermont Cavalry, which served in 1861–1865, flew this battle flag.

✦ Vineland Historical and Antiquarian Society

Founded in 1864, New Jersey's oldest local historical society maintains several rooms of artifacts, including a Grand Army of the Republic relic room featuring donated accouterments from various veterans from around the state.

LOCATION: **108 S. 7th St., Vineland, 856-691-1111, www.vinelandhistory1864.org.**

✦ Walt Whitman Mausoleum

Whitman's most popular Civil War–era poem may be his elegy to President Lincoln in "O Captain! My Captain!" but the poet composed many more pieces that captured the effects of the war on 1860s America. He is buried here in a tomb of his own design.

LOCATION: **Harleigh Cemetery, 1640 Haddon Ave., Camden, 856-963-3500, www.harleigh cemetery.org.**

FURTHER READING

Civil War Letters of George Washington Whitman
Letters chronicling the wartime experience of Walt Whitman's younger brother

New York

New York was a major economic, political, and social hub during the Civil War, and as the Union's most populous state, it contributed more troops to the Northern cause than any other. Despite its unequaled military support, however, the state wasn't free of its political divisions, and tension came to a head during the New York City Draft Riots of 1863. The state today is heavily populated with monuments and museums.

✦ Battery Park

Battery Park is home to a statue of John Ericsson, who designed the U.S.S. *Monitor.*

LOCATION: **Southern tip of Manhattan Island, New York, 212-344-3491, www.thebattery.org.**

✦ Castle Williams

Castle Williams initially served as a Union training ground and recruiting depot. As the war dragged on, however, the obsolete sandstone fortress was adapted to house Confederate prisoners of war.

LOCATION: **Governors Island National Monument, 212-825-3045, www.nps.gov/gois. Reachable by ferry.**

✦ Central Park

Constructed between 1858 and 1873, much of the park's development took place during the Civil War. Important monuments include Saint-Gaudens's equestrian monument of Sherman, the 7th Regiment Memorial, and Frederick Douglass Circle, which is inscribed with quotes attributed to the abolitionist, statesman, and former slave.

LOCATION: **For maps and tours of the park, visit www.centralparknyc.org or call 212-310-6600.**

✦ Elmira Prison/Woodlawn National Cemetery

For a period of 15 months from 1864 to 1865, Elmira Prison—dubbed "Hellmira" by its inmates for its brutal conditions—held

The Secret Six

Before John Brown could lead his infamous raid and slave revolt at Harpers Ferry in 1859, he needed financial support. Help came in the form of the Secret Six, a group of six abolitionists, most of whom had Massachusetts ties, who secretly funded Brown's raid, agreeing with Brown that the end of slavery would not likely be brought about peacefully. In the years after Brown's failed revolt, only one member of the group remained in the United States, Thomas Wentworth Higginson, who, despite publicly claiming his support of Brown, avoided arrest himself.

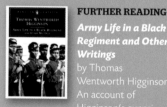

FURTHER READING
Army Life in a Black Regiment and Other Writings
by Thomas Wentworth Higginson An account of Higginson's experience as an officer in one of the first regiments of African-American soldiers

more than 12,000 Confederate prisoners of war. Nearly 3,000 died while incarcerated because of the overcrowding, inadequate shelter, and disease; many were buried at Woodlawn National Cemetery, about two miles north of the original prison site.

LOCATION: **1200 Walnut St., Elmira, 607-732-0151, www.friendsofwoodlawnelmira.org.**

FURTHER READING
Elmira: Death Camp of the North
by Michael Horigan A history of the infamous Union prison

✦ Fort Totten

Fort Totten in Queens was constructed in the 1860s to defend New York City from a potential naval attack. Today, New York City's Urban Park Rangers offer tours of the fortress, which was never completed, and the surrounding grounds.

LOCATION: **422 Weaver Ave., Bayside, 718-352-4793.**

✦ General Grant National Memorial

As commanding general of the Union Army and the only Union general to receive the surrender of three Confederate armies—including Lee's final surrender of the Army of Northern Virginia at Appomattox—Ulysses S. Grant was largely recognized as a hero throughout the war. Yet over the course of his military career, the man who would eventually serve two terms as the 18th president of the United States also received considerable criticism for the high number of casualties seen under his command. Mosaics of the general's Civil War victories can be viewed throughout the mausoleum, where both he and his wife, Julia Dent Grant, are entombed.

LOCATION: **W. 122nd St. and Riverside Dr., New York, 212-666-1640, www.nps.gov/gegr.**

FURTHER READING

The Complete and Personal Memoirs of Ulysses S. Grant
by Ulysses S. Grant
Completed by Grant shortly before his death in 1885

The Personal Memoirs of Julia Grant Dent
by Julia Grant Dent and John Simon
Attempts to correct misconception about her husband

✦ Great Hall of the Cooper Union

The Great Hall was the site of Abraham Lincoln's famous Cooper Union Address in 1860. The future president used his lengthy speech to expound upon his position on slavery and its expansion into future American territories. The speech made Lincoln the immediate front-runner for the 1860 Republican nomination.

LOCATION: **7 E. 7th St., New York, 212-353-4100, www.cooper.edu.**

FURTHER READING

Lincoln at Cooper Union: The Speech That Made Abraham Lincoln President
by Harold Holzer
An in-depth analysis of the famous speech and its impact

✦ Green-Wood Cemetery

A National Historic Landmark, Green-Wood Cemetery is the final resting place of at least 3,000 veterans of the Civil War, including Henry Halleck, Henry Slocum, and Robert Selden Garnett.

LOCATION: **500 25th St., Brooklyn, 708-768-7300, www.green-wood.com.**

✦ Harriet Tubman Home

The famed abolitionist spent much of her time at this house in Auburn, where her parents lived during the Civil War and which also served as Tubman's home until her death in 1913.

LOCATION: **180 South St., Auburn, 315-252-2081, www.harriethouse.org.**

✦ Horace Greeley House

The house of *New York Tribune* editor and literary giant Horace Greeley is now home to the New Castle Historical Society, which, in

Anthony Burns

A Virginia slave who escaped to Boston in 1854, Anthony Burns was captured just a few months later and returned to his slave master under the Fugitive Slave Act of 1850. Outraged Bostonians rallied in support of Burns's freedom, storming the courthouse where he was held, and an estimated 50,000 people lined the streets of Boston to watch him walk in shackles to the ship that would return him to Virginia. Less than a year later, however, the minister of a black Baptist church in Boston purchased Burns's freedom with $1,300 raised by church members. Burns's story was circulated widely as an example of the injustices plaguing the nation.

addition to preserving and providing tours of the Greeley home also holds maps, photographs, and artifacts documenting the history of the local community.

LOCATION: 100 King St., Chappaqua, 914-238-4666, www.newcastlehs.org.

FURTHER READING

Lincoln and Greeley
by Harlan Horner
A history and comparison of the two men

✦ John Brown Farm State Historic Site

Following his raid on Harpers Ferry, abolitionist John Brown was tried and hanged in Virginia in December 1859, but his body was returned here. Surrounded by a network of trails, Brown's home is open seasonally.

LOCATION: 115 John Brown Rd., Lake Placid, 518-523-3900, www.nysparks.com.

✦ Mount Hope Cemetery

It is only fitting that Mount Hope Cemetery serves as the final resting place for famed suffragist, abolitionist, and women's rights activist Susan B. Anthony, as well as for Frederick Douglass—who was famous not only for his devotion to the abolitionist movement but also for his support of women's suffrage.

LOCATION: 1133 Mt. Hope Ave., Rochester, 585-428-7999, www.cityofrochester.gov/mounthope.

✦ National Baseball Hall of Fame and Museum

As the Civil War escalated during the early 1860s, young men who knew the game of baseball played it in countless soldier's camps, introducing it to new communities along the way. Visitors to the Hall of Fame's three-floor museum in Cooperstown can learn about the origins of America's pastime and much more.

LOCATION: 25 Main St., Cooperstown, 888-HALL-OF-FAME, www.baseballhall.org.

✦ New-York Historical Society

The items here include a wide range of Civil War artifacts and a special collection of items related to the Underground Railroad. Life-size bronze statues of Abraham Lincoln and Frederick Douglass stand at either entrance to the building.

LOCATION: 170 Central Park W., New York, 212-873-3400, www.nyhistory.org.

✦ New York State Capitol

Here at the seat of government for New York State, visitors can tour the capitol building and its Hall of Governors, which contains exhibits on President Grant, state history, and New York's role in the Civil War.

LOCATION: Between State St. and Washington Ave., Albany, 518-474-2418, www.ogs.ny.gov.

✦ New York State Military Museum and Veterans Research Center

Housed in a historic armory, this museum contains more than 10,000 military artifacts including nearly 2,000 Civil War flags. The Veterans Research Center includes unit histories, Civil War newspaper clippings, and a sizable collection of Civil War photographs.

LOCATION: 61 Lake Ave., Saratoga Springs, 518-581-5100.

✦ Seward House Historic Museum

As secretary of state under President Lincoln, William Seward spent most of his wartime efforts managing international affairs and preventing foreign countries from entering the war. This house museum preserves his life story and accomplishments.

LOCATION: 33 South St., Auburn, 315-252-1283, www.sewardhouse.org.

✦ Ulysses S. Grant Cottage State Historic Site

Although a native of Ohio, Grant died here in this cottage of throat cancer in 1885. The cottage provided Grant with an opportunity to finish his memoirs, and the site has been preserved, with original furnishings and personal items. The visitor center offers interpretive displays and exhibits.

LOCATION: 1000 Mt. McGregor Rd., Wilton, 518-584-4353, www.grantcottage.org.

✦ Weeksville Heritage Center

As Brooklyn's largest African-American cultural institution, this museum and historic institution is dedicated to preserving the history of the 19th-century African-American community of Weeksville—one of America's first free black communities.

LOCATION: 158 Buffalo Ave., Brooklyn, 718-756-5250, www.weeksvillesociety.org.

FURTHER READING

The New York City Draft Riots: Their Significance for American Society and Politics in the Age of the Civil War
by Iver Bernstein
An in-depth study of the riots and the people who participated in them

✦ West Point Museum

Spanning more than 200 years of conflict, this museum features several galleries of artifacts, paintings, weaponry, and information related to the history of the U.S. Army, American wars, and West Point itself, whose long list of graduates includes Union leaders Ulysses S. Grant, William T. Sherman, and George Meade, as well as Confederate leaders Robert E. Lee, Jefferson Davis, J. E. B. Stuart, and Stonewall Jackson.

LOCATION: 2107 New South Post Rd., West Point, 845-938-3590, www.usma.edu /museum.

Augustus Saint-Gaudens

Irish-born Augustus Saint-Gaudens came to be recognized as one of America's greatest sculptors not only for his historical monuments of President Lincoln, General Sherman, and Robert Louis Stevenson but also for his numismatic designs, including the 1907 $20 gold piece, commissioned by Theodore Roosevelt in 1905. Saint-Gaudens was raised in New York from the age of six and later studied art at the Cooper Union, the National Academy of Design, and the prestigious École des Beaux-Arts in Paris. In his later years, he helped establish the Cornish Art Colony —a collective of artists, sculptors, writers, and politicians that gathered in Cornish, New Hampshire, to hone their respective crafts.

Rhode Island

The smallest state in the Union contributed more than 25,000 men to the Union cause. Fort Adams in Newport also played a significant role, serving as the temporary home for the U.S. Naval Academy. Key figures include Ambrose Burnside, the commander who oversaw the Union defeat at the Battle of Fredericksburg.

✦ Burnside Park

An equestrian statue of Ambrose Burnside was erected here in 1887, six years after the death of Rhode Island's most famous Civil War general.

LOCATION: **Near the intersection of Exchange St. and Exchange Terrace in Providence.**

The Confederate Constitution

The constitutions of the United States and the newly formed Confederacy were quite similar, but there were differences. The most obvious difference occurs in Article 1, Section 9 (4), of the Confederate Constitution, which specifically upheld the right to own slaves.

Other revolutionary differences included giving states the power to impeach federal officials and judges and a directive that all legislative actions must relate to only one subject, thus eliminating huge omnibus bills and special interest "riders" that weren't connected to the original bill. Since the core of the new government was to emphasize the rights of the states, the legislators restricted the executive branch by limiting the Confederate president to a single six-year term and prohibiting him from appointing someone, as a recess appointment, who had been rejected by the Senate.

FURTHER READING
Burnside
by William Marvel
A biography of the general and his maligned career

✦ Fort Adams

Wishing to avoid conflict with Southern sympathizers in Maryland, the U.S. Naval Academy moved its base of operations from Annapolis, Maryland, to Fort Adams in 1861. The campus grounds also included the nearby Atlantic House Hotel, which served as the academy's headquarters until 1865. Tours of the fortress show the quarters where officers and their families lived, and interpretive markers tell the fort's history.

LOCATION: **84 Fort Adams Dr., Newport, 401-841-0707, www.fortadams.org.**

✦ Hard Scrabble and Snow Town Riots

Though loyal to the Union, Rhode Island had historically been a major hub in the American slave market, and the state's population was composed of a large number of free African Americans. Racial tensions persisted, however, and more than 30 years before the Civil War, riots broke out in Hard Scrabble and Snow Town—two predominantly black Providence neighborhoods.

LOCATION: **The Hard Scrabble Riot marker is in Providence in the median formed by N. Main St. (RI Rte. 1), Canal St., and Mill St. The Snow Town Riot marker is about 400 feet south, near the intersection of N. Main St. and Smith St.**

✦ Rhode Island Historical Society

The society oversees two museums. The John Brown House Museum (named for the slave trader, not the abolitionist) tells the story of 18th-century life in Rhode Island, while the Museum of Work and Culture

Fort Adams in Newport, Rhode Island, served as the wartime home of the U.S. Naval Academy.

focuses on the late 19th and early 20th centuries. The society's collections also include military records and other documents related to the Civil War.

LOCATION: **John Brown House Museum, 52 Power St., Providence, 401-273-7507; Museum of Work and Culture, 42 S. Main St., Woonsocket, 401-769-9675; Rhode Island Historical Society Library, 121 Hope St., Providence, 401-273-8107, www.rihs.org.**

✦ Rhode Island Soldiers and Sailors Memorial

This memorial honors both black and white soldiers who fought and died in defense of the Union.

LOCATION: **In the plaza across from City Hall, 25 Dorrance St., Providence, 401-421-7740.**

✦ Rhode Island State House

On display in the lobby are several Civil War flags and a cannon known as "the Gettysburg Gun." This piece of Union artillery helped repel Pickett's Charge (see p. 355–356).

LOCATION: **82 Smith St., Providence, 401-222-3983, www.ri.gov.**

FURTHER READING
The Rhode Island Home Front in the Civil War Era
by Frank J. Williams and Patrick T. Conley, editors
An examination of the war's impact on Rhode Island society

✦ Second Freewill Baptist Church

An interpretive plaque commemorates this historic church, which was led by Edward Scott—an escaped slave from New Orleans who served as pastor from 1846 to 1864. The church also served as a station on the Underground Railroad.

LOCATION: **75 Chester Ave., Providence, 401-331-4681, www.sfwbc.org.**

✦ South County Museum

Rural and coastal life in the Ocean State is preserved at this museum, which was once the estate of William Sprague—Rhode Island's Civil War–era governor and postwar senator. Sites include the 19th-century one-room schoolhouse, blacksmith shop, and print shop.

LOCATION: **115 Strathmore St., Narragansett, 401-783-5400, www.southcountymuseum.org.**

✦ Swan Point Cemetery

Those buried here include Union veterans Ambrose Burnside and William Sprague IV; Medal of Honor recipients Benjamin Ham Child and Edward Parsons Tobie; and Elisha Hunt Rhodes, whose diary was excerpted in Ken Burns's documentary *The Civil War.*

LOCATION: **585 Blackstone Blvd., Providence, 401-272-1314, www.swanpointcemetery.com.**

FURTHER READING
Kate Chase and William Sprague: Politics and Gender in a Civil War Marriage
by Peg A. Lamphier
A biography of the most publicized union and divorce of the Civil War era

Vermont

No state had a bigger day at the Battle of Gettysburg than Vermont. Soldiers from the Nutmeg State played the leading role in breaking up Pickett's Charge, and their courage and tenacity were recognized with due honors. As a whole, the state has commemorated her sons, daughters, and even horses of the Civil War with a number of notable monuments, museums, and historical sites.

FURTHER READING
Something Abides: Discovering the Civil War in Today's Vermont
by Howard Coffin
An extensive guide to Civil War sites in Vermont

✦ Brandon Museum at the Stephen A. Douglas Birthplace

The museum provides information on the local antislavery movement, as well as Stephen A. Douglas, who lost to Lincoln in the 1860 presidential election.

LOCATION: **4 Grove St. (Rte. 7), Brandon, 802-247-6401, www.brandon.org/the-brandon-museum.**

✦ Equinox Resort and Spa

Over its 200 years of history, this hotel has hosted many distinguished guests, including First Lady Mary Todd Lincoln, who stayed here with her two sons in mid-1864.

LOCATION: **3567 Main St. (Rte. 7A), Manchester Village, 800-362-4747, www.equinoxresort.com.**

✦ Hildene

The only son of the Lincoln family to live to adulthood, Robert Todd Lincoln built this home at the turn of the 20th century. Direct descendants lived at the property until 1975.

LOCATION: **1005 Hildene Rd., Manchester, 802-362-1788, www.hildene.org.**

✦ Lakeview Cemetery

A host of Vermont's Civil War greats have been laid to rest here, including Lakeview's most famous resident, George Stannard, who commanded the flank attack that broke up Pickett's Charge at Gettysburg. Other notable burials include Medal of Honor recipients William Wells, George Evans Davis, and William W. Henry.

LOCATION: **South of Burlington High School off North Ave. in northwest Burlington.**

✦ National Museum of the Morgan Horse

Due to its stamina, endurance, and muscular structure, the Morgan horse was preferred by many cavalrymen on both sides of the war. This unique museum features extensive information on its vital role in the Civil War.

LOCATION: 34 Main St., Middlebury, 802-388-1639, www.morganhorse.com/museum.

✦ Norwich University, Sullivan Museum and History Center

Outside of West Point (see p. 379), no Northern school produced more officers than Norwich University, whose museum has rotating displays on the Civil War.

LOCATION: 158 Harmon Dr., Northfield, 802-485-2183, http://academics.norwich.edu/museum.

✦ President Calvin Coolidge State Historic Site

The historically preserved village of Plymouth Notch gives visitors a better sense of the 30th president, who was profoundly influenced by the Civil War.

LOCATION: 3780 Rte. 100A, Plymouth, 802-672-3773, www.historicsites.vermont.gov.

✦ Rokeby Museum

This museum houses Vermont's most extensive display on antislavery activities in the Civil War. A permanent exhibit on the Underground Railroad tells the story of two slaves who found shelter at Rokeby, which served as a Vermont station, in the 1830s.

LOCATION: 4334 Rte. 7, Ferrisburgh, 802-877-3406, www.rokeby.org.

✦ St. Albans Historical Society and Historical Museum

This museum commemorates the enthralling story of the St. Albans Raid, a plot orchestrated by the Confederate Secret Service in retribution for the Union's burning of several Southern cities.

LOCATION: 9 Church St., St. Albans, 802-527-7933, www.stamuseum.org.

FURTHER READING
The St. Albans Raid: Confederate Attack on Vermont
by Michelle Sherburne
An historical account of the infamous raid

✦ Tunbridge

This small town—a must-see 19th-century time capsule listed on the National Register of Historic Sites—was home to Union officer Frank Haskell, who wrote the most famous eyewitness account of the Battle of Gettysburg. Today, it is home to the most widely read monthly newspaper about the Civil War, *Civil War News.*

LOCATION: About 30 miles south of Montpelier in Orange County, Vermont, on VT Rte. 110, www.tunbridgevt.com.

✦ Vermont Heritage Galleries

Featuring flags, photographs, and impressive panoramas of Civil War battle scenes, the permanent exhibit here explains how the Civil War dramatically changed the villages of Vermont.

LOCATION: 60 Washington St., Barre, 802-479-8500, www.vermonthistory.org.

Civil War graves at the First Congregational Church of Bennington in Vermont

The Midwest

"Hardscrabble" was the name of
the cabin home built by Ulysses S.
Grant in St. Louis, Missouri.

Milestones

> JANUARY 12, 1863
In response to the Emancipation Proclamation, Davis promises to return captured black soldiers to slavery.

> MARCH 6, 1863
Riots in Detroit target blacks, who are blamed for the war and viewed as a threat to whites' jobs.

> APRIL 2, 1863
Facing hostile women during the Richmond Bread Riot, Davis turns out his pockets to show he is giving them everything he has.

> APRIL 24, 1863
The U.S. government issues General Orders No. 100, the Lieber Code, which defines permissible conduct in war.

> JULY 3, 1863
Lee's offensive is turned back at Gettysburg, his first important battlefield defeat.

> JULY 4, 1863
The surrender of Vicksburg reopens the Mississippi River for commerce.

> JULY 13-17, 1863
New York Draft Riots again target blacks, who replaced striking Irishmen on New York docks.

> AUGUST 21-22, 1863
Confederate guerrilla William Quantrill sacks Lawrence, Kansas, murdering 180.

> SEPTEMBER 5, 1863
England seizes Laird rams being built in Liverpool for the Confederate Navy.

> NOVEMBER 19, 1863
In declaring a "New Birth of Freedom" at Gettysburg, Lincoln publicly redefines his war aims.

Go West, Young Man

By the controversial 1850s, the focus of national growth and prosperity had turned decisively to the western boundaries of the country. What army the United States had was sparsely distributed along the western divide that was Illinois, Missouri, Arkansas, Texas, Iowa, and Minnesota. The discovery of gold in California ushered in rapid and practically uncontrolled expansion westward. A compromise in 1850 played the few political wild cards still available on the national stage.

Not surprisingly, issues such as slavery and commerce dominated the national dialogue. An old and venerated party, the Whigs, disappeared and were replaced by a new progressive party known as the Republicans, whose standard-bearers were Westerners. The dominant senator, Stephen A. Douglas of Illinois, was head of the territories committee. The great debate of the ages took place between Douglas and a new Republican, Abraham Lincoln.

Dred Scott, "Bleeding Kansas," John Brown, and the transcontinental railroad all took center stage—the issues of the West were the issues of America, and it was here that the Civil War began to percolate.

The 630-foot Gateway Arch in St. Louis, Missouri, frames the Old Courthouse, where the Dred Scott case was heard.

North Dakota

Killdeer Mountain ✴

Dead Buffalo Lake ✴ ✴ **Big Mound**
Stony Lake ✴

Whitestone Hill ✴

Minnesota

Wood Lake ✴   St. Paul ●

✴ **Fort Ridgely**

MAP KEY
✴ Confederate victory
✴ Union victory
✴ Inconclusive
● City

0 mi   200
0 km   200
Present-day boundaries are shown.

Iowa

Des Moines ●

Mt. Zion Church

Lexington I   **Kirksville** ✴
Lexington II

Independence I   **Roan's**
Independence II   **Tan Yard**
                          Glasgow ✴
Liberty
Little Blue River ✴
Lawrence ✴   **Lone Boonville**
Westport ✴   **Jack**
Byram's Ford
Marais des Cygnes ✴   Missouri
Mine Creek ✴   **Marmiton River**
                          Springfield I
Dry Wood Creek ✴   **Springfield II**

K a n s a s

Carthage
Baxter Springs ✴
Newtonia II ✴   **Wilson's Creek** ✴
Chustenahlah ✴   **Newtonia I** ✴
Cabin Creek ✴   **Clark's Mill** ✴
Round Mountain ✴ ✴**Chusto-**   **Old Fort Wayne**
              Talasah   **Hartville**

Honey Springs ✴

O k l a h o m a

Middle Boggy Depot ✴

388

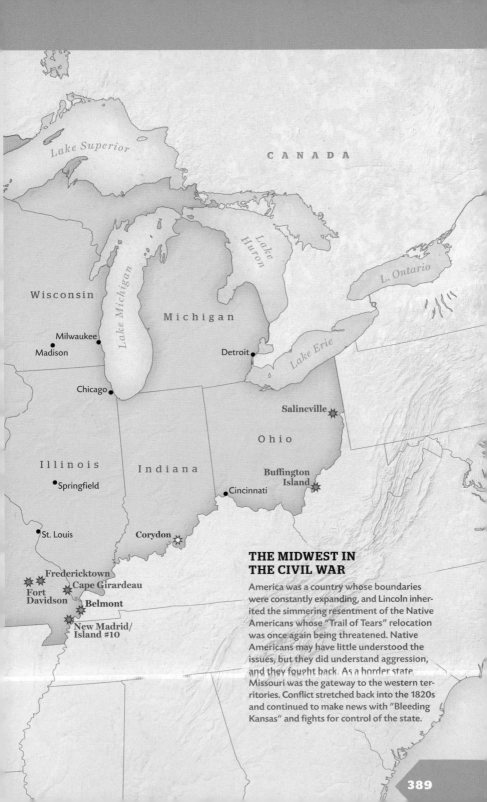

Lake Superior

CANADA

Lake Huron

L. Ontario

Wisconsin

Michigan

Lake Michigan

Milwaukee

Madison

Detroit

Lake Erie

Chicago

Salineville

Ohio

Illinois

Indiana

Springfield

Buffington Island

Cincinnati

St. Louis

Corydon

Fredericktown

Cape Girardeau

Fort Davidson

Belmont

New Madrid/ Island #10

THE MIDWEST IN THE CIVIL WAR

America was a country whose boundaries were constantly expanding, and Lincoln inherited the simmering resentment of the Native Americans whose "Trail of Tears" relocation was once again being threatened. Native Americans may have little understood the issues, but they did understand aggression, and they fought back. As a border state, Missouri was the gateway to the western territories. Conflict stretched back into the 1820s and continued to make news with "Bleeding Kansas" and fights for control of the state.

Indiana and Ohio

A RIVER OF DREAMS AND A PRIMARY VEHICLE FOR COMMERCE, the Ohio River represented the dividing line between North and South. President Lincoln, recognizing the difficult problem he would face if Confederate forces crossed the river into the Midwest, focused on Kentucky, playing the state until the Confederates made a misstep and violated its neutrality. Sealing Kentucky to the Union provided a critical buffer between this economically prolific region and the rebellious South.

Indiana and Ohio represented something else: a land of freedom and opportunity for refugee slaves, conducted here by courageous and morally troubled Americans who were primarily Quakers. The two states were also significant sources of leadership, manpower, and anxiety for the Lincoln Administration. With men such as Grant, Sherman, and others, Ohio was the new Virginia and fountain of victory. As the South closed off economic traffic downriver, Lincoln worked with Midwestern governors to keep their states in the Union. In the end, Indiana and Ohio proved critical to the Union's victory.

The "Freedom Stairway" leads from the Ohio River up to the Rankin House, a station on the Underground Railroad.

INDIANA BATTLES

✳ Corydon

CAMPAIGN: Morgan's Raid in Kentucky, Indiana, and Ohio

DATE(S): July 9, 1863

The Confederacy counted many flamboyant and successful cavalry officers among its ranks, one of whom was General Morgan. One of the romantic figures of the war, Morgan married in the midst of the conflict in a much celebrated nuptial event attended by high-ranking Confederate officers.

With Federal troops penetrating the Cumberland Plateau on what is known as the Tullahoma Campaign, Morgan attempted to derail the Union plan by entering on an extended raid north of the Ohio River. Accompanied by more than 2,000 Confederate cavalrymen, Morgan rode into Kentucky, where he and his men encountered Union troops at Tebb's Bend on July 4. They went on to capture the garrison at Lebanon, Kentucky. On July 8, Morgan

crossed the Ohio River at Mauckport, Indiana, defying orders to stay in Kentucky. The next day, near Corydon, Indiana, Morgan's force met about 400 Indiana Home Guards. In the battle, the Rebels captured more than 300 Yankees, who were greatly outnumbered. Resupplied and confident, the Confederates headed toward Ohio.

The battlefield is now a small county park with interpretive signs. Take an easy wooded walk and see a replica Civil War cannon. The park has no facilities.

LOCATION: Battle of Corydon Memorial Park, 100 Old Hwy. 135 S.W., Corydon, 812-738-8236, www.harrisoncountyparks.com.

FURTHER READING

The Longest Raid of the Civil War
by Lester V. Horwitz
Recounts Morgan's little-known raid into Kentucky, Indiana, and Ohio

✷ Buffington Island

CAMPAIGN: Morgan's Raid in Kentucky, Indiana, and Ohio

DATE(S): July 19, 1863

General Morgan's raid—conducted in contravention of the orders of his commanding officer, General Bragg—crossed the Ohio River on July 8, 1863. Following a skirmish at Corydon, Indiana (see p. 392), Morgan's troops worked across southern Ohio, causing panic and confusion about their destination while destroying supplies, food, and bridges. On July 19, having found little support for their cause in Ohio, Morgan's men began looking for an exit from the state. They found just that in Meigs County at a ford in the Ohio River known as Portland. Ohio soldiers held the crossing, and Morgan planned an attack. Pursuing Union cavalry caught up with the column, however, and, as

Morgan's men began to cross, they attacked. It was a disaster for Morgan, who lost two-thirds of his men—nearly 900. The Federals lost about two dozen. Morgan escaped upriver with about 400 men but without his supply wagons.

The small park has interpretive markers.

LOCATION: Buffington Island State Memorial Park, 55890 State Rte. 124, Portland, 866-363-2652, www.stateparks.com/buffington_island .html.

FURTHER READING

Rebel Raider: The Life of General John Hunt Morgan
by James A. Ramage
A balanced biography of the famous Confederate general as a revolutionary guerrilla chief

Patriarch of the Fighting McCooks of Ohio

✳ Salineville

CAMPAIGN: Morgan's Raid in Kentucky, Indiana, and Ohio

DATE(S): July 26, 1863

After a week under pursuit, General Morgan and his Confederates approached Smith's Ford in the hopes of finally crossing the Ohio River. Union troops surrounded them before they could reach it, and Morgan had to surrender. The general and several of his key subordinates were sent to the state penitentiary in Columbus, from which they escaped in November 1863.

During the raid, Morgan and his men diverted tens of thousands of troops from other duties, captured and paroled about 6,000 Union soldiers and militia, destroyed 34 bridges, and disrupted the railroads in more than 60 locations.

LOCATION: Markers commemorating Morgan's raid can be found in Monroeville, at the intersection of OH Rte. 164 and County Rd. 55, and on Salineville Rd. N.E. (OH Rte. 39), east of Oasis Rd. N.E., approximately 3.4 miles west of Salineville. A marker commemorating Morgan's surrender can be found in West Point, on OH Rte. 518, a quarter mile east of local Hwy. 784.

Other Battles and Beyond

Indiana

✦ General Lew Wallace Study and Museum

General Lew Wallace fought in several important battles of the Civil War, including a much maligned role at Shiloh (see pp. 199–202). After the war, he served the government in various ways, including as governor of the New Mexico Territory, where he encountered Billy the Kid, in addition to writing the best-selling novel of the 19th century, *Ben-Hur: A Tale of Christ*. His study and carriage house in Crawfordsville are now a museum exhibiting artifacts both personal and related to his literary legacy.

LOCATION: **200 Wallace Ave., Crawfordsville, 765-362-5769, www.ben-hur.com.**

FURTHER READING

Shadow of Shiloh: Major General Lew Wallace in the Civil War
by Gail Stephens
A biography of this fascinating, multifaceted American character with a spotlight on Shiloh

✦ Lincoln Boyhood National Memorial

This National Park Service site is where President Abraham Lincoln lived from age 7 to 21. See a short film and exhibits at the visitor center, visit the cabin site, enjoy the (seasonally open) Lincoln Living Historical Farm (which includes rangers in period clothing depicting life in the 1820s), and walk the path to see the grave of Nancy Hanks Lincoln, his mother.

LOCATION: **Off IN Hwy. 162, 43 miles from Evansville, 812-937-4541, www.nps.gov/libo.**

Ohio

✦ *Morgan's Raid Across Ohio: The Civil War Guidebook of the John Hunt Morgan Heritage Trail*

Read and follow the official guide, written by Lora Schmidt Cahill and David L. Mowery, to this dramatic Ohio Civil War story. You will pass 56 interpretive signs and travel more than 557 miles. Interesting anecdotal information rounds out the experience. To order a copy, visit www.lulu.com.

✦ John P. Parker Museum

Born a slave, John P. Parker purchased his freedom and moved north. He became a successful businessman who doubled as an

The General Lew Wallace Study and Museum spotlights the writing of *Ben-Hur*.

agent and conductor on the Underground Railroad, of which the museum was once an important station.

LOCATION: **300 N. Front St., Ripley, 937-392-4188, www.johnparkerhouse.org. The Rankin House is nearby, at 6152 Rankin Hill Rd.**

✦ Johnson's Island

The Confederate officers' prisoner-of-war camp here held more than 15,000 men during its three years. In response to rumors of Confederate secret agents plotting to raid prison camps from Canada, field artillery was set up in an earthen fort and aimed at the camp. Easily reached from Ohio Route 2, the island is now a private residential area accessible by causeway (and toll). The site has been preserved, but the only area currently open to the public is the cemetery (no facilities). See the website for detailed driving directions.

LOCATION: **Visit the Johnson's Island information center at the Ohio Veterans Home, 3416 Columbus Ave., Sandusky, www.johnsonsisland .org.**

Underground Railroad

Kentucky was a slave state, and Ohio was a free state. The Ohio River divided slaves from freedom. Ohio has a major series of sites related to the Underground Railroad, a network of secret routes and safe houses that allowed blacks to escape from slavery and make their way to free states or Canada.

✦ National Underground Railroad and Freedom Center

The nation's premier Underground Railroad museum was founded on the banks of the Ohio River in 2004. Any serious effort to understand slavery, its role in the Civil War and American history, and its modern impact should include this site.

LOCATION: **50 E. Freedom Way, Cincinnati, 513-333-7739, www.freedomcenter.org. The Harriet Beecher Stowe House, where Stowe gathered inspiration to write *Uncle Tom's Cabin*, is located nearby, at 2950 Gilbert Ave.**

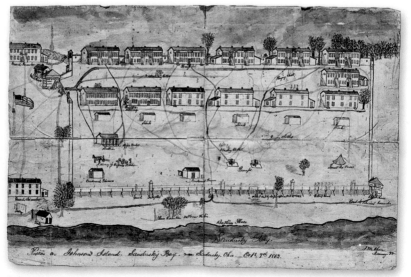

A drawing of the Johnson's Island prison, where more than 15,000 Confederates were held.

This humble house in Point Pleasant, Ohio, was the birthplace of Ulysses S. Grant.

✦ Oberlin College and Conservatory

The first American institution of higher learning to regularly admit blacks and women, this liberal arts college and music conservatory was also the intellectual center for the abolitionist movement. Oberlin's first black student graduated in 1844.

LOCATION: **173 W. Lorain St., Oberlin, 440-775-8411, www.oberlin.edu.**

✦ Rutherford B. Hayes Presidential Center

President Hayes was the beneficiary of the 1876 Tilden-Hayes deal, which ended Radical Reconstruction. The House of Representatives elected Hayes in exchange for ending Reconstruction in the South and reconstructing the states. This center includes Hayes's home as well as his and his wife's graves.

LOCATION: **Spiegel Grove State Park, Hayes Ave., Fremont, 419-332-2081, www.rbhayes .org.**

✦ Sherman House Museum

Both William T. Sherman, Grant's trusted subordinate and one of the most important officers in the Union service, and his brother, John Sherman, a U.S. senator, were born in this frame home originally built in 1811. After the death of their father in 1829, the Sherman brothers were adopted by Thomas Ewing, whose family includes several Civil War generals.

LOCATION: **137 E. Main St., Lancaster, 740-687-5891, www.shermanhouse.org. The privately owned Ewing house is located nearby.**

✦ Ulysses S. Grant's Birthplace

The man who won the war for the North was born on April 27, 1822, in a humble one-room house on the banks of the Ohio River. He grew up in nearby Georgetown on East Grant Avenue and attended a school on Water Street.

LOCATION: **1551 OH Rte. 232 (US 52), Point Pleasant, 513-553-4911, www.historicnr.org /grantsbirthplace.html.**

Kansas

"BLEEDING KANSAS" DRAMATICALLY AFFECTED THE MOOD of the country. The Kansas-Nebraska Act of 1854 brought to prominence the aspirations and political acuity of the "Little Giant," Senator Stephen A. Douglas. He became the darling of the South by advocating that the residents of territories should decide the issue of slavery for themselves.

Pro-slavery forces poured across the border to stuff ballot boxes, while high-principled abolitionists funded settlers who opposed slavery. The result was a menagerie of like-minded people clustered around Lawrence and Lecompton. In defiance of Douglas and the popular sovereignty principles he advocated, President James Buchanan accepted and supported a fraudulent pro-slavery constitution. Douglas's opposition cost him the backing of the South and the presidency in 1860.

The real tragedy is that innocent men and women bled. John Brown and his sons murdered slaveholding farmers, and pro-slavery men sacked Lawrence and brought a degree of lawlessness that gripped the nation.

Notorious abolitionist John Brown advocated and practiced armed insurrection as a means to overthrow the institution of slavery.

KANSAS BATTLES

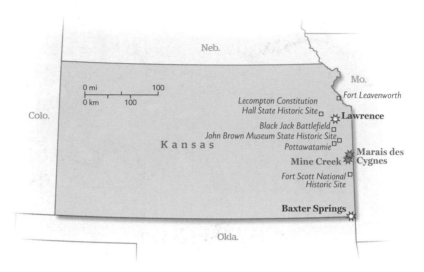

☀ Baxter Springs

CAMPAIGN: Occupation of Indian Territory North of the Arkansas River

OTHER NAME(S): Baxter Springs Massacre

DATE(S): October 6, 1863

Notorious Confederate raider William Quantrill and his band of about 400 men decided to attack a post called Fort Blair (also known as Baxter). Quantrill sent one column to attack the fort, which was defended by mostly black Union soldiers. Refusing demands to surrender, the post commander repulsed the attack using a field howitzer. Quantrill's second column happened upon an unprepared column of Union soldiers moving from Fort Scott to Fort Smith in Arkansas and massacred more than 100 of them. Realizing he could not take Fort Baxter, Quantrill continued toward Texas. This vicious encounter was indicative of the Kansas-Missouri border warfare.

LOCATION: Marker located on Frontier Military Byway (US 69 Alt.), 2 miles north of Baxter Springs. For a driving tour related to this battle, see page 402.

☀ Lawrence

CAMPAIGN: Quantrill's Raid Into Kansas

DATE(S): August 21, 1863

Lawrence was the center of the Free State movement in the Kansas Territory. Before dawn on August 21, 1863, Quantrill and about 400 of his Confederate raiders surprised the town. They ransacked homes, burned a quarter of the town's buildings (including the Eldridge Hotel, center of life in antebellum Lawrence), looted stores, and killed nearly 200, mostly unarmed, civilian men and boys. They specifically targeted Free State leaders and blacks but indiscriminately killed many others. The bloodiest incident in Kansas history, Quantrill's raid was purportedly in retaliation for a raid on Osceola, Missouri, by U.S. Senator James H. Lane and his infamous Jayhawkers.

LOCATION: Marker located at a roadside turnout on Tennessee St. (US 40) in Lawrence. Other markers and monuments can be found in town. Today, there is also a walking tour of the raid (see p. 402).

FURTHER READING

Bloody Dawn: The Story of the Lawrence Massacre
by Thomas Goodrich
A spellbinding recounting of this brutal raid

❉ Marais des Cygnes

CAMPAIGN: Price's Missouri Expedition
DATE(S): October 25, 1864

In October 1864, Confederate General Price entered Missouri on an extended raid. After several weeks of riding, he was defeated at the Battle of Westport. Short of supplies and support, Price turned back toward Arkansas. While attempting to cross the Marais des Cygnes River, he was fired on by artillery. This is also the location of the Marais des Cygnes Massacre of 1858, an ugly and representative action of the period and region (see p. 403).

LOCATION: **Marker located on Frontier Military Byway (US 69), half a mile north of Trading Post.**

FURTHER READING

Jennison's Jayhawkers: A Civil War Cavalry Regiment and Its Commander
by Stephen Z. Starr
A fine account of the genesis, activities, and character of the 7th Kansas Volunteer Cavalry

❉ Mine Creek

CAMPAIGN: Price's Missouri Expedition
DATE(S): October 25, 1864

General Price extracted himself from the banks of the Marais des Cygnes River only to be attacked as he tried to cross Mine Creek. After losing more than 600 men and supply wagons, he hurried out of Kansas and back to Arkansas. Well-interpreted Mine Creek

"Bleeding Kansas"

The Kansas-Nebraska Act of 1854 authorized the organization of new states from spacious federal lands. In a major departure from the Missouri Compromise of 1820, it was left up to the individual states to determine whether slavery would be permitted. Southerners, who saw new opportunities in the ore-rich territories, welcomed the idea of popular sovereignty. Implementation was chaotic as pro-slavery supporters from bordering Missouri (a slave state) flooded into Kansas on election days, setting up a rivalry with antislavery proponents. The conflict escalated into the violence known as "Bleeding Kansas."

Civil War Battlefield State Historic Site has a visitor center and self-guided trail.

LOCATION: **Mine Creek Civil War Battlefield State Historic Site, 20845 K52, Pleasanton, 913-352-8890, www.kshs.org/mine_creek.**

FURTHER READING

General Sterling Price and the Civil War in the West
by Albert Castel
An excellent introduction to the war in the West

This seal emblematizes popular sovereignty.

Other Battles and Beyond

✦ Baxter Springs Massacre and Fort Blair Driving Tour

This self-guided driving tour will take you to 12 different spots, ending at the cemetery (for battle details, see p. 400). Pick up a tour map and check out the exhibits at Baxter Spring Heritage Center and Museum (740 East Ave., Baxter Springs, 620-856-2385, www.baxterspringsmuseum.org).

✦ Quantrill's Lawrence Raid Walking Tour

This self-guided walking tour starts at the Miller Farm site, where the first person was killed. For a map and brochure, stop at the Lawrence Visitor Center (402 N. 2nd St., Lawrence, 758-856-3040), or visit www.kansastravel.org/quantrillslawrence raid.htm for a partial guide.

✦ Black Jack

Many people believe the Civil War began here on June 2, 1856. Free State forces under the command of radical abolitionist John Brown attacked a camp of pro-slavery forces who had been hunting Brown since the Pottawatamie Massacre (see p. 403). Partially interpreted, this site features a self-guided walking tour.

LOCATION: **Adjacent to Robert Hall Pearson Memorial Park, 163 E. 2000 Rd., Wellsville, 785-883-2106, www.blackjackbattlefield.org.**

✦ Fort Leavenworth

Established in 1827, this is one of the Army's oldest and most important outposts. Check in at the Visitor Control Center, and then start your tour at the Frontier Army Museum. From there, visit Leavenworth National Cemetery, where General Custer's brother Tom, a double Medal of Honor recipient, is buried. A self-guided tour of

Buffalo Soldier Memorial Park is available online or at the museum.

LOCATION: **881 McClellan Ave., Fort Leavenworth, 913-684-3523, http://garrison.leaven worth.army.mil.**

✦ Fort Scott National Historic Site

One of the most important frontier fortifications, Fort Scott was headquarters of the Union Army of the Frontier and refuge for settlers threatened by Confederate raiders. Here, Free Soil Senator James Lane recruited and fielded the 1st Kansas Colored Infantry, the first to fight in the war at nearby Battle of Island Mound State Historic Site (see p. 429).

LOCATION: **Downtown Fort Scott, intersection of US 54 and US 69, www.nps.gov/fosc.**

✦ John Brown Museum State Historic Site

Museum displays tell the story of John Brown, the Adairs, and local abolitionists.

Quantrill's raid on Lawrence, Kansas, left the town in ruins.

John Brown and followers massacre five slave owners at Pottawatamie Creek, Kansas, in 1856.

Highlights include a John Brown statue and the Adair Log Cabin, where Brown lived.

LOCATION: **John Brown Park, 10th and Main Sts., Osawatamie, 913-755-4384, www.kshs .org/john_brown.**

✦ Lecompton Constitution Hall State Historic Site

In the fall of 1857, a convention here drafted a constitution that would have admitted Kansas as a slave state. After intense national debate, the Lecompton Constitution was rejected. However, the controversy helped stoke the fire that flamed into the Civil War. At this well-preserved site, you can see the constitution and other exhibits relating to the Kansas Territorial government.

LOCATION: **319 Elmore St., Lecompton, 785-887-6520, www.kansastravel.org /constitutionhall.htm.**

✦ Marais des Cygnes Massacre State Historic Site

On May 19, 1858, a band of pro-slavery raiders crossed into Kansas from Missouri, capturing 11 Free Staters along the way. Five were shot and killed here. This event was the last significant act of violence in "Bleeding Kansas" prior to the outbreak of the Civil War.

LOCATION: **Four miles northeast of Trading Post via K52 E., 913-352-8890, www.kshs.org /marais.**

✦ Pottawatamie

Kansas was called "Bleeding Kansas" for good cause. Here on May 24, 1856, John Brown and his sons killed five pro-slavery farmers in retaliation for the sacking of Lawrence. Three years later, Brown brought his harsh vengeance to the East and Harpers Ferry (see p. 314).

LOCATION: **This unmarked site is in Franklin County, just north of Pottawatamie Creek and the town of Lane.**

FURTHER READING

Bleeding Kansas: Contested Liberty in the Civil War Era by Nicole Etcheson Sheds light on the ideological origins of the Civil War

Minnesota and North Dakota

WHILE THE UNITED STATES FACED THE TURBULENT 1850s, the country was expanding. In 1858, Minnesota became the 32nd state. Minnesota was wild country, popular for hunting and trapping. Fort Snelling was created to protect settlers, who moved to the state when treaties were made with the Dakota Indian tribes.

Motivated by fear, the government offered rewards for good behavior to local Indians, who came to rely on the cash and supplies provided by Uncle Sam. Once the Civil War reached Minnesota, however, shipments and payments to the tribes were sometimes delayed. In 1862, after another treaty payment was late, the Dakota rebelled. Soon, more than 500 settlers were massacred along the Minnesota River. Order was eventually restored and the renegades forced into the unorganized territory (North Dakota). Within a year, the white soldiers would also force them from these remote environments. The Great Sioux War had begun.

Sitting Bull, chief of the Sioux, had to flee Sibley's raid at Killdeer Mountain.

❋ Fort Ridgely

CAMPAIGN: Operations to Suppress the Sioux Uprising

DATE(S): August 20, 22, 1862

The federal government had failed to pay annuities, and the ration quality was poor, so the Santee Sioux under Chief Little Crow went on the offensive in August 1862. They killed approximately 500 settlers and soldiers, took many prisoners, and caused extensive property damage. White settlers sought refuge at Fort Ridgely. When post commander Captain Marsh and his men set out for the Lower Sioux Agency, a large Sioux force surprised them. Half the white men, including Marsh, were killed. The Sioux attacked the fort again on August 20 and 22 but were repulsed.

Well-interpreted Fort Ridgely State Park boasts excellent views across the plains.

LOCATION: Fort Ridgely State Park, 72158 County Rd. 30, Fairfax, 507-426-7840, www.dnr.state.mn.us/state_parks/fort _ridgely/index.html.

FURTHER READING

The Dakota War of 1862: Minnesota's Other Civil War by Kenneth Carley A balanced account with ancillary materials

❋ Wood Lake

CAMPAIGN: Operations to Suppress the Sioux Uprising

DATE(S): September 23, 1862

On September 19, Colonel Sibley and 1,500 volunteers set out from Fort Ridgely to put down the Santee uprising. Chief Little Crow and his men ambushed their encampment.

White settlers took refuge from the Santee Sioux at Fort Ridgely, Minnesota, in 1862.

On September 23, Sibley inflicted heavy casualties on the Sioux and was promoted to brigadier general.

Wood Lake Battlefield, an uninterpreted site, consists of a memorial stone and an area indicating Sibley's encampment.

LOCATION: **Wood Lake Battlefield, 4210 57th St. N.W., Rochester, 507-280-9970, www.wood lakebattlefield.com.**

FURTHER READING

Little Crow
by Gary Clayton Anderson
The biography of Little Crow, who led his people in war for self-preservation

The Last Full Measure: The Life and Death of the First Minnesota Volunteers
by Richard Moe
A wonderfully told regimental history

Dakota War of 1862, or the Sioux Uprising

The bloody firefight that erupted in September 1862 required Abraham Lincoln's attention, the dispatch of a general, the trial of more than 400 Indians, and the largest mass execution in American history (38 Dakota). For years, late or unfair annuity payments and treaty violations had increased the hardship of the Dakota. The uprising was an escalation of an incident in which several Dakota Sioux murdered settlers near Acton. Many white men, women, and children were killed along the Minnesota River. Up to 800 civilians, 100 soldiers, and 150 Indians were murdered or killed in combat during this period. Ultimately, the Dakota were banished from Minnesota. And in an 1863 punitive expedition, they were also chased from what is today the state of North Dakota.

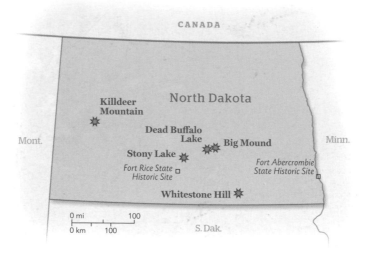

✳ Big Mound

CAMPAIGN: Operations Against the Sioux in North Dakota

DATE(S): July 24–25, 1863

The Dakota War was over, and the Sioux had been removed from Minnesota. Still, Federal forces were determined to drive the surviving Indian population from the Dakota Territory. General Pope sent out two columns, one along the Minnesota River under command of General Sibley and one along the Missouri River under command of General Sully. Sibley was to be the hammer, and Sully the anvil.

On July 24, 1863, Sibley caught up with a smaller force of Dakota. During a parlay, the Indians opened fire on the troops and killed the translator. Then Sibley's artillery dominated. The Indians fled toward Canada and the Southwest. U.S. soldiers lost 7, and the Indians nearly 100.

LOCATION: Big Mound Battlefield State Historic Site, 10 miles north of Tappen, off Country Rd. 71 (unpaved road, no interpretation), www.history.nd.gov/historicsites/sibleysully/bmb.html.

✳ Dead Buffalo Lake

CAMPAIGN: Operations Against the Sioux in North Dakota

DATE(S): July 26, 1863

On July 26, 1863, General Sibley continued his pursuit and found himself under attack by the Indians. Their attempts to get at Sibley's flanks failed when Sibley used his artillery. Casualties were light, and the Sioux were on the run.

LOCATION: Kidder County; no interpreted site.

✳ Killdeer Mountain

CAMPAIGN: Sully's Expedition Against the Sioux in Dakota Territory

DATE(S): July 28–29, 1864

Unsatisfied with the results of the 1863 expeditions, General Sibley returned. When he and the group of gold speculators who accompanied him came across an Indian encampment, they opened fire and destroyed the camp. The Indians—including Sitting Bull—fled. Killdeer Mountain both broke the back of the Sioux resistance and helped to foment the conflict that erupted on the northern plains in the late 1860s.

The pristine battle site has a marker and several headstones but no interpretation.

LOCATION: **Dunn County, located about 8.5 miles northwest of Killdeer.**

✴ Stony Lake

CAMPAIGN: Operations Against the Sioux in North Dakota

DATE(S): July 28, 1863

While General Sibley rested his troops and their horses, he discovered a large number of Sioux moving upon him. He pursued them to the Missouri River, where some Indians trying to cross were slaughtered or drowned. Sibley's indiscriminate engagement of Indians who were not part of the Dakota removal inflamed attitudes and contributed to the subsequent Northern Plains Indian wars that would consume the region for another three decades.

LOCATION: **Burleigh County; no interpreted site.**

✴ Whitestone Hill

CAMPAIGN: Operations Against the Sioux in North Dakota

DATE(S): September 3–5, 1863

General Sully and 1,200 men arrived after General Sibley had left for Minnesota. Sully's scouts, accompanied by members of the 6th Iowa Cavalry, entered a Sioux camp and demanded they surrender. As the Sioux families fled, soldiers engaged the men, later destroying foodstuffs, supplies, and tepees. Hundreds of Sioux and a small number of soldiers were killed. This engagement weakened Native American resistance in the area.

Today, there are memorials to the Sioux and soldiers, as well as a small museum.

LOCATION: **Just off Rte. 56 in Dickey County, about 6 miles southwest of Merrricourt. Use caution on the severe turn before the entrance.**

The Battle of Killdeer Mountain helped foment conflict with the Sioux in the late 1860s.

Other Battles and Beyond

Minnesota

✦ Minnesota River Valley Mobile Tour

The Minnesota Historical Society has highlighted 13 stops relating to Dakota life and the U.S.-Dakota War of 1862. To download the 32-page brochure, visit www.usdakota war.org/mobiletour. Or call 888-601-3010 to listen to the stories.

✦ Birch Coulee

This was one of the hardest fought and most decisive battles of the U.S.-Dakota War of 1862. The battlefield and vegetation are fully preserved. A self-guided tour with a paved path and interpretive signs explains the action from the perspectives of both the U.S. soldiers and the Dakota.

LOCATION: **Birch Coulee Battlefield, intersection of Hwy. 2 and Hwy. 18, Morton, 800-657-3773, www.mnhs.org.**

FURTHER READING
Birch Coulie: The Epic Battle of the Dakota War by John Christgau Provides insight into this critical historic moment in the American West

✦ Camp Release State Monument

The Dakota Uprising ended here, with the release of 280 hostages and the surrender of 1,200 Dakota. A military tribunal held here condemned 303 Dakota to death, many after trials as short as five minutes. President Lincoln commuted all but 39 of the death sentences.

LOCATION: **Just off Hwy. 212 in Montevideo.**

✦ Fort Snelling and Fort Snelling National Cemetery

This well-maintained fortification was a staging area for soldiers fighting in the Dakota War and the Civil War. While originally the location of an Indian agency, it became a camp to hold some 1,600 Dakota prisoners. This seasonal site has a visitor center, costumed staff, and interpretive signs. Don't miss Dred Scott's Quarters (see sidebar below). More than 200,000 people are buried in the 1870 cemetery, including 7 Medal of Honor recipients.

LOCATION: **200 Tower Ave., St. Paul, 612-726-1171, www.historicfortsnelling.org.**

✦ Lower Sioux Agency (Redwood Agency)

Here, the Dakota Uprising accelerated. The failure of the U.S. government to provide

---

Dred Scott at Fort Snelling

The fort has a direct and important connection to the famous *Dred Scott* court decision. Throughout the 1820s and 1830s, there were about 15 to 20 slaves at the fort at any given time, violating the Missouri Compromise of 1820. After living for four years as officers' slaves, the Scotts eventually ended up as slaves in St. Louis. There, they sued for their freedom based on the fact that they had lived as enslaved people in a free territory. After an initial ruling that freed them, the Scotts were declared slaves once again when the Supreme Court heard their case on appeal. This decision inflamed the national debate about slavery and helped push the nation toward the Civil War.

the food needed and owed under treaty led the Sioux to riot and murder the sutlers encamped around the agency. This site has three walking trails with interpretive signs.

LOCATION: 32469 Hwy. 2, Morton, 507-697-6321, http://sites.mnhs.org/historic-sites/lower-sioux-agency.

✦ Minnesota Military Museum

This museum is located on the site of the old Fort Ripley, which sheltered settlers during the 1862 uprising. Also currently a National Guard Bureau headquarters, the site honors the long and glorious history of fighting Minnesotans.

LOCATION: Camp Ripley, 15000 Hwy. 115, Little Falls, 320-616-6050, www.mnmilitarymuseum.org.

✦ New Ulm

Here, the U.S.-Dakota War of 1862 came to the very streets of the town. Interpretive signs with instructive paintings help visualize the drama. Three structures remain: the Forster House (117 N. Broadway), used as a fortified defensive point by the residents of the town; the Kiesling House (220 N. Minnesota St.), part of the earthworks at the edge of the town; and the Erd Building (108 N. Minnesota St.). Other points of interest include the Brown County Historical Society and the New Ulm Monument.

LOCATION: Visit the Chamber of Commerce at the intersection of Center St. and Minnesota St. to find out about historical podcasts and to borrow an iPod. Just outside town are two massacre sites: Milford on CR 29 has an impressive monument to the 52 settlers slaughtered there (8 miles west of New Ulm). At the Ravine, also on CR 29, a small stone monument marks the spot where soldiers crossing a bridge were ambushed by rampaging Indians (5 miles west of New Ulm).

✦ Sibley Historic Site

A successful fur trader and the first governor of Minnesota, Henry Hastings Sibley also played a critical role in the U.S.-Dakota War

of 1862. This historic site includes four structures that illustrate the history of the state.

LOCATION: 1357 Sibley Memorial Hwy., Mendota Heights, 651-452-1596, http://sites.mnhs.org/historic-sites/sibley-historic-site.

✦ Upper Sioux Agency (Yellow Medicine Agency)

Here is where Little Crow, leader of the rebellious Dakota, met with other Indian tribes but was unable to convince them to join his war. His next move was to ambush troops camped near Wood Lake. Failure there forced him to abandon the offensive, however, and escape toward current-day North Dakota. This multiuse state park has preserved the remains of the old agency.

LOCATION: Upper Sioux Agency State Park, on State Hwy. 67, 8.5 miles southeast of Granite Falls, 320-564-4777, www.dnr.state.mn.us/state_parks/upper_sioux_agency.

North Dakota

✦ Fort Abercrombie State Historic Site

During the Dakota Uprising of 1862, only four soldiers were killed at this fort, the westernmost outpost built to protect fearful settlers. Today, it has a museum, rebuilt buildings, and the original guardhouse.

LOCATION: Hwy. 22, Abercrombie, 701-328-2666, www.history.nd.gov/historicsites/abercrombie.

✦ Fort Rice State Historic Site

Fort Rice symbolized the escalation of the Indian fighting in the Dakota Territory. The site now is a series of ruins abandoned in 1878; building footprints are marked with stones. A single interpretative marker and a map are on-site (no facilities).

LOCATION: Off ND 1806 about 30 miles south of Mandan, 701-328-2666, www.history.nd.gov/historicsites/rice.

Missouri

CLAIMED BY BOTH SIDES, MISSOURI EMBODIED THE DIVISION of the Civil War, and Missourians fought on both sides. In fact, Julia Grant—wife of Ulysses S. Grant—was from a slaveholding Missouri family, and she owned slaves during the war. The state had long been a flash point. In St. Louis, Dred Scott sued for his freedom, leading to the infamous 1857 Supreme Court decision, which held that blacks had no rights that whites were obliged to respect and that slavery could not be restricted, directly inflaming passions in both North and South. When war broke out, Missouri had two separate governments, and neighbors and friends were pitted against one another to a degree found in few other states.

The wounds of the Civil War did not heal easily, and nowhere was this truer than in Missouri. Some argue that the Civil War did not fully end in Missouri until 1882 when Jesse James—the famous outlaw and Confederate guerrilla—was killed. Today, Missouri contains a wealth of Civil War–related sites, a lasting testament to this bloody and divisive conflict.

Border ruffians from Missouri enter "Bleeding Kansas" in an attempt to secure it as a slave state. Missouri was riven with division between Free-Soilers and slave owners.

MISSOURI BATTLES

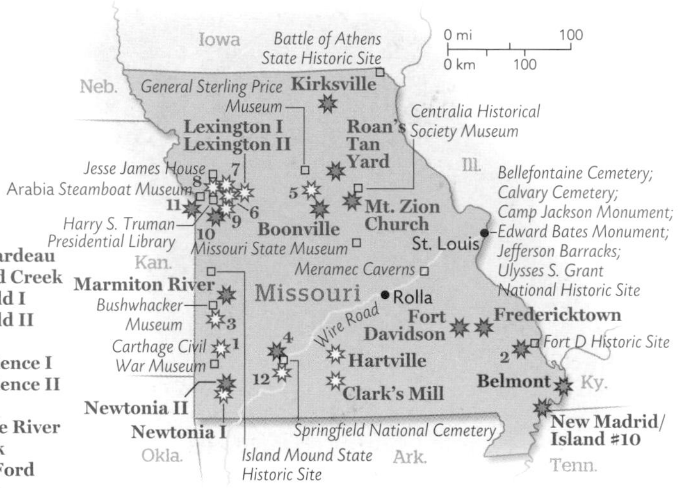

1 Carthage
2 Cape Girardeau
3 Dry Wood Creek
4 Springfield I
Springfield II
5 Glasgow
6 Independence I
Independence II
7 Liberty
8 Little Blue River
9 Lone Jack
10 Byram's Ford
11 Westport
12 Wilson's Creek

✲Belmont

CAMPAIGN: Operations at the Ohio and Mississippi River Confluence

DATE(S): November 7, 1861

General Grant intercepted Confederates at Belmont, Missouri, routing them and destroying supplies. A Southern counterattack forced Grant back to Paducah, Kentucky. The battlefield has not been interpreted nor is it open to the public.

LOCATION: Marker located at the intersection of Rte. 501 and Rte. 80 in Belmont. Head east on Rte. 80 for about 3.5 miles and then make a slight right. If you miss the slight right, do not fear. The road ends shortly thereafter, and you can simply turn around.

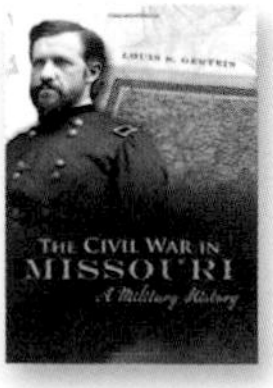

FURTHER READING

The Civil War in Missouri: A Military History

by Louis S. Gerteis

A look at Missouri's role in the war

✱ Boonville

CAMPAIGN: Operations to Control Missouri

DATE(S): June 17, 1861

Missouri, a slave border state, had significant secessionist leanings, from Governor Claiborne Jackson on down into the legislature. To quash any moves to join the rebellion, Union General Lyon moved to pacify the Missouri State Guard, led by Sterling Price. Union men attacked and defeated the Confederates at Boonville, helping ensure that Missouri would remain a Union state.

LOCATION: Markers located on E. Morgan Dr., just east of the intersection with Riverside Dr., in Boonville.

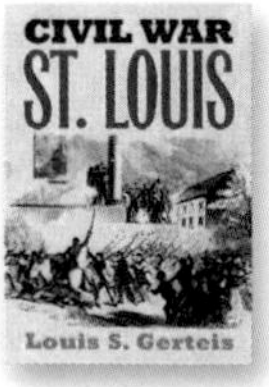

FURTHER READING

Civil War St. Louis

by Louis S. Gerteis

The history of St. Louis in the war between the states

* Byram's Ford

CAMPAIGN: Price's Missouri Expedition
DATE(S): October 22–23, 1864

Hoping to hurt Lincoln's reelection chances and restore his adopted state, General Price and his army of Confederate soldiers advanced toward Kansas City in an attempt to seize Missouri. Price's supply wagons, nearly 500 of them, safely forded the Big Blue River at Byram's Ford, while General Shelby's Confederates attacked Union lines in a diversion. General Pleasonton was hot on the Rebels' trail, however. The next day, his Union cavalry assaulted General Marmaduke's men at Byram's Ford and within three hours had pushed them back toward Westport. These actions, in addition to the contemporaneous Battle of Westport (see pp. 425–426), meant that Price was forced to retreat south and Confederate power in Missouri was forever broken.

LOCATION: **Marker and walking trail located in Big Blue Battlefield Park, E. 60th St., a fifth of a mile to the east of Colorado St. in Kansas City. A walking tour is available. Two other markers are located on Manchester Trafficway, just after the intersection with E. 63rd St. in Kansas City.**

* Cape Girardeau

CAMPAIGN: Marmaduke's Second Expedition Into Missouri
DATE(S): April 26, 1863

General McNeil, pursued by Confederate General Marmaduke, moved into fortifications near Cape Girardeau. Marmaduke, attempting to ascertain Federal strength, sent Colonel Shelby's brigade into a demonstration. The maneuver escalated into an attack that McNeil's Union troops repulsed. Marmaduke retreated to Jackson, having failed in his attempt not only to crush McNeil but also to relieve the pressure on other Confederate forces.

Today, Southeast Missouri State University occupies the core of the battlefield—Fort B. Although the preserved Fort D Historic Site (see p. 430) saw no action in this battle, it is nonetheless representative of similar defenses in the city and well worth a visit.

LOCATION: **Fort B marker located on the campus of Southeast Missouri State University, between Kent Library and Academic Hall, 1 University Plaza, Cape Girardeau, 573-651-2000, www.semo.edu.**

Although designed to sabotage Lincoln's reelection, the Confederate defeat at Byram's Ford instead meant that Missouri was solidly in Union hands.

The Battle of Carthage was the first major engagement for German revolutionary Franz Sigel, who was serving as a Union colonel at the time.

✳ Carthage

CAMPAIGN: Operations to Control Missouri

DATE(S): July 5, 1861

Although he had been chased from Jefferson City and Boonville, Secessionist Governor Claiborne Jackson still commanded a 6,000-man force of secessionists. Colonel Sigel and 1,000 Union troops pursued him. Realizing he outnumbered the Union force, Jackson enticed Sigel to attack.

As the fight ebbed and flowed into and out of the town center, Sigel received a report of a Confederate flanking movement that would overwhelm his force. Not knowing that the Confederate troops were unarmed, he pulled back into Carthage. Content with the victory, the Rebels did not pursue him.

The eight-acre Battle of Carthage State Historic Site has preserved the battlefield's Civil War appearance and features interpretive signs.

LOCATION: Battle of Carthage State Historic Site, Chestnut St. just east of the intersection with S. River St., Carthage, 417-751-3266, www.mostateparks.com/park/battle-carthage-state-historic-site.

FURTHER READING

The Battle of Carthage: Border War in Southwest Missouri, July 5, 1861 by David C. Hinze and Karen Farnham
An insightful look at the Battle of Carthage

✳ Clark's Mill

CAMPAIGN: Operations North of Boston Mountains

DATE(S): November 7, 1862

Hiram Barstow and approximately 100 men moved to meet the Confederates southeast of Clark's Mill. They skirmished with an initial force, which they pushed back. At Clark's

Mill, Barstow learned that another Confederate force was pursuing them from the northeast. Barstow placed artillery to protect himself from attack on two sides, but after five hours of fighting, he finally surrendered to the much larger, approximately 1,000-man, Rebel force.

LOCATION: **No public access.**

✸ Dry Wood Creek

CAMPAIGN: Operations to Control Missouri

DATE(S): September 2, 1861

Approximately 600 Union cavalry under politician turned colonel James H. Lane moved out of Fort Scott to find the Confederates who were supposedly nearby. They found 6,000 men, and despite taking the Rebels by surprise, the Union troops numbered too few and were forced to retreat.

LOCATION: **Marker referencing the battle (although not at the true battle location) located at the intersection of Old US 54 and US 54 in Deerfield.**

FURTHER READING
Jayhawkers: The Civil War Brigade of James H. Lane by Bryce Benedict A fascinating look at Lane's raids

✸ Fort Davidson

CAMPAIGN: Price's Missouri Expedition

DATE(S): September 27, 1864

General Price's Confederate forces intended to take the city of St. Louis; however, they encountered General Ewing's men near Fort Davidson. Numbering only 184, the Federals were outnumbered more than eight to one by the 1,500 Confederates, and so the Northerners retreated into the fort, which Price's men repeatedly attacked without the help of artillery, suffering many needless casualties. The Federals retreated during the night.

Today, the battlefield site has a visitor center, earthworks, and burial trenches.

LOCATION: **Battle of Pilot Knob State Historic Site, 118 E. Maple, Pilot Knob, 573-546-3454, www.mostateparks.com/park/battle-pilot -knob-state-historic-site.**

✸ Fredericktown

CAMPAIGN: Operations to Control Missouri

DATE(S): October 21, 1861

Confederate General Thompson moved out of Fredericktown as two columns of Union troops approached. Twelve miles from town, he parked his supplies and moved back, attacking the now Union-occupied town without first doing proper reconnaissance. Overwhelmed by the larger Union numbers, the Confederates retreated. This solidified the Union's control in southeastern Missouri.

LOCATION: **Battle of Fredericktown Civil War Museum, 156 S. Main St., Fredericktown, 573-576-8528, www.visitmo.com. No battlefield interpretation.**

✸ Glasgow

CAMPAIGN: Price's Missouri Expedition

DATE(S): October 15, 1864

Confederate forces sent by General Price moved to take Union supplies and arms in Glasgow, besieging the city and beginning an artillery barrage on the morning of October 15, 1864. Union forces were hard-pressed and moved to fortifications on Hereford Hill, above the town. Believing that further resistance was impossible, Union Colonel Harding surrendered to the Confederates.

The raid was valuable to the Rebels not only as a morale boost but also as a crucial supply cache. Despite this victory, the resulting campaign was still a failure as the Southerners were defeated at Westport (see pp. 425–426) one week later.

Stump Island Recreation Park preserves a relatively small portion of the battlefield,

"Bloody Bill" Anderson knotted a string after each kill. At his death he had 53 knots.

with no interpretation. A general marker in Glasgow briefly explains the battle.

LOCATION: **Stump Island Recreation Park, intersection of Old Hwy. 87 and Stump Island Dr., Glasgow. Marker located at the intersection of Bridge St. and Randolph St. in Glasgow.**

✴ Hartville

CAMPAIGN: Marmaduke's First Expedition Into Missouri

DATE(S): January 9–11, 1863

Colonel Porter's Confederate Missouri Cavalry Brigade attacked Union forces near Hartville, seizing the town before moving toward Marshfield. On January 10, Colonel Merrill's Union forces moved to Hartville and attacked the Rebels. Although they pushed back the Union forces, the Southerners suffered heavy losses and had to return to Confederate-held territory.

LOCATION: **Marker and Confederate mass grave located at Steele Cemetery, S. Main Ave., just south of the intersection with W. Marshfield St. in Hartville.**

✴ Independence I

CAMPAIGN: Operations North of Boston Mountains

DATE(S): August 11, 1862

Union forces under Colonel Buel occupying Independence were attacked by Confederate troops led by Colonel Hughes and Colonel Thompson, who assaulted the city from two directions. Buel and some of his Federals attempted to hold out in a building but were forced to surrender when the structure next to them caught on fire. After surrendering, around 150 Union soldiers were paroled.

LOCATION: **Marker located at the intersection of Truman Rd. and N. Main St. in Independence.**

✴ Independence II

CAMPAIGN: Price's Missouri Expedition

DATE(S): October 22, 1864

Union forces under General Pleasonton seized Independence before being met by General Marmaduke's Confederates just west of the city. The Rebels attacked the Federals with vigor, pushing them back.

LOCATION: **Marker at Jackson County Truman Historic Courthouse, 112 W. Lexington, Independence, 816-881-3000.**

✴ Kirksville

CAMPAIGN: Operations North of Boston Mountains

DATE(S): August 6–9, 1862

Union Colonel McNeil and his 1,000 troops had been searching for Colonel Porter and his 2,500 Confederate soldiers for more than a week. On August 6, 1862, they found what they were looking for and attacked the Confederates, some of whom were hiding among crops or in homes and stores in Kirksville. In the end, the Federals defeated the Southerners. Three days later a Union force killed Porter himself. The preserved battlefield is now part of Thousand Hills State Park. The 3,215-acre park features trails, a marina, dining facilities, and Native American petroglyphs.

LOCATION: **Thousand Hills State Park, 20431 MO 157, Kirksville, 660-665-6995, www.mostateparks.com/park/thousand-hills -state-park. Marker located at Adair County Courthouse, 106 W. Washington St., Kirksville.**

✴ Lexington I

CAMPAIGN: Operations to Control Missouri
DATE(S): September 13–20, 1861

General Price's Confederates moved on Lexington, skirmishing with Union troops on September 13, 1861. Union forces, behind fortifications, were not attacked again until September 18, when an artillery barrage and further attacks pushed the Federals back into their innermost defenses. Assaults on September 19 and 20 convinced Union forces to surrender, boosting the Confederate cause in the Missouri Valley. The battlefield has been preserved and today offers interpretive signs and a visitor center.

LOCATION: **Battle of Lexington State Historic Site, 1101 Delaware St., Lexington, 660-259-4654, www.mostateparks.com/park /battle-lexington-state-historic-site.**

✴ Lexington II

CAMPAIGN: Price's Missouri Expedition
DATE(S): October 19, 1864

Confederate soldiers under General Price moved to Lexington, dispersing Union pickets along the way and ultimately driving back Federal forces along the Independence Road. Under strength, the Union troops were unable to hold back the Confederates, but they did slow their advance, while also gaining information about the size and nature of the opposing forces.

The battle took place primarily in southern Lexington and along the bank of the Missouri River, but modern development means there are no commemorative areas open to the public.

LOCATION: **No public access.**

✴ Liberty

OTHER NAME(S): Blue Mills
CAMPAIGN: Operations to Control Missouri
DATE(S): September 17, 1861

Late in the morning, as Colonel Scott and his men moved toward Liberty, scouts found the Confederates. By 3 p.m., a full-scale battle was under way. Although Union troops had made the first strike, the Confederates rallied and pushed them back in a mere hour. Located at a bend in the Missouri River, eight miles northeast of Kansas City, the battlefield is now a mix of residential subdivisions and industrial-use areas.

LOCATION: **No public access.**

"Bloody Bill" Anderson

Infamous raider and somewhat of a mentor to a young Jesse James, William T. "Bloody Bill" Anderson (1840–1864) truly deserved his nickname. Born in Kentucky, Anderson began his streak of lawlessness in his home state, before moving to Missouri after his father was killed. He joined Quantrill's Raiders, a notorious bushwhacker group, and eventually came to command his own group of raiders, who wreaked havoc on Union soldiers and sympathizers in Missouri. He was responsible for the Centralia Massacre, in which more than 100 Union soldiers or militiamen were slaughtered. Although he died in battle in 1864, his bloodthirsty legacy was carried on by Jesse James, who also participated in the Centralia Massacre.

FURTHER READING

Guerrilla Hunters in Civil War Missouri
by James W. Erwin
The story of irregular warfare in the Show Me State

✳ Little Blue River

CAMPAIGN: Price's Missouri Expedition

DATE(S): October 21, 1864

Union forces failed to destroy General Price and his troops as they moved slowly along the Missouri River. Nevertheless, they did succeed in slowing down the Confederate advance. This pattern continued at Little Blue River, eight miles east of Independence. On October 21, 1864, Union troops commanded by General Blunt engaged the Confederates. At first, the Federals successfully pushed back the Rebels, but in the end the numerical superiority enjoyed by Price's Confederate soldiers forced the Union men to retreat back to Independence. Today, part of the battlefield is still visible at Little Blue Trace Park.

LOCATION: **Little Blue Trace Park, 13498 E. 87th St., Kansas City, 816-503-4800, www.visitmo .com/little-blue-trace-park.aspx.**

✳ Lone Jack

CAMPAIGN: Operations North of Boston Mountains

DATE(S): August 15–16, 1862

Confederates under the command of Colonel Coffee were attacked on the evening of August 15, 1862, by an 800-man Union force led by Major Foster. Defeated, they dispersed into the night. The next day, a 3,000-man-strong force of Rebels engaged the Union forces in a pitched battle. Coffee and his men regrouped and joined the assault against the Union forces. This was more than the Yankees could bear, and they withdrew in an orderly retreat to Lexington. Although a notable Confederate victory, it was short-lived, as Union forces retook the area shortly thereafter.

Lone Jack Battlefield Museum and Soldiers Cemetery has preserved the battlefield and tells the story of those who

Price's victory at the Little Blue River was pyrrhic, as he was delayed by a Union Army that was rapidly growing in strength.

Sterling Price was famous for his victories during the Mexican-American War.

perished in the battle. Call in advance to arrange a special tour of the battlefield.

LOCATION: **Lone Jack Battlefield Museum and Soldiers Cemetery, 301 S. Bynum Rd., Lone Jack, 816-697-8833, www.historiclonejack.org /museum.html.**

✻ Marmiton River

CAMPAIGN: Price's Missouri Expedition
DATE(S): October 25, 1864

Following Price's loss at the Battle of Mine Creek in Kansas (see p. 401), he continued his retreat toward Arkansas. Near Fort Scott, he was attacked by General McNeil. McNeil had not realized the extent of attrition that Price had suffered on the extended march and with the fighting near Kansas City and southward. Instead of attacking with his full force, McNeil used only a portion of his manpower. Had he known that many of the retreating Confederates were unarmed, he could have turned an advantage into a crushing defeat for Price.

LOCATION: **Marker located at the intersection of Hwy. 54 and Old Hwy. 54 in Deerfield.**

✻ Mount Zion Church

CAMPAIGN: Operations in Northeast Missouri
DATE(S): December 28, 1861

To protect the North Missouri Railroad and quash any secessionist sympathies in the area, General Prentiss led two companies of sharpshooters and five mounted companies to Boone County. On December 26, 1861, a skirmish between a detachment of Union men and Rebels near Hallsville bloodied the Northerners. Two days later, Prentiss returned in force, routing the Confederates led by Colonel Dorsey. The victory helped dampen secessionist activities in the area.

LOCATION: **Mount Zion Church, intersection of Mt. Zion Church Rd. and Hartley Rd., Hallsville.**

✻ New Madrid/Island No. 10

CAMPAIGN: Joint Operations on the Middle Mississippi River
DATE(S): February 28–April 8, 1862

The Confederates needed to hold the Mississippi River, lest their nation be torn in two. Union forces decided to do just that, and after Forts Henry and Donelson fell, the

Sterling Price

Born in Virginia, Sterling Price (1809–1867) moved to Missouri, where he farmed, owned a general store, and speculated on real estate before moving into politics, soon becoming speaker of the Missouri House. Service in the Mexican-American War catapulted him into the governorship. Supporting the South, Price used the Missouri State Guard and other forces he would raise with a dream of "liberating" Missouri. Alas, Missouri didn't want that kind of liberation. After the war, he fled to Mexico. He returned to St. Louis in 1867, dying in September of that year.

Rebels moved forces to Island No. 10, a strong defensive position at a double bend in the river. Sadly for the Confederates, the island could be supplied only along a single road, and when Union General Pope laid siege to nearby New Madrid on March 3, 1862, that line was in jeopardy.

With the Union threat looming, the Rebel commander quickly evacuated New Madrid, leading his forces to Island No. 10. Seeing the opportunity, the Federal infantry and navy cooperated to tighten the vice around the island. The doomed Confederate garrison surrendered on April 8, opening up the Mississippi River south to Fort Pillow in Tennessee.

LOCATION: Markers located on the Mississippi River Observation Deck, 560 Mott St., New Madrid, 573-748-2866, www.new-madrid .mo.us. Markers also located in nearby Tennessee, at the intersection of Rte. 22 and Cates Landing Rd. N., north of Tiptonville.

John McNeil

Born to American parents in Halifax, Nova Scotia, John McNeil (1813–1891) moved to Boston, then New York City, before finally settling in St. Louis. There he became a member of the Missouri Legislature and, later, the captain of a volunteer company, eventually advancing to brigadier general. Ironically for a man descended from Loyalists in the American Revolution, McNeil became famous for his ruthlessness against secessionists. "He openly proclaimed that where a Union man could not live in peace, a secessionist should not," noted *Harpers Weekly*. On October 18, 1862, in Palmyra, Missouri, McNeil—avenging the death of a Unionist—killed ten Confederate prisoners in an incident that came to be known as the Palmyra Massacre. After the war he held a number of minor government jobs before his death in St. Louis in 1891.

FURTHER READING

Island No. 10: Struggle for the Mississippi Valley by Larry J. Daniel and Lynn N. Bock The seminal account of the fight for Island No. 10

✳ Newtonia I

CAMPAIGN: Operations North of Boston Mountains
DATE(S): September 30, 1862

Hearing of the resurgent Confederate threat in southwest Missouri, Union forces moved to confront Colonel Cooper's Confederate forces, who had occupied Newtonia, the site of a mill. The battle began near Newtonia on the morning of September 30, 1862. The Rebels stopped initial Union attacks, and then Confederate reinforcements drove the Federals back upon themselves. Additional Union troops slowed the retreat but soon were bloodied as well. Pushing ever more aggressively, the Confederates eventually routed the Yankees from the field, winning the day. The victory proved hollow, however, as the Confederates simply did not have enough soldiers to gain additional land or hold what they had won. They fell back, and the battle for Missouri decisively ended in northwestern Arkansas in December with the Confederate defeat at Prairie Grove (see pp. 48–49). Today, the battlefield is partially preserved, and the Matthew Ritchey Mansion and Newtonia Civil War Cemetery are open for visitors.

LOCATION: Matthew Ritchey Mansion, 520 Mill St., Newtonia, 417-451-3415, www.newtonia bpa.webs.com. For the Newtonia Civil War Cemetery, follow Market St. north until it ends.

✳ Newtonia II

CAMPAIGN: Price's Missouri Expedition
DATE(S): October 28, 1864

Union forces continued to hound Price's men, who were now disorganized and worn

Both the Union and Confederacy used Ritchey Mansion as a headquarters and hospital.

out by the extended raid. Although the end was within sight, Price was not yet safe. At Newtonia, General Blunt's Union forces caught the Rebels unprepared. They were met by General Shelby's men, who dismounted and held off the Northerners while the rest of their Southern compatriots continued to retreat. Union reinforcements soon forced Shelby to retreat, but not before buying the Confederates desperately needed time. This conflict is notable as one of the few battles where Native Americans fought on both sides. The Matthew Ritchey Mansion and Newtonia Civil War Cemetery are open for visitors at the partially preserved battlefield.

LOCATION: **Matthew Ritchey Mansion, 520 Mill St., Newtonia, 417-451-3415, www.newtonia bpa.webs.com. For the Newtonia Civil War Cemetery, follow Market St. north until it ends.**

✳ Roan's Tan Yard

CAMPAIGN: Operations in Northeast Missouri

DATE(S): January 8, 1862

Union forces scoured Randolph County looking for small bands of Confederates. On January 8, 1862, the Northerners found their camp and achieved a decisive victory in only 40 minutes, sending many Confederates fleeing and killing or capturing others. They would have captured more Rebels were it not for heavy fog, which aided their escape. This action increased the Union grip on Randolph County.

LOCATION: **Portions of the battle took place along Hwy. B from Roanoke to just after Yates, although it is not interpreted. The core of the battle took place around 1 mile north of Hwy. B's intersection with Rte. 2945, although it is not publicly accessible.**

✳ Springfield I

CAMPAIGN: Operations to Control Missouri

DATE(S): October 25, 1861

Following the defeat at Wilson's Creek (see p. 426), Fremont moved to take Springfield with more than 20,000 men. A smaller vanguard of 5,000 cavalry marched ahead of Fremont, looking to seize the city if possible. Although ambushed by around 1,000 men under Confederate Colonel Frazier, the larger Union forces prevailed and sent them

William Tecumseh "Cump" Sherman

"Many a boy here today . . . looks on war as all glory, but, boys, it is all hell," said Sherman.

William Tecumseh "Cump" Sherman (1820–1891) achieved lasting fame in the North—and infamy in the South—for his hard war tactics in Mississippi, Georgia, and the Carolinas. Using a strategy designed to break the South's will and fighting ability, he burned towns and bridges, destroyed railroads, confiscated military supplies, seized food, and expelled civilians from their towns. His seizure of Atlanta won Lincoln reelection.

At the outbreak of secession, Sherman had predicted the course of the war, telling one Southerner, "This country will be drenched in blood . . . At first you will make headway, but . . . your cause will begin to wane. If your people will but stop and think, they must see in the end that you will surely fail."

Considered to be an alarmist, Sherman was removed from command in Kentucky before being assigned to serve under Grant in the west. He survived being surprised at Shiloh (see pp. 199–202) and mediocre performances elsewhere to eventually accept the surrender of General Joe Johnston's army in North Carolina.

Uninterested in politics, Sherman famously said, "I will not accept if nominated and will not serve if elected." After the war, the wounds healed, and Johnston served as a pallbearer at Sherman's funeral. Despite the cold, he refused to wear a hat, noting, "If I were in [his] place, and he were standing in mine, he would not put on his hat." Johnson died of pneumonia a month later.

FURTHER READING

Sherman: A Soldier's Passion for Order
by John F. Marszalek
The definitive biography of Sherman

fleeing. The Union vanguard briefly took Springfield, before Fremont finally occupied the city in force a few days later. This battle is notable for Zagonyi's Charge, a famed charge by vastly outnumbered cavalry.

LOCATION: **Zagonyi's Charge Marker at Zagonyi Park, intersection of Mt. Vernon St. and Park Ave., Springfield.**

✴ Springfield II

CAMPAIGN: Marmaduke's First Expedition Into Missouri

DATE(S): January 8, 1863

Looking to cut off Springfield, an important supply and communications center, General Marmaduke moved to take the town. With only one day to prepare his Union troops for the Rebel assault, General Brown rounded up extra soldiers and made ready for battle, which began the next morning. Intense fighting throughout the day ended only when the Confederates retreated under cover of darkness.

LOCATION: **First battle marker located at Park Central Square in Springfield. There is a 12-stop walking tour in the city. For the driving tour, stop at the visitors bureau at the Route 66 Tourist Information Center, 815 E. St. Louis St.,**

Suite 100, Springfield, 417-881-5300, www.springfieldmo.org, or visit www.nps.gov/wicr/planyourvisit/nearbyattractions.htm. Springfield National Cemetery (see p. 431) is nearby and also worth a visit.

✴ Westport

CAMPAIGN: Price's Missouri Expedition

DATE(S): October 23, 1864

By mid-October, Price's Missouri raid had failed in every instance. Turning away from St. Louis, he moved toward Kansas City, pursued by General Pleasonton's cavalry and General Curtis's Army of the Border. Price knew he had to take on the Union forces—perhaps a victory would change the karma of the raid and bring fruit to a barren expedition. Realizing he stood a better chance of defeating the Yankees in detail, he sought to tackle them separately. He struck Curtis's men at Westport, resulting in a pitched battle. The strong Union lines were more than a match for Price, despite his soldiers' brave charges. This battle disabused Price of any illusions of success in this raid, and he now determined to leave Missouri and return to Arkansas.

LOCATION: **Multiple markers located in Jacob L. Loose Park, 5200 Pennsylvania Ave., Kansas**

Westport was a decisive blow against Price and his dreams of a Confederate Missouri.

City, 816-784-5300, kcparks.org. Another marker located one block south of the park, at the intersection of 56th St. and Pennsylvania Ave. Also visit the Battle of Westport Visitor Center and Museum, 6601 Swope Pkwy., Kansas City, 913-345-2000, www.battleofwest port.org; open seasonally, call for updated hours. The visitor center website has a 32-mile driving tour and walking tour. The *Arabia* Steamboat Museum (see p. 429) is nearby.

✳ Wilson's Creek

CAMPAIGN: Operations to Control Missouri

DATE(S): August 10, 1861

Both Confederate and Union strategists were intent on securing Missouri. General Lyon's men moved to strike the Confederates at Wilson's Creek at daybreak on August 10, 1861. After initial success, Rebel reinforcements stabilized the Southern lines, counterattacking the Union forces. Despite three attempts to break through, the Union lines held. Yet the Federals had lost much. Lyon was killed in action and replaced by Major Sturgis. Ammunition was low, and the oppressive August heat had exhausted the

men. Unable to hold against continued pressure, the Union forces withdrew, even though the Confederates had already done the same. This victory strengthened the secessionist cause in Missouri.

Replete with a wide range of interpretive activities and walking trails, this is among the best preserved battlefields in the nation. A significant portion of the battlefield is located outside the park boundary; a park ranger can explain how to follow the Confederates' flank attack.

LOCATION: **Wilson's Creek National Battlefield, 6424 W. Farm Rd. 182, Republic, 417-732-2662, www.nps.gov/wicr.**

FURTHER READING

Wilson's Creek: The Second Battle of the Civil War and the Men Who Fought It by William Garrett Piston and Richard W. Hatcher III
A thorough look at this important battle

Rebel reenactors load and prepare to fire an artillery piece at a Wilson's Creek reenactment.

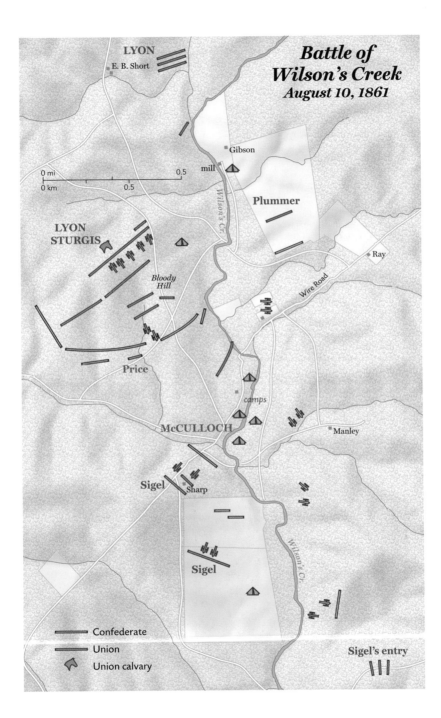

Battle of Wilson's Creek
August 10, 1861

LYON
E. B. Short

Gibson

mill

Plummer

Ray

LYON
STURGIS

Bloody
Hill

Wilson's Cr.

Wire Road

Price

camps

McCULLOCH

Manley

Sigel

Sharp

Sigel

Wilson's Cr.

Sigel's entry

0 mi   0.5
0 km   0.5

— Confederate
— Union
⮞ Union calvary

Other Battles and Beyond

✦ Civil War Traveler

With free maps, driving tours, and information on nearby sites, Civil War Traveler is an invaluable resource and traveling companion. For information on all important engagements in Missouri and beyond, visit www.civilwartraveler.com.

✦ Missouri Civil War Sesquicentennial

A companion to Missouri's commemoration of the 150th anniversary of the war, the sesquicentennial website includes a trip planner, historical information, videos, and more. Access it at www.mocivilwar150.com.

✦ Missouri's Civil War

Run by the Missouri Civil War Heritage Foundation, this valuable resource for any itinerary lists the latest on Civil War–related events in the Show Me State and includes interactive maps of the Gray Ghosts Trail and the U.S. Grant Trail. Visit it at www.mocivilwar.org.

✦ Ozarks Civil War

This is the premier website for information about the war in the Ozarks. For primary sources, resources for educators, battle information, and more, visit www.ozarks civilwar.org.

✦ Visit Missouri

The official state tourism website offers information on Civil War battles, shopping, hotels, and more. An interactive map makes journey planning more convenient. Access it online at www.visitmo.com/civil-war.aspx, or call 800-519-2100.

Union reenactors wave their hats—a gesture used by Civil War soldiers to taunt their enemies—at the 150th anniversary of the Battle of Lexington.

✦ *Arabia* Steamboat Museum

The *Arabia* was a steamboat that snagged and sank in the Missouri River in 1856. Discovered in 1987 in an old riverbed in a farmer's field, the wreck produced the world's largest collection of antebellum American artifacts, including all manner of goods used on the frontier, such as pickles, linens, china dishware, and toys.

LOCATION: 400 Grand Blvd., Kansas City, 816-471-1856, www.1856.com.

✦ Battle of Athens State Historic Site

In 1861, in the northernmost battle west of the Mississippi, outnumbered Union soldiers defeated separatist Missouri State Guards. The Thome-Benning House, struck by a cannonball in the battle, is open to visitors.

LOCATION: At the intersection of Rte. 81 and CC, take CC east, following the highway until its terminus just before the Des Moines River (the park is on the left), 660-877-3871, www.mostateparks.com.

✦ Battle of Island Mound State Historic Site

The 1st Kansas Colored Infantry entered Missouri on a mission to suppress guerrillas. Encountering Rebel forces on October 29, 1862, at Toothman Farm, they killed 30 Confederates and suffered only 8 losses. This small victory is noteworthy as the first participation of black troops in the war. An interpretive trail includes Fort Africa.

LOCATION: Eight miles southwest of Butler off Rte. K at N.W. 1002 Rd., www.mostateparks.com.

✦ Bellefontaine Cemetery

Bellefontaine Cemetery features the graves of gunboat builder James B. Eads, who built the *Cairo*, *Mound City*, and other city-class

ironclads for service in western waters, in addition to Edward Bates, Generals Blair and Price, and explorer William Clark.

LOCATION: 4947 W. Florrisant Ave., St. Louis, 314-381-0750, www.bellefontainecemetery.org.

✦ Bushwhacker Museum

Located in an old jail that was one of the few buildings to survive an 1863 Yankee raid, this eclectic museum is the only one dedicated to this unique form of lawlessness. Open seasonally; call for hours.

LOCATION: 212 W. Walnut St., Nevada, 417-667-9602, www.bushwhacker.org.

✦ Calvary Cemetery

Established in 1854 on 470 acres, this site has a large range of notable internments, including Dred Scott, William Tecumseh Sherman (see p. 424), and Don Carlos Buell.

LOCATION: 5239 W. Florissant Ave., St. Louis, 314-792-7738, www.archstl.org/cemeteries/content/view/91/233.

✦ Camp Jackson Monument

On May 10, 1861, pro-secessionist men gathered here in an attempt to take St. Louis but were driven away by Union soldiers, who killed at least 28 men who had already surrendered. Confederate sympathizers used the occasion as a rallying cry.

LOCATION: Lyon Park, 3100 S. Broadway, St. Louis, 314-622-4800.

✦ Carthage Civil War Museum

This museum features an impressive, although not completely accurate, wall-size mural of the battle, multiple artifacts and displays, and even a video describing the Civil War and its effects on the Ozarks.

LOCATION: 205 Grant St., Carthage, 417-237-7060, www.visitmo.com/carthage-civil-war-museum.aspx.

✦ Centralia Historical Society Museum

Exhibits in the museum's Civil War room explore the history of the Centralia Massacre, in which "Bloody Bill" Anderson and his men killed 24 unarmed Union soldiers (see p. 419). Open seasonally; call or check online for the latest information.

LOCATION: 319 E. Sneed St., Centralia, 573-682-5711, www.centraliamo museum.org.

The skirmish at Island Mound saw the first action of a black regiment in the war.

✦ Edward Bates Monument

Drafter of Missouri's first constitution, and also the state's first attorney general, Bates is perhaps most famous as a rival to Lincoln at the 1860 Republican Convention. Having lost the nomination, he faithfully served Lincoln as attorney general of the United States.

LOCATION: Intersection of Fine Arts Dr. and Lagoon Dr., within Forest Park, 5595 Grand Dr., St. Louis, 314-367-7275, www.forestpark forever.org.

✦ Fort D Historic Site

Of the four forts built in Cape Girardeau by John Fremont, Fort D is the only one that remains. Well preserved and beautifully interpreted, this is the best place to learn about the Battle of Cape Girardeau (see p. 415). Guided tours are available and reenactments are held.

LOCATION: 920 Westport St., Cape Girardeau, 573-335-5421, www.fortdhistoricsite.com.

✦ General Sterling Price Museum

Two-time governor of Missouri, Mexican-American War leader, and Confederate general in the Civil War, Sterling Price left his mark on Missouri. This museum,

which includes a period re-creation of a parlor and textiles of the time, can be visited seasonally. Be sure to call ahead to confirm.

LOCATION: 412 W. Bridge St., Keytesville, 660-288-3204.

✦ Harry S. Truman Presidential Library

One of the founding members of the Kansas City Civil War Roundtable, President Truman was deeply interested in the Civil War. You can follow in his tradition by attending meetings, which are still held. The library and his nearby home are a humble tribute to the man who "gave 'em hell!"

LOCATION: 500 W. U.S. Hwy. 24, Independence, 800-833-1225, www.trumanlibrary.org. Find out more about the Civil War Roundtable he co-founded at www.cwrtkc.org.

✦ Jefferson Barracks

Active as a major hospital during the Civil War, this important army post has seen luminaries like Lee and Grant. It was downsized after World War II, and now the grounds host the Missouri National Guard, a national cemetery, and multiple Civil War–era buildings. The Missouri Civil War Museum and other artifacts make this a pleasant and worthwhile visit.

LOCATION: **222 Worth Rd., St. Louis, 314-845-1861, www.mcwm.org.**

✦ Jesse James House

Among the most famous outlaws of all time, Jesse James was one of Quantrill's Raiders, notorious pro-Confederate bushwhackers. James was killed in this house.

LOCATION: **15918 James Farm Rd., Kearney, 816-736-8500, www.claycountymo.gov /Historic_Sites/Jesse_James_Farm.**

✦ Meramec Caverns

Union ordnance technicians used this large, beautiful natural formation as a saltpeter resource and gunpowder storage facility. It was captured by William Quantrill in 1864 and later used by Jesse James (a member of Quantrill's troop) as a hideout during his postwar bank-robbing days.

LOCATION: **1135 State Hwy. W., Sullivan, 573-468-2283, www.americascave.com.**

✦ Missouri State Museum

Covering the complete history of the Show Me State, this museum boasts an impressive collection of regimental battle flags, as well as other artifacts and information on Missouri's role in the war.

LOCATION: **201 W. Capitol Ave. No. 2, Jefferson City, 573-751-2854, www.mostateparks.com /park/missouri-state-museum.**

✦ Rolla

Home to the terminus of the southwest branch of the Pacific Railroad and now several buildings on the National Register of Historic Places, the town of Rolla was secured by Union forces and used as a supply base throughout the conflict.

LOCATION: **Visitor Center at 1311 Kings Hwy., Rolla, 573-364-3577, www.visitrolla.com.**

✦ Springfield National Cemetery

Created in 1867 as the final resting place for Union soldiers, Springfield National Cemetery now holds the graves of soldiers from a number of wars, including World War II and the Spanish-American War. An adjacent section containing the remains of Confederate veterans was added in 1911. Five recipients of the Medal of Honor are buried here.

LOCATION: **1702 E. Seminole St., Springfield, 417-881-9499, www.cem.va.gov/cems/nchp /springfield.asp.**

✦ Ulysses S. Grant National Historic Site

An important stop on any Civil War itinerary, this site preserves White Haven, the family home of Julia Dent, the wife of Ulysses S. Grant. Grant lived here with his wife from 1854 to 1859. Ironically for a man fighting for the Union, slaves worked the plantation at White Haven until the end of the Civil War. Indeed, Julia had a slave with her when she visited her husband at Oxford, Mississippi, in December 1862. Free guided tours of White Haven are available.

LOCATION: **7400 Grant Rd., St. Louis, 314-842-1867, www.nps.gov/ulsg.**

✦ Wire Road

Known as the "wire road" for the telegraph wire that ran alongside it, this route was an important pathway between Springfield, Missouri, and Fayetteville, Arkansas. The Battle of Wilson's Creek (see pp. 426–427) was fought along the road, as was the Battle of Pea Ridge (see pp. 45–46). Today, one of the few places where the road still exists is at the Wilson's Creek Battlefield. Be sure to ask the historians there about other stretches of the road that you can visit.

LOCATION: **Wilson's Creek National Battlefield, 6424 W. Farm Rd. 182, Republic, 417-732-2662, www.nps.gov/wicr.**

Oklahoma

EARLY AMERICANS FEARED NATIVE AMERICANS, AND DURING the presidency of Andrew Jackson they began a systematic and ruthless effort to remove them from their native lands to newly designated Indian Territory (today known as Oklahoma).

The majority of the prewar U.S. Army was stationed at fortifications along the boundaries of western states and territories. Riches and opportunities lay in the West, and military expeditions escorted settlers along various routes, such as the Santa Fe Trail, to protect them from Indians. Dustups and encounters were frequent, and relations between the Indians and white men suffered. When the war came, however, both Confederates and Federals attempted to recruit Native Americans to fight on their side. Indians fought in small numbers in places like Pea Ridge in March 1862, Second Manassas in August 1862, and Spotsylvania in May 1864. Native Americans such as John Ross, Stand Watie, and Ely Parker were prominent participants. Combat actions in Indian Territory were few but noteworthy.

General Stand Watie led the Cherokee Indians, who allied themselves with the Confederacy.

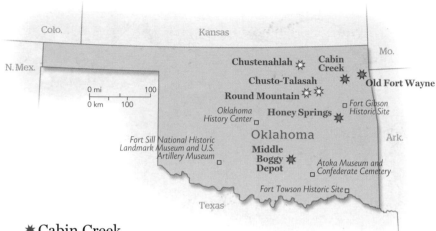

✳ Cabin Creek

CAMPAIGN: Operations to Control Indian Territory

DATE(S): July 1–2, 1863

With the removal of Unionist Indians from Indian Territory, the Federals sought to reestablish their position by returning 1,000 refugees via Fort Gibson. At Cabin Creek, Indian Confederates under the command of Colonel Watie intercepted the Union supply train on its way from Fort Scott. After two days of fighting, the Federals forced the ford and delivered the supplies. A choke point on the southern supply route, Cabin Creek would see more fighting later in the war.

LOCATION: Cabin Creek Battlefield, 442370 E. 367 Rd., Big Cabin, 405-521-2491, www.ok history.org/sites/cabincreek.

FURTHER READING

Between Two Fires: American Indians in the Civil War
by Laurence M. Hauptman
A thorough depiction of Indian service

✳ Chustenahlah

CAMPAIGN: Operations in the Indian Territory

DATE(S): December 26, 1861

After two indecisive encounters, Colonel Cooper received 1,400 new Confederate soldiers. He used them to strike a camp of Creeks and Seminoles. In hand-to-hand fighting, the Unionist Indians were routed, with Colonel Watie's Indians leading an aggressive pursuit. The Union encampment suffered more than 200 casualties. By the end of December 1861, the Confederates controlled Indian Territory.

LOCATION: Marker located on OK 20, 3 miles west of Skiatook Sportsman Club. The actual battle took place along Hominy Creek.

✳ Chusto-Talasah

CAMPAIGN: Operations in the Indian Territory

DATE(S): December 9, 1861

Confederate forces continued to pursue Chief Opothleyahola's Unionist Indians. The

Chief Opothleyahola led Unionist Indian forces at the Battle of Chusto-Talasah.

harsh campaign caused more than 400 Confederate Cherokees to desert or join with the Unionists. Confederate Colonel Cooper attacked the Unionist camp at Chusto-Talasah. Opothleyahola found excellent defensive grounds at Horseshoe Bend along Bird Creek and held for nearly four hours. That evening, the Unionist Indians moved to Shoal Creek. Nearly 500 casualties (mostly defenders) were suffered.

LOCATION: Stone marker located near the intersection of 86th St. N. and Delaware Ave. Battlefield located on private land 1 mile north of 86th St. N. on Delaware Ave., 5 miles northwest of Tulsa along Bird Creek.

☀ Honey Springs

CAMPAIGN: Operations to Control Indian Territory

DATE(S): July 17, 1863

This was by far the largest battle of the Civil War in Indian Territory, with nearly 9,000 men engaged, including Native Americans on both sides, blacks from the 1st Kansas Infantry, and white troops. Bolstered by its numerical superiority and the promise of substantial reinforcements from Arkansas, General Cooper intended to reestablish Confederate control of the territory by capturing the 3,000 men stationed at Fort Gibson.

Warned of the Confederate advance, General Blunt struck Cooper before he was reinforced at Honey Springs. Enjoying superior firepower and training, Blunt's men deployed in a 1,000-yard-wide line of battle. After desultory firing, Blunt ordered the 1st Kansas to assault. The attack bogged down, and the Confederates launched a counterattack. This was a big mistake as the Kansans mowed them down.

Cooper withdrew, hoping to link with the promised reinforcements from Arkansas. The retreat bottlenecked at the bridge over Dirty Elk Creek, and superior Federal marksmanship inflicted a heavy toll on the Confederates. The pursuit continued to Honey Springs. There, Cooper's line was broken. Victorious, Blunt returned to Fort Gibson. The Union had proved it could stay in Indian Territory.

The 1,110-acre Honey Springs Battlefield Park has six walking trails and Civil War interpretive signs.

LOCATION: Honey Springs Battlefield Park, 1863 Honey Spring Battlefield Rd., Checotah, 918-473-5572, www.okhistory.org/sites /honeysprings.

This Plains Indian pipe tomahawk dates to the mid-19th century.

With nearly 9,000 Native American, black, and white troops engaged, Honey Springs was the largest battle of the Civil War in Indian Territory.

✳ Middle Boggy Depot

CAMPAIGN: Operations in the Indian Territory
DATE(S): February 13, 1864

With Choctaw, Chickasaw, and Seminole Indians serving in the Confederate cavalry, Federal forces were determined to enlist Indians in the Union Army. An expedition, under Colonel Phillips from Fort Gibson encountered Confederate troops, which were primarily Native American. The Confederates, poorly trained and armed, were routed, with 47 men killed. Rumors of Confederate reinforcements caused the expedition to withdraw, and Indian loyalty was unaffected.

LOCATION: **Unmarked and generally inaccessible site located on B&L Rd., about 4 miles south-southwest of Allen and 500 yards east of the Richard V. Wallace Memorial Bridge crossing Little Sandy Creek.**

✳ Old Fort Wayne

CAMPAIGN: Operations North of Boston Mountains
DATE(S): October 22, 1862

On October 4, 1862, the Indians fighting under Confederate Colonels Cooper and Watie during the first battle of Newtonia (see p. 422) retreated into Indian Territory, pursued by a division of General Schofield's Army of the Frontier led by General Blunt. Near dawn on October 22, the Confederates were attacked in their camps near Old Fort Wayne. The uneven fight caused them to abandon much of their equipment and artillery and flee across the Arkansas River.

LOCATION: **The historical marker for the battle in Oklahoma is missing. An informative battle marker is located in nearby Maysville, Arkansas, on the west side of AR Rte. 43 near AR 72.**

✳ Round Mountain

CAMPAIGN: Operations in the Indian Territory
DATE(S): November 19, 1861

Early in the Civil War, both Union and Confederate representatives sought treaties with Indian tribes. This battle occurred when unaligned or Unionist Indians attempted to move to Kansas and were attacked in camp by approximately 500 Confederate troops and 900 sympathetic Indians. The fleeing Indians set fire to the prairie, causing the Confederate commander to fear for his supply trains. By the next day, the Indians had moved on.

LOCATION: **Unidentified camp site located at the foot of Round Mountain.**

Other Battles and Beyond

✦ Atoka Museum and Confederate Cemetery

Originally the site of a Confederate camp, this museum includes exhibits relating to the Civil War in Indian Territory. The small cemetery is for Confederate soldiers who perished in a measles epidemic.

LOCATION: 258 N. Hwy. 69, Atoka, 580-889-7192, www.okhistory.org/sites/atokamuseum.

✦ Fort Gibson Historic Site

A starting point for expeditions exploring the West, this fort was later used as a staging area during the Civil War. The site includes a reconstruction of the early log fort and other interesting buildings. Walking tours are offered by the Oklahoma Historical Society.

LOCATION: 907 Garrison Ave., Fort Gibson, 918-478-4088, www.okhistory.org/sites /fortgibson.

✦ Fort Sill National Historic Landmark Museum and U.S. Artillery Museum

Dedicated to the preservation of the history of field artillery and Fort Sill, the museums

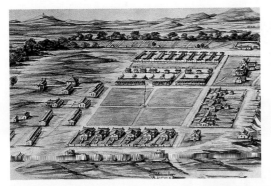

Built during the Indian Wars, Fort Sill is an active U.S. field artillery school.

Tonkawa Massacre

On the morning of October 24, 1862, pro-Union Indians attacked the camp of the Tonkawa tribe, who were loyal to the Confederacy. They killed more than 130 Tonkawa, a tragedy from which their population never recovered.

include exhibits such as a cavalry barracks and many types of field artillery. Because the fort is actively training U.S. Army soldiers, you must check in with I.D. before entering.

LOCATION: 437 Quanah Rd., Fort Sill, 580-442-5123, www.fortsillmuseum.com.

✦ Fort Towson Historic Site

Established in 1824, this fort served as a gateway for settlers, a dispersal point for displaced Indian tribes, a staging area for the Mexican-American War of 1846, and headquarters for Confederate forces in Indian Territory. General Watie surrendered his command nearby, the last Confederate general to do so. The Fort Towson visitor center opened nearby in June 2015.

LOCATION: 1 mile east of Fort Towson and three-quarters of a mile north of Hwy. 70 E., 580-873-2634, www.okhistory.org /sites/forttowson.

✦ Oklahoma History Center

Learn the history of Oklahoma with an emphasis on the Civil War.

LOCATION: 800 Nazih Zuhdi Dr., Oklahoma City, www.okhistory .org.

Other Midwestern States

Illinois, Iowa, Michigan, and Wisconsin

THE FOREST OF MEN WHO ANSWERED THE NATION'S CALL from Illinois, Iowa, Michigan, and Wisconsin were as sturdy as oaks, hewn into the greatest fighting force ever seen to that time.

The 1st Brigade, 1st Division of the I Corps from Michigan and Wisconsin wore Hardee hats and after the Battle of South Mountain were known as the Black Hats—the Iron Brigade. At Vicksburg no one was braver than the Iowans, whose service is honored with one of the grandest monuments seen anywhere save one other—the Illinois Memorial, also at Vicksburg.

The West was the future. It took a diminutive giant, Stephen A. Douglas, to bring forth popular sovereignty, and another even greater to lead the country through its greatest trial—Abraham Lincoln, who rededicated the country to a "New Birth of Freedom."

The monument marks Abraham Lincoln's tomb at Oak Ridge Cemetery in Springfield, Illinois.

The Custom House in Cairo, Illinois, was a port of delivery after goods were shipped through New Orleans, as well as an important post office for mail traveling farther west.

Illinois

✦ Looking for Lincoln/ Abraham Lincoln National Heritage Area

A statewide guide to Lincoln sites in 42 counties and six important gateway communities is available online at www.lookingfor lincoln.com.

✦ Abraham Lincoln Presidential Library and Museum

This exceptional site includes dozens of personal Lincoln artifacts, rotating exhibits, a high-tech digital movie experience, and a holographic presentation.

LOCATION: **212 N. 6th St., Springfield, 217-558-8844, www.illinois.gov/alplm.**

✦ Alton Civil War Prison

This infamous Union prison site on the banks of the Mississippi was originally a state penitentiary. More than 11,000 prisoners passed through these gates with an above-average mortality rate (more than 1,500), mostly due to disease. The site features interpretive panels with contemporary photography.

LOCATION: **Uncle Remus Park, 214 William St., Alton.**

✦ Cairo Custom House Museum

Situated at a key location on the Ohio River, this small but satisfying museum contains the desk Grant used while headquartered in Cairo, a scale model of a gunboat, and more.

LOCATION: **1400 Washington Ave., Cairo, 618-734-9632, www.illinoisbeautiful.com/southern -illinois-tourism/cairo-custom-house-museum -cairo-illinois.html.**

✦ Decatur

Numerous sights in this town relate to Abraham Lincoln. Highlights include the Lincoln family's first Illinois home, the site of Lincoln's first political speech, and the site where Lincoln was nominated to run for president. Download the "Shadows of Lincoln" brochure or visit 15 wayside exhibits around town.

LOCATION: **Decatur Convention and Visitors Bureau, 202 E. North St., Decatur, 217-423-7000, www.decaturcvb.com/abraham-lincoln.**

✦ Elijah Lovejoy Monument

In November 1837, this martyred abolitionist and newspaper editor had his presses destroyed and thrown in the river by pro-slavery protesters. The 110-foot monument over his grave has been richly inscribed with tributes to his courage.

LOCATION: **Alton Cemetery, Monument Ave., Alton.**

✦ John A. Logan Museum

This museum is dedicated to the compelling life of John A. Logan, who was one of Illinois's most powerful senators, General Grant's favorite officer, and a man who very publicly changed his views from actively racist to civil rights advocate.

LOCATION: **1613 Edith St., Murphysboro, 618-684-3455, www.loganmuseum.org.**

FURTHER READING

Black Jack: John A. Logan and Southern Illinois in the Civil War Era
by James P. Jones
Details the extraordinary political clout of this man and his region in the growing United States

✦ Lincoln-Herndon Law Office

Lincoln practiced law here with his partner, William Herndon, from about 1843 until 1852. There is a 20-minute guided tour. At publication time, the site was closed for renovations, so check before visiting.

LOCATION: **Old State Capitol Plaza, 6th and Adams Sts., 217-785-7960, www.illinois.gov /ihpa/experience/sites/central/pages/lincoln -herndon.aspx.**

✦ Lincoln Home National Historic Site

Stroll through the historic Lincoln-era neighborhood and get a glimpse into the daily life of Lincoln. At the visitor center, see a film and pick up a site brochure and a free ticket to see the interior of the home. A cellphone tour is also available.

LOCATION: **426 S. 7th St., Springfield, 217-492-4241, www.nps.gov/liho.**

✦ Lincoln's New Salem

This is a reconstruction of the village (log buildings, workshops, and a school) where Abraham Lincoln spent his early adulthood and first ran for office. Staff is attired in period costume.

LOCATION: **15588 History Ln., Petersburg, 217-632-4000, www.lincolnsnewsalem.com.**

✦ Lincoln Tomb State Historic Site

A stunning granite monument marks the site of the Lincoln Tomb, where Abraham Lincoln, Mary Todd Lincoln, and three of their children are interred.

LOCATION: **Oak Ridge Cemetery, 1500 Monument Ave., Springfield, 217-782-2717, www.lincolntomb.org.**

✦ Mother Bickerdyke Memorial

This monument shows a compassionate Mother Bickerdyke (see sidebar p. 443) kneeling beside a wounded soldier.

LOCATION: **In front of the Knox County Courthouse, 200 S. Cherry St., Galesburg.**

✦ Old Lincoln Courtroom and Museum

This is the only courtroom still in use today in which Lincoln actually tried a case. A museum provides other important details.

LOCATION: **101 W. 3rd St., Beardstown, 217-323-3225, www.lincolninbeardstown.org.**

✦ Old State Capitol State Historic Site

Take a guided tour to see where Lincoln delivered his famous "House Divided" speech, served as a member of the Illinois State Legislature, and argued cases in front of the Illinois Supreme Court.

LOCATION: **5th and Adams Sts., Springfield, 217-785-7960, www.illinois.gov/ihpa /Experience/Sites/Central/Pages/Old -Capitol.aspx.**

✦ Rock Island Arsenal and Museum

Originally a Confederate POW camp, this site later produced weapons for the army.

The museum has an extensive collection of small arms and also chronicles the site's history. A Confederate cemetery houses nearly 2,000 victims of incarceration, and an adjoining national cemetery is the burial place for Union prison guards and other veterans.

LOCATION: **1 Rock Island Arsenal, Bldg. 60, Rock Island, 309-782-5021, www.arsenal historicalsociety.org/museum.**

✦ U.S. Grant Home State Historic Site

In 1865, the residents of Galena gave this home to General Grant in thanks for his war service. Many artifacts from his public life are here, including furniture he used during his presidency.

LOCATION: **500 Bouthillier St., Galena, 815-777-3310, www.granthome.com.**

✦ U.S. Grant Museum

This museum contains important artifacts from General Grant's service and features a

Learn about life in the 1840s at Lincoln Log Cabin State Historic Site near Lerna, Illinois.

majestic painting of the Confederate surrender at Appomattox.

LOCATION: 211 S. Bench St., Galena, www.galenahistorymuseum.org.

✦ Vermilion County Museum

Once a home where Lincoln stayed while practicing law in the county, his bedroom remains intact. The balcony was used for a speech before the war.

LOCATION: 116 N. Gilbert St., 217-442-2922, www.vermilioncountymuseum.org.

Iowa

✦ Iowa Civil War Monuments

The state has compiled a comprehensive list of monuments, plaques, and facilities honoring Iowa's Civil War soldiers. Access it online at www.iowacivilwarmonuments.com.

✦ Camp McClellan

In 1863, this site—once the training grounds for Iowa's Union recruits and a hospital for the wounded—served as a prison for the 278 Indians convicted of participating in the Sioux Uprising of 1862 (see Camp Release, p. 410). Today, it is the McClellan Heights Historic District, where you can enjoy a splendid view of Rock Island Arsenal. Lindsay Park includes the former parade grounds and the area where the barracks once stood.

LOCATION: 2200 E. River Dr., Davenport, 563-326-7812, www.cityofdavenportiowa.com.

✦ Iowa State Capitol

Home of the Iowa Legislature, this building displays battle flags of the Iowa Regiments on the main floor. A cell-phone audio tour is also available.

LOCATION: 1007 E. Grand Ave., Des Moines, 515-281-5591, www.legis.iowa.gov/resources/tourcapitol.

Mother Bickerdyke, Union Nurse

Mary Ann Bickerdyke, known fondly as Mother Bickerdyke to the grateful enlisted men, was a tireless member of the Corps of Union Nurses. Adamant about cleanliness, she was unafraid to step on any toes in the course of her self-appointed duties. Present at 19 battles, she tended to the wounded, directed kitchens, and introduced and managed army laundries. After the war, she became an attorney advocating for Union veterans. Galesburg Public Library houses many of her papers and artifacts.

✦ Todd House

This historic house museum was a key spot on the Underground Railroad as well as a staging area for supplies, such as rifles (known as Beecher Bibles) being shipped to abolitionist settlers in the Kansas Territory. The infamous John Brown visited here many times, as did abolitionist Kansas Senator Jim Lane.

LOCATION: 705 Park St., Tabor, 712-629-3164, www.taboriowahistoricalsociety.org/todd.html.

Michigan

✦ Dearborn Historical Museum

An arsenal here supplied arms to Union troops during the Civil War.

LOCATION: 915 Brady St., Dearborn, 313-565-3000, www.thedhm.com.

✦ Fort Mackinac

The oldest building in Michigan, this scenic fort briefly served as a Confederate POW camp during the war.

LOCATION: A ferry ride is required to access the site. Mackinac Island, 904-847-3328,

www.mackinacparks.com/parks-and
-attractions/fort-mackinac.

✦ Fort St. Joseph Museum

The museum's collection includes an exhibit
about the story of the Underground
Railroad in southern Michigan.

LOCATION: 508 E. Main St., Niles, 269-683-
4700, www.nileshistorycenter.org/fort
-st-joseph-museum-home-page.html.

✦ Fort Wilkins Historic State Park

This pristine fortification overlooking Lake
Superior was manned throughout the war
but never tested. Living-history presenters
give a sense of life in the 19th century.

LOCATION: 15223 US 41, Copper Harbor,
906-289-4215, www.michigandnr.com.

✦ Henry Ford Museum

Ford was a collector of historic artifacts, and
this world-class museum contains among its
priceless collection the chair President
Lincoln was sitting in at Ford's Theatre when
he was assassinated on April 14, 1865. Other
items on display include slave quarters and
works of art depicting the Civil War.

LOCATION: 20900 Oakwood Blvd., Dearborn,
313-982-6001, www.thehenryford.org.

Sojourner Truth, Slave Turned Abolitionist

Born into slavery in New York,
Sojourner Truth escaped to freedom with her infant daughter in
1826. Later, she sued to recover her
young son, who had been illegally
sold in Alabama. She became the
first black woman to win such a case
against a white man. Truth traveled
the country speaking passionately
as an abolitionist and advocate of
women's rights.

The Legend of the Iron Brigade

Composed of regiments from
Wisconsin, Indiana, and
Michigan, the Iron Brigade was one
of the toughest infantry units in the
Union Army. It was known for its
strong discipline and unique uniform,
which included black, soft-brimmed
Hardee hats. The Iron Brigade fought
fiercely in many encounters of the
Civil War, including the first day of
the Battle of Gettysburg, when it
repulsed the first main Confederate
attack at McPherson Ridge, capturing General Archer and most of his
brigade. The Iron Brigade was soon
decimated, another bloody statistic
in a bloody war.

✦ Monroe County Historical Museum

Built as a post office in 1910 on the site of
George Armstrong Custer's home, this site
is unabashedly about Custer, who met his
wife, Libbie, here. An exhibit focuses on
Custer from his days at West Point through
the Civil War. The museum also boasts one
of the largest collections of artifacts related
to life and history in southeast Michigan.
While in town, don't miss the monument
dedicated to Custer.

LOCATION: 126 S. Monroe St., Monroe,
734-240-7780, www.co.monroe.mi.us
/government/departments_offices/museum
/index.html.

✦ Oakhill Cemetery

Many abolitionists lived in Battle Creek,
including Sojourner Truth (see sidebar this
page), who is buried here alongside most of
the town's earliest pioneers. The cemetery is
open daily.

LOCATION: 255 South Ave., Battle Creek,
269-964-7321, www.battlecreekvisitors.org
/oakhill-cemetery-battle-creek.

Wisconsin

✦ Camp Randall Memorial Park

More than 70,000 Wisconsin Union troops trained here. A 36-foot memorial arch is dedicated to the state's soldiers.

LOCATION: 132 N. Randall Ave. (near Camp Randall Stadium, University of Wisconsin), Madison.

✦ Little White School House

The Republican Party was born here on March 20, 1854.

LOCATION: 305 Blackburn St., Ripon, 920-748-6764, www.littlewhiteschoolhouse.com.

✦ Civil War Museum

This well-developed museum houses an impressive number of artifacts and a high-tech digital movie experience focused on the Civil War experience in the Midwest.

LOCATION: 5400 1st Ave., Kenosha, 262-653-4141, www.kenosha.org/wp-civilwar.

✦ "The Victorious Charge"

Created in 1898, this dramatic bronze sculpture pays tribute to the courage of Union soldiers. It depicts a fallen color-bearer as his mates sweep past him on the charge.

LOCATION: Court of Honor, W. Wisconsin Ave., downtown Milwaukee.

The Arch at Camp Randall commemorates the Union soldiers trained there during the Civil War. Today, it's also an entrance to the University of Wisconsin football stadium.

The West

The only Texas troops to fight in the East, Hood's Texas Brigade was often the tip of Lee's spear.

Milestones

› JANUARY 2, 1864
General Cleburne's proposal to arm slaves to fight for the South is rejected.

› FEBRUARY 15, 1864
Prior to the presidential election, the Confederate Congress allots $5 million to fund secret service operations in the North.

› FEBRUARY 27, 1864
The first Union prisoners arrive at a camp to be known as Andersonville. Extreme mortality will plague prisoners here and at other prisons.

› MARCH 9, 1864
Grant is made general in chief of the Union armies.

› MARCH 13, 1864
Lincoln declines a petition from Louisiana blacks asking for the vote but sets the stage for blacks to vote in future presidential elections.

› MAY 7, 1864
After the costly Battle of the Wilderness, Grant advises Lincoln he will keep moving forward if it takes all summer—and it will.

› JULY 12, 1864
General Early unsuccessfully attacks the fortifications of Washington, D.C.

› SEPTEMBER 2, 1864
The fall of Atlanta signals to the North that Lincoln can win the war.

› OCTOBER 18-19, 1864
General Sheridan extinguishes the last offensive spark of the Confederacy.

› NOVEMBER 30, 1864
The Confederate invasion of Tennessee comes to an abrupt halt at Franklin.

A Vast Opportunity

Even as the country flowed inexorably toward the Pacific Ocean, the American victory in the Mexican-American War opened vast new lands that had been part of the Mexican Empire. Starting with Texas, which had passed through a period as a Lone Star Republic, the United States had ceded lands it brought away from the Texas War of Independence to form the New Mexico and Arizona Territories; California had also been a prize.

In 1861, the southwestern routes to California and the discovery of gold and silver in the New Mexico and Colorado Territories guaranteed the mutual interest of the white man in the now threatened Indian territories. Soon men such as Kit Carson would meet Mangas Coloradas, Cochise, and Geronimo in battle.

With the Confederates facing a blockade, suddenly Mexico and her ports became attractive outlets for their trade and cotton. The Southern power brokers had foreseen the competition in these areas, and this greater consideration set many Southern minds on an independent existence. In this region, as well as the others, however, Southern hopes were dashed.

This painting by Robert Lindneux shows the massacre of Arapahoe and Cheyenne Indians at Sand Creek by Federal troops under the command of John Chivington.

THE WEST IN THE CIVIL WAR

The Republican Party had come into being philosophically opposed to the expansion of slavery into the territories. The Southern power structure railed at the intended containment of their means of prosperity—when legal precedent swung their way after the 1854 Kansas-Nebraska Act and the 1857 Dred Scott Supreme Court decision, they believed the Constitution was on their side. With secession, the South unsuccessfully attempted to control the southern access to California and develop friendly relations with the Apaches. Elsewhere where Indians got in the way, white men slaughtered them.

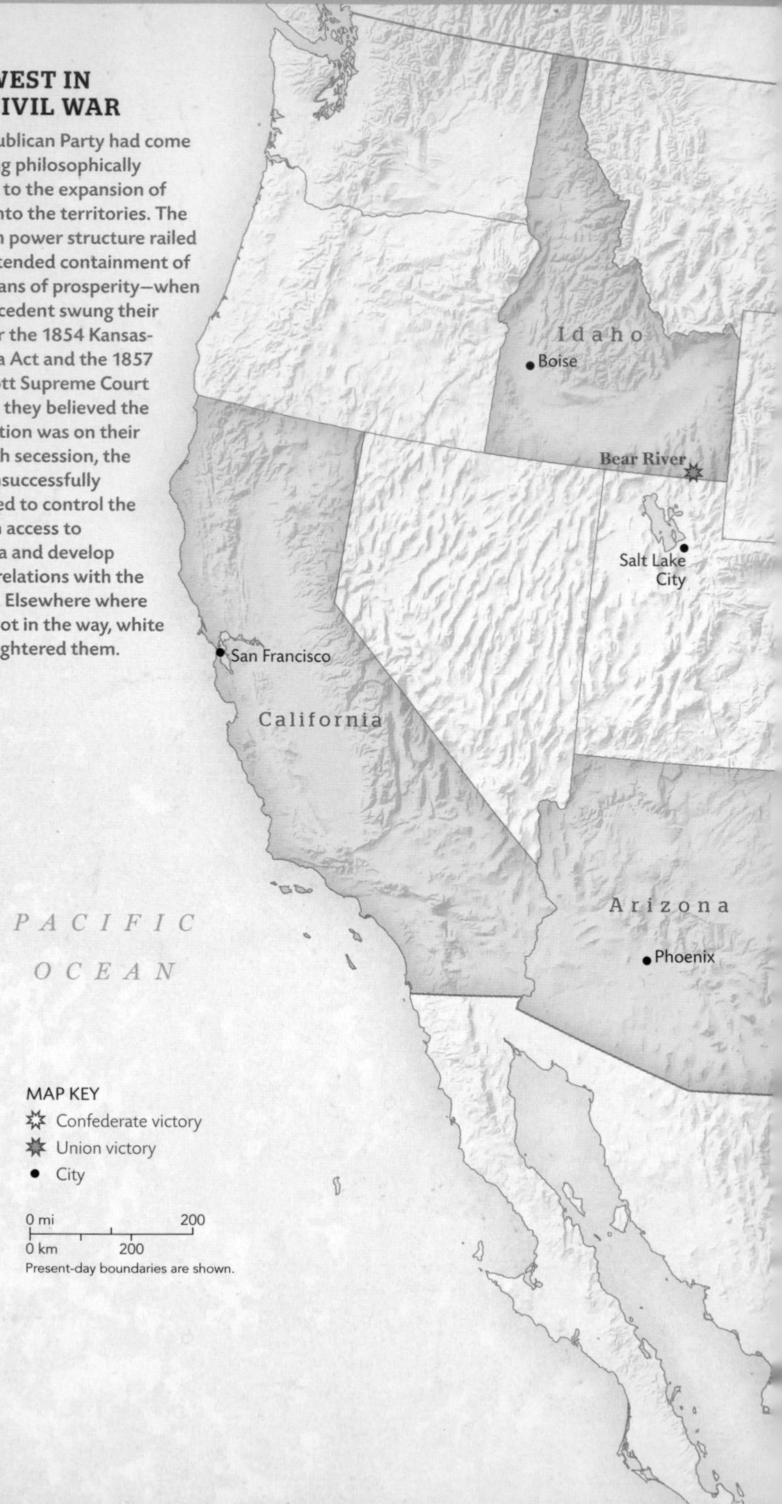

Idaho

• Boise

Bear River ✳

Salt Lake City •

• San Francisco

California

PACIFIC

OCEAN

Arizona

• Phoenix

MAP KEY

✳ Confederate victory

✳ Union victory

• City

0 mi   200

0 km   200

Present-day boundaries are shown.

CANADA

Lake Superior

Colorado

Sand Creek ✳

Santa Fe ●
✳ Glorieta
Pass
● Albuquerque

New Mexico

✳ Valverde

Texas

Fort Worth ●

Sabine Pass I ✳
✳ Sabine Pass II
✳ Galveston I
Galveston II

GULF OF
MEXICO

MEXICO

✳ Palmito Ranch

451

Colorado

AS AMERICAN EYES TURNED WESTWARD IN THE EARLY 19TH century, the work of ages was revealed—the Rocky Mountain chain and the other massive land masses that were formed by shifting tectonic plates below the surface of the Earth, creating nature's great barrier. And it was the nature of the American settler to accept the challenge and to climb the mountain. As explorers ventured into the harsh and unforgiving environment, the land gave up its rewards to the heartiest among them—gold and silver, the coin of the realm. Unlike the products of labor-intensive plantations and factories, this natural bounty made people wealthy fast, and those with the drive and means risked all for limitless wealth.

What would the United States do about the slave labor that would begin pouring into the territories within a matter of years? The Republican Party knew—no slavery in the territories, "free soil for free labor." Gold and silver were coming out of the ground; who would benefit and who would suffer? At Sand Creek and Bear River, we found out.

The rugged terrain around Pike's Peak in Colorado yielded gold deposits that were of great interest to both the Confederate and Union Armies.

COLORADO BATTLES

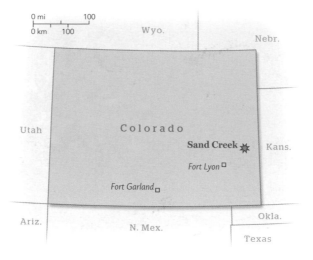

✳ Sand Creek

CAMPAIGN: Sand Creek Campaign
DATE(S): November 29, 1864

Tensions between whites and Indians had been mounting since the late 1850s, when prospectors struck gold near Pike's Peak. The country had fallen in love with the lure of quick wealth, and thousands of settlers streamed onto lands that had been set aside for the Cheyenne and Arapaho.

Confederate forces had invaded the New Mexico Territory in 1862 with dreams of effecting a partnership with Native Americans and disrupting the Santa Fe Trail traffic. Had they succeeded, they would have been well positioned to move into and control the Colorado Territory and gold fields.

The 1861 Treaty of Fort Wise had greatly diminished tribal lands in the region. Resentful Cheyenne and Lakota warriors ignored the new boundaries, however, and through the spring and summer of 1864 fought a series of skirmishes with the Colorado militiamen. On November 29, 1864, hoping to make peace, Cheyenne

Chief Black Kettle encamped with about 700 Cheyenne and Arapaho Indians at Sand Creek, 40 miles north of Fort Lyon. After a night of drinking, 675 troops from the Colorado home guard, commanded by Colonel Chivington, attacked the peaceful encampment and killed 200 Indians, many of them women, children, and elderly. Although the army and Congress condemned the event, which became known as the Sand Creek Massacre, Chivington was never court-martialed. Nonetheless, his reputation was forever stained by the massacre.

LOCATION: Sand Creek National Historic Site, County Rd. W., 1 mile east of County Rd. 54 (off Colorado State Hwy. 96), 719-438-5916 or 719-729-3003, www.nps.gov/sand.

FURTHER READING
The Sand Creek Massacre
by Stan Hoig
An exhaustive account of the massacre and events that lead up to it

Other Battles and Beyond

✦ Fort Garland

Built in 1858 to protect settlers in the San Luis Valley from the Ute Indians, Fort Garland had a garrison of more than 100 men and was at one point commanded by the famous Western frontiersman Kit Carson. The fort is a museum today, with re-created commandant headquarters, exhibits on the Battle of Glorieta Pass (see pp. 462), a parade ground, and original adobe buildings.

LOCATION: **29477 Hwy. 159, Fort Garland, 719-379-3512, www.historycolorado.org/museums.**

✦ Fort Lyon

Even before Colonel Chivington staged the Sand Creek Massacre from here, the fort had gone through an embarrassing identity crisis in the early years of the war. The U.S. Army built the fort in 1860 to provide a military link along the Santa Fe Trail between Fort Leavenworth in Kansas and Fort Union in New Mexico. Initially it was named Fort Wise, after Henry A. Wise, the governor of Virginia, but once the Civil War broke out, the Army decided it was inappropriate for a Union fort to be named after a Confederate. They renamed it Fort Lyon, for Nathaniel Lyon, the first Union general killed in the Civil War. The fort's garrison marched south to help defeat the Confederate Army at Glorieta Pass in New Mexico in 1862, but then spent the rest of the Civil War guarding emigrant trails and headquartering the Army's dealings with the local Plains Indians. The original fort was abandoned in 1867.

LOCATION: **No public access.**

Confederate Resistance

As many as 40 percent of the miners who ended up in Colorado prospecting for gold in the late 1850s were Southerners. When the Civil War started, many headed home to fight for the Confederacy, but some remained behind and formed partisan units that practiced a shadowy resistance against Federal forces throughout the Colorado Territory. In 1862, George T. Madison and a group of about 35 soldiers called the Brigands worked to disrupt Federal mail and communication lines in southern Colorado. They targeted Fort Garland in particular, and managed to capture a mail train on its way to the fort. Betrayed to Union forces, Madison and his Brigands escaped and headed south to join Confederates in Texas.

Federal Fort Lyon was the staging point for the Sand Creek Massacre.

Idaho

MANIFEST DESTINY WAS INTERRUPTED BY THE CIVIL WAR. Independent-minded dreamers sought places where they might be free to pursue happiness, but America in the mid-19th century showed little tolerance for religious difference. In New York, another sect had arisen to the consternation of the white, Anglo-Saxon power structure: Mormonism.

The Mormon faith follows the teachings of the modern holy man Joseph Smith, and thousands of followers had accompanied Brigham Young to a remote and barren section of Utah where they could practice their unique way of life, which included polygamy. In 1857, President Buchanan dispatched an army column to bring democracy to what he perceived as a growing religious threat.

As Mormons adapted to life in the desert, some settlers found their way into what would become Idaho. In 1863, Lincoln formally established the Idaho Territory, from which the states of Montana, Wyoming, and Idaho eventually emerged. Once again, Indians paid the price.

Civil War reenactors play the roles of Union infantry soldiers standing guard at an encampment near Boise, Idaho.

CANADA

Wash.

Mont.

0 mi 100

0 km 100

Idaho

Oreg.

★ Boise
Fort Boise;
Idaho Soldier's Home/
Veterans Memorial Park

Wyo.

Bear River ⚹

Nev.

Utah

Fort Douglas ☐

⚹ Bear River

CAMPAIGN: Expedition From Camp Douglas, Utah Territory, to Cache Valley, Idaho Territory

DATE(S): January 29, 1863

During the Civil War, the American government was as wary of Mormons in the western territories of Utah and Idaho as it was of American Indians. It feared that the Mormons—who had never acknowledged the sovereignty of the federal government—might cooperate with Confederate sympathizers to threaten Union interests. In 1862, Union Army Colonel Patrick E. Connor established Camp Douglas near Salt Lake City in Utah with volunteer troops from Nevada and California. His assignment was to guard the overland mail route and to keep an eye on the Mormons.

A few years earlier, in 1860, Mormon emigrants—mistakenly believing they were still in Utah—had settled Franklin, the first town of present-day Idaho's southern Cache Valley. The Shoshone Indians in the area had begun to feel crowded in the 1840s, when the Oregon and California Trails brought floods of pioneers across their lands; the arrival of the Mormons added to their discomfort. The discovery of gold farther north in Idaho brought yet another wave of white settlement in the early 1860s. Their resources depleted and their lands encroached on, the Shoshone began to fight back, raiding ranches and towns and attacking settlers.

In early 1863, Colonel Connor learned that a party of Shoshone had attacked a mining party in southern Idaho. He advised the War Department that he would "chastise them, if possible." He and 200 California Volunteers set out from Camp Douglas for the Cache Valley in midwinter, moving through deep snow. On January 29, 1863, they attacked a Shoshone winter village at the confluence of Bear River and Beaver Creek. Of the 400 Indians encamped, 250 were killed, about 90 of them women and children. It was the largest massacre of American Indians in the history of the American West, but Civil War headlines elsewhere in the country—the attack on Charleston, Chancellorsville, and the death of Stonewall Jackson—overshadowed the event, which remains a little-known brutality in Western history.

LOCATION: Marker located off Hwy. 91, about 5 miles northwest of Preston, Idaho.

FURTHER READING

The Shoshoni Frontier and the Bear River Massacre by Brigham D. Madsen Detailed account of the conflict between the Shoshoni and white settlers and soldiers

Other Battles and Beyond

✦ Fort Boise

Built by the Hudson Bay Fur Company in 1834, Old Fort Boise was a fur-trading post at the confluence of the Boise and Snake Rivers. The company eventually abandoned the fort because of Indian attacks, and the Union Army built a new Fort Boise—a permanent military cavalry fort—in 1863. Its purpose was to protect miners from Indians and to guard the interests of the U.S. government in the region's gold and silver mines. The town that sprang up around it became present-day Boise. Fort Boise has become part of the Boise VA Medical Center complex today, but three sandstone buildings from the 1863–1864 Union cavalry fort still stand, and are among the oldest surviving architecture in Idaho. Nearby on a hill is the Fort Boise Military Cemetery, which contains the remains of Civil War veterans, the identity of some forever unknown.

LOCATION: 500 W. Fort St., Boise.

✦ Fort Douglas

The first troops to arrive at Camp Douglas in 1862 lived in dugouts covered by tents; the next year more permanent buildings of log or adobe were constructed for living quarters and supply buildings. The camp continued to function as an important U.S. Army post after the Civil War and received the grander title Fort Douglas in 1878. In the 20th century, it was used in both world wars, and parts of the fort are still in use today as Army Reserve offices. The Fort Douglas Military Museum preserves photographs of an excavation of one of the original 1862 dugouts (though the site itself is gone), and an original adobe building from 1863 still stands—the former post commander's quarters. Patrick E. Connor—who ordered the Bear River Massacre and became a brigadier general in the Union Army—is buried in Fort Douglas Cemetery.

LOCATION: 32 Potter St., Salt Lake City, 801-581-1251, www.fortdouglas.org.

✦ Idaho Soldier's Home/ Veterans Memorial Park

Although no Idaho militia served in the Civil War, in the years after the war more than a thousand veterans of the Union and Confederate Armies moved to the state. The Idaho Soldier's Home, a state-run home for aging and disabled veterans of the Civil War, was built and opened in 1895. It was a grand, chateau-style building that housed veterans until 1966. Though it no longer stands, the site of the Soldier's Home is now Veterans Memorial Park, which has memorials to veterans of all wars and a brick Patriots' Walk that honors Idaho veterans.

LOCATION: 930 Veterans Memorial Pkwy., Boise.

Mormons in the Civil War

In Utah Territory, relations between the U.S. government and the Mormons had been tense since 1857, when President James Buchanan had tried unsuccessfully to assert federal authority by attempting to replace Brigham Young as Utah's territorial governor. Resentful of Buchanan's interference, Young decided that the Mormons would not participate in the Civil War. Nonetheless, at the request of the U.S. Army in 1862, Young did permit Lot Smith—also a Mormon—to muster a company of 100 volunteers to help the Union Army guard the overland mail route and telegraph lines in northern Utah and present-day southwestern Wyoming from Indian attack. This constituted Utah's only real military contribution—to either side—in the Civil War.

New Mexico

KNOWN AS THE LAND OF ENCHANTMENT, NEW MEXICO WAS a central element of American expansionism talks throughout the 1850s. The prewar history of the New Mexico Territory—which included Arizona, Nevada, and part of Colorado—involved pacifying Mexican residents and reconciling the interests and lifestyle of the Native Americans. Frontier officer General Stephen Kearny had gone far in Americanizing the region, which had been used as the stepping-off point for operations against Mexico.

Like many of the western territories, life in New Mexico could be harsh; however, the territory was the most promising route to California, now a growing, prosperous state. A number of U.S. fortifications sprung up in the intervening years so that, by the start of the Civil War, Confederate and Texas troops were able and ready to move into established forts.

When the war began, Southerners saw the potential of taking the territories and spreading across the southwestern plains to the mineral-rich territories. The dream was over in less than a year.

The red adobe ruins of Fort Union still guard the remains of the Santa Fe Trail in New Mexico—now protected as a national monument.

✳ Glorieta Pass

CAMPAIGN: Sibley's New Mexico Campaign

DATE(S): March 26–28, 1862

Once he had occupied Santa Fe, Confederate General Sibley turned his sights on Fort Union, a critical military garrison that protected the Santa Fe Trail. It was reached via a strategic part of the trail—Glorieta Pass. His intent was to control the pass so the Confederates would have access to the high plains and to Fort Union (see p. 464).

Under the command of Major Charles Pyron, a Rebel force of 200 to 300 men camped at Johnson's Ranch, at one end of the pass. On March 26, Major Chivington, with a force of 400 Union soldiers, advanced on the Confederates, eventually forcing Pyron's men to retreat to a narrow section of the pass, where they formed a defensive line. Chivington's men attacked and again forced them to retreat.

A cannonball from the Glorieta Pass battlefield in New Mexico

On March 27, reinforcements arrived for both sides, with Colonel William Scurry in command for the Confederates and Colonel John Slough for the Union. The next day, the two sides skirmished through the afternoon. Slough eventually retired to a way station on the Santa Fe Trail, and Scurry left the battlefield soon after, thinking he had won the battle. Chivington, however, had located the Confederate supply train at Johnson's ranch and destroyed it. Without supplies, Scurry was forced to retreat, and Sibley soon abandoned Santa Fe. The battle was the high-water mark of the Rebel advance in the New Mexico Territory.

LOCATION: Pecos National Historical Park, 2 miles south of Pecos Village on Hwy. 63, 505-757-7241, www.nps.gov/peco. The park has a 2.25-mile self-guided trail across the actual battlefield. Access the site via the park visitor center.

FURTHER READING

The Battle of Glorieta: Union Victory in the West by Don E. Alberts Draws on little-used sources to create the first full battle account

✳ Valverde

CAMPAIGN: Sibley's New Mexico Campaign
DATE(S): February 20–21, 1862

The Battle of Valverde was an important victory in the Confederate campaign to occupy the New Mexico Territory, gain access to Colorado's mineral wealth, and eventually expand west to the Pacific.

In early 1862, General Sibley and his Texan army—hoping to cut off communication between Union Fort Craig and its military headquarters in Santa Fe—advanced up the east side of the Rio Grande River. Sibley planned to cross the river at Valverde Ford and bypass the fort. When Sibley loitered in the area north of the fort, however, Colonel Canby left Fort Craig with 3,000 men (only 1,200 of whom were experienced soldiers) to drive the Confederate forces away from his supply lines. Kit Carson commanded a small regiment of volunteers, which augmented Canby's force. The Federal soldiers

opened fire and soon forced Sibley's army to retreat. The Confederates took up a strong position in the Old Rio Grande riverbed and from there made a frontal attack on Canby's forces, scattering the Union battle line and forcing them to retreat. With the arrival of reinforcements, Sibley began to organize for another attack, but Canby, realizing his position was collapsing, asked for a truce and Sibley agreed. The Confederates held on to the battlefield and an open road to Santa Fe; however, they lost a large number of supply wagons.

LOCATION: No public access. Battle is interpreted at nearby Fort Craig (see p. 464).

FURTHER READING

Bloody Valverde: A Civil War Battle on the Rio Grande, February 21, 1862
by John Taylor
Definitive account of the battle

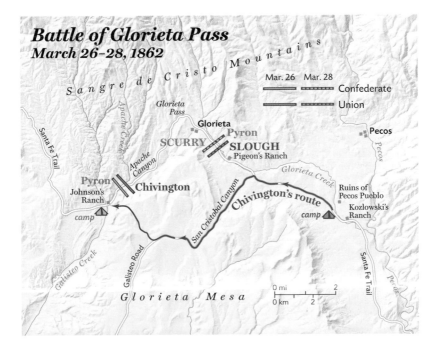

Battle of Glorieta Pass
March 26–28, 1862

Sangre de Cristo Mountains

	Mar. 26	Mar. 28
			Confederate
			Union

Glorieta Pass
Glorieta
SCURRY
Pyron
SLOUGH
Pigeon's Ranch
Pecos
Pyron
Johnson's Ranch
Chivington
camp
Glorieta Creek
Chivington's route
camp
Ruins of Pecos Pueblo
Kozlowski's Ranch
Apache Creek
Apache Canyon
San Cristobal Canyon
Santa Fe Trail
Galisteo Creek
Galisteo Road
Glorieta Mesa
Pecos
Santa Fe Trail

0 mi 2
0 km 2

Other Battles and Beyond

✦ Albuquerque Museum

Albuquerque was twice occupied by Confederate forces during the Civil War—once when General Sibley's troops were headed north to attack Fort Union in March 1862, and then again when they retreated back to Texas in April. During the latter occupation, Union and Confederate forces lobbed artillery shells at each other, but there were no casualties. When Sibley and his men withdrew from the city, they buried eight brass howitzer cannons to conceal them from the Union Army. These are now preserved in the Albuquerque Museum in Old Town; two replica cannons grace the Old Town Plaza.

LOCATION: **2000 Mountain Rd. N.W., Albuquerque, 505-242-4600, www.albuquerquemuseum.org.**

✦ Cañada Alamosa

Concerned about a Confederate movement on Fort Craig after the Battle of Mesilla, a Union reconnaissance force, under the command of Captain Minks, set up an encampment at the town of Cañada Alamosa—about 40 miles southwest of the fort—on September 24, 1861. They were attacked by a party of more than 100 Confederates and defeated; the main force withdrew, but the rear guard surrendered and was taken prisoner by the Confederates.

LOCATION: **Nothing remains of the battlefield.**

✦ Fort Craig Historic Site

In 1862, as Confederate troops under General Sibley advanced up the Rio Grande River, Colonel Canby staged his attack on them from Fort Craig. The Union lost the battle but held the fort, which was afterward used mostly to control Indian raids. It was abandoned in 1885. Established in 1854, the site is now managed by the Bureau of Land

Management. It is open to the public and contains well-preserved ruins of the fort and signs that interpret it, as well as self-guided walking tours.

LOCATION: **35 miles south of Socorro on Rte. 1, 575-835-0412, www.blm.gov/nm/fortcraig.**

✦ Fort Stanton

Fort Stanton was built in 1855 in south-central New Mexico to control Indian raids. The Confederates captured and occupied it for about a month in 1861; they burned it when they left it, but the stone walls stayed standing. In 1862, Kit Carson and Union New Mexico volunteer forces reoccupied the fort. Fort Stanton was rebuilt after the war and today comprises 88 buildings, some of which date back to 1855. The fort—which is now a state monument and museum—is open to the public. There is a nice visitor center and short movie telling the fort's history.

LOCATION: **Off the Billy the Kid Scenic Byway (Hwy. 380) on Hwy. 220 at the Bonito River, 575-354-0341, www.fortstanton.org.**

✦ Fort Union National Monument

Known as the "guardian of the Santa Fe Trail," the Federal Fort Union was one of the targets of General Sibley's forces during the New Mexico Campaign. Established in 1851, Fort Union saw three different fortifications built over its 40-year existence. Today, the adobe ruins of the last and largest fort (built in 1867)—and the largest visible network of Santa Fe Trail ruts still extant—are protected as a national monument and open to the public. A visitor center at the site has interpretive talks and programs, and a self-guided 1.6-mile loop gives visitors access to the ruins.

LOCATION: **NM 161 (exit 366 off I-25), 505-425-8025, www.nps.gov/foun.**

✦ Mesilla

After Texas seceded from the Union, a battalion of Confederates under the command of Colonel John Baylor moved into the New Mexico Territory in July 1861 to launch an attack on Union forces at Fort Fillmore, outside the town of Mesilla. Major Isaac Lynde was informed of the Confederate movement, however, and led Union troops from the fort to attack the Confederates at Mesilla. The Confederates repulsed the attack and Lynde and his troops abandoned the fort; they later surrendered to the Confederates at Augustine Springs. Baylor then established the short-lived Confederate Territory of Arizona with Mesilla as its capital. About a year later, after a second short skirmish at Mesilla, Rebel forces withdrew toward Texas.

LOCATION: **Nothing remains of Fort Fillmore today, though Mesilla has adobe buildings that date from the Civil War and earlier.**

✦ Peralta

As the Confederates retreated toward Texas after General Sibley's failed New Mexico Campaign, the Union Army under Colonel Canby overtook them at the town of Peralta on April 14, 1862. Members of the 5th Texas Mounted Volunteers under Colonel Green took cover behind the low adobe walls of the town's buildings as the Union forces attacked. A dust storm blew in that afternoon and gave the Confederates the chance to retreat across the Rio Grande, though the town was left a shambles.

LOCATION: **Nothing of the battlefield is preserved today.**

✦ Santa Fe National Cemetery

General Sibley occupied Santa Fe in March 1862 at the high point of the Confederate New Mexico Campaign; after the Battle of Glorieta Pass (see p. 462), with his supply trains destroyed, he retreated back to Texas. Santa Fe National Cemetery holds the remains of hundreds of U.S. soldiers who died at the Battle of Glorieta Pass and at other remote southwestern outposts.

LOCATION: **501 N. Guadalupe St., Santa Fe, 505-988-6400, www.cem.va.gov.**

The Fort Stanton Museum exhibits the fort's frontier history, including its occupation during the Civil War.

Texas

THE GREAT STATE OF TEXAS HAD BARELY SETTLED INTO ITS
new relationship with the United States when it was thrust into the
Civil War. Texas statesman Sam Houston did not want to see the
country divided and did not want the state to secede; however, he
refused to accept an offer from Abraham Lincoln that would have
kept Texas in the Union.

When Texas seceded, U.S. military installations in the state were
turned over to Texas officials, and regiments were recruited, perhaps
the most famous being Hood's Texas Brigade. Overall, as many as
90,000 men entered Confederate service, but significantly, perhaps
2,000 entered Union regiments.

The intrigues of politics made Texas an interesting and powerful member of the Confederacy. Governor Francis Lubbock, General
(Senator) Louis Wigfall (head of the opposition to Jefferson Davis),
General Sam Houston, cotton, cattle, Indians, German immigrants,
loyalists, and Prince John Magruder—all created a fascinating four
years in the Lone Star State.

**The 1st Texas Regiment of the Confederate Army charges into battle under
the colors of Texas in this painting by Don Troiani.**

TEXAS BATTLES

✳ Galveston I

CAMPAIGN: Operations to Blockade the Texas Coast

DATE(S): October 4, 1862

The U.S. Navy blockade of Galveston Harbor began in July 1861, but not until October 1862 did the Union manage to take control of the port. Union Commander William Renshaw—in charge of the naval blockade—sent the U.S.S. *Harriet Lane* into the harbor on October 4 to inform Colonel Joseph Cook, the Confederate military commander, that unless his forces surrendered the town of Galveston, the navy would attack. Initially Cook refused, and the Confederate forces at Fort Point and the navy ships in the harbor exchanged fire. The Confederates then negotiated a four-day truce with Renshaw so that women and children could be evacuated from Galveston. Renshaw agreed, and over the next several

days, the Confederates left the city altogether, taking with them their weapons, ammunition, and supplies. Renshaw felt this evacuation exceeded the terms of the truce he had agreed to, but since it had never been committed to paper, he permitted it. The Galveston port was taken over by the Union Army for the next several months.

LOCATION: Marker located at the Galveston Yacht Club, on 4th St., between Holiday Dr. and Albacore Ave., in Galveston.

✳ Galveston II

CAMPAIGN: Operations Against Galveston

DATE(S): January 1, 1863

Confederate General Magruder, who took over as commander of Confederate forces in Texas in late 1862, was anxious to retake Galveston from the Union. On January 1, 1863, Magruder executed a daring raid that earned him much praise. As part of the plan, the Confederate gunboats C.S. *Bayou City* and C.S. *Neptune* approached the harbor and engaged the Union fleet, which consisted of six ships. The *Neptune* was sunk, but the C.S. *Bayou City* managed to capture the U.S.S. *Harriet Lane.* Commander William Renshaw blew up the U.S.S. *Westfield* rather than have it fall into Confederate hands, but an error in the timing of the explosion killed him and several other Union sailors. The rest of the Union ships sailed out to sea, ignoring the Confederate demand that they surrender. The Union forces in Galveston—operating under the command of Colonel Isaac Burrell—surrendered. The Union blockade of Galveston Harbor remained in place, but the Confederate Army held the port for the rest of the Civil War.

LOCATION: **Marker located at the Galveston Yacht Club, on 4th St., between Holiday Dr. and Albacore Ave., in Galveston. Magruder's grave is an obelisk along an outer wall of Episcopal Cemetery, between 40th St. and 43rd St.**

✳ Palmito Ranch

CAMPAIGN: Expedition From Brazos Santiago

OTHER NAME(S): Palmeto Ranch, Palmetto Ranch

DATE(S): May 12–13, 1865

More than a month after General Lee surrendered at Appomattox, the Civil War's final

battle was fought near Brownsville, Texas, and ironically, it was a Confederate victory. On May 11, a Union expedition under the command of Colonel David Branson set out from Brazos Island to attack Confederate outposts along the Rio Grande. The expedition encamped that night near White's Ranch, a Confederate outpost that was found abandoned. The next day Branson and his men attacked a Confederate camp at Palmito Ranch, dispersing the Rebels. Later that afternoon, a larger force assembled and forced the Union troops to retreat back to White's Ranch.

At daybreak, Union Colonel Theodore Barrett arrived with reinforcements for the Union Army. The bolstered Union force returned to Palmito Ranch and destroyed the remaining Confederate supplies. After another skirmish with Confederate troops, Barrett's forces encamped at a bluff over the river, where they were attacked by Confederate cavalry commanded by Colonel John S. Ford. The Union formed a battle line that the Confederates pounded with artillery until Barrett ordered a retreat back across the river to Brazos Island. So concluded the Civil War on land, and a few days later, Federal officers from Brazos Island arranged a truce with Colonel Ford and Confederate General James Slaughter.

LOCATION: **Marker located 12 miles east of Brownsville on Texas Hwy. 4.**

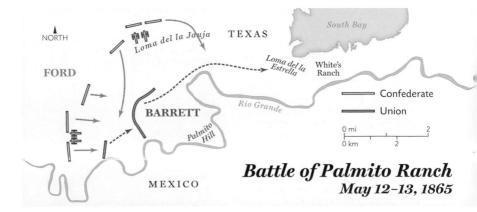

Battle of Palmito Ranch
May 12–13, 1865

FURTHER READING

The Last Battle of the Civil War: Palmetto Ranch
by Jeffrey Wm. Hunt
Letters and military records help re-create the battle

✳ Sabine Pass I

CAMPAIGN: Operations to Blockade the Texas Coast

DATE(S): September 24–25, 1862

Sabine Pass, on the northern end of the Texas Gulf Coast, was an important Union objective because it could help the U.S. Navy strengthen its blockade on the coast and would give the army access to the Texas interior. The U.S.S. *Kensington,* U.S.S. *James Henry,* and U.S.S. *Rachel Seaman* entered Sabine Pass on the morning of September 24, 1862, and began firing on the Confederate position on the shore. At first, the shots from both the Union ships and the Confederates on the shore fell short of their targets, but as the Union flotilla moved closer, its superior firepower prevailed, and the Confederates evacuated the post overnight. The Union forces took control in the morning.

LOCATION: Sabine Pass Battleground State Historic Site, 6100 Dick Dowling Rd., Port Arthur, 512-463-7948, www.visitsabinepass battleground.com.

✳ Sabine Pass II

CAMPAIGN: Operations to Blockade the Texas Coast

DATE(S): September 8, 1863

Four Union gunboats steamed through Sabine Pass and up the Sabine River on September 8, 1863, with Lieutenant Frederick Crocker in command. Their objective was to attack Fort Griffin and begin an invasion of Texas. The fort, however, was occupied by 44 Confederate gunners, who had been conducting artillery practice on

targets in the river to sharpen their accuracy. Under the command of Lieutenant Dick Dowling, the small Confederate force fired on the Union flotilla when it came within range, destroying two ships and forcing the rest to retreat. The Union suffered hundreds of casualties in the fight; the Confederates, not one. The defeat effectively ended Union efforts to launch an invasion in east Texas.

LOCATION: Sabine Pass Battleground State Historic Site, 6100 Dick Dowling Rd., Port Arthur, 512-463-7948, www.visitsabinepass battleground.com. A bronze statue of Lieutenant Dowling stands on the site, and an interpretive pavilion tells the story of the battle. Walking trails offer visitors self-guided tours of the battleground.

FURTHER READING

Sabine Pass: The Confederacy's Thermopylae
by Edward T. Cotham, Jr.
Award-winning portrait of the battle that draws on often overlooked sources

Hood's Texas Brigade

Texas may have seen only marginal fighting during the Civil War, but it produced one of the fiercest fighting units in the Confederate Army. In February 1862, General Hood was put in charge of the 1st, 4th, and 5th Texas Infantry regiments, along with the 3rd Arkansas Infantry. These Texas troops were the only Texans to fight in the East, and fight they did, with great distinction in nearly every major battle of General Lee's Army of Northern Virginia. These included Antietam, Gettysburg, Fredericksburg, and Second Manassas. Hood remained in command of the brigade for only six months, but his leadership produced a fighting unit of great tenacity and bravery—one that had, by the end of the war, suffered more than a 60 percent casualty rate.

Other Battles and Beyond

✦ "Texas in the Civil War"

The Texas Historical Commission developed this essential map in 2001. To order, call 512-463-6100 or visit www.thc.state.tx.us.

✦ Camp Ford

At its peak in 1864, Camp Ford housed more than 5,300 prisoners of war. The Confederates struggled to supply the prisoners and guards with adequate rations and supplies and, as a result, conditions were deplorable during the last year of the war. The prison compound was destroyed in 1865, but Camp Ford Historic Park now sits on the site. It has walking trails and signs that interpret the history of Camp Ford.

LOCATION: **Hwy. 271, three-quarters of a mile outside Loop 323, Tyler, 903-592-5993, www.smithcountyhistoricalsociety.org/camp-ford.**

✦ Eagle Pass

This town on the Rio Grande River served as a crossover point into Mexico for Confederate leaders seeking to escape the collapsed Confederacy. Diehard Confederates hoped to align with Emperor Maxmilian's government and perhaps find a new way to resurrect the moribund Confederate experiment.

LOCATION: **Just east of the Mexico border, at the junction of Hwy. 277 and Hwy. 57.**

✦ Fort Bliss

In 1861, General Sibley used Fort Bliss as the staging point for his invasion of New Mexico, which was repulsed by the Union Army in 1862. The fort retained a variety of military uses over succeeding decades and remains an active U.S. Army base today. On the base, a replica of Old Fort Bliss is built with adobe structures that house period rooms representing life on the post in 1857.

Exhibits, artifacts, and demonstrations give visitors a sense of how the military installation operated between 1853 and 1868.

LOCATION: **Bldg. 5054, Pleasonton Rd., Fort Bliss, 915-568-4518 or 915-588-8482.**

✦ Fort Davis National Historic Site

After Texas seceded, Confederate troops occupied this 1854 fort until 1862, when the Union Army briefly took possession again. After the Union troops departed, it sat vacant until after the war. Today, it is one of the best remaining examples of a frontier military post in the Southwest.

LOCATION: **101 Lt. Henry Flipper Dr., Fort Davis, 432-426-3224, www.nps.gov/foda.**

✦ Fort Worth Texas Civil War Museum

The largest Civil War museum west of the Mississippi contains artifacts from infantry, cavalry, navy, medical, and musical divisions of both the Northern and Southern armies. Another collection focuses on the Texas home front and Texas soldiers, and a third on domestic artifacts.

LOCATION: **760 Jim Wright Freeway N., Fort Worth, 817-246-2323, www.texascivilwarmuseum.com.**

✦ Texas State Cemetery

Located a mile from the state capitol in Austin, this cemetery holds the remains of more than 2,000 Confederate veterans and their widows. A smaller plot holds the graves of prominent Texans including Stephen F. Austin and Confederate General Albert Sidney Johnston, who died at the Battle of Shiloh. A small chapel houses Johnston's death mask.

LOCATION: **909 Navasota St., Austin, 512-463-0605, www.cemetery.state.tx.us.**

Other Western States

Arizona and California

GOLD AT SUTTER'S MILL PROPELLED CALIFORNIA INTO THE
midst of American politics. In 1850, barely a year later, the expansive
region qualified for statehood. In the absence of slaves, the state
entered as a free state; however, there was no southern territory
ready for statehood, and so Maine was also admitted.

Faced with the need to give the South something of value, the
government agreed to a more robust enforcement of the Fugitive
Slave Law. Soon the concept of "popular sovereignty" gave hope that
the South could preserve its electoral balance.

To maintain law and order in the new West, U.S. army units were
assigned to, and many names of note were stationed in, California
before coming east to join in the war. Many of those treks were
through the wild and unorganized Arizona Territory, defended by
snakes, heat, and Apaches.

Arizona's upthrust Picacho Peak loomed over the scene of a skirmish between
the Union California Column and Confederate Rangers in 1862.

Arizona

The Civil War brought hard decisions to the westernmost Confederacy. With Texas the only Confederate state on the western border, and with an active incursion of white settlers into the New Mexico and Arizona Territories, the Confederates sought to control the routes west by developing a friendly Indian policy. They hoped to take advantage of the bad relations that had festered between the United States and the Native American tribes. They would find that the Apaches considered them no better than the Yankees.

✦ Dragoon Springs

In early May 1862, the Confederates were in their final days of occupying Tucson. On May 5, a Confederate patrol was rounding up cattle near Dragoon Springs, 50 miles east of Tucson and near an Old Butterfield Stage Coach station. A group of Apaches

After the skirmish at Picacho Pass, the California Column retreated west.

attacked them, killing several Confederates. The Rebel graves and the ruins of the old station can be visited via a three-mile round-trip hike outside the town of Dragoon (or you can drive another mile toward the trailhead in a high-clearance vehicle). The site is very rural, and visitors should beware of rattlesnakes at the station ruins.

LOCATION: **Take the Dragoon Rd. exit off I-10, to Old Ranch Rd. and follow the signs for the Butterfield Stage Coach station. Detailed instructions and a map to the site can be found at www.bensonvisitorcenter.com.**

✦ Fort Bowie National Historic Site

Captain Sherod Hunter and his Confederate Rangers pulled out of Tucson on May 14, 1862, and the Union Army occupied the village several days later. In July, the California Column continued its march east, headed for New Mexico. On July 15, an advance guard under the command of Captain Thomas Roberts approached the springs at Apache Pass, thirsty and sorely in need of rest. The detachment was ambushed by a party of Apache Indians, led by the warriors Cochise and Mangas Coloradas. Roberts and his men fought back, using artillery fire to scatter the Apaches and close in on the springs. By the next morning, the Apaches had fled and the Union Army took possession of the springs. After the incident, Colonel James Carleton thought it necessary to erect a permanent military outpost there, and Fort Bowie was constructed.

LOCATION: **3327 S. Old Fort Bowie Rd., Bowie, 520-847-2500, www.nps.gov/fobo. Fort Bowie is accessed via a 1.5-mile trail that takes visitors past Apache Springs and the ruins of the 1862 fort to a very nice visitor center.**

✦ Picacho Pass

The California Column continued to march toward Tucson. On April 15, 1862, a patrol unit from the column under the command of Lieutenant James Barrett encountered a

Only ruins remain of Fort Bowie, built at Apache Pass in 1862 following the ambush of Federal troops by Apache Indians at nearby springs.

group of Confederate Rangers near Picacho Peak, 50 miles northwest of Tucson. During an encounter that lasted more than an hour, Barrett was killed and his patrol was forced to retreat. Alarmed by the skirmish and thinking it foretold a heavily fortified Tucson, the Union forces retreated 100 miles west to Pima Indian villages and delayed their occupation of the city for more than a month. Today, the site of the skirmish falls within Picacho State Park, and though interpretation on the site is limited, an annual reenactment is held there each March. The park also features hiking trails, campgrounds, and a visitor center.

LOCATION: Picacho State Park, 70 miles south-east of Phoenix, off I-10, 520-466-3183, www .azstateparks.com/parks/pipe.

✦ Stanwix Station

After the Battle of Mesilla in New Mexico (see p. 465), the Confederates headed farther west and occupied Tucson in February 1862. Their goal was to eventually expand to the Pacific. To drive them back, Union General James Carleton headed east from California with a force of volunteers known as the California Column. They headed slowly across the desert along the old Butterfield Overland Stage Road toward Tucson. On March 30, 1862, a vanguard of the column encountered a Confederate raiding party at Stanwix Station, in the act of burning supplies that had been pre-staged there for the Union Army. This sparked the westernmost encounter of the Civil War, a firefight in which shots were exchanged but no Confederates were injured. They escaped to Tucson to alert Captain Hunter—in command of the Arizona Rangers occupying the city—that the U.S. Army was on the move.

LOCATION: Kiosk only, 110 miles southwest of Phoenix, near Ave. 76 E. off I-8.

California

With the discovery of gold in 1849, California quickly achieved statehood, and its admittance, along with that of Maine, disrupted the balance of power in the U.S. Congress. The wealth that was created demanded U.S. Army presence in the growing frontier towns to maintain order. Many U.S. officers—such as Henry Halleck and William T. Sherman—left the service and became businessmen. A homesick Ulysses S. Grant drowned his sorrows in liquor and resigned his commission. With the advent of war, Southern-born officers such as Albert Sidney Johnston found themselves facing perilous journeys to return home and join the Confederacy.

✦ Fort Alcatraz

In the late 1850s, Fort Alcatraz was still the only completed military fort on the San Francisco Bay. During the early years of the Civil War, the U.S. Army expanded and

Alcatraz Island was the site of the only federal fort on the San Francisco Bay completed by the time of the Civil War. It later gained notoriety as a federal prison.

San Francisco National Cemetery, located in the Presidio of San Francisco, contains the remains of Civil War soldiers and the plucky Union spy Pauline Cushman.

strengthened the fort, and used it as a training ground for soldiers headed to the southwest and east to fight for the Union. Alcatraz later famously became a federal penitentiary for almost 30 years. Today, Alcatraz Island is part of the Golden Gate National Recreation Area and is accessed by ferry from San Francisco. It can be explored on guided or self-guided tours.

LOCATION: **Alcatraz Island, Golden Gate National Recreation Area, San Francisco, 415-561-4700, www.nps.gov/alca.**

✦ Fort Point National Historic Site

Built beginning in 1855, Fort Point is a pristine example of the third system of fortifications built to protect U.S. harbors. With the Civil War looming, the U.S. Army became more concerned about the possibility of a Confederate assault. In 1861, 55 guns were mounted and the fort's first garrison was assembled. Although its guns were never fired in anger during the Civil War, the fort

gave the Union a strong hold on the Pacific Coast. The preserved site features exhibits, guided tours, and demonstrations. It is part of the old army Presidio.

LOCATION: **Marine Dr., Presidio, San Francisco, 415-556-1693, www.nps.gov/fopo.**

✦ Fort Yuma

Before the Civil War, Fort Yuma was used to protect emigrant travel routes from Yuma Indians, and later as a stage station on the Butterfield Overland Mail route. The Union Army retained control of it after war broke out, and in 1862, the California Column under General James Carleton set out from Fort Yuma to expel the Confederates from Arizona and New Mexico. For the duration of the war, the fort acted as a Union supply point. Buildings from the original fort still exist and are found in the Yuma Crossing National Heritage Area.

LOCATION: **Located on 149 acres near Winterhaven, California, and Yuma, Arizona; no public access.**

International

The Civil War ended in England at Liverpool Town Hall with the surrender of the commerce raider C.S.S. *Shenandoah* on November 6, 1865.

Milestones

> JANUARY 11, 1865
The Missouri Constitutional Convention abolishes slavery, the first slave state to do so.

> JANUARY 15, 1865
Fort Fisher in North Carolina falls, closing the last port in the Confederacy.

> JANUARY 23, 1865
Robert E. Lee is made general in chief of the Confederate forces—too little and too late.

> JANUARY 31, 1865
The U.S. House of Representatives passes the 13th Amendment, which, when ratified by states in December, abolishes slavery.

> APRIL 2, 1865
Grant breaks Lee's lines around Petersburg, compelling the evacuation of Richmond.

> APRIL 9, 1865
Lee surrenders at Appomattox, effectively ending the war.

> APRIL 14, 1865
John Wilkes Booth assassinates President Lincoln at Ford's Theatre.

> MAY 23-24, 1865
Federal eastern and western armies parade down Pennsylvania Avenue in triumph.

> JULY 7, 1865
Four conspirators are executed in Washington for the assassination of Lincoln.

> NOVEMBER 6, 1865
C.S.S. *Shenandoah* is the last Confederate unit to surrender in the Civil War.

ABRAHAM

International
England, France, Australia, Bahamas, Bermuda, and Canada

IN THE MID-19TH CENTURY, AMERICA WAS BECOMING AN increasingly important player on a global scale. The nation had taken Ireland's poor and starving and provided them with jobs, and it had given refuge for survivors of the German wars of unification. Large enclaves of Slavs had settled in the north. Internationally, America had taken a leading role in Central American affairs, and European ports from Gibraltar and Bordeaux to Cherbourg and Liverpool welcomed American vessels. While the full import of the Monroe Doctrine had yet to discourage European adventurism, the dustup between the North and the South, accompanied by a naval blockade of Southern ports, had everyone's attention.

In 1778, the long-standing Anglo-French dispute had spilled over to America's advantage. Now the possibility of a similar intervention threatened to break apart the nation before it replaced the European powers on the world stage.

This statue of Abraham Lincoln stands in Parliament Square, London, opposite the Houses of Parliament, a rare and moving international tribute.

England

The American Civil War affected nations around the world, not the least of which was our major international trading partner, England. Immigration and trade filled the docks of the ports of London and Liverpool, and both the Thames and Mersey Rivers were sites of international intrigue. As England was a major sea power, its naval bases at Spithead near Portsmouth and merchant navy port of Liverpool at the mouth of the Mersey were supported by a robust shipping industry in Birkenhead. English cotton looms were major sources of employment. Diplomacy and mercantilism were cut from the same cloth.

FURTHER READING

A World on Fire: Britain's Crucial Role in the American Civil War
by Amanda Foreman
Best-selling account of Britain's role in the war

✦ Liverpool and Wirral

Before the war, cotton agents and financiers set up offices in Liverpool. Most prominent among them was the agency of Fraser and Trenholm at 10 Rumford Place. Trenholm would become the Confederacy's treasurer, and his Liverpool offices would serve as a central clearinghouse for funds being raised for the Confederacy. The U.S. Consul in Liverpool, who reported to Charles Francis Adams, the U.S. minister (ambassador) in London on Confederate activities, was Thomas Haines Dudley, whose offices were at 69 Tower Building. When Grant visited Liverpool in 1877, he was feted at Liverpool Town Hall. Jefferson Davis also spent considerable time in Liverpool after his release from imprisonment in 1868. Make sure to visit the Merseyside Maritime Museum, which also houses the International Slavery Museum at Albert Dock. Many items of interest relating to the Civil War are located in each set of galleries.

Downtown, St. George's Hall was the site of a great Confederate aid bazaar in

H.M.S. *Warrior* was the first iron-hulled, armored warship powered by steam and sail. The pride of Queen Victoria's fleet can be visited at Portsmouth Historic Dockyard.

September 1864 that raised more than 20,000 pounds. One mile away is the home of Fraser and Trenholm senior manager Charles Prioleau of South Carolina, who lived at 19 Abercrombie Square.

Across the Mersey River in Wirral, you will find more of the maritime story of the region. The Confederate raider C.S.S. *Alabama* was built for Confederate service here, and the C.S.S. *Shenandoah* returned here to strike her flag—the last Confederate military unit to surrender on November 6, 1865. The captain surrendered his ship to British authorities at the Liverpool Town Hall.

Today, from the tower of St. Mary's Church on the grounds of Birkenhead Priory, visitors can look down into the No. 4 dock at Laird Shipyard, where the *Alabama* was built. Looking toward the west you will see the grave of John Laird, founder of the shipyard. Also constructed in the yards were oceangoing ironclad vessels known as Laird Rams that were being built for the Confederacy in violation of the neutrality agreements. The rams to be named *Mississippi* and *North Carolina* were eventually bought by the British government, after Minister Adams complained, and were placed in the Royal Navy.

Downtown, the Williamson Art Gallery and Museum features a Civil War exhibit and carefully constructed model of the *Alabama*. Laird's family ensured he would not be forgotten by funding a monument to him in Hamilton Square, opposite the Birkenhead Town Hall. At 28 Argyle Street (known as the Argyle Rooms), abolitionist Englishmen met and gave speeches calling for the end of American slavery, while along Canning Street, 30 potential sailors for Confederate privateers sang "Dixie" before taking the ferry to Liverpool.

Don't miss the Quarry Bank Mill and Styal Estate, ten miles south of Manchester near Wilmslow off the B5166. Well worth a day visit, this preserved antebellum cotton mill and village show the tremendous financial and social impact of the cotton crop on the livelihood of English workers.

About 3.5 hours north of Liverpool, Glasgow, Scotland, has the Riverside Museum at 100 Pointhouse Place. This great museum on the River Clyde has a powerful display on the Clyde River shipbuilders, who built many of the blockade-runners used by the Confederacy during the war, including the *Robert E. Lee, Herald, Juno,* and *Advance.*

FURTHER READING

The Secret Service of the Confederate States in Europe; or, How the Confederate Cruisers Were Equipped
by James D. Bulloch
Memoir originally published in 1884

Around the World With General Grant
by John Russell Young
Traces Ulysses S. Grant's around-the-world tour after leaving the presidency in 1877

Lifeline of the Confederacy: Blockade Running During the Civil War
by Stephen R. Wise
Detailed history of blockade-running during the Civil War

✦ London

As the center of government, London boasts multitudinous and diverse Civil War–related sites. In addition to the walking tour of London (see pp. 484–485), you may want to see the U.S. legation's (embassy's) two locations at 22 Mansfield Street and 98 Portland Place. This was the location of the U.S. minister (ambassador) to the Court of St. James, Charles Adams. You will find a monument of Abraham Lincoln in

Civil War on Foot: London

London was an ocean away from the battlefields of the American Civil War, yet American politics, especially of the Confederate sort, were still alive and well in this city in the 1860s. Follow this tour to trace the footsteps of spies, politicians, and other agents of the Confederacy.

❶ St. James Church (*197 Piccadilly*) This church looks very much like it did in August 1864, when it was filled with guests to witness and celebrate the marriage of celebrated spy Belle Boyd (see p. 319), also known as the Cleopatra of Secession. Boyd famously advised Stonewall Jackson in Virginia in 1862.

❷ Home of Rose O'Neal Greenhow (*34 Sackville St.*) In this fashionable housing area resided the famous Confederate spy turned diplomat Rose O'Neal Greenhow. Credited with ensuring the Confederate victory at the first Battle of Manassas (see pp. 254–256), Greenhow was imprisoned before bringing her guile and charm to the parlors of London in an effort to encourage recognition of the Confederacy. Greenhow drowned in the surf near Wilmington, North Carolina, in 1864.

❸ Home of Dr. Richard King (*17 Savile Row*) Key Confederate agents involved in many aspects of commerce, political lobbying, and shipping rented rooms here, including C. J. McRae, Henry Hotze, and John R. Thompson.

❹ Home of Matthew Fontaine Maury (*162 New Bond St.*) A noted American oceanographer, Maury was also a Confederate officer intimately interested in the acquisition of naval vessels from the British. This was Maury's London home during the American Civil War.

❺ Jefferson Davis House (*36 Clarges St.*) After being released from Federal custody, former Confederate president Jefferson Davis traveled abroad. He stayed here during his 1868 visit.

❻ Cambridge House (*94 Piccadilly*) This former royal residence

At Cambridge House, Confederates petitioned the British prime minister.

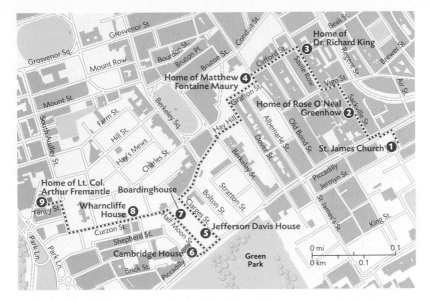

was the official home
of Prime Minister
Lord Palmerston,
on whose shoulders
rested the question of
Southern recognition.
Palmerston was visited
by Confederate agent
Edwin De Leon in 1862,
and by James Mason in
1865. He carefully kept
his distance to avoid
the appearance of offi-
cial recognition, which
would have angered the
queen and the Lincoln
Administration. He
received a petition urging
English mediation in the
war as late as July 1864.

❼ Boardinghouse
(15 Half Moon St.) The
first Confederate rep-
resentative to Britain,

William Lowndes
Yancey, stayed here in
1861. Yancey was a fire-
eater and politician from
Alabama. After James
Mason and John Slidell
were released following
their brief detainment
and sent on to England
and France, Yancey
returned to Richmond,
where he served as a
senator from Alabama
until he died in 1863.

❽ Wharncliffe House
(15 Curzon St.) In the
1860s, this building
was the home of Lord
Wharncliffe, an influ-
ential member of the
British House of Lords.
The president of the
Southern Independence
Association, Wharncliffe

hosted many Southern
representatives during
the war and advocated
on their behalf.

❾ Home of Lt. Col. Arthur Fremantle
(5 Tilney St.) This was
the home of the most
famous of all English
Civil War observers,
Arthur Fremantle of Her
Majesty's Coldstream
Guards. Fremantle's
diary, Three Months in the
Southern States, is widely
quoted and predicted
a Southern victory.
Fremantle has since
found immortality in the
1993 movie Gettysburg
as an observer who
interacts with Generals
Longstreet and Hood
and other figures.

Parliament Square. British Foreign Secretary Lord John Russell's House is at 37 Chesham Place—here he informally welcomed Confederate envoys. British author Thomas Carlyle hosted Rose Greenhow and other Confederates at 24 Cheyne Row. The Reverend Francis Tremlett, a vocal Confederate partisan, hosted Rafael Semmes, the famous captain of the *Alabama,* among others at his home at 35 Buckland Crescent. He was buried in Hampstead Cemetery.

Charles Prioleau, who managed Fraser and Trenholm in Liverpool, had his London home at 47 Queen's Gate Gardens. He is buried in Kensal Green Cemetery. James Spence, a Liverpool merchant who wrote an impassioned defense of the South's right to secede, titled *The American Union,* lived at 20 Chepstow Place. Alexander Collie and Thomas Begbie, two successful blockade-running merchants, reaped the rewards of their risky business practices in mansions at 12 Kensington Palace Gardens and Wantage House, 14 Ladbrook Road, respectively.

The firm Firmin and Sons, at 153–154 The Strand, sold buttons for uniforms to both sides, while Goody and Jones, at 40 Pall Mall, loomed and sold Confederate gray linen for uniforms.

FURTHER READING

The London Confederates: The Officials, Clergy, Businessman and Journalists Who Backed the American South During the Civil War
by John D. Bennett
Examines Confederate activity in London

Blue and Gray Diplomacy: A History of Union and Confederate Foreign Relations
by Howard Jones
Important exploration of wartime foreign relations

✦ Portsmouth and Southampton

The might of the Royal Navy centered on Spithead and Portsmouth. At Portsmouth Naval Yard, in the shadow of Nelson's H.M.S. *Victory* and Henry the VIII's *Mary Rose,* is H.M.S. *Warrior,* an iron-hulled behemoth. At the time of the Civil War, it was the most powerful ship ever built—the largest in the Royal Navy—and it would have been a key weapon had the British government decided to go to war with the United States over the diplomatic incident known as the Trent Affair. This emotional event that involved a U.S. warship taking passengers off an unarmed British ship on the high seas caused Britain to mobilize for war. Lincoln and Secretary of State Seward quickly ordered the diplomats released. Still impressive today, *Warrior* is open to visitors.

A day trip from London to Southampton brings you to the Radley Hotel at the corner of Terminus Terrace and Queen's Terrace. It was the place to stay if you were a Confederate officer or diplomat transiting the area. After the rescue and docking of the

The Civil War in England Today

For more than 50 years, the American Civil War Roundtable (ACWRT) of the United Kingdom has maintained a meticulous eye on preservation and education issues. Members receive an informative magazine and a newsletter. An annual conference in April brings more than 100 participants, and many members are experts on aspects of the war in England. Interested tourists can contact the ACWRT at www.acwrt.org.uk for help in acquiring tour guides for more detailed looks at Civil War–related sites in England and France. Visitors are welcome to attend the group's conferences and meetings.

Deerhound with officers of the *Alabama,* including Raphael Semmes and John Kell, a number of Southern sympathizers and overseas agents—including James Mason, Reverend Francis Tremlett, and James Bulloch—came to visit them in the nearby Kelway's Hotel at 29 Queen's Terrace. Take a trip to the Old Cemetery to see the graves of Doctors James Ware and John Wiblin, who treated the wounded of the *Alabama* once they landed at Southampton.

France

French interests in the United States and the Civil War found fruit in Mexican adventurism. Napoleon III hoped to install a friendly regime that would provide France a large landmass in Central America—Mexico fit that bill. Napoleon, however, was reluctant to find himself overextended and vulnerable if the English were not equally distracted. Some people believe that Napoleon was sympathetic to the Confederates, as were many key Englishmen and politicians, but he did not see enough potential in their effort to commit his resources.

✦ Paris

Then as now the center of intrigue and leadership orbited around Paris and the Palace of the Tuileries. U.S. Minister (Ambassador) William Dayton was at 6 rue Presbourg. Dayton died in December 1864 while at the Hôtel du Louvre (currently the Louvre des Antiquaires at place du Palais Royal). Confederate and Union representatives coming from and going to London departed after 1864 from Gare du Nord, which was the main train station. Confederate naval officers attempting to acquire warships operated from the Grand Hotel at 2 rue Scribe, next to the Paris Opera House. The head of Confederate naval forces in Europe, Flag Officer Samuel Barron, had offices at 172 rue de Rivoli, which was the Hôtel des Trois Empereurs. Confederate diplomats

The bells of Basilique Sainte-Trinité rang during the naval battle near Cherbourg.

stayed at 28–30 rue Jean-Mermoz, which was the Hôtel Montaigne. Envoy John Slidell and agent turned author Edwin DeLeon arrived in Paris and stayed at the Hôtel du Rhin at 4–6 place Vendôme.

After the war, Confederate Commissioner John Slidell died in France and was buried at Villejuif Cemetery. The Confederacy's Belgium envoy, Ambrose Dudley Mann, lived in France after the war, as did the versatile Confederate cabinet minister Judah P. Benjamin. Both died and were buried in French soil, Mann at Montparnasse Cemetery and Benjamin at Père Lachaise Cemetery.

FURTHER READING

Secret History of Confederate Diplomacy Abroad
by Edwin DeLeon
DeLeon's memoir, first
published in 1867–1868

✦ Cherbourg

Here on June 19, 1864, was the hottest ticket on the coast. After a successful raiding career in the North and South Atlantic and Gulf of Mexico, the Confederate raider *Alabama* put in for overhaul at Cherbourg and was discovered by the U.S.S. *Kearsarge,* whose captain, John Winslow, was awaiting the ship's departure. Semmes accepted the implied challenge. The *Alabama* was quickly defeated and sunk; however, much of the crew was gathered up by English observers and delivered to Southampton, England.

The town has a number of important sites. St. Clement Church at rue du Val de Saire held a special mass for Semmes and his crew the morning of June 19. The Confederate agent in port, Adolphe Bonfils, lived at 40 rue du Val de Saire; his Union counterpart, Édouard Liais, lived at the Hotel de la Horie at 1 rue de Val Sarie. Each captain met separately with Admiral Augustin Dupouy of the French navy at the Prefecture Maritime on rue des Bastions. Winslow maintained he was there only to pick up prisoners who had been landed by the *Alabama;* however, to the French admiral it was clear that *Kearsage* was waiting for *Alabama* to come out. Semmes knew that and was ready to fight, asking for permission to coal his ship. When Winslow advised he would leave French territorial waters, the stage was set.

As the *Alabama* sailed and reached West Pass, her crewmembers recall hearing church

Jacob Thompson led the Confederate Secret Service, which was based in Canada.

The Unfulfilled Journey of the C.S.S. Stonewall Jackson

After much lobbying, the Confederates succeeded in acquiring a new ironclad ram that was built in 1863–1864 at the Arman Shipyard in Bordeaux. U.S. protests caused the vessel to be sold to Denmark, and the Confederates acquired it in Copenhagen. Named the C.S.S. *Stonewall Jackson,* the ship sailed under orders to disrupt the blockade at Wilmington and destroy merchant shipping. Two U.S. warships, fearing *Stonewall Jackson's* firepower, refused to engage on the open seas. After the war, the ship was sold to the Cubans. Then the U.S. acquired the ship and docked it at the Washington Naval Yard for two years before selling it to Japan.

bells strike the hour. The bells were those of Ste-Trinité church. Citizens anticipating the confrontation lined the shoreline and every available vantage point. Included in the number was William Lewis Dayton, Jr., son of the U.S. minister (ambassador) to France, and French Consul Édouard Liais, who accompanied him. They watched the battle from the chapel of St. Germain in Querqueville. The wounded were taken to two hospitals, the Caserne de l'Abbaye and the Abbaye du Voeu on rue de l'Abbaye. Three burials, two from *Alabama* and one from *Kearsarge,* exist in the Old Cemetery. In 1994, divers on the *Alabama*'s wreck brought up a Blakely naval gun that is on display at the Cité de la Mer Museum.

FURTHER READING

The Alabama and the Kearsage: The Sailor's Civil War
by William Marvel Riveting account of the face-off at sea

Australia

The land down under got quite a surprise when the Confederate raider C.S.S. *Shenandoah* arrived in Melbourne on January 25, 1865. The ship had completed its Indian Ocean transit and was en route to the rich fishing grounds where Yankee whalers were bringing in fish, blubber, and oil. In its course around the globe, the ship captured or destroyed 38 vessels from the mid-Atlantic across the Indian Ocean on up through the Caroline Islands into the Bering Sea. After the war, the *Shenandoah* was refitted to appear as a merchant vessel. The ship made its way back across the Atlantic Ocean to Liverpool, surrendering its colors on November 6, 1865.

✦ Melbourne

Undermanned, the *Shenandoah* recruited as many as 40 sailors while in port; the recruitment office was at 125 Flinders Lane East. During the visit, Shenandoah's officers posed for photographs at the studio of Batchelder and O'Neil at 41 Collins Street East. Nearby, at 36 Collins Street, a gala dinner was held at the Melbourne Club. The officers stayed ashore at the Scott Hotel at 440 Collins Street, which is now the Royal Insurance Building, and they were entertained at places such as the Haymarket Theatre on Bourke Street East. A walking tour of Civil War sites is available at www.auscivilwar.com.

FURTHER READING

Sea of Gray: Around-the-World Odyssey of the Confederate Raider Shenandoah
by Tom Chaffin
Detailed history of the *Shenandoah*'s trip around the globe

The Alabama Claims

The *Shenandoah*'s Australian visit was not without repercussions. The U.S. government took great exception to the English role in producing five commerce raiders for the Confederates. Secretary of State William Seward wanted to acquire the Alaska Territory (which he eventually did), and Senator Charles Sumner wanted to annex Canada as reparations; however, by early 1870 the Grant Administration and the British agreed in claim and counter-claim to accept a $13,600,000 British payment to the United States.

Bahamas

Nassau saw significant blockade-running. Indeed, the Confederate ironclad ram C.S.S. *Stonewall Jackson* docked there in May 1865. Most assuredly the mythical blockade-running captain Rhett Butler frequented the Bahamas. Stephen Wise's book *Lifeline of the Confederacy* addresses operations from here and other spots like Bermuda and Havana, Cuba.

Bermuda

Bermuda also served as a major port of exchange for blockade-runners going into Wilmington and Charleston. The Bermuda National Trust Museum, Globe Hotel, King's Square on St. George's Island has a major exhibit on the American Civil War. Diving companies will take you out to dive on blockade-runner wrecks around the island.

Canada

An excellent book to identify Canadian Civil War sites is John Boyko's *Blood and Daring: How Canada Fought the American Civil War and Forged a Nation*. Famous Canadians who fought in the war include Robert Knox Sneden, whose diary, *Eye of the Storm*, and drawings, *Images From the Storm*, are among the most informative and graphic extant.

In Their Footsteps: Great Campaigns of the Civil War

Few Civil War battles were fought in isolation. Most were part of a larger campaign with specific objectives. Here are the most significant campaigns in chronological order, along with the page numbers where you can find information on each battle.

✧ Burnside's North Carolina Expedition

DATE(S): February 7, 1862–June 5, 1862

Fearing for the security of their naval construction program at Gosport Shipyard in Portsmouth, Virginia, the Confederates perceived Ambrose Burnside's expedition to North Carolina's Outer Banks as a backdoor move on Gosport. In reality, it was a good deal more complex: Burnside intended to secure eastern North Carolina for further operations and to support blockading operations along the upper Atlantic seaboard.

BATTLES: Roanoke Island (p. 151), New Bern (p. 150), Fort Macon (pp. 147–148), South Mills (pp. 151–152), Tranter's Creek (p. 152)

✧ Sibley's New Mexico Campaign

DATE(S): February 20, 1862–March 28, 1862

With aspirations to dominate western routes to California, the Confederates created a territory and a plan to occupy the civilized areas of New Mexico, create an alliance with the southwestern Indian tribes, and perhaps gain access to the silver and gold mines of Colorado. It failed.

BATTLES: Valverde (p. 463), Glorieta Pass (p. 462)

✧ Jackson's 1862 Valley Campaign

DATE(S): March 23, 1862–May 17, 1862

Stonewall Jackson's Army of the Valley was an independent force; however, when called upon to join a larger cause to maneuver in a way that would keep Federal forces in the Shenandoah Valley and away from operations near Richmond, Virginia, they performed brilliantly and vastly exceeded expectations.

BATTLES: Kernstown I (p. 250), McDowell (pp. 259–261), Front Royal (pp. 242–244), Winchester I (p. 291), Cross Keys (pp. 230–232), Port Republic (p. 272)

✧ Peninsula Campaign

DATE(S): March 8, 1862–July 1, 1862

In response to President Lincoln's General War Order No. 1, George McClellan moved against the Confederate capital via the Virginia peninsula. By the end of June 1862, however, Robert E. Lee had seized the initiative from McClellan in a relentless series of attacks that chased the Union commander's forces from a broad front to a new encampment under the cover of gunboats on the James River.

BATTLES: Hampton Roads (p. 246), Yorktown (p. 291), Williamsburg (p. 290), Eltham's Landing (p. 234), Drewry's Bluff (p. 234), Hanover Court House (p. 246), Seven Pines (pp. 279–280), Oak Grove (p. 265), Beaver Dam Creek (pp. 218–219), Gaines' Mill (p. 244), Garnett's and Golding's Farm (p. 244), Savage's Station (p. 277), Glendale/White Oak Swamp (p. 245), Malvern Hill (p. 254)

✧ Confederate Heartland Offensive

DATE(S): June 7, 1862–October 8, 1862

Under the less than watchful eye of Henry Halleck, Braxton Bragg had extracted himself and his Confederate troops from northern Mississippi and moved on to Chattanooga, the gateway of Tennessee, via Mobile and

Atlanta. There he intended to cooperate with Confederate forces in eastern Tennessee in "liberating" Kentucky from Union dominance. Kentucky was not interested, however, and Bragg withdrew later under much criticism.

BATTLES: **Chattanooga I (pp. 178–179), Murfreesboro I (p. 197), Richmond (pp. 94–95), Munfordville (p. 89), Perryville (pp. 92–94)**

✦ Northern Virginia Campaign

DATE(S): August 9, 1862–September 1, 1862

After his mediocre performance during the Seven Days Battles, Stonewall Jackson was dispatched to confront the newly constituted Federal Army of Virginia under the command of John Pope. Pope was operating on the Orange and Alexandria Railroad and had disrupted the countryside with a much firmer policy toward Southern civilians. The South would win a decisive victory.

BATTLES: **Cedar Mountain (p. 223), Rappahannock Station I (p. 273), Manassas Station Operations (pp. 258–259), Thoroughfare Gap (p. 284), Manassas II (p. 257), Chantilly (p. 227)**

✦ Maryland Campaign

DATE(S): September 12–20, 1862

In less than nine weeks, Robert E. Lee had reversed the Confederacy's fortunes and taken the war from the gates of Richmond across the Potomac River, where he fought the bloodiest single-day battle in American history at Antietam.

BATTLES: **Harpers Ferry (pp. 312–313), South Mountain (pp. 344–345), Antietam (pp. 340–341), Shepherdstown (pp. 316–317)**

✦ Grant's Operations Against Vicksburg

DATE(S): April 29, 1863–July 4, 1863

Ulysses S. Grant's successful plan to open the Mississippi River was the greatest Union achievement in the first 27 months of the war.

BATTLES: **Grand Gulf (pp. 127–128), Snyder's Bluff (p. 134), Port Gibson (p. 130), Raymond (pp. 130–131), Jackson (pp. 128–129), Champion Hill (p. 125), Big Black River Bridge (pp. 122–123), Vicksburg (p. 136), Milliken's Bend (p. 110), Goodrich's Landing (p. 107), Helena (p. 42)**

U.S. naval firepower on the rivers quickly reduced Rebel fortifications.

The war produced military mobilization on an unimagined scale.

✧ Gettysburg Campaign

DATE(S): June 9, 1863–July 23, 1863

Robert E. Lee's spring offensive took on added importance when he convinced President Davis and his cabinet to support this operation instead of sending away two divisions to contest Federal operations at Vicksburg. It resulted in dual defeats for the Confederacy, one at Gettysburg on July 1–3 and the other at Vicksburg on July 4.

BATTLES: Brandy Station (p. 221), Winchester II (p. 291), Aldie (p. 215), Middleburg (p. 261), Upperville (p. 285), Hanover (p. 357), Gettysburg (pp. 352–357), Williamsport (p. 345), Boonsboro (pp. 341–342), Manassas Gap (p. 258)

✧ Tullahoma or Middle Tennessee Campaign

DATE(S): June 24–26, 1863

This nearly bloodless operation dislodged Confederate forces from a position just south of Murfreesboro, Tennessee, and forced them back across the Cumberland Plateau to Chattanooga, thus freeing the state of active Confederate occupation and making it much easier for loyalists in eastern Tennessee to support the Union. Sadly for William S. Rosecrans, the operation's architect, the dual victories at Gettysburg and Vicksburg caused this liberation to be largely overlooked.

BATTLES: Hoover's Gap (p. 195)

✧ Red River Campaign

DATE(S): March 14, 1864–May 18, 1864

In an effort to completely restore Louisiana, Federal troops and transports moved along the Red River in a coordinated campaign to capture the state capital at Shreveport, gather cotton for New England mills, and demonstrate to the French, who were engaged in Mexico, that the United States would not tolerate European adventurism in Texas. The military operations were a disaster, however, tying up troops needed elsewhere, delaying the capture of Mobile, and nearly destroying the Federal fleet.

BATTLES: **Fort DeRussy (p. 105), Mansfield (p. 109), Pleasant Hill (p. 112), Blair's Landing (p. 103), Monett's Ferry (p. 110), Mansura (p. 109), Yellow Bayou (p. 114)**

✧ Camden Expedition

DATE(S): April 3–30, 1864

Designed as a supportive movement to the Red River Campaign (see above), Federal forces found themselves unable to supply their movements toward Louisiana. The problem became so severe that, with Nathaniel P. Banks in retreat from Mansfield, Frederick Steele abandoned the campaign in an effort to save his own forces.

BATTLES: **Elkin's Ferry (p. 41), Prairie D'Ane (pp. 47–48), Poison Spring (pp. 46–47), Marks' Mills (p. 44), Jenkins' Ferry (p. 43)**

✧ Grant's Overland Campaign

DATE(S): May 5, 1864– June 24, 1864

Ulysses S. Grant and the Army of the Potomac endeavored to destroy Robert E. Lee's Army of Northern Virginia during continuous and sustained combat.

BATTLES: **Wilderness (pp. 288–289), Spotsylvania Court House (pp. 280–283), Yellow Tavern (p. 291), North Anna (p. 263–265), Wilson's Wharf (p. 290), Haw's Shop (p. 247), Totopotomoy Creek/Bethesda Church (p. 285), Old Church (pp. 265–266), Cold Harbor (p. 228), Trevilian Station (p. 285), Saint Mary's Church (p. 275)**

✧ Bermuda Hundred Campaign

DATE(S): May 6–20, 1864

Federal forces under the command of Benjamin Butler squandered an opportunity to cut Confederate supplies into Richmond and perhaps end the war in May 1864 by allowing themselves to be bottled up on the peninsula known as Bermuda Hundred, near

where the James River and Appomattox River meet.

BATTLES: **Port Walthall Junction (p. 272), Swift Creek (pp. 283–284), Chester Station (p. 227), Proctor's Creek (p. 273), Ware Bottom Church (p. 286)**

✧ Atlanta Campaign

DATE(S): May 7, 1864–September 1, 1864

William T. Sherman, acting in concert with Ulysses S. Grant's plan to prevent Confederate armies from reinforcing one another, moved against the Army of Tennessee to cut off the central transportation hub of Atlanta.

BATTLES: **Rocky Face Ridge (p. 79), Resaca (p. 78), Adairsville (p. 62), New Hope Church (p. 76), Dallas (p. 66), Pickett's Mill (p. 77), Marietta (p. 76), Kolb's Farm (p. 75), Kennesaw Mountain (pp. 72–75), Peachtree Creek (p. 77), Atlanta (pp. 63–64), Ezra Church (pp. 67–68), Utoy Creek (p. 79), Dalton II (pp. 66–67), Lovejoy's Station (pp. 75–76), Jonesborough (p. 72)**

The 15th New Jersey Memorial at Spotsylvania's Bloody Angle

❖ Lynchburg Campaign

DATE(S): May 15, 1864–June 21, 1864

This portion of Ulysses S. Grant's grand plan for 1864 threatened farming in the bountiful Shenandoah Valley, snapped the Virginia Central Railroad, and carried the war to the key city of Lynchburg, where the Tennessee & Virginia Railroad met a spur of the Orange & Alexandria Railroad, the James River, and Kanawaha Canal.

BATTLES: New Market (pp. 262–263), Piedmont (p. 271), Lynchburg (pp. 251–254)

❖ Richmond-Petersburg Campaign

DATE(S): June 9, 1864–March 25, 1865

Having tied Robert E. Lee to the essential railroad hub at Petersburg and covered the capital at Richmond, Ulysses S. Grant made numerous attempts to destroy Lee's line or flank him out of the city, which he finally did on April 2, 1865. Lee surrendered a week later.

BATTLES: Petersburg I (p. 268), Petersburg II (pp. 268–270), Jerusalem Plank Road (p. 249), Staunton River Bridge (p. 283), Sappony Church (p. 277), Ream's Station I (pp. 273–274), Deep Bottom I (p. 233), The Crater (p. 230), Deep Bottom II (p. 233), Globe Tavern (pp. 245–246), Ream's Station II (p. 274), Chaffin's Farm and New Market Heights (p. 224), Peebles' Farm (pp. 267–268), Darbytown and New Market Roads (p. 232), Darbytown Road (p. 233), Boydton Plank Road (p. 220), Fair Oaks and Darbytown Road (p. 234), Hatcher's Run (p. 247), Fort Stedman (pp. 236–237)

❖ Forrest's Defense of Mississippi

DATE(S): June 10, 1864–August 21, 1864

Nathan Bedford Forrest and his cavalry had been so successful throughout the war that William T. Sherman feared they might disrupt Federal supply lines during his Atlanta Campaign. So Sherman dispatched cavalry to occupy him during the move south. All the battles that Forrest and his men fought in defense of Mississippi—including Shiloh in April 1862 and Okolona in February 1864—make an interesting driving tour and teach much about his military skill and impact.

BATTLES: Brice's Cross Roads (p. 123), Tupelo (pp. 134–136), Memphis II (p. 196)

❖ Early's Raid and Operations Against the B&O Railroad

DATE(S): July 9, 1864–August 7, 1864

After defeating David Hunter at Lynchburg, Jubal Early and a remnant of the old Army of the Valley moved north to threaten the security of Washington, D.C., and draw forces away from the siege at Petersburg.

BATTLES: Monocacy (p. 343), Fort Stevens (p. 332), Cool Spring (pp. 228–230), Rutherford's Farm (p. 275), Kernstown II (p. 251), Folck's Mill (p. 342), Moorefield (p. 315)

❖ Sheridan's 1864 Valley Campaign

DATE(S): August 16, 1864–October 19, 1864

Jubal Early's early successes were soon overwhelmed by the aggressive Union leadership of Phillip H. Sheridan, who reversed Early's fortunes and ultimately destroyed the Confederate commander's military force and the Shenandoah Valley as a source of supplies.

BATTLES: Guard Hill (p. 246), Summit Point (p. 317), Smithfield Crossing (p. 317), Berryville (p. 219), Opequon (pp. 266–267), Fisher's Hill (p. 235), Tom's Brook (pp. 284–285), Cedar Creek (pp. 222–223)

❖ Price's Missouri Expedition

DATE(S): September 27, 1864–October 28, 1864

Confederate Sterling Price's final effort to liberate Missouri from Union control was a disastrous failure.

BATTLES: Fort Davidson (p. 417), Glasgow (pp. 417–418), Lexington II (p. 419), Little Blue River (p. 420), Independence II (p. 418), Byram's Ford (p. 415), Westport (pp. 425–426), Marais des Cygnes (p. 401), Marmiton River (p. 421), Mine Creek (p. 401), Newtonia II (pp. 422–423)

Black cooks and teamsters were soon augmented by black troops.

✧ Franklin-Nashville Campaign

DATE(S): October 5, 1864–December 16, 1864

After failing to hold Atlanta, John B. Hood met with President Davis to advocate a bold move into Tennessee and perhaps as far as the Ohio River. Once implemented, Hood's plan caused William T. Sherman to chase him and redeem the ground just contested by Sherman, Johnston, and Hood. Sherman followed a bit and then left the task to George H. Thomas, the "Rock of Chickamauga." Hood missed a golden opportunity and then had his army operationally destroyed at Nashville, effectively ending the war in the West.

BATTLES: Allatoona (pp. 62–63), Decatur (pp. 29–30), Johnsonville (p. 196), Columbia (p. 184), Spring Hill (p. 202), Franklin II (pp. 190–191), Murfreesboro II (pp. 197–198), Nashville (pp. 198–199)

✧ Carolinas Campaign

DATE(S): February 3, 1865–March 21, 1865

William T. Sherman moved north from Savannah to join Ulysses S. Grant in the final push to crush Robert E. Lee's army. His orders were changed in late March while in North Carolina.

BATTLES: Rivers Bridge (p. 168), Wyse Fork (p. 153), Monroe's Cross Roads (pp. 149–150), Averasboro (pp. 144–145), Bentonville (pp. 145–146)

✧ Appomattox Campaign

DATE(S): March 29, 1865–April 9, 1865

Under extreme duress and with his lines ruptured on every front, Robert E. Lee conducted a masterful withdrawal from the Petersburg lines and crossed the Appomattox River en route to Danville, Virginia. Cut off by Union forces, he turned west and was captured at Appomattox, Virginia.

BATTLES: Lewis's Farm (p. 251), White Oak Road (pp. 286–288), Dinwiddie Court House (p. 233), Five Forks (p. 236), Petersburg III (p. 271), Sutherland's Station (p. 283), Namozine Church (p. 261), Amelia Springs (pp. 215–216), Sayler's Creek (pp. 277–279), Rice's Station (p. 275), High Bridge (pp. 247–248), Cumberland Church (p. 232), Appomattox Station (p. 217), Appomattox Court House (p. 216)

In Their Footsteps:
Key Cities of the Civil War

A number of cities were central to transportation networks or in key locations relative to military interests and, thus, saw a number of battles or engagements. The following cities are great locations to see multiple Civil War sites. Battles associated with each city are listed in chronological order.

◇ Atlanta, Georgia

The objective of Sherman's 1864 campaign, which would sever the Confederate communications network in Georgia

BATTLES: New Hope Church (p. 76), Dallas (p. 66), Pickett's Mill (p. 77), Kolb's Farm (p. 75), Kennesaw Mountain (pp. 72–75), Peachtree Creek (p. 77), Atlanta (pp. 63–64), Ezra Church (pp. 67–68), Utoy Creek (p. 79), Jonesborough (p. 72), Allatoona (pp. 62–63), Buck Head Creek (p. 64)

◇ Chattanooga, Tennessee

Key communications hub that also served as a gateway to Virginia and Atlanta

BATTLES: Chattanooga I and II (pp. 178–179), Chickamauga (pp. 64–66), Wauhatchie (p. 205), Chattanooga III (pp. 179–183), Ringgold Gap (pp. 78–79), Dalton I (p. 66), Rocky Face Ridge (p. 79), Resaca (p. 78), Dalton II (pp. 66–67)

◇ Corinth, Mississippi

Home to a vital railroad junction

BATTLES: Shiloh (pp. 199–202), Corinth I (pp. 126–127), Iuka (p. 128), Corinth II (p. 127), Hatchie's Bridge (pp. 194–195), Holly Springs Raid (p. 139)

◇ Frederick, Maryland

Saw action throughout the war

BATTLES: Harpers Ferry (pp. 312–313), South Mountain (pp. 344–345), Antietam (pp. 340–341), Shepherdstown (pp. 316–317), Hanover (p. 357), Gettysburg (pp. 352–357), Hagerstown (p. 348), Williamsport (p. 345), Boonsboro (pp. 341–342), Monocacy (p. 343), Fort Stevens (p. 332)

◇ Fredericksburg, Virginia

Located along the Rappahannock River, halfway between Washington, D.C., and Richmond

BATTLES: Fredericksburg I (pp. 237–242), Chancellorsville (pp. 224–227), Fredericksburg II (p. 242), Salem Church (pp. 275–276), Wilderness (pp. 288–289), Spotsylvania Court House (pp. 280–283), North Anna (pp. 263–265), Cold Harbor (p. 228)

◇ Mobile, Alabama

The key blockade-running port on the Gulf Coast coveted by Grant

BATTLES: Santa Rosa Island (pp. 57–58), Mobile Bay (pp. 30–32), Spanish Fort (p. 33), Fort Blakeley (p. 30)

◇ Petersburg, Virginia

Focus of war efforts from June 1864 until April 2, 1865

BATTLES: Drewry's Bluff (p. 234), Norfleet House/Suffolk (p. 263), Hill's Point/Suffolk (p. 249), Port Walthall Junction (p. 272), Swift Creek (pp. 283–284), Chester Station (p. 227), Proctor's Creek (p. 273), Ware Bottom Church (p. 286), Petersburg I and II (pp. 268–270), Jerusalem Plank Road (p. 249), Ream's Station I (pp. 273–274), The Crater (p. 230), Globe Tavern (pp. 245–246), Ream's Station II (p. 274), Peebles' Farm (pp. 267–268), Boydton Plank Road (p. 220), Hatcher's Run (p. 247), Fort Stedman (pp. 236–237), Lewis's Farm (p. 251), Dinwiddie Court House (p. 233), White Oak Road (pp. 286–288), Five Forks (p. 236), Sutherland's Station (p. 283), Petersburg III (p. 271), Namozine Church (p. 261), Amelia Springs (pp. 215–216), Sayler's Creek (pp. 277–279)

✧ Richmond, Virginia

Confederate capital with battlefields aplenty

BATTLES: Williamsburg (p. 290), Eltham's Landing (p. 234), Hanover Court House (p. 246), Seven Pines (pp. 279–280), Beaver Dam Creek (p. 218–219), Oak Grove (p. 265), Gaines' Mill (p. 244), Garnett's and Golding's Farm (p. 244), Savage's Station (p. 277), Glendale/White Oak Swamp (p. 245), Malvern Hill (p. 254), Yellow Tavern (p. 291), North Anna (pp. 263–265), Wilson's Wharf (p. 290), Haw's Shop (p. 247), Totopotomoy Creek/Bethesda Church (p. 285), Old Church (pp. 265–266), Cold Harbor (p. 228), Saint Mary's Church (p. 275), Deep Bottom I and II (p. 233), Chaffin's Farm and New Market Heights (p. 224), Darbytown and New Market Roads (p. 232), Darbytown Road (p. 233), Fair Oaks and Darbytown Road (p. 234)

✧ Savannah, Georgia

Key supply port and destination for both blockade-runners and General Sherman's March in November and December 1864

BATTLES: Fort Pulaski (p. 69), Fort McAllister I (p. 68), Honey Hill (pp. 167–168), Fort McAllister II (p. 68)

Fixed fortifications were rendered obsolete during the Civil War.

✧ Vicksburg, Mississippi

Key point on the Mississippi whose fall would permit commercial trade on the river for Northern states

BATTLES: Chickasaw Bayou (p. 125), Grand Gulf (pp. 127–128), Snyder's Bluff (p. 134), Port Gibson (p. 130), Raymond (pp. 130–131), Jackson (p. 128–129), Champion Hill (p. 125), Big Black River Bridge (pp. 122–123), Vicksburg (p. 136)

✧ Warrenton, Virginia

Integral to the battles found at Manassas and along the Rappahannock River line

BATTLES: Manassas I (pp. 254–256), Ball's Bluff (p. 218), Front Royal (pp. 242–244), Cedar Mountain (p. 223), Rappahannock Station I (p. 273), Manassas Station Operations (pp. 258–259), Thoroughfare Gap (p. 284), Manassas II (p. 257), Kelly's Ford (pp. 249–250), Brandy Station (p. 221), Aldie (p. 215), Middleburg (p. 261), Upperville (p. 285), Manassas Gap (p. 258), Auburn I and II (p. 218), Buckland Mills (p. 222), Rappahannock Station II (p. 273), Mine Run (p. 261), Morton's Ford (p. 261), Wilderness (pp. 288–289), New Market (pp. 262–263), Guard Hill (p. 246)

✧ Wilmington, North Carolina

The final port open in the Confederacy, a key source of European supplies for Lee's army

BATTLES: Fort Anderson (p. 146), Fort Fisher I and II (pp. 146–147), Wilmington (p. 153)

✧ Winchester, Virginia

Shenandoah Valley town that heard the constant tramping of soldiers' boots

BATTLES: Hoke's Run (pp. 313–315), Kernstown I (p. 250), Front Royal (pp. 242–244), Winchester I (p. 291), Harpers Ferry (pp. 312–313), Antietam (pp. 340–341), Shepherdstown (pp. 316–317), Winchester II (p. 291), Williamsport (p. 345), Boonsboro (pp. 341–342), Manassas Gap (p. 258), New Market (pp. 262–263), Cool Spring (pp. 228–230), Rutherford's Farm (p. 275), Kernstown II (p. 251), Guard Hill (p. 246), Berryville (p. 219), Opequon (pp. 266–267), Fisher's Hill (p. 235), Tom's Brook (pp. 284–285), Cedar Creek (pp. 222–223)

Acknowledgments

No book is ever written to make money; this book is a labor of love based on 40 years of studying the Civil War. I would like to thank my wife, Pam, daughter, Kat, and my parents, Janet and Bill, and in-laws, Billie and Julian (a WW II Veteran), for their exceptional support. Brothers Karl and Dave accompany me on many tours, while Jim and sister Katy have been constant sources of support. My brother Don passed in 2012 but was a dedicated volunteer.

More than 200 historians have contributed to making me a historian over the years. I cannot name them all, but Richard McMurry, Harold Wilson, Ed Bearss, A. Wilson Greene, Mary and Richard Hatcher, Kenneth Noe, and Kendall Gott are some of the best.

Lisa Thomas and Bill O'Donnell at NGS proposed this book and a partnership with the BGES. My board of directors—Jim Davis, Mike Chesson, David Dubose, Bert Dunkerly, Joe Overstreet, and Ben Buckley—led with their checkbooks to match the generous project leadership of Jim Anderson of Mentone, Indiana.

Over 100 BGES members helped fund this effort; of particular note were Frank Roberts, Laurie and Corky Lowe, Jim Sagerholm, Bill McKinnon, Bryan Hagen, Pat and Mike Stevens, Jeanette and Carl Christman, and Janet and Bill Riedel. Becky, Bill, and Chantel Hollen have given hundreds of volunteer hours keeping the headquarters ship-shape during my countless absences.

NGS put an exceptional team of players on this project, with senior editorial project manager Susan Straight in the lead. The team of writers—Ann Siegal, Olivia Garnett, Amy Sklansky, Alex Webb, and Jeff Waraniak—provided great copy to work with. They were aided by Mike Gorman, Jenna French, Matt Wendling, Mike Bailey, Shane Bernard, Paul Branch, Julie Burks, Dan Fullenwider, Mark Christ, William H. H. Clark, Dale Cox, Charlie Crawford, Scott Dearman, Stacye Hathorn, Richard Holloway, Tim Cavannaugh, Rodney Kite-Powell, James Madere, Jim Mckee, Jon Miller, David Ogden, Jim Ogden, Tres Seymour, Roland Stansbury, and Michael Zatarga—thank you. Designer Linda Makarov created beautiful pages, text editor Mary Stephanos made it all fit, Patrick Bagley assisted with photographs and rights clearance, Elisa Gibson art directed, and Marty Ittner created the design. Greg Ugiansky and Carl Mehler created outstanding maps. Photo editor Jane Martin's selections included images by BGES members such as Jeff Fioravanti, Charles Lee, Michael Green, Bart Allen, Parker Hills, and Harry Thaete, and Michael O'Connor was the production editor.

Stephen Wise, Gloria Swift, Kent Masterson Brown, Keith Gibson, Chris Fonvielle, and Doug Waters all provided tour outlines. We had international support from Barry Compton, Len Ellison, John Bethell, Charles Rees, Peter Lockwood, and Greg Bayne. Charles Priestley allowed us to adapt his Piccadilly walking tour for this book. The English and Australians are true Civil Warriors, and Compton, Ellison, Lockwood, and Priestley are all part Sherlock Holmes and superb tour leaders. I hope one day you will be as lucky as I have been to walk the sites with them.

Before going out to visit battlefields, I would check *Civil War News,* a monthly newspaper with up-to-date feature stories and lots of information about activities. Kay Jorgenson in Tunbridge, Vermont, edits it. Next I would call Dave or Jason Roth at *Blue and Gray Magazine* in Columbus, Ohio, to see if they have done a "General's Tour" of the site you want to visit. It will be time and money well spent.

This book grew from 384 to 512 pages and could have easily filled 100 more pages. I had the final word on historical interpretation and have reviewed all 256 spreads; any mistakes that exist are mine alone. BGES is proud of this work, and I hope you enjoy it.

—Len Riedel
Chatham, Virginia
October 5, 2015

The Blue and Gray Education Society

The Blue and Gray Education Society is a tax-exempt, nonprofit educational organization chartered in 1994 in Chatham, Virginia.

BGES is funded by membership donations that are generally tax deductible. Membership is open to all. Sign up online or call 434-250-9921.

BGES is focused on short-term projects that are quickly funded by member and supporter donations. Projects generally attracts 30 percent or higher participation from the membership.

BGES plans and executes a variety of field studies of battlefields and campaigns known as BGES' Civil War Field University or BGES Weekend Warriors. Each program is a one-of-a-kind experience purposely designed to reach areas not generally known to or open to the public. Programs are open to all and can be found under Civil War tours on the BGES website.

This book has been inspired and based on the BGES' tour program.

BGES is a working, results-oriented nonprofit, and members should expect to participate in preservation and educational projects that have included:
• Restoration of the flags at President Lincoln's Box in Ford's Theatre
• Placement of 17 restored artillery pieces at Raymond, Fort Clinch, Pelham's Corner, and Pamplin Historical Park's Adventure Camp
• Placement of over 115 interpretative signs at Bermuda Hundred, South Mountain, Perryville, North Anna, Holly Springs, and Cedar Creek
• Completion of National Park Service battlefield preservation conferences for the Vicksburg Campaign, Price's Raid in Missouri, and Mobile Bay in Alabama
• Completion of 19 scholarly monographs and 4 books
• More than 80 tours during 9 years of supporting America's Wounded Warriors
• Execution of over 300 study tours visiting more than 400 different battlefields over the past 22 years

Visit these sites with the group that knows them best—join BGES today! Join the BGES Internet mailing list for free by emailing and asking to join the list.

Help us grow: Contact us at www.blueandgrayeducation.org with recommended additions and updates to sites.

Blue and Gray Education Society (BGES)
9 Ridge Street
P.O. Box 1176
Chatham, VA 24531-1176

Phone: 434-250-9921 Fax: 434-432-0596
www.blueandgrayeducation.org
Email: blueandgrayeducation@yahoo.com
Facebook: www.facebook.com/blueandgray

Illustrations Credits

COVER Danita Delimont/Getty Images **FRONT MATTER** 2-3, AP Photo/Matt Rourke; 6, Library of Congress Prints and Photographs Division; 8, Evan McCaffrey/Shutterstock.com; 9, Don Troiani/Corbis; 11, Jeff Fioravanti, BGES; 13, Michael Byerley **THE SOUTHEAST** 20-21, Parker Hills, BGES; 22, Andre Jenny/Alamy; 26, Library of Congress Prints and Photographs Division; 29 Medford Historical Society Collection/Corbis; 31, RosaBetancourt/Alamy; 32, Farragut on the Hartford at Mobile Bay, August 5th 1864 (color litho), Ogden, Henry Alexander (1856-1936)/Private Collection/The Stapleton Collection/Bridgeman Images; 33, The American Civil War Museum/Museum & White House of the Confederacy; 34, Library of Congress Prints and Photographs Division/Carol M. Highsmith Archive; 35, RosaBetancourt/Alamy; 36, Andy Thomas/Maze Creek Studio; 39 (UP), The American Civil War Museum/Museum & White House of the Confederacy; 39 (LO), Library of Congress Prints and Photographs Division; 40, Library of Congress Prints and Photographs Division; 41, Library of Congress Prints and Photographs Division; 43, Courtesy of the Old State House Museum, Little Rock, Arkansas; 44, Library of Congress Prints and Photographs Division; 47, National Park Service; 48, Andy Thomas/Maze Creek Studio; 50, Courtesy of the Arkansas Historic Preservation Program; 51, Library of Congress Prints and Photographs Division; 52, Robert Harding Picture Library Ltd/Alamy; 55, Dave G. Houser/Alamy; 56, Historic Florida/Alamy; 57, Jason Meyer/Alamy; 58, Confederate paper money, 1st March, 1863 (litho), American School (19th century)/Private Collection/Peter Newark Military Pictures/Bridgeman Images; 60, Library of Congress Prints and Photographs Division; 63, Library of Congress Prints and Photographs Division; 67, Ebyabe/https://en.wikipedia.org/wiki/Fort_McAllister_Historic_Park#/media/File:GA_Richmond_Hill_Fort_McAllister_inside01.jpg/http://creativecommons.org/licenses/by-sa/3.0/legalcode; 69, Library of Congress Prints and Photographs Division; 70, Anthony T. Nigrelli; 76, Library of Congress Prints and Photographs Division; 77, George Puvvada/http://en.wikipedia.org/wiki/Pickett%27s_Mill_Battlefield_Site#/media/File:Pickett%27s_Mill_Battlefield_Site,_Paulding_County,_Georgia_by_George_Paul_Puvvada.jpg/http://creativecommons.org/licenses/by-sa/3.0/legalcode; 78, Library of Congress Prints and Photographs Division; 79, National Park Service; 80, Library of Congress Prints and Photographs Division; 81, Kevin Fleming/Corbis; 82, Library of Congress Prints and Photographs Division; 83, Joseph Sohm/Shutterstock; 84, Jim Lane/Alamy; 87, Michael Byerley; 88, Library of Congress Prints and Photographs Division; 89, Battle of Mill Spring, Ky. Jan 19th 1862 (color litho), Currier, N. (1813-88) and Ives, J.M. (1824-95)/Gilder Lehrman Collection, New York, USA/Bridgeman Images; 90, Daderot/https://commons.wikimedia.org/wiki/File:Lexington_Cemetery_-_Lexington,_Kentucky_-_DSC09071.JPG/https://creativecommons.org/publicdomain/zero/1.0/legalcode; 92, Library of Congress Prints and Photographs Division; 95, Jim Lane/Alamy; 96, Greg Hume/https://en.wikipedia.org/wiki/Washington,_Kentucky#/media/File:MeffordsFort.jpg/http://creativecommons.org/licenses/by-sa/3.0/legalcode; 98, Abraham Lincoln Birthplace National Historical Park; 99, Stephen Saks Photography/Alamy; 100, SeanXu/iStockphoto; 103, Don Troiani/Corbis; 104, William Joseph Bozic, Jr.; 105, Library of Congress Prints and Photographs Division; 106, Capture of New Orleans: The Fleet Passing Forts on the Mississippi, ca. 1862 (engraving), Parsons, Charles (1821-1910) (after)/Free Library of Philadelphia/Print and Picture Collection, Free Library of Philadelphia/Bridgeman Images; 108, Brad Clark; 109, U.S. War Department/Public Domain; 110, Everett Collection Inc/Alamy; 112, Don Troiani/Corbis; 113, Corbis; 114, Dave G. Houser/Alamy; 115, Corbis; 116, Stephen Saks Photography/Alamy; 117, John Elk III/Alamy; 118, Eric James/Alamy; 119, age fotostock/Alamy; 120, Dimitry Bobroff/Alamy; 123, Wilson44691/https://commons.wikimedia.org/wiki/File:BricesCrossroads2010.jpg/; 126, The Granger Collection, NYC—All rights reserved; 128, Parker Hills, BGES; 129, *Harper's Weekly*, issue of October 4, 1862; 133, Gene Ahrens/Alamy; 135, Michael Green, BGES; 136, Don Troiani/Corbis; 138, RSBPhoto/Alamy; 139, Library of Congress Prints and Photographs Division; 140, Buddy Mays/Alamy; 141, Steve Nudson/Alamy; 142, National Park Service; 145, Everett Collection Historical/Alamy; 147, Library of Congress Prints and Photographs Division; 149, Library of Congress Prints and Photographs Division; 151, Library of Congress Prints and Photographs Division; 154, Billy Hathorn/http://en.wikipedia.org/wiki/Wilmington,_North_Carolina_in_the_American_Civil_War#/media/File:Confederate_Monument,_Wilmington,_NC_IMG_4320.JPG/http://creativecommons.org/licenses/by-sa/3.0/legalcode; 157, Michael Verville/Alliance for Historic Hillsborough; 158, MarkVanDykePhotography/Shutterstock; 164, Bill Fitzpatrick/http://en.wikipedia.org/wiki/Colleton_County_Courthouse#/media/File:Colleton_County_Courthouse.jpg/http://creativecommons.org/licenses/by-sa/3.0/legalcode; 166, Library of Congress Prints and Photographs Division; 169, Library of Congress Prints and Photographs Division; 171, A K Nicholas/Shutterstock; 172, National Park Service; 174, Michael Byerley; 178, Library of Congress Prints and Photographs Division; 179, Michael Byerley; 180, Library of Congress Prints and Photographs Division; 181, Library of Congress Prints and Photographs Division; 183, Michael Byerley; 184, Library of Congress Prints and Photographs Division; 185, Tennessee Dept. of Tourist Development; 189, copyright Bradley Schmehl, all rights reserved. www.bradleyschmehl.com; 190, The American Civil War Museum/Museum & White House of the Confederacy; 191, Tennessee Dept. of Tourist Development; 192, Skye Marthaler/https://en.wikipedia.org/wiki/Lotz_House#/media/File:Lotz_House.JPG/http://creativecommons.org/licenses/by-sa/3.0/legalcode; 194, Michael Green, BGES; 197, Picture Collection, The New York Public Library, Astor, Lenox, and Tilden Foundations; 199, Tennessee Dept. of Tourist Development; 200, Michael Byerley; 206, Library of Congress Prints and Photographs Division; 207-11, Tennessee Dept. of Tourist Development; 212, Charles F. Lee, BGES; 217, Furniture used by Grant and Lee at Appomattox, ca. 1861-65 (mixed media), American School (19th century)/National Museum of American History, Smithsonian Institution, USA/Bridgeman Images; 219, Medford Historical Society Collection/Corbis; 220, Library of Congress Prints and Photographs Division; 221, The American Civil War Museum/Museum & White House of the Confederacy; 222, Library of Congress Prints and Photographs Division; 226 (UP), The American Civil War Museum/Museum & White House of the Confederacy; 226 (LO), The death of Stonewall Jackson, pub. by Currier & Ives, 1872 (litho), American School (19th century)/American Antiquarian Society, Worcester, Massachusetts, USA/Bridgeman Images; 228, Don Troiani/Corbis; 232, Library of Congress Prints and Photographs Division; 235 (UP), *Harper's Weekly*, issue of October 29, 1864; 235 (LO), Don Troiani/Corbis; 236, Library of Congress Prints and Photographs Division; 237 (UP), Alan Thompson/The American Civil War Museum/Museum & White House of the Confederacy; 237 (LO), Buddy Secor/Fredericksburg and Spotsylvania National Military Park; 239, Library of Congress Prints and Photographs Division; 240, Hand Colored Postcard by W. L. Bond Druggist, Fredericksburg, VA., published by The Albertype Co., Brooklyn, NY; 243, The Granger Collection, NYC—All rights reserved; 245, Library of Congress Prints and Photographs Division; 247, Library of Congress Prints and Photographs Division; 248, Library of Congress Prints and Photographs Division; 250, Library of Congress Prints and Photographs Division; 251, The American Civil War Museum/Museum & White House of the Confederacy; 252, Josh Filo; 258, Library of Congress Prints and Photographs Division; 259, The Granger Collection, NYC—All rights reserved; 260 (UP), Library of Congress

Index

Boldface indicates illustrations;
page numbers in *italics* indicate maps.

H

I

J